PRINCIPLES OF INTERNATIONAL FINANCIAL LAW

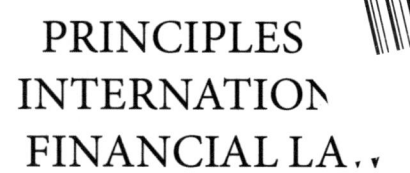

THIRD EDITION

PRINCIPLES OF INTERNATIONAL FINANCIAL LAW

THIRD EDITION

COLIN BAMFORD
Barrister
Hon. Fellow, Society for Advanced Legal Studies
Former Visiting Senior Fellow, London School of Economics and Political Science

OXFORD
UNIVERSITY PRESS

OXFORD
UNIVERSITY PRESS

Great Clarendon Street, Oxford, OX2 6DP,
United Kingdom

Oxford University Press is a department of the University of Oxford.
It furthers the University's objective of excellence in research, scholarship,
and education by publishing worldwide. Oxford is a registered trade mark of
Oxford University Press in the UK and in certain other countries

© Oxford University Press 2019

The moral rights of the author have been asserted

First Edition published in 2011
Second Edition published in 2015
Third Edition published in 2019

Impression: 1

All rights reserved. No part of this publication may be reproduced, stored in
a retrieval system, or transmitted, in any form or by any means, without the
prior permission in writing of Oxford University Press, or as expressly permitted
by law, by licence or under terms agreed with the appropriate reprographics
rights organization. Enquiries concerning reproduction outside the scope of the
above should be sent to the Rights Department, Oxford University Press, at the
address above

You must not circulate this work in any other form
and you must impose this same condition on any acquirer

Crown copyright material is reproduced under Class Licence
Number C01P0000148 with the permission of OPSI
and the Queen's Printer for Scotland

Published in the United States of America by Oxford University Press
198 Madison Avenue, New York, NY 10016, United States of America

British Library Cataloguing in Publication Data

Data available

Library of Congress Control Number: 2019947399

ISBN 978–0–19–883270–6 (pbk.)
ISBN 978–0–19–883271–3 (hbk.)

Printed and bound by
CPI Group (UK) Ltd, Croydon, CR0 4YY

Links to third party websites are provided by Oxford in good faith and
for information only. Oxford disclaims any responsibility for the materials
contained in any third party website referenced in this work.

CONTENTS

Table of Cases	vii
Table of Legislation	xv

1 Introduction
The Special Position of Financial Law	1.03
The Choice of Topics	1.16

2 Money
The Importance of Understanding Money	2.01
The Nature of Money	2.09
The Statutory Treatment of Money	2.16
Money in the Courts	2.52
The European Single Currency	2.84
The Ability of States to Control the Use of Their Money	2.187

3 Payment
Payment as the Discharge of an Obligation to Pay Money	3.04
Payment as the Transmission of Money	3.27
New Payment Technologies	3.113

4 Personal and Property Rights
The Importance of the Distinction	4.01
The Nature of the Distinction	4.18
The Distinction in Practice	4.54
Multiple Ownership	4.90
Structuring Security Arrangements	4.100

5 Intangibles as Property
Choses in Action and *Choses in Possession*	5.04
Things which are *Choses in Action*	5.12
The Nature of a *Chose in Action*	5.25
Dealings with *Choses in Action*	5.53
Hybrid Rights	5.106

6 The Legal Nature of the International Bond Market
Introduction	6.01
The Bond Market Pre-History	6.11
Post-World War II	6.26
Immobilization and the Modern Era	6.56
Legal Analysis of Bond Structures	6.72
Dematerialization	6.115

7 Fiduciary Duties and How They Arise
The Perceived Risk	7.01
The Fiduciary Relationship	7.18
The Existence of a Fiduciary Relationship	7.31

	The Nature of Fiduciary Duties	7.79
	Summary	7.98
8	Fiduciary Duties in Financial Markets	
	Introduction	8.01
	Fiduciary Duties in Commercial Transactions	8.13
	Fiduciary Duties in Financial Transactions	8.83
	Regulatory Rules for Retail Customers	8.118
9	Credit Support in Financial Markets	
	Multiple Obligors	9.05
	Contracts of Suretyship	9.22
	'Almost Guarantees' and Comfort Letters	9.39
	Commercial Credit Support	9.58
	Subordination	9.112
10	Security Interests	
	Reasons for Taking Security	10.01
	Terminology	10.04
	Registration	10.26
	Kinds of Security	10.37
	Reverse Security	10.106
11	The Construction of Financial Contracts	
	The Meaning of Contracts	11.04
	The Common Law and Civil Law Approaches	11.18
	The Difference between Meaning and Effect	11.44
	Implied Terms	11.94

Index   337

TABLE OF CASES

Abbott v Philbin [1959] 2 All ER 270 ....5.19
ABN Amro Commercial Finance PLC v McGinn & others [2014] EWHC 1674 (Comm)........9.37
Actionstrength Ltd v International Glass Engineering INGLEN SpA [2001] EWCA Civ 1477....9.32
Aectra Refining & Manufacturing Inc v Exar N.V. [1995] All ER 641 ....3.10
Agip SpA v Navigazione Alta Italia SpA [1984] 1 Lloyd's Rep 353 .... 11.86
Agnew v Inland Revenue Commissioner [2001] 2 AC 710 .... 4.87, 11.65, 11.67
AIB Group (UK) Ltd v Martin [2001] UKHL 63 ....9.21
Akbar Khan v Attar Singh [1936] 2 All ER 545..6.86
Alberta Statutes, Re (1938) SCR 100...2.13
Alderson v White [1858] 2 de G & J 97.. 10.79
Amalgamated Investment & Property Co. Ltd v Texas Commerce International Bank Ltd
    [1982] QB 84... 11.93
Antaios Compania Neviera SA v SalenRederierna A.B. [1985] AC 191 ....11.05, 11.95
Anthracite Rated Investments (Jersey) Ltd v Lehman Brothers Finance SA in Liquidation
    [2011] EWHC 1822 (Ch).. 11.70
Arab Bank Ltd v Barclays Bank (Dominion Colonial & Overseas) Ltd [1954] AC 495 ....3.73
Arm Asset Backed Securities SA, In re [2013] EWHC 3351 (Ch) 10.119
Arnold v Britton & others [2015] UKSC 36...11.15, 11.75
Atlantic Computers plc (in administration), Re, National Australian Bank Ltd v Snowden
    [1995] BCC 696 ....9.55
Australian Securities & Investments Commission v Citigroup Global Markets Australia Pty
    Ltd (CAN 113 114 832) (No 4) [2007] FCA 963 .... 7.05, 8.99–8.100

Bainbridge, Re, ex parte Fletcher (1878) 8 Ch D 218 .... 5.16, 5.22
Bank of Scotland v Dunedin Property Investment Co. Ltd [1998] SC 657 .... 11.10
Banco de Portugal v Waterlow & Sons Ltd [1932] AC 452.............. 2.11, 2.40, 2.62, 2.100, 2.112
Banco Santander SA v Bayfern Ltd [2000] 1 All ER (Com) 776 ....9.16
Bank of Credit & Commerce International S.A. (No 8) [1998] AC 214.............4.75, 4.85–4.86,
    4.88, 5.110, 10.31, 10.33–10.34, 10.37, 10.85, 10.115
Bankers Trust International plc v PT Dharmala Sakti Sejahtera [1996] CLC 518 ....7.04, 8.89
Banque Belge v Hambrouck [1921] 1 KB 321 .... 5.102
Banque Bruxelles Lambert SA v Australian National Industries Ltd [1989] 21 NSWRL 502 ......9.54
Banque Bruxelles Lambert SA v Eagle Star Insurance Co. Ltd [1997] AC 191 ....7.87
Barnard, Re (1886) 32 Ch D 447..9.19
Barnes v Addy (1874) 9 Ch App 244...8.69
Bechuanaland Exploration Company v London Trading Bank [1898] 2 QB 658..................6.41
Beconwood Securities Pty Ltd v Australia & New Zealand Banking Group Ltd [2008]
    FCA 594..10.78, 10.82
Beecham Group plc v Gist-brocades NV [1986] 1 WLR 51..5.24
Belmont Park Investments Pty Ltd v BNY Corporate Trustee Services Ltd & Lehman Brothers
    Special Financing Inc [2011] UKSC 38 ...... 9.116, 9.122, 9.124, 10.101–10.102, 10.104–10.105
Birknyr v Darnell (1805) 1 Salk 27..9.34
Boardman v Phipps [1967] 2 AC 46, [1965] Ch 992..7.64–7.75
Bolkiah v KPMG [1999] 2 AC 222 ....8.101–8.102
Borden (UK) Ltd v Scottish Timber Products Ltd [1981] Ch 25..................................... 10.72
Borland's Trustee v Steel Brothers Co. Ltd [1901] 1 Ch 279..6.15
Boston Deep Sea Fishing v Ansell (1888) 39 Ch D 339 ....8.21
Bourne v Colodense Ltd [1985] ICR 291..5.20
BP Refinery (Westernport) Pty Ltd v Shire of Hastings [1978] 52 ALJR 20..............11.98, 11.107
Bradeo v Barnett (1846) 3 CB 519 HL 5.42

viii TABLE OF CASES

Brice v Bannister (1878) 2 QBD 569. ....5.20
Brightlife Ltd, In re [1987] Ch 200 .... 11.59
British & Commonwealth Holdings plc (No 3) [1992] 1 WLR 672 .... 9.120
British Eagle International Airlines Ltd v Compagnie Nationale Air France
    [1975] 1 WLR 758. .... 9.114, 9.116–9.118, 9.122
British Oil & Cake Mills Ltd v IRC [1903] 1 KB 689. .... 10.04
Bristol & West Building Society v Mothew [1998] Ch 1. .... 7.01, 7.43, 7.81, 8.38
Buchnel v Buchnel [1969] 2 All ER 998 ....5.16
Buller v Crips (1703) 6 Mod. 29 ....6.88
Butters v BBC Worldwide Ltd [2009] EWCA Civ 1160 .... 10.96, 10.98–10.99

California v State Street Corp 34-2008-00008457-CU-MC-GDS 8.117
Cambridge Antibody Technology Ltd v Abbot Biotechnology Ltd [2005] FSR 590. .... 11.89
Carey Value Added SL v Grupo Uvesco SA [2010] EWHC 1905 (Comm) 9.73
Carillion Construction Ltd v Hussain [2013] EWHC 685 (Ch) 9.44, 9.47
Carmichael v National Power plc [1999] 1 WLR 2042. .... 11.189
Chaplin v Leslie Fruin (Publishers) Ltd [1966] Ch 71 ....5.23
Charge Card Services Ltd, In Re [1987] 1 Ch 150. .... 3.05, 3.18, 4.05, 4.54, 4.58, 4.66, 4.73–4.74,
                               4.77, 4.79, 4.83, 4.85–4.88, 5.28, 5.35, 10.31, 10.34, 10.57
Charington & Co. Ltd v Wooder [1914] AC 71. .... 11.08
Chartbrook Ltd v Persimmon Homes Ltd [2009] UKHL 38 .... 11.04, 11.19, 11.75, 11.78–11.79,
                                                                            11.89, 11.93
Charter Reinsurance Co. Ltd v Fagan [1997] AC 313. .... 3.01–3.02, 11.04, 11.12
Christopher Charles Dixon & EFI (Loughton) Ltd v Blindley Heath Investments Ltd &
    others [2015] EWCA Civ 1023 .... 11.90
Clarke v Martin (1701) 2 Ld. Raym. 757 ....6.88
Claydon v Bradley [1987] 1 WLR 521 ....6.86
Clement v Clement (1996) 71 P&CRD 19. ....9.36
Coastplace Ltd v Hartley [1987] QB 948 ....5.19
Colonial Bank v Whinney (1885) 30 Ch D 261. .... 5.06, 5.09–5.10, 5.13, 5.31, 6.13
Colonial Bank v Whinney (1886) 11 App Cas 426 .... 2.168, 5.07, 5.21, 5.28
Concord Trust v Law Debenture Trust Corporation plc [2006] 1 BCLC 616 .... 11.107
Coomber, In re [1911] 1 Ch 723 .... 7.44, 7.52 7.56, 7.68, 7.74, 7.96
Coslett (Contractors) Ltd, Re [1998] Ch 495. .... 10.41, 10.58, 10.67, 10.110
Countess of Rutland's Case (1604) 5 Co. Rep 25b. 11.73
Cowper v Smith (1838) 4 M & W 519 ....9.28
Credit Lyonnais Bank Nederland N.V. v Export Credit Guarantee Department [1998]
    1 Lloyd's Rep 10. ....9.78

D & C Builders v Rees [1966] 2 QB 617. ....3.05
Dalton v Midland Counties RLY Co. (1853) 13 CB 474. ....5.18
Dear v Reeves [2001] EWCA Civ 277. ....5.19
Derry v Peak [1889] 14 App Cas 337 ....7.23
DHL International (NZ) Ltd v Richmond Ltd [1993] 3 NZLR 10 ....8.13
Don King Productions Inc v Warren [1998] 2 All ER 608. .... 5.51, 5.56, 5.68–5.69, 5.80
Doosan Babcock v Comercializadora De Equipos Y Materiales Mabe Limitada [2013]
    EWHC 3201 (TCC) 9.71
Downs v Chappell [1997] 1 WLR 426. ....7.87
Downsview Nominees Ltd v First City Corporation Ltd [1993] AC 295. .... 10.59–10.60
Drummond v Austin Brown [1985] Ch 52 ....5.19
Dublin City Distillery (Great Brunswick Street, Dublin) Ltd v Docherty [1915] AC 823, HL. 10.63
Dundas v Dutens (1790) 1 Bes 196. ....5.21

East v Pantiles (Plant Hire) Ltd [1981] 263 EG 61. .... 11.85
Edelstein v Schuler & Co. [1902] 2 KB 144 ....6.36

Edie v East India Company (1761) 2 Burr 1216 . . . . 5.39, 5.44, 6.41
Edward Owen Engineering Ltd v Barclays Bank International Ltd [1978] QB 159 . . . . 9.68, 9.70
Elektrim SA v Law Debenture Trust Corporation plc [2008] EWCA Civ 1178 . . . . 8.112, 8.115
Evans v Rival Granite Quarries Ltd [1910] 2 KB 979 . . . . 11.66

FHR European Ventures LLP & others v Cedar Capital Partners LLC [2014] UKSC 45 . . . . .4.16
Foley v Hill (1848) 2 HLC28 . . . . 2.10, 7.06, 7.78, 8.87
Fons (HF) (In Liquidation) v Corporal Ltd & Pillar Securitisation Sarl [2014] EWCA Civ 304 . . . . 6.22
Fouad Bishara Jabbour v Custodian of Absentee's Property State of Israel [1954] 1 All ER 145 . . . . 5.19
Frame v Smith [1987] 2 SCR 99 . . . . .8.71
Franklin v Westminster Bank, The Times 17 July 1931 . . . . .2.92
Frederick E Rose (London) Ltd v William H Pim Jnr & Co. Ltd [1953] 2 QB 450 . . . . 11.88
Fuji Finance Inc. v Aetna Life Insurance Co. [1997] Ch 173 . . . . 9.109

George Cohen Sons & Co. Ltd v Docks & Inland Waterways Executive
    (1950) 84 Lloyd's Rep 97 . . . . 11.88
George Inglefield Ltd, Re [1933] 1 Ch D 1 . . . . 10.79
Geys v Societe Generale [2013] 1 AC 523 . . . . 11.96
Gibbs v Merrill (1810) 3 Taunt 307 . . . . .9.10
Girardet v Crease & Co. (1987) 11 BCLR (2d) 361 . . . . .7.93
Goldcorp Exchange Ltd, Re [1995] 1 AC 74 . . . . 3.145, 4.07, 8.27, 8.78–8.79
Goodwin v Robarts (1875) 10 Exch 337 . . . . 5.99, 5.101, 6.36, 6.39, 6.88
Goring v Bickerstaff (1662) 1 Cas 5.43
Graiseley Properties Ltd & others v Barclays Bank plc [2013] EWCA Civ 1372 . . . . .5.90
Griffith v Pelton [1958] Ch 205 . . . . .5.19

Hadley v Baxendale (1854) 9Exch 341 . . . . .2.70
Halesowen Presswork v Westminster Bank [1972] AC 785, [1971] 1 QB 1 . . . . 3.21, 3.25–3.26, 4.57
Halliday v Holgate (1868) LR 3 Exch 299 . . . . 10.10, 10.38, 10.41, 10.62
Hambleton v Brown [1917] 2 KB 93 . . . . .5.18
Harris v Tremenheere 15 Ves.34.39 . . . . .7.46
Hedley Byrne v Heller & Partners [1964] AC 465 . . . . .9.57
Henderson v Merrett Syndicates Ltd [1995] 2 AC 145 . . . . 7.29, 7.35, 7.43, 7.80
HIH Casualty & General Insurance Ltd v Chase Manhattan Bank [2003] 2 Lloyd's Rep 61 . . . . . .9.92
HMRC v Benchdollar Ltd [2009] EWHC 1310 (Ch) 11.92
Horn & others v Commercial Acceptances Ltd [2012] EWCA Civ 958 . . . . 5.82, 5.85
Hosni Tayeb v HSBC Bank plc [2004] EWHC 1529 (Comm) 3.32, 3.104–3.105
Hospital Products Ltd v United States Surgical Corporation (1984) 156 CLR 41 . . . . .8.46
Humble v Mitchell (1839) 11 Ad & El 205 . . . . .5.21

Ilich v the Queen (1987) 162 CLR 110 . . . . 5.98, 6.44
Imageview Management Ltd v Kelvin Jack [2009] EWCA Civ 63 . . . . 8.16–8.20, 8.26, 8.37
IIG Capital LLC v Van Der Merwe [2008] EWCA Civ 542 [2008] 2 Lloyd's Rep 187 261
Inglis v John Buttery & Co. (1878) 3 App Cas 552 . . . . 11.75
International Air Transport Association v Ansett Australia Holdings Ltd [2008]
    HCA 3, (2008) 234 CLR 151 . . . . 9.116
Investors Compensation Scheme v West Bromwich Building Society [1998] 1 All ER 98 . . . . . 5.20, 5.29,
                                                    5.37, 5.38, 11.04–11.05, 11.09–11.13, 11.72
Irving, Re, ex parte Brett (1877) 7 Ch D 419 . . . . .5.18

Jay, ex parte (1880) 14 Ch D 19 . . . . 10.89
Jones v IRC [1895] 1 QB 484 . . . . 10.04
Josclyne v Nissen [1970] 2 QB 86 . . . . 11.87
JP Morgan Chase Bank v Springwell Navigation Corporation [2008]
    EWHC 1186 (Comm) 7.05, 8.93–8.96, 8.98, 8.114

TABLE OF CASES

K (Restraint Order), In re [1990] 2 QB 298 .... 3.22, 3.102, 4.64
K Ltd v National Westminster Bank plc [2007] 1 WLR 311 .... 3.107
Keenan Bros. Ltd [1986] BCLC 242 .... 11.66
Kelly v Cooper [1993] AC 205 .... 8.39–8.48, 8.51, 8.79, 8.113
Keppel v Wheeler [1927] 1 KB 577 .... 8.48, 8.50, 8.51
King v Hoare (1844) 13 M&W 494 .... 9.09, 9.14
Kleinwort Benson Ltd v Malaysian Mining Corp. Bhd [1989] 1 WLR 379 .... 9.53–9.54
Kookmin Bank v Rainy Sky SA [2010] EWCA Civ 582 .... 11.06, 11.14
KPMG LLP v Network Rail Infrastructure Ltd [2007] Bus LR 1336 .... 11.85

Lac Minerals Ltd v International Corona Resources Ltd [1989] 2 SCR 574 (Canada) 7.01, 8.64–8.77,
 8.79, 8.82, 8.102
Lehman Brothers International (Europe) (in administration), Re 11.92
Levy v Sale (1877) 37 LT 709 .... 9.20
Libyan Arab Foreign Bank v Bankers Trust Co. [1989] 1 QB 728 .... 3.60–3.61, 3.63, 3.72,
 3.75, 3.95–3.97
Linden Gardens Trust Ltd v Lenesta Sludge Disposals Ltd [1994] 1 AC 85 .... 5.43, 5.46, 5.80
Lines Brothers Ltd, In re [1983] Ch 1 .... 3.69
Lister v Romford Ice & Cold Storage Co. Ltd [1956] AC 555 .... 11.96
Lloyd's & Scottish Finance Ltd v Prentice (1977) 121 SJ 847 .... 10.82
Lloyd's Bank Ltd v Bundy [1975] 1 QB 326 .... 7.58–7.63, 7.75–7.78, 8.05, 8.60, 8.83, 8.90, 8.118
Lomas & others v JFB Firth Rixon Inc & others [2010] EWHC 3372 (Ch) 11.70
Lomas & others v RAB Market Cycles (Master Fund Ltd) & Hong Leong Bhd [2009]
 EWHC 2545 (Ch) 4.10
Luxor (Eastbourne) Ltd v Cooper [1941] AC 108 .... 11.96

M (Kenya) v Secretary of State for the Home Department [2008] EWCA Civ 1015 .... 5.19
Macmillan Inc. v Bishopsgate Investment Trust plc (No 3) [1996] WLR 387 .... 3.116, 3.151
Mainwaring v Newman (1800) 2 Bos. & P 120 .... 9.11
Mannai Investment Co. Ltd v Eagle Star Life Assurance Co. Ltd [1997] AC 749 .... 11.04–11.05
Mardorf Peach & Co. Ltd v Attica Sea Carriers Corporation of Liberia (The Laconia)
 [1977] AC 850 .... 1.11, 3.47, 3.54–3.56, 3.58, 3.82, 3.89, 3.91
Mareva Compania Naviera SA v International Bulkcarriers SA [1975] 2 Lloyd's Rep 509 ...... 3.108
Marks & Spencer Group plc v Freshfields Bruckhaus Deringer [2004] EWCA Civ 741 .... 8.105–8.109
Marks & Spenser plc v BNP Paribas Securities Services Trust company (Jersey) Ltd
 [2015] UKSC 72 .... 11.95, 11.107
Marley v Rawlings [2014] UKSC 2 .... 11.15
Marley Laboratories Ltd's Application, Re [1952] 1 All ER 1057 .... 5.20
Marubeni Hong Kong & South China Ltd v The Mongolian Government [2005]
 EWCA Civ 395 .... 9.26
Master v Miller (1791) 4 Term Rep 320 .... 5.18
Matthew v Sutton Ltd [1994] 4 All ER 793 .... 10.61
Maye, Re [2008] UKHL 9 .... 5.20
Maxwell Communications Corporation plc (No 3) [1993] 1 WLR 1402 .... 9.119, 9.121–9.122
Mikeover Ltd v Brady [1989] 3 All ER 618 .... 9.07
Miller v Race (1815) 3 M & S 562 .... 2.54
Miller v Rice (1758) 1 Burr 452 .... 5.94
Millers v Miller (1822) 1 Sh App 309 .... 11.74
Mirehouse v Rennell 1 Clark & Finnelly 527 .... 1.11
Modern Engineering (Bristol) Ltd v Gilbert-Ash (Northern) Ltd [1974] AC 689 .... 3.11
Momm v Barclays Bank Int. Ltd [1977] QB 790 .... 3.53–3.56, 3.82
Moorcock, The (1889) 14 PD 64 .... 11.100
Moore, Re, ex parte Ibbetson (1878) 8 Ch D 519 .... 5.19
Morgan v Gibson [1989] STC 568 .... 5.19
Morritt, Re (1886) 18 QBD 222 .... 10.61

Mortgage Express Ltd v Bowerman & Partners [1996] 2 All ER 836 . . . . .7.87
Moschi v Lep Air Services Ltd [1973] AC 331. . . . . 9.24, 9.36
Moss v Hancock [1899] 2 QB 111 . . . . 2.19, 2.53, 2.55, 2.59, 2.61
Mosvolds Rederi A/S the Food Corp of India [1986] 2 Lloyd's Rep 68 . . . . 11.105
Motemtronic Ltd v Autocar Equipment Ltd, unreported, 20 June 1996 . . . . .9.32
Mulliner v Florence (1878) 3 QBD 484 . . . . 10.65
Murad v Al-Saraj [2005] EWCA Civ 959, [2004] EWHC 1235 (Ch) 7.17, 8.55, 8.80, 8.82, 8.118
Mutton v Peat [1900] 2 Ch 79 . . . . 3.21, 3.24–3.25
MW High Tech Products v UK Ltd v Biffa Waste Services Ltd [2015] EWHC 949 (TCC) 9.72

NML Capital, Ltd v Republic of Argentina (Southern District of New York) 3.80
National Bank of Sharjah v Dellborg [1997] EWCA Civ 2070 . . . . 11.42
National Provincial Bank v Ainsworth [1965] AC 1175 . . . . 2.160-2.161
National Westminster Bank v Halesowen Presswork [1972] AC 785. . . . . 3.26, 4.57, 10.09
New Bullas Trading Ltd, In re [1994] 1 BCLC 485 . . . . 11.62
New Zealand Netherlands Society 'Oranje' Inc. v Kuys [1973] 1 WLR 1126. . . . . .8.48
Nocton v Lord Ashburton [1914] AC 932 . . . . 4.40, 7.17, 7.19–7.28, 7.30

OBG Ltd v Allan [2008] 1 AC 1. . . . . 2.163
Oceanbulk Shipping & Trading SA v TMT Asia Ltd & others [2010] UKSC 44 . . . . 11.86
Ogdens Ltd v Weinberg [1906] 95 LT 567 . . . . .5.20
Olympic Pride (Etablissements) Georges et Paul Levy v Adderley Navigation CoPanama
    S.A. [1980] 2 Lloyd's Rep 67 . . . . 11.88
Other v Iveson (1855) 3 Drew 177 . . . . .9.19
Oxford v Moss [1979] Crim LR 119 . . . . 2.164

Peek v Gurney L.R. 13 Eq.79 . . . . .7.27
Peekay v Australia & New Zealand Banking Group [2006] 2 Lloyd's Rep 511 . . . . 8.98, 8.114
Permanent Building Society v Wheeler (1994) 14 ACSR 109 . . . . .7.93
Perpetual Trustee Company Ltd v BNY Corporate Trustee Services Ltd [2009]
    EWCA Civ 1160 . . . . 10.96, 10.100–10.102
Perry v National Provincial Bank [1910] 1 Ch 464. . . . . .9.28
Philips Electronique Grand Public S.A. v British Sky Broadcasting Ltd [1995]
    EMLR 472 . . . . 11.104, 11.106–11.107
Piggott v Stewart [1875] WN 69 . . . . 5.16, 5.22
Prenn v Simmonds [1971] 1 WLR 1381. . . . . 11.75–11.76
Private Equity Insurance Group SIA v Swedbank AS. 10.09
Proctor & Gamble Company v Bankers Trust Company & BT Securities Corp.,
    Civil Action No C-1-94-735 (S.D. Ohio). 7.05
Prudential Insurance Co. v Inland Revenue Commissioners [1904] 2 KB 658. . . . . 9.109

Quistclose Investments Ltd v Rolls Razor Ltd (in liquidation) [1970] AC 567 . . . . .4.08

R v Golechha [1989] 3 All ER 908. . . . . .5.18
R v Marland, R v Jones (1985) 82 Cr App Rep 134 . . . . .5.18
R v Preddy [1996] AC 815 . . . . 2.05–2.06, 2.77, 2.154, 3.28, 3.126
Ralli Bros v Compagnia Naviera Sola Aznar [1920] 2 KB 287. . . . . 2.117, 3.64–3.66, 3.68–3.69,
                                                                                                     3.72, 3.150
Read v Brown (1888) 22 QBD 128 . . . . .5.58
Reading v Attorney-General [1951] AC 507. . . . . 7.51, 7.57, 7.72, 7.74
Reading v The King [1949] 2 KB 232 . . . . 7.14, 7.17, 7.51, 7.73, 7.75
Rehman v Santander UK plc & BNP Paribas Real Estate Advisory & Property Management
    UK Ltd [2018] EWHC 748 (QB). 8.83
Reigate v Union Manufacturing Co. [1918] 1 KB 592 . . . . 11.102
Rhodes v MacAlister (1923) 29 Com Cas 19 . . . . 8.24–8.25

xii TABLE OF CASES

Robson v Drummond (1831) 2 B & Ad 5.45
Robinson v R [1974] SCR 573 ....2.57

Santley v Wilde [1899] 2 Ch 474, CA 10.48
Satnam Investments Ltd v Dunlop Heywood & Co. Ltd [1999] 3 All ER 652 ..... 7.12, 7.14, 7.37, 8.79
Scarf v Jardine (1882) 7 App Cas 345 ....5.88
Scottish Power plc v Britoil (Exploration) Ltd, The Times, 2 December 1997 .... 11.10
SEC v Chenery Corp. (1943) 318 HS 80..7.79
Shah v HSBC Private Bank (UK) Ltd [2012] EWHC 1283 (QB).....................3.103, 3.107
Sharif v Azad [1967] 1 QB 605 .... 2.190
Sheldon v Hentley 2 Show 160 ....5.100, 6.40
Sigma Finance Corporation, Re [2009] UKSC 2.......................11.04, 11.11, 11.39, 11.42
Sirius International Insurance Company v FAI General Insurance Ltd [2003] EWCA Civ 470 ....9.71
Société des Hotels Le Touquet Paris-Plage v Cummings [1922] 1 KB 451.....................3.45
Sookraj v Samaroo [2004] UKPC 50 .... 10.66
Space Investments Ltd v Canadian Imperial Bank of Commerce Trust Co. (Bahamas)
    Ltd [1986] 3 All ER 75 ....5.22
Sparks v Biden [2017] EWHC 1994 (Ch)... 11.107
Squirrell Ltd v National Westminster Bank plc (Customs & Excise Commissioners
    intervening) [2005] EWHC 664 (Ch) 3.101
State of Florida, The v Michell Almer Espinoza (Fla. 11th Ct. 2016) Case No. F14-2923 .... 2.155
Steet v Mountford [1985] AC 809... 11.66
Stevens v Benning (1855) 6 De Gm & G 233..5.45
Swainland Builders Ltd v Freehold Properties Ltd [2002] 2 EGLRM 71 .... 11.92

Tailor v London & County Banking Co. [1901] 2 Ch 231 ....5.18
Tan Wing Chuen v Bank of Credit & Commerce Hong Kong Ltd [1996] BCC 388........... 10.111
Tancred v Delagoa Bay & East Africa Railway Co. (1889) 23 QBD 239 ....5.60, 10.52
Target Holdings Ltd v Redferns [1996] 1 AC 421 ....7.16
Temax Steamship Co. Ltd v The Brimnes (Owners)[1975] QB 929 ....2.17
Titan Steel Wheels Ltd v Royal Bank of Scotland plc [2010] EWHC 211 (Comm) 8.97, 8.99,
                                                                                   8.114, 8.122
Tolhurst v Associated Portland Cement Manufacturers (1900) Ltd [1903] AC 414...............5.56
Toprak Mahsulleri Ofisi v Fiagrain Compagnie Commerciale Agricole et Financiere S.A.
    [1979] 2 Lloyd's Rep 98 ....3.68
Torkington v Magee [1902] 2 KB 427...5.63
Torre Asset Funding Ltd & another v The Royal Bank of Scotland plc [2013]
    EWHC 2670 (Ch).. 8.113
Total Gas Marketing Ltd v Arco British Ltd [1998] 2 Lloyd's Rep 209 .... 11.27
TSB Bank of Scotland Ltd v Welwyn Hatfield District Council & Council of the London
    Borough of Brent [1993] 2 Bank LR 267 .... 3.46, 3.90
Transtrust SPL v Danubian Trading Co. Ltd [1952] 2 QB 297..............................5.18
Trevor v Whitworth [1887] 12 App Cas 409..6.14
Trident Turbo Prop (Dublin) Ltd v First Flight Couriers Ltd [2008] 2 Lloyd's Rep 581...........8.99
Tritton, Re, ex parte Singleton (1889) 61 LT 301......................................5.16
Trollope &Colls Ltd v North West Metropolitan Regional Hospital Board (1982)
    149 CLR 337 .... 11.95
Tufton v Sperni [1952] 2 TLR 516..7.62
Turcan, Re (1888) 40 Ch D 5 ....5.48, 5.67

United City Merchants (Investments) Ltd v Royal Bank of Canada [1983] 1 AC 168 ....9.70
United Dominions Corporation Ltd v Brian Pty Ltd 91985) 157 CLR 1 ....8.53
United Pan-Europe Ltd v Deutsche Bank AG [2000] 2 BCLC 461..........................8.63
United Railways of Havana & Regla Warehouses Ltd [1961] AC 1007 .... 2.193
Union Bank of Manchester (Ltd) v Beech (1865) 3 H & C 672 ....9.28

Wait, In re [1927] 1 Ch 606 ....8.78
Walsh v Lonsdale (1882) 21 Ch.D.9 .... 4.39, 4.43
Warmestrey v Tanfield (1628) 1 Rep Ch 29 ....5.43
Wells v Middleton (1784) 1 Cox 112 ....7.03
Western Credit Ltd v Alberry [1964] 1 WLR 945 ....9.28
White v Tyndall (1888) 13 App Cas 263 ....9.13
Wilmer v Currey (1884) 2 De G &Sm 347 ....9.20
Wilson & another v Hurstanger Ltd [2007] EWCA Civ 299 .... 8.26, 8.37
Wilson, Smithett & Cope Ltd v Terruzzi [1976] 1 QB 683..............2.192–2.194
Wirth v Weigel Leygonie & Co. Ltd [1939] 3 All ER 712 ....6.84
Wood v Capita Insurance Services Ltd [2017] UKSC 24 ....11.16–11.17
Wookey v Pole 4 B &Ald 1 .... 5.101

Your Response Ltd v Datateam Business Media Ltd [2015] 1 QB 41; [2014]
    EWCA Civ 281 ....2.167, 2.176
Yuill v Fletcher (Inspector of Taxes) [1984] STC 401 ....5.18

TABLE OF LEGISLATION

TABLE OF STATUTES

Bank Charter Act 1844 . . . . .2.33
   s 1 . . . . .2.28
   s 11 . . . . .2.27
Bank of England Act 1946 . . . . .2.30
Bank Notes (Scotland) Act 1845 . . . . .2.33
Bankers (Ireland) Act 1845 . . . . .2.33
Banking Act 2009
   Pt 6 . . . . .2.33
   s 208 . . . . .2.25
Bankruptcy Act 1883
   s 44(iii) 5.10
Bill of Exchange Act 1704, 3&4 Anne, c.8 . . .6.88
Bills of Exchange Act 1882 . . . . 5.57, 5.103–5.104,
         6.81–6.82, 6.84, 6.87–6.88, 6.120
   s 83 . . . . 6.101
   s 83(1) 6.82
   s 85(1) 9.19
   s 85(2) 9.19
Bills of Sale Act 1878 . . . . 10.27, 10.49–10.50
Bills of Sale Act 1882 . . . . 10.27, 10.49–10.50
Bretton Woods Agreement
   Act 1945 . . . . .2.189, 2.191
Carriage of Goods by Sea Act 1992
   s 2(1) 5.42
Civil Liability (Contribution) Act 1978
   s 3 . . . . .9.14
Coinage Act 1971 . . . . .2.23
   s 2(1) 2.22
   s 2(1A) 2.22
   s 2(1B) 2.22
   s 9(1) 2.23
Companies Acts 6.12, 10.60
Companies Act 1862
   s 16 . . . . .6.15
Companies Act 1877
   s 3 . . . . .6.14
   s 4 . . . . .6.14
Companies Act 1928 . . . . 3.139
Companies Act 1929 . . . . .6.22
Companies Act 1948
   s 95 . . . . .4.62
Companies Act 1985 . . . . .4.66
Companies Act 1989
   s 207 . . . . 6.123
Companies Act 2006 . . . . 4.89, 6.24,
       10.28–10.29, 10.32, 10.36, 11.54–11.55
   s 738 . . . . .6.24

   s 755(5) 6.24
   s 783 . . . . .6.24
   s 859A 4.66, 4.86, 10.51
   s 859A(4) 10.32
   s 859A(7) 10.08, 10.32
   s 859H(3) 10.08
   s 860(7)(f) 9.127
Copyright, Designs and Patents Act 1988
   s 1(1) 5.23
Criminal Justice Act 1988
   s 93A 3.104
Currency Act 1983
   s 2 . . . . .2.29
   s 3 . . . . .2.29
   s 3(2) 2.50
   s 3(4) 2.50
Currency and Bank Notes Act 1928
   s 3 . . . . .2.28
   s 6 . . . . 2.29, 2.30
Currency and Bank Notes Act 1954
   s 1(1) 2.20
   s 1(4) 2.46
   s 1(5) 2.48–2.49
Drug Trafficking Offences Act 1986 . . .3.22, 3.102
Exchange Control Act 1947 . . . . .6.37
Exports and Investment Guarantees
   Act 1991 . . . . .9.72
Factors Act 1889
   s 2 . . . . 11.48
Finance Act 1899
   s 5(2) 6.36
Finance Act 1986
   s 79 . . . . .6.37
Financial Services Act 1986 . . . . .7.09
Financial Services Act 2012 . . . . 8.119
Financial Services and Markets Act 2000 . . . . 9.110
   s 138D 8.121–8.123
   s 138D(1) 8.119
   s 150 . . . . 8.122
   s 417(1) 8.119
Forgery and Counterfeiting Act 1981
   Pt II 2.20
   s 14 . . . . .2.20
   s 19 . . . . .2.20
   s 27 . . . . .2.20
Insolvency Act 1986
   s 40(2) 11.54
   s 107 . . . . 9.112
   ss 175–176A 11.54

Land Charges Act 1972 .... 10.27
Land Registration Act 1925 .... 3.141
Land Registration Act 2002
   Pt 5............................... 10.27
   s 23............................... 10.54
   s 51............................... 10.54
Larceny Act 1861
   s 100................................2.54
Law of Property Act 1925..... 5.45, 10.52–10.53
   s 82..................................9.11
   s 85............................... 10.53
   s 87(1)............................. 10.07
   s 136......... 5.11, 5.14, 5.43, 5.56, 5.58–5.59,
          5.61–5.64, 5.69–5.70, 5.103, 10.52
   s 136(1).............................5.55
   s 205(1)(xvi) 10.08, 10.53
Law Reform (Frustrated Contracts)
   Act 1943
   s 1............................ 3.63, 3.72
Life Assurance Act 1774........... 9.104–9.105
   s 1................................ 9.104
   s 4................................ 9.101
Limitation Act 1980 ....4.16
Local Government Act 1933 ... 10.11–10.12, 10.15
   s 13............................... 10.56
Local Government Act 2003
   Pt 1, ch 1............................9.83
   s 2(3)...............................9.83
   s 13......................... 10.16, 10.56
   s 13(1).......................10.14–10.15
   s 13(3)............................ 10.15
   s 13(4)............................ 10.16
Marine Insurance Act 1906
   s 1................................ 9.105
   s 4................................ 9.105
   s 5................................ 9.106
   s 5(1)............................. 9.106
   s 5(2)............................. 9.106
Misrepresentation Act 1967
   s 2..................................8.94
Partnership Act 1890
   s 9..................................9.13
Patents Act 1977
   s 30(1)........................2.159, 5.24
Proceeds of Crime Act 2002 ...... 2.196–2.197,
               3.103, 3.107–3.108
   s 328.............................. 3.101
   s 328(1)........................... 3.100
Provisions of Oxford 1258 ....4.34
Sale of Goods Act 1979.................. 11.96
   ss 21–25 .... 11.48
Social Security Administration Act 1992
   s 187(i) 5.45
Stamp Act 1891
   s 109................................6.36

Statute of Frauds 1677 .... 9.32–9.33
   s 4............................. 9.31–9.34
Supreme Court of Judicature
   Act 1873....... 4.38–4.39, 4.41–4.42, 4.51,
              5.15, 5.43, 5.55, 5.103
   s 25(6)..............................5.43
Supreme Court of Judicature
   Act 1875....... 4.38–4.39, 4.41–4.42, 4.51,
                   5.15, 10.38
Theft Act 1968..................... 2.05, 2.164
   15(1)................................3.28
Trademarks Act 1994
   s 22.................................5.23

STATUTORY INSTRUMENTS

Bretton Woods Agreements Order 1946
   (SR&O 1946/36).................. 2.189
Business Contract Terms (Assignment
   of Receivables) Regulations 2018
   (SI 2018 No 1254)...................5.46
   r 3..................................5.46
Civil Procedure Rules 1998
   (SI 1998/3132)......................9.12
   r 16.6...............................3.12
   r 25.1............................. 3.108
Companies Act 2006 (Amendment
   of Part 25) Regulations 2013
   (SI 2013/600)..................... 10.32
Exchange Control (General Exemption)
   Order 1979 (SI 1979/1660) 6.37
Financial Collateral Arrangements
   (No 2) Regulations 2003
   (SI 2003/3226)............... 10.09, 10.32
   reg 3 ....5.56
   reg 4 .... 4.101
   reg 16 .... 10.03
Financial Markets and Insolvency
   (Settlement Finality) Regulations
   1999 (SI 1999/2979)..........2.117, 3.112
Financial Services and Markets Act 2000
   (Right of Action) Regulations 2000
   (SI 2001/2256)
   Art 3............................. 8.121
Insolvency (England and Wales) Rules
   2016 (SI 2016/1024)
   r 14.24............................ 13,16
   r 14.25..................... 3.13–3.14, 3.16
Insolvency Rules 1986
   (SI 1986/1925).................... 10.92
   r 4.90...............................4.77
   r 4.181(1)........................ 9.112
Insolvency (England and Wales) Rules
   2016 (SI 1986/1925)
   r 14.25........................ 4.77, 10.92

Merchant Shipping (Registration of Ships)
  Regulations 1993 (SI 1993/3135) 10.27
Mortgaging of Aircraft Order 1972
  (SI 1972/1268)..................... 10.27
Uncertified Securities Regulations 2001
  (SI 2001/3755)
  reg 3(i) 5.56
Uncertified Securities (Amendment)
  (Eligible Debt Securities) Regulations
  2003 (SI 2003/1633) 6.123

OTHER LEGISLATION

Australia
Bills of Exchange Act 1909.............. 6.119

Canada
Criminal Code
  s 391(b)(1)..........................2.58
  s 392................................2.58

France
Civil Code
  Art 1156C 11.21

New Zealand
Sale of Goods Act 1908
  s 18............................4.09, 8.31

United States
Banking Act 1933 ....6.31
Banking Act 1935 ....6.31
Constitution 4.19
Dodd-Frank Wall Street Reform and
  Consumer Protection Act 1.22
Interest Equalisation Tax Act 1964 ....6.29
New York State Insurance Law
  s 6902(a)(1) 9.83
  s 6904(a)............................9.83
Securities Act 1933 ....6.48
  s 5..................................6.49
Uniform Commercial Code
  Art 8.......... 5.30, 5.106, 5.109–5.111, 5.113

Art 8-501 .... 5.111
Art 8-502 ....5.111–5.112
Art 8-1501 ....5.30
Art 8-1582 ....5.30

EUROPEAN UNION

Council Regulation (EC) No 1103/97 ......2.88
  Art 2................................2.96
  Art 3................................2.96
Council Regulation (EC) No 974/98 ....2.88
  Art 2............................. 2.100
Council Regulation (EC) No 1346/2000
  on Insolvency Proceedings 10.19, 10.23
  Art 5............................. 10.23
Directive on Financial Collateral
  Arrangements (EC) 2002/47........ 10.03,
                                10.09, 10.62
Regulation (EU) 2015/848 on
  Insolvency Proceedings...... 10.19–10.20,
                                10.23, 10.43
Recital (68) 10.20
Art 8............. 10.20, 10.23–10.25, 10.33
  Art 8.1 .... 10.21
  Art 8.2 .... 10.22
  Art 8.3 .... 10.22
Settlement Finality Directive (EC)
  98/20/26....................2.117, 3.112
Treaty establishing the European
  Community.........................2.88
  Art 105a.....2.102, 2.104, 2.110–2.111, 2.115
  Art 123.4 ....2.99
Treaty establishing the European
  Stability Mechanism............... 2.123
Treaty on European Union (Maastricht
  Treaty) 2.86–2.99, 2.102, 2.114,
                                2.126, 6.67

INTERNATIONAL PROVISIONS

Agreement establishing the International
  Monetary Fund (Bretton Woods
  Agreement) 1945 ....2.191, 2.193
  Art VIII, s 2(b) 2.189–2.192
Security Council Resolution 661 .... 2.198

1
INTRODUCTION

> When I first visited ... Washington some three years ago accompanied only by my secretary, the boys in your Treasury curiously inquired of him – where is your lawyer? When it was explained that I had none – 'Who then does your thinking for you?' was the rejoinder.
>
> John Maynard Keynes[1]

1.01 Lord Keynes did not like lawyers. His words are heavy with irony. However, despite Keynes' distaste, in modern financial markets it often falls to the lawyers to do the thinking about the nature and consequences of the structures and products that their clients have invented. The purpose of this book is to help the lawyers who advise clients on financial law in this task of analysis.

1.02 It might be thought that the same aim could be made for any legal textbook, with the substitution of the relevant area of law for the reference to the law of financial transactions. However, financial law, in its current stage of development, is different from many other areas of legal practice in some important ways. The cumulative effect of these differences is to make it important that practitioners have a clear understanding of the concepts and principles that underlie the applicable legal rules, in addition to a knowledge of the detailed rules themselves.

The Special Position of Financial Law

Legal advice in financial markets

1.03 The first characteristic which distinguishes the legal advice given in financial markets from that given in most other areas concerns the objectives of clients in asking for legal advice. Litigation lawyers, asked to advise a client in relation to a dispute which has already arisen with another party, or with a regulator or other public authority, have two questions to address:

1. What facts will the court decide are relevant?
2. How will the court apply the law to those facts?

Both questions invoke the lawyer's evaluation of the relevant rules of law. This evaluation, however, is heavily influenced by the lawyer's knowledge of the particular court which will hear the case and of the prevailing judicial and social attitudes. Deciding what the law is, and

---

[1] Speech made to the US delegation to the Bretton Woods Conference, recorded by Sir Roy Harrod in *The Life of John Maynard Keynes*.

predicting what a particular court will do, are not necessarily the same exercise. The skill of the litigator lies as much in the organization and presentation of facts and in the understanding of judicial thinking and attitudes as it does in a detailed knowledge of the law.

1.04 Financial lawyers operate in a different climate. Their advice is usually sought in connection with the structuring of financial transactions or the documenting of agreed proposals. The client is looking for a way to set up arrangements so that disputes will not arise or, if they do, there should be as little doubt as possible that they will be resolved in favour of the client.

1.05 In some respects, the task of the financial lawyer is much simpler than that of the litigator: he or she does not need to deal with any vagaries of evidence or other factual matters; nor are the sensitivities of particular courts or judges relevant. The question facing a legal advisor dealing with a financial transaction is simpler, but also wider: 'If something goes wrong with the operation of this transaction, and the matter comes before a court for decision, what will the judge do?'

1.06 The financial lawyer need not be concerned with the need to prove or disprove allegations of fact, nor with the attitudes of particular judges. However, he or she cannot avoid facing the much wider questions which arise from the possibility that all sorts of things might go wrong, the nature of which cannot be foreseen, and that any resulting dispute might come to be considered by one or more courts in different places. The nature of financial law is now transnational and any document which is drafted on the basis that it is to be governed by the law of England and Wales (or that of any other country) might, in the event, fall to be interpreted and enforced by a court where the judge has no qualification or experience in the chosen governing law.

Legal developments and economic change

1.07 The common law develops in response to changes in behaviour which produce new situations and disputes. In the commercial sphere, developments in the law have normally been preceded by changes in technology, which have, in turn, brought about changes in trading patterns. A clear example is the change that followed the invention of the marine steam engine. With the introduction in the mid-nineteenth century of ships which were much faster than the standard sailing cargo vessels, a major change in trading activity came about. A bill of lading, representing the goods loaded on a vessel, could be dispatched by steamer at the time when the cargo left on a sailing ship. The documents of title would reach their destination long before the cargo itself. This meant that the goods could be traded and financed on the basis of the bill of lading, without the goods being in the same country. This produced a large number of cases, and a great deal of new law about the nature of ownership and possession of goods, in the context of international trade.

1.08 The explosion in the use and the sophistication of computer technology in the late twentieth century has had a similar effect on financial activity. Not only has the technology enabled the creation of increasingly sophisticated financial instruments. More importantly, it has allowed trading activity to take place through the exchange of digital information, rather than physical book entries. More recently, Distributed Ledger Technology has the potential in some areas of activity to replace the use of centralized records altogether.² Geography has become, in many cases, irrelevant in financial trading. It is just as easy to effect a transaction with a counterparty on the other side of the world as it is to do it with someone who is sitting next door.

For the financial lawyer, one of the most complex consequences of globalization is that for many transactions the draftsman must assume that any future problems might occur, or be litigated, in a foreign jurisdiction. Private international law, once considered the preserve of the more academically minded practitioners, has become a central area of focus for all financial lawyers. **1.09**

The process of development of the common law

Human beings are creatures of habit. They feel most comfortable, when presented with a problem, in dealing with it as they have dealt before with similar problems. To the extent that a problem has novel characteristics, the human instinct is to find the nearest proven approach, and to make only such changes as are necessary to deal with the novelty. Our instinct is to adapt to change incrementally. **1.10**

Common lawyers are no different from other people. In 1833[3] James Parke J explained how the common law would approach the problem which was then before the court, and for which there was no precedent: **1.11**

> The case ... is in some sense new, as many others are which continually occur; but we have no right to consider it, because it is new, as one for which the law has not provided at all; and because it has not yet been decided, to decide it for ourselves, according to our own judgment of what is just and expedient. Our common law system consists in the applying to new combinations of circumstances those rules of law which we derive from legal principles and judicial precedents; and for the sake of obtaining uniformity, consistency and certainty, we must apply those rules, where they are not plainly unreasonable and inconvenient, to all cases which arise; and we are not at liberty to reject them, and to abandon all analogy to them, in those to which they have not yet been judicially applied, because we think that the rules are not as convenient and reasonable as we ourselves could have devised. It appears to me to be of great importance to keep this principle of decision steadily in view, not merely for the determination of the particular case, but for the interests of law as a science.

More recently, Lord Simon of Glaisdale made the same point more succinctly:[4]

> ... English law develops by applying an established rule of law to new circumstances which are analogous to the circumstances in which the established rule was framed.

When new circumstances come before a court for decision, the closer those facts are to those of a previous case, the easier it is to see how the court will make the analogy with **1.12**

---

[2] Discussed below at paras 3.113 *et seq.*
[3] *Mirehouse v Rennell* 1 Clark & Finnelly 527.
[4] *Mardorf, Peach & Co. Ltd v Attica Sea Carriers Corp of Liberia* [1977] AC 850.

previous circumstances, and so predict the way in which rules of law will be applied to the new facts.

The challenge for financial lawyers

1.13 When drafting the documentation for a transaction, or advising clients on how to design trading systems or operating systems, the financial lawyer has a task which is made more complex by the combination of the three factors described above. He or she is asked to predict how the proposed arrangements will be viewed by a future court, which may or may not be in the jurisdiction of the lawyer's own expertise. The area of activity involved may well be one where there is little or no decided case law or statutory guidelines. There may be no closely related decisions which have an obvious analogy to the situation under review.

1.14 The lawyer must therefore predict how a court might apply to the new circumstances principles and rules of law devised to cover quite different factual circumstances. The courts may well be obliged to apply an analogy across a large factual gap. The wider the gap which must be jumped, the harder it is to predict where the court will land.

1.15 It is not enough, therefore, for financial lawyers to have a thorough knowledge of the rules of law relating to the activity with which they deal. There may well be situations where there are no specific rules to be derived from decided cases, nor even any rules that are almost on the point. In predicting the future approach of the courts, the financial law practitioner must have a sound understanding of principles and concepts which underpin the existing rules of law in areas which are removed from areas of current market activity, because these principles are the foundations on which future decisions will be built.

The Choice of Topics

1.16 It is not possible to draw up a list of 'foundation concepts' which can be confidently forecast to be those which will underpin future decisions in cases involving financial transactions and markets. There are, however, a number of legal principles which have already been shown to be central to issues in this field, and which can be predicted to arise again in different circumstances. It is possible to put these into a number of categories, examples of each of which form the subject-matter of one or more chapters of this book.

1.17 First, there are those concepts which have not needed, as a matter of English domestic law, to be analysed in any great detail in the past, but which are likely to become more significant in the context of globalized financial trading. Among these are the concepts of money and of payment. Payment, for example, has been regarded traditionally as a mechanical matter, relevant only to the determination of whether a particular payment obligation had, or had not, been performed. However, when payments in large amounts are made internationally, the mechanical process involves many steps being taken by a number of institutions, perhaps in several different countries. The legal consequence of the failure of this complicated chain is much more complex than the determination simply of whether A did, or did not, make a payment to B.

Second, there are core legal concepts which are different in common law and civil law countries. As long as disputes are factually confined to a single jurisdiction, these differences are unimportant in practice. When several countries are involved, the differences become crucial. Each system of law has its own concepts of property and of the nature of personal rights. In each case, this understanding determines the way in which rights may be exercised or dealt with. There is a fair degree of harmony between systems, when they deal with physical property. However, when legal systems consider intangible assets, such as debt or intellectual property, their understanding of the legal nature of those assets differs very widely. When intangible property is traded across national boundaries or moves its location from one jurisdiction to another, complex issues of conflicts of laws regularly arise. Before a financial lawyer can begin to address these issues, he or she must have a clear understanding of the nature of property rights and obligations under the law of his or her own jurisdiction. **1.18**

Some issues in financial law involve not only an understanding of the legal rules which now apply, but also knowledge of how they developed. Some international markets, and in particular the international bond market, have developed (rather like the common law) incrementally. The form and structure of the market and of transactions which take place in it are the creature of a number of small steps, each of which prompted a minor change to the legal arrangements of the market. When there is a major shift in the way in which the market operates, for example by the move to electronic trading instead of the transmission of pieces of paper which represent the items sold, problems arise. The legal effect of the new methods of dealing has to be analysed against the backdrop of a structure which was designed for a different era. In order to address these issues at all, it is necessary to understand where the present structure came from and why it evolved as it did. **1.19**

In structuring or documenting transactions, the financial lawyer must often choose how best to secure his or her client's interests. The possible mechanisms available, whether by way of property-based or contract-based security or by way of credit support, are all familiar. However, lawyers are usually taught about these mechanisms in connection with specific areas of law. For example, they learn about mortgages and charges in connection with their study of land law and about guarantees as part of a contract law course. For a financial lawyer deciding upon a structure or documenting a transaction, it is important to see these disparate concepts as belonging to the same available tool kit. The ability to see the use of these concepts in combination is an important skill in structuring financial transactions. **1.20**

Some legal concepts, which at first sight appear to have little to do with international financial markets, regularly present themselves as potential problems. The most persistent of these is probably the issue of fiduciary relationships and fiduciary duties. To many in the financial markets, fiduciary duties belong to the law of trusts and are designed to protect the interests of vulnerable individuals. They cannot see that this branch of law should have anything to do with international financial markets, which are populated by large and supposedly sophisticated organizations. To others, the claim that a fiduciary duty exists has the **1.21** effect of shifting commercial responsibility for the actions of one of the parties onto to the shoulders of the other.[5] The concept of fiduciary relationships is just as relevant in financial markets as it is in any other walk of life. However, in order to understand why this is so, and why it need not be a matter of concern for responsible market participants, one needs to understand in some depth the origins of the doctrines and the way in which they are now applied.

1.22 The chapters which follow aim to bring to the attention of financial law practitioners the concepts which underpin some of the more difficult and important issues in financial law. No chapter claims to be the definitive treatment on the topic which it discusses. Indeed, most of the topics are the subject of complete textbooks in their own right. It must be remembered that these topics are not matters on which it is possible simply to 'look up the law'. Each lawyer must form his or her own understanding of the concepts and issues, in order to apply that understanding to the facts of new transactions and arrangements. The aim of the ensuing chapters is to point practitioners towards their own understanding.

---

[5] For example, the Dodd-Frank Wall Street Reform and Consumer Protection Act, designed as a regulatory response to the banking crisis of 2008, contains provisions which impose specific duties on those who conduct swaps business with 'special entities'. 'Special entities' are, broadly, state and municipal bodies and pension plans. The original draft of the Bill proposed in rather simpler terms that the swaps dealers, when dealing with such bodies, should have fiduciary duties. The phrase was an inappropriate term to use, in order to achieve the effect sought, and was changed before the final text was agreed. Its use does, however, illustrate the very broad-brush misunderstanding which many have of the term.

2
MONEY

There is no sphere of human thought in which it is easier for a man to show superficial cleverness and the appearances of superior wisdom than in discussing questions of currency and exchange.

Sir Winston Churchill[1]

The Importance of Understanding Money

2.01 Almost all commercial transactions involve money. In trade, property is sold for money; in finance, money is loaned and repaid; and in foreign exchange dealings money is exchanged for money. But English law and other common law systems have little to say about the nature of money, or the way in which it is created, disappears, and is transferred. Other legal systems, notably those of France and Germany, pay much more attention to money. Indeed, a separate discipline of 'monetary law' is firmly established within the body of their commercial law.

2.02 This distinction between common law and other systems has no explanation in jurisprudence. The reason for the difference is probably historical. The stresses that led to the French Revolution of 1789 included a struggle with the king about his habit of changing the value, in terms of the French currency unit, of coins in circulation. The king claimed the right to declare that a particular coin was now worth fewer *livres* than it had been worth before the decree. By this device, he reduced the number of *livres* that he owed to his subjects, and consequently the amount of money held by his subjects. The struggle ended when the king was forced to accept that coins should bear the stamp of their nominal value (the principle now known as 'nominalism') so that their value could not be changed after the coins were issued.

2.03 In Germany, the hyper-inflation under the Weimar Republic, which contributed to the rise of the Nazi party, was thought to have been exacerbated by the practice of index-linking prices in commercial contracts. As inflation eroded the value of money, the contract price automatically increased. This acceptance of inflation was thought to encourage its acceleration. Accordingly, the post-war constitution prohibited such monetary indexation as a fundamental safeguard of political stability. This measure has had practical consequences. In the days before monetary union and the introduction of the euro, the European Communities accounted internally through the medium of the European Currency Unit (ECU), a composite measure, the value of which was determined by combining the values of a basket of the currencies of some of the individual Member States. In the 1980s German

[1] Hansard, Vol 468, Col 160 (28 September 1949).

banks, recognizing a commitment among their customers to the European project, began to offer retail bank accounts denominated in ECUs. However, a German constitutional court declared that it was unlawful for banks to maintain ECU accounts: the ECU was not money; it was a composite of the values of its constituent currencies. Accordingly, it was an index and fell foul of the constitutional prohibition. Although, in response, the Bundesbank authorized the use of the ECU for certain monetary purposes,[2] the principle was unaffected.

2.04 In the common law world, money has not been a focus of political attention. While the English had a civil war about the raising of taxation, and the United States declared independence for the same reason, no common law country has faced a major constitutional crisis about the nature or control of its currency. A characteristic of the common law is that it develops piecemeal, in response to events. In the absence of practical problems that find their way to the courts, or issues that prompt Parliament into action, no rules are created. The common law has, therefore, developed no organized approach to the concept of money. A few statutory provisions dealing with specific and somewhat random details, and a very few cases, are all that can be found.

2.05 This approach has been sufficient in the past, but it no longer is. Large-scale transfers of money or monetary value are now made by electronic means, very often without reference to national boundaries. It is not enough for lawyers to understand the mechanics of the transfer system. They must also understand the nature of the subject-matter and of the rights and obligations that are created by the transfer process. In *R v Preddy*,[3] the question arose whether an electronic transfer of funds, procured by fraud, resulted in the fraudster receiving 'property belonging to another' within the meaning of the Theft Act 1968. The House of Lords analysed the steps in the process of transfer through the banking system. The electronic messages between the payer, its bank, the payee's bank, and the payee each created and/or cancelled a legal relationship. Thus, when the payer's bank transferred money to the payee's bank, the transaction in law was that it created itself a debtor of the payee's bank for the amount concerned, and ceased to owe a corresponding amount to its customer, whose instructions it was fulfilling. As far as the fraudulent payee was concerned, he received an acknowledgement that his own bank had now become a creditor of the payer's bank and a debtor of the payee (its own customer) for the amount concerned.[4] Thus, the only thing that the payee could be said to have 'acquired' as a result of the transfer of money was the debt payable to him from his bank. That debt was a new creation, which did not exist before the money transfer had taken place. It could not be said, therefore, that the payee had acquired 'property belonging to another'. Similar issues of analysis have arisen again in relation to so-called 'cryptocurrencies' that have recently been invented.[5]

2.06 In international transactions, money transfers involve more steps than were taken in the transfer in the *Preddy* case, and book entries and electronic messages are made and sent in more than one jurisdiction. Events in any of the countries through which a transfer passes

---

[2] Communications Nos 1010/87 and 1002/90.
[3] [1996] AC 815.
[4] An additional step in the process is needed to clear the money transfer across the books of the central bank. See paras 3.31 *et seq*.
[5] See paras 2.150 *et seq*.

(eg the blocking of a bank account by local legislation) might affect the rights and obligations of the parties involved. It is no longer possible to see the process of money transfer as a simple mechanical issue without legal consequences.[6]

2.07 In both personal and corporate taxation, the location of assets is often central to questions of liability. This is particularly so when the asset concerned is money. The question *where* it is cannot be answered without first knowing *what* it is.

2.08 Sovereign governments increasingly view the control of the use of their currency as a foreign policy issue. By imposing sanctions and freeze regulations they can restrict the ability of other countries to have access to international trade. They can also deny the use of their currency to those of whom they disapprove. The United States in particular has imposed freeze regulations with dramatic effects on international financial dealings.[7] On occasion, United Nations resolutions have resulted in widespread action by individual states, notably in relation to the Iraqi invasion of Kuwait in 1990 and the wars in the Balkans in 1993.[8] More recently, the response of the United States and the European Union to the tension between Russia and Ukraine in 2014 has been the imposition of economic sanctions on individuals and organizations in Russia, the principal effect of which is to deny them the use of the currencies of the sanctioning states. An understanding of how such regulatory action operates and its effect on the international flow of funds is often essential in financial transactions. In turn, an understanding of the nature of the monetary transactions involved, and how they are treated at law, is also essential.

The Nature of Money

2.09 Like most attempts to define intellectual constructs, purported definitions of money have described what it does and some of the characteristics that it has, rather than delineating the thing itself.

2.10 The word 'money' is used by economists, by lawyers, and by the general population to indicate a number of different tangible things and intangible concepts:

1. It can be used to refer to the notes and coins that represent monetary obligations of a sovereign issuer.
2. When people speak of 'having money in the bank' they are referring to the debt owed to them by their bank.[9]
3. Politicians may speak of a growth in the 'supply of money' when they mean an increase in the value of debts owed between members of the public.
4. Central bankers draw a distinction between 'central bank money' and other kinds of money; the one being represented by or derived from a debt owed by the issuing central bank (either in the form of bank notes or on accounts maintained with the central

---

[6] And see Chapter 3 for a discussion of the legal consequences of the use of Distributed Ledger Technology in the transfer of money and other assets.
[7] See paras 3.75 *et seq* and 3.61 *et seq* respectively in relation to the consequences of regulations on Iran and Libya.
[8] UN Security Council Resolutions 661 and 942 respectively.
[9] See *Foley v Hill* (1848) 2 HL Cas 28.

bank by commercial banks), the other comprising debts created between individuals or non-bank institutions.

2.11 It would be possible to put forward an acceptable definition of money, if one was prepared to think only at a conceptual level. One might, for example, say that money is the total value of the assets owned by a sovereign entity, measured by units (the currency) chosen by that sovereign. Such a definition finds support in the words of Lord Macmillan in *Banco de Portugal v Waterlow & Sons Ltd*[10] in describing the 'quantity theory of money':

> The only effect of the increase in the currency of Portugal by the introduction of ... [additional currency] notes was to diminish the value of each unit of the currency and to increase correspondingly the value in terms of the currency of all the assets in the country.

It has support in Roman law. By the time of Justinian the *fiscus*, or imperial treasury, was given legal personality, as being a symbol of the abstract conception of the claims by and on the emperor.[11]

2.12 However, if one looks for a more concrete definition, the target becomes elusive. Economists identify a number of characteristics of money. It is a medium of exchange; it is a measure of value or a standard of contractual obligations; it is a store of wealth; and it is a unit of account. Useful as they are, these statements do not tell us what money is; they describe some of its uses. Understanding is further confused by the identification of a number of different 'measures' of money. In the UK, M0 is the aggregate value of sterling coin and notes in circulation and commercial banks' deposits with the Bank of England. M4 is the sum of all sterling cash held by non-banks, private-sector retail bank and building society deposits, and private-sector wholesale bank deposits (including the nominal value of Certificates of Deposit in issue). In the United States, a different set of definitions is used. It is misleading to describe these different classifications as separate measures of money, in the sense that 1 mile and 1.6 kilometres are different measures of the same distance. The economists' 'measures of money' are, in reality, descriptions of different things.

2.13 It is not for common lawyers to criticize economists for their lack of precision in the use of the word. Its use by lawyers suffers from the same defect. Blackstone, in his *Commentaries on the Laws of England*, defined money by reference only to its use as a measure of value:

> Money is a universal medium, or common standard, by comparison with which the value of all merchandise may be ascertained.

More recently, the Supreme Court of Canada defined money by reference only to its use as a means of exchange:[12]

> Any medium which by practice fulfils the function of money and which everyone will accept as payment for a debt is money in the ordinary sense of the word even though it may not be legal tender.

---

[10] [1932] AC 452, 510 and see paras 2.62 *et seq* below.
[11] See T. C. Sanders, *The Institutes of Justinian* (Longmans, 1927), Introduction.
[12] *Re Alberta Statutes* (1938) SCR 100.

In England, Professor Goode[13] has used the word to denote only coin and notes:

> … much of the debate on what constitutes money in law is rather sterile and has few implications for the rights of parties to commercial transactions, where payment by bank transfer is the almost universal method of settlement.

2.14 It is not often necessary in legal practice to find a definition of the word 'money'. The crucial point is to understand that it can mean different things in different contexts and to be clear about the specific meaning with which one is confronted. A working model might be to start from the premise that money is first an intellectual concept. In relation to each state it represents the aggregate measurable obligations of that state, owed to its nationals and to others. These obligations are measured and expressed in terms of a yardstick (a currency) selected and controlled by that state. This conceptual money (sometimes called by central bankers and economists 'fiat money', because it exists by virtue of the will of the issuer) has emanations in the real world in a number of forms: as coin, as bank notes (whether issued by the state itself or by others), by accounting balances shown in the books of the state's central bank, commercial banks, and other institutions, and in amounts owed between private individuals. When the word is encountered in commercial life, it will refer to one of these emanations of the concept. The important point is to be clear which emanation is involved.

2.15 Discussion of questions involving money has been complicated by the emergence of so-called 'cryptocurrencies'. The nature of cryptocurrencies and their implications for the monetary system are discussed below.

The Statutory Treatment of Money

Legal tender

2.16 In popular perception, whether particular notes or coins are 'legal tender' is taken to denote their status as money. For example, while shopkeepers in the parts of England closest to the Scottish border will readily accept Scottish bank notes, in most other places in England and Wales shopkeepers will refuse Scottish and Northern Irish notes, on the grounds that they are not legal tender, as if that implied that they were of no value, or that accepting them would be illegal.

2.17 In English law, 'legal tender' is an expression with a technical and very limited meaning. In the UK it defines those money tokens (notes and coin) which, if they are tendered by an obligor in discharge of a monetary obligation, the obligee is bound to accept as good discharge. In practice, the concept has little significance. First, it does not apply where the obligation to pay money requires that it be discharged by a specified method other than the payment of cash. For example, most loan agreements of any size will require discharge of the payment obligations to be made by credit to a specified bank account by transfer through the banking system. Further, courts are ready to imply into contracts terms that payment of monetary

---

[13] *Goode on Commercial Law* (2nd edn, LexisNexis Butterworths), 49.2.

sums may be made in ways that are commercially sensible. In *Temax Steamship Co Ltd v The Brimnes (Owners)*,[14] the court held that, even though the contract stipulated that payment should be 'in cash', the transfer of funds to the payee's bank account was sufficient properly to discharge the debt.

2.18 In everyday transactions, the issue rarely arises. Shops and petrol stations routinely display the stickers of credit card companies, as indicators of their willingness to accept payment by those methods. Tender of one of the advertised cards will be sufficient to relieve the payer of any liability for breach of his or her payment obligations, should the shopkeeper refuse to accept payment by that method.

2.19 As far as concerns the use of cash in everyday transactions, the significant point is not whether the particular tokens are 'legal tender' but whether they are 'currency in circulation', a term used in *Moss v Hancock*[15] and defined as:

> ... that which passes freely from hand to hand throughout the community in final discharge of debts and full payment for commodities, being accepted equally without reference to the character or credit of the person who offers it and without the intention of the person who receives it to consume it or to apply it to any other use than in turn to tender it to others in discharge of debts or payment for commodities.

Northern Irish and Scottish bank notes are not accepted commonly in England and Wales. They are not 'currency in circulation'; accordingly, shopkeepers in London and Cardiff will not accept Scottish notes. If the notes fell within the definition in *Moss v Hancock*, as they do in Carlisle and Berwick, it would be irrelevant whether or not they were legal tender. They would be accepted, and in most cases of contractual payment the law would imply a term that they should be so accepted.

2.20 The same point arises in Part II, Forgery and Counterfeiting Act 1981. Section 14 makes it a criminal offence to counterfeit a 'currency note' or a 'protected coin', intending that it should be passed as genuine. By s 27 an element of the definition of both terms is that the genuine note or coin should be (or, in the case of notes, be or have been) 'customarily used as money'. The status of the tokens as legal tender is not relevant.[16]

2.21 Whether particular notes or coins are given the status of legal tender depends on statute. The notes and coins included in the list are surprisingly few, and there are a number of areas where no provision at all is made for monetary tokens to have the status of legal tender. The fact that it has not been found necessary to extend or rationalize the provisions in this area indicates, of course, that their practical importance is very limited.

2.22 The notes and coins that are legal tender in the UK are as follows:

1. Bank of England notes are legal tender in England and Wales (s 1(1) Currency and Bank Notes Act 1954). There is specific provision for such notes to be put into

---

[14] [1975] QB 929.
[15] [1899] 2 QB 111.
[16] Curiously s 19 of the Act, which makes it an offence to reproduce British coins as imitations in connection with an advertising campaign, restricts the definition to coins that are legal tender.

circulation in Scotland and Northern Ireland, but they are not legal tender there, unless their value is below £5. There are now no Bank of England notes with a face value below £5.
2. There is no provision that bank notes issued by Scottish or Northern Irish banks are legal tender, even in the place where they are issued. It follows that, in Scotland and Northern Ireland, no bank notes have the status of legal tender.
3. Throughout the UK, coins produced by the Royal Mint are legal tender, but only in respect of debts which are within specified limits:
    (i) gold coins are legal tender for debts of any amount (s 2(1) Coinage Act 1971). It should be noted that in the case of all sterling gold coins, the value of the metal content far exceeds their nominal value;
    (ii) coins of £1, £2, and £5 value are legal tender for debts of any amount (s 2(1B) Coinage Act 1971);
    (iii) 'silver' coins of 5p or 10p denomination are legal tender for debts of up to £5 (s 2(1A) Coinage Act 1971);
    (iv) 'silver' coins of more than 10p nominal value are legal tender for debts of up to £10 (s 2(1A) Coinage Act 1971); and
    (v) 'bronze' coins of 1p or 2p denomination are legal tender for debts up to 20p (s 2(1A) Coinage Act 1971).

Notes and coin

Coins and notes, although they both represent money, and indeed are both often referred to as money, do not share the same legal structure in English law. Coins are produced by the Royal Mint. The monopoly of issue of coins by the Crown is embodied in s 9(1) Coinage Act 1971:

2.23

> No piece of gold, silver or bronze, or any metal or mixed metal, of any value whatsoever, shall be made or issued except with the authority of the Treasury, as a coin or token for money, or as purporting that the holder thereof is entitled to demand any value denoted thereon.

This prohibition gives an indication of what money is. Although it is not a statutory definition of money, it is possible to say that money, in the sense that the term is used in the Coinage Act, is a claim against the Crown denominated in the Crown's own currency, and which is represented by the coin which the Crown issues.

Bank notes serve the same function as coins. They represent money and are used to transfer value between holders in exactly the same way as coins. In English law, however, their structure is very different. It should be stressed that the analysis below relates to the position in the United Kingdom, and the legal status of bank notes is different in some other jurisdictions.[17]

2.24

---

[17] In particular, see paras 2.110 to 2.116 below in relation to the status of euro bank notes.

2.25 In the eighteenth century, as the industrial revolution expanded trade and commerce, the number of banking businesses in the UK grew very rapidly. Individuals, partnerships, and corporations began to trade as bankers in the newly-industrialized towns and cities to service the expanding industrial base. One of the services they provided to customers was the issue of bank notes. These were promissory notes made by the banker as principal, which the banker sold to its customers in exchange for coin or other assets with a monetary value. The portable and transferable bank notes were much more convenient for the commercial community than were bags of coins. A definition of 'bank note' is now contained in s 208 Banking Act 2009:

> ... 'bank note' means a promissory note, bill of exchange or other document which
> (i) records an engagement to pay money,
> (ii) is payable to the bearer on demand, and
> (iii) is designed to circulate as money.

2.26 The major distinction between the obligation represented by a coin and that represented by a bank note is that the promise contained in a bank note is that of the maker of the note, while the implicit promise in a coin is that of the Crown. The issuers of bank notes were businesses that varied widely in size and financial standing. Accordingly, some 'private money' was considerably more valuable than other. In addition, bank notes were easy prey for fraudsters, because there were so many issuers, using different formats and security devices. More importantly, from the point of view of the Crown, there was no control over the issue of bank notes, nor any requirement that the money represented by the promise should be held by the issuer in the form of coin. Private bankers had the ability to increase the amount of money in circulation at will, without the consent of the Crown.

2.27 The issue of paper currency was brought under state control by the Bank Charter Act 1844. Section 11 gave a monopoly on the issue of bank notes to the Bank of England, a private corporation which had acted as the government's banker since the late seventeenth century. Section 11 prohibited any banker other than the Bank of England from issuing in England and Wales:

> ... any bill of exchange or promissory note or engagement for the payment of money payable to bearer on demand ...

2.28 On its own, the granting of the monopoly would have done no more than concentrate the problems in one institution. There would still have remained the difficulty that a private body was able, in effect, to issue the Crown's money on its own account. This difficulty was solved by s 1 of the Act, which required the Bank of England to keep its note issue business 'wholly distinct' from the rest of its business and to establish a separate Issue Department, which would deal only with the issue of bank notes. The Act further required that the Bank of England should hold in the Issue Department gold or other specified securities (which might include, in particular, debt securities issued by the UK government itself) in order to cover the value of the notes which were issued. This provision is now contained in s 3 Currency and Bank Notes Act 1928.

2.29 As time has passed, some of the arrangements for the Bank of England's issue of notes have been formalized. For example, ss 2 and 3 Currency Act 1983 provide that the amount of notes to be issued by the Bank of England should be controlled directly by HM Treasury.

Perhaps most importantly, s 6 Currency and Bank Notes Act 1928 provides that the profits and expenses of the Issue Department of the Bank of England are for the account of HM Treasury.

2.30 The Bank of England has been wholly owned by the state since 1946.[18] This fact, combined with the consequence of s 6, that the Bank of England is, in effect, a nominee of HM Treasury for the purpose of the issue of bank notes, means that the status of Bank of England notes in economic and financial terms is the same as that of coin issued directly by the Crown.

2.31 When the Bank of England puts bank notes in circulation, it does so by selling its notes to commercial banks which maintain accounts with it, and which need bank notes in order to satisfy the requirements of their own customers. The price payable by those banks is represented by a debit to their account with the Bank of England. On this account, the central bank will charge interest to the commercial bank on the amount of the debit (or will avoid the need to pay interest, if the account is in credit). The Bank of England itself, acting as nominee of the Crown, pays no interest on the money represented by the face value of the notes that it has issued. It has created the money, rather than borrowed it from someone else. This ability to charge interest without incurring any cost is a happy consequence of being a central bank and is known by the sonorous word 'seigniorage'. This aspect of central banking is possibly the only business in which it is impossible not to trade at a profit.

2.32 The process of the issue of notes within the Bank of England can perhaps best be represented by the book entries involved:

Issue Department	
Assets	Liabilities
Cover for notes issued consisting of government securities, bullion, etc	Value of notes issued
Banking Department (so far as concerns note issue)	
Assets	Liabilities
Obligations owed by customers to pay for the Bank of England notes sold	Obligation owed by the Bank of England on the notes issued and delivered to customers

The position in Scotland and Northern Ireland

2.33 The arrangements effected by the Bank Charter Act 1844 in England and Wales were mirrored in the provision made for Scotland and Ireland by the Bank Notes (Scotland) Act 1845 and the Bankers (Ireland) Act 1845. The position is now governed by Part 6 of the Banking Act 2009.

2.34 Certain commercial banks in Scotland and Northern Ireland are permitted to issue their own bank notes. As in the case of Bank of England notes, HM Treasury is given power to

---

[18] Bank of England Act 1946.

make regulations which set out the way in which issues are to be made and the amount and timing of them.

2.35 Issuing banks are required to hold covering assets for the notes they issue. In practice, the covering assets consist of Bank of England notes, which are created for the purpose in multiples of £1 million face value. The special notes are retained by the Bank of England on behalf of the commercial issuing bank concerned.

2.36 Regulations provide that, on the insolvency of an issuing Scottish or Northern Irish bank, the Bank of England notes which cover the issue of that bank's currency notes will be used to fund the replacement of the insolvent bank's notes with new Bank of England notes. Thus, the holders of such notes are shielded from the consequence of the insolvency of the issuing bank.

2.37 Because the issuing bank has to buy from the Bank of England a note to cover the issue it is to make, the seigniorage on those notes stays with the Bank of England.

Demonetization

2.38 As bank notes circulate they become worn out or defaced. They are routinely replaced. As commercial banks receive over their counters worn-out notes, they hand them back to the Bank of England, which replaces them with freshly printed notes. The Bank of England then destroys the surrendered notes. This process has no legal consequence. Because the bank notes are not, in a conceptual sense, money, but merely represent the money to which they refer, replacing the piece of paper has no effect on the identity or amount of the money represented.

2.39 There are, however, circumstances where a central bank or government might wish to break the link between bank notes that represent money, and the money that they represent, even though the pieces of paper are still in circulation. The purpose of this process is to render worthless the circulating bank notes concerned. In the true sense, they no longer represent money. In another, more mundane sense, they no longer are money.

2.40 There are several reasons why a central bank might wish to do this. First, it might simply wish to replace one design or format of notes with a newer, perhaps more secure, design. By announcing that the notes will cease to be money at some point in the future, holders will be encouraged to surrender the notes in exchange for notes of the new issue. Another reason to demonetize an issue of notes is illustrated in the *Banco de Portugal* case (see paras 2.62 *et seq* below). In that case, a large number of forgeries were detected within the system. In order to preserve confidence in the currency, the only course was to remove the genuine notes of that issue from the monetary system (removing the forgeries at the same time) and to replace all the notes with fresh notes.

2.41 A third reason to demonetize an issue of notes would be to deny value to those who have stolen large numbers of those notes. Before Christmas 2004, thieves broke into the vaults of Northern Bank Limited in Belfast and stole notes to the value of £26 million. Northern Bank Limited is one of the commercial banks permitted to issue bank notes in Northern Ireland. The theft included £10 million in unissued Northern Bank notes and £5.5 million in used Northern Bank notes. In response to the theft, Northern Bank recalled all of its notes in circulation with a value of £10 and above, totalling some £300 million. These were replaced by fresh notes of a different design.

2.42 A fourth reason why a government might wish to demonetize notes in issue lies in its wish to control the use of its currency by those of whom it disapproves. If it became aware, for example, that foreign governments of whom it disapproved were holders of large amounts of its currency in cash form, an obvious response would be to break the link between those notes and the money which they represented, therefore rendering them valueless in the hands of the holder.

2.43 The extent to which demonetization in these circumstances is possible, and the means by which it might be achieved, depend on the laws of the state that issues the notes concerned.

2.44 The position in the United Kingdom is that it is not in law possible to break the link between a bank note that has been issued by the Bank of England (ie a note that is not a forgery) and the money that it represents.

2.45 A Bank of England note is an unconditional promise to pay an amount of money to bearer on demand. The corollary of this is that the holder of the note is entitled to be paid, as is the holder of any promissory note. The crucial point is to determine what is meant in substance by 'the obligation to pay' in these circumstances.

2.46 The Currency and Bank Notes Act 1954 s 1(4) provides that the holder of a bank note is entitled on demand:

> ... to receive in exchange for the notes bank notes of such lower denominations ... as he may specify.

He is given no other right (eg the right to demand payment in coin or in gold, or even to demand a new note of the same denomination).

2.47 It is perhaps more fruitful to look at the question from the other side—what must or may the Bank of England do in order to discharge its obligation to pay? The answer is to be found in the rules relating to legal tender (see paras 2.16 to 2.22 above). In practice, if the holder of a note presented himself at the Bank of England, produced a £10 note, and demanded that the Bank pay him £10, the Bank would discharge its obligation by handing him another £10 note.

2.48 The Bank of England is given no statutory right to avoid its obligation to pay. It cannot simply declare that it will not perform the promise set out on one of its notes. A power is given, however, in s 1(5) Currency and Bank Notes Act 1954 for the Bank of England to 'call in' any bank notes:

> ... on payment of the face value thereon ...

In other words, the Bank of England has the ability to crystallize its obligation to pay.

2.49 However, if the holder of the note does not comply with the calling-in request, and continues to hold the old note, the Bank of England's obligations in respect of that note do not cease. Section 1(5) provides only that, on the expiry of the calling-in notice, unpresented notes should cease to be legal tender. As shown above (para 2.19) the fact that a note may have ceased to be legal tender does not affect its identity as money.

2.50 The Currency Act 1983 s 3(2) provides that, ten years after the end of a calling-in period, the Bank of England may write off in the accounts of the Issue Department the value of the called-in notes that have not then been presented. However, it is specifically provided in subsection (4) that the writing off does not affect the liability of the Bank of England to pay, in its capacity of maker of the note.

2.51 Thus, there is power for the Bank of England, using the statutory calling-in procedure, to cause specified notes to cease to be legal tender. In practice, once an issue has been called in, notes in that series will cease to be usable as tokens for money in everyday transactions. They will no longer be 'currency in circulation'. They will not, however, cease to represent money, in the conceptual sense, and the Bank of England will remain liable indefinitely to pay their face value on presentation.

Money in the Courts

2.52 The courts in England (and elsewhere in the common law world) have been called upon only rarely to consider the nature of money. Such few cases as there are tend to be unhelpful in finding an understanding of the term. Usually the courts are asked to consider the meaning of a particular emanation of money, in a very specific circumstance. Nonetheless, consideration of some of the cases is helpful, in illustrating the point that 'money' can mean many different things in different contexts.

2.53 In *Moss v Hancock*[19] a butler stole from his employer a five-pound gold coin. The coin was issued by the Royal Mint and would have been legal tender for its face value. In reality, it had a much greater value as a collector's item. The thief sold the coin to a dealer. The case concerned the employer's attempt to recover the coin from the dealer.

2.54 The Larceny Act 1861 s 100 provided for the court to make an order directing the return of stolen property to its true owner. The coin dealer, who claimed to have bought the gold piece in good faith, argued that no such order could be made. Since the gold coin was legal tender, and was therefore to be regarded as money, title to the physical item passed to him as a *bona fide* purchaser. In relation to physical items that are 'money', there is an exception to the rule *nemo dat quod non habet* where the physical money token is transferred for value to an acquirer who is acting in good faith. In *Miller v Race*,[20] Lord Mansfield said:

> So, in the case of money stolen, the true owner cannot recover it, after it has been paid away fairly and honestly upon a valuable and bona fide consideration: but before money has passed in currency, an action may be brought for the money itself.

2.55 The judge in *Moss v Hancock*, Darling J, held that the purchasing coin dealer did not acquire title in this case. His argument was in two stages: first, he identified two separate meanings of the word 'money', even when it was used in relation to a specific coin:

---

[19] [1899] 2 QB 111.
[20] (1815) 3 M & S 562.

apply it to any use other than in turn to tender it to others in discharge of debts or payment for commodities. Money as currency, and not as medals, seems to me to have been well defined ... as 'that which passes freely from hand to hand throughout the community in final discharge of debts and full payment for commodities, being accepted equally without reference to the character or credit of the person who offers it and without the intention of the person who receives it to consume it or to apply it to any use other than in turn to tender it to others in discharge of debts or payment for commodities.

Having drawn the distinction between money as currency, and money as a medal, he went on to hold that the transfer of ownership of the gold coin to the dealer in the case before him did not pass an indefeasible title to the dealer:

... the mere fact that the stolen gold piece was money would not render it unfit for the application to it of an order for restitution. The true question seems to me to be whether by the manner of dealing with it which the thief adopted the gold piece passed in currency.

2.56 The crucial point about the gold coin in this case was not its status in law as legal tender, or even the fact that it could have been used as a means of payment, had its owners so wished. The point on which the judge's decision turned was the intention of the transferor and the transferee and the purpose for which they used the coin. They had not used it as money in the sense of currency, but as a chattel, which had value quite separate from its worth as a means of exchange.

2.57 Many years later, a similar point came before the Supreme Court of Canada in *Robinson v R*.[21] A Canadian coin dealer was caught in possession of a number of United States 'dimes', marked 1941/42. The evidence was that this particular issue of dimes was lawful currency in the United States, but because of production errors, the coins had a numismatic value far in excess of their face value.

2.58 The dimes which Mr Robinson held were, however, counterfeit, and he was charged under s 392 of the Canadian Criminal Code, which made it an offence for anyone to have in his possession 'counterfeit money'. That phrase was said by s 391(b)(1) to include

... a false coin ... that resembles or is apparently intended to resemble or pass for current coin ...

According to the Code, 'current' means lawfully current in Canada or elsewhere.

2.59 The trial judge acquitted the defendant, relying heavily on the reasoning of Darling J in *Moss v Hancock*. He said that the 1941/42 dimes could not be said to be money, because the accused did not intend to use them as currency but was holding them to sell them for their numismatic value.

2.60 The Supreme Court reversed the decision. The majority concluded that the trial judge had no justification in finding that the coins concerned 'are not money'. The statute was clear. In order for an offence to have been committed, the statute required a finding that the dimes were 'counterfeit money'. That phrase is said to include counterfeits of things which are 'current coin' in the United States. Genuine 1941/42 dimes were within that

---

[21] [1974] SCR 573.

category (even if no-one with any numismatic knowledge would dream of using them as a medium of exchange at their face value). Accordingly the appellant should have been convicted.

2.61 The decision, although at first sight it appears to take a different view from that taken in *Moss v Hancock*, in fact supports the distinction drawn by Darling J between money as currency and money as 'medals'. The Supreme Court of Canada merely found that, although Mr Robinson may have been holding the coins as 'medals' the offence merely required that genuine coins of the description concerned might have fallen within the definition of 'current coin'. For the purposes of the Code, it did not matter whether the holder intended to use the coins as currency.

2.62 Although most cases concerning money deal with very detailed issues about a particular use of the word, there is one case in which the House of Lords examined in detail the nature of money and the obligations which it represents. The case, *Banco de Portugal v Waterlow & Sons Ltd*,[22] arose from one of the largest frauds in history perpetrated against Banco de Portugal in 1925 and masterminded by a 25-year-old man called Alves dos Reis.

2.63 Banco de Portugal was, like the Bank of England at that time, a privately owned company which acted as the issuer of bank notes for its government. The structure of the legal relationships between the Portuguese central bank, its government, and the public is, in all practical senses, the same as the structure in the UK at the time, and at the present day. Banco de Portugal decided to make a large issue of new 500 escudo notes, bearing the portrait of Vasco de Gama, the famous navigator. The decision was to print 600,000 of these notes (making an issue worth 300,000,000 escudos in total).

2.64 It arranged for the notes to be printed in London by Waterlow & Sons, Limited, who were well-known security printers at the time. The plates were made, the notes printed, delivered to Banco de Portugal, and put in circulation, replacing existing escudo notes. At this point the fraudsters intervened. They persuaded Waterlow & Sons, Limited that they were acting with the authority of the Portuguese central bank. They arranged for Waterlow to print a further 600,000 Vasco de Gama 500 escudo notes, and deliver them to the fraudsters.

2.65 The fraudsters, who had set up their own bank in Portugal for the purpose, then began to pass the false notes into circulation. The fraudsters' notes, having been printed from the genuine plates owned by Banco de Portugal, were indistinguishable by members of the public from the genuine notes.

2.66 The fraud was eventually uncovered when someone noticed that the fraudsters' bank appeared to have very large amounts of money to lend, although it did not seem to be accepting any deposits. By the time the plot was uncovered, 290,000,000 escudos, represented by false Vasco de Gama notes, had been placed in circulation. The conspirators had used the proceeds of the fraud, among other things, to amass a holding of over 10 per cent in the shares of Banco de Portugal itself.

---

[22] [1932] AC 452.

Banco de Portugal, in order to preserve public confidence in the currency, called in all of the Vasco de Gama notes, consisting of the 600,000,000 escudos which it had itself issued and the 290,000,000 escudos put into circulation by the fraudsters. It replaced all of the notes with new Banco de Portugal notes. It then sued Waterlow & Sons, Limited in England for breach of contract, in failing to exercise the degree of care implied in their contract with Banco de Portugal.

2.67

By the time the case reached the House of Lords in 1932 only one issue remained to be considered. It had been accepted that Waterlow had been negligent and that the action taken by Banco de Portugal in calling in both the genuine and the false Vasco de Gama notes and replacing them with new notes had been a reasonable way to respond to the problem created by Waterlow's negligence, and that it was foreseeable that Banco de Portugal would behave in this way.

2.68

The question, therefore, was the amount of the loss suffered by Banco de Portugal. It was accepted that the Bank had been involved in expenditure, in calling in the genuine and false Vasco de Gama notes and in printing and distributing new notes to the value of 590,000,000 escudos. The point at issue was whether Banco de Portugal, in issuing its own notes to the value of 290,000,000 escudos, to replace the false notes circulated by the fraudsters (referred to in the case as 'Marang' notes, after the name of one of the conspirators), had incurred a monetary liability for that amount. If so, its loss would include the amount of that liability.

2.69

On this point, the case is most unusual. There were no authorities on the point, nor any general established principles which would have pointed towards a particular conclusion. The judges were on their own. Each of them had to work out for himself the financial consequences, based on an analysis at what happened when a central bank issues notes. As Lord Warrington put it:

2.70

> There are no principles applicable except such as are expressed in *Hadley v Baxendale*, nor are there any authorities which are of help.

Lord Russell phrased the question posed to each of the judges as follows:

2.71

> ... when the Bank gave a good unissued note in exchange for a Marang note did they become poorer to the amount of 500 escudos either by parting with 500 escudos or by incurring an immediate liability to part with 500 escudos? That appears to me to be the crucial question; and the answer seems to me to depend upon the correct appreciation of what happened when the Bank issued the good note to the holder of a Marang note, and a correct statement of the obligations which the Bank assumed by the issue of that good note.

Of the judges who sat on the case, Wright J at first instance, Greer and Slesser LJJ in the Court of Appeal, and in the House of Lords Viscount Sankey LC, Lord Atkin, and Lord Macmillan found that the Bank did suffer a loss of 500 escudos in the note exchange. Scrutton LJ in the Court of Appeal, and Lords Russell and Warrington in the House of Lords, held that the Bank suffered no loss.

2.72

When looking at the reasoning adopted by the judges, it is useful to think of the consequences of the fraudulent issue, in terms of its effect on the balance sheet

2.73

position of Banco de Portugal. If there had been no negligence and the Vasco de Gama notes had been issued as Banco de Portugal intended, the effect would have been as follows:

Banco de Portugal	
Assets	Liabilities
300,000,000 Escudos (debts owing from the banks to whom Banco de Portugal sold the Vasco de Gama notes)	*300,000,000* Escudos (liability of Banco de Portugal to the holders of the Vasco de Gama notes, as maker of the notes)

In the event, the Bank's balance sheet after it had effected the exchange of the genuine and false Vasco de Gama notes would be as follows:

Banco de Portugal	
Assets	Liabilities
300,000,000 Escudos (debts owing from the banks to whom it sold genuine Vasco de Gama notes)	*300,000,000* Escudos (its own obligations in respect of notes issued to replace 'genuine' Vasco de Gama notes) *290,000,000* Escudos (its obligations on notes issued to replace 'spurious' Vasco de Gama notes)

The fraud creates a deficit which will need to be filled in some way; either by an injection of capital or, much more likely, by a transfer from reserves.

2.74 Two judges in the House of Lords felt that Banco de Portugal suffered no loss when it issued replacement notes for the false Vasco de Gama notes surrendered to it. Lord Warrington addresses the question very shortly:

> The whole question in my opinion turns on the nature of the obligation incurred by the issuing Bank under the notes it issues. They are in effect promissory notes payable to bearer on demand. So long as they remain in the possession of the Bank they are merely pieces of paper, and if, for example, they were lost or destroyed while in their possession they could be replaced by printing other notes at the cost of the paper and the printing.
>
> As soon as a note is issued it imposes an obligation on the Bank to pay to the bearer on demand 500$ ...
>
> It is proved by the evidence of witnesses called on behalf of the Bank itself that the only material obligation is satisfied by exchanging the note in question for another note of like denomination.

2.75 He then refers to the judgment of Wright J at first instance, who had said of Banco de Portugal:

> They are damaged by having to assume liability on these notes without getting anything in return. I think this argument is correct, and I think these notes must be taken for this purpose at their face value, just as they would be if they had been issued by some other institution that is not a Bank of issue.

Lord Warrington takes issue with this conclusion:

> With all respect, I cannot accept the conclusion of the learned judge. It seems to me that by treating the Bank on the same footing as 'any other institution' he ignores the vital distinction – namely, that the obligation incurred by the Bank is merely to pay in other currency which it has power to create for the purpose ...

2.76 The other dissenting judgment is given by Lord Russell. His argument is more complex. He records the view taken by the trial judge, and by the majority in the Court of Appeal, quoting the words of Greer LJ:

> Every time they issued good notes to the value of 500 escudos in place of worthless notes, they lost the market value of 500 escudos.

However, Lord Russell does not think that this represents a correct analysis of the situation:

> But in my opinion this view does not represent the facts, but overlooks the exceptional situation which arises when a bank of issue issues notes constituting an inconvertible currency.

2.77 He then explains his analysis in terms that are similar to the reasoning adopted many years later in *R v Preddy*.[23] Lord Russell argues that a bank note, before it is handed over to a recipient by the issuing bank, is simply a piece of paper. It contains a promise to pay bearer. If the bearer is the promisor him- or herself, the promise simply becomes circular and has no monetary value. When the issuing bank hands the note to an outsider, the promise becomes valuable. This, however, does not constitute a loss to the bank, in the sense that it has ceased to own something of value which it owned before. Rather, it amounts to the creation of a fresh obligation on the part of the bank. When the newly-issued bank note is presented to the bank for payment, the bank's obligation is simply to replace the then existing bank note with a fresh note. That transaction does not change the bank's position at all.

2.78 He then makes the point that, in assessing damages, one must draw a distinction between the cost to the defendant of repairing the breach of contract that he has committed, and the detriment that has been suffered by the plaintiff as a result of that breach. He accepts that, if Waterlow were to buy the replacement notes that Banco de Portugal had been forced to issue, in order to destroy them and thereby return the Bank to the position it should have been in, had there been no breach of contract, the cost would be equal to the face value of the notes. However, it did not follow that the loss to Banco de Portugal had the same value. This would be true only if Banco de Portugal had:

> ... parted with 500 escudos with each note it issued in exchange for a Marang note.

2.79 There is a degree of attraction in Lord Russell's view that the mere issue of the note does not itself involve Banco de Portugal in any loss. It is the assumption of a liability which will result in detriment only when it is performed. To see this more clearly, one might perhaps think of an individual who has been induced by fraud to make out a cheque, which is then negotiated. The damages he could claim from the fraudster would not be based merely on the fact that he had written out a cheque with a particular face value. He would have to show

---

[23] See para 2.05 above.

that he had subsequently been obliged to pay on the cheque. If the cheque had, for instance, been destroyed before presentation, he would have suffered no loss.

2.80 The flaw in Lord Russell's argument lies elsewhere. Because the bank's obligation on the note is to pay the value of it, and because the bank may, if presented with the note, merely replace it with a freshly printed one, he concludes that the payment on the note does not result in any cost to the bank. In reality an issuing bank does not fulfil its liability to pay on its notes by replacing each note with a fresh one. Bank notes are not issued across the counter of the central bank to individual members of the public. They are placed in circulation through the system of commercial banks which maintain accounts with the central bank. The central bank pays its liability on its notes, when they are returned to it through the banking system, by crediting the account of the commercial bank which makes the presentation.

2.81 It has to be remembered that, although it is open to the central bank to pay its liability on a note by tendering a fresh note,[24] that is not the only way in which it can discharge its obligation to pay. In practice, it pays through the banking system. It is reasonable to assume that, after the replacement issue by Banco de Portugal, the value of the notes issued would in due course be replaced by credits made to the accounts of commercial banks in the books of the central bank. Accordingly, Banco de Portugal would ultimately have paid out the value of the replaced notes, although it would not have paid by the issue of replacement notes, but by making credits in its own books in favour of its commercial bank customers.

2.82 The leading judgment for the majority is that of Lord Atkin. He takes a much more robust view of the arrangements than does Lord Russell. His central point is that the bank, in issuing its note, is in the same position as any other merchant who issues a cheque or promissory note. It has an obligation to pay on presentation. The fact that it may pay by assuming a fresh obligation of the same amount does not affect the position:

> Now in the case of a private trader it appears to be conceded that his loss in similar circumstances would be measured by face value. On this analysis the obligation of the Bank would appear to be the same. That it meets its obligation on its note by issuing a further note seems to have no effect upon the nature or amount of the original obligation; the original obligation is met by renewal, the Bank have only gained time, not increased or decreased an obligation which would be measured just as before. They have in fact done exactly what the merchant has done: they have paid in currency; and their obligation is measured in the same way.... I therefore find the position to be that the Bank by issuing its note like the trader issues its promise to pay a fixed sum; issues a bit of its credit to that amount; like the trader, it is bound to pay the face value in currency; like the trader, it is liable on default to judgment for the face value exigible out of its assets; and, like the trader, if it is compelled by the wrong of another to incur that liability, its damages are measured by the liability it has incurred.

2.83 The reasoning of Lord Atkin and the other majority judges is persuasive. The debate, however, indicates the conceptual difficulty involved in understanding the effect of the process of issuing currency obligations. That difficulty follows from the problem of understanding the nature of money itself.

---

[24] As in the case of the Bank of England, see para 2.47 above.

The European Single Currency

2.84 The introduction of the euro as the single currency of many of the Member States of the European Union was an event which, it might have been supposed, would do much to clarify the nature of money and of its various manifestations as notes, coin, and book entries. For reasons that appear below, this did not happen. The process of EMU (Economic and Monetary Union) has raised questions at this level, rather than answered them. In reviewing the nature of money and its significance to lawyers in the financial markets, the process of EMU is important first because of the practical issues which financial markets lawyers had to address, and second because these issues flowed from the nature of money itself and from uncertainties about what that nature might be.

2.85 The world financial crisis of 2008 exposed more issues about the nature of the single currency and the relationship between the Member States that had adopted it. The decision taken on the introduction of the euro, to leave these questions unanswered, resulted in doubts that made resolution of the problems more difficult than it needed to be. A great deal of time and energy has been expended in the process of agreeing measures to support the single currency project. A clearer understanding of the nature of the euro would have avoided much of this. The 'solutions' are, in many cases, the inevitable consequence of the nature of the euro. They did not need agreement, but only acknowledgment.

The introduction of the euro

2.86 The Member States of the EU committed themselves to the process of EMU in the Treaty on European Union, signed at Maastricht on 7 February 1992 (referred to below as the 'Maastricht Treaty'). The process of monetary union had at its core the introduction of a single currency throughout the EU, to replace the currencies then issued by individual Member States. All Member States committed themselves to the process, although Denmark was granted an 'opt-out' and it was agreed that the United Kingdom would not adopt the single currency until it decided to 'opt-in'.

2.87 The Maastricht Treaty gave the name of the new currency as the 'ECU' (sometimes rendered in lower case as 'ecu'), the name previously used to denote the European Currency Unit, used as a unit of account between EU institutions. The name, however, proved controversial. 'Ecu' was the name of an old French coin. Although this fact made it popular in France as a choice of name, it had the opposite effect elsewhere. Accordingly, the Member States decided to change the name given in the Treaty to 'euro'.[25]

2.88 The issue of euros is controlled by the European Central Bank, based in Frankfurt, which was established by the Maastricht Treaty. The ECB is itself part of the wider European System of Central Banks, which comprises the ECB and the central banks of all the Member

---

[25] The Presidency Conclusions after the Madrid summit in December 1995, when the name 'euro' was chosen, said that the Maastricht Treaty, when giving the name of the currency as 'ECU' had used the term as a 'generic' reference to European currency units. The name 'euro' was therefore an 'interpretation' of the Treaty name. The legality of the approach, in terms of Community law, was questioned (see The Delegation of French Bars, *Aspects Juridiques du Passage a la Monnaie Unique* (September 1996), pp 31–3), but to no avail.

States that have adopted the euro as their currency (the 'Participating Member States'). In addition to the high level provisions introduced into the Treaty establishing the European Community (referred to below as the 'Treaty of Rome') by the Maastricht Treaty, the legislative framework for the introduction of the euro was contained in two Council Regulations, referred to below as 'the 1997 Regulation' and the '1998 Regulation'.[26] The 1998 Regulation provided for a 'transitional period' of up to three years. During that period the euro became the currency of all the Participating Member States, but the units of their former currencies continued to exist for some purposes. In particular, currency notes and coins denominated in the 'old' currencies remained in circulation. Their value was fixed as against the euro, of which the 'old' currency units were now said to be a sub-division.

2.89 On 31 December 2001 the transitional period ended, and from that date the 'old' currency units were no longer used. Any reference to those units was deemed to be a reference to euro units, converted at the fixed rate agreed at the beginning of the transitional period. In the weeks immediately after the beginning of 2002, 'old' national currency notes and coins were withdrawn from circulation and replaced by euro notes and coins.

2.90 The operations involved in replacing the national currencies with the euro were on an enormous scale, not least in relation to the physical production of new notes and coin and their introduction into circulation in a very short space of time across most of the EU. The fact that this operation was conducted without any major hitch was a remarkable achievement on the part of the Commission, the ECB, and the central banks of the Participating Member States.

2.91 In the period before the introduction of the euro, a great deal of thought was given to the consequences for commercial contracts of a change in currency. In most cases, the change of currency from, say, deutschmark to euro was not likely to cause significant legal disturbance. First, the change in currency was signalled several years in advance, and the vast majority of contractual arrangements could be tailored to accommodate the change. Second, in those circumstances where the change could not have been foreseen (eg very long-term supply contracts concluded before the EMU process had begun), all developed legal systems have established principles and mechanisms to cope with unexpected changes in the identity of the currency of payment or account.

2.92 In English law, if a monetary contractual obligation is expressed in the currency of a foreign country, the exact nature and definition of that obligation is determined by reference to the law of the country concerned. If, for example, a party to an English law contract has an obligation to pay US dollars, the meaning of the term 'US dollars' is decided by looking at its meaning in the law of the United States. This is often described as the rule of *lex monetae*. It is not unknown for countries to change their currencies in accordance with their national law. This national law will then provide for the substitution of a new currency, so that obligations undertaken in the old currency continue to have a legal meaning.[27] English law will take those provisions into account, if asked to determine the meaning of an obligation

---

[26] Respectively, Council Regulation (EC) No 1103/97 on certain provisions relating to the introduction of the euro, and Council Regulation (EC) No 974/98 on the introduction of the euro.
[27] An example of such change in the 1990s was the abolition by Brazil of the cruzeihro, and its replacement by the real.

originally undertaken in the old currency. The matter is a question of fact, rather than law. An obligation in a contract to pay an amount expressed in old currency means, at the time when performance falls to be made, that payment must be made in the new currency.[28] In this way, English law permits the contractual obligations to continue, notwithstanding a significant change in the identity of the currency of payment or account: the *meaning* of the obligation changes with the circumstances.

The question which faced financial markets lawyers in the context of EMU was whether this doctrine would be sufficient to overcome problems that might arise in financial contracts, where the currency was not only the means of payment, but was the essence of the contract. For example, in a forward currency contract, the identity of the currencies concerned is the point of the agreement. Several potential difficulties were identified which, on analysis, did not relate to the currency as such, but rather to the economic circumstances surrounding the currency. For example, it was pointed out that commitments undertaken by pension providers throughout the EU were predicated on the basis of long-term interest rates at the time that the commitment was undertaken. If, say, ten years into a 30-year contract period, the currency of account was replaced by the euro, which had a very different interest rate structure, the economic consequences of the contract for the parties could be very different from those which they had contemplated when the contract was made. More obviously, long-term fixed-rate borrowings undertaken in 'old' currency that traditionally had interest rates in excess of the level expected to be commanded by the euro would change dramatically in economic terms. If a borrower was committed to paying interest at, say, 10 per cent per annum on a bond issued in an 'old' currency, it would be disadvantaged if, following the change of currency to the euro, it was obliged to pay interest at the same rate, when euro borrowings might then cost only 3 or 4 per cent per annum.   2.93

In the event, it does not seem that these issues caused any major concern or disruption which needed response from the relevant legal system. The reason is probably that commercial markets were given sufficient notice of the advent of the change to be able to re-organize their affairs so that adverse consequences could be avoided, or hedging strategies put in place.   2.94

There were, however, three situations identified by the financial markets[29] where adverse or unpredictable consequences could flow from the change of the identity of the currency itself: 2.95

1. During the three-year transitional period, the 'old' currency units were to remain in use, although they would now be units of the euro. Many financial contracts, loan agreements, bond issues, and derivatives contracts fixed the amount payable by reference to currency indexes. For example, the interest rate might be expressed to be a percentage above 'three month deutschmark LIBOR'. During the transitional period, although a rate would continue to be quoted which had that designation, it would in fact refer to the cost of borrowing euros, rather than deutschmarks, which would no longer exist as a separate currency.

---

[28] See *Franklin v Westminster Bank*, The Times, 17 July 1931.
[29] See Financial Law Panel, *Economic and Monetary Union: Continuity of Contracts in English Law* (January 1998).

2. In a small number of cases, particularly in the derivatives markets, the disappearance of the national currencies might undermine the commercial rationale of a contract. For example, a long-term forward contract to sell Italian lira against the delivery of French francs would become meaningless, once both currencies had converted to the euro.

3. Particular problems arose in relation to contracts denominated in ECU. The ECU was used not only as the unit of account of the EU itself. It had also become quite common for private entities, particularly in the bond market, to raise debt denominated in ECU. Under the terms of these issues, payment was to be made in one or more of the currencies which constituted the ECU basket, at the market rate then prevailing.[30] The assumption of the Commission was that, on the disappearance of the ECU, all obligations denominated in ECUs would become euro obligations on a one-for-one basis. There was concern in the markets that this would change the economic value of the obligations. The ECU basket was a weighted average of some, but not all, of the EU currencies, and the euro would reflect the value of a slightly different group of EU currencies.[31] An arrangement which changed an obligation to pay one ECU into an obligation to pay one euro might therefore change the economic size of the obligation.

2.96 From the point of view of market stability, the danger was that substantial numbers of contracts would be affected by these issues, and one or other of the parties would seek to argue that performance had been frustrated or otherwise made impossible. Although all legal systems had mechanisms in place to address such a situation, their operation was not easily predictable. The important point, therefore, was to avoid uncertainty. The 1997 Regulation did this in Article 3, by overriding any argument that contracts might have been avoided or terminated by events:

> The introduction of the euro shall not have the effect of altering any terms of a legal instrument or of discharging or excusing performance under any legal instrument, nor give a party the right unilaterally to alter or terminate such an instrument. This provision is subject to anything which parties may have agreed.

As far as the ECU was concerned, parties were simply told to ignore the change in economic value. Article 2 provided:

> Every reference in a legal instrument to the ECU ... shall be replaced by a reference to the euro at a rate of 1 euro to 1 ECU.

2.97 Although the approach involved the use of a very blunt instrument, it was effective. There was enough time between the position being known, and the euro being introduced, to allow the markets to adopt consensus views about the way in which they would deal with the kinds of contracts that might be adversely affected by the change. The fact that no major disruption occurred demonstrates the ability of the markets to adapt to change, provided that the change does not happen unexpectedly.

---

[30] Although there was in addition a small but active clearing system in ECUs, under which certain banks would settle ECU-denominated transactions by the creation or reduction of ECU-denominated balances.
[31] The ECU basket did not include, for example, the Finnish maaka and the euro was unlikely to reflect the value of sterling or the Danish kroner.

2.98 Although the contractual issues arising from the act of introduction of the euro are now matters of history,[32] the status of the euro and the terms on which it was introduced left a number of open questions that complicated the arrangements needed to deal with the financial crisis of 2008.

The open questions

2.99 One might have thought that the EU, when introducing a new currency, would have taken the opportunity to establish its nature and status in legislation. Not only did the Member States fail to do this; the legislation went out of its way to avoid describing the nature of the currency and its basis. The provision which creates the euro is to be found in Article 123.4 of the Treaty of Rome:[33]

> ... the Council shall, acting with the unanimity of the [Participating] Member State ... adopt the conversion rates at which their currencies shall be irrevocably fixed and at which irrevocably fixed rate the ECU[34] shall be substituted for these currencies, and the ECU will become a currency in its own right.

It was accepted that the ECU was not, because of its nature as an index which measured value in terms of currencies, capable of itself being a currency.[35] The euro was a new creation which replaced the ECU as well as relevant national currencies, rather than being a changed version of the ECU. Article 123.4 must be interpreted in the light of this.

2.100 The status of the euro was referred to again in Article 2 of the 1998 Regulation:

> As from 1 January 1999 the currency of the participating Member States shall be the euro. The currency unit shall be 1 euro. 1 euro shall be divided into 100 cent.

This statement is very straightforward and superficially simple. However, it hides a fundamental issue of great political significance. There are, among monetary lawyers, two theories about the nature of money. The 'societal theory' concentrates on the identity of the thing which serves the purposes for which money is used: if a particular society uses an item (or a concept) to fulfil the functions of money, then that thing is money. The competing 'state theory' of money requires that, before something can be described as 'money', it should be established that it is issued by and controlled by a sovereign state.[36]

2.101 The 'state theory' of money, taken to its conclusion, leads to the view that the ownership and control of its own currency is an essential mark of a state's sovereignty. Those in the UK who were opposed to the idea of a single currency on ideological grounds focused their

---

[32] Of course, as new countries accede to the euro and replace their existing currencies, issues could arise, both under the law of the country concerned and under the laws of other countries whose law has been chosen as the governing law of relevant contracts.
[33] As amended by the Maastricht Treaty.
[34] It will be remembered that the word 'ECU' was 'interpreted' to mean 'euro'.
[35] See Financial Law Panel, *The Need for the ECU* (December 1995) and also the comment of M. de Silguy, the Commissioner for Economic & Monetary Affairs, quoted in *The Times* on 27 November 1995: 'It is ... important not to confuse the present basket ECU with the future single currency ... the two are economically very different.'
[36] See, eg, Lord Macmillan's view in the *Banco de Portugal* case that the currency of Portugal represented a share of all the assets of that state.

objection on the view that giving up sterling and adopting a supranational currency necessarily involved ceding the UK's sovereignty. It will readily be seen that this issue would be bound to be one of great sensitivity throughout the EU, and it is suggested that this was the main reason why the question of the nature of the single currency and in particular the fundamental question 'whose currency is it?' was avoided.

2.102 The legislation is cryptic, not only at the conceptual level. When dealing with the physical emanations of the euro (ie notes and coin) the Treaty of Rome (as amended by the Maastricht Treaty) has little to say. Article 105a says:

1. The ECB shall have the exclusive right to authorise the issue of bank notes within the Community. The ECB and the national central banks may issue such notes. The bank notes issued by the ECB and the national central banks shall be the only such notes to have the status of legal tender within the Community.
2. Member States may issue coins subject to approval by the ECB of the volume of the issue . . .

It is easy to see why the Member States would not wish to discuss in detail the question of issue of notes and coins. Although arguments about the 'state theory' of money might attract economists and lawyers, public concern about money inevitably centres on its physical emanations; on the notes and coins in issue. Not only is the national central bank seen as a symbol of national sovereignty; in some Member States (and particularly in Germany) the central bank was regarded as the guardian of financial stability and integrity. Suggestions that the national central banks would simply disappear, to be replaced by an entirely new body, based in another country, would raise difficult political arguments. It was felt to be better to avoid these arguments by leaving the wording of the legislation vague or ambiguous.

2.103 Understandable as it is, the vagueness of the legislation has left unanswered three important questions. The first is, perhaps, political and economic. The remaining two, however, have very obvious implications for financial markets.

Question 1: Whose currency is it?

2.104 It is fundamental to the identity of the euro that it should be a 'single' currency. In other words, the same underlying concept should apply in each of the Member States which adopts the euro as its currency. The euro, as far as the law of Greece is concerned, should be exactly the same as a euro, so far as the law of France is concerned. If, as the 'state theory' of money dictates, money is in essence an obligation of a sovereign entity, one must be able to identify the sovereign concerned.

2.105 It is very hard to identify a satisfactory candidate for the role. Clearly, one must rule out the possibility that each of the Participating Member States is alone the sovereign, in relation to the euros circulating in its territory. If this were the case, then a French euro would be different from a Spanish euro and an Irish euro. In the case of a single currency, this cannot be.

2.106 It is tempting to think that the European Central Bank might itself be the sovereign issuer. This does not, however, bear examination. The ECB is created specifically by legislation to fulfil the function of a central bank. Its role is to decide and implement a monetary policy, to issue bank notes like any other central bank, and to control the issue by others. Like any other central bank, it is an agency of the sovereign whose currency it administers. It cannot be the sovereign itself. Moreover, Article 105a of the Treaty of Rome gives the ECB no power to issue euro coins. It merely has the right to approve the volume of issue of such coins by Participating Member States.[37]

2.107 A third candidate might be the European Union itself. Conceptually, all euros in existence would be a claim on all Member States of the EU in much the same way as one might describe the United States dollar as a claim on all of the states of the Union. Unfortunately, this argument does not hold. If it were the case that the European Union was the sovereign, whose money the euro was, it would necessarily follow that the euro conceptually represented a liability for those countries who have not yet adopted it, and who instead maintain their own currency, which itself represents the country's obligations.

2.108 The only solution which accords with the facts is that the euro represents the collective obligation of the Participating Member States. Anti-federalists will no doubt take such a conclusion to mean that the Participating Member States have each surrendered their sovereignty, or at least exchanged individual sovereignty for collective sovereignty as far as their money is concerned. The implications of this analysis for a wider political view of the European Union depend very much on the observer.

2.109 An alternative approach to the question 'Whose currency is it' is to say that the Participating Member States have not ceded any political sovereignty by adopting the euro. The search for a sovereign who is conceptually liable in relation to the currency issued in his name is an illusion. All that matters is that there should be a mechanism for accounting, for storing, and for transferring value which has the confidence of the population; what it is, as a matter of intellectual concept, is irrelevant. In other words, one can argue that the 'state theory' of money is wrong, and that the 'societal theory' is correct; all that one needs to do is to establish that the identified monetary entity fulfils certain uses and commands confidence. This view, however, does not help to explain the status of euro coins (see para 2.115 below).

Question 2: Who issues euro notes and coins?

2.110 As far as bank notes are concerned, the position is deceptively simple. Article 105a of the Treaty of Rome (as amended) says:

1. The ECB shall have the exclusive right to authorize the issue of bank notes within the Community. The ECB and the national central banks may issue such notes.

Ambiguity arises because of the use of the word 'issue'. In relation to bank notes, it could refer to the act of making the bank note, and thereby assuming liability as drawer in respect of it, or it could refer simply to the ministerial act of putting a bank note into circulation.

---

[37] See paras 2.115 and 2.116 below.

2.111 When the euro was introduced, there was political pressure in a number of Member States for the government to reassure the local population that their central bank would continue to 'issue' currency notes and that the euro notes put into circulation would be as sound and dependable as the former national currency notes. The wording of Article 105a allowed such statements to be made. However, it is quite clear that, if the currency was to be a single currency, and that one euro unit was to have exactly the same status as every other euro unit, the physical emanation of the euro, in the form of bank notes, must all be identical in legal terms. If it were the case that a euro bank note 'issued' by the Banque de France was the obligation of that institution, and a euro note issued by the Bundesbank was the obligation only of that bank, the two notes would not represent the same obligation. They would represent obligations undertaken by different legal entities.

2.112 In physical form, all euro notes are the same. They bear the initials of the ECB and the signature of the ECB's President. In legal form, they are the promissory note of the European Central Bank.[38] The notes are 'issued' by the national central banks only in the sense that those institutions arrange the mechanics of printing the notes and of distributing them through the commercial banking systems in their own countries. The liability on the promise contained in the notes is that of the European Central Bank.

2.113 While this is interesting, from the point of view of monetary law, it also has practical significance. The Banque Nationale de Belgique, the Belgian central bank, is a public company, the majority of whose shares are owned by the Belgian state. Under the terms of its constitution, its reserves are not capable of being paid out to shareholders so long as it remains the 'issuer' of Belgian currency. Following the introduction of the euro, a group of minority shareholders brought proceedings on the basis that the central bank was no longer the issuer of the currency within the meaning of its constitution. Since it had no liability on the notes which it put into issue, it had no need for reserves against that liability. Those reserves could therefore be released to shareholders as dividends.

2.114 In July 2013, the Belgian Cour de Cassation ruled against the shareholders. The decision, of course, turns on a matter of interpretation of the central bank's statutes, which is itself a matter of Belgian law. However, the 11-year dispute illustrates the problems caused by the ambiguity in the Maastricht Treaty.

2.115 As far as coins are concerned, Article 105a of the Treaty of Rome (as amended) provides that euro coins may be issued by Member States. No other issuer is contemplated. The ECB has no power to issue coin or to direct its issue. Its only power is to approve or disapprove the amount that any particular state proposes to issue. In practice, euro coins bear the name of the individual state which put them in issue. They are, of course, fungible. They are all tokens that represent the same currency. The identity of the country which originally minted the coin makes no difference to the holder.

2.116 This structure conforms with the traditional arrangements for the issue of a national currency: the coin is issued by the sovereign power as its coin, while notes are issued by a separate entity (the central bank) as its own promissory notes backed by assets provided by the state. In the case of the euro, the unanswered question is the identity of the sovereign which issues

---

[38] See the explanation of Lord Atkin in the *Banco de Portugal* case [1934] AC 452, at 487.

euro coins and whose agent (the ECB) issues euro notes. The discussion of the issue of notes in para 2.112 above left open the possibility that there might be no sovereign issuer of euro notes; that one need look no further than the ECB, as maker of the notes. Such a view of the nature of the euro does not accommodate the position of euro coins. The identity of the Participating Member State which issued a particular coin is not relevant to the value of that coin or to its acceptability as currency in circulation. The coin does not represent the money of the state concerned. Nor does it represent the obligation of the ECB. But it must represent something; otherwise it is merely a piece of metal. It is suggested that the only analysis which matches the facts is that all coins represent the money (ie the obligation) of Participating Member States, acting collectively.

Question 3: Where do payments in euros settle?

As will be seen in Chapter 3,[39] the question when (or whether) a payment has been completed depends on the mechanics of the settlement process for the currency concerned. The settlement arrangements for the euro are complex, and consideration lies outside the scope of this chapter. For most practical purposes, the situation is put beyond doubt by legislation.[40] However, there may be circumstances where it is important to know the location in which settlement takes place, rather than where it is deemed by legislation to have occurred. An example, in the case of the euro, might be a situation where regulations made in Germany prohibited the transfer of money to the credit of particular individuals, or nationals of a country that is outside the EU. The ECB is based in Germany, although it is not part of the German government or a German national. There is a rule of English law[41] that the performance of a contract will be excused, if that performance necessarily involves the doing, in a foreign country, of an act, the performance of which is unlawful by the law of that state. If a contract governed by English law stipulated that payment was to be made in euros to a national of the embargoed state, it would be essential to know whether, as a matter of law, a payment of euros through the banking system must necessarily settle on the books of the ECB in Frankfurt (where the payment would be caught by the German freeze regulations), or might settle when the payment was reflected in the books of a national central bank located elsewhere. Discussion of this question is outside the scope of this chapter, but it is addressed in Chapter 3, paras 3.33 to 3.40.

2.117

The crisis of 2008

In 2008, most Western countries, including almost all EU Member States, underwent a financial crisis. In some cases, this resulted from excessive government borrowing. In other cases, private sector banks had lent unwisely, acquiring as cover assets that turned out to be worth much less than the value of the loans they supported. At the onset of the crisis,

2.118

---

[39] Chapter 3, paras 3.30 to 3.36.
[40] See in particular the Settlement Finality Directive 98/26 (EC) and, in the UK, the Financial Markets and Insolvency (Settlement) Finality Regulations 1999.
[41] *Ralli Bros v Compagnia Naviera Sola y Aznar* [1920] 2 KB 287.

commercial banks were forced to write down the value of their assets. In many cases, the losses were great enough to threaten insolvency. Governments had to step in, lending huge sums in support of the banks' balance sheets. To fund this support, the governments themselves incurred debts that their taxpayers will repay over many years.

2.119 This is clearly a major issue for each of the Member States affected. However, in the case of the eurozone, the crisis has had a novel impact. It is widely said that the problems of each eurozone Member State infect all other eurozone members. By extension, the problems of the eurozone Member States become the problems 'of the euro'.

2.120 The question at the heart of the issue was said to be whether the stronger eurozone countries would decide to support the borrowing obligations of the weaker. If such support was to be given, there were two obvious mechanisms through which it could be delivered. First, the ECB might buy the euro-denominated debt of the endangered states in return for newly-created euros. At the maturity of the debt so purchased, the face value of the debt instrument would become a euro debt owing by the state concerned to its own central bank (the ECB). At this point, the problem becomes one not of default, but of accounting between the eurozone Member States, to be adjusted through the books of the ECB.

2.121 The second method of support would be for the stronger eurozone Member States to lend euros to the troubled ones to fund repayment of the latter's maturing debt.

2.122 The issue engendered long and loud debate. The establishment of support mechanisms was resisted strongly in some of the eurozone Member States. The uncertainty about whether the eurozone would or would not adopt the measures necessary to support the troubled Member States contributed to the crisis and to the economic difficulties of the eurozone. In the event, both of the support methods referred to in paras 2.120 and 2.121 above were adopted. The first mechanism was the authorization of debt purchase by the ECB (the 'OMT' programme).[42]

2.123 The second mechanism was created in the form of the European Stability Mechanism (the 'ESM').[43] The ESM is a body that is administratively separate from the EU Commission.[44] The eurozone Member States have committed capital of 702bn euros, of which 80bn euros have been paid in. It has the capacity to lend up to 500bn euros, which it obtains by borrowing in the markets.

2.124 The form taken by the two mechanisms gives the impression that each of the eurozone Member States has limited the amount of its support – to its pro rata share of the committed capital of the ECB, in the case of the OMT programme, and to its pro rata share of the callable capital of the ESM, in the latter case. In reality, it is hard to see that there is any such limit. In the case of the OMT programme, if the ECB held a very large amount of the euro debt of a troubled eurozone Member State, and that state defaulted in payment, the result might be a deficit on the ECB's own balance sheet. The eurozone Member States would

---

[42] Decision of the Governing Council of the European Central Bank of 6 September 2012 on Technical Features of Outright Monetary Transactions.
[43] Established by treaty between the eurozone Member States signed on 12 February 2012. The ESM supersedes the earlier European Financial Stabilisation Mechanism, under which loan assistance to Ireland and Portugal was disbursed.
[44] It is described on its own website as an 'intergovernmental institution under public international law'.

in practice have no alternative but to fund the deficit, whether or not this took individual Member States beyond the limit of their capital commitments. The statement that the ECB would 'do whatever it takes' to prevent a default by a eurozone Member State is, in practice, saying that each eurozone Member State will do the same.

The same is true of the ESM. Although its constitution places a limit on the amount of capital committed by each eurozone Member State, in reality each such state is bound to provide whatever is needed to keep the ESM solvent. It is interesting to note that the EU Commission's website, when describing the European Financial Stabilisation Mechanism, which operates through the agency of the Commission itself, says:

2.125

> Under EFSM, the Commission is allowed to borrow up to a total of 60bn euros in financial markets on behalf of the Union under an implicit EU budget guarantee.

In the case of the ESM, it is hard to see that its market activities are not also conducted 'under an implicit guarantee' of the eurozone Member States.

The practical effect of the mechanisms is that each of the eurozone Member States guarantees to external lenders (although not to other such states) repayment of the euro-denominated debts of all other eurozone Member States. This is not surprising. It is inherent in their decision to issue the same currency. The decision at the time of the Maastricht Treaty to leave unanswered the three questions posed in paras 2.104 to 2.117 above has proved unhelpful. The drawn-out process of negotiating and drafting the 'solutions' to the problems caused by the crisis of 2008 could have been avoided if it had been made clear that the solution was itself part of the structure and identity of the euro.

2.126

Cryptoassets

The world of cryptoassets[45] was created in October 2008. A paper was published, under the name of Satoshi Nakamoto,[46] entitled *Bitcoin: A Peer-to-Peer Electronic Cash System*. The paper described the creation and operation of Bitcoin, which was claimed to be a new form of digital electronic money. A central feature of Bitcoin was that the individual units were to come into existence as a result of the operation of mathematical formulae, rather than as the result of a declaration (the 'fiat') of a government or central bank. The units would not represent obligations of any government.[47]

2.127

Movements of Bitcoins and their ownership would be recorded, not in the books of a bank or government agency, but in an accumulating history of transactions called a 'blockchain'.

2.128

---

[45] 'Cryptoassets' is a term that is now widely used instead of 'cryptocurrency' or 'virtual currency'. It is slightly wider in meaning than those terms, since it includes other concepts, in addition to the 'digital cash' which was the original intention. These wider concepts are discussed below in this chapter at paras 2.178 *et seq*.

[46] Satoshi Nakamoto has not been identified. There is even doubt about whether he or she is a single person or a group of people working together.

[47] Nor, indeed, of anyone else. According to an important announcement made on 8 June 2017 by Bitcoin.com:

> Bitcoins exist as records of Bitcoin Transactions ... There are no physical bitcoins anywhere – not on a hard-drive, or a spreadsheet, or a bank account, and not even a server somewhere.

The original Nakamoto White Paper said:

> We define [Bitcoin] as a chain of digital signatures ...

36 MONEY

Each new activity would be checked, to verify that it had been properly made. A number of transactions would be dealt with at the same time. The transactions so verified would then be added as a 'block' to the 'chain' that recorded all previous activity involving the same Bitcoin. The digital record of the blockchain would be held in identical form on each of a large number of separate computers around the world, owned by participants in the system. The transfer of a Bitcoin would be effected by the transferor adding to the relevant block a message moving the Bitcoin to the digital address of the transferee. The participants in the system, who all held the history of the Bitcoin concerned on their computers (because the history was part of the blockchain), would confirm the action. The blockchain would then be altered to incorporate the new transfer. The fact that the information given by the digital message between the parties had been accepted and recorded by numerous other participants made it as secure, at least, as a transaction that was confirmed by a central registry.

2.129 This Distributed Ledger Technology ('DLT')[48] was the innovation that gave Bitcoin its unique characteristic: it enabled the transfer of Bitcoins outside the payment structures operated and controlled by commercial banks, central banks, and governments. If users so wished, they could operate with almost complete anonymity. It appealed to libertarians. It also appealed to money-launderers and others who wished to operate away from the gaze of regulators and government agencies.

2.130 In the decade since Nakamoto's paper introduced Bitcoin, more than 4,000 other systems of cryptocurrency and other cryptoassets have been created. Because of the anonymity that lies at the heart of the systems, it is not possible to say with any certainty how widespread is the use of cryptocurrencies in trade or payment systems. However, it seems clear that the economic importance of cryptocurrencies lies in their use as a medium of investment. Investors exchange fiat currency for cryptocurrency in the hope that the latter will appreciate in value, and they will be able to sell their holding for more fiat money than they spent on the acquisition.

2.131 This section examines the legal nature of cryptoassets and their potential uses and limitations in international finance. DLT, on which dealings in cryptoassets depend, has potential uses outside the world of cryptoassets, and is discussed in Chapter 3.

The language used in the crypto world

2.132 Over 2,000 years ago, Confucius gave advice to those in government, on being asked what he would do if required to run the country:

> Correct the language. If language is not correct then what is said is not what is meant and what ought to be done remains undone; morals and the arts will deteriorate; justice will go astray; and the people will stand about in helpless confusion.[49]

2.133 The language used to describe a thing often shapes the way in which the thing is understood. The promoters of the crypto world have chosen to describe its processes and transactions

---
[48] DLT is discussed in more detail in Chapter 3.
[49] *The Analects of Confucius.*

by using terms and names that are taken directly from the world of money. The effect is to create the assumption that the world of cryptoassets is analogous to the real world of money; that the concept in the crypto world which is under discussion is, perhaps, a variation of something in the real world which is very familiar. The crypto concept thus seems credible and understandable.

The use of names and terms from the field of money and banking, in particular 'currency', 'own', 'hold', 'transfer', 'wallet', and 'coin', have the effect of pre-empting analysis of the process or concept involved. How can it be doubted that something is a currency, when it is called 'cryptocurrency'? **2.134**

For this reason, in examining the legal nature of cryptoassets and of dealings in them, this chapter tries to avoid the use of money-analogous language. Where this is inconvenient, the misleading word is used between inverted commas. The exception is the word 'cryptocurrency' itself. Its use without any qualification should not be taken as an acceptance that the concept to which it relates is a form of currency. **2.135**

The operation of a cryptosystem

The following paragraphs describe the operation of a system for the creation, maintenance, and operation of a cryptocurrency. The aim is to highlight those aspects that raise questions about the legal nature of the system. The description is necessarily simplified. It is based on the model of Bitcoin, but is applicable to many other cryptosystems. **2.136**

If an individual, A, wishes to participate in the cryptosystem, he or she must establish an address on the system. The word 'address'[50] does not denote a place, but only a unique digital identifier. Each address on the system has a randomly assigned 'private key' that is uniquely associated with it. A selects his address by choosing a private key and computing the corresponding address. This is an easy task to perform. However it is, in practice, impossible to carry out the computation in reverse (ie to compute the private key when only the corresponding address is known). It is safe for A to disclose his address to others without fear that they might be able to work out his private key. **2.137**

Once he has an address, A may receive 'Inputs', digital messages sent by other participants that refer to a specified amount of the cryptocurrency. Receipt of an Input puts A in a position to make an 'Output'. He may himself send a message to B using his own private key.[51] That message indicates in turn that B has received an Input corresponding to A's Output. The cryptosystem will permit the Input and Output messages to be made only if there is an independent verification that: **2.138**

(i) A has, in the past, received Inputs that are at least as great in amount as the Output that he wishes to make to B's address; and

---

[50] The phrase 'public key' is often used to mean the same thing as 'address'.
[51] No Output can be made without the private key associated with the address. If A loses his record of his private key, he will not be able to make any further Outputs in respect of Inputs received at his address. There have been press reports of instances when individuals lost a laptop on which the only record of their private keys was stored. The cryptocurrency associated with their address were no longer available. On the other hand, if a record of the private key were stolen, the thief might be able to make an Output, thereby 'stealing' the cryptocurrency concerned.

38 MONEY

(ii) A has not made Outputs (including the Output that he proposes to make in favour of B) in a greater amount than the Inputs that he has received.

A must have a surplus of Input messages to his address before an Output to B's address will be accepted.[52]

2.139 This process of verification is carried out through the operation of a 'Distributed Ledger'. The first element in the verification process is that the transaction (ie the Output by A and the corresponding Input to B) is recorded on the system by being added, as part of a 'block' of data to the record of the series of transactions that resulted in A receiving the Input on which his Output is based. The transaction thus becomes part of the chain of transactions that records the history of the message concerned and its passage around the cryptosystem. A's message has a 'chain-of-title' associated with it. This chain shows A's capacity, under the rules of the system, to transmit the message to B. It contains a record of A's receipt of the message and shows the Output to B in respect of the same message. Thereafter, A cannot make another Output in respect of the same Input received by him. He cannot use any Input more than once.

2.140 The second key feature of the Distributed Ledger system is that the record of the Output/Input between A and B is not held on a central register maintained by a trusted third party. Rather, the record, in the form of the chain-of-title blocks, is available to all system participants.

2.141 In order that the record constituted by the block of data held by all participants should be accurate and complete, some participants, known as 'nodes', also take part in the verification process. Each Output by A is broadcast to all system participants. The nodes try to compute the answer to a complex mathematical question. The question is associated with a group of transactions (a 'block') that is waiting to be confirmed. Answering the question will automatically confirm the validity of the transactions which constitute the block. When one of the nodes answers the question, the Output/Input transactions in the block are added to the chain and thereafter form part of the record held by all participants.

2.142 The computing power needed to solve each of these validation problems is vast. It is very expensive to be a node, and participants take on the task only because the cryptosystem rewards the node that wins the race to solve the puzzle (and incidentally to verify the transactions on the data-block concerned) by generating an Input in his favour. Such an Input is not received by the successful node as a consequence of an Output by another participant. It is the creation of the cryptosystem. It has the effect of increasing the number of cryptocurrency units that are available to be transmitted, without requiring anything to be added to the pool of cryptocurrency.[53]

2.143 Many of those who wish to participate in the cryptosystem as investors do not want to take an active part in managing their operations on the system. There has grown up a body of participants who provide services as exchanges who will make Outputs to a user in return

---

[52] In the language of the cryptoworld, A cannot 'spend' more 'currency' than he has 'received'.
[53] The units of cryptocurrency do not represent any property or the obligation of any issuer. Their creation, therefore, does not involve anyone putting value into the system to 'back' the issue.

for the payment of money (ie fiat money), or will pay money to the user against receipt by the exchange of an Input from the user.

Other participants act as so-called 'wallet-holders' on behalf of system users. The customer entrusts to the 'wallet-holder' his system address and private key and appoints him to receive Inputs for him and, on his instructions, to generate Outputs. The danger in this is obvious. The (almost) inevitable disaster came to pass in 2018, when Gerald Cotton,[54] the Canadian controller of QuadrigaCX, a 'cold wallet-holding'[55] company, was reported to have died in India. No-one else, it seemed, knew where he kept the private keys of the customers. Without the private keys, no-one could make Outputs from the customers' addresses.[56]

2.144

A strange phenomenon in the world of cryptocurrencies is the process of 'forking'. This happens when a consensus develops among some (but not all) of the participants that a change should be made to the rules that govern the validation of transactions. From then on, transactions that follow the 'old' rules will not be recognized by nodes that have accepted the 'new' rules. On the other hand, nodes that have chosen to stay with the old rules will not recognize transactions that follow the new rules.[57]

2.145

Because a recognized transaction becomes part of the Distributed Ledger, a transaction that has been accepted by the old protocol, but not by the new, cannot thereafter be the subject of an Output that uses the new rules. The converse also applies. The cryptosystem thus splits in two, creating two distinct steams of transactions or, as it is often described, creating two separate cryptocurrencies. Each participant who 'holds' units at the time of the fork will thereafter be recorded as the 'holder' of units of both new cryptocurrencies. The number of units attributed to him will be, in the case of both new cryptocurrencies, the number that he 'held' in the original cryptocurrency.

2.146

There have been many forks in cryptoasset systems. The best-known are the split in June 2016, when Ethereum forked to become Ethereum and Ethereum Classic, and that on 4 August 2017 when Bitcoin forked to become Bitcoin Core and Bitcoin Cash.[58]

2.147

The legal nature of cryptoassets

In considering the nature of cryptoassets, it is important to separate the thing under consideration (the cryptocurrency or other cryptoasset itself) from the way in which it is evidenced and through which it is transferred. The platform on which cryptoassets are recorded is based on DLT. In the case of Bitcoin, the variant of DLT used is called Blockchain. The significance of DLT for financial markets is discussed below.[59] For present purposes it is enough to note that a DLT platform can be used to record the existence and history of any

2.148

---

[54] Sometimes rendered as 'Cotten'.
[55] This term describes an arrangement in which the service provider retains the details of clients' passwords on a computer that is not connected to the internet.
[56] Reported in The Financial Times, 7 February 2019.
[57] This paragraph describes a 'hard fork'. There are sometimes 'soft forks', where the protocols after the fork will recognize transactions on both forks.
[58] Confusingly, Bitcoin Core is now often called simply 'Bitcoin'.
[59] See Chapter 3.

kind of asset. The information on it, like the entries on a manually kept register, can refer to things in many different classes.

2.149 In the case of cryptoassets, the systems on which they are recorded and on which they move refer to (i) cryptocurrencies which, it is claimed, can be used as money. Some proponents claim that they *are* money; and (ii) securities that exist only in digital form and which have been created to be transferable only on the DLT platform concerned. The analysis below deals only with systems that relate to cryptocurrencies.

2.150 The first question that must be answered is:

What is the nature of a unit of the cryptocurrency under consideration?

The answer is needed before it can be decided how (or whether) the unit can be transferred, used in commerce as security, or used as a payment medium. The answer also affects the tax treatment of dealings that employ the unit and other public law interactions with the unit. For example, is it possible to steal a unit of cryptocurrency?

2.151 Paras 2.138 to 2.141 describe a hypothetical transaction between two people, A and B. The nature of the cryptocurrency in which they deal can be considered by reference to that transaction. Before the transaction takes place, A has received an Input in the form of a message from a third party. This message amends the digital record relating to a particular unit of cryptocurrency. The record now shows that A has received the message and is thereby empowered (provided that he remembers the digital code that is his private key) to send a similar message to B. Such a message will amend the record relating to the unit to record the transmission to B's system address and will enable B, in turn, to send has own message. A will no longer be able to make an Output that refers to the unit concerned.

2.152 In the terms normally used, it is said that A 'acquired' (or 'was paid') a unit of cryptocurrency. He then became the 'owner' of the unit and subsequently 'transferred it' to B. However, this language is misleading. Before something can properly be 'held' or 'owned', 'acquired', or 'transferred' it must be recognized as property.

2.153 Whether a unit of cryptocurrency would be recognized at law as property is a surprisingly complex question. The first point to make is that cryptocurrencies, as described in this chapter, should not be confused with 'stablecoins'. A 'stablecoin' is a digital representation of value that is issued by a corporate entity, and 'backed' by fiat currency held by that entity.[60] The value of the 'stablecoin' is tied to that of the reference fiat currency, usually by a provision that a unit of the 'stablecoin' may be redeemed by payment of a unit of the 'backing' currency. In law, the 'stablecoin' is a *chose in action*, a debt obligation of the issuer. The fact that the 'stablecoin' is transferred through a DLT system does not make it, by nature, a cryptocurrency.

2.154 Second, although there are cases that provide help in determining the legal nature of cryptocurrency, they must be approached with caution. Courts are not usually asked to consider highly technical issues in an academic vacuum. There is often a practical consequence to the answer that helps shape the court's approach. The importance of the context

---

[60] 'Stablecoin' is not a term of art, and the structure may vary from one 'stablecoin' to another. The description given here is a generalization only.

can be seen in the House of Lords' decision in *R v Preddy*,[61] where a very technical analysis of the process for transmission of money electronically was adopted. The case involved a criminal charge of theft. If convicted, the defendant would have faced a long prison sentence. If the context of the case had instead been, for example, a claim by the constructor of an elaborate tax-saving scheme to rely on an exemption in a taxing statute, where his eligibility depended on the fact that money had not moved from one account to another, the court might not have been so ready to take such a technical view of the transaction.

2.155 In the US there have been a number of cases in which individuals have been charged with money laundering offences involving cryptocurrency. In most cases, the court did not need to consider the legal nature of the cryptocurrency concerned, because the legislation concerned focused on the activity that was undertaken, rather than the asset involved. However, in one case[62] the judge at first instance considered the nature of a Bitcoin. In describing the process of 'mining', by which Bitcoins are created, she said succinctly:

> Bitcoins are bits of data that the miner receives in exchange for the use of their computer processor.

2.156 This view is not controversial. The *Bitcoin Whitepaper* published by Satoshi Nakamoto in October 2008 says:

> We define [Bitcoin] as a chain of digital signatures.

The explanation of the working of Bitcoin which is given on the website of Bitcoin.org, an organization established at the time of Bitcoin's creation, includes:

> There are no physical bitcoins anywhere—not on a hard-drive, or a spreadsheet, or a bank account, and not even a server somewhere.

2.157 The bits of data created in the 'mining' process are pure information. The data refers to nothing other than itself. It says merely 'This is a Bitcoin'. It confers no right on its 'holder' and does not imply that the 'holder' has any right. This contrasts with an entry on a bank statement, which records the fact that the bank owes an amount of money to the customer, or that he owes a debt to the bank. The rights and obligations of bank and customer are embodied in the *chose in action* to which the account record refers (the debt owing between the bank and the customer). The account record is, in itself, no more than evidence of the existence of the debt.

2.158 In the case of cryptocurrency, its value to the address-holder is not found in the debt to which the record refers (because it does not make any such reference), nor in any other claim or asset. The value lies only in the fact that a third party might be prepared to pay the address-holder (in fiat money or in kind) to make an Output in his favour.

2.159 A number of cases in England have considered the legal nature of complex intangible assets. None of the cases concerned cryptocurrency, but they show the courts' view of assets that, in some respects, resemble cryptocurrency. A later chapter discusses the division made by English law of property into real property, *choses in possession* and *choses in*

---

[61] [1996] AC 815 and see paras 2.05 *et seq.*
[62] *The State of Florida v Michell Almer Espinoza* (Fla. 11th Ct. 2016) Case No. F14-2923.

action.[63] However, there exists the possibility that this classification system might not be comprehensive; that there might exist something which is property, but which does not fall within any of the categories that together comprise all property. A clear example is a patent. By statute[64] a patent is declared to be an item of personal property, but excluded from the class of *choses in action,* the only class of personal property in which it could fit:

> Any patent or application for a patent is personal property (without being a thing in action).

It is possible, therefore, that a unit of cryptocurrency might be property, and capable of being owned, even though it neither embodies nor represents a right capable of enforcement or protection.

Is a unit of cryptocurrency property?

2.160   The first case to consider, when looking for the rules that determine whether a right or interest can be properly described as 'property' or 'proprietorial', is the House of Lords decision in *National Provincial Bank v Ainsworth.*[65] The point at issue was whether the rights of a deserted wife to occupy her husband's house were property rights (ie whether they operated to give the wife a property interest in the house itself), or were personal (ie were exercisable only against the husband who owned the house). Lord Wilberforce said:

> Before a right or an interest can be admitted into the category of property, or of a right affecting property, it must be definable, identifiable by third parties, capable in its nature of assumption by third parties, and have some degree of permanence or stability.

2.161   It has been said that, because units of cryptocurrency might be said to satisfy this test, the *National Provincial Bank* case supports the argument that cryptocurrencies are property, as a matter of law. However, it must be remembered that Lord Wilberforce was addressing the nature of the wife's interest in the husband's house. There was no doubt that the house was property; the point was whether the wife's rights in respect of it were purely personal, or whether they gave her property rights in respect of the house. The case may be helpful in deciding whether a holder's rights in respect of cryptocurrency units received by way of an Input at his address are proprietary in nature. It does not help in deciding whether the cryptocurrency units are themselves property.

2.162   As argued in paras 2.155 to 2.158 above, units of cryptocurrency consist only of information. That information does not refer to anything else. The digital record, which shows that the unit exists at the stated address, does not imply or describe any right or claim of the person who controls the activity at that address through the use of the private key associated with the address. The digital record constitutes the cryptocurrency unit, and is no more than information.

---

[63] See paras 5.04 to 5.24.
[64] Patents Act 1977 s 30(1)
[65] [1965] AC 1175.

It has long been settled in English law that pure information is not property. In *OBG Limited v Allan*[66] Lord Walker, when discussing the information contained in a photograph, said: **2.163**

> information ... cannot properly be regarded as a form of property.[67]

The point is illustrated most clearly in *Oxford v Moss*.[68] A student at Liverpool University acquired a proof copy of a paper for an examination that he was about to sit. It was accepted that he had no intention to steal the proof paper, but only to read it before returning it. He was charged with the theft of an item of intangible property (ie the information recorded on the paper). The stipendiary magistrate in Liverpool took the view that the information in the paper, as opposed to the paper itself, was not property. It was not capable of being stolen, within the terms of the Theft Act 1968. He acquitted the defendant. **2.164**

On appeal, the Divisional Court was robust. Smith J said: **2.165**

> ... we have to consider whether there is property in the information which is capable of being the subject of a charge of theft. In my judgement, it is clear that the answer must be no.

The other judge, Wein J, went further: **2.166**

> ... the right to confidential information is not intangible property within the meaning of section 4(1) of the Theft Act 1968.[69]

The information was not property. Further, the University's right in respect of that information was not property either.

In *Your Response Ltd v Datateam Business Media Ltd*[70] the Court of Appeal considered a dispute between a magazine publisher and the contractor which maintained the database of the magazines' subscribers. The dispute between them led to the publisher terminating their contract. The contractor, among other things, claimed to exercise a lien over the database until the outstanding invoices were paid. One of the questions to be answered concerned the legal nature of the database, held by the contractor in digital form on its computers. Was the database property, and, if it was property, was its nature such that it could be the subject of a possessory lien?[71] **2.167**

Moore-Bick LJ doubted whether information of the kind that constituted a database could be 'possessed': **2.168**

> Indeed, I do not think that the concept of possession in the hitherto accepted sense has any meaning in relation to intangible property.

> In addition, there are indications elsewhere that information of the kind that makes up a database (usually, but not necessarily, maintained in electronic form), if it constitutes property at all, does not constitute property of a kind that is susceptible of possession ...

---

[66] [2008] 1 AC 1.
[67] At para 275.
[68] [1979]Crim LR 119.
[69] '(1) "Property" includes money and all other property, real or personal, including things in action and other intangible property.'
[70] [2015] 1 QB 41; [2014] EWCA Civ 281.
[71] As to the nature of a lien and its effect see paras 10.65 to 10.68 below.

He addressed directly the argument that a database was a form of intangible property different from a *chose in action*. He rejected the argument, holding that the decision in *Colonial Bank v Whinney*:[72]

> ... makes it very difficult to accept that the common law recognizes the existence of intangible property other than *choses in action* (apart from patents, which are subject to statutory classification) ...

2.169 Floyd LJ dealt with the same argument:

> An electronic database consists of structured information. Although information may give rise to intellectual property rights such as database rights and copyright, the law has been reluctant to treat information itself as property. When information is created and recorded there are sharp distinctions between the information itself, the physical medium on which the information is recorded and the rights to which the information gives rise. Whilst the physical medium and the rights are treated as property, the information itself has never been.

2.170 On the basis of English law as it now stands, it seems likely that the courts would take the view that units of cryptocurrency are not property.

What happens when cryptocurrency is traded?

2.171 It is common to see references to cryptocurrency units being 'sold', 'bought', 'owned', 'held', or 'traded', as if they were items of property. If the analysis above is correct and units of cryptocurrency are not items of property, the language used is misleading. Such linguistic inaccuracy might well have dismayed Confucius,[73] but financial lawyers are not wrong-footed.[74] They are used to language that, at a technical level, gives a misleading impression.

2.172 The 'holder' of an amount of cryptocurrency has an address on the cryptosystem and a private key that identifies that address to the system. When he receives an Input, a message arrives at his address that alters the distributed database to record the information that his address is now associated with the item of cryptocurrency concerned. That message does not give the 'holder' any rights of property or any claim against any other person. The only thing that the receipt gives him is the ability to make an Output in favour of a different address. Such an Output will alter the database, so far as the relevant units of cryptocurrency are concerned, to show their link to the new address, in place of his own address.

2.173 The 'holder' hopes that a third party will be prepared to pay him, either with money or with the transfer of goods, to make this kind of Output. Then, instead of describing accurately what has happened, the 'holder' will probably say that he has 'sold' or 'transferred' the units concerned.

---

[72] (1886) 11 App Cas 426 and see paras 5.04 to 5.09 below.
[73] See para 2.132.
[74] For example, the market practice of 'stock lending' does not involve a loan, but rather an absolute transfer of ownership, with an agreement to transfer in the opposite direction at a future date stock of the same type and amount, and a 'pledge' of stock usually describes a transaction that is, in law, a charge.

In what other ways may a holder deal with his cryptocurrency?

2.174 If cryptocurrency is not property, it follows that it is not possible to deal with it as property. In particular, it is not possible to give to a third party a property interest in it, by creating a charge over it, or by declaring a trust in respect of it.

2.175 This is not to say that a holder of cryptocurrency cannot deal with his holding in a way that reflects its economic value. That value lies in the holder's ability to make an Output. He has a piece of information, his private key, that is the only thing which allows the digital record to be amended, so as to pass economic value to a third party. The value of his cryptocurrency to him lies in his knowledge of his private key.

2.176 For the same reason that the cryptocurrency is not property (because it consists only of information), knowledge of the code that constitutes a key cannot be classified as property. Thus, for example, if a holder entrusts his key to a 'wallet-holder', it is hard to build an argument that the 'wallet-holder' is a trustee of the key, any more than it could be claimed that he was the trustee of the cryptocurrency that the key controls. That does not mean that, if the trusted third party misbehaved by losing the key or by using it to make an unauthorized Output, the person who had entrusted the key to the 'wallet-holder' would have no claim to legal redress against him. There would almost certainly be claims under the terms of the contract between the parties. There might well be claims framed in restitution, quasi-contract or tort. But there could be no claim based directly on ownership of, or a property interest in, the cryptocurrency or the key.[75]

2.177 The nature of cryptocurrencies and the law's reluctance to recognize them as property must severely limit their economic uses, and make them less useful as assets in the financial markets than they would otherwise be. One might speculate that this is one of the reasons for the relaxed view that many governments and regulators have taken to cryptocurrencies. Their nature is such that they are unlikely to find a use in the mainstream financial system. The defects that are inherent in them will not infect that system.

Cryptoassets other than cryptocurrencies

2.178 The Cryptoassets Taskforce[76] in its final Report of October 2018 defined cryptoassets as:

> … a cryptographically secured digital representation of value or contractual rights that uses some type of DLT and can be transferred, stored or traded electronically.

This definition includes cryptocurrencies[77] and 'stablecoins'. It also includes many other things that do not claim to be currency or money-substitutes. These other things are called 'cryptosecurities' below.

---

[75] See the *Your Response* case, where one of the points in issue was whether it is possible, in relation to a database, to commit a tort which depends on the concept of possession (eg conversion).
[76] A working Group established by the UK Government, and comprising representatives of HM Treasury, the Financial Conduct Authority and the Bank of England.
[77] Although it is argued above that cryptocurrencies do not represent value or, indeed, anything. And see para 2.153 for a description of 'stablecoins'.

46 MONEY

2.179 The Cryptoassets Taskforce estimated that, as at October 2018, there were around 2,000 kinds of cryptosecurities in existence. These can be divided into two broad categories. First, there are 'security tokens' which are issued by a company and which give the holder rights to payment of money or delivery of some other asset at a future date, or represent ownership of (or other property interest in) assets that belong to the issuer. Second is a class of 'utility tokens' which are issued by a company and give the holder the right to receive some product or service from the issuer at a future date.

2.180 These cryptosecurities are different from cryptocurrencies in one fundamental respect: the cryptosecurities represent a contractual right against the issuer and this right embodies the value of the cryptosecurity. Cryptocurrencies, on the other hand, represent nothing and contain no rights or claims against anybody.

2.181 Seen in this light, cryptosecurities are not, at a conceptual level, revolutionary or even novel. The form that a cryptosecurity takes and the ways in which it is issued and traded will have consequences in each jurisdiction according to the law and regulations in that state. It may or may not be classified as a security or a collective investment for regulatory purposes. It may be outside the scope of the regulatory regime altogether.

2.182 The major difference in practice between cryptosecurities and traditional corporate securities is that ownership of the former is recorded and transferred on a distributed ledger and the latter usually employs a central register kept by the company itself. While this feature may make cryptoassets seem attractive in concept, it is actually a throwback to former practice in the financial markets. Chapter 6 deals with the history and development of the international bond market. A major breakthrough was the creation of bearer securities. Here, a debt obligation was 'chattelised' by embedding it in a piece of paper, thereby allowing it to be traded along with the ownership of the paper, following the legal rules applicable to tangible assets. However, bearer securities had two drawbacks for market participants. First, the issuer often did not know to whom it owed its obligations, because there was no record of the ownership of bearer bonds. Second, the institutional investors who came to make up the majority of market participants found the pieces of paper inconvenient. Accordingly, the market has reached a position where the movement of pieces of paper has been eliminated and the records of the bonds have been centralized on an electronic trading platform.

2.183 The use of DLT in the issue and structure of corporate securities is not a very dramatic change in conceptual terms. It remains to be seen if it is one that the markets really want.

Governmental and regulatory response

2.184 In 2018 a leading central banker described cryptocurrencies as:

> ... the evil spawn of the financial crisis.[78]

---

[78] Benoit Coeure, Executive Member of the Board of the ECB, reported in The Financial Times on 12 May 2019.

The Governor of the Bank of England adopted language more usually associated with that institution. Cryptocurrencies were, he said:

...inherently risky.[79]

Some countries, notably China, have prohibited dealings in cryptocurrencies. Most jurisdictions, reluctant to strangle the spawn at birth, when its ultimate destiny is not knowable, have been more cautious. The Cryptocurrency Taskforce's report concluded that:

[Cryptocurrencies] present new challenges to traditional forms of financial regulation.

It then announced a series of further consultations on the regulatory treatment of all cryptoassets.

2.185 Although they are cautious about future action that might be taken, the position of the UK authorities on some questions is clear. The Cryptoassets Taskforce was clear that cryptocurrencies are not currency. Nor are they money. The reason given is not that their nature precludes them qualifying. Rather, it is that cryptocurrencies do not perform the functions of currency or money.[80] They are not widely accepted as means of exchange, are not used as units of account, and are too volatile to be a good store of value.

2.186 Tax authorities have been more forthright in their response. In the UK, HMRC takes the view that cryptoassets (including cryptocurrencies) are property. The tax treatment of dealings in them and of payments of salary or earnings expressed in cryptocurrency largely follows the treatment of their 'hard copy' relatives.[81] In the US, the IRS takes a similar approach.[82]

The Ability of States to Control the Use of Their Money

2.187 Whether or not they consciously accept the 'state theory' of money, most states hold firmly to the view that the state 'owns' its own money and may legitimately take action to safeguard its value against interference by outsiders.[83] Further, states feel that they have the right to prevent enemies, or others of whom they disapprove, from using the state's currency.

2.188 Chapter 3 examines the consequences for payers when states seek to control the processes of payment in order to control the use of their currency by foreigners.[84] It is worth examining here states' understanding of the nature of their own money, since it colours their attitude to its use.

Exchange control

2.189 One of the mechanisms that states have traditionally used to manage their economies is exchange control; that is, the prohibition on residents against transferring the national

---

[79] Ibid.
[80] See Cryptoassets Taskforce Report para 2.13.
[81] See HMRC Policy Paper: *Cryptoassets for Individuals* 19 December 2018.
[82] IRS Notice 2014-21.
[83] As evidenced by the number of signatories to the Bretton Woods Agreements.
[84] See paras 3.58 to 3.97.

currency to non-residents, or holding foreign monetary assets. After World War II, it was accepted that such tight control by sovereign states of their own currencies was necessary in order to promote recovery from the effects of the war. A conference convened at the New Hampshire town of Bretton Woods in 1945 resulted in a treaty under which the participating states agreed to support each other's imposition of controls over their own currencies. The Agreement establishing the International Monetary Fund (Bretton Woods Agreement) 1945, article VIII, s 2(b) reads:

> Exchange contracts which involve the currency of any member and which are contrary to the exchange control regulations of that member maintained or imposed consistently with this agreement shall be unenforceable in the territories of any member ...

At first sight, the provision seems fairly clear. The treaty parties were recognizing each other's right to introduce national laws which prevented or restricted the circumstances in which, or the terms on which, its currency could be used. The states would reinforce their mutual rights. If a contract contravened the exchange control regulations of another signatory state, they would each ensure that it was treated as unenforceable under their own law. In the UK, effect was given to this provision by the Bretton Woods Agreements Act 1945 and the Bretton Woods Agreements Order 1946.

2.190 However, the courts have had considerable difficulty in deciding how far the treaty states intended to go. The questions of the meaning of section 2(b) came before the English Court of Appeal in 1967 in *Sharif v Azad*.[85] The parties were Pakistani nationals resident in the UK. Mr Azad was a travel agent, who also had facilities for dealing in currency. The plaintiff asked for his help in providing funds for a friend who was visiting the UK from Pakistan. In return for a blank cheque for 6,000 rupees, drawn on a bank in Pakistan by the friend, Mr Azad wrote sterling cheques in favour of the plaintiff. Payment of the rupee cheque was contrary to the exchange control regulations in Pakistan, a signatory to the Bretton Woods Agreement. The proceeds of the rupee cheque were blocked by the Pakistan authorities. The defendant stopped his own sterling cheques, and Mr Sharif sued him on the cheques.

2.191 The defence was that the arrangement was a single 'exchange contract' within the meaning of Article VIII 2(b) and therefore unenforceable. The question turned on the meaning of the phrase 'exchange contracts'. Lord Denning MR saw the position clearly. 'Exchange contracts' were:

> ... any contracts which in any way affect the country's exchange resources.

Diplock LJ agreed:

> The expression 'exchange contract' is nowhere defined in the Act or the Order or even in the Bretton Woods Agreement itself. I think that it should be liberally construed having regard to the objects of the Bretton Woods Agreement to protect the currencies of the states who are parties thereto.

However, the plaintiff succeeded in his action on the sterling cheques, because the court held that the action on the cheques was a separate cause of action, and was not tainted by the agreement to buy the sterling cheques for rupees. Mr Sharif was not seeking to enforce

---

[85] [1967] 1 QB 605.

the 'exchange contract'. Importantly, the statements about the definition of the phrase in the treaty were *obiter*.

When the question came before the court again, some nine years later, Lord Denning MR changed his mind. In *Wilson, Smithett & Cope Ltd v Terruzzi*,[86] Mr Terruzzi, an Italian resident who dealt in metals, placed orders with the plaintiffs, who were members of the London Metal Exchange. When his account was almost £200,000 in debit, he refused to pay. He said that, under Italian exchange control regulations, permission was needed before such contracts could be concluded. He had obtained no permission, and the contracts were unenforceable by the plaintiff, because they were 'exchange contracts' within Article VIII 2(b). **2.192**

The court here took the view that the treaty parties had not intended the class of contracts, which were to be supported by the 'global unenforceability' provision, to be so wide. Instead, 'exchange contracts' had been intended to cover only those contracts for the exchange of one currency against another (ie only FOREX dealing). The court relied heavily on a statement by Lord Radcliffe in *In re United Railways of Havana and Regla Warehouses Ltd*,[87] in a quite different context, referring to: **2.193**

> ... a true exchange contract, which is a contract to exchange the currency of one country for the currency of another...

It is difficult to understand the change of attitude of the courts. The purpose of the signatories to the Bretton Woods Agreement was clearly to give mutual support to their efforts to control the use of their currencies. The decision in *Terruzzi*, that they intended only to support each other's efforts to control foreign exchange dealing, is surprising. The reason for the change of approach may lie in the fact that, by the mid-1970s, economic policy had shifted strongly towards free trade and away from centralized control of economies. Exchange control had become unfashionable, and there was perhaps a reluctance on the part of the courts to enforce a system which had the effect of restricting international trade and the free movement of capital. It should be noted that exchange control was abolished entirely in the UK in 1979.

Questions of exchange control, so far as the UK is concerned, are now behind us. However, the difficulty faced by the courts in interpreting the phrase 'exchange contracts' is a useful reminder of the problems that arise when lawyers have to address questions of money and economic policy. As Kerr J said at first instance in *Terruzzi*: **2.194**

> I was referred to a large number of foreign decisions, text books and learned articles spanning some 20 years. They nearly all proceeded on the basis (with which I wholeheartedly agree) that these are vexing and doubtful questions.

Interdiction and sanctions regulations

A separate issue from the wish of states to control the flow of their currency and the ownership of it in economic terms, exemplified by the use of exchange controls, is the wish to deny **2.195**

---

[86] [1976] 1 QB 683.
[87] [1961] AC 1007.

the use of its currency or the enjoyment of its monetary assets to those of whom it disapproves. It has been quite common, in time of war, for states to confiscate assets within their territory, which belonged to nationals of enemy states, and to impose trading sanctions on their enemies.[88]

2.196 Since the 1990s, there has been an increasing trend for states to adopt legislation or pass regulations that affect not states, but individuals and classes of individuals. The apogee of this approach can be seen in the Proceeds of Crime Act 2002, which makes it an offence to assist a suspected criminal (whether the suspected crime was committed in the UK or abroad) to use or retain the proceeds of crime. In practice, once the criminality is suspected, the assets should be frozen.

2.197 Under the Proceeds of Crime Act, if a bank, or other intermediary, does not fulfil its obligations under the statute, it commits a criminal offence itself. The legislation, and its counterparts in other jurisdictions, has expanded a long way beyond its original aim, to deny access to assets belonging to drug dealers and terrorists. It now covers the 'proceeds' of all criminal offences (including offences relating to the payment of tax) whether the offence was committed in the UK or abroad. The operation of legislation of this kind, known generically as 'interdiction legislation', is a serious problem for all banks, but particularly for those dealing with the international movements of funds. The operation of interdiction legislation is discussed in Chapter 3.[89]

2.198 A separate issue is the use of economic and monetary sanctions as a weapon of foreign policy. The weapon is now used regularly both by individual states and by states acting collectively through international organizations. In August 1990 UN Security Council Resolution 661 called upon all states to freeze the assets of Kuwait and Iraq 'located within their territories', following the invasion of Kuwait by Iraq. The purpose was to prevent the government of Iraq dissipating the assets of Kuwait and also to deny Iraq the use of its own assets. Since 1990, the use of financial and economic sanctions has become common. Further, regulations often target the assets and activities not only of states that are thought to be hostile to the policy of the country that is imposing the sanctions. Individuals and companies thought to be instrumental in devising or implementing the activities disapproved may be targeted by name. The sanctions imposed by the United States and separately by EU Member States in 2014 on Russian corporations and nationals, following the troubles in eastern Ukraine, are examples of the specific nature of modern sanctions regulations.

2.199 Regulations may prohibit commercial activity between those subject to the terms of the legislation and the sanctioned state or persons, for example by banning the export or import of some kinds of goods. The most far-reaching provisions, however, are those which prohibit the giving of financial assistance to the sanctioned persons. This will usually cover not only the making or arranging of loans, but also the processing of payment transactions. Examples of the terms of such regulations, and the problems that compliance with them can

---

[88] As early as 225 BC, Rome forbade anyone from selling gold or silver to the Gauls, or buying those commodities from them: W. V. Harris, *War and Imperialism in Republican Rome 327–70 BC* (Oxford University Press, 1979), p 198, n. 3.
[89] At paras 3.99 to 3.107.

pose for banks involved in processing payments and for their customers, are discussed in Chapter 3.[90]

2.200 It is worth pausing here to consider another aspect of the operation of sanction regulations. In order to give teeth to its sanctions, a state will usually provide that anyone on whom obligations are imposed by the regulations should be guilty of a criminal offence (or subject to a regulatory penalty) if those obligations are broken. In recent years, there have been a number of well-publicized examples of non-US banks being subjected to financial penalties for assisting activities that were prohibited by US regulation.

2.201 In January 2009 Lloyds TSB Bank plc, a UK bank, agreed to pay a penalty of US$350 million, to settle claims that it had violated sanction regulations relating to Iran and to Sudan. In both cases, the regulations prohibited the 'exportation of services' to residents of the counties concerned. Lloyds, acting though branches in London or Dubai, had transmitted to correspondent banks in New York requests for the transfer of US dollar funds, the requests being made on behalf of customers who were residents of Iran or Sudan.[91] The New York banks involved would not have been prepared to process the payments had they been aware that the customers of Lloyds were residents of sanctioned countries. However, it was alleged that Lloyds removed from all messages sent to correspondents in New York all references that might have shown a connection with the state concerned.

2.202 The US Department of Justice argued that, even though Lloyds had done nothing through its branches in the US, it had nonetheless 'exported services' from the US by virtue of its use of the services of US banks.[92] As a separate claim, it was said that Lloyds' manipulation of the information in the messages sent to its correspondents in New York amounted to a falsification of the records of those banks, an offence under New York law.

2.203 A number of other European banks were subsequently accused of violations of US sanction regulations, on facts similar to the Lloyds case.[93] This has culminated in criminal charges being brought against BNP Paribas, SA, the major French bank, in New York, relating to a rather more sophisticated course of action. The allegation was that BNPP had conspired with banks and other entities in Sudan, Iran, and Cuba to mislead banks involved in processing US dollar payments in New York about the source of the payments concerned. The allegations covered activities over the course of eight years, involving almost US$9 billion. In July 2014, BNPP pleaded guilty to the charges against it, and agreed to pay fines of US$8.9 billion in total.

2.204 The cases have caused some disquiet outside the United States, mainly because, it was said, the acts complained of took place outside the United States. Michel Sapin, Finance minister of France, noted the 'extraterritorial' nature of the claims. It is often said that the courts of the United States are far more ready than their counterparts elsewhere to claim jurisdiction over parties who are located abroad and/or in respect of things which happen abroad.

---

[90] See paras 3.61 to 3.98.
[91] For a description of the process by which US dollars are transferred, see para 3.33.
[92] This allegation seems slightly odd. While it is easy to see that the alleged activities might have caused the US banks to export services, it is not easy to see how Lloyds could be said to have exported the services itself.
[93] For example, in June 2012, ING Groep NV of the Netherlands paid US$619 million to settle allegations against it, and Standard Chartered Plc paid US$327 million in December of the same year.

Whether or not this is correct, there is a strong argument that the accusation is misplaced, in the case of controls over payment transactions. Chapter 3 explains the mechanics needed to effect a substantial payment of US dollars from a non-US payer to a non-US payee.[94] The way in which a payment *must* be made involves US residents carrying out part of the process in the US. This is not an accident. It follows inescapably from the nature of the US dollar.

2.205 It appears to be common ground that sovereign states have the right, in pursuit of their foreign policy ends, to deny to other states and foreign individuals access to their territory and to their assets. There is no reason why this principle should not extend to the infrastructure of the country's financial system. Put simply, if the UK decided that the residents of Ruritania should not be allowed to have access to British manufactured goods or agricultural produce, there is no reason why the denial of access should not extend to the sterling clearing services of the Bank of England.

2.206 States see their currencies, and the infrastructure for dealing in them, as part of their national identity. Their wish to control the use of their currency by foreigners is not an interference with the rights of non-residents. They see it only as an assertion of their own rights.

---

[94] See para 3.33.

3
PAYMENT

> The word 'paid' is ... slippery.
>
> Lord Mustill[1]

Almost all financial transactions involve a payment. One might have thought that this would be one of the least problematical statements that could be made in the area of financial law; it should be simple to work out what a payment should be, and whether it has been made. This is far from being the case. Particularly in international transactions, there can be great difficulty in analyzing what is meant by 'payment' in the context of the particular contract, and in predicting the consequences for the parties if, for some reason, the payment process is prevented or fails. Many of the disputes that find their way into the commercial courts centre on the issue whether payment was made or was not made. Sometimes the problem is about more than mere money. In the Iran debt crisis of 1979 a dispute about whether payments had been made, and if not, where the responsibility for failure lay, triggered a major international political crisis, settled only by concerted action by a number of governments and their central banks.[2]   **3.01**

The word 'payment' is used in this chapter in two separate senses: **3.02**

1. to describe the process of money transmission, whether by the delivery of money tokens (notes and coins) or by the posting of entries in the accounts of banks, so that the transferee has the benefit of the money transferred. This use of the word can apply whether the transfer is made under a contract, by way of gift, or otherwise; and
2. to denote the performance or other discharge of an obligation to pay, which may or may not involve the transfer of money.

These categories encompass a very wide range of activities. However, they do not cover all of the situations in which the word 'pay' is used. In *Charter Reinsurance Co. Ltd v Fagan*[3] the House of Lords interpreted the phrase 'actually paid' to include the process of calculating the sum to be brought into account under an insurance contract, whether or not money was transferred as a result.[4]

Problems relating to payment in commercial transactions, in the sense of money transmission, frequently arise out of the relationship between payer and payee. Such issues have been the subject of much case law over the years. Some are described below. More important to a financial markets lawyer are the problems that occur when the process of money transmission is disrupted by a third party or by events. The making of large international payments   **3.03**

---

[1] *Charter Reinsurance Co Ltd v Fagan* [1997] AC 313.
[2] See paras 3.75 *et seq* below.
[3] [1997] AC 313.
[4] And see the examples of the use of the word 'pay' given by Lords Mustill and Hoffmann in their speeches.

may involve the active participation of a number of banking institutions and organizations and rely upon the governments in several jurisdictions to permit (or at least not to prevent) part of the payment process taking place in their territory. Many events can disrupt the process. One of the transmitting banks might become insolvent, or have its own commercial reasons for wishing to block the payment; or governmental action may make the payment illegal, or prevent the process taking place in a timely manner. One of the principal concerns of the financial markets lawyer is the possibility of such a failure of the payment process.

Payment as the Discharge of an Obligation to Pay Money

3.04 Before turning to the issues that arise in money transmission, it is useful to consider in outline the first sense of the idea of payment. There a number of ways in which an obligation to pay money (which will, in financial markets, normally arise under the provisions of a contract) may be discharged. The most common is, of course, by the transmission of money to the payee, either through the banking system or by delivery of notes and coins. However, there are a number of ways of effecting payment (or its equivalent) which do not involve money being received by the obligee.

Agreed method of payment

3.05 A contract under which an obligation to pay money arises may stipulate the way in which that obligation is to be, or may be, settled. In *Re Charge Card Services Ltd*[5] Millett J described the common situation where a garage displays a sign indicating that it will accept a particular brand of credit or charge card. In such a case, it is a term of the contract between the garage and the customer that payment for the petrol purchased may be made by tendering a valid card issued by the relevant card provider. The acceptance of the card discharges the customer's obligation to pay for the fuel. If the card company becomes insolvent before it has paid the garage, the garage cannot look to the customer for payment. The customer has discharged his payment obligation by the use of the card. It should be noted, in passing, that payment by cheque does not have the same effect in law as payment by credit card. In *D & C Builders v Rees*[6] Lord Denning MR described the position when a payee accepts a cheque in payment of a contract debt. He said:

> The cheque, when given, is conditional payment. When honoured, it is actual payment. It is then just the same as cash.[7]

3.06 Commonly, a contract for the sale of land in the UK will provide that payment at completion should be made by handing over a banker's draft in favour of the payee drawn by a specified bank, or one of a category of banks. A banker's draft is a promissory note made by a bank. It is an obligation undertaken by the bank as a primary obligor. The seller of the land accepts that obligation in the place of the purchaser's obligation to pay for the land. Handing

---

[5] [1987] 1 Ch 150.
[6] [1966] 2 QB 617.
[7] See also the discussion in *In re Charge Card Services Ltd* [1987] 1 Ch 150 at 166 *et seq*, and the cases there cited.

over the banker's draft at completion is performance of the purchaser's obligation to pay for the land, and discharges him from any further obligation. If, following completion of the sale, but before payment of the banker's draft, the bank should become insolvent, the risk would be borne by the seller of the land.

Set-off

If A owes £100 to B, and B owes £50 to A, then (unless the parties have agreed otherwise) A can discharge his payment obligation to B by paying £50 to B, and forgiving the £50 debt owed from B to him. For his part, B may treat his debt to A as paid, by setting it off against £50 of the debt that A owes to him, so that the only claim left unsatisfied is a debt of £50 from A to B. Although the concept is simple, the detail is not. **3.07**

In English law, set-off has been seen for hundreds of years as essential to the operation of free markets.[8] With the rapid expansion of trade in the late eighteenth and early nineteenth centuries, imported commodities were traded on exchanges in all of the major cities in England. Many of the traders were individuals, whose creditworthiness could not be assessed by reference to published accounts or any other public information. The only way in which one trader could safely conduct business with another was to be sure that the payment obligations which arose from their trading could be set off against each other, so that the maximum amount that either of the traders could be made to pay the other (or the other's trustee in bankruptcy) was the net amount owing. The ability to control credit exposure in this way was seen as essential to the growth and functioning of exchanges. **3.08**

The same view was not taken in all other jurisdictions. In many civil law countries, for example in Scotland, the idea of set-off, at least in the context of an insolvency, was seen as unfair. A creditor of an insolvent trader, who also happened to owe money to the bankrupt could, in effect, obtain payment of the debt that was owed to him. He could use the money that he owed to the bankrupt by setting this payment obligation against the debt owed to him, thereby arranging payment of the debt that was owed to him. This, it was thought, gave him an unfair advantage over other creditors of the bankrupt who did not have access to any means of payment. Whatever view one takes of the morality of the issue, it is certainly now the case that the mechanism of set-off, and concepts closely related to it, such as netting, are seen as indispensable tools for the control of risk in financial and other traded markets. **3.09**

'Set-off' is a phrase used to describe several related but distinct concepts. It is important to bear the distinctions in mind. In *Aectra Refining and Manufacturing Inc v Exmar NV*,[9] Hoffmann LJ simplified the classifications by adopting the analysis used by Philip Wood.[10] It was possible to reduce the types of set-off to three categories: transactional set-off; independent set-off; and insolvency set-off. **3.10**

---

[8] See Philip R. Wood, *English and International Set-off* (Sweet & Maxwell, 1989).
[9] [1995] All ER 641.
[10] In *English and International Set-off*, above.

Transactional set-off

3.11 Transactional set-off occurs where a party (the payer) has an obligation to make a payment to another party (the payee) under a contract, and the same contract (or something very closely connected to it) also gives rise to a money claim by the payer against the payee. In such a case, the payer gives to the payee a release of the debt (or part of the debt) owed by the payee to the payer. This release operates to satisfy the payment obligation that the payer would otherwise owe to the payee. Transactional set-off is not merely a defence which a payer may use to avoid the need to make a payment; it has the same effect at law as the payment of the debt.[11]

Independent set-off

3.12 Independent set-off is not a matter of substantive law, but of procedure. Under the Rules of Civil Procedure,[12] if an obligor is sued for payment, he may ask that the action against him should be consolidated with a claim that he has against his creditor, even if that claim relates to an entirely different subject. If the two claims are decided by the court at the same time, the court will then make an order requiring that only the net amount should be paid.

Insolvency set-off

3.13 Insolvency set-off is one of the most important protections offered by English law in relation to commercial and financial activity. Rule 14.25 of the Insolvency Rules[13] says, in relation to the winding up of companies:[14]

(1) This Rule applies in a winding up where, before the company goes into liquidation there have been mutual dealings between the company and a creditor of the company proving or claiming to prove for a debt in the liquidation.
(2) An account must be taken of what is due from the company and the creditor to each other in respect of their mutual dealings and the sums due from the one must be set off against the sums due from the other.

3.14 Unlike transactional set-off, which applies only when the claims between payer and payee relate to the same contract or subject-matter, Rule 14.25 applies on the winding up of a company in relation to all dealings between the company and a creditor which can be described as 'mutual'. All the debts that arise from the mutual dealings of the parties are aggregated, and only the net balance is payable to (or from) from the insolvent company. In financial markets, large institutions may have hundreds of unsettled transactions with each other at any time, all involving large amounts of money. The great fear in risk management is that, if the counterparty should become insolvent, its liquidator might be able to demand payment of all sums due from the solvent party to the bankrupt, but tell the solvent counterparty that it must prove in the liquidation for the amounts which are payable the other way. Rule 14.25 prevents this from happening. It is, perhaps, the single most important rule of English law, so far as the security of financial transactions is concerned.

---

[11] See Lord Diplock in *Modern Engineering (Bristol) Ltd v Gilbert-Ash (Northern) Ltd* [1974] AC 689, at 717.
[12] Civil Procedure Rules 73rd Update r 16.6.
[13] The Insolvency (England and Wales) Rules 2016.
[14] Rules in similar terms apply to administration and to the insolvency of individuals.

Netting

Netting is a contractual mechanism which, like set-off, has the effect that payment obligations are satisfied by the forgiveness of payment obligations owed in the opposite direction. The idea has been in use for a long time, but has grown in importance, so far as financial markets are concerned, since the early 1990s. It lies at the heart of the operation of the various master agreements published by the International Swaps and Derivatives Association, which are used to govern most of the relationships between institutions in the international derivatives markets. It is fundamental also to other standard market arrangements. Again, the concept is simple: the parties who intend to enter into a number of transactions of the same sort with each other (eg banks who propose to enter into a number of derivatives contracts), under which sums of money will fall to be paid on a number of dates, agree that the payment obligations which arise under the individual transactions should be subject to an overall netting arrangement. This falls into two parts. First, the parties agree that all payments which fall due on a particular date should be aggregated, so that only the net amount is payable, one way or the other. This is called 'payment netting'. Second, they agree that, if one of the parties is in a position which indicates it may become insolvent, the other party has the option to close out all of the arrangements then in existence. This procedure (called 'close-out netting') has the effect of terminating each of the underlying contracts, resulting in a sum of money becoming immediately payable from one party to the other, in relation to each contract. These individual sums are then aggregated, to produce a single net figure, payable one way or the other.

3.15

Payment netting is a matter of commercial convenience and has comparatively little significance, so far as market security and risk management are concerned. Close-out netting is a different matter. It is possible to view the mechanism as a form of contractual pre-insolvency set-off, which produces a result similar to that of Rule 14.25, without having to wait for insolvency. Moreover, it must be remembered that Rule 14.25 and its equivalent in administration, Rule 14.24, apply only to insolvency procedures in the UK. Contractual netting is designed to produce the same result, even in jurisdictions that do not have a rule in insolvency providing for global set-off.

3.16

The difficult question for lawyers working in the derivatives field is the extent to which the contractual netting provisions in market master agreements (which are usually governed by either English or New York law) will operate if the failing party to the arrangement enters into insolvency proceedings in a jurisdiction which does not accept the concept of insolvency set-off. Will the contractual netting arrangements be effective, if the relevant insolvency legislation has contradictory provisions? This is a very complex issue, the nuances of which are different in every jurisdiction.

3.17

Running accounts

A running account arises when two parties enter into a number of transactions with each other, each of which would, except for the arrangement, result in an immediately payable debt. It is agreed that each of those 'debts', as it arises, should be credited or

3.18

debited (as the case may be) to a single account. The entry either increases or reduces the balance on the account. The agreement is that, at any time, only one debt should be payable from one party to the other, that debt being the balance on the running account. The most common form of the running account is a retail bank account. The bank makes credits to the account in respect of cheques it has collected for its customer, or other payments received on his behalf, and debits the account with sums for which it is entitled to reimbursement, because of money it has paid on the client's instructions. None of the individual transactions gives rise to a payment obligation, but each results in an amount being credited or debited to the running account. The figure on that running account is the only debt.[15]

3.19 It should be remembered that the running account mechanism is different from the netting mechanisms adopted in market-based master agreements. A running account can operate only where all the debts are presently payable. Where the transactions between the parties give rise to individual debts which are payable at future dates, it is not possible to deal with them collectively in this way.

Consolidation of accounts

3.20 In the context of a banking relationship, another method by which a debt might be satisfied is the process called variously 'banker's lien', 'banker's right of set-off', 'banker's right of combination', and 'banker's right of consolidation'. The concept is that a bank which maintains two or more accounts for a particular customer may, unless there is an agreement that the accounts should be treated as separate, take the credit balance on one (a debt owed by the bank to its customer) and transfer it to the account which is in deficit (a debt owed by the customer to the bank). The process, like transactional set-off, has the effect of satisfying the two debts, to the extent of the combination. In this sense, it is a form of payment.

3.21 The mechanism is long established. In *Halesowen Presswork v Westminster Bank*[16] Lord Denning MR referred to:

> ... the long line of cases which show that a banker is entitled to combine two accounts unless there is an agreement to keep them separate.

However, the basis for the mechanism is obscure. One might assume that, because the relationship of banker and customer is based on contract, the banker's right of set-off arises from an implied term of that contract. This may not be so. In *Mutton v Peat*,[17] a bank had two accounts for a bankrupt stockbroker customer. One was in credit and the other in debit. It also held security from a third party for the indebtedness of the customer. It wished to use the security from the third party to satisfy the debt owing from the customer on its overdrawn account, and to pay the customer's trustee in bankruptcy

---

[15] See the explanation given by Millett J in *Re Charge Card Services Ltd* [1987] 1 Ch 150, at 173G–174F.
[16] [1971] 1 QB 1.
[17] [1900] 2 Ch 79.

the amount owing by the bank on the account that was in credit. This payment would then have been available for the general creditors, while the third-party security provider would have paid the debt owed to the bank. The Court of Appeal held that the bank could not do this. It must combine the two accounts and only then use the third-party security to satisfy the balance outstanding. It was not a matter on which the bank had a choice:

> It seems to me that it does not matter in the least whether they appropriated [the credit balance] or not ... they were bound to allow the [credit balance] in account whether they appropriated it or not, and even if they endeavoured not to appropriate it.[18]

The mandatory nature of the consolidation is incompatible with the idea of a right, which implies that the owner of the right may choose whether or not he should exercise it.

The view that the process is mandatory is supported by the decision of Otten J in *In re K (Restraint Order)*.[19] The case concerned an order made under the Drug Trafficking Offences Act 1986, freezing accounts of a customer with the bank. The bank wished to combine accounts, and the question was whether the act of combination would amount to 'disposing of or diminishing' assets belonging to the customer. Otten J first considered the 'banker's right of combination': **3.22**

> In my judgment, the right of a bank to combine is well established and is fundamental to the bank/customer relationship. It is a means of establishing the indebtedness of the customer to the bank and the bank to the customer. In exercising this right the bank ... is merely carrying out an accounting procedure so as to ascertain the existence and amount of one party's liability to the other.

However, the judge goes on to contrast this process of 'combination' with the 'contractual set-off' contained in an agreement which had been concluded in this case between the bank and the customer. The agreement gave an explicit right to the bank to combine the accounts and set off the balances. He concludes that the 'contractual' right of set-off does not involve 'disposing' of the assets or 'diminishing' the assets. The reason for this is that the account balances are 'encumbered' by the contractual right of set-off, so that the exercise of the right does not affect the value of the assets.

It is hard to see how the analyses of the two sets of rights are reconcilable. The 'contractual' arrangements clearly show that each of the balances on the individual accounts constitutes a debt, which is then 'encumbered' by the existence of the right of set-off. In the court's analysis of the 'banker's right of combination', however, the individual account balances are no more than items which must be aggregated in order to determine what is the debt. **3.23**

The better view would seem to be that the right to consolidate accounts does involve dealing with individual debts, even if they are 'encumbered' by the existence of the right itself, and that *Mutton v Peat* should not be taken as holding that the account balances were not **3.24**

---

[18] Rigby LJ, at 86.
[19] [1990] 2 QB 298.

individual debts. Rather, the decision is explicable on the basis that the security given to the bank by the third party operated to secure the ultimate balance due after consolidation of the separate debts, and therefore required that the right of consolidation be exercised, before the security could be applied.

3.25 A further difficulty arises in deciding whether the 'banker's right of consolidation' is an accurate description. In the *Halesowen* case Lord Denning MR, after confirming the existence of the bank's rights, added:

> Conversely, the customer has a right to call on the banker to combine the two accounts, and to set off one against the other unless there is some agreement, express or implied, to the contrary.

He then cites *Mutton v Peat* as authority for this proposition.

3.26 Accordingly, although the right of consolidation of accounts is clearly established, it is not clear whose right it is, whether it operates as a way of satisfying debts or only as a method of calculating a debt, or even what it should be called.[20] It is common now for banks to include an explicit right of set-off in their standard forms of contract. In conformity with the normal caution of lawyers, the drafting often begins with the words 'in addition to any other rights the bank may have', in order to preserve the implied right of consolidation. For the sake of clarity, it might be safer to exclude the implied right (both for the bank and for the customer) and to rely on the explicit contractual terms.

Payment as the Transmission of Money

3.27 The primary sense in which the word 'payment' is used, to mean the act of money transmission, gives rise to a number of difficult and important issues for financial lawyers. Before turning to these, it is important to understand the mechanics by which money is transmitted through the banking system.

3.28 There is a preliminary point to be made. Except where a payment is made by the physical delivery of money tokens (notes and coin), the payment of money does not involve the transfer of any physical thing, nor even of personal rights and claims.[21] Rather, it is a series of transactions in which rights and claims are extinguished, to be replace by new rights and claims in favour of other parties. In *R v Preddy*[22] the question was whether a transfer of money through the UK banking system, obtained by deception, fell within the wording of s 15(1) of the Theft Act 1968, which required that the fraudster should have acquired

---

[20] The phrase 'banker's lien' was rejected in the *Halesowen* case as inaccurate. In the House of Lords ([1972] AC 785, sub nom *National Westminster Bank v Halesowen*, Lord Cross said, 'I agree with Lord Denning MR and Buckley LJ ... that a debtor cannot sensibly be said to have a lien on his own indebtedness to his creditor ... to describe the right to consolidate several accounts as an example of the banker's lien is, I think, a misuse of language.'
[21] It is important to remember that this discussion relates to the transfer of money, properly so called. In a system which used Distributed Ledger Technology (see paras 3.117 *et seq*) the message of transfer might, in some cases, have the effect of transferring rights and claims.
[22] [1996] AC 815.

'property belonging to another'. Lord Jauncey[23] explained the way in which the procedure operates in law:

> ... there falls to be drawn a crucial distinction between the creation and extinction of rights on the one hand and the transfer of rights on the other ... I start with the proposition that the money in a bank account standing at credit does not belong to the account holder. He has merely a chose in action which is the right to demand payment of the relevant sum from the bank. I use the word money for convenience but it is, of course, simply a sum entered into the books of the bank. When a sum of money leaves A's account his chose in action quoad that sum is extinguished. When an equivalent sum is transferred to B's account there is created in B a fresh chose in action being the right to demand payment of that sum from his bank. Applying these simple propositions to the cases where sums of money are transferred from the lender's account to the account of the borrower ... either by telegraphic transfer or by CHAPS the lender's property which was his chose in action in respect of the relevant sum is extinguished and a new chose in action is created in the borrower ... Thus although the borrower has acquired a chose in action quoad a sum of money of equal value to that which the lender had right, he has not acquired the property of the lender which was the latter's right against his own bank.

Lord Jauncey speaks only of the position of the lender and the borrower (the originator of the payment and the ultimate recipient). At each step in the payment process a similar analysis will apply. For any step to be complete a right to a money claim is extinguished and a fresh one created in favour of a different party.

3.29 It is possible to make a payment which results in the payee receiving a credit to his bank account without involving any party other than the payer, the payee, and the bank concerned. For example, the payer might go into the payee's bank and hand over a number of bank notes with instructions that the money they represent should be credited to the payee's account. The bank will then have possession of the bank notes, which become its property, and are accordingly its asset. This asset will be balanced by the fact that it has accepted an obligation to give credit in the same amount to the nominated payee. It has credited the payee's account, and has become his debtor. In any payment process which involves more than one bank, however, the accounting procedures will need to be reflected in the books of all of the banks concerned. The consequence of this is that all the entries must be reflected in the accounts which the individual banks hold with the central bank which is the issuer of the currency. In the terminology used by bankers, all payments must settle across the books of the central bank.

3.30 Set out below are diagrammatic descriptions of the entries that would be made to reflect the payment process in three situations. It should be stressed that the diagrams are a greatly simplified representation of the relevant processes involved.

Payment through the UK banking system

3.31 Customer A instructs his bank C to pay a sum in sterling to the credit of customer B's account with building society F as shown in Figure 3.1.

---

[23] At 841.

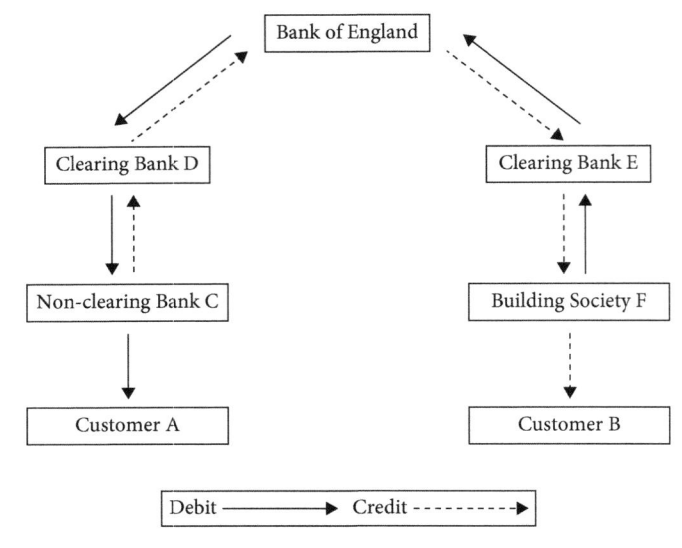

Figure 3.1 Sterling Domestic Payment

3.32 In this case, neither bank C nor building society F maintains an account with the Bank of England. They must settle sterling payments through the agency of another bank which does maintain such an account with the central bank. The steps in the book entries involved in the process can be described as follows:[24]

1. Customer A gives instructions to his bank C. C debits the account of customer A with the amount concerned, and credits its own clearing bank D with the same amount.
2. Clearing bank D, having received the instruction, debits non-clearing Bank C, and credits the Bank of England in its own books.
3. The Bank of England debits clearing bank D, and credits the same amount to the account in its books of clearing bank E.
4. Clearing bank E debits the Bank of England in its own books and credits building society F.
5. Building society F debits clearing bank E and credits the account of customer B in its books.

Each of the credits represents a new legal claim to a monetary amount in favour of the party credited, against the party making the credit. Conversely, each debit represents the extinguishment of a claim which the debited party previously had against the party which makes the debit.

International payments

3.33 E, resident in Iran, who holds a US dollar bank account with Bank C in Paris, wishes to pay US dollars to F, an Egyptian resident, who maintains a US dollar account with bank D in London. The process follows the same system of debits and credits, and the same process of extinguishing claims and creating new claims, as did the domestic arrangement shown in Figure 3.2. The major difference is, of course, that the process crosses four national boundaries and potentially involves the laws of five different sovereign states.

---

[24] See also the description of the operation of CHAPS given by Colman J in *Hosni Tayeb v HSBC Bank Plc* [2004] EWHC 1529 (Comm), at para 14.

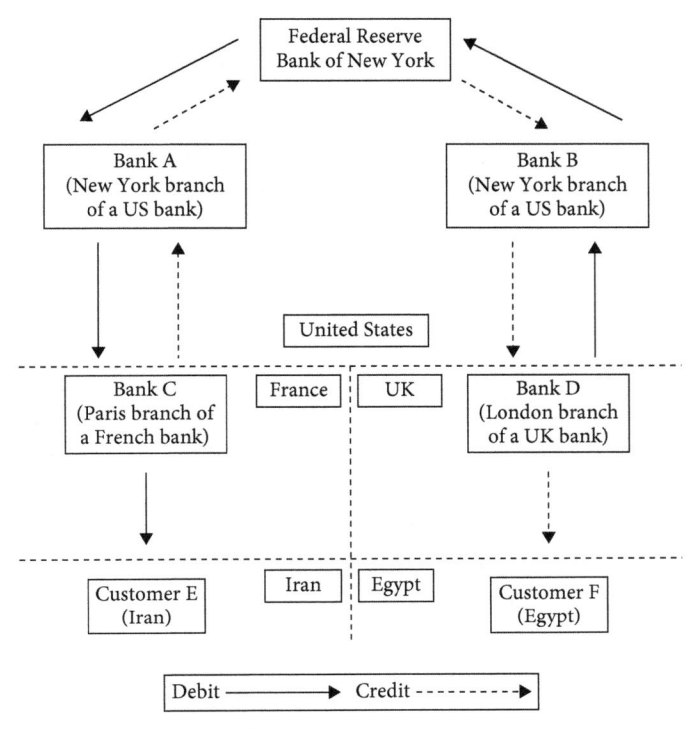

```
                    Federal Reserve
                    Bank of New York

   Bank A                                Bank B
(New York branch                     (New York branch
 of a US bank)                        of a US bank)

                    United States

   Bank C          France    UK        Bank D
(Paris branch of                    (London branch
 a French bank)                      of a UK bank)

                    Iran    Egypt

  Customer E                          Customer F
    (Iran)                              (Egypt)

           Debit ⟶    Credit ----▶
```

Figure 3.2 US Dollar International Payment

TARGET2

3.34 The process for making payments in euros is slightly different from that which applies to other currencies. The difference arises because the euro is the currency of a number of states. Although there is one central bank (the European Central Bank) each of the EU Member States which participate in the euro has its own national central bank, which participates in the clearing process. Indeed, even the central banks of those Member States that have not adopted the euro play a part in the settlement process for euros. The system for transmitting payments in euros is TARGET2 (the second generation of the system known as Trans-European Automated Real-time Gross-settlement Express Transfer). The legal framework for the operation of TARGET2 is a Guideline issued by the ECB,[25] which binds the central banks of the Member States which participate in the euro. As regards the central banks of the Member States which have not adopted the euro, the Guideline applies as a matter of contract under the terms of the TARGET2 Agreement which each of them has with the ECB.

3.35 The system links the ECB and all of the national central banks, so that a payment can be made direct between any two national central banks, without passing directly across the books of the ECB itself at the time the payment is made. Article 6 of the Guideline says that settlement of any payment between two central banks gives rise to an 'intra-Eurosystem obligation' of the paying central bank to the payee central bank. At the end of each day the 'intra-Eurosystem obligations' of each central bank are subject to a netting process, and replaced by a single obligation to or from the ECB.

---

[25] ECB 2012/27 made on 5 December 2012 (as amended). This replaced the Guideline that governed the operation of the first generation TARGET (ECB/2001/3 made on 26 April 2001).

3.36 Suppose, for example, that during the course of a trading day the Bank of England makes 100 credit entries in favour of Banque de France, to a total value of 100 billion euros, and Banque de France credits the Bank of England with 200 payments of 80 billion euros in aggregate. At close of business, the obligations between the central banks are netted off to produce a figure of 20 billion euros 'owing' from the Bank of England to Banque de France. That net figure is then replaced by the figure of 20 billion euros owing from the Bank of England to the ECB.

3.37 This looks like a classic clearing structure, except that a normal clearing system includes a provision that the debts owing between the participants should be extinguished and replaced by two new debts between the clearing house, on the one hand, and each of the two participants, on the other. Such a novation provision is unnecessary in the case of TARGET2. The reason for this is that the 'intra-Eurosystem obligations' are not debts. They are accounting entries that reflect the position between the ECB, on the one hand, and the customer of the relevant national central bank, on the other. Another way of explaining this position is to say that the national central banks are acting as agents for the ECB.

3.38 This explains the apparently relaxed attitude adopted by the ECB to one of the events that happened during the crisis period of 2012. Some residents in the so-called periphery countries were concerned about the potential break-up of the eurozone. One of the consequences might be that their country of residence ceased to use the euro and adopted its own unique currency. In all likelihood, euro deposits with banks in the country concerned would be converted by law to deposits in the new currency. This new currency would then decline in value against the euro. To avoid this currency redesignation, the depositors transferred their euro cash balances from their accounts with local banks to their accounts with banks in the 'core' countries, where there was little chance that the euro debts would be redesignated. Some commentators claimed that this was creating a significant systemic risk, because the flows of money through TARGET2 resulted in large unsecured debts from the central banks of the periphery countries to the central banks of the core countries. The ECB had no concern about this 'problem'. The reason for its sanguinity was that the 'intra-eurozone obligations' created by the operation of TARGET2 are not debts owing between the participating national central banks, but only accounting entries.

3.39 The agency relationship between the national central banks and the ECB explains another facet of the TARGET2 arrangements that would otherwise be hard to understand. The system is said to provide for settlement 'in real time'. On the face of it, this cannot be so. A payment between two national central banks during the course of a day is not reflected on the books of the ECB until after the close of business. This seems to ignore the basic requirement of central bank money, that payments should be reflected in the books of the issuing central bank before they can be regarded as complete. However, the apparent problem disappears when one realizes that each of the participating central banks, other than the ECB, acts for the purposes of TARGET2 as agent for the ECB. Thus, in the example given above, each payment message passing between the Bank of England and Banque de France constitutes a completed payment at the time it is made, irrespective of the netting processes carried out at the end of the day. The effect is the same as if the two national central banks were branches of the ECB.

3.40 A payment in euros made by a UK resident payer to a French resident payee (leaving aside the subsequent accounting entries) can be represented as follows:

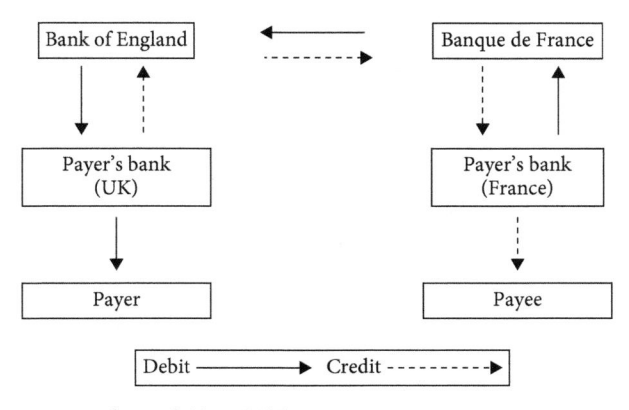

Figure 3.3 Euro Payment through TARGET2

At the end of the day, the obligation created by the payment from the Bank of England to the Banque de France will be included in the netting of all payments between them made on the same day. The net figure will then be extinguished and replaced by an entry of the same amount shown in the books of the ECB as 'owing' to it from the Bank of England or Banque de France (according to which one of them is the net obligor after the netting process has been carried out) as shown in Figure 3.3.

Payment between payer and payee

3.41 The most important payment issues for international financial transactions are to be found in those situations where the payment process is interrupted or blocked. These situations are discussed below. However, most payment disputes before the courts have not been caused by problems in the transmission system but by differences between the payer and the payee. These situations can arise in financial contracts as well as in other commercial arrangements. Such potential difficulties are often overlooked when financial contracts are drafted.

3.42 If a contract under which payment is to be made specifies the exact form of payment (eg that payment should be made by credit to a particular account of the payee) then, unless payment is made in the agreed manner, the contractual obligation will not have been performed. If the contract requires that a particular sum be paid, without specifying the detailed method of payment, the payer may choose to pay by offering legal tender. Alternatively, a court might be willing to imply a term that payment could be effected by a method contemplated by the circumstances.[26]

3.43 In commercial transactions, and particularly in financial transactions, it is usual to set out in detail the payment method that is required. Failure to comply with that requirement will result in a breach of contract, even if the payer has chosen to do an act which results in the payee receiving monetary value equal to that contemplated by the contract. At first sight, it might be thought that a payee who receives value, even if it is not in the payment form required by the contract, would have no wish to complain. There are, however, circumstances in which a payee might wish to claim a breach of contract by the payer, notwithstanding that the payer had transferred monetary value in the amount required. In reported cases

---

[26] See para 2.17.

this arises most often in relation to payment of charterhire. The rates of charterhire for ships can be volatile. The owner of a ship may wish to terminate a charter early, so that he or she might re-charter the ship at a higher rate. Under the terms of some of the standard charter contracts, one of the grounds on which the owner may terminate is the non-payment of charterhire in accordance with the terms of the contract. Disputes focus on two issues: first, whether the charterer paid in accordance with the contract; and second, if he did not, whether the owner waived his right to terminate the charter by accepting late payment of charterhire.

3.44 The process of payment as between payer and payee involves action by both: the payer must tender payment in the form required by the contract, and the payee (or his agent) must accept the payment for the purpose of the contract. If the payer duly tenders payment, but the payee or his agent refuses to accept it, no payment has been made. The obligor still remains liable to pay. The refusal of payment does not have the effect of discharging the obligation. A valid tender does, however, mean that the obligee cannot, having refused a valid tender, then claim that the payer has committed a breach of contract which allows the payee to terminate, or take other action in consequence of the payer's breach. The payer's obligation is duly to tender payment. He cannot make the payee accept. If the obligor has properly offered payment and it has been declined, he cannot be said to have failed to perform his payment obligation.

3.45 The question of whether payment has been accepted depends on the facts. The dividing line between acceptance and non-acceptance is often a fine one. In *Société des Hotels Le Touquet Paris-Plage v Cummings*,[27] Mrs Cummings had been a guest of a hotel in Le Touquet in the early summer of 1914. She did not pay her bill when she left, intending to visit again later in the year. World War I intervened, and at the end of the war she had still not paid her bill. Meanwhile, the French franc had declined dramatically in value against sterling. The hotel began proceedings against Mrs Cummings in England for the amount of the bill outstanding. At the time, it was not possible to sue in England for a liquidated sum expressed in a foreign currency. The claim had to be in sterling, converted at the rate applicable at the time the cause of action arose. The amount of sterling which could be claimed by the hotel on this basis was considerably more valuable, in terms of the French franc, than it had been at the time the franc debt was contracted. To pre-empt the position, Mrs Cummings went to the hotel, and handed over the amount in French francs that she owed. This involved her paying, in sterling terms, far less than she would be required to pay if judgment were given against her. The hotel manager was aware of a dispute with Mrs Cummings, and knew that she owed money to the hotel. He did not have access to the books and was not sure of the amount that she owed. He accordingly took the French francs from her and gave her a receipt. In the words of the Law Report the receipt was 'as for money deposited with him'. Although the manager was clearly reluctant to accept the money as discharging the indebtedness, the court nonetheless held that the payment (which was in fact payment of the full amount outstanding in French francs) had been accepted.

3.46 Even in circumstances where the recipient specifically reserves his position, payment will be deemed to have been accepted, if the recipient subsequently treats the money as his own.

---

[27] [1922] 1 KB 451.

See *TSB Bank of Scotland Ltd v Welwyn Hatfield District Council and Council of the London Borough of Brent*.[28]

3.47 In *Mardorf Peach & Co Ltd v Attica Sea Carriers Corp of Liberia (The Laconia)*,[29] the agreement to charter a ship required payment of hire to be made on specified dates:

> in New York in cash in US currency ... to be paid to owners ... into their account with First National City Bank of New York, 34 Moorgate, London EC2 to the credit of OFC Account No 705586.

In default of punctual payment, the owners had the right to terminate the charter. One of the dates for payment of charterhire was a Sunday, when the banks in London were closed. The charterers tried to make the relevant payment on the following day. The House of Lords held that there was no implicit extension in English law for a payment date which fell due on a non-banking day. The payer could have avoided default by ensuring that payment was made on the previous Friday.

3.48 The charterer had a further argument. In any event, it said, the payment had been accepted when tendered on the Monday, and the breach of the payment obligation had been waived. It was, therefore, not open to the owner to terminate the charter for non-payment of hire. The House of Lords held that the owner was able to terminate.

3.49 The relevant facts are as follows:

1. The charterer's bank, Midland, sent to FNCB a payment order drawn on the London Dollar Clearing System. This is an arrangement between banks in London which make payments to each other in US dollars, under which they account between themselves for payments made on a particular day, the net result of the payments being reflected later in New York through clearing across the books of the Federal Reserve Bank of New York.[30] A payment order on the system drawn by a participating bank operates to produce a credit in favour of the payee bank as soon as the recipient bank presents it to the system for settlement. After this time, the payment cannot be rejected by the receiving bank. Its effect can, however, be reversed by the recipient bank drawing its own payment order in the opposite direction.
2. The payment order was received by FNCB at 3.10pm and stamped by it as received at that time.
3. FNCB then put in train the process of collection through the clearing system. In the ordinary course of events, this would have resulted in the payee's account being credited by FNCB 24 hours later.
4. Having activated the system, FNCB then telephoned the commercial agent of its customer (the payee/owner). The agent told it to refuse the payment and to return it.
5. FNCB wrote on the payment order 'beneficiary has refused payment' and the next day sent to Midland a payment order for the same amount.

---

[28] [1993] 2 Bank LR 267.
[29] [1977] AC 850.
[30] A process similar (as far as its mechanics are concerned) to that which is used within the European System of Central Banks for payments in euros, as described in paras 3.34 to 3.40 above.

68 PAYMENT

3.50 The court was clear that, on the facts, the owner had not accepted payment, in a sense that amounted to a waiver of its right of withdrawal. This was so, even though its bank had received the money. The decision is, perhaps, a little surprising. The payment mechanism selected by the parties involved an act of acceptance, in that the payee's bank was required to present to the clearing system a payment order drawn by the payer's bank, in the same way that a cheque might be presented for payment. FNCB, by activating the process, clearly intended that a debt should arise in its favour (as it did), for the account of its customer. Unless it could be shown that FNCB was acting outside the normal scope of authority of a collecting banker, one might have expected that its acceptance of the payment from Midland would have constituted acceptance by its customer.

3.51 The decision is explained by Lords Salmon and Fraser, though in slightly different terms. Lord Salmon takes the view[31] that the bank had authority to accept only *punctual* payment. Once a payment was overdue, FNCB had no authority to accept the payment:

> Certainly it was not within the banker's express or implied authority to make commercial decisions on behalf of its customers by accepting or rejecting late payments of hire without taking instructions.

Lord Fraser makes a similar point:

> ... the bank was, in my opinion, the agent of the owners only to receive payment for hire but it had no authority, actual or ostensible, to waive the owners' rights.

He reinforces his point:

> In the second place, the actions [of FNCB] ... were not of a character that could have operated as a waiver of the owners' right of withdrawal. A waiver would have required an overt action.

3.52 The explanation is not that the payment was not accepted. FNCB had participated in an arrangement that resulted in it becoming a creditor of Midland. That debt was created in its favour on behalf of the owners. To say that the payment was not made (on the basis that FNCB did not have authority to accept, a requisite element of payment) is wrong, or at least misleading. As Lord Russell said:[32]

> ... a payment order being as between banks the equivalent of cash ... it should suffice for punctual payment that such cash equivalent be tendered in due time to the nominated bank to be credited to the named account: this was the method of payment laid down: you cannot pay 'into' an account, whether you are tendering cash or its equivalent.

Rather, receipt and acceptance by FNCB of the payment did not amount to its acceptance by the owners for the purposes of determining whether they had decided to exercise their right of withdrawal. The question was not whether payment had been made. It concerned instead the contractual consequences of the payment.

3.53 The important, but rather nebulous, position of the payee's bank in the process of transmission is illustrated by the facts in *Momm v Barclays Bank Int Ltd*.[33] This was one of the

---

[31] At 880 B–C.
[32] At 889 F–G.
[33] [1977] QB 790.

cases which resulted from the collapse of a small German bank called Herstatt. Momm and Herstatt both held accounts at Barclays Bank International Ltd in London. H had an obligation to pay to M the sum of £120,000. On 25 June 1974 H instructed BBIL to transfer money from its account to Momm's account with BBIL 'value 26th'. BBIL set in train the making of the relevant book entries during working hours on the 26th. The entries were processed and made some time in the overnight period between close of business on the 26th and the opening of business on the 27th. The effect of debiting H's account and crediting the account of M was that H's account with BBIL went into overdraft. At 4:15pm on the 26th H entered into liquidation in Germany. BBIL staff became aware of this at the opening of business on the 27th and they then reversed the entries that had been made overnight. Their motivation for this was that the effect of the entries made on the instructions of H would have been to make BBIL the creditor of H to the extent of the overdraft. It would have had to prove for this debt in the liquidation of H. If the payment from H to M had not been made, however, H's account would have remained in credit and the bank would lose nothing. M, of course, would probably fail to recover all of the £120,000 owed to it, as a consequence of the reversal of the entries.

3.54 The court held that the payment was complete when BBIL accepted H's instructions and set in motion the accounting process. This situation is clearly different from that in *The Laconia*, because both payer and payee used the same banker. The decision by BBIL to accept payment instructions from H would result in BBIL debiting the account of H (thereby recording that its debt to H was extinguished) and crediting M (thereby acknowledging the creation of a new debt from it to M). Acceptance of a payment instruction given by H necessarily implied the acceptance of the payment by the bank, as agent for M. The payment was therefore complete when BBIL accepted instructions from H.

3.55 At first sight it is hard to see that this case is consistent with *The Laconia*. If H had been a charterer, and M a shipowner, and the payment of £120,000 had been in respect of charterhire, the decision in *The Laconia* would seem to indicate that acceptance of the payment would not have happened, if M had refused the payment on being aware that it had been made. In *The Laconia*, FNCB had accepted the payment order received from Midland and had set in process the arrangements which would necessarily have resulted in a credit entry in FNCB's books in favour of the shipowner.

3.56 There are two ways in which it is possible to reconcile the two decisions. The first is to say that the banks' authority in the two cases was different: in *The Laconia*, FNCB did not have the authority of its customer to accept a payment on the customer's behalf, while in *Momm*, BBIL did have such authority. There is, however, nothing in either decision that indicates any factual difference in the mandate of the two banks. The second, and more convincing, course is to take the reasoning of Lord Fraser in *The Laconia* and to say that in both cases the payment was made and accepted, but that the payment in *The Laconia* did not amount to a waiver by the owners of their rights under the charter.

3.57 The conclusion has to be that the point of acceptance of a payment is difficult to predict and is sensitive to the facts of individual cases. This is, of course, a significant difficulty for any lawyer structuring a transaction in which the point of payment might be a critical factor.

Disruption in the money transmission process

3.58 The transmission of any money payment through the banking system involves a number of stages. In many cases, the detail of the steps involved will not be known to the payer and payee. For example, it is unlikely that the charterer and shipowner in *The Laconia* case were aware that their banks would use the London Dollar Clearing System, and would certainly not have known the details of the operation of that arrangement. Between the payer's decision to perform his payment obligation and the receipt by the payee of the contemplated payment, there are many opportunities for something to go wrong.

3.59 Some of the events which might derail performance of the payment obligation in a contract are the same, or of the same nature, as those which might disrupt the performance of other contractual obligations. A strike by bank employees or the breakdown of a bank's computer systems might mean that a payment obligation is not performed, in the same way that a shipping company's computer failure might result in cargo not being loaded as required by contract of affreightment. The same principles of contract law will apply in both cases. The lawyers drafting the contracts will address the same points and concerns when considering the terms of *force majeure* clauses. In financial contracts, where the payment of money is often the central purpose of the arrangement, there are additional potentially disruptive events which need to be addressed by the lawyers who design financial operating systems and draft financial contracts.

3.60 Some of these disruptive events – the terms of legislation designed to block the assets of criminals or terrorists, governmental freeze regulations relating to particular countries or their residents, freezing injunctions granted by local or foreign courts, insolvency that affects one of the banks in the payment chain, are outlined below. The list is not exhaustive. In addition, the disruptive event, in the case of an international payment, might occur in, or under, the laws of any state through which the payment passes, or to the jurisdiction of which one of the parties might be subject.[34] It is not possible to draw up a checklist of things that might go wrong, and to draft with reference to this list. It is suggested that the draftsman should examine the payment mechanisms involved in the transaction with which he or she is dealing, and try to identify the events that might disrupt the payments contemplated. He or she should then ask three questions that would be relevant if the disruptive event happened:

1. Has payment been made?
2. If not, has payment been tendered but not accepted?
3. If payment has not been tendered, does the disruptive event provide the payer with an excuse for non-payment, and if so, what are the contractual consequences?

In order to test this approach, a useful exercise is to examine two sets of events from the late twentieth century, both of which involve governmental embargo legislation, and a more recent case where the disruptive event is a court injunction against payment.

---

[34] In the *Libyan Arab Foreign Bank* case discussed below, the executive order which imposed the freeze was addressed to 'US persons' wherever they were operating. The order therefore applied (as a matter of US law) to Bankers Trust Company, operating through its London branch.

The Libyan Arab Foreign Bank case

3.61 The Libyan Arab Foreign Bank was incorporated in Libya and wholly owned by the Libyan state. It acted as the main channel of payments for Libya's overseas trade. It maintained a US dollar account with Bankers Trust Co, a New York bank. The terms of the contract under which the account was operated were disputed. For the purposes of his judgment, however, the trial judge in proceedings in England found that, in addition to an account with BT's head office in New York, LAFB had a US dollar account with BT's London branch, that the contract between banker and customer in respect of that account was governed by English law, and that one of the terms of the contract was that the amount outstanding at any time was payable to the customer on demand.

3.62 On 8 January 1986, the President of the United States issued an executive order in the following terms:

> I, Ronald Reagan, President of the United States, hereby order blocked all property and interests in property of the Government of Libya, its agencies, instrumentalities and controlled entities and the Central Bank of Libya that are in the United States that hereafter come within the United States or that are or hereafter come within the possession or control of US persons including overseas branches of US persons.

BT was a US person. The requirement to 'block' the property of LAFB was therefore binding on the London branch of BT, as a matter of the law of New York and all other US states.

3.63 Following the Presidential Order, LAFB demanded payment of the balance of US$131.5m standing to the credit of the account in London, or alternatively payment of the sterling equivalent. Payment was demanded by way of banker's draft or in cash. When the money was not forthcoming, LAFB issued proceedings, which came before Staughton J in June 1987.[35] In the proceedings, LAFB claimed the US$131.5m demanded; its claim was for the contract debt. It further argued that, if the effect of the Presidential Order was to prevent performance of the contract, it had been frustrated, and accordingly it was entitled to be repaid all sums flowing into the account, on the basis of s 1 of the Law Reform (Frustrated Contracts) Act 1943.[36]

3.64 The defence of BT to these points rested on the rule of English law established in *Ralli Brothers v Compania Naviera Sota y Aznar*.[37] The rule is that if, in a contract governed by English law, an obligation is required to be carried out in a foreign country where the act concerned is illegal, performance of the contractual obligation is excused. The BT argument was that the payment of the sums claimed in US dollars in accordance with the contract would necessarily involve actions being carried out in New York[38] that were illegal under the law of New York. The rule in the *Ralli Brothers* case excused compliance with the demand for payment in dollars. BT denied that LAFB had the right to demand payment in sterling as an alternative.

---

[35] *Libyan Arab Foreign Bank v Bankers Trust Co* [1989] 1 QB 728.
[36] It also claimed US$161.3m, in respect of a further sum which should have been transferred from New York to the London account, but which had been blocked in New York.
[37] [1920] 2 KB 287.
[38] See para 3.33 above and the diagram set out there.

3.65 In the *Ralli Brothers* case an English firm chartered a ship from Spanish owners to carry a cargo of jute from Calcutta to Barcelona at a freight of £50 per ton. Half was payable (and was paid) on loading. The balance was to be paid on arrival in Barcelona in pesetas in cash or bills, converted at the then current rate of exchange. Before the ship reached Barcelona, a decree had been passed in Spain limiting the amount of freight that could be paid for jute to 857 pesetas per ton. When the ship landed, the company that received it paid the balance of the freight outstanding, up to 875 pesetas per ton. The owners claimed in London the difference between the sterling equivalent of 875 pesetas per ton and the contract rate of £50 per ton. The Court of Appeal held that the obligation of the charterers with respect to payment had to be performed in Spain, according to the contract. Since, by the law of Spain, the payment of freight above 875 pesetas per ton was illegal, that part of the contract which required the payment of freight in excess of this figure was invalid and could not be enforced against the charterers. The claim therefore failed. The grounds were put succinctly by Scrutton LJ:

> ... where a contract requires an act to be done in a foreign country, it is, in the absence of very special circumstances, an implied term of the continuing validity of such a provision that the act to be done in the foreign country should not be illegal by the law of that country. This country should not in my opinion assist or sanction the breach of the laws of other independent States.

3.66 The court was at pains to limit the observations that it made. The charterers had paid freight at the maximum level permitted by Spanish law. The claim against them had related to the difference between this figure and the contract price. The court was not asked to decide what would have been the situation, if the charterers had declined to pay at all. Scrutton LJ said:

> I understand our decision only to settle the point whether the Spanish shipowner can claim freight from the charterer at the rate of 50l. per ton in spite of the law of Spain, and hold that he cannot. What freight he can claim, in view of the actual facts which are not fully before us, we do not decide.

3.67 In the *LAFB* case, BT's argument was that its obligation to pay to its customer the amount of the debt standing to the credit of the London account could be performed only by using a method that involved something being done in New York. The only payment process contemplated by the contract was to follow a procedure which involved banks in New York making payments between themselves, 'across the books' of the Federal Reserve Bank of New York. LAFB's rights as a customer were to demand payment only by a method that involved a transfer being made in New York.

3.68 Before deciding this point, the court looked at each of the ways in which the debt constituted by the London account might have been discharged, commenting on whether the particular method was something which necessarily involved an act being carried out in New York.

  1. In-house transfer
     If LAFB had wished to pay the money away to a third party which held an account at BT's London branch, it could have demanded that BT debit its account and credit

that of the third party. Complying with this request would have amounted to payment by BT to LAFB.

This had not been requested by LAFB. In any event, it would not have been helpful to LAFB to have the funds transferred to a friendly nominee which happened to hold an account at BT's London branch. When that nominee tried to transfer the money away, BT would have suffered from exactly the same problem as it had, when the account was in the name of LAFB itself.

However, if such an in-house transfer had been carried out, the court held that it would not have involved any action being taken in the United States.

2. Correspondent bank transfer

This involved a similar situation, where another bank located outside the United States held an account for BT and also for LAFB (or its nominee). Provided that BT had a credit balance at the correspondent bank in excess of US$131.5m, it could have instructed the correspondent bank to debit its account and credit that of LAFB. BT could then have exercised its right of consolidation, to debit the amount standing to the credit of LAFB in its books in London and to set off against LAFB's reimbursement obligation arising from the transfer made at the correspondent bank.

Again, the court held that this would not have involved any act being done in New York.

3. CHIPS or Fedwire

These are the two systems used to effect transfers between banks across the books of the Federal Reserve Bank of New York, and are the only forms of settlement that, on BT's argument, were permitted by the contract.

Of course, using either of these methods would have involved the doing of an act in New York which was unlawful under local law.

4. Banker's draft

When making its demand for payment on BT, LAFB had demanded that it be paid by a negotiable banker's draft for US$131m 'drawn on Bankers Trust London payable in London to ourselves (Libyan Arab Foreign Bank) or to our order'. As an alternative, it demanded payment in cash, although expressing the view that a banker's draft would be preferred.

Staughton J thought that the provision of a banker's draft in London would not have involved anything being done in New York. However, he observed, the provision of the draft would not have solved the problem, but would only have postponed it. The question then would have arisen how the bank would honour the draft when called upon to do so. As he put it:

> The Libyan Bank would receive no credit until the draft had been honoured; and Bankers Trust would have to use another means of transfer in order to honour it.

One might question whether this analysis is correct. The effect of the issue of a banker's draft is that the bank undertakes a completely new obligation when it makes the promissory note which is the banker's draft. The consideration for the bank assuming this new primary liability is the payment by the customer to the bank of an amount equal to the face value of the bank's new obligation. Indeed, bankers often describe the act of issuing a banker's draft at a customer's request as 'selling' a banker's draft to the customer. Further, the normal practice of banks is to debit the customer's account as soon as the draft is delivered, rather than at the point when the bank honours its obligation on the draft. Accordingly, had BT provided its banker's draft as demanded, it would have discharged its payment obligation in respect of the account at that time.

At a later date, if it had declined to honour the draft, because of the existence of the freeze order in the US, an action against it in London (whether by LAFB or by someone else, to whom the draft had been negotiated) would have been an action on the bill itself. The terms of the original account, and the implied terms relating to payment on the account would no longer have been relevant.

It is, perhaps, inaccurate to say that the issue of a draft would merely have postponed the problem; it would have replaced the problem with a slightly different one. And it might be that the answer to that second problem would have been different.

5. Banker's payments and use of clearing systems outside US

In practice, it would not have been possible to effect payment of such a large amount through the London Dollar Clearing System or any of the other arrangements that existed outside the US for clearing dollar payments between banks. These systems are designed to deal with comparatively small payments. It is assumed, in the design of such systems, that large dollar payments will settle through New York.

6. Certificates of deposit

A CD is a document which acknowledges the existence of a debt in favour of the holder by the bank and, in many respects, is the same as a banker's draft. Again, Staughton J points out that the problem is merely postponed until the point when repayment of the CD needs to be made. The analysis gives rise to the same objection as that made in relation to the banker's draft. If LAFB had asked for a CD of US$131m, payable in, say, six months' time and BT had acceded to the request, the obligation to pay US$131m on the call account would have been discharged. Six months later, a question would arise about the method of payment of the CD. It would, however, be a different question.

7. Cash-dollar bills

The court found that it would be possible in practice for BT to obtain US$131m in US dollar bills, although this would have to be done in New York. The dollar bills could then be shipped over to London so the payment could take place there. The obtaining of the notes in New York and shipping them from there would not in itself be enough to invoke the rule in *Ralli Brothers*. The shipping of the dollar bills from New York to London is not part of the act of making payment. The shipment should properly be regarded as a preparatory act under which BT would 'equip itself for performance'.[39]

3.69 Having set out the ways in which payment might be effected, the court went on to decide which of the methods could, under the terms of the account contract, have been demanded by LAFB. It should be remembered, of course, that no method of payment had been explicitly agreed between the parties. The terms of repayment had to be implied.

---

[39] *Toprak Mahsulleri Ofisi v Fiagrain Compagnie Commerciale Agricole et Financiere SA* [1979] 2 Lloyd's Rep 98.

1. CHIPS and Fedwire

    The right of demand on a call account included the right to demand payment through the use of CHIPS or Fedwire. A demand for payment by one of these methods would not have been met, because the steps involved in New York were illegal there, and the rule in *Ralli Brothers* would have excused performance by BT as a matter of English law.

2. Non-US dollar clearing systems

    As regards the use of dollar clearing systems outside the United States, a payment instrument of US$131m would have been too large to be handled under the rules of the systems concerned. LAFB had no right to demand that payment be made in this way.

3. Banker's draft

    The court held, perhaps surprisingly, that one of the terms of the account contract in a case such as this is that the customer was entitled to demand payment by way of banker's draft. In fact, Bankers Trust, London branch, in common with many other branches of overseas banks in London, did not issue its own drafts.[40] BT's custom, if asked to produce a draft, would be to produce a cheque drawn on Lloyd's Bank plc. The court regarded this as making no difference, and therefore held that LAFB was entitled to demand that BT issue such a cheque, but added the proviso that the cheque should be capable of being cleared through the London Dollar Clearing System (ie so that the payment of it need not clear through New York, where it would be caught by the illegality). It is easy to see why LAFB, in the circumstances, would not want to receive a cheque or other instrument which cleared in New York. It is difficult to understand the court's view that, under the implied terms of the contract, the customer was not entitled to demand a draft of a nature which the customer would not have wanted, but was entitled to demand only one that would better suit its purposes.

    LAFB did, in fact, demand that a banker's draft be issued in payment. The judge found that BT was not obliged to comply with the demand (on the basis of the rule in *Ralli Brothers*). However, he left open the question whether, if a banker's draft of the kind requested had been capable of being cleared though the London Dollar Clearing System, that settlement would have involved the doing of an act in New York, when the consequences of the London system cleared through New York later in the day. Had he addressed the question, the answer might well have been affirmative. The transfers made through a US dollar settlement system based outside the United States are netted offshore and then reflected in net settlements in New York. A settlement bank in New York which was aware that its settlement figures included the payment of funds which belonged to the Libyan government would be unable to process the net settlement payments. Assuming full disclosure of the facts, settlement though an offshore settlement system would be no more possible than payment directly through New York.

---

[40] The reasons for this are largely based on regulatory and tax issues. Since the issue of a draft involves the assumption of liability by the legal entity making it, rather than it being a liability of the branch only, there is a risk that the corporate entity might be held to be carrying on a business in London, separate from the business of the branch.

It is interesting to consider what would have been the position, if BT had (presumably with the consent of the relevant authorities in the United States) complied with LAFB's demand, and drawn a cheque for US$131m on Lloyd's Bank. Such a cheque would necessarily have cleared through New York, and payment would have been blocked there. But in that situation, would not BT have complied with its contractual obligations to LAFB?

4. Certificate of deposit

As far as certificates of deposit are concerned, the court held that the customer had no right to demand that one be issued as way of making payment for the debt owing to him. The making of a certificate of deposit involved agreeing a maturity period and a rate of interest. It must, of its nature, be negotiated separately. It could not be implied that the terms would be agreed.

5. Cash–dollars

The judge then turned his attention to whether the customer had the right to demand payment of the US$131m in cash, in the form of dollar bills. He held that he did. This was, he said, a fundamental right of a customer under the terms of a London call account. This right can, of course, be ousted by the specific terms of a contract, but in the absence of contrary agreement:

> ... every obligation in monetary terms is to be fulfilled, either by the delivery of cash, or by some other operation which the creditor demands and which the debtor is either obliged to, or is content to, perform.

He explains the statement by drawing an analogy to commodity futures. In practice, such contracts are settled by the payment of the cash value of the commodities concerned, and not by delivery of the commodity:

> ... but an obligation to deliver and accept the appropriate commodity, in the absence of settlement by some other means, remains the legal basis of these transactions.

The flaw in this comparison is that cash, in the form of bank notes (ie promissory notes issued by a central bank) represents money rather than being, in a true sense, money. Even on its face, a bank note does not claim to be money, but to be a promise to pay money.

It is, perhaps, questionable that a right to demand payment in cash in dollars should have been seen as an implied term of the account contract. The implication of a term in a contract is not a casual matter.[41] The term must be one which is necessary to give commercial efficacy to the contract and which the parties, if asked at the time the contract was made, would have agreed on the basis that 'it goes without saying'.[42] In this case, the account was in foreign currency and regularly handled amounts far in excess of the amounts of cash available in London. The judge accepted that producing the amount of cash concerned in London would have needed the help of the US authorities. Further, the account was established so that sums in LAFB's New York account could be 'parked' in London when markets in New York

---

[41] See Chapter 11 below.
[42] See para 11.98.

were closed overnight and could continue to earn interest. On the facts, it seems highly unlikely that, at the time when the London account was established, the parties would have contemplated withdrawals in cash from the account.

6. Sterling

Staughton J then considered whether LAFB was entitled to demand payment of the dollar sum in sterling. He held that it was. His starting point was the rule in *Dicey & Morris*:[43]

> Where a debtor owes a creditor a debt expressed in foreign currency ... the general rule is that the debtor may choose whether to pay in the foreign currency in question or in sterling.

This statement, he found, had the support of the Court of Appeal in *In re Lines Brothers Ltd*.[44] On this basis, the judge held that the bank had an option to discharge its dollar debt by payment either in dollars or in sterling. If payment by one route is not possible for some reason, he must choose the other route. He took this thought one step further, and considered the question from the point of view of the customer. He concluded:

> When ... there is (as I have held) no express or implied term that the obligation must be discharged only in dollars, I hold that the customer is entitled to demand payment in sterling if payment cannot be made in dollars.

3.70 The analysis used in the case deals with two separate issues: first, it examines the ways in which a bank might discharge an obligation to pay in dollars; and second, it considers the ambit of the customer's right to demand payment. In this latter respect, the judgment is, in some respects, a little unclear. For example, the judge holds that the customer is entitled to demand payment by production of a banker's draft, provided that the draft is capable of being cleared in London. It is, no doubt, true that the customer would not wish to have a draft unless it could clear in London. That is not the same, however, as to say that he has a right to demand payment of a banker's draft only if it will clear in London. There is not a clear distinction drawn between what the contract entitles the customer to demand, and what he would want to demand.

3.71 The outcome, however, is clear. In the absence of agreement to the contrary, a bank account in London in respect of which balances are payable on demand will entitle the customer to demand that the payment be satisfied in a number of different ways, at the customer's option.

3.72 A further important point emerging from the case relates to question 3 set out in para 3.60 above. If the judge had held that the sum could not be repaid without an act being done in New York which was illegal by New York law, what would have been the consequences? In the *Ralli Brothers* case, the members of the Court of Appeal were at pains to point out that they had decided that the payer could not be obliged to pay an amount which was unlawful by the law of the place of payment. They specifically declined to say what the consequences of this decision might be. In the *Libyan Arab Foreign Bank* case, one of the claims by LAFB

---

[43] Dicey and Morris, *The Conflict of Laws* (11th edn, Stevens, 1987), p 1453 (now, Dicey, Morris, and Collins, *The Conflict of Laws* (15th edn, 5th Suppl, 2018), p 2361)
[44] [1983] Ch 1.

was that the contract of deposit was frustrated as a result of the Presidential Order, which made performance impossible. Accordingly, they said, they were entitled to be repaid the amounts standing to the credit on the account, under the terms of s 1 of the Law Reform (Frustrated Contracts) Act 1943, which provides:

> (1) Where a contract governed by English law has become impossible of performance or been otherwise frustrated, and the parties thereto have for that reason been discharged from the further performance of the contract ...
> (2) All sums paid or payable to any party in pursuance of the contract before the time when the parties were so discharged ... shall, in the case of sums so paid, be recoverable by him ...

As an alternative claim, LAFB asked for a restitutionary remedy on the basis of total failure of consideration.

3.73 Staughton J dismissed these claims. Although he had said, earlier in the judgment, that it was possible for a banking contract to be frustrated,[45] this had not happened in the present case:

> ... the obligation of Bankers Trust was suspended but not discharged: *Arab Bank Limited v Barclays Bank (Dominion Colonial & Overseas)Ltd* [1954] AC 495 ... Accordingly I would hold that the contract as a whole has not become impossible at performance or been otherwise frustrated; or at any rate that the parties have not been altogether discharged from further performance.
>
> ...
>
> As to the alternative restitutionary remedy at common law, the consideration given by Bankers Trust has not wholly failed. They are still obliged to repay one day, and meantime to credit interest to the account.

3.74 The *LAFB* case is the only decided case in England to consider in detail the mechanics of international payments and the consequences of those operations. Although the conclusions were not examined by an appeal court, they serve as a useful checklist for anyone who is drafting contact documents or designing the legal basis of a structure which involves the transmission of money across borders.

The 1979 Iranian debt crisis

3.75 The *Libyan Arab Foreign Bank* case was, in one sense, quite simple. The bank had an obligation to pay. It did not pay. It did not tender payment. The only question was whether this failure to pay amounted to a breach of contract, or whether BT was excused performance of its obligation in the circumstances. A rather more fundamental question had arisen some six years earlier.

3.76 In 1979, the revolution in Iran deposed the Shah and installed a new regime, headed by Ayatollah Khomeini. A short time later, President Jimmy Carter allowed the Shah to enter the US in order to be treated for cancer. When this happened, student militants in Tehran stormed the US embassy and took hostage 69 members of staff. In response to this, the US

---

[45] At 749 C.

imposed sanctions against Iran. Executive Order 12170 of 14 November 1979 was in terms even wider than those of the corresponding order in relation to the Libyan assets:[46]

> I, Jimmy Carter, President of the United States ... hereby order blocked all property and interests in property of the Government of Iran, its instrumentalities and controlled entities and the Central Bank of Iran which are or become subject to the jurisdiction of the United States or which are or come within the possession or control of persons 'subject to the jurisdiction of the United States.

At the time, Iranian public sector entities owned large amounts of financial and other assets in the US and held substantial balances with US banks outside the US. In addition, Iranian state entities were heavy borrowers in the euromarkets. They had obligations to make payments under a number of so-called jumbo syndicated loans, which had been organized in London. Under these arrangements, interest was payable, and principal repayable, by credit to a nominated account at a bank in London. In many cases, the London bank concerned was the local branch of a US bank and the borrowings were in US dollars. **3.77**

One of the immediate effects of the Executive Order was that, when Iranian public sector borrowers gave instructions to their bankers in New York to transfer US dollars to the relevant agent bank for the loan concerned, for credit to the designated account with that bank's London branch, the payer's bank would decline to carry out the instruction. No credit appeared in the designated bank account of the London branch. In some cases, the agent bank in London then declared a default under the terms of the syndicated agreement. These declared defaults then triggered the operation of cross-default clauses in many other Iranian borrowing arrangements. **3.78**

Although litigation was started in respect of several loans, it was all terminated by settlement arrangements reached in 1981 between Iran and the United States under which it was agreed that Iranian assets would be returned by the US, and outstanding claims settled by an international tribunal formed for the purpose. **3.79**

The Argentinian bond case

Although the Iranian hostage and the Libyan freeze crises were very unusual and extreme events, they show the way in which the operation of international payment systems can be brought to a juddering halt by external events. The same issue is illustrated by the litigation in New York that surrounds a US dollar bond issue made by Argentina in 2001, expressed to be governed by the law of New York.[47] Argentina found itself unable to pay under the terms of the bond issue, and offered a settlement to the bondholders. They should surrender their bonds in exchange for new bonds. Although the interest rate on the 'exchange bonds' would be lower than that on the original bonds, there was a higher probability that it would be paid. Ninety-seven per cent of holders accepted the settlement, and received new 'exchange bonds'. A minority of holders (the 'holdout bondholders') refused to settle, and began a **3.80**

---

[46] See para 3.62 above.
[47] *NML Capital, Ltd v Republic of Argentina*, filed in the Southern District of New York.

course of litigation, in New York and elsewhere, to enforce payment of the original bonds that they held.

3.81 One of the many claims made by the holdout bondholders was that the bond documentation precluded Argentina from making interest payments to the exchange bondholders, unless it also paid interest due on the original bonds (which Argentina refused to do). In July 2014, Argentina paid to Bank of New York Mellon, the trustee for the exchange bonds, US$539m, the aggregate amount of interest then due, for distribution to those bondholders. This is the primary payment methodology stipulated by the bond indenture.[48] The holdout bondholders then applied for, and were granted, an injunction addressed to the trustee, prohibiting the distribution of the funds to the exchange bondholders.

3.82 One of the many questions for consideration was whether Argentina did fulfil its payment obligation to the exchange bondholders, notwithstanding that the funds were not credited to the accounts of the individual registered bondholders. The answer to this question would involve the court in detailed examination and construction of the bond indenture, and of the facts. It would also raise the questions discussed in the English courts in *The Laconia*[49] and *Momm v Barclays Bank Int. Ltd.*[50] Did the trustee accept the payment on behalf of its beneficiaries, even though it was unable to credit their accounts? If so, has not payment been made?

3.83 In February 2016, Argentina reached a settlement with its bondholders, and the US courts were not required to answer the thorny questions raised by the events. However, the case shows the problems that can arise from such simple issues as the determination of whether a payment has been made.

3.84 The drafting of the documentation for an international financial transaction (indeed, for any large transaction that involves cross-border payment) must address the problems caused by a disruptive event, such as those shown in the three cases discussed above. Assuming that the transaction in question is a syndicated loan agreement, the borrower will wish to be sure that, after it has taken all available steps to pay, it cannot be held to have failed to honour its payment obligation. The lenders, on the other hand, will wish to be clear that, if they do not receive the payment they expect, they will be free to take action to obtain reimbursement (eg by looking to a guarantor or by realizing security).

3.85 The process for the draftsman involves predicting the facts that might emerge in the future. Of its nature, this will be an inexact exercise. However, the most significant faults that might occur with the payment process are now fairly obvious. One can, therefore, put forward a hypothetical set of facts, in this case based upon those of the Iranian debt crisis discussed above, and then examine how an English court might react to them. Drafting can then take account of any pitfalls exposed.

---

[48] The documentation contained a provision that Argentina's payment obligation:

... shall not have been satisfied until such payments are received by registered holders of the [exchange bonds].

It was not clear, however, whether this provision applied to payments made through the trustee. The construction of this provision was one of the issues in dispute.

[49] See para 3.47 *et seq*. above.
[50] See para 3.53 *et seq*. above.

3.86 This example assumes the existence of a hypothetical loan. The facts are sufficiently close to reality for any discrepancies to be unimportant. The loan agreement is one under which A, an Iranian public sector entity, has borrowed US$500m from a syndicate of banks in London. The agent bank for the loan agreement is the London branch of B, a New York bank. The lending banks under the agreement, for whom the London branch of B is acting as agent, are 50 banks, incorporated and operating in a number of different countries. Under the terms of the agreement, A is to make payment of interest at the specified rate every three months. Payment is to be made by credit to an account at B's London branch, identified in the agreement by its number. On 16 November 1979 (two days after the date of the Executive Order[51]), A instructs C, a French bank in Paris, with whom A has a US dollar account which is substantially in credit, to make a payment of the amount then due under the agreement. The instructions are to pay the money to bank B, for the credit of the nominated account at its London branch.

3.87 Assume now two different, but equally plausible steps:

1. Bank C happens to use bank B as its New York correspondent bank. It instructs bank B to debit the account of bank C in its books, and to credit the nominated account at bank B's London branch. Bank B in New York declines to comply with the instructions, because it is prevented from doing so by the Executive Order.
2. Bank C's correspondent bank in New York is bank D. Bank C instructs bank D to debit bank C's account with it and to credit bank B for the credit of the nominated account of bank B's London branch. Bank D debits the account of bank C, but declines to credit bank B, believing that to do so would involve a breach of the Executive Order. Instead, it takes the amount concerned to a suspense account.

3.88 The legal consequences which, as a matter of English law, flow from this situation are far from simple. The most helpful way to consider them might be to examine the facts in the light of the three questions posed in para 3.60 above:

3.89 **1. Has the payer paid?** At first sight, the answer seems simple. Bank B has not credited the nominated account in London. Accordingly, bank B, through its London branch, has not become the debtor of the syndicate banks who are the beneficiaries of that nominated account. On the face of it, payment has simply not been made. However, A might be able to argue that it had been paid. In *The Laconia*, Lord Russell addressed the question of payment into a nominated account, effected through the delivery of a payment order between banks. He said:

> ... it should suffice for punctual payment that such cash equivalent be tendered in due time to the nominated bank to be credited to the named account: this was the method of payment laid down: you cannot pay 'into' an account, whether you are tendering cash or its equivalent.

It should be noted that Lord Russell does not refer to this merely as a good tender of payment. He regards the tender in this case as discharging the debt.

---

[51] See para 3.76 above.

3.90 Again, in *TSB Bank of Scotland v Welwyn Hatfield District Council and Council of the London Borough of Brent*,[52] Hobhouse J drew a distinction between a one-off payment, which requires an act of acceptance by the payee, and a payment made under a contract which provided specifically for the method of payment, in relation to which no acceptance was required of the payee for the payment to be complete. In the passage below, taken from the judgment, the words 'creditor' and 'debtor' appear to have been transposed in some places:

> The physical or ministerial aspect of payment involves the delivery of money by one person to another. Where the two persons meet together face-to-face and the debtor seeks to hand to the creditor legal tender the physical act of delivery (in the absence of some misrepresentation or mistake) will not be achieved without the concurrence of the [debtor]. Where the relevant contract or terms of the debt requires payment to be made in a particular way, as for example by payment into an identified branch of a named bank, the payment will be effected by payment into that account. Prior authority has been given to discharge the debt or other obligation in that way: the [debtor] has authorised the bank (or other relevant person) to receive and accept the money on his behalf. No further act of concurrence or assent is required from the [debtor]. The [creditor] discharges his obligation by making the contractual payment in the contractually stipulated manner.

3.91 In the case where bank C held an account with bank B in New York, A might argue that the instruction to B to debit C's account and credit the nominated account in its specific London branch amounted to payment. Bank B, as agent for the syndicate banks, had authority to receive the payment on their behalf, and to credit the nominated account. A might argue, adopting Lord Fraser's point in *The Laconia*, that the act of bank B in crediting the account of the syndicate banks at its London branch was an administrative matter between the beneficiary banks and their agent. As far as the payer is concerned, the position is the same as if bank B, having received the instruction to credit the account, had decided to appropriate the payment in discharge of obligations owed to bank B by the beneficiary banks on another account. The blocking of the account is a problem that falls on the beneficiary banks, not on the payer, who has performed his contractual obligations.

3.92 It is, of course, true that, under the law of New York, bank B is precluded from making the transfer concerned. A would argue, however, that the Executive Order did not affect the position. Put baldly, bank B had the money, and had been told to make it available to the beneficiary banks. A's payment obligation was to give the money to bank B. It was bank B's task to make it available to the beneficiary banks. A had fully performed its obligation.

3.93 It seems that the argument could not run in the situation where bank C's correspondent bank was bank D. If the account was blocked in bank D, so that no credit was ever received by bank B in New York, it does not seem possible to argue that payment was made.

3.94 2. **If payment was not made, was it tendered?** In the case where bank C's correspondent bank in New York was bank B, A would seem to be on strong ground. Even if A did not succeed with its argument that the payment had been completed by the instruction from C to bank B to credit the London account, A had offered payment in a way that would have

---

[52] [1993] 2 Bank LR 267.

discharged its payment obligation. The fact that bank B was precluded by the Executive Order from accepting the tender would not alter the fact that it had been duly tendered.[53] In the situation where A's correspondent bank in New York was bank D, the inability of bank D to make a credit in favour of bank B would result in the fact that A had not tendered payment to bank B in accordance with the agreement.

3. If A had neither paid nor tendered payment, would it be excused as a matter of law from the consequences of that failure? In looking at this question, a court would be faced with the reverse situation to that in the *Libyan Arab Foreign Bank* case. A would argue that it should be excused the consequences of failure to pay on the basis that payment required things to be done in New York, and those things were illegal by the law of New York. One would expect that the court would consider whether any means was open to A to pay the London branch of B. A would, presumably, run the same argument that Bankers Trust ran in the *Libyan Arab Foreign Bank* case, that the only contractual method of payment for the purposes of the contract was settlement through New York. It would seem that the case here would have a greater chance of success.

3.95

In the *Libyan Arab Foreign Bank* case the account was a London current account with no written terms. In the theoretical Iranian case, there is a very detailed contract, in the form of a syndicated loan agreement. The relationship between A, bank B and the beneficiary banks under the syndicated loan agreement is of a very different nature from the general banker/customer relationship under English law, which applied in the *Libyan Arab Foreign Bank* case. There might well be a strong case that the operations of the syndicated eurodollar loan market contemplated that all payments should be made through New York and that the payer was obliged to settle in no other way.

3.96

If this argument failed, one would assume that the court would take the view, as Staughton J took in the *Libyan Arab Foreign Bank* case, that there were a number of methods open to A to discharge its debt. It could, for example, in the case of interest payments, arrange for the credit of dollars to the account of the London branch of bank B through the London Dollar Clearing System, or through the presentation of a dollar banker's draft drawn by another bank, or by the payment of cash. Whether these options would have been open in the case of payment of principal in a very large amount indeed, is another matter. Moreover, one would have thought it unlikely that the court would take the view that, on the facts, the debt could be discharged in sterling. The eurodollar market is a specialized wholesale market. The participating banks would have funded their loans by themselves borrowing dollars in the euromarket. They would be unlikely to accept, at the time when the contract was concluded, the possibility that the borrower should have the option to repay in a different currency, leaving the banks to bear the risk and cost of converting the sterling into dollars. A would certainly argue that the contract contemplated payments only in dollars. Indeed, it is usual for such loan agreements to provide that payments must be made in the currency selected for the loan.

3.97

---

[53] It does not follow, of course, that because A was not in breach of its payment obligation, the banks in the syndicate would not be able to accelerate payment under the terms of the loan agreement. It might well be that the facts would fall within one of many circumstances (usually called 'events of default') which could trigger such an acceleration. An 'event of default' does not necessarily involve a breach by the borrower of any of its obligations.

3.98 None of the disputes that flowed from the Iranian debt crisis found their way to the courts. Nonetheless, the issues that are raised are clear and require close scrutiny by those who draft financial contracts that call for international payments through the banking system.

Interdiction legislation

3.99 In the last 30 years, governments throughout the world have looked for ways to control organized crime, drug trafficking, and terrorist activities by denying criminals the ability to move funds through the banking system, by freezing assets within the system that might be the fruits of crime, and then by confiscating those assets through legal process. The mechanics of these legislative processes are usually to place an obligation on banks and others concerned with the movement of money to report suspicious activity and to refrain from helping to move suspected funds. An examination of money laundering legislation lies outside the scope of this work. It is, however, relevant to look at examples of the way in which 'interdiction legislation' might disrupt the flow of payments in legitimate transactions.

3.100 An example of the kind of legislation concerned is the Proceeds of Crime Act 2002. By s 328(1):

> A person commits an offence if he enters into or becomes concerned in an arrangement which he knows or suspects facilitates (by whatever means) the acquisition, retention, use or control of criminal property by or on behalf of another person.

The terms are very wide. As far as banks are concerned, they prohibit a bank from carrying out normal banking transactions for a customer, for example by honouring cheques or otherwise paying money away from an account that is in credit, if the bank suspects that the money in the account may be the fruits of criminal activity somewhere in the world.

3.101 The unfortunate effects for the customer can be seen clearly in the facts of *Squirrell Ltd v National Westminster Bank plc (Customs & Excise Commissioners intervening)*.[54] Squirrell was a company which dealt in various items, including mobile telephones. The bank suspected that money in its account might be the fruits of a so-called 'carousel fraud' under which small high-value items were imported and exported from the UK in such a way as to evade the payment of Value Added Tax. The activity was a criminal offence. Once the bank's suspicion was aroused, it had no alternative but to freeze the account in accordance with section 328. Squirrell applied for an order that its account be unfrozen. There was no evidence before the court of any wrongdoing by Squirrell. The judge held that, although he sympathized with Squirrell, he could not make the order sought. Section 328 applied to the bank as soon as it had a suspicion that money in the account might be the proceeds of crime. As soon as the suspicion entered its mind, it was obliged to report the matter to the relevant authorities, and to decline to carry out instructions of the customer in relation to the account.

3.102 In *In re K (Restraint Order)*,[55] an order had been made under the Drug Trafficking Offences Act 1986, freezing a customer's account with its bank. In this case, the bank wished to use

---
[54] [2005] EWHC 664 (Ch).
[55] [1990] 2 QB 298.

the balance on the frozen account to offset against sums it was owed on other accounts by the same customer. It relied on the banker's right of consolidation of accounts at common law[56] and on a specific letter of set-off signed by the customer. The court allowed the bank to combine accounts, on the basis that the exercise of this right did not amount to 'disposing of or diminishing' assets of the customer, the act prohibited by the restraint order imposed upon the bank. The court's reasoning was that the asset concerned (the credit balance on the account) was 'encumbered' by the set-off agreement, and that the exercise of the rights of the bank, whether at common law or under the terms of the agreement, did not have the effect of diminishing the value of the asset so encumbered.

3.103 Although interdiction legislation usually provides statutory defences for the bank against criminal liability if it complies with the obligations imposed on it by the statute, the question remains whether it might incur liability to its customer for breach of its contractual obligations in relation to the account concerned. Normally, the issue would not arise. If the bank is prevented by statute from complying with its contractual obligations, its contractual obligations will be suspended during the period when it is under statutory constraint. Indeed, in *Shah v HSBC Private Bank (UK) Ltd*,[57] the court held that there was an implied term in the contract between bank and customer that relieved the bank of contractual liability in such a case. If the bank was required by the Proceeds of Crime Act to report to the relevant authorities that it held suspicions that money in its customer's account might include the proceeds of crime, it was relieved of its contractual obligations to comply with its customer's instructions and to tell the customer what it had done, unless the appropriate consents had been given.

3.104 However, a case in 2004 illustrated the problems for a bank if it does not tread carefully in this particular minefield. In *Tayeb v HSBC Bank plc*,[58] the claimant, a Tunisian national who did not live in the UK, opened an account with the Derby branch of HSBC. He was about to conclude a business deal and needed an account to receive payment. He had relatives who lived in Derby and who recommended the bank to him. His business transaction involved the sale of certain intellectual property rights to a Libyan corporation for the sterling equivalent of US$1.5m. The sale was completed and the purchase price, of just under £1m, was transferred through CHAPS from Barclays Bank in Westminster to HSBC in Derby. Upon receipt, the assistant manager of HSBC's branch became suspicious that the transaction might involve some criminal activity. If the bank assisted, it might have been at risk of committing an offence under s 93A of the Criminal Justice Act 1988.

3.105 The bank's assistant manager put a 'marker' on the account. This was an internal HSBC procedure which indicated that no transaction was to take place without the consent of the assistant manager concerned. After unsuccessful attempts to find out more facts, HSBC decided that it was unhappy with the whole transaction, and sent the payment back to Barclays through CHAPS, for the account of the payer, Barclays' customer. The funds from the Barclays account were subsequently remitted abroad. The claimant sued HSBC for the sum that it had sent back to Barclays without his instructions. He succeeded. HSBC argued, somewhat optimistically,[59] that it had not accepted the payment from Barclays for the

---

[56] See paras 3.20 *et seq*.
[57] [2012] EWHC 1283 (QB).
[58] [2004] EWHC 1529 (Comm).
[59] See paras 3.41 to 3.57 above.

account of their customer, and therefore remitting the payment to Barclays did not involve paying away the customer's money without his consent. This argument was rejected. As soon as the money was received by HSBC it was accepted on behalf of the customer under an authority implicit in the operation of the account. HSBC thereupon became indebted to the customer for the amount of the payment. Accordingly, when it later remitted the sum to Barclays, it did so without the authority of its customer and was not entitled to debit the customer's account in order to reimburse itself. In this case, the bank clearly made a mistake. It is, however, easy to see how such a mistake could be made by a bank that was simply trying to comply with its obligation.

3.106 It is easy to see the danger that interdiction legislation poses for innocent payers who are suspected, reasonably but wrongly, of involvement in criminal activities. They may find that payment instructions are declined, causing them to commit a breach of a payment obligation that they are trying to fulfil. They may find that they have no claim for recompense against the bank that declined to make the payment concerned.

3.107 This uncomfortable fact is recognized by the courts. In the *Shah* case, the judge said:

> … the reporting regime under POCA, necessarily in my view, makes inroads into the contractual duty of bankers to comply with a customer's payment instructions. It is plain that POCA has intervened in the contractual relationship between banker and customer in a way which may cause the customer prejudice. This has been recognized by the courts. However, the courts also recognize that it is a price Parliament has deemed worth paying in the fight against money laundering.[60]

This will be of scant comfort to a company or individual that finds itself paying the price the Parliament has decided needs to be paid.

Freezing orders

3.108 In 1975, the High Court in England issued an order requiring a defendant not to dispose of assets within the jurisdiction, pending the outcome of the claim against it.[61] The Mareva injunction, named after the claimant in the case where it was first granted, has been adopted in many Commonwealth counties and has expanded in its scope. It is now embodied in the Civil Procedure Rules 1998, r 25.1, under which the court may grant as an interim remedy:

> an order (referred to as a 'freezing injunction')—
> (i) restraining a party from removing from the jurisdiction assets located there; or
> (ii) restraining a party from dealing with any assets whether located within the jurisdiction or not.

From the point of view of a payment transaction, the dangers for an innocent payer posed by a freezing injunction are similar to those that might arise if a suspicion on the part of one of the banks involved in the payment process triggers the operation of a statutory freeze under the Proceeds of Crime Act 2002 or other interdiction legislation.

---

[60] See also the remarks of Longmore LJ in *K Ltd v National Westminster Bank plc* [2007] 1 WLR 311 at para 22.
[61] *Mareva Compania Naviera SA v International Bulkcarriers SA* [1975] 2 Lloyd's Rep 509.

Herstatt risk

3.109 Insolvency of other parties is an unavoidable risk in any commercial activity. Any payment process that involves a number of steps between different parties involves the risk that, before the process is complete, one of the parties may become insolvent. Such an insolvency may affect either the payer or the payee. If a payment reaches the payee's bank and the payee's account has been credited, the subsequent insolvency of the receiving bank might result in the payee not receiving full value for the payment made and credited to its account. The payer, however, has discharged his payment obligations. At the other end of the transaction, if the payer gives instructions to his bank to make a payment and, before it carries out those instructions, the bank becomes insolvent, the payee will never receive the payment. The payer will remain liable on its underlying obligation to pay. The detailed analysis of the payment process, will, in such a case, determine whether the underlying obligation has been performed or not, and will also show where the loss has fallen.

3.110 A particular kind of insolvency risk was shown in the case of the collapse of Bankhaus Herstatt, a small German bank active in the foreign exchange market. On 26 June 1974, the bank's licence was withdrawn at the end of the banking day (4.30pm local time). In New York the time was 10.30am. Herstatt immediately ceased trading and instructed its correspondent banks in New York to make no further payments. Herstatt had foreign exchange contracts with various counterparties in which Herstatt had agreed to buy deutschmarks in exchange for US dollars, which were to settle on 26 June. Settlement of the deutschmark leg of the contract (ie the payment to Herstatt by the counterparty of deutschmarks) had already taken place across the books of the Bundesbank by 4.30pm German time. However, payment of the dollar leg by Herstatt was not due to happen until the end of banking hours in New York. Accordingly, its counterparties in the trades concerned found themselves in the position where they had paid out the deutschmarks, but did not receive the US dollar equivalent.

3.111 The problem has been solved, so far as large payments are concerned, by the creation, almost 30 years after the event, of continuous linked settlement. This is an arrangement under which some of the world's largest banks settle foreign exchange transactions among themselves, either for their own account or for that of customers. The process is managed by CLS Group Holdings AG and payments settle through a settlement bank owned by the Group. The central feature of the system is that settlement takes place on a payment-versus-payment basis. In other words, payment of the two currencies concerned happens simultaneously.

3.112 Within the EU, security for payment systems is provided by legislation made under the Settlement Finality Directive[62] of 1998. This was implemented in the UK by the Financial Markets and Insolvency (Settlement Finality) Regulations 1999.[63] The purpose of the legislation under the Directive is to ring-fence designated payment systems and systems for settlement of securities trades. The consequence is that, once a payment has been entered into a designated system, the insolvency of any participant in that system should have no effect on the payment. From the point of view of the payer and payee, it is not simply a

---

[62] Directive 98/20/26/EC.
[63] SI 2979/1999.

matter that the payment is deemed to have been made when it enters the payment system. The consequence of the Directive's provisions is that the payment will actually pass through the system and into the hand of the payee, notwithstanding that the system participant concerned was in insolvency at the time the payment was passing through its hands. This provision is of importance in respect of the payment of money. It is of even more importance in relation to the settlement of trades in securities.

New Payment Technologies

3.113 The invention and development of new technologies can have a profound effect on the way in which business is conducted. In turn, this may lead to the development of new legal concepts or the adaption of old ones. A well-known example is the introduction of the marine steam engine in the mid-nineteenth century. Steam ships were much faster than sailing vessels. After their advent it was possible for a bill of lading for the cargo on a sailing ship to be sent by steam ship to the port of destination of the cargo, where it would arrive weeks before the goods themselves. This gave traders and financiers opportunities for trading in the goods that would not have existed in times when the documents of title arrived at the same time as the cargo. The law was forced to develop new rules of law to deal with issues that arose out of that new trading activity.

3.114 The invention of the telephone, and later of the computer and satellite communication, allowed ways of trading that before had not been possible. In the securities industry dealers established offices in different time-zones. When the sun went down at the end of a trading day in Tokyo or Singapore, the dealer could pass its 'book' to the London or Frankfurt office by sending the records of the day's trading by computer link. The European office could then deal with the same assets and contracts until the end of its day, when it would pass the 'book', in its amended state, to its New York office. This raised a question: if the Tokyo office bought stock and the same asset was sold a few hours later by the New York office at a profit, where was the profit made? This was of interest not only to the trader (and its individual employees whose bonuses would be affected) but also to the tax authorities in Japan and the US.

3.115 Such conceptual problems have been complicated further by the development of the internet. In a world of overlapping jurisdictions, most of which assert competence and authority on the basis of geography, the issue of where an event occurred is often the first to be confronted. Lawyers must find the answer before they can take the next step. To the developers and users of the internet, to ask where an event to place might be as irrelevant as asking what colour it was.

3.116 The area of activity where there is the greatest mismatch between modern trading procedures and the legal concepts and rules relating to them is, perhaps, the area of securities trading. The Court of Appeal faced this problem in *Macmillan Inc. v Bishopsgate Investment Trust plc (No 3)*.[64] This case, which arose out of the collapse of the Maxwell publishing empire in the early 1990s, turned on the determination of the correct governing law for

---

[64] [1996] WLR 387.

deciding a dispute about the ownership of shares in a US company. It is instructive to follow the judges through the labyrinth of legal argument that tried to make the facts of modern share-trading practice fit within the framework of established legal rules. It is hard not to think of the old Irish story of the man who asked a stranger for directions to Dublin, and met with the reply:

> If you want to go to Dublin, you shouldn't be starting from here.

Against this confused background a new technology is rapidly developing. The idea of Distributed Ledger Technology (DLT) saw the light of day in 2008 in the White Paper posted on the internet in the name of Satoshi Nakamoto. It was part of the infrastructure of Bitcoin, the first cryptocurrency. Its form, so far as it relates to cryptocurrencies, is discussed in Chapter 2.[65]   **3.117**

DLT is not confined in its application to the world of cryptoassets. It was developed as a method for dealing with the transfer of assets in that area, but has the potential for much wider application.[66] It is, in essence, a way of sending messages. The messages might relate to a variety of issues. In the finance industries, many projects have begun with the aim of identifying activities in which the adoption of DLT can add security or speed to current processes. In particular, banks have established projects to look at the making of payments in the wholesale markets. The current way in which cross-border payments are made involves a number of steps,[67] each of which takes time (and, therefore cost) and is a source of security risk. The simplification of this process will be a great prize for those who devise it. The same is true for processes to deal with the transmission of messages about other assets, in particular securities and commodities.   **3.118**

At its simplest, DLT can be described as a system for sending messages over the internet to a number of recipients, each message including its own history. Thus, each recipient sees not only the current sender and destination of the message but also every previous sender and recipient of the same message. This information is sent to all participants in the relevant system.[68] This makes the subject-matter of the message very secure. It is impossible for any outsider to alter the information included in the message, because the correct information has been disseminated throughout the system, and appears on the computer of every participant. Any alteration would be instantly noticed.   **3.119**

Since DLT is a system for sending messages, it might be used to carry messages about a number of different things. The message might be, for example, '*The controller of this system address is the owner of one unit of stock in X plc.*' In this case, the message has become the digital equivalent of a bearer share certificate. Or, DLT might be used to transfer between A and B sums owing to A from Bank C, without the need to have the transfer effected by Bank C altering its own account records.   **3.120**

---

[65] Paras 2.136 to 2.147.
[66] The form of DLT adopted for the purposes of the Bitcoin structure was called 'blockchain' and that name is often used, confusingly, to describe forms of DLT that have different characteristics.
[67] See para 3.33 and Figure 3.2 above.
[68] The identities of the parties will usually be in encrypted form so that, even though the code is seen by all, it is impossible to identify the people to whom it relates.

3.121 A DLT system does not need to be open to the public, as is the case with cryptocurrencies. Instead, the system might be 'permissioned'—available only to a selected group of participants. The 'public keys' that constitute the system addresses of participants might be made available only to other participants who have been chosen because they belong to a particular group (eg the clients of a particular stockbroker, or account-holders with an individual bank). The system could then be confined in its operation to transactions between the members of that class. A good example of this kind of 'closed' system is the JPM Coin, a system that allows the transmission of US dollars directly between institutional customers of JP Morgan, the US bank. This system is described in paras 3.125 to 3.127 below.

The potential uses of DLT

3.122 It is too early to say where the exploration of DLT's potential will lead. But it is likely that successful applications will emerge in the area that has been the Philosophers' Stone[69] of financial markets for many years. That is the search for 'disintermediation' or, as it is now commonly called, 'decentralization'. The underlying idea is that much of what happens in finance is concerned with moving capital from those who have it to those who need it. Thus, banks take money on deposit from customers and then lend it to other customers who wish to borrow. This 'intermediation' is inefficient. It takes time and costs money. In addition, the transmission process involves the routing of transactions through central bodies that control the system. This routing is inefficient. The road to improvement, it is said, lies in finding methods for bypassing the intermediaries and central bodies.

3.123 The growth of the internet has led to much greater ease of communication and opened up the possibility of direct contact between the consumers of capital and the providers. From this has grown, for example, peer-to-peer lending, in which individuals lend money to small companies, receiving a higher rate of interest than they would receive from a bank, while the borrower pays less than a bank would charge. It has to be said that the growth in these areas has not been spectacular. In lending transactions, banks do not merely act as conduits for funds. They also take the credit risk of the transactions.

3.124 Nonetheless, there are functions which are essentially mechanical. Examples might be the transfer of money across national borders, or the settlement of securities trades by the transfer of securities and the payment of the price. If DLT can provide a way of simplifying the steps that are needed, at the same time eliminating the risk of something going wrong during the process, it will reduce cost and increase security.

3.125 An indication of one of the possible courses of development is the prototype system of internal money transmission announced by JP Morgan.[70] The system described is a way in which large-scale US dollar payments may be made between customers of the bank, without the need to use the bank's standard internal accounting and recording process. When a customer wishes to pay dollars to another customer, it initiates the transaction by buying JPM

---

[69] The mythical catalyst that could change base metal to gold, the search for which occupied many alchemists in medieval Europe.
[70] *J.P. Morgan Creates Digital Coin for Payments*: Announcement published by JP Morgan on 14 February 2019.

Coins for dollars on a one-for-one basis. These 'stablecoins' are then transmitted through the 'permissioned' DLT system to the payee, who sells them to the bank on receipt for dollars, again on a one-for-one basis. The seller's dollar account with the bank is debited and the recipient's account credited instantaneously.

The potential benefits of this are quite clear, particularly if the system can be widened to include payments made to accounts at other banks. The attenuated chain of message transmission that is involved in an international payment[71] would be dramatically shortened, reducing cost, time, and risk. However, to call the system a 'cryptocurrency' or to name the message sent as a 'coin' is unnecessary. In *R v Preddy*[72] Lord Jauncey[73] explained the numerous steps taken in a simple transmission of a bank balance, by extinguishing the *chose in action* that constitutes the account balance and subsequently creating a new debt to replace it. If one wishes to create a function under which the account-holder can make the transfer without the involvement of any other party, it cannot be done by enabling him to deal with the *chose in action* that is the bank balance. One must instead convert that *chose* into a message that is capable of transmission through the system without the involvement of the bank, or of any other outside party.   **3.126**

This is what the JP Morgan system seems to do. If a customer wishes to send dollars to another customer, he initiates a process under which the debt owing to him from the bank is extinguished and replaced by a message which is sent by DLT to the account of the payee. On receipt, the message is deleted and a new debt, from the bank to the payee, is created. The system seems very neat. Its benefits will probably be realized only when it is expanded to permit payments to other banks, when the transmission process that is avoided will be more complex. Its core is the creation of a message that can be sent by DLT. There is no reason to complicate matters by calling that message a 'cryptocurrency' or a 'stablecoin'.   **3.127**

There are clearly going to be activities in which DLT will prove beneficial. On the other hand, there are reasons to predict that in some areas the outcome is likely to be less exciting than is hoped. The assumption that is often made is that participants in financial markets will always choose a product or course that increases speed or reduces cost. This is not always true. Intermediaries often perform functions which their clients value highly, in addition to their principal activity. In securities markets, for example, custodian banks do not only keep their clients' assets safe. They also provide services connected with the ownership of assets, such as making claims for tax refunds, collecting dividend income or interest and maintaining the clients' own records of the assets, which the clients would need to undertake themselves if there were no custodian.   **3.128**

It is noticeable that in the world of cryptocurrencies, the genesis of which was the wish to create peer-to-peer payment systems, without the need for any intermediary to be involved, middlemen have emerged to meet the wishes of the users. There are large numbers of 'exchanges' and 'wallet-holders', who act on behalf of participants in the systems to deal with the assets and take the actions that are needed to operate the system. It may well be that areas will be found in which DLT could be used to simplify or speed up transactions, but in   **3.129**

---

[71] Described in para 3.33 above.
[72] [1996] AC 815.
[73] At 841, quoted in para 3.28 above.

92 PAYMENT

which the market users will prefer to retain the participation of intermediaries, because of the ancillary benefits that they bring.

3.130 The proposal which has received the greatest amount of attention in the press has been the intended creation of Libra, described in its 'official White Paper'[74] as 'a new kind of digital currency built on the foundation of blockchain technology'. The intention is that the currency will be issued and controlled by a not-for-profit membership organization based in Switzerland. Libra will be 'backed by' baskets of fiat currencies and government securities held for it by custodians in various locations (called 'the Reserve'). When new Libra are issued, it will be against payment of fiat currency. Wholesale holders of Libra (eg currency exchanges) will be able to demand that their holdings be redeemed at a value equal to a proportionate part of the Reserve. Redeemed Libra will be destroyed. It appears to be expected that Libra will be freely exchangeable for currencies in the marketplace, and that the price will reflect the value of the Reserve.

3.131 According to the White Paper:

> Libra's mission is to enable a simple global currency and financial infrastructure that empowers billions of people.

The project is promoted by a number of very large technology organizations including Facebook, and several leading payment organizations. However, questions about the project's ability to satisfy regulators and governments on a number of fronts have led many of the original promotors to withdraw. Nonetheless, Libra has not been closed down and may develop as proposed. It is intended to run on a newly developed DLT system. At the outset, access will be on a 'permissioned' basis, restricted to users of the supporting organizations. But the stated intention is to move to an 'open' system within a few years. Since the potential initial users are numbered in billions, it is clear that Libra, if it comes to maturity, will become a major force, not only in payment systems but also in finance throughout the world.

3.132 The White Paper is understandably short on detail. However, it is clear that the intention is to produce a concept that fulfils all the functions of a currency. The only structural differences between Libra and a 'traditional' fiat currency are that Libra will not be issued in token (ie coin or note) form[75] and that the issuer will not be a sovereign entity. Libra, as proposed, is very different from the cryptocurrencies already created. Its development poses major policy questions for governments across the world. They will need to address these questions very quickly.

The regulatory challenge

3.133 It is the irony of DLT that a system in which each transaction carries its own audit trail, where every message has attached to it every previous message about the asset concerned, should be seen as difficult in concept and, perhaps, obscure. The anonymity of DLT systems

---

[74] Released 18 June 2019.
[75] There is no reason that this functionality could not be added later, if the issuer wished.

makes them difficult to regulate and, for this reason, makes them attractive to those who do not wish to be observed. In principle, this ought to signal to regulators and governments that DLT systems could be dangerous. The Financial Stability Board,[76] in its Report on this issue,[77] echoes this concern. The problem that regulators and legislators face is that applications of the new technology are proposed, but the issues which they will raise cannot be assessed until the proposals reach an advanced stage of development. Since most proposals have not reached a detailed stage, they remain untested. The one exception to this is probably the Libra proposal discussed in paras 3.130 to 3.132 above, which has clear political and financial implications that will need to be addressed.

3.134 With this one exception, it is possible to predict that, so far as the integrity of financial markets is concerned, the problems raised by DLT will probably not be as great as might be thought at first.

3.135 First, the potential for DLT lies most obviously in 'permissioned' systems, where a closed group of users transfer money or financial assets among themselves. In these cases, it is likely that the participants in the system will be already subject to financial regulation and supervision. They will be under an obligation to maintain their own records of their dealings and to make these available to supervisors. To the extent that there is a gap in the network, it can be easily closed. One might expect that this will apply to almost all of the wholesale markets.

3.136 At the retail level, there is no reason to believe that the majority of participants will wish to take advantage of the anonymity afforded by 'open' DLT systems. The growth of 'wallet-holders' and 'exchanges' in the cryptocurrency world suggests that many, probably most, participants have no wish to hide their participation. There will be, of course, a constituency of participants whose members wish to use the opacity of an anonymous transfer system to hide their affairs from revenue and police authorities. The demand for this kind of facility is as old as financial crime and taxation. Ways have always been found to cater for the demand. The use of companies with bearer shares, whose ownership cannot be traced through public records, and of bank accounts in jurisdictions where banking law prevents the disclosure of information about the holder of an account has long been common among tax evaders and money launderers. Indeed, the early growth of the international bond market was fuelled by the wish of individuals in Europe to hide their assets from their national tax authorities.[78]

3.137 The development of structures that permit the anonymous transfer of financial assets will be a weapon in the armoury of those who are intent on evading tax or hiding the proceeds of crime. But there is little to suggest that new structures will attract new participants to illegal activity. It may well be that the effective regulation of decentralized structures will be achieved only piecemeal and with great effort. However, the prospect of the growth of such structures does not, in principle, threaten the integrity of the financial system.

---

[76] A body whose members consist of national regulators, central banks, and international bodies active in the area of financial regulation and monetary policy.
[77] *Decentralised financial Technologies: Report on financial stability, regulatory and governance implications*, 6 June 2019.
[78] See para 6.33.

The effect of DLT on legal principles and practices

3.138 DLT introduces into dealings in financial assets the apparently novel idea that each transfer of an asset includes details of all previous transfers in that asset. Of course, the information about historical transactions identifies the parties only by a line of computer code. External evidence is needed to connect that coded identity to a real person. Nonetheless, an audit trail exists, waiting to be decrypted. Indeed, it is a fundamental feature of DLT that, once a piece of information is added to the chain, it cannot thereafter be removed or altered. In contrast, the central records of, say, the ownership of assets held in a clearing system are unlikely to allow tracing of the transactional history of a particular asset.

3.139 In the UK, until the passage of Companies Act 1928, all shares in a company had an individual number, so that the transfers of each share could be traced through the Register of Members. This made the maintenance of the Share Register of large companies very complex and onerous. The 1928 Act removed the need to number shares individually.[79] The underlying rationale was that shares are fungible (ie each share is exactly the same as, and interchangeable with, every other share of the same class) and there is no need to have a record of the ownership of individual securities. The records of a DLT system might, surprisingly, offer more information of past activity in some cases than would the records of an (apparently) more transparent system.

3.140 The idea that the act by which an asset is transferred should carry with it the whole of the asset's history seems, at first sight, innovative. However, it has an echo of legal practice from an earlier age. Until the early twentieth century, when land in England and Wales was transferred, the seller executed and delivered a 'conveyance' of the land that he was selling. In addition, because there was no centralized record of land ownership, the seller had to show to the buyer that he owned the land that he claimed to sell. Without this proof, the buyer could not be sure that he would be acquiring ownership. The process of 'making title' involved producing to the buyer all the documents that formed a chain of title which stretched back in time sufficiently far to assure the buyer that the seller was the owner of the land. It was not unusual for a conveyance to be delivered with a trunkful of old deeds.

3.141 In 1925[80] a statutory system of title registration was introduced. An official body. HM Land Registry, issues a certificate that a named person is the owner of the land concerned, after satisfying itself that such is the case. The certificate also notes any charges and other major encumbrances that affect the owner's title. On a transfer, the document of transfer is delivered to the Land Registry, along with the certificate, and a new certificate is issued that reflects the transaction that has just taken place.

3.142 It is possible to see DLT as a digitalized version of the old system of land conveyancing, without the trunkful of documents. Financial markets have grown used to arrangements under which a central registry or depositary is involved in the transfer of interests and assets, to add a level of security to transactions in those assets. But, as a matter of legal principle,

---

[79] Before 1928, some public companies had taken the step of converting their shares into units of stock. Stock units did not need to have individual numbers.
[80] Land Registration Act 1925.

the use of a central register is not always necessary. A DLT system might equally well suffice to assure the title to assets that are being transferred.

3.143 However, there are challenges for the designers of DLT systems. In particular, although the DLT concept easily deals with the task of showing the ownership of an asset, it will also need to be able to disclose the interests of third parties that affect the asset and the legal rights of the owner. The simple message that '*A transfers the asset to B*' does not indicate that A has the legal authority to pass title. Nor does it assure that there is no other set of legal rules that might conflict with the message. If the asset that is the object of the transfer is, say, a bearer instrument, a message from the holder transferring the asset to another party will not prevent the holder (or a different person who subsequently has possession of the bearer instrument) from obtaining payment by presenting the instrument to the maker of it.[81] The task of devising legal safeguards to ensure that the message does mean what it appears to say may prove to be a difficult one, depending on the nature of the assets concerned.

3.144 A number of projects have been discussed recently that have as their purpose the making of large payments of currency or the transfer of securities within a 'permissioned' system, in order to avoid the complex web of correspondents and intermediaries that must normally be navigated.[82] The process, often called 'tokenisation', usually includes the creation of a digital token that is the object of the transfers, with the issuer undertaking to ensure that the tokens are 'backed' by the currency or other assets that they are said to represent. This might mean that a stock of the assets concerned, equal in value to the tokens issued, would be held by the issuer. These might be held in the same way that the Bank of England holds assets to balance the liabilities that it incurs on the issue of sterling currency.[83] The tokens could then be passed round the system between participants. Any participant could withdraw money or assets from the system by asking for the redemption of his tokens, at a rate pre-determined by the value of the assets that 'back' the issue. For this reason, the tokens are often called 'stablecoins'. The trading of tokens in this way, it is claimed, would speed up and simplify international payments and securities settlement.[84]

3.145 The idea has a digitalized echo of other schemes that facilitate investment in illiquid assets that are inconvenient or cumbersome to hold. In particular, it resembles the schemes set up to allow investment in gold bullion or coins. An example of the dangers in such schemes and the consequences when they go wrong can be seen in the fact behind the *Goldcorp* case.[85]

3.146 In addition, there are political problems associated with the idea of tokenization. Such schemes that were based on the representation of money would seem to bypass controls over the use of national banking systems (and, indeed, the use of national currencies) which are used by states for policy purposes.[86] Once the system has been established and primed with the currency that 'backs' the tokens, there is no effective control over the movement

---

[81] The transferee in the DLT system may, of course, acquire rights in equity in these circumstances.
[82] See para 3.33 and Figure 3.2 above for an example of a typical payment path for international currency transfers.
[83] See paras 2.28 to 2.32 above.
[84] These ideas are essentially more complicated versions of the JPM Coin system described at paras 3.125 to 3.127 above.
[85] *Re Goldcorp Exchange Ltd* [1995] 1 AC 74, discussed at paras 8.27 to 8.36 below.
[86] See paras 2.195 *et seq* above.

between participants of the tokens that represent the currency. Indeed, the system may be designed to be anonymous, so that no-one can tell when a transaction occurs or the identity of the participants.[87]

3.147 This issue could doubtless be addressed by legislation and regulation in the countries whose currency is involved. The problem is that this process will create a further layer of bureaucracy that will cancel out the gains in time that are offered by the DLT system, or will simply make the system unworkeable. A similar issue arose in the UK in the late nineteenth century. The government then, as now, earned revenue by charging stamp duty on documents that transferred the ownership of securities. The practice of companies in issuing bearer shares threatened this, because the transfer of a bearer share certificate by delivery did not involve any document on which stamp duty could be levied. So the UK government simply banned the issue of bearer shares by companies incorporated in the UK. It is easy to foresee similarly drastic action being taken by governments, if they felt that tokenization was nullifying one of their most effective tools of foreign policy.

3.148 The greatest challenge that DLT presents to the principles on which financial markets work is one of location. When an asset is transferred from one participant in a DLT system to another, where does the transfer take place; and where is the asset?

3.149 All developed systems of law have rules of private international law, the purpose of which is to decide in each situation the identity of the national legal system that should be applied to decide the question in issue. The rules of private international law are largely the same in all legal systems.

3.150 As far as financial markets are concerned, the place where a payment was made, or is to be made, may be critical for a number of purposes. As an example, the rule in the *Ralli Bros* case[88] excuses non-performance of a contractual obligation, if performance of that obligation would have been unlawful in the place where it needed to be performed. In the case of an obligation to pay through a DLT system, the term would require payment by reference to a specified system address (often referred to as a 'public key').[89] The key does not have a geographical location.

3.151 In the case of systems designed for dealings in securities, the *Bishopsgate Investment Trust plc* case[90] shows that a problem already exists. In determining the governing law that should be applied to the question before it, the Court of Appeal was faced with a choice between the law of the place where the securities were dealt in, and the place where the issuer was incorporated. If dealings take place in cyberspace, it may be that the law of the place of incorporation of the issuer is the only possibility. In any event, the ability of DLT to remove geography from the picture will make questions of private international law harder to answer.

3.152 The development of DLT-enabled systems in the financial markets will without doubt present challenges to regulatory structures and to legal principles. It is equally clear that, until the technological applications are more advanced, it is impossible to say with any certainty what the challenges will be.

---

[87] This issue presents itself on a large scale with the Libra project described at paras 3.130 to 3.132 above.
[88] *Ralli Bros v Compagnia Naviera Sola y Aznar* [1920] 2 KB 287, discussed at paras 3.64 to 3.66 above.
[89] See para 2.137 and also the explanation of the transmission process at paras 2.138 to 2.143 above.
[90] *Macmillan Inc. v Bishopsgate Investment Trust plc (No 3)* [1996] WLR 387, and see para 3.116 above.

4
PERSONAL AND PROPERTY RIGHTS

> To a civil lawyer 'property' is a thing; to a common lawyer 'property' is a relationship to a thing.
>
> Lord Hoffmann

The Importance of the Distinction

Financial transactions give rise to two separate sets of relationships in English law. First, a transaction may give rise to claims that are based on the ownership of assets. Second, transactions create obligations and rights in the participants, which are owed directly to each other and are capable of being realized only by court action against the relevant individual. Most of these personal relationships arise out of a contract between the parties. However, personal rights may be created out of other circumstances surrounding a financial transaction. For example, the transaction might give rise to a claim by one party against a third party on the basis that the defendant is a constructive trustee because of the way in which it has chosen to interfere in the transaction. 4.01

A single transaction may produce both personal and property rights. For example, a simple loan gives the lender a right to claim personally against the borrower for payment of the debt. At the same time, the lending of the money creates an asset (the debt) capable of being owed. The lender has both a personal right against the borrower and a property right in respect of the asset. 4.02

This much is simple. In financial transactions, the picture becomes much less clear when the transaction involves parties or activities in a jurisdiction where the law looks at rights and obligations differently. If, for example, a London-based mutual fund contracts with a Ruritanian broker to buy shares in a Ruritanian company, and the holding of such shares is recorded on the books of the broker, conceptual problems may well arise if their factual relationship becomes a matter of dispute. The English purchaser may claim to own the underlying securities, as well as being able to claim personally against the broker to compel delivery of the securities. It may be, however, that Ruritanian law does not recognize the relationship as creating rights for the English client which an English lawyer would see as proprietary. Local law may take the view that the broker owns the property registered in its name, since property can have only one owner. On this view, the broker's obligations to the English client arising out of the relationship would be personal. In the event of a dispute or insolvency, this difference of legal view might be crucial, particularly if the English owner had purported to transfer the ownership of the securities to a purchaser, or to give a proprietary interest to a chargee. 4.03

4.04 As far as English law is concerned, the significance of the distinction between property rights and personal rights becomes important when a party cannot in practice protect his or her interests by the assertion of one only of the sets of rights. An example would be where A has agreed to safeguard property belonging to B but has dishonestly sold it to C. If A can be sued (ie has not fled abroad) and is good for the money, B will be satisfactorily served by claiming a breach of A's personal obligation to him. If, however, A has disappeared or is insolvent, that personal claim is worth little or nothing. In this case, B's only hope will lie in asserting his ownership rights in relation to the property, and claiming the property back from C.

4.05 It does not follow that property rights are always more valuable than personal claims. If, in the above example, A was completely creditworthy, and the item had been stolen from him by a thief, who sold it to C in circumstances in which title passed to C, the position would be the other way around. B could not assert any rights to the property against C. He would instead need to look for a personal claim against A (perhaps based on A's failure to fulfil his contractual obligation to look after the property). Further, there may be circumstances where a property right, in the form of a charge or mortgage, might be void for want of registration, while personal rights which in practice lead to the same result would not suffer from the same defect. An example of this can be seen in *In re Charge Card Services Ltd*,[1] where a common form of debt factoring agreement gave the factor the right to retain balances due to the counterparty against the possibility that amounts might become owing in the opposite direction. The liquidator of the counterparty argued that the agreement gave the factor a charge (a proprietary interest) which was void against him for want of registration. The factor contended successfully that the agreement gave it only personal rights, so that no question of registration arose.

4.06 The question of whether the rights of an aggrieved party are personal or proprietary lies at the heart of many financial disputes. This is particularly true in insolvency. The counterparty of an insolvent company often finds itself in a position where, if it relies on its undoubted claim to be paid money, whether in debt or as a matter of damages, it will recover little of what it is owed. If, however, it can successfully claim ownership of assets held by the insolvent company, it will escape without loss. Although this result will be very satisfactory for the claimant, it has the effect of shifting the loss elsewhere. If the claimant to the insolvent company's property can take that property out of the liquidation, its value will not be available to other creditors, whether they are secured or unsecured. Such a claim is, therefore, likely to be contested, if not by the administrator or liquidator of the insolvent company, then by the other creditors who stand to lose. Insolvency litigation often involves a fight over assets between unsecured creditors (who have only personal rights against the insolvent company), creditors who have both personal rights and some form of proprietary claim as well (eg banks which are owed money and which also have a charge over the assets of the company), and claimants who rely on their claim to ownership of assets in the company's possession.

4.07 In insolvency, claims for proprietary interests are often constructed with great complexity and ingenuity. A good example of such a case is *Re Goldcorp Exchange Ltd*,[2] a Privy Council

[1] [1987] 1 Ch 150.
[2] [1995] 1 AC 74.

decision on appeal from the Court of Appeal of New Zealand. Goldcorp was a dealer in gold and other precious metals. It had sold gold bullion and coins to members of the public, on terms that the gold would be retained by the company for safekeeping on a 'non-allocated' basis. In other words, the gold sold to a particular client would be retained in a pool along with gold which had been sold to other clients. The company went into liquidation. The court described it as 'hopelessly insolvent'. It had insufficient assets even to satisfy the claims of the Bank of New Zealand, which held a floating charge. The company had a certain amount of gold, though far less than it had purported to sell to customers, and some cash. The customers, who had undoubted personal claims for damages or for the repayment of sums paid in advance, would recover nothing, unless they could successfully assert ownership rights in respect of Goldcorp's assets.

4.08 The customers put forward a number of ingenious arguments to support their claim to be the owners of the company's various assets:

1. Each customer acquired the ownership of gold equal to that which he had contracted to buy, as soon as he bought it.
2. If a customer had not acquired ownership of gold at the point of sale, he acquired ownership of any gold subsequently bought by the company of an amount necessary to satisfy his contract.
3. When a customer paid over money in order to buy gold, the money was received by the company on trust to apply it for the particular purpose of buying gold, and the money (to the extent that the company still had it) belonged to the customer.[3]
4. The customers were entitled to a restitutionary remedy of a proprietary character in respect of the purchase monies (ie the assets should be treated as belonging to the customers, because the company had breached its fiduciary duties to them).

4.09 The claimants did not succeed. As regards the principal proprietary claim, that they became the owner of gold on paying the purchase price, the position was very simple. The contract was a contract for the sale of goods. Since the goods had never been appropriated to the contract, title had not passed.[4] The alternative claims also failed. The result of the case was not remarkable. The important point about it is the ingenuity and effort deployed in the claimants trying to find a property claim, as giving them their only hope of recovery, even though they had a very clear and undoubted personal claim.

4.10 The importance of the distinction between personal and property claims is illustrated starkly in the decision of the High Court in *Re Lehman Brothers International (Europe) (in administration), Lomas and others v RAB Market Cycles (Master Fund Ltd) and Hong Leong Berhad*.[5] RAB was a hedge fund which had entered into a so-called Prime Brokerage Agreement with LBIE. Under that agreement LBIE advanced money, to be used by RAB for the purchase of securities, acted as a broker in arranging the purchase of securities, and arranged for their retention by custodians. The agreement provided that the securities so purchased would belong to RAB, and RAB granted a charge over them to LBIE to secure amounts owing to LBIE. The securities concerned would produce cash while they were held by LBIE. LBIE

---

[3] See *Quistclose Investments Ltd v Rolls Razor Ltd (in liquidation)* [1970] AC 567.
[4] Section 18 Sale of Goods Act 1908 of New Zealand.
[5] [2009] EWHC 2545 (Ch).

would receive dividend payments in respect of shares, or interest payments in respect of bonds in the portfolio. In relation to debt securities, the assets concerned would ultimately turn into cash as the bonds or government securities matured and were redeemed.

4.11 As far as the cash 'fruits' of the securities were concerned, the agreement contained a rather confusing provision:

> The parties acknowledge and agree that any cash held by us [LBIE] for you [RAB] is received by us as collateral with full ownership under a collateral arrangement and is subject to the security interest contained in the agreement.

When cash was received by the broker (say, by way of interest on a bond held for RAB) it would take the form of a credit in a bank account of LBIE with another bank. LBIE would then, having received that credit to its favour, credit RAB in its own books. The correct analysis of the position is that LBIE acquired an asset (the debt owed to it from the third-party bank concerned), and RAB acquired a different asset (the debt to it from LBIE).[6] The clear intention of the agreement was that the asset acquired by LBIE should not be held by LBIE on trust for RAB. It could not be correct, however, to say that the asset concerned had been *'received by us as collateral . . . and is subject to the security interest contained in the Agreement'*. The draftsman was confusing two separate assets. The intention, on which basis the court proceeded, was that LBIE had acquired the debt from the third-party bank in its own right. The asset which RAB owned, and which it charged back to LBIE as security, was the debt owing to it from LBIE.

4.12 The result was that RAB had a proprietary claim to securities held for it by LBIE. To the extent that cash had been received by LBIE, and was constituted by a debt owed by a third-party bank to LBIE, RAB had no proprietary interest in it. That asset of LBIE was reflected in the books of LBIE as a credit in favour of RAB. It is, of course, true that RAB 'owned' the debt due from LBIE. In practice, however, the ownership of that debt gave it no different rights than were involved in its personal claim against LBIE to be paid the money standing to the credit of its cash account.

4.13 Put starkly, RAB had a proprietary claim to securities in its portfolio held by LBIE. As those securities were transformed into cash, that claim disappeared and was replaced by a personal claim to be paid an amount equal to the sum concerned. When LBIE went into administration, it stopped paying money out to customers, even when it was clear that they were entitled to be paid. All of RAB's securities were, in fact, debt securities. As time passed and the debt securities held for RAB matured, the assets owned by RAB (the securities) would be replaced by cash. RAB was thus faced with the prospect of its proprietary rights simply dissolving, to be replaced by personal rights.

4.14 In the event, the court held that cash received by LBIE after the date of administration should be held on trust for the customers to whom the securities concerned belonged. In effect, the court gave to RAB a property right in the debts owed by third-party banks to LBIE, to replace the property rights in the redeemed securities.

---

[6] See para 3.28 above.

4.15 The case is significant, not because of its result, but because it illustrates the way in which the parties to a very sophisticated agreement had not addressed, at the outset, the consequences that might flow from drawing a distinction between property rights and personal rights. Or it may be, of course, that they had simply not contemplated the possibility that a bank of the size of Lehman Brothers might fail.

4.16 The need to find an advantage, as against other creditors in an insolvency, is not the only reason that a claimant might look for a proprietary claim, in addition to a personal claim against a delinquent counterparty. There may be circumstances in which a personal claim would be time-barred by statute, but in which a property claim would not.[7] More widely, the establishment of a claim based on ownership of assets might open access for the claimant to a greater range of remedies than would otherwise be available.[8]

4.17 In the financial markets, the distinction between personal and property rights is often significant, and is of critical importance in almost every insolvency situation. The arguments and analysis are usually very complex and difficult. Moreover, in an international setting the position is made even more difficult by the fact that other legal systems may draw the demarcation line between personal and property rights in a different place, with fundamentally different consequences.

The Nature of the Distinction

Civil law and common law

4.18 Civil law systems, as a generalization, find it comparatively easy to draw a clear distinction between legal rights that relate to property, and those which are personal. Before examining the process by which the common law draws distinctions, we need to consider the alternative approach adopted by the major civil law systems.

4.19 The civil law approach looks back to Roman law for its inspiration. More accurately, it looks back to the analysis of Roman law carried out by jurists at the end of the eighteenth century and in the early nineteenth century. In particular, it relies heavily on the work of the German jurist, Friedrich Carl Von Savigny (1779 to 1861). It does not matter that Savigny's explanation of the thought processes of the Roman jurists might have come as a surprise to the Romans. The effect of Savigny's work is what matters.[9]

4.20 Savigny's analysis was based on a study of the Code and Digest of Justinian, published respectively in ad 529 and 533. The former work consists of a codification of statutes, and the latter on the writings of jurists. Savigny saw these works as pointing to a legal system that was logically complete and interconnected. To Savigny, law was the science of the

---

[7] See *Limitation Act 1980*.
[8] For example, it might be possible to 'trace' the proceeds of a proprietary claim into the hands of a third party, or to obtain a freezing injunction to prevent a defendant's assets being removed from the jurisdiction. For a detailed review of this very complex area of law, see *FHR European Ventures LLP and others v Cedar Capital Partners LLC* [2014] UKSC 45.
[9] A similar process occurred when the draftsmen of the US constitution followed the analysis by the Frenchman, Montesquieu, of the structure of the British constitutional system, and adopted it as a model. The fact that Montesquieu's analysis misdescribed the British system in a number of respects is no longer of any importance.

relationship between persons defined by rules of law. Private law is therefore the aggregate of the positive legal rules which determine the relations between individuals in their private capacity. Those rules of law assigned each relationship to a particular sphere or province of operation. Each relationship operates within its own sphere of influence, unaffected by other relationships.

4.21 At the level of the individual citizen, the concept of a legal right was closely allied to the concept of power. Thus, a right of ownership in a thing gave the individual complete power (*dominium*) over it. A legal right against another person gave the owner of that right a partial power over the person concerned, to the extent of the obligation to which the counterparty was subject.

4.22 The Roman law structure led first to a division of the world into distinct areas where different legal rules operate. Each of these areas was then sub-divided into other divisions, through a series of tiers. The result was a pyramid in which legal authority descended logically from the top, to shape at the base a specific legal rule for each factual situation.

4.23 In Roman private law, the operation of the rights of an individual was first allocated to one of two spheres of influence: first, the sphere of the individual himself (including his family, and matters of inheritance and succession); and second, the external world.

4.24 The external world was sub-divided into two. First, there was the sphere which contained unreasonable (ie non-human) things over which complete control could be exercised. Second, there was the area occupied by reasonable things (persons).

4.25 As regards unreasonable things, the right of an individual could be classified into rights of ownership (*jus in rem*) or personal rights (*jus ad rem or jus in personam*). In the latter case, there was another person who was the subject of the right, and who was required to do something in relation to the unreasonable thing concerned. For example, an individual might have a right to walk over a field which belonged to someone else. This was seen as a personal right. Although the owner of the field had complete *dominium* over the field, he was subject to an obligation. That obligation was the correlative of the right of the person with the claim to walk across the field. Roman law did not see this arrangement as fragmenting the ownership of the field. The rights of the two individuals lay in different spheres, and the existence of one did not affect the nature of the other.

4.26 As far as rights against persons were concerned, the right of an individual against another individual (eg a right to require a sum of money to be paid under a contract) was seen as a partial *dominium* of the owner of the right over the person who had the obligation to fulfil it. As one commentator put it:

> The object of the vast majority of obligations is the acquisition or the transitory enjoyment of *dominium*.[10]

4.27 Thus, according to Savigny, the Roman law concept of ownership of unreasonable things was very clear. A person had ownership if he had complete legal power over the thing concerned. If his rights in relation to a thing were only to oblige the owner of it to use it in a

---

[10] J. B. Moyle, *Justinian's Institutes* (1883), General Introduction.

certain way, or to permit the claimant to do something in relation to the thing, his rights were treated as personal. Equally, the owner who was subject to someone else's claim (eg to walk across the owner's land) did not have his rights of ownership of the thing diminished by the fact that he had a personal obligation in relation to it.

Most civil law systems, which derive their structure from Roman law, take this position as a starting point. They therefore draw a clear distinction between the idea of ownership of a thing and the fact that someone other than the owner might have rights that affect the way the thing is dealt with. In English law, and other common law systems based on it, the position is more complex. In particular, the common law recognizes different kinds of ownership of the same thing. Viewed from one point of view, the law may regard A as the owner (the legal owner) while, looking at the situation from a different view point, the law may see B as the owner (the owner in equity). Moreover, there are certain kinds of personal rights (eg a claim to be paid a sum of money) which the common law treats, for some purposes, as if they were also items of property. The subject-matter of almost all financial transactions, money, securities, and contract claims, are things that would have been regarded by Roman lawyers (or at least by Savigny) as matters giving rise only to personal rights. **4.28**

The difference between a civil law classification and a common law classification of a particular right can cause difficulty when obligations are created and assets transferred across national boundaries. The way in which, and the circumstances in which, an individual can enforce a property claim may be very different from the enforcement action open to him in respect of a personal claim. An attempt to enforce in a civil law jurisdiction a right created in a common law jurisdiction and regarded there as being of a proprietary nature may be impossible, because the law of the place where the claim must be enforced does not recognize that claim as being one of property, and a personal claim in respect of the same subject-matter may in practice fail. **4.29**

Legal and equitable ownership

Common lawyers like to say that the common law has developed pragmatically, in response to changing circumstances and the practical needs of society. Those who, like Savigny, look for order and logical development from a principled foundation, might say that the development of the common law has been haphazard and fragmented. Whichever view one takes of the common law's process of development, it is certainly true that, in order to understand the common law's classification of different kinds of property rights, and in particular the distinction between legal ownership and equitable ownership, one must understand the evolution of this branch of the law over the last 800 years.[11] **4.30**

From the end of the Roman occupation of Britain until shortly before the Norman Conquest in 1066, England had been fragmented into different kingdoms, each of which had its own law and its own legal system. As part of the drive to unify the country, English kings after 1066 concentrated on unifying the forms of procedure and the administration of the court system, rather than concentrating on the rules of law that the system administered. **4.31**

---

[11] See generally J. H. Baker, *An Introduction to English Legal History* (4th edn, Butterworths, 2002).

4.32 Medieval England had a multiplicity of courts and local administrations. The attempt at standardization was centred on the idea of the writ, a formal instruction prepared by the King's officials, under the guidance of the Chancellor. A claim by a subject against another subject was initiated by the drafting of a writ, which would authorize the impleading of the adversary before a royal tribunal, and would instruct that tribunal to enquire into the complaint made and to order a remedy, if the facts alleged were found to be true. In this context, legal rights were meaningful and remedies were available only to the extent that the procedure set out in the writ gave them form.

4.33 During the late eleventh century and twelfth century, the drafting of writs was not subject to any stringent control. Writs were issued that called upon the court to decide matters of complaint where a similar complaint had never been lodged before, without any explanation or justification of its legal basis. It reached the point in the mid-thirteenth century where complainants petitioned the King, claiming that the Chancellor was issuing writs 'against justice'.

4.34 In order to bring a sense of order to the law which was being administered, rather than the method in which it was administered, the Provisions of Oxford in 1258 forbade the Chancellor from issuing any unprecedented writ without the consent of the King's Council. The effect of this simple administrative instruction was dramatic, and probably unexpected. The categories of claim that could be brought before the courts were now fixed by reference to the wording of writs which had already been issued before 1258. The wording of these writs, which had been drafted principally for administrative purposes to begin court proceedings, came to define the rights and remedies recognized by the common law, and thereby froze the common law within the framework of the verbal formulae set out in the writs.

4.35 This, of course, produced injustice. Claimants who had legitimate claims to compensation or damages or to the recovery of property from another were not able even to bring their adversary before a court, because the facts of their claim did not fit within the wording of one of the available writs.

4.36 Fortunately, there was a way out of the Kafkaesque nightmare. The King, as the fount of all justice, retained a residual power to overreach his own court system, if justice demanded it. In the fourteenth century, therefore, it became common for frustrated claimants to petition the King, seeking a remedy that was denied them by the rigid wording of the writs available in the law courts. The King routinely passed these petitions, or 'bills', on to Parliament for consideration and decision. By the middle of the century, however, they had become so numerous that they were usually passed to individual counsellors, and in particular, the Chancellor, for consideration. In time, petitioners found it easier to miss out one step in the process, by addressing their petitions directly to the Chancellor. The Chancellor did not have the time or capacity to deal with the large number of petitions himself. Accordingly, he set up his own system of courts, the courts of Chancery. The system of justice administered by the Chancery courts was not a competitor to the justice administered by the common law courts. The Chancery courts, or courts of equity, would deal with cases only when the common law courts were unable to provide a remedy, because of the administrative shortcomings produced by the writ system. The principles and rules of equity developed by the Chancery courts were a gloss on the common law. The courts of equity saw their rulings as operating upon the conscience of the parties, in circumstances where the law was unable to provide a remedy.

Lord Dunedin, in 1914, explained why rules of equity, rather than those of the common law, governed the duties of parties in situations where there was no contractual relationship (eg the position between a trustee and a beneficiary):[12]   **4.37**

> It is in this latter class of cases that equity has been particularly dominant, not, I take it, from any scientific distinction between the classes of duty existing and the breaches thereof, but simply because in certain cases where common justice demanded a remedy, the common law had none forthcoming, and the common law (though there is no harder lesson for the stranger jurist to learn) began with the remedy and ended with the right.

The administrative distinction between Chancery courts and the common law courts continued until the late nineteenth century, when the Supreme Court of Judicature Acts 1873 and 1875 fused the two streams of law and equity. The effect of this combination was not to merge the two sets of rules and remedies, but to fuse the administration of the two different processes. Every court was now able to look at situations both from the point of view of the common law and also from the viewpoint of the rules and procedures of equity, if it was necessary to do so.   **4.38**

The relationship of common law and equity

The way in which the rules of the common law and the rules of equity combine in practice is illustrated in a case which came before the courts shortly after the Judicature Acts combined the two jurisdictions. In *Walsh v Lonsdale*,[13] Lonsdale had agreed with Walsh to grant a lease of a cotton mill. The agreement said that the lease was to be for a period of seven years, at a stated rent. The other terms were to be determined by reference to those used in the lease of another mill, identified in the agreement. Solicitors were to be instructed to draw up the lease immediately. Walsh entered into possession of the property immediately, but the draft lease was never produced. Despite the fact that the agreement for the lease said that the rent would be payable annually in advance, Walsh began paying the rent quarterly in arrears. At common law, an agreement for lease did not, by itself, create a lease, or any other property interest. However, the act of allowing someone into possession of a property and accepting rent had the effect at law of creating a tenancy 'from year to year'. Under such a tenancy, the law stipulated that the rent was payable in arrear, rather than in advance.   **4.39**

After two and a half years, Lonsdale wrote to Walsh, demanding immediate payment of one year's rent in advance, as provided in the agreement for lease. Two days later, Lonsdale distrained for rent (that is, he went into possession of the mill and took possession of the contents, which belonged to Walsh, with the intention of selling them in order to pay the rent). Walsh applied to the court for: (a) damages on the basis that Lonsdale had wrongfully distrained for rent; (b) an injunction to restrain Lonsdale from selling the mill's contents; and (c) specific performance (an equitable remedy) of the agreement for lease.   **4.40**

---

[12] *Nocton v Lord Ashburton* [1914] AC 932, at 964.
[13] (1882) 21 Ch D 9.

4.41 Before the Judicature Acts, a common law court would have considered only the question of whether Walsh was a yearly tenant, by virtue of his being allowed into possession and paying rent quarterly in arrears. It would have concluded that Walsh was a yearly tenant, and that Lonsdale had no right to distrain for rent, since no rent was payable in advance under the terms of the deemed tenancy. The term of the lease, however, would have been for only one year. If Lonsdale had wished to remain in possession for the seven years agreed, he would have needed to apply to a different court, a court of equity, for an order for specific performance of the agreement for lease.

4.42 The Court of Appeal explained how the two systems worked together following the Judicature Acts. Sir George Jessell, MR said:

> There is an agreement for lease under which possession has been given. Now since the Judicature Acts the possession is held under the agreement. There are not two estates as there were formerly, one estate at common law by reason of the payment of the rent from year to year, and an estate in equity under the agreement. There is only one Court, and the equity rules prevail in it. The tenant holds under an agreement for a lease. He holds, therefore, under the same terms in equity as if a lease had been granted, it being the case in which both parties admit that relief is capable of being given by specific performance. That being so, he cannot complain of the exercise by the landlord of the same rights as the landlord would have had if a lease had been granted. On the one hand, he is protected in the same way as if the lease had been granted; he cannot be turned out by 6 months' notice as a tenant from year to year ... that being so, it appears to me that being a lessee in equity he cannot complain of the exercise of the right of distress merely because the actual parchment has not been signed and sealed.

4.43 The process by which the courts today combine the rules of equity and the rules of common law is the same. The difference now is that the process of application has become so deeply established that it is rarely found necessary, as the court felt in *Walsh v Lonsdale*, to explain how two sets of rules relate to each other.

The trust and equitable ownership

4.44 A trust is an arrangement in which one person is regarded by the common law as the owner of property, while another, or others, are seen by equity as the owners of the same property. The legal owner is obliged to hold the property for the benefit of the equitable owners. The ability of common law systems to accept this divided ownership provides great scope for the structuring and arrangement of transactions involving property, both in the areas of family property and land, and in commercial and financial transactions. So pleased are common lawyers with the arrangement (which, in truth, probably arose by historical accident) that most of them will readily agree with Maitland that the trust is:

> ... the greatest and most distinctive achievement performed by Englishmen in the field of jurisprudence.

Not everyone is so eulogistic. Some civil lawyers see the concept of the trust as being designed to hide the true ownership of assets behind the 'front' of a legal owner. Thus, they see the trust as a perfect vehicle for money laundering, insider trading, and other property-based wrongdoing.

4.45 Like most of the concepts in common law systems, the trust was not invented by jurists and adopted fully formed. It evolved over hundreds of years in response to particular societal needs. In order to understand the place that the concept of the trust now plays in financial markets and other commercial dealings, it is necessary to follow its growth from its medieval beginnings.

4.46 A particular problem arose in the Middle Ages when a nobleman went off on crusade. He would certainly be gone for many years, and might never return. He was the owner of large amounts of land, which needed to be managed and organized during his absence. With the owner away, however, there would be no-one capable of defending the land at law from adverse claims or trespassers. The common law recognized the owner as the only person who could bring the claims necessary to defend the land.[14] With the owner abroad, therefore, there was no-one to protect the interests of his family in respect of the land that constituted the family wealth.

4.47 The practice arose that, in order to protect the interests of his family in these cases, an owner would transfer the land to a trusted friend, perhaps the abbot of a monastery which the transferor had endowed. At the time of transfer, the transferor would state in writing that the transfer was to be 'to the use of' the transferor's family. The transferee became the owner of the land in law, and so could manage and protect it. However, he was expected by the transferor to use his property rights for the benefit of the object of the 'use'.

4.48 The common law was unable to take account of uses. From its point of view, the owner of the land (the transferee) had full rights of ownership, unfettered by any instructions given or expectations held by the former owner. The system worked well, provided that the transferee behaved as he had been instructed and had agreed. If he did not, the law could do nothing to protect the members of the family for whose benefit the land had been transferred to the new owner.

4.49 Inevitably, problems arose. From the late fourteenth century, the Chancellor began to intervene, if petitioned by beneficiaries who complained that the owner of property transferred for their use was not protecting their interests. The courts of equity were prepared to enforce the use which had accompanied the transfer of land to the current owner. At this stage, there was no divergence from the position taken by the common law. The courts of equity did not interfere with the common law view that the transferee was the only owner of the property, and entitled at law to deal with it as he thought fit. Instead, the courts of equity looked to the owner personally to behave as he had been instructed at the time of transfer. Its approach was to ensure that the owner behaved in good conscience, and the courts of equity were prepared to make orders that the owner should behave in accordance with the terms of the use. If he did not obey that order, he would be in contempt of court. The focus was on compelling the owner to behave properly, rather than on conferring rights on, or granting remedies to the beneficiaries.

---

[14] See paras 4.32 and 4.33 above.

4.50   Over time, the attitude of the courts of equity changed. The most important element of the transformation of the use into the trust is that equity came to see the beneficiaries of the trust as being the owners of the property concerned. Accordingly, the courts of equity were prepared to make orders to protect the interests of the beneficiaries as property owners. This was in addition to personal claims that they might have against the trustee to enforce the trust, or to claim compensation for a breach of the trust. Crucially, the view of the courts of equity that the beneficiaries were the owners of the property did not displace the position at common law, where the trustee was seen as the only owner of the property.

4.51   Following the Judicature Acts and the fusion of the administration of law and equity, every court would see the trustee as the owner of the property, when it viewed the situation from the point of view of the common law, and would see the beneficiaries as the owners, when adopting the viewpoint of equity.

4.52   The recognition of the beneficiaries as owners of the property, rather than merely the object of fiduciary duties owed by the trustee, has two important practical consequences which are of fundamental importance in the financial and commercial markets. First, if the trustee becomes insolvent, the beneficiaries' position as owners in equity means that the property, even though it is owned by the trustee as a matter of law, will not be available to the trustees' creditors. Second, if the trustee transfers the property to a third party, the transferee will become the owner, as a matter of law. The beneficiaries remain the owners in the eyes of equity, and their rights as owners will survive the transfer. They will be able to enforce their property position as against the new legal owner, who takes over the same position as the original trustee. Equally, a beneficiary can, in some circumstances, transfer his equitable ownership to a third party, who will be able to enforce his newly acquired ownership rights against the trustee.

4.53   These statements are, of course, subject to many caveats and exceptions. In particular, a transferee of the legal title to an asset will not usually need to take account of the equitable ownership of someone else, if he acquires the asset in good faith, for value, and without notice of the existence of the interest of the equitable owners. As basic rules, however, they are vitally important in the structuring of financial transactions and operating systems.

The Distinction in Practice

Charge-backs

4.54   One of the best ways to understand the significance that financial lawyers attach to the distinction between property and personal rights, and to see the conceptual difficulties produced in practice, is to follow the debate which lasted for ten years following a remark made by Millett J in *In re Charge Card Services Ltd*.[15] Although the controversy prompted by the case has now been laid to rest, it is worth considering in detail because the issues about the nature of property rights and personal rights which were debated, and the conclusions reached, will rise again in other contexts. Practitioners in the financial law field need to understand the detail of this area of law in order to deal with future problems.

---

[15] [1987] 1 Ch 150.

4.55 The issue concerns the nature of the rights that arise in a form of security that is central to commercial banking relationships and also to many other forms of financial transactions and business. A debt, including the debt owed by a banker to his customer, is a *chose in action* and is treated by common systems as a form of property. It is capable of being transferred. It is also possible, in equity, to charge a debt. By this, it is meant that the owner of the debt (the creditor) agrees to dedicate the property (his claim to be paid) to a particular purpose (eg the payment of money that he owes to a third party). Thus, for example, A may agree to charge in favour of C a debt owed to A by B, to secure sums owing from A to C. The charge is an invention of equity, allied in concept to the trust. In equity, the chargee is recognized as having a proprietary interest in the debt.[16]

4.56 The difficulties begin when the owner of the debt (the creditor) wishes to give a security interest, not to a third party to whom he owes money, but to the institution which is his debtor. The paradigm case is where the creditor has deposited money with a bank (and is accordingly the creditor of the bank for the amount of the deposit) and then agrees that the bank should have security over the deposit (ie over the debt which the bank itself owes to the depositor) to secure an obligation of the depositor to the bank (eg as guarantor of the obligation of a company with which the depositor is connected). This arrangement, sometimes called a 'charge-back', is common, and has been regarded by commercial bankers for many years as one of the most desirable forms of security. One of the leading textbooks for the banking profession says:

> It is impossible to envisage a more satisfactory security than this. It can never depreciate in value, and, if the customer defaults, the bank will be able to realise the security without trouble and without the expense of any legal proceedings.[17]

A bank's ability to look to a customer's deposit as security is not only well established. There is implied into the ordinary contract between the banker and customer a right for the bank to use money it owes to the customer as security for sums owing in the opposite direction. This is the so-called banker's right of set-off, or banker's right of consolidation.[18]

4.57 A banker's right to take security over sums that it owes to a customer has long been unquestioned. The courts had not, before 1987, been called upon to consider in detail whether the rights created by the arrangement (whether the implied right of consolidation or a specific agreement) were property rights or personal rights, or even to consider whether that was a question of any significance. The only discussion had arisen in the *Halesowen* case.[19] In that case judges in both the Court of Appeal and in the House of Lords commented on the fact that the banker's right to combine accounts was sometimes referred to as a 'banker's lien'. A lien is a possessory remedy relating to tangible assets, under which the person in possession has a right to retain possession, as against the owner of the asset, pending payment of an amount owing.[20] The judges were agreed that the phrase was an inappropriate one. A lien

---

[16] For a more detailed discussion of the nature of a charge, see paras 10.46 to 10.60 below.
[17] J. Milnes Holden, *The Law of Practice of Banking, volume 2, Securities for Bankers' Advances* (Pearson Education, 8th edn 1993).
[18] See paras 3.20 *et seq* above.
[19] *Halesowen Presswork v Westminster Bank* [1971] 1 QB 1, Court of Appeal and *National Westminster Bank v Halesowen Presswork* [1972] AC 785, House of Lords; see paras 3.21 and 3.25 above.
[20] See paras 10.65 *et seq* below.

could relate only to physical tangible assets, and not to a debt. A suggestion was that the word was commonly used because the right of consolidation was associated in the minds of bankers with a bank's right to retain physical things belonging to its customer (eg title deeds or securities left for safekeeping). This latter right could properly be called a 'lien'. In any event, the judges described the use of the phrase in relation to the right of consolidation as 'a misuse of language'. There was no doubt, however, that the concept was effective, even if the technical description was not.

The *Charge Card* case

4.58 The *Charge Card* case is an important decision because of the court's explanation of the legal effect of using a charge or credit card for payment of a consumer debt.[21] It is more famous, however, for a remark made by the judge, Millett J, in the context of the second question which the court was asked to consider.

4.59 Charge Card Services Limited was a company which issued cards to commercial organizations, who gave them to their employees, to use when buying petrol from service stations with whom the charge card company had payment arrangements. The method was that the driver holding the charge card would present it for payment to the participating garage. When the card was accepted, the garage would then look for payment to the charge card company, rather than to the individual to whom it had supplied petrol or his employer. The charge card company, in turn, would look to be paid by the employer of the individual to whom petrol had been supplied. Thus, the trade receivables of the charge card company consisted of a number of debts from the companies to whom it supplied cards, in respect of reimbursement of sums spent by the charge card provider in paying garages for the supply of petrol to its customers' employees.

4.60 As part of its financing arrangements, Charge Card factored its debts to a company called Commercial Credit. Debt factoring is a common form of financing. Charge Card agreed to sell all of its receivables (ie the debts to it arising from its cardholding customers) to Commercial Credit. Charge Card, when it sold the receivables, warranted that they would be paid in full at the end of the credit period granted by Charge Card to its customer. The purchase price for each debt was its face value, less a discounting charge to reflect the fact that Commercial Credit would pay Charge Card for the receivable before the date when Charge Card's customer was expected to settle its debt. The purchase price was also subject to deduction in respect of an administration fee. Under the contract, Charge Card agreed to repurchase from Commercial Credit any receivable which was not settled by the cardholder on or before its due date. All of these accounting entries were to be reflected on a running account maintained by Commercial Credit. Charge Card was allowed to draw down on the credit balance in its favour, attributable to the purchase of the receivables, subject to Commercial Credit's right to retain part of the credit balance, against the possibility that debits might fall to be made in the future (eg because Charge Card might become obliged to buy back receivables that it had sold).

---

[21] See para 3.05 above.

4.61 When Charge Card went into liquidation, its liquidator challenged the terms of the factoring agreement. At the time, there was a considerable credit balance in favour of Charge Card on the running account in the books of Commercial Credit. This represented, in part, sums that Commercial Credit had retained against the possibility that some of the receivables purchased from Charge Card might not be paid by the cardholders. In this event, Commercial Credit would transfer the unpaid debts back to Charge Card under the terms of the factoring agreement, and would debit the face value of the failed receivables to the running account.

4.62 The principal argument on behalf of the liquidator of Charge Card was that Commercial Credit's right of retention set out in the factoring agreement amounted to a charge by Charge Card in favour of Commercial Credit over the credit balance shown in the books of the factoring company as owing to Charge Card. The alleged charge was to secure amounts which might become owing to Commercial Credit as a result of the operation of the agreement. That charge, so the argument ran, was a charge over a book debt of the insolvent company (ie the debt owing from Commercial Credit to Charge Card under the terms of the factoring agreement). This charge had not been registered, as required by the Companies Act.[22] Accordingly, the charge was void as against the liquidator of Charge Card, and Commercial Credit had no right to withhold payment of the balance shown on the running account.

4.63 It should be noted that the factoring agreement did not purport to create a charge over any debts. The word 'charge' was not used. The charge which was alleged to exist was one which arose by virtue of the legal analysis of the arrangements between the parties, not because of any stated intention of their part that a charge should be created.

4.64 The court rejected the argument put on behalf of the liquidator. There was no charge over the debt concerned and there could accordingly be no question that the arrangement in the factoring agreement was void for want of registration. The agreement set up a running account between the parties. The particular matters which gave rise to an obligation to pay (eg the obligation of Commercial Credit to pay for debts purchased, and the obligation of Charge Card to pay for any debts which were resold to it) simply constituted entries on a running account. They were factors which went towards establishing the size of a single debt, represented by the balance on the account. The individual entries were matters of accounting, rather than separate debts, subject to an arrangement where they were set off against each other. The terms of the agreement could not constitute a registrable charge:

> ... for there is no relevant property capable of forming the subject matter of the charge. The only asset which the company could charge is its chose in action, ie the right to sue Commercial Credit for the sum due under the agreement, but this already contains within it the liability to suffer a retention.[23]

4.65 However, this was not the end of the matter. It had been conceded in argument by counsel for Commercial Credit that the obligation of Charge Card to buy back any purchased

---

[22] Section 95 Companies Act 1948, the registration requirement then in force.
[23] See also the comment of Otten J in *In re K (Restraint Order)* at para 3.22 above, that a banker's right of combination involved the fact that balances due to the customer were 'encumbered' by the banker's legal right to combine.

receivables which subsequently turned out to be bad was not part of the running account mechanism but was a separate matter. Whether this concession should have been made is not relevant. The court was faced with the position that it had to deal with the fact that the agreement gave Commercial Credit the right to set off sums that might become owing to it in the future from Charge Card (in respect of Charge Card's repurchase obligations) against the amount owing from Commercial Credit to Charge Card on the running account. Did this contractual right of set-off amount to a charge over a book debt owing to Charge Card?

4.66 The first step in the argument addressed the question whether the debt owing to Charge Card was a book debt, so as to give rise to a registration requirement, if that debt had been charged. Since 2013, this question has been irrelevant, since charges created by a company over any property (with limited exceptions) are registrable.[24] It was, however, a live issue at the time the case was decided. The court in the *Charge Card* case thought it obvious that the balance of a running account due from a factoring company would be a book debt within the meaning of the Companies Act (as it then stood).

4.67 The second part of the court's reasoning is the statement which has caused the controversy. Millett J asked and then answered a simple question:

> But is it a charge at all? The sum due from Commercial Credit to the Company under the agreement is, of course, a book debt of the company which the company can charge to a third party. In my judgment, however, it cannot be charged in favour of Commercial Credit itself, for the simple reason that a charge in favour of a debtor of his own indebtedness to the chargor is conceptually impossible.

4.68 He explained why this was so. First, a debt, although it is capable of being assigned to a third party, cannot be assigned to the debtor. Because a debt (although it might be treated as property for some purposes) is a personal right to make a claim, it must follow that the assignment of that right to the person against whom the claim can be made must operate as a release of the claim. In other words, as soon as the debt is assigned to the debtor, it disappears. Second, a debt cannot be made the subject of a mortgage in favour of the debtor. A mortgage involves the transfer of the property, subject to the right of re-transfer when the debt, in respect of which the mortgage is made, is discharged. In the case of a mortgage of a debt in favour of the debtor, therefore, the mortgage assignment must also operate as a release of the debt.

4.69 The question remained whether it was possible to grant a charge over a debt in favour of the debtor, even if one could not transfer it by assignment. After reviewing authorities dealing with the nature of a charge, Millett J concluded:

> Thus the essence of an equitable charge is that, without any conveyance or assignment to the chargee, specific property of the chargor is expressly or constructively appropriated to or made answerable for payment of a debt, and the chargee is given the right to resort to the property for the purpose of having it realised and applied in or towards payment of the debt. The availability of equitable remedies has the effect of giving the chargee a proprietary interest by way of security in the property charged.

---

[24] Companies Act 2006 s 859A. Also see paras 10.29 *et seq*.

The judge took the view that, just as it is impossible to assign to the debtor the right to sue himself, it is equally impossible to 'appropriate or make available to the debtor' the right to sue himself.

4.70 The reasoning centres on the fact that a debt is seen both as property and also as a personal right. To grant to the debtor proprietary rights in respect of the property necessarily involves the release of the personal claim. Once the personal claim ceases to exist, the property disappears with it.

4.71 It is important to remember that the court did not say that a debt could not be used as security for the debt. The point was that any security created in favour of the debtor in respect of the debt must relate to the personal claim of the creditor against the debtor, rather than follow from the character of the debt as property. However, even a purported attempt to create a mortgage or a charge would have the effect of creating personal rights which could confer the security sought:

> It does not, of course, follow that an attempt to create an express mortgage or charge of a debt in favour of the debt would be ineffective to create a security. Equity looks to the substance, not the form; and while in my judgment this would not create a mortgage or charge, it would no doubt give a right of set-off which will be effective against the creditor's liquidator ...

4.72 In short, the reasoning was that, because of the essential nature of a debt as a personal claim of the creditor against the debtor, any attempt to create a property right in favour of the debtor must fail, because such a proprietary right, if created, would destroy the personal right on which it was based. However, it is perfectly possible to create security by changing the nature of the personal right of the creditor. For example, the right to claim payment might be made subject to a right of set-off, or some other encumbrance that affected the nature of the claim itself. Indeed, even a purported attempt to create a proprietary interest would be construed as having that effect on the personal claim.

4.73 In the *Charge Card* case itself the effect of this reasoning was helpful to the security-taker. The upshot was that, since the security created was personal, and not by way of charge, there could be no question of it being void for want of registration.

4.74 For a period of ten years following Millett J's decision, a heated debate was conducted through the pages of legal periodicals. Some commentators took the view that the reasoning in the *Charge Card* case was wrong, and seriously undermined the ability of banks and other institutions to take effective security over cash balances which they held on behalf of customers. Others took the view that the reasoning was correct, and in any event the security available was every bit as effective as proprietary rights would have been. However, the concern of many practitioners remained that, notwithstanding the benign picture painted by the case itself, there might turn out to be situations where a proprietary right might be of more value than purely personal rights. There was no reason, they said, for the common law to deny to practitioners the ability to create such property rights, if they wished to do so.

In re Bank of Credit and Commerce International SA (No 8)[25]

4.75 Despite the concern among financial lawyers about the importance of the point, the issue did not arise in any reported case for a decade. In 1997, however, the issue came before the

---
[25] [1998] AC 214.

Court of Appeal, and subsequently the House of Lords, in a case arising out of the liquidation of Bank of Credit and Commercial International SA. In *BCCI (No 8)* an individual had granted to the bank security over a cash deposit which he maintained with the bank. This security was in respect of indebtedness owed to the bank by a company with which the individual depositor was associated. The depositor had given no personal guarantee of the obligations of the company to the bank. Nor had he explicitly undertaken any personal liability in respect of the company's debt to the bank. His agreement with the bank, under which the claimed security was granted, contained the following provisions:

> I ... hereby give a lien/charge on the balances maintained by me in my accounts with you for all of the outstanding liabilities of the borrower in respect of the banking facilities and so that you shall have the power to withdraw and utilise the proceeds thereof ... for the reduction or adjustment of the outstanding liabilities of the borrower with the bank without reference to me.
>
> ...
>
> It is understood that the balances held in the accounts under the lien/charge are not to be released to me, my heirs or assignees unless and until the entire outstanding liabilities of the borrower whether actual or contingent are fully repaid ...

4.76 When the bank became insolvent, the liquidators demanded that the company repay its loan to the bank. At the same time, without addressing the fact that the deposit had been held as security for the debts of the company, the liquidators told the depositor that he would, like all creditors of the bank, need to prove in the liquidation for the amount of his deposit. He would certainly receive less than its full value. The depositor retorted that the bank must set off the amount of the deposit owed to him against the debt due to the bank from the company. In this way, although the depositor would receive nothing back from the bank, his company would be relieved of its debt to the extent of the unpaid deposit.

4.77 The depositor's argument was an ingenious one. Relying on the statement made by Millett J in the *Charge Card* case, he said that it was conceptually impossible that the letter could have created a proprietary interest in the deposit, in favour of the bank. He accepted (indeed, he insisted) that the letter created a security for the bank in respect of the deposit. However, because the security could not be proprietary in nature, it must take effect by giving the bank a personal right of set-off. Before there could be a set-off of the deposit, there must be a debt from the depositor to the bank, against which the deposit could be set. Therefore, the security document must have the effect of creating a personal liability from the borrower to the bank. There was thus a personal liability from the bank to the depositor (in respect of the amount of the deposit) and a personal liability from the depositor to the bank (ie to pay an amount up to the value of the deposit). On the insolvency of the bank, the mandatory set-off under the Insolvency Rules[26] operated to cancel both the depositor's right to repayment of his deposit and the bank's right to claim the debt due from him. Since the debt from him to the bank must be the same as the debt from the company to the bank, it followed that the company's liability to the bank was discharged *pro tanto*. Because the arrangement created

---

[26] Insolvency Rules 1986 Rule 4.90, now replaced by Insolvency Rules 2016 Rule 14.25.

only personal rights, rather than proprietary rights, the bank did not have the option of claiming repayment from the company, while sitting on its property rights as a chargee.

4.78 It is interesting to note, in passing, that the argument for the depositor did not claim that the bank had no security over the deposit. Quite the opposite, the argument was that the bank had been granted personal rights under the so-called letter of charge/lien which were perfectly sound. The argument was that the statutory intervention of the Insolvency Rules required that those rights be exercised, through the mandatory set-off in r 4.90.[27] On the facts of the case, it better suited the liquidators' interests not to exercise their rights. They would, in the event, have been happy to have no security at all. They would simply have claimed the money from the debtor company, which was solvent, leaving the depositor, like all other depositors, to prove in the liquidation for what he was owed. The liquidators' argument was that, if they had any security at all, it was not a personal right of set-off (which would be caught by the mandatory set-off provisions of the Insolvency Rules). They did not care whether they had proprietary rights or not; only that there should be no debt owing from the depositor to the bank.

4.79 When the case reached the Court of Appeal, the reasoning in the *Charge Card* case was affirmed. However, the Court of Appeal did not accept the argument that the effect of the letter of lien/charge was to create a personal liability from the depositor to the bank, in respect of the money owed by the company. Accordingly, they held that the agreement provided perfectly good security to the bank, since it provided that the deposit should not be repayable until such time as the company's liability to the bank had been completely discharged. In the present case, the mandatory set-off provisions in r 4.90 had no effect. The liquidators could demand repayment of the loan from the company. After the loan was repaid, the depositor would be entitled, under the terms of his letter, to ask for his deposit back. When he did, he would be told to prove in the liquidation for the debt.

4.80 When the appeal came before the House of Lords, the only substantive speech was made by Lord Hoffmann, the other four judges concurring. Lord Hoffmann accepted the reasoning of the Court of Appeal that the terms of the letter did not create a personal liability from the depositor to the bank, and accordingly mandatory set-off would not apply. He further accepted the reasoning that the agreement created an effective security for the bank by requiring that the deposit was not repayable until the company's debt had been discharged. However, because the question of 'conceptual impossibility' had been argued in full and was a matter of great interest in the financial law community, he felt he should go on to deal with it.

4.81 Lord Hoffmann begins by addressing the nature of a charge. He refers to the fact that there are several cases where descriptions of a charge have been given. None of them, however, gives a complete definition, and he says specifically that he has no intention of trying to give such a definition. He contents himself with saying only that an equitable charge:

> … is a proprietary interest granted by way of security … A proprietary interest provided by way of security entitles the holder to resort to the property only for the purpose of satisfying some liability due to him …

---

[27] Now Rule 14.25 Insolvency Rules 2016.

There is no doubt that a proprietary interest over a debt can be granted in favour of a third party. In the case of a proprietary interest granted to the debtor himself, the only difference in effect between that situation and the grant of a charge to a third party is that the method of realization of the charged property would be slightly different. That difference is not a matter of any significance. Therefore, it is possible to create a charge over a debt in favour of the debtor.

4.82 Lord Hoffmann is addressing the question from the opposite end of the chain of logic from that chosen by Millett J. The effect of a debtor being able to have a proprietary interest in his own debt by way of charge is no different in substance from the effect of any other security-taker having a proprietary interest in the same asset. Therefore, there is no reason why the law should not allow the definition of a charge to include such an arrangement. He is prepared to expand the definition of charge to encompass the result which is sought. Millett J, on the other hand, started from the position of an existing definition of a charge, and concluded that that definition could not lead to the result sought. Lord Hoffmann explains his approach succinctly:

> ... the law is fashioned to suit the practicalities of life and legal concepts like 'proprietary interest' and 'charge' are no more than labels given to clusters of related and self-consistent rules of law. Such concepts do not have a life of their own from which the rules are inexorably derived.

4.83 Curiously, Lord Hoffmann's explanation has echoes of Millett J's words in the *Charge Card* case:

> ... the essence of an equitable charge is that, without any conveyance or assignment to the chargee, specific property of the chargor is expressly or constructively appropriated to or made available for payment of a debt, and the chargee is given the right to resort to the property for the purpose of having it realised and applied in or towards payment of the debt. The availability of equitable remedies has the effect of giving the chargee a proprietary interest by way of security in the property charged.

> ... The objection to a charge in these circumstances is not to the process by which it is created, but to the result ... The debtor cannot, and does not need to, resort to the creditor's claim against him in order to obtain the benefit of the security; his own liability to the creditor is contractually discharged or reduced.

Millett J's point is that, in a common law system, in contrast to the Roman law system, the question of whether an interest or right is personal or proprietary depends on the nature of the remedy available for its enforcement. Because, in this case, no equitable remedy is needed to enforce the rights of the security-taker, his interest is not proprietary in nature, but consists of a personal right, inherent in the nature of the debt itself.

4.84 One might think that Lord Hoffmann would have agreed with this, the only difference being that he would go one step further by adding that the method of enforcement in this case was not important. The fact that the enforcement method was not based on ownership was not a bar to describing the right itself as 'proprietary'; it was a label that did not affect the substance of the right itself.

The current position

From the point of view of banks wishing to take security over cash deposited with them, or other debts which they owe to the security-giver, the position is benign. The *Charge Card* case itself, and both the Court of Appeal and House of Lords in *BCCI (No 8)* were clear that contractual arrangements which give the security-taker rights of set-off, or the ability not to repay the indebtedness until it has itself been paid, are effective as security in accordance with their terms. Further, the House of Lords has now said that it is possible as a matter of legal concept to create a charge over indebtedness in favour of the debtor. More accurately, the House of Lords accepted that the rights created in these circumstances are proprietary in nature, and therefore capable of being described as a charge. Given the effectiveness of the rights in the view of the Court of Appeal, and of Millett J in the *Charge Card* case, it is difficult to see how they are changed by applying the adjective 'proprietary'. Categorizing rights in these circumstances as proprietary may be a matter of form rather than substance.

4.85

The House of Lords' decision in *BCCI (No 8)* has been welcomed generally by financial lawyers. Even those who felt that it was unnecessary to classify rights given to security-takers in these circumstances as 'proprietary' accept that the additional flexibility which this brings to the design of security structures and systems is desirable. However, no silver lining is without one or two clouds. The possibility that a charge can exist in favour of a debtor over its own indebtedness raises a potential problem. The disadvantage of any security structure which is a charge is that it will be void against liquidators and creditors if the charge is not registered under the terms of the Companies Act 2006, s 859A. The *Charge Card* case formulation, that a charge in these circumstances was 'conceptually impossible' had one very clear and beneficial effect. If the creation of a charge was not possible, failure to register a charge was equally impossible. Following *BCCI (No 8)*, one must envisage the possibility that a structure produced to provide security might be interpreted by a court to amount to a charge, even though that was not the intention of the parties. Failure to register the charge might mean that the structure was void against a liquidator of the security-giver.

4.86

The question of the correct classification of the legal effect of an arrangement is a matter for the court rather than the parties. If what the parties have agreed upon amounts in law to a charge, it does not matter that they have described it differently.[28] It must be remembered that, in the *Charge Card* case itself, the factoring agreement under consideration did not purport to create a charge over the indebtedness of the factoring company. It was the argument of the liquidator that, whatever the intention of the parties might have been, the effect of what they had done was to create a charge. Although the argument failed in that case, draftsmen in future need to bear in mind the possibility that such an argument might in appropriate cases succeed.

4.87

It has been the practice for some years, because of the legal uncertainties surrounding the question of registration of security, for institutions to draft security documents to include the so-called 'triple cocktail'. Under this arrangement, the bank which wishes to take security over a deposit in its own hands expresses its security interest as being first a charge

4.88

---

[28] See *Agnew v Inland Revenue Commissioner* [2001] 2 AC 710.

over the deposit; second, it takes a specific right of set-off of the deposit against debts owed to it; and third, it is agreed with the depositor that the deposit will not be repayable so long as any indebtedness is outstanding. The thinking, put simply, is that one of these arrangements must be effective, whatever the uncertainties in the law surrounding the area.

4.89 Perhaps a caveat should be put on this. If a court were to hold that the provisions of the Companies Act meant that a charge over the indebtedness was void for want of registration, it is possible that such a defeat might taint the other mechanisms involved. It is possible that a judge would take the view that the purpose of the Companies Act provisions was, as a matter of public policy, to prevent the taking of security (or certain kinds of security) without public disclosure. The 'triple cocktail' contained in a single document, and often in a single clause, might be seen as a composite arrangement. To allow the enforcement of, say, the contractual right of set-off, in circumstances where the charge was void as a matter of public policy, might be seen as giving effect to an arrangement specifically avoided by statute. If there is any doubt at all, therefore, that a purported arrangement might amount to an unregistered charge, the interests of the security-taker might be better served by declining to take a proprietary interest.

Multiple Ownership

4.90 The view taken by English law, and other common law systems, of the nature of ownership and the difference between personal rights and property rights is formed by its response to practical situations. At the most fundamental level this pragmatism gave rise to the creation of the trust and the division of property interests into legal and equitable ownership. On a very specific level, it allowed the House of Lords to extend the idea of a proprietary interest to arrangements which might be seen in logic as giving rise to only personal rights. As far as financial lawyers are concerned, this flexibility of approach makes common law systems ideal for the structuring of complex arrangements in financial and commercial markets.

Syndicated lending

4.91 Under the usual forms of syndicated lending, each of a number of banks in the syndicate makes available a separate loan to the borrower. The borrower makes its payments of interest and principal to an agent bank, which acts for the lenders under the terms of an agency agreement or under contractual terms in the lending documentation. Issues arise, however, if the syndicated loan is to be secured. In this case, the security will need to be given to each of the banks in the syndicate, to secure the loan it has made. It might be possible at the outset of the syndicated loan for charges or mortgages to be given to each of the banks to secure its loan, and for contractual arrangements to be reached between them for the enforcement of their individual charges. However, this position will become very complex if, as is often the case, the individual loans are capable of assignment or transfer in whole or in part. In relation to each transfer, new arrangements would have to be made to cope with the change in security interests and alteration of the enforcement arrangements.

4.92 The concepts of legal and equitable ownership allow a common law system to deal with the situation very easily. A trustee can be appointed at the outset on behalf of all the banks. The security is given to that trustee. It has one charge giving it a single proprietary interest in the assets concerned. It then declares that it holds its ownership interests as a chargee on trust for the banks who form the syndicate. As the extent of the lending interest of those banks change, and new banks are introduced, the trusts will vary so that the security trustee will hold the benefit of the charge for the syndicate banks, in accordance with the terms of their agreement. This arrangement allows for flexibility in the documentation and for clarity in the practical arrangements.

Bond issues

4.93 One of the difficulties with the structure of the bond market is that, when a company issues a bond, it may be owned by hundreds or thousands of individual bondholders. The bond documentation will give the holders rights not only to be repaid the principal and to be paid interest. In addition, they will have the benefits of large numbers of warranties, representations, and covenants by the company. Under a structure where each bondholder simply owns his own bond, and has the benefit of the undertakings and covenants given to him, there are practical difficulties, both from the point of view of the company and of the bondholders. Bond issues typical last for many years. If during that period the company needs to rearrange the terms of the bond issue, perhaps because of a change in its corporate structure, it can have great difficulty in obtaining the consent of its bondholders. It has no idea who they are, at least if the bonds are evidenced by negotiable definitive certificates. Attempts to obtain the consent of all bondholders to change the terms of the documentation are likely to be unsuccessful. From the point of view of the bondholders, each will face a difficulty if he wishes to take action to enforce the terms of the bonds. There is no easy mechanism for collective action, and few bondholders will face the prospect of beginning expensive litigation on their own, when they stand to reap only a tiny proportion of the benefit.

4.94 The ability of common law systems to split ownership rights is especially useful in this situation. It is common for the bond documentation to appoint a trustee, typically a specialist trust corporation, to hold the contractual rights, other than the right to payment, on trust for the bondholders. The trustee holds the benefit of the contractual promises as legal owner, the equitable ownership of those promises being vested in the individual bondholders. As the bonds are traded, the identity of the equitable owners of the rights changes automatically. There is, however, only one person who, as a matter of law, is in a position to enforce the rights, or agree to any change in them.

4.95 This provides a mechanism both for change and enforcement. Arrangements set out in the bond documentation deal with the way in which bondholders may request or require that the trustee bring proceedings against the issuer. These will usually involve the calling of meetings and provisions for majority voting on behalf of the equitable owners of the promises. On the other side, if the company wishes a change to any of the terms, it need negotiate only with the trustee. The trustee will normally not act with discretion, but will put any proposals to a meeting of the bondholders, and will do as instructed by them at the meeting.

The distinction between equitable and legal ownership, therefore, allows the drafting of consistent and sensible arrangements for dealing with the administration of the contractual arrangements, in circumstances which would otherwise be very difficult.

Project finance

4.96 Project financing arrangements are typically very complicated. Often they provide for complicated security arrangements, not only to secure finance granted to the project by outside lenders, but between participants themselves to secure the obligations which they owe each other. Further, interests in project arrangements often change, sometimes frequently, as new partners are introduced and/or old ones drop out, or as the project develops.

4.97 The flexibility of common law principles, and particularly the ability to use the trust mechanism to deal with the holding of the benefit of security interests is critical to the smooth operating of project documentation.

Fund management

4.98 In English practice, and that of most other common law jurisdictions, the collective management of funds has traditionally drawn on the ability to create trust interests, as part of its administration. The assets of the collective fund are held by the trustees. The trustees may be the managers of the fund, or may simply hold the assets which are dealt with by those managers. The trustees hold the assets for the equitable owners. The classic form of such an arrangement is the unit trust. In a unit trust arrangement the beneficial investors own, in equity, a share of the assets. They do not merely, as in the case of a corporate collective investment vehicle, hold shares in a company which in turn holds the assets.

4.99 The benefit of the trust arrangement is that the assets of the trust are quite separate from the property of the trustees. In the event of the insolvency of the trustees for any reason unconnected with the trust, the assets would simply fall outside the insolvency. The trustees would be replaced by a new trustee and the investment vehicle would carry on regardless. In the case of a corporate collective investment vehicle, careful steps have to be taken to ensure that the affairs of that vehicle cannot in any way contaminate the assets of the investment scheme. While this is, of course, possible and is very common in the investment world, it is arguably more complicated than the traditional trust route.

Structuring Security Arrangements

4.100 The approach taken by common law systems to the recognition of property rights and the distinction between proprietary and personal rights follows the flexible approach of equity in recognizing the interests of those entitled to the benefits of ownership and in providing remedies to protect those interests. For a financial lawyer, the facilities provided by this approach can be used to structure commercial and financial transactions with flexibility, to provide protection of the rights of participants without inhibiting the effective operation of the transaction. This is one of the principal reasons for the dominance of common law systems as the governing regimes for international trade and finance.

As far as taking security is concerned, the same flexibility can be of great advantage. However, the drafting of security arrangements must be approached with care. Whether a security-taker's interests will be best served by his having a proprietary interest cannot always be judged in advance. There may even be circumstances where taking a security interest by way of charge can cause problems for the security-taker. For example, clearing systems usually require that participants grant security to the system itself to collateralize their obligations as members. Such security usually involves the system having a right to retain and set off sums owing to the member from the system. If the system's rights are proprietary in nature, there is a risk that the security might be void against a liquidator of the participant, unless registered. Registration might not be possible in practice. In these circumstances, a draftsman must take great care to ensure that the arrangements do *not* involve the creation of a proprietary interest.[29] The courts have shown a readiness to give effect to the clear commercial intentions of parties. Draftsmen must play their part, by stating clearly what the parties have agreed, and the effect of the rights they intend to create. If they do not, they run the risk that the courts might produce an answer that the parties (or some of them) do not wish.

4.101

---

[29] In the UK, this problem has been overcome by legislation that specifically exempts such arrangements from registration requirements. See The Financial Collateral (No 2) Regs 2003 Reg 4 (as amended).

5
Intangibles as Property

> Property in chattels personal may be either in possession ... or else it is in action; where a man hath only a bare right, without any occupation or enjoyment.
> Sir William Blackstone[1]

The subject-matter of most international commercial contracts has traditionally consisted of physical property. A search through the commercial law reports will show masses of cases dealing with the sale of manufactured goods and commodities, the transportation of those items, and the hire of ships for that purpose. To a large extent, the legal problems which can arise are defined and limited by the nature of the physical subject-matter and the events and accidents that might befall it.   5.01

In contrast, financial law contracts are concerned with a subject-matter which consists entirely of intangible property, rights, and claims. A financial lawyer spends his or her career dealing with contracts and transactions that relate to one or more of the following things: debts; contract rights; equity securities; debt securities (whether in the form of bonds, commercial paper, or notes); or money. Usually, of course, there will be more than one intangible asset involved. A commercial loan agreement includes a large number of contractual rights which fall to be dealt with in connection with the principal debt and which on occasion can be dealt with as separate items. Debt securities are often issued on terms which contain an obligation on the issuer to pay a sum of money at a future date (a debt), together with 'warrants', an option for the holder to require the company to issue securities (whether debt securities or equity securities) at a stated price. The warrants will usually be tradable and transferable separately from the main debt repayment obligation. In addition, it may be that the subject-matter of a financial transaction is not the underlying intangible asset itself, but rather an interest in the asset recognized in equity, but not at law. An example of this would be the rights of a bondholder against the issuer under a traditional common law form of bond issue, where the right to demand repayment and to enforce covenants in the issue documentation is vested in a trustee, and the bondholders themselves have an equitable interest in the rights owned, at law, by the trustee. In this context, the problems that might befall a financial contract between inception and discharge are more likely than is the case with other commercial arrangements to involve factors which relate to the legal nature of the asset itself, in addition to the external events which generate the problem.   5.02

The nature of the subject-matter of financial law is difficult. In addition, the rules dealing with the way in which the subject-matter can be dealt with are complex. The approach of the common law is to deal with legal relationships as they arise and operate in practice, rather than to establish principles from which detailed rules can be deduced as a matter of   5.03

---

[1] W. Blackstone, *Commentaries on the Laws of England*, Book 2 (Clarendon Press, 1765–69), Ch 25, p 389.

logic. The law relating to the way in which intangibles are created, transferred, and extinguished has, therefore, developed piecemeal, and forms a patchwork of rules which cannot be viewed as a cogent and self-contained system. An understanding of this area of the law requires that the different kinds of intangible asset should be examined separately, and the different ways of dealing with those assets should be considered one by one.

Choses in Action and *Choses in Possession*

5.04 An obvious way to categorize the world of things which are capable of being owned, but do not consist of land or relate to land, would be to divide the group into those which are tangible and those which are intangible. However, the common law did not develop in such a way. Its evolution followed the form and wording of the writs which were issued in connection with the enforcement of legal rights. The availability of legal remedies from the courts dictated the nature of the rights which those remedies enforced.[2]

5.05 The common law, from its earliest times, categorized property other than real property as being either a *chose in possession* or a *chose in action*.[3] The difference between the two lay in the method by way the owner could assert or enforce his rights. According to Blackstone, a *chose in possession* was:

> ... where a man hath not only the right to enjoy, but hath the actual enjoyment of, the thing.[4]

Thus, someone who owned a physical object, such as a book, could exercise the benefits of his rights of ownership simply by having physical possession of the book. On the other hand, someone who owned a contractual right (eg the right to require that another man pay him a sum of money) could enjoy the fruits of that right, in the absence of co-operation by the debtor, only by bringing an action at law for its enforcement. He had, in Blackstone's words:

> ... only a bare right, without any occupation or enjoyment.

5.06 In 1885, in *Colonial Bank v Whinney*,[5] Fry LJ explained the meaning of the 'bare right' when considering whether shares in a company were *choses in action*:

> Such a share appears to me to be closely akin to a debt, which is one of the most familiar of choses in action; no action is required to obtain the right to the money in the case of the debt, or the right to the dividends or other accruing benefits in the case of the share; but an action is the only means of obtaining the money itself or the other benefits in specie, the right to which is called in one case a debt and in the other a share. In the case alike of the debt and of the share, the owner of it has, to use the language of Blackstone, 'a bare right without any occupation or enjoyment'.

---

[2] See paras 4.30 to 4.35 above.
[3] These expressions, a mixture of Norman French and English, have been called 'antiquated Franglais', and modern statutes sometimes use the terms 'things in possession' and 'things in action'. Unfortunately, the anglicized version is no clearer than the Franglais. In the interests of Anglo-French relations, the original terms are used in this chapter.
[4] W. Blackstone, *Commentaries on the Laws of England*, Book 2 (Clarendon Press, 1765–69), Ch 25, p 389.
[5] (1885) 30 Ch D 261, at 286, 287.

When *Colonial Bank v Whinney* reached the House of Lords on appeal,[6] Lord FitzGerald defined *chose in action* as: **5.07**

> ... all those incorporeal rights which are not visible or tangible or capable of manual delivery or of actual enjoyment in possession in the ordinary sense, and which, if denied, can be enforced only by action or suit.

The definitions are clear. However, the task of assigning a particular right to one of the two available categories is not necessarily simple. The court must first analyse the right or rights involved, and on this analysis will depend the answer to the question whether the right is a *chose in action* or a *chose in possession*. **5.08**

If one accepts the proposition of Fry LJ in *Colonial Bank v Whinney* that all things capable of being owned, and which are not real property, are either *choses in possession* or *choses in action*, attention must turn to the process by which it is determined into which category a particular item of property falls. This question, when presented to the court, normally arises as a quest to determine whether a particular item of property is, or is not, a *chose in action*. For this, there are probably two reasons: first, if something is a *chose in possession*, it will probably be obvious. Since *choses in possession* are items which are capable of physical transfer, their identification as such will normally require very little effort. In contrast, *choses in action*, being intangible, are less easy to identify. First, a court will need to decide what exactly is the nature and character of the alleged item of property; and thereafter, it may need to decide whether the purported *chose in action* is an item of property at all, or whether it might be only a right to seek a legal remedy and accordingly not classified as property at all, dismissed as a *mere chose*. **5.09**

Most often, the question arises when a statutory provision makes specific reference to *choses in action* as being included in or excluded from the operation of particular provisions, or requires that they be dealt with in a particular way. For example, the discussion in *Colonial Bank v Whinney* took place in the context of the provisions of s 44(iii) The Bankruptcy Act 1883, which excluded *choses in action* from the ambit of the 'reputed ownership' provisions of the section. The property concerned was a share in a limited liability company. The question for decision, therefore, was whether a share in such a company was a *chose in action*. **5.10**

Most importantly, s 136 Law of Property Act 1925 creates a regime for the legal assignment of a debt 'or other legal thing in action'.[7] The consequences of the statutory regime created by s 136 are available only in respect of *legal choses in action*. The question, therefore, is always to determine whether the item under consideration can be said to fall within that category. **5.11**

Things which are *Choses in Action*

In identifying the things which fall into the category of *choses in action*, the test is, as a matter of logic, deceptively simple. First, the item concerned must be property (ie something capable of being owned, and not merely the ability of a person to ask a court for a **5.12**

---

[6] (1886) 11 App Cas 426.
[7] See paras 5.53 to 5.63 below.

remedy); second, it must not be real property (ie land or property relating to land); and third, it must not be a *chose in possession*. The complexities shown by the decided cases lie not in any difficulty in answering these questions, but rather in the initial analysis of the particular item under review. When the court has decided the nature of the rights with which it is dealing, it is a straightforward task to assign those rights to the correct category. The analytical problem arises in the first stage. For this reason, it is possible to compile a list of accepted *chose in action* only by reference to a large number of cases, where the courts have held that a particular item is, or is not, a *chose in action*.

5.13 *Colonial Bank v Whinney* decided that a share in a joint stock company was a *chose in action*. It is worth remembering, however, that although the view of Fry LJ was confirmed by the House of Lords, his was the dissenting voice in the Court of Appeal. In his judgment[8] he draws attention to the then conflicting authority on the point. His analysis, therefore, is rather more important for defining the nature of a share, rather than for deciding that the consequence of that nature was that a share is a *chose in action*. He says:

> What, then, is the character of a share in a company? Is it in its nature a *chose in possession*, or a *chose in action*? Such a share is, in my opinion, the right to receive certain benefits from a corporation, and to do certain acts as a member of that corporation; and if those benefits be withheld or those acts be obstructed, the only remedy of the owner of the share is by action. Of the share itself, in my view, there can be no occupation or enjoyment; though of the fruits arising from it there may be occupation, enjoyment, and manual possession. Such a share appears to me to be closely akin to a debt, which is one of the most familiar of *choses in action*; no action is out any occupation or enjoyment required to obtain the right to the money in the case of the debt, or the right to the dividends or other accruing benefits in the case of the share; but an action is the only means of obtaining the money itself or the other benefit in specie, the right to which is called in one case a debt and in the other case a share. In the case alike of the debt and of the share, the owner of it has, to use the language of Blackstone, 'a bare right with

5.14 The most useful way to classify *choses in action* is by grouping them under a small number of headings, relevant to a particular type of property. Before doing so, however, it is important to be clear about a distinction which is drawn between types of *chose in action* and which affects the way in which they may be dealt. *Choses in action* can be divided into *legal choses in action* and *equitable choses in action*. This is not an easy distinction to make. It is, however, important because s 136 Law of Property Act 1925, which provides a specific regime for the transfer of certain kinds of *choses in action*, is restricted in its operation to *legal choses in action*. It is necessary to decide whether a particular *chose in action* is legal or equitable, before one can know whether s 136 will apply to its transfer.

5.15 *Legal choses in action* are those which, before the fusion of the administration of equity and law by the Supreme Court of Judicature Acts 1873 and 1875[9] could be recovered or enforced by action at law. This category would include in particular debts, bills of exchange, claims under insurance policies, and rights which are created by statute and are capable of being owned (eg shares in a company formed under companies legislation).

---

[8] At pp 287 and 288.
[9] See para 4.38 above.

Equitable choses in action, on the other hand, are those which before 1873 were enforceable only through the courts of equity. *Equitable choses in action* are those which relate to the property and rights which were created by equity, or in respect of which the courts of equity had an exclusive jurisdiction. This would include for example a share in a partnership,[10] an interest on money held on trust,[11] a reversionary interest under a will,[12] or the right of a mortgagor to claim the surplus of any funds left after the exercise by a mortgagee of its power of sale.[13]

5.16

Financial assets which are *choses in action*

Because rights have been classified in decided cases as being (or not being) *choses in action* on a case-by-case basis, there is no formal or systematic categorization.[14] The most helpful approach for financial lawyers is, perhaps, to consider the kind of financial assets which are the subject-matter of financial transactions, and to examine whether those assets have been classified by the courts as *choses in action*. It should be remembered that, in the list which follows, an individual asset might well fall under more than one heading. This is of no significance: what matters is to know whether the item with which one is dealing is, or is not, a *chose in action*. One might classify financial assets as follows.

5.17

Debts

Debts are perhaps the most important single type of *chose in action*. They have been accepted as such in law since the reign of Henry VI.[15] The category embraces all kinds of debts, and in particular:

5.18

- mortgage debts;[16]
- contractual rights to present or future payments;[17]
- balances on a bank account, whether owing to or from the banker;[18]
- the balance owing on a building society or savings bank account;[19]
- debentures;[20]
- dividends declared on company shares;[21]
- dividends declared on a bankruptcy;[22]
- negotiable instruments, including bills of exchange, promissory notes, and cheques;[23] and
- money payable under a banker's confirmed credit or performance guarantee.[24]

---

[10] *Re Bainbridge, ex p Fletcher* (1878) 8 Ch D 218.
[11] *Piggot v Stewart* [1875] WN 69.
[12] *Re Tritton, ex p Singleton* (1889) 61 LT 301.
[13] *Buchnel v Buchnel* [1969] 2 All ER 998.
[14] But see *Halsbury's Laws of England* (5th edn), Vol 13, paras 3 *et seq* for a comprehensive review of the rights which have been classified as *choses in action*.
[15] See *Halsbury's Law of England* (5th edn), Vol 13, para 4, fn 1.
[16] *Tailor v London & County Banking Co* [1901] 2 Ch 231.
[17] *Yuill v Fletcher (Inspector of Taxes)* [1984] STC 401.
[18] *R v Golechha* [1989] 3 All ER 908.
[19] *R v Marland, R v Jones* (1985) 82 Cr App Rep 134.
[20] *Hambleton v Brown* [1917] 2 KB 93.
[21] *Dalton v Midland Counties RLY Co* (1853) 13 CB 474.
[22] *Re Irving, ex p Brett* (1877) 7 Ch D 419.
[23] *Master v Miller* (1791) 4 Term Rep 320 and see paras 5.42 and 5.54 below.
[24] *Transtrust SPL v Danubian Trading Co Ltd* [1952] 2 QB 297.

Accordingly, most of the financial assets which could be described as 'debts', and others which are likely to arise in financial contracts, would fall within the description of items already held to be *choses in action* by decided cases.

Contractual rights

5.19 Rights which arise by virtue of a contract have long been held to be *choses in action*. Of particular relevance to financial contracts are contractual rights in respect of:

- insurance policies;[25]
- a claim to be indemnified under the terms of an insurance policy;[26]
- a contractual right to a future sum;[27]
- a contingent right to receive a capital sum;[28]
- an option to purchase land[29] or shares;[30]
- the benefit of a covenant of a suretyship under a lease;[31]
- a right of pre-emption;[32] and
- rights under a licence of intellectual property rights.

It should not be assumed, however, that any entitlement that arises under a contract will necessarily be regarded as a *chose in action*. For example, some of the obligations under a contract which calls for the performance of personal services will not be so regarded.[33]

Rights of action

5.20 As would be expected, rights to claim at law are regarded as *choses in action*. For example, *choses in action* would include:

- a right of action arising under a contract;[34]
- a claim for unliquidated damages for breach of contract;[35] and
- a right of action to damages in tort.[36]

Other items of property which might be classified as *choses in action* under this heading would include a claim to be indemnified, which arises as a matter of law, rather than as a term of a contract.[37] It does not follow, however, that every individual who has the right to apply to the court for an order is necessarily the owner of a *chose in action*. For example, a right to apply for an order for costs has been held not to be a *chose in action*.[38] In addition, certain kinds of claim can be brought only by a particular individual. For example, a claim to rescind a mortgage can be made only by the owner of the property. In that case, it would not be right to regard the ability to claim for rescission as being a *chose in action*.[39]

---

[25] *Re Moore, ex p Ibbetson* (1878) 8 Ch D 519.
[26] *Fouad Bishara Jabbour v Custodian of Absentee's Property State of Israel* [1954] 1 All ER 145.
[27] *Drummond (Inspector of Taxes) v Austin Brown* [1985] Ch 52.
[28] *Morgan (Inspector of Taxes) v Gibson* [1989] STC 568.
[29] *Griffith v Pelton* [1958] Ch 205.
[30] *Abbott v Philbin (Inspector of Taxes)* [1959] 2 All ER 270.
[31] *Coastplace Ltd v Hartley* [1987] QB 948.
[32] *Dear v Reeves* [2001] EWCA Civ 277.
[33] In *M (Kenya) v Secretary of State for the Home Department* [2008] EWCA Civ 1015, rights under a continuing contract for the provision of medical services were held not to be a *chose in action*.
[34] *Brice v Bannister* (1878) 3 QBD 569.
[35] *Ogdens Ltd v Weinberg* [1906] 95 LT 567
[36] *Re Maye* [2008] UKHL 9.
[37] *Bourne v Colodense Ltd* [1985] ICR 291.
[38] *Re Marley Laboratories Ltd's Application* [1952] 1 All ER 1057.
[39] See *Investors Compensation Scheme v West Bromwich Building Society* [1998] 1 All ER 98, and see para 5.38 below.

Shares

5.21 Shares in joint stock companies were recognized as being *choses in action* as early as 1839.[40] *Colonial Bank v Whinney*[41] extended the range to include all kinds of company. To the extent that they would not be classified as *choses in action* under the heading of debts, stock in public funds and government stock would be included within this category.[42]

Equitable rights

5.22 Certain kinds of equitable rights have been held to be *choses in action*. Of course, these items must be *equitable choses in action*. They cannot be classified as a *legal choses in action*, because they could not, by their nature, have been enforced by action at law (rather than in equity) before the fusion of the jurisdictions in 1873.[43] Most importantly, this category would include beneficial interests under trusts and in trust funds,[44] and a share in a partnership.[45]

Intellectual property

5.23 Intellectual property rights, consisting principally of copyright, patents, registered designs, etc have always been regarded as anomalous in legal terms. Their classification as *choses in action* or their exclusion from this list does not seem to follow any principled structure. In 1848, the author of *Williams' Personal Property* said:

> For want of a better classification, these subjects of personal property are now usually spoken of as choses in action. They are, in fact, personal property of an incorporeal nature, and a recurrence to the history of their classification amongst choses in action will help to explain some of their peculiarities.

Copyright is stated in s 1(1) Copyright, Designs and Patents Act 1988 to be 'property' and has been held to be a *chose in action*.[46] Design rights are similarly described as 'property', and a registered trademark is, in s 22 Trademarks Act 1994 described as 'personal property'. Both would, presumably, be regarded as *choses in action*.

5.24 However, the position in relation to patents is rather confusing. In *Beecham Group plc v Gist-brocades NV*,[47] Lord Diplock said:

> An English patent is a species of English property of the nature of a chose in action and peculiar in character.

However, the Patents Act 1977 specifically states that, while a patent and an application for a patent are items of personal property, neither is a thing in action.[48] While this position seems to be somewhat anomalous, it is not thought that, in the present context, anything turns on it.

---

[40] *Humble v Mitchell* (1839) 11 Ad & El 205.
[41] (1886) 11 App Cas 426.
[42] *Dundas v Dutens* (1790) 1 Bes 196.
[43] See para 4.38 above.
[44] *Piggott v Stewart* [1875] WN 69; *Space Investments Ltd v Canadian Imperial Bank of Commerce Trust Co (Bahamas) Ltd* [1986] 3 All ER 75.
[45] *Re Bainbridge, ex p Fletcher* (1878) 8 Ch D 218.
[46] *Chaplin v Leslie Fruin (Publishers) Ltd* [1966] Ch 71.
[47] [1986] 1 WLR 51, at 59.
[48] Patents Act 1977 s 30(1).

The Nature of a *Chose in Action*

5.25 The nature of a *chose in action* is not a matter which is of concern to practitioners as a subject of enquiry for its own sake. What matters in practice is whether, and how, assets which are classified as *choses in action* may be dealt with. In particular, practitioners need to know whether *choses in action* may be transferred, realized, mortgaged, or charged, and, if so, what are the legal requirements necessary to ensure that such dealings are effective. The answers to these questions may, however, depend on the nature of the *chose in action* itself. It is, therefore, important to consider the legal nature of a *chose in action*, and also whether all assets classified in this way have the same legal constitution.

5.26 There is no formal definition of a *chose in action*. However, one might start with *Blackstone's* explanation[49] that it is:

> Property ... where a man hath only a bare right, without any occupation or enjoyment.

This formulation has stood the test of time, and the definition in *Snell's Equity*[50] is to the same effect:

> ... all personal rights of property which can only be claimed or enforced by action, and not by taking physical possession.

Helpful though this definition is, it does not say what the property is; it refers only to the method by which the property may be realized.

Choses in action and other kinds of property

5.27 *Choses in possession* have an objective existence. A tangible asset exists, whether or not it is owned by a particular individual, or even if it is not owned at all. If the owner of, say, a pen decides to throw it away, and drops it in a litter bin, he ceases to be the owner of the pen by abandoning his ownership rights. Another person may become the owner of the pen by retrieving it from the bin, with the intention of acquiring ownership in it. During the period between the abandonment and the acquisition, the pen has no owner. However, it still exists. Ownership is the relationship between the individual who is the owner and the asset which is owned. Ownership of a *chose in possession* may arise, be extinguished, or be transferred without affecting the nature of the object concerned.

5.28 The position in relation to a *chose in action* is different. It is common for lawyers to refer to a *chose in action* as being 'a right to sue'.[51] This is, however, a form of shorthand. The *chose in action* is not a right to bring an action. It is rather a claim to have something happen (eg to be paid a sum of money or to have a counterparty under the contract perform an obligation undertaken in that agreement), where that claim is capable of being realized through

---

[49] Blackstone's *Commentaries on the Laws of England*, Book 2, Ch 25, p 389.
[50] (33rd edn, 2015) Sweet & Maxwell Ch 3-001.
[51] See, eg, Millett J in *In Re Charge Card Services Ltd* [1987] Ch 150.

the medium of a court action. In the House of Lords in *Colonial Bank v Whinney*,[52] Lord FitzGerald drew this distinction. *Choses in action* were:

> ... those incorporeal rights which are not visible or tangible or capable of manual delivery or of actual enjoyment in possession in the ordinary sense and which, if denied can be enforced only by action or suit.

The fact that a *chose in action* can only be enforced by suit is merely one of its characteristics.

5.29 Likewise, in *Investors Compensation Scheme v West Bromwich Building Society*,[53] Lord Hoffmann, when discussing the question of assignment of a *chose in action*, draws a distinction between the property which constitutes the *chose in action*, and the process by which it is enforced:

> ... what is assignable is the debt or other personal right of property. It is recoverable by action, but what is assigned is the chose, the thing, the debt or damages to which the assignor is entitled. The existence of a remedy or remedies is an essential condition for the existence of the chose in action but that does not mean that the remedies are property in themselves, capable of assignment separately from the chose.

He then gives the example of a debt or other *chose in action* where the obligors are two individuals who have assumed joint and several liability.[54] In this case the owner of the *chose in action* who is owed, say, £100, can sue either of the obligors for £100. He has two potential claims open to him; he may sue either of the obligors for the whole of the debt. This does not mean, however, that there are two *choses in action*. There is only one debt, of £100. The right to be paid £100, which is the only *chose in action*, is not the same as the capacity to bring a claim against either of the obligors for the realization of the *chose in action*.

5.30 A further illustration of this distinction between the *chose in action* and the process by which it is enforced is shown in the operation of Article 8 of the United States Uniform Commercial Code, which is discussed below.[55] This Article creates a special statutory regime of claims based on 'security entitlements', where securities are held within a chain of holdings in the securities markets. This regime can operate as intended only if it does not conflict with legal claims which might arise outside the terms of the regime. In particular, it is necessary that those who claim to own an equitable interest (an equitable *chose in action*) in securities which are subject to the regime should not be able to enforce their rights as owners in equity in competition with those entitled to the statutory rights conferred by the regime. Accordingly, Article 8-1582 provides:

> An action based on an adverse claim to a financial asset, whether framed in conversion, replevin, constructive trust, equitable lien or other theory, may not be asserted against a person who acquires a security entitlement under section 8-1501 for value and without notice of the adverse claims.

---

[52] (1886) 11 App Cas 426, at 446.
[53] [1998] 1 All ER 98.
[54] For a general description of the nature of joint and several liability, see paras 9.05 *et seq*.
[55] Paras 5.106 *et seq* below.

Article 8 operates by drawing a distinction between a legal claim and the procedure by which that claim may be turned to account. An outsider may own a *chose in action* in the form of an equitable interest in the securities. The section does nothing to affect the existence of that right or the claimant's ownership of it. It does, however, stop him using the process of legal action by which that property might be realized.

5.31 Likewise, in the Court of Appeal in *Colonial Bank v Whinney*,[56] Fry LJ draws, both in relation to debts and shares, a clear distinction between the right to receive money or other benefits, which comprises the *chose in action*, and the process of litigation by which that right is realized:

> Such a share is, in my opinion, the right to receive certain benefits from a corporation, and to do certain acts as a member of that corporation; and if those benefits be withheld or those acts be obstructed, the only remedy of the owner of the share is by action. Of the share itself, in my view, there can be no occupation or enjoyment; though of the fruits arising from it there may be occupation, enjoyment and manual possession. Such a share appears to me to be closely akin to a debt, which is one of the most familiar of *choses in action*; no action is required to obtain the right to the money in the case of the debt, or the right to the dividends or other accruing benefits in the case of the share; but an action is the only means of obtaining the money itself or the other benefits in specie, the right to which is called in one case a debt and in the other case a share.

5.32 It is clear, therefore, that a *chose in action* is a thing which is separate from the court process by which it is realized. This is not to say, however, that *choses in action* are things which have an objective existence unconnected with the identity of the person who owns them. There are a number of *choses in action*, the very existence of which depends upon the identity or status of the person who is the owner, or who was the owner at the time of creation of the *chose in action*.

5.33 In some cases, a *chose in action* will not come into existence at all if the purported first owner of it has certain characteristics, or lacks certain characteristics. For example, certain kinds of debt are void, either as a result of statute, public policy, or otherwise. An example would be a right to payment under a contract, where the purpose of the contract was to perform an illegal act. In these circumstances the debt purportedly arising under the contract would be void (ie would not come into existence at all). Whether a debt falls within that category depends on whether the contract is illegal. This in turn may depend on the intention or purpose of the parties at the time of the creation.[57] In other words, the question whether there is a *chose in action* at all, whether the property exists at all, depends on the characteristics of the first owner rather than on the characteristics of the property itself.

5.34 Another example of the same relationship between the owner of the *chose in action* and the *chose in action* itself can be seen in the case of a negotiable instrument expressed to be payable to the bearer.[58] In this case, the bearer instrument embodies a *chose in action*, a claim against the maker of the instrument. That claim is owned by any person who is the holder

---

[56] (1885) 30 Ch D 261.
[57] N. Enonchong, *Illegal Transactions* (LLP Professional Publishing, 1998), pp 29 *et seq*.
[58] See paras 5.100 *et seq* below.

of the physical instrument. If the instrument is destroyed, so that no one can thereafter be the holder of the piece of paper, the *chose in action* ceases to exist. There can be no right to be paid by the maker of the instrument, because no one can thereafter fall within the category of persons who can own that claim. Again, the very existence of the *chose in action* (the claim to be paid) depends upon the characteristics of the owner (ie he must be the 'bearer' of the piece of paper).

A further example is that given in the *Charge Card* case by Millett J, when he said that: **5.35**

> ... a debt cannot be assigned in whole or in part to the debtor, since an assignment operates wholly or partially as a release.

If the person who becomes the owner of a debt as a result of assignment is also the person who is under the obligation to pay, the result must be that the debt ceases to exist, on the basis that an individual cannot owe obligations to himself. Although the case caused much controversy, this particular proposition has not been doubted.[59]

Assignability

There are many situations where an individual or corporation has a legal entitlement to bring proceedings in order to enforce an obligation, which would not be thought of as involving any 'property'. For example, a statute might give all residents of a particular area the ability to bring proceedings against the local authority to enforce duties imposed on the local authority by the statute. One would not expect a resident's right to sue in those circumstances to be described as his 'property'. It is very hard to identify a factor which turns a right to claim which someone 'has' into a right which he 'owns'. In other words, it is difficult to see the line which is crossed when a '*mere chose*' becomes a *chose in action*.   **5.36**

In the *Investors Compensation Scheme* case,[60] Lord Hoffmann said that: **5.37**

> ... a *chose in action* is property, something capable of being turned into money.

The fact that a *chose in action* is property means that it has a monetary value which is capable of being realized by the owner ('turned into money') otherwise than by simply allowing the claim to be met in due course. The point of describing a debt as 'property' is that it indicates that the owner of the debt not only has a right to be paid by the debtor, but can transfer the benefit of that right to someone else in return for money or otherwise for value. If he cannot do this, if the right which he has is purely personal and is of no value to anyone else, it is of no benefit to describe that right as 'property'.

It is for this reason that Lord Hoffmann in the *Investors Compensation Scheme* case says that the right of rescission of a mortgage, which the mortgagor might have in certain circumstances, is not a *chose in action*:   **5.38**

> Now it is important to notice that a claim to rescission is a right of action but can in no way be described as a chose in action or part of a chose in action. It is a claim to be relieved of

---

[59] See paras 4.54 *et seq* above for a detailed discussion of the propositions in the *Charge Card* case.
[60] [1998] 1 All ER 98, at 117b.

a mortgage, and such a claim can be made only by the owner of the mortgaged property. The owner cannot assign a right to recession separately from his property because it would make no sense to acquire a right to have someone else's property relieved of a mortgage.

Thus, a characteristic of a *chose in action* which distinguishes it from a mere right of action is the ability for the owner of it to transfer it to someone else, who will regard it as having value for him.

5.39 In recent years a curious mirror-image of this analysis has arisen. So-called 'cryptocurrencies' have been created. The existence of a digital entry in a 'wallet' of an individual, indicating that he is the 'owner' of a stated quantity of the cryptocurrency, gives him the ability to procure that the entry concerned should be deleted and replaced by a similar entry in the 'wallet' of another person. This process is referred to as 'transferring ownership' of the cryptocurrency. In Lord Hoffmann's phrase,[61] the first individual can 'turn into money' the cryptocurrency in his 'wallet', by carrying out the process of replacement in return for a payment of cash by the second person.

5.40 However, the cryptocurrency is not a *chose in action*. Indeed, it is hard to see that it has any substance, or even existence, other than as a digital impulse which manifests itself in someone's 'wallet'. Cryptocurrencies are created by an algorithm. They do not represent or constitute a claim by the holder against any other person (unlike coins or book-entries relating to real currencies). Without the ability to cause an entry to appear in someone else's 'wallet' in respect of the cryptocurrency, the 'holder' has nothing at all. In particular, he has no right to claim against any issuer or creator of the cryptocurrency, because there is no such person.

5.41 It seems, at first blush, that the digital world has created its own version of the phenomena that are found in quantum mechanics: an entity the only characteristic of which is its ability to be transferred. On examination, this turns out not to be so. In legal terms cryptocurrency has no existence. It cannot be a *chose in action*; it is not even a *mere chose*. The process of replacing one digital entry with another, described in para 5.39 above, is no more than that. It is not, and does not represent, the transfer of any *chose* or other legal right. The use in this context of the description 'transfer' is misleading and incorrect.[62]

5.42 The standard method by which the rights of the owner of a *chose in action* are transferred is by way of assignment. Although it is tempting to think of this word as denoting a specific process of transfer, it is used without much legal precision. In early cases it is often used interchangeably with 'negotiability'.[63] To find a meaning for the word, it might be useful to look to one of the statutes that makes assignable specific kinds of *choses in action*. Section 2(1) Carriage of Goods by Sea Act 1992 describes the effect of a transfer of a bill of landing. That effect is to constitute the transferee the owner of the *chose in action* which the bill represents. The section states that the holder shall:

> ... have transferred to and vested in him all rights of suit under the contract of carriage as if he had been a party to that contract.

---

[61] See para 5.37 above.
[62] This topic is discussed in more detail in Chapter 2, especially para 2.160 *et seq.*
[63] See, eg: *Bradeo v Barnett* (1846) 3 CB 519 HL; and *Edie v East India Company* (1761) 2 Burr 1216, at 1226.

It may be useful to take this formulation as a statement of the nature and effect of the process of assignment.

5.43 The law relating to the assignability of *choses in action* has developed slowly. Originally it seems that almost all *choses in action* were, at law, incapable of assignment.[64] However, equity recognized from the earliest times assignments of all kinds of *choses in action*.[65] After the fusion of the administration of common law and equity by The Supreme Court on Judicature Act 1873,[66] the assignee of a *legal chose in action* was allowed to bring an action in his own name, provided that certain statutory conditions had been met.[67]
In addition, statutory provisions permit the transfer of other specific kinds of *chose in action* such as shares, contracts of marine insurance, bills of exchange, and intellectual property rights.

5.44 Even before the passage of statutes permitted the assignment of *choses in action* connected with international trade, some *choses in action* were treated as being assignable in England by virtue of the law merchant (ie the universal law and customs applied to the trading of goods throughout the world). In particular, the law merchant recognized the assignability of bills of exchange promissory notes and drafts payable to bearer, bills of lading, and policies of marine insurance. In the eighteenth century, in the case of *Edie v East India Company*,[68] Lord Mansfield said of a bill of exchange:

> When the payee assigns it over, he does it by the law of merchants; being a chose in action, not assignable by the general law ... The custom of merchants is part of the law of England; and courts of law must take notice of it as such.

5.45 The position now is that *legal choses in action* are capable of assignment under the terms of the Law of Property Act 1925, and certain types of *chose in action* can be assigned under the terms of specific statutes. There are, however, some classes of *chose in action* which are not capable of assignment at all. As a matter of public policy, certain pensions and salaries payable by the state are non-assignable, as are social security benefits.[69] In addition, rights under a contract which provides for the exercise of personal skill or confidence are not assignable.[70]

5.46 In relation to financial transactions, an important exception to the general rule that *choses in action* are assignable is the situation where a contract under which a *chose in action* arises specifically prohibits its assignment or transfer. Consideration of the effect of such an arrangement came before the House of Lords in *Linden Gardens Trust Ltd v Lenesta Sludge Disposals Ltd and Others*.[71] That case involved a building contract on standard industry terms, which included a provision that the employer should not assign the benefit of the

---

[64] See Lord Browne-Wilkinson in *Linden Gardens Trust Ltd v Lenesta Sludge Disposals Ltd and others* [1993] 1 AC 85, at 109B.
[65] See *Warmestrey v Tanfield* (1628) 1 Rep Ch 29; *Goring v Bickerstaff* (1662) 1 Cas in Ch 4.
[66] See para 4.38 above.
[67] Section 25(6) of the Act was the predecessor of s 136 Law of Property Act 1925, as to which see para 5.55 below.
[68] (1761) 2 Burr 1216.
[69] Social Security Administration Act 1992 s 187(i) (as amended).
[70] *Stevens v Benning* (1855) 6 De Gm & G 233; *Robson v Drummond* (1831) 2 B & Ad; and, in relation to the non-assignability of *choses in action* generally, see *Halsbury's Laws of England* (5th edn), Vol 13, title Choses in Action, paras 92 *et seq*.
[71] [1994] 1 AC 85.

contract without the consent of the contractor. The employer sold the property and, as part of the sale, purported to assign to the purchaser the benefit of the building contract. When a claim arose for a breach of the terms of the building contract, the contractor argued that the purported assignment was ineffective to transfer to the purchaser the *chose in action* (the rights under the contract). The House of Lords agreed. Lord Browne-Wilkinson said:

> Therefore the existing authorities establish that an attempted assignment of contractual rights in breach of a contractual prohibition is ineffective to transfer such contractual rights. I regard the law as being satisfactorily settled in that sense. If the law were otherwise, it would defeat the legitimate commercial reason for inserting the contractual prohibition, viz, to ensure that the original parties to the contract are not brought into direct contractual relations with third parties . . .
>
> Therefore in my judgment an assignment of contractual rights in breach of a prohibition against such assignment is ineffective to vest the contractual rights in the assignee.

The inclusion in the contract of a specific prohibition against assignment appears to bring the contract concerned within the same category as contracts for personal services, where the identity of the parties is a crucial factor in the existence of the claims created by the contract. The inclusion of the provision does not merely prevent the owner of the *chose in action* from dealing with it in a particular way; it defines the nature of the *chose in action* itself, so that it is incapable of being transferred.[72]

5.47 The fact that a *chose in action* may be incapable of assignment does not necessarily mean that the benefit of it cannot be transferred. Although the word 'assignment' (used in the sense set out in para 5.42 above) implies the transfer of ownership of the *chose in action*, as a matter of law, from one person to another, someone other than the legal owner may become entitled in equity to the benefit of a *chose in action*. For example, the owner of the *chose in action* may make a declaration of trust of his property for the benefit of someone else. This ability extends to situations where the *chose in action* is the benefit of a contract, and even where the contract itself prohibits assignment, provided that the contract does not also prohibit a declaration of trust.[73]

5.48 In *Re Turcan*,[74] Mr Turcan, on his marriage in 1884, entered into a marriage settlement. He covenanted to 'convey or assign his estate and interest' in all after-acquired property to trustees, to be held on the terms of the trust. He then took out three policies of insurance on his life, one of which was subject to a condition that 'it should not be assignable in any case whatever'. In 1887 he was drowned, and his executors received the proceeds of all three policies. The court at first instance held that the executor was bound by Mr Turcan's covenant, and ordered that the proceeds of all three policies be transferred to the trustees.

---

[72] The Business Contract Terms (Assignment of Receivables) Regulations 2018 (SI 2018 No 1254) have the effect of rendering void a contract term that prohibits the assignment of trade debts. The Regulations are intended to ensure that the markets for invoice discounting, factoring and other forms of receivables financing are available to small and medium-sized companies, and accordingly do not apply in relation to debts owed to companies that are members of large groups or Special Purpose Vehicles used in financing transactions. There are numerous other exemptions to the application of the Regulations, set out in Regulation 3.

[73] As to which, see para 5.51 and 5.52 below.

[74] (1888) 40 Ch D 5.

5.49 On appeal, the question arose whether the benefit of the policy which included the prohibition on assignment should be included within the trust property subject to the marriage settlement, notwithstanding that the policy could not be assigned. The Court of Appeal held that the effect of the non-assignability provision was to prevent the policy being assignable at law. It did not, however, inhibit the settlor's ability to deal with the beneficial interest in the *chose in action*. The explanation of Cotton LJ was as follows:

> ... I think the condition was inserted in order to prevent the insured from availing himself of his power to assign the policy and to give the assignee a right to receive the money from the office. But though he could not assign the policy, I think it would have been a sufficient compliance with the covenant if he had executed a declaration of trust for the trustees of the settlement ...Then he could not have assigned the policy or given the trustees the power to receive the money, but he might have given them all the benefit of the money when it was received. And I think he could have given them the same benefit in the present case by executing a declaration of trust.

5.50 The reasoning is that there is a distinction between the *chose in action* itself (ie the claim against the person who owes the obligation) and the fruits of that property (ie the money that is paid over when the obligation is performed). The decision emphasizes that the policy did not prohibit a declaration of trust of the policy. Although the wording made clear that the policy could not be assigned, it accepted that the benefit might be transferred in other ways:

> But the policy contained another condition, shewing that the insurance office recognised the right of the insured to part with his interest, for it provided that the company should not be bound by notice of liens and charges on the policy.

In other words, the policy did not prevent all dealings with the benefit of it; only those dealings that would have changed the position of the insurer. If the trustees had sued Mr Turcan during his lifetime to enforce his promise to 'convey or assign' the benefit of the policy to them, a court of equity would have enforced that promise by ordering Mr Turcan to execute a declaration of trust. Accordingly, he should be deemed to have done so. The court did not address the position that would have come about, if the policy had prohibited all dealings with the policy or the creation of beneficial interests in it.

5.51 The same point was made, and taken further, in the case of *Don King Productions Inc v Warren and others*.[75] In that case, Don King and Frank Warren, two leading boxing promoters, entered into two partnership agreements relating to the promotion of boxing in Europe. In the first contract, Mr Warren purported to assign to the partnership the benefit of management contracts which he had with individual boxers. In fact, some of the contracts contained an express prohibition against assignment. The second contract provided that the parties should hold all relevant management contracts for the benefit of the partnership. When the relationship between the two promoters broke down, and the partnership was wound up, the question arose as to the status of the contracts which had purportedly been assigned in breach of the prohibition contained in them. The contracts were, in any event, non-assignable because of the personal nature of the subject-matter.

---

[75] [1998] 2 All ER 608.

5.52 The court held that, in principle, there was no objection to a party to a contract which contained non-assignment provisions becoming the trustee, not only of the benefit of the rights conferred on him (the 'fruits of the contract'), but also the benefit of his being a contracting party. This was so, even if the contract was one which involved skill and confidence, and which would accordingly by non-assignable at law. Further, it was not necessary that the transferor should have made an express declaration of trust. Since it was the intention of the parties that the boxers' contracts should be held by the partners for the benefit of the partnership, the purported assignment, although ineffective to transfer ownership of the contractual rights at law, would be effective to make the owner of the *chose in action* trustee of that property for the benefit of the partnership. In an *obiter* statement, Lightman J went even further:

> I should add that, even if for some technical reason there could not be created in this case a trust relationship in respect of the ...agreements, I would reach the same practical result by another means. For it seems to me that, if parties agree to enter into a partnership and bring about the vesting of the benefits of certain agreements in a partnership, (public policy considerations apart) they will be constrained by the terms of that contract to bring about the same substantive consequence if it lies within their powers to do so, even if the anticipated means of doing so is blocked.

Dealings with *Choses in Action*

5.53 The most important consequence of the fact that a *chose in action* is an item of property is that its owner can treat it as the subject-matter of transactions with third parties; in particular he can transfer it to someone else or grant someone else a property interest in it by way of mortgage or charge. The majority of financial transactions, other than simple loans, involve some form of dealing with a *chose in action*. The basis on which dealings in financial *choses in action* take place and the ways in which they are effected are summarized below.

Legal assignment

5.54 Assignments of *choses in action* are classified as *legal* or *equitable*. This distinction is slightly misleading, since it gives the impression that there are two different forms of transfer. More accurately, there are a number of forms of transfer sanctioned by statute, each of which relates to a specific kind of *legal chose in action*, or to *legal choses in action* generally. In addition to these statutory forms of assignment, there are other methods of transfer of *choses in action* which are recognized in equity. This recognition is conferred by equity on non-statutory transfers of *legal choses in action*. In addition, it is the only way in which it is possible to transfer *equitable choses in action*. To make the distinction clearer in the text below, the transfers which are usually referred to as 'legal assignments' will be called 'statutory assignments'.

5.55 When the administration of common law and equity was merged by the Supreme Court of Judicature Act 1873,[76] a provision was inserted to provide a standard method of transferring

---

[76] See para 4.38.

ownership of *legal choses in action*. That provision was repealed and replaced by s 136(1) Law of Property Act 1925, which reads:

> Any absolute assignment by writing under the hand of the assignor (not purporting to be by way of charge only) of any debt or other legal thing in action, of which express notice in writing has been given to the debtor, trustee or other person from whom the assignor would have been entitled to claim such debt or thing in action, is effectual in law (subject to equities having priority over the right of the assignee) to pass and transfer from the date of such notice –
>
> the legal right to such debt or thing in action;
>
> all legal and other remedies for the same; and
>
> the power to give a good discharge for the same without the concurrence of the assignor . . .

5.56 Section 136 applies not only to debts, but also to any 'other legal thing in action'. To this there are important exceptions. First, the section does not apply in the case of securities which are held within clearing systems or to *choses in action* that have been given as part of a financial collateral arrangement.[77] For both of these cases separate arrangements are made. Further, although s 136 makes assignable those *legal choses in action* which, before 1873, were not assignable in law, but only in equity, it does not operate to make assignable any *legal chose in action* that was not previously assignable in equity.[78] For these purposes, a *legal chose in action* is 'assignable in equity' if an attempted transfer would have been recognized in equity as having achieved that object. It would not include a situation such as that in the *Don King* case, where an agreement to transfer a non-assignable *legal chose in action* (in that case, the rights under a contract for personal services) was treated as a declaration of trust over the asset, rather than a transfer of it.

5.57 Other statutory provisions deal with the transfer of specific kinds of *legal choses in action*. An example is the regime for the transfer of bills of exchange established by the Bills of Exchange Act 1882. The statutory forms of transfer are not mutually exclusive, and should be seen as alternatives.

5.58 The effect of a statutory transfer made in accordance with s 136 is that the transferee becomes the owner of the *chose in action* at law. Under the terms of the section, the assignee is entitled to the *chose in action*, and to all remedies for it, and has the ability to acknowledge that it no longer exists, by giving a discharge in respect of it. It has been made clear in case law[79] that the effect of transferring these rights to the assignee is to deprive the assignor of them. He is no longer the owner of the *chose in action* and cannot bring an action to enforce it. It does not follow that, because the ownership of the *chose in action* has been completely transferred from one person to another, no third party can have an interest in equity. It is perfectly possible that the transferee may acquire ownership of the *chose in action* in law, but be a trustee in equity of the benefit of it. An example is where rights under a bond issue are vested in a trustee to hold for the bondholders. If the identity of the trustee changes, the assignment to the new trustee of the claims under the bond documentation will make the

---

[77] See respectively Uncertificated Securities Regulations 2001 (SI 2001/3755), Reg 3(i); and Financial Collateral Arrangements (No 2) Regulations 2003 (SI 2003/3226), Reg 3.
[78] *Tolhurst v Associated Portland Cement Manufacturers (1900) Ltd* [1903] AC 414, at 424.
[79] *Read v Brown* (1888) 22 QBD 128, at 132.

new trustee the only owner in law of that *chose in action*. He will, however, hold all rights as trustee for the bondholders, as did his predecessor.

5.59 An important issue in relation to s 136 statutory assignments is the extent to which transfers within the section can be used in the establishment of security arrangements. An assignment which brings about complete transfer of ownership at law, as described in s 136, must be:

> absolute ... not purporting to be by way of charge only) ...

At first sight, this might be taken to mean that the section could not be relied upon to create a security interest over a *legal chose in action*. This is not so. One of the purposes and consequences of a s 136 assignment is that the debtor, or other obligor, is placed in the position where he is quite clear that, following the assignment, his obligation is to pay the transferee rather than the assignor, and that the assignor has no longer any right to demand payment from him. The stipulation that the assignment must be absolute, and must not 'purport to be by way of charge only', is aimed at this point. The benefits of the section are not available if the transfer is conditional, or is said to create only a limited form of ownership in the transferee. If such partial assignments were permitted within the terms of the section, the debtor would not know, without detailed enquiry, which of the transferor and the assignee was entitled to be paid at any given time. As long as the *chose in action* is owned, at law, by one person only, the section's objective of clarity is met. Accordingly, a security interest created by the 'traditional' method of outright transfer by the security-giver to the security-taker, with an agreement for retransfer on satisfaction of the secured obligation, will be within the terms of the section.

5.60 Shortly after the predecessor of s 136 came into effect, the point came to be considered in *Tancred and others v Delagoa Bay and East Africa Railway Co*.[80] In that case a debt had been assigned by way of mortgage. The assignment deed contained a provision for reassignment when all moneys due under the mortgage had been paid. The argument was made that such a mortgage was not an absolute assignment, and was indeed 'purporting to be by way of charge only'. There was no doubt that the transaction was a security arrangement. However, it followed the form of a traditional mortgage, rather than a charge. It transferred the legal title to the property, with an arrangement for retransfer of that title in due course. A charge, on the other hand, would create a proprietary interest for the chargee in the property concerned, without that property actually being transferred.

5.61 The court considered that the assignment under the mortgage deed was an absolute assignment:

> Now the document in this case does not appear to us to purport to be 'by way of charge only', either expressly or by necessary inference from its provisions, within the meaning of section; it is an absolute assignment of the debt; a document given by way of 'charge' is not one which absolutely transfers the property with a condition or re-conveyance, but is a document which only gives a right to payment out of a particular fund for particular property, without transferring that fund or property.

---

[80] (1889) 23 QBD 239.

5.62 Accordingly, s 136 assignments can be used in order to create security over financial assets which are *legal choses in action*. As long as the transfer is stated to be absolute, or it is otherwise clear that the assignment is absolute, that is sufficient for the purposes of this section. If it is absolute in form, the debtor can be sure about the identity of the person to whom he must pay the debt, and who can give him a discharge of his indebtedness.

5.63 It is a requirement of s 136 that notice of the assignment should have been given in writing to the debtor. It does not matter who gives the notice, only that the debtor receives it. In practice, it will usually be the assignee who gives notice, since he is the one concerned to gain the benefits of the section. If no notice is given, an assignment which, in other respects, complies with the requirements of s 136, will not have the effects set out in that section. This is not to say, of course, that it will be without effect. It may well take effect as an equitable assignment.[81] The commercial disadvantages of an equitable assignment, as compared to a statutory assignment, are first, that the debtor will be unaware of the change in identity of the person entitled to the debt. If he pays the assignor, in ignorance, he will have discharged his debt, and the assignee will need to look to the assignor to recoup his money. Second, the assignee of a *chose in action* takes 'subject to equities'. These equities are the encumbrances and reservations to which the debt is subject (eg the possibility of a transactional set-off made by the debtor in respect of a claim that he has under the contract under which the *chose in action* arises).[82] The transferee takes subject to any claim under the contract that would have been good against the assignor.[83] In the case of a statutory assignment under s 136, the assignee will take subject to these reservations existing when notice of the transfer is given. If no notice is given, the possibility will exist of further 'equities' arising, so that potential claims of the debtor against the transferor, which come into existence only after the debt has been transferred, may still be available to reduce the amount payable to the transferee, if the debtor has no notice of the assignment.

Equitable assignment

5.64 Statutory assignments are possible only within the terms of the statute concerned. In particular, s 136 applies only if the *chose in action* is a *legal chose in action*. The section does not apply if the assignment is of part only of the debt, nor if the assignment is one 'purporting to be by way of charge only'. However, even before the common law courts had began to accept the principle that *legal choses in action* could be assigned, and well before there had been any statutory provisions dealing with the transfer of particular *choses in action*, the courts of equity had recognized the ability to transfer ownership of *choses in action*.

5.65 The transfer of *choses in action* in the eyes of equity, called equitable assignment, is available in many circumstances when a statutory assignment would not be possible. The first point to make is that, in this context, the phrase 'equitable assignment' does not refer to a particular method or form of transfer of ownership rights in the *chose in action*. Rather, it refers

---

[81] See paras 5.64 to 5.71 below.
[82] See para 3.11 above.
[83] *Torkington v Magee* [1902] 2 KB 427, at 432.

to a process by which one person becomes entitled, in the eyes of equity, to property rights in the *chose in action*.

5.66 However, one must be careful in the use of the expression. A number of different processes may be seen by equity as effective to transfer the benefit of a *chose in action*, even though the process does not purport to transfer ownership of the *chose in action* concerned, and even if the *chose* was not capable of being assigned.

5.67 In *Re Turcan*,[84] a settlor covenanted in a marriage settlement to transfer to trustees all after-acquired property. He subsequently became the owner of a life assurance policy, which contained a prohibition against assignment. The Court of Appeal took the view that, although the *chose in action* could not be assigned, in the sense of the ownership being transferred in the eyes of the common law, a court of equity could compel the settler to bring about the intended result in another way, by declaring that he held the benefit of the property on trust for the person to whom he had agreed to assign it.

5.68 In *Don King Productions Inc v Warren and others*,[85] two boxing promoters had agreed to form a partnership. One of them agreed to assign to the partnership certain existing contracts which he had with boxers. When the partnership was dissolved and account taken, the question arose as to the status of certain contracts with boxers which, although it had been agreed by the parties that they would be assigned to the partnership, were incapable of assignment in their terms. The court held that, although the contracts concerned prohibited the transfer of ownership of the *choses in action*, they contained no provision prohibiting the owner of the *choses in action* from declaring himself trustee of the benefits of the agreements for other parties. Accordingly, the agreements had at all times been held by the owners of the *choses in action* as trustees for the partnership.

5.69 In both cases, someone who intended to transfer the *chose in action* and had agreed to do so was treated by a court of equity as if he had declared himself a trustee of the property concerned, thereby transferring the economic and beneficial interest in the property, even though the property could not, as a matter of law, be transferred. It must be noted that the willingness of equity to recognize the transfer of the beneficial interest in a *legal chose in action* in this way does not have the effect of bringing within the ambit of s 136 a *legal chose in action* that would otherwise be non-assignable.[86] Perhaps the best way to look at the position is to see the *Don King* case as deciding that the beneficial interest in the contracts (which must necessarily be an *equitable chose in action*) was transferred through the medium of a trust declaration. There was, therefore, an equitable assignment of an *equitable chose in action*; the *legal chose in action* (the right in law to the contract claim) did not move. Therefore, s 136 was not relevant.

5.70 The application of the concept of equitable assignment is wider than that of a statutory assignment. It looks to the effect of the transfer of the benefit of the *chose in action*, rather than the formal procedure of transfer of ownership set out in s 136. It is, therefore, relevant in relation to the transfer of a *legal chose in action* where a statutory assignment is not possible

---

[84] (1888) 40 Ch D 5 and see para 5.48 above.
[85] [1998] 2 All ER 608; and see paras 5.51 and 5.52 above.
[86] See para 5.56 above.

(eg because the *chose in action* itself is stated to be non-assignable) or where the conditions of s 136 have not been satisfied (eg because notice has not been given to the debtor). It is also relevant where the property concerned is an *equitable chose in action*, an assignment of which could not come within the terms of s 136 in any event. From the point of view of financial contracts, the most important difference between equitable assignments and the statutory transfers which come within s 136 is that equitable assignments may be effective, even if they are made expressly by way of charge[87] or where the assignment is of part only of a debt or other *chose in action*.

5.71 As between the assignor and the assignee, an equitable assignment is complete when made, and no notice is required to be given to the debtor. However, in order to make the transfer effective, from the point of view of the assignee, he must give notice to the debtor at some point. Without this, he runs the risk that the debtor will, in ignorance of the assignment, pay the assignor rather than the assignee. In addition, he runs the risk that further equities will arise between the assignor and the debtor after the date of the transfer, which will bind him, if they arise before the date on which notice is given.

Sub-participation

5.72 Large corporations, governments, and government-owned entities have a great appetite for borrowing money. There are a number of quite separate markets: borrowers may use the so-called capital markets by issuing securities which evidence a debt, in the form of bonds; or they may issue negotiable instruments in the forms of 'commercial paper'. The form of the instrument used in these markets lends itself to trading, so that the obligations created by the original instrument can be transmitted from one holder to another with the minimum of effort. The biggest single source of international finance, however, is probably direct lending from banks to borrower, creating a *chose in action* in the form of a debt.

5.73 Bank lending in large amounts, say US$100 million or above, is rarely undertaken by a single bank. It is more usual for the loan to be syndicated. In this process, a number of banks make separate loans under the terms of the same document. The administration of the loans is conducted through a single bank, which acts as agent for itself and all the others. Once the loans have been made, each of the banks is the owner of a *chose in action*, the debt owed to it individually by the borrower.

5.74 An individual bank which has participated in a syndicated loan and has lent, say, US$20 million out of an aggregate loan of US$200 million, may be perfectly happy to leave that situation as it is, collecting interest on its US$20 million during the life of the loan, and expecting to receive repayment of US$20 million in due course. On the other hand, it may wish to arrange to dispose of the economic risk of the loan or part of it to another bank or banks in the secondary market. There are a number of reasons why a bank may wish to dispose of all or part of a loan which it has made. The bank may have internal limits on the amount which it

---

[87] Strictly speaking, a charge, as opposed to a mortgage, creates a new property interest in the item charged, rather than being a transfer to the chargee of an existing interest. See *Halsbury's Laws of England* (5th edn), Vol 13, para 26.

may lend to companies in a particular sector or in a particular country, and disposal of part of the loan which it has made may be necessary in order for it to keep within those limits or in order to free up capacity within those limits for it to enter into new business. The bank may make a periodical reassessment of risk which requires it to reduce its exposure to the particular borrower or type of borrower. The constraints of the capital requirements imposed upon the bank by regulators may require that it reduces certain categories of risk on its balance sheet. The costs which the bank incurs in borrowing the money which funds the loan may be such that it is profitable for the bank to dispose of the loan and use the proceeds to reduce its own borrowings.

5.75 The process by which banks dispose of all or part of a *chose in action* constituted by the debt created in a loan agreement is generally called 'sub-participation'. This is not a term of art, rather a description of the effect brought about by the use of several different techniques. There is a variety of arrangements which have the effect of transferring some or all of the economic consequences of being the owner of a *chose in action* in these circumstances. The most commonly used are:

1. Funded participation

    Bank A, which is proposing to enter into a US$20 million loan as part of a large syndicated credit, may have decided before the loan is made that it does not wish to carry on its balance sheet an asset of that size. It may, therefore, have agreed with Bank B that Bank B will take a sub-participation of $5 million. Not only will Bank B acquire the benefit of $5 million of the *chose in action* which Bank A is to acquire; in addition, Bank B will fund part of the loan to be made by Bank A to the borrower by depositing US$5 million with Bank A before the loan is made to the borrower.

    The legal relationship created between Banks A and B is that Bank B deposits $5 million with Bank A, on terms that interest will be paid at the same rate as interest payable on the loan to the borrower which is to be made by Bank A. The interest on Bank B's deposit, however, will be payable only if and to the extent that the borrower pays interest on its loan from Bank A. As regards principal, the deposit placed by Bank B with Bank A will be repayable only when, and to the extent that, the borrower repays the principal under the syndicated loan to Bank A.

    Economically, Bank A has disposed of 25 per cent of the risk of the loan it is to make. If the borrower defaults on interest or principal on the part of the loan which is participated to Bank B, Bank A's obligations to Bank B will abate by the same amount. From Bank B's point of view, the economic effect is the same as if it had lent US$5 million to the borrower, provided of course that Bank A is solvent and able to perform its obligations. If it is not, the legal position becomes problematical.[88]

2. Participation by guarantee

    Under this arrangement, Bank A, having already made the loan to the borrower, agrees with Bank B that Bank B will guarantee to Bank A the payment by the borrower of sums due under the syndicated loan agreement to Bank A. The guarantee is expressed to extend to 25 per cent of every payment to be made to Bank A. In return for the guarantee, Bank A agrees to pay to Bank B an amount equal to 25 per cent

---

[88] See para 5.81 below.

of sums received from the borrower, less a sum to reflect the cost to Bank A of borrowing from the market the sums which it used to lend on to the borrower. In effect, Bank B receives half of the margin earned by Bank A (the difference between Bank A's borrowing costs and the amount payable under the loan agreement) in return for Bank B accepting 25 per cent of the risk of non-payment by the borrower.

This method does not involve any attempt to transfer or otherwise deal directly with the *chose in action* owned by Bank A. It produces instead a parallel effect by establishing the guarantee arrangements. The obvious problem with this technique is that it involves the assumption by Bank A of all the risks connected with the existence of a guarantee. For example, any variation of the terms of the loan agreement between Bank A and the borrower (or by the agent bank on behalf of Bank A) might have the effect of releasing the guarantor, Bank B, from its obligations. Whilst these difficulties can be overcome by careful drafting, this method of risk sharing is inherently difficult.

3. Sale of part of the debt

The simplest approach commercially is for Bank A to agree with Bank B that it will sell to Bank B 25 per cent of the debt in return for a capital sum. Consequently, Bank A agrees to pass on to Bank B 25 per cent of the amounts received from the borrower. The effect of such a sale is to put Bank A in funds, so that it may repay 25 per cent of the money it borrowed from the market, in order to lend under the syndicated credit, and that the risk of non-payment is thereafter borne as to 25 per cent by Bank B. Often, the documentation of these transactions is cryptic, and little thought is given to the detailed legal consequences. Probably, a participation by way of sale amounts to an equitable assignment of 25 per cent of the debt concerned, although that should not be assumed without reference to the other circumstances surrounding the transaction.

5.76 In recent years the form of documentation used in sub-participation has improved dramatically. In particular, trade associations such as the Loan Market Association have produced standard form documentation which incorporates into loan agreements mechanisms for the transfer of interests in those agreements. Nonetheless, there are still many transactions which are documented in rudimentary terms, and which do not address the legal issues which arise in relation to transactions which purport to deal with *choses in action*.

5.77 Many modern syndicated credits contain explicit provisions for the transfer of the benefit of debts arising under the agreement. The mechanisms vary, but typically are based on a form of novation[89] in which the transferee of the interest is substituted for the transferor, as if it had been an original party. However, many credits have no embedded arrangements for transfer, and many actually prohibit the transfer of an interest. It is common, therefore, to find that a transfer of an interest by way of sub-participation happens without the borrower being aware of its occurrence, and often in breach of specific prohibitions against its occurrence. In practice, this can lead to difficulties in two different sets of circumstances. In each case, the analysis of the legal rights and obligations produced by the sub-participation technique is vital, but often difficult to make.

---

[89] See paras 5.88 to 5.91 below.

5.78 The first contentious situation is where the borrower seeks to reorganize and renegotiate the terms of the original credit agreement. The clearest examples of the difficulties that can arise were shown in the 1980s, when a number of sovereign borrowers threatened to default, or actually defaulted, on bank loans. For these purposes, state enterprises were usually treated as part of the sovereign borrower, even if they were separate legal entities. In order to prevent a major crisis developing when default was threatened, the procedure adopted was for the sovereign government to enter into negotiations with all of the banks with whom it had relationships ('the lenders of record') in order to agree that the loans should be renegotiated. This often involved the forgiveness of interest, the reduction in interest rate, and the extension of repayment dates. In order to vary effectively the terms of the existing credit agreement, the consent of all lenders of record to each agreement was necessary. Problems were encountered because, in many cases, lenders of record had sub-participated their interest to other banks, which were not party to the negotiations. Often, the existence of these sub-participant banks was not even disclosed by the lender of record which had sub-participated its involvement.

5.79 The other situation in which problems are likely to arise is that where a borrower appears to be close to the point at which it will default. It might, for example, have breached covenants in the agreement or have committed acts which would entitle the lenders of record to declare the loan in default, if they wished to do so. In those circumstances, banks which have bought participations might feel very uneasy that they are being ignored in any consideration of action to be taken and cannot in any event negotiate with the borrower, who is unaware of their existence. The sub-participants might therefore put pressure on the lenders of record to take action to recover the loan or to protect the position of the lenders. The lenders of record, on the other hand, might be more sympathetic to the position of the borrower, have a long-term relationship with it, and be naturally inclined not to take aggressive action.

5.80 In both situations the same questions arise. If the sub-participation is by way of sale, the sub-participant might claim that it has taken an equitable assignment of part of the debt and is therefore in a position to sue, joining the seller bank as a party. If the loan agreement contains a prohibition against assignment or other dealing, the prohibition will, on the authority of the *Linden Gardens* case, operate to prevent the transfer of any property interest to the sub-participant. However, the agreement to sell will be effective as between the selling and buying banks, even though it does not bind the borrower. Applying the reasoning adopted in the *Don King* case, it could be argued that the selling bank holds the debt on trust for itself and the sub-participant.

5.81 In the case of a funded sub-participation, where there was no purported transfer of the benefit of the *chose in action* to the sub-participant, the lender of record might argue that the matter was purely one of deposit between the sub-participant and the lender of record. The loan agreement with the borrower was relevant only because the receipts under that agreement defined the amount payable by the lender of the record under the funding arrangements with the sub-participant. The sub-participant, on the other hand, would argue that the terms of the loan agreement were not simply a way of measuring the amount that was payable under the funding arrangements. The receipts under the loan agreement provide the source of funds to be used to pay amounts due under the funding arrangement. The sub-participant would therefore argue that there was an implied trust of the benefit of the loan agreement for the sub-participant. This argument would also be relevant in the event that the lender of record itself became insolvent. The sub-participant could argue that the debt from the borrower was held on trust, to be used for the purpose of satisfying amounts due under the funding arrangements. That particular asset of the lender of record was therefore not within its ownership when it went insolvent.

5.82 The difficulties involved in establishing funded participation arrangements are illustrated in the Court of Appeal decision in *Horn and others v Commercial Acceptances Ltd*.[90] Commercial Acceptances was a company that lent money on mortgage. It had an arrangement with the trustees of a corporate pension scheme that the trustees would co-lend with the company. The company would advance the majority of the loan and the trustees the remainder. It was agreed between them that the company would have priority in recoveries, so that the trustees bore the first risk of loss. One of the loans so advanced defaulted. The recoveries were sufficient to repay in full the sums advanced by the company. The trustees, however, recovered only part of their advance. They then discovered that the company had entered into an arrangement with an associate, Mr Goldstein, under which Mr Goldstein had provided 50 per cent of the money which the company had told the trustees was its share of their joint loan to the borrower. The borrower, of course, was unaware of any of the arrangements between the company and Mr Goldstein. As far as it was concerned, its creditor was the company, which had taken a charge on behalf of itself and the trustees.

5.83 The agreement between the company and Mr Goldstein did not describe very clearly the relationship between them. However, it did recite that the company's share of the total loan had been lent by Mr Goldstein and itself 'in equal shares and proportions', and that the company would hold its share of any recoveries 'on Trust to divide the same in shares equally between itself and Mr. Goldstein'.

5.84 The question for the court related to the interpretation of the priority arrangements between the company and the trustees. It was clear that the arrangements between the company and the trustees contemplated that each of them would be lending on its own account and at its own risk. But the court had to decide whether the company was lending its own money to the borrower, having itself borrowed part of it from Mr Goldstein, or was lending part of the money as agent for Mr Goldstein. If the latter were the case, the company could not rely on its priority arrangements with the trustees to cover that part of the loan provided by Mr Goldstein, because the contract between the company and the trustees did not provide priority to the company in respect of recoveries of funds advanced as agent for Mr Goldstein. Importantly, the question of interpretation did not turn on the technical question of whether the funds advanced by Mr Goldstein had been expressed to be a limited-recourse loan to the company or had been advanced to the borrower through the company's agency. The matter was one of commercial substance. The arrangements between the trustees and the company contemplated that each would bear the risk of the loan it was making. Rimer LJ said:

> Of course they could borrow from a third party in order to make their loans, but in that event they would still be lending their own money. What, however, I regard as clear is that

---

[90] [2012] EWCA Civ 958.

[the company]—which stood first in the queue—could not syndicate its senior lending slice with others so as to share any risk with them.

5.85 It is important to note that the decision does not cast doubt on the validity of the syndication arrangements, as between the company and Mr Goldstein. Its effect is on the wider relationship between the lender of record and third parties (in this case, the trustees with whom the lender had negotiated priority arrangements). Lenders often organize their sub-participation arrangements on the assumption that they are of no concern to other lenders or the borrower. The *Commercial Acceptances* case is a reminder that this is not necessarily so, and that the structuring of the arrangements needs great care.

5.86 As far as concerns sub-participations by way of guarantee, the sub-participant would argue that any attempt by the lender of record to change the terms of the loan agreement, or to grant any waiver of its terms by failing to enforce them, would amount to a variation of the agreement between the lender of record and the borrower, which would have the effect of terminating the guarantee from the sub-participant, if it did not consent to the action being taken by the lender of record.

5.87 These arguments are very far from clear-cut. In practice, the lack of clarity in the legal situation might result in the lender of record, which has purportedly disposed of a percentage of its exposure and risk, being forced to buy it back or otherwise take the risk back onto its own books. In practice, the combined effect of the legal complexities involved in dealing with *choses in action*, and lack of precision in the methods adopted for carrying out those dealings, may result in failure to achieve the straightforward objective sought.

Novation

5.88 Novation is a mechanism that is widely used in the transfer of interests in syndicated loans. The name describes a form of transfer of contractual obligations effected by the replacement of one party by a new one. In *Scarf v Jardine*,[91] the process was said to be one in which a new contract was substituted for an existing contract, either between the same parties or different parties. The consideration for the new contract was the discharge of the old. It is, however, more usual now to confine the term to situations where the parties to the new contract are not the same as the parties to the old contract. When the parties are the same, it is usual to regard the change as a variation of the original contract, rather than the substitution of a new one.

5.89 Under old common law rules, *legal choses in action* could not be assigned (although most could, of course, be assigned in equity).[92] Novation was a way of transferring the benefit of a debt at law, without the need for an assignment. The contract under which the debt arose was cancelled and replaced by a new contract, under which the obligation to pay was owed to the transferee.

5.90 The factor that prevents general use of novation as a way of transferring *choses in action* is that the consent of all parties to a contract is required before the transfer is effective.

---

[91] (1882) 7 App Cas 345.
[92] See paras 5.43 *et seq* above.

However, it is possible to use the mechanism as a way of transferring interests in loans made under a syndicated loan agreement. Standard forms used in the market contain terms whereby all parties to the agreement consent in advance to any bank transferring its debt under the agreement to a third party, subject to specified conditions being met. The mechanism of transfer, when followed, is said to have the effect of discharging the contract at that point and replacing it with a new contract on exactly the same terms, but with the substitution of one lending bank for another.[93] However, while such a mechanism can be set up to operate simply and effectively when documentation is first entered into, it is more complicated when an arrangement is already in existence and it is sought to effect a transfer of a *chose in action* that has arisen under the contract. The need to obtain the consent of all parties can make the matter very complex, if they have not agreed in advance.

No particular form need be used for novation to be effected. However, if the subject-matter of the contract is such that a particular form is required by statute in order for the contract to be operative (eg a statute requires that the contract concerned be in writing) then the substituted contract must comply with that requirement. Since the process of novation involves the formation of a new contract, the new contract must, unless it is made by deed, be supported by consideration. Usually, the consideration for the new contract will be the arrangement of the discharge of the old contract. **5.91**

Chattelization

A *chose in action* is a difficult item of property with which to deal. It is a claim by one person against another, which needs the intervention of court proceedings for its enforcement. The claim itself may involve a number of obligations which might become subject to dispute. There are obvious problems in establishing a regime for the transfer of the property concerned. For this reason, the common law did not generally recognize the ability of parties to transfer *choses in action* at all. Equity was more inventive and accommodating. However, the transfer of *choses in action* in equity might well involve the participation of several parties, if enforcement proceedings were necessary. If the *chose in action* had been transferred several times before the matter came before the court, it might be necessary for all parties to the dealings to be involved in the action. **5.92**

Choses in action are, therefore, inherently unsuited for use in commerce. Their transferability is so complex, and subject to so many unknown adverse interests, that their value often cannot be calculated without a great deal of information, which would not normally be available in a trading situation. There is, however, one example of an incorporeal claim which has always been freely transferable. Since the earliest civilizations, sovereigns have **5.93**

---

[93] In *Graiseley Properties Ltd and others v Barclays Bank plc* [2013] EWCA Civ 1372, the Court of Appeal cast some doubt on whether the wording used in a market standard loan agreement, purportedly bringing about the novation of a loan obligation, did have that effect. The point of concern was that the borrower in the case was claiming the right to rescind the agreement for misrepresentation by the original lender. If the transfer of that lender's interest had been by way of novation, it must follow that a new contract had been formed between the borrower and the transferee. The alleged misrepresentation would be irrelevant, since it had been made in relation to a different contract. The point did not need to be decided in the case, which subsequently settled. The decision does, however, draw the attention of practitioners to the point that use of the word 'novation' may lead to consequences that are not intended.

issued coins to represent monetary obligations which they owe. Coins have been accepted within the territory concerned as transferring the right to the claim, from holder to holder. The monetary claim against the sovereign is annexed to the piece of metal, and the ownership of that claim passes with the ownership of the coin itself. In effect, the incorporeal claim had been turned into a physical object.

5.94 An illustration of this can be seen in the leading case of *Miller v Rice*.[94] In this case, a highwayman had robbed a mail coach. He had stolen, among other things, a bank note issued by the Bank of England. The note could be easily identified by its serial number. The owner of the note informed the Bank of England and asked them to refuse payment. The highwayman used the bank note to pay for accommodation at an inn. When the innkeeper presented the note to the Bank of England for payment, the Bank of England refused to pay and retained the note, on the basis that it still belonged to the original owner.

5.95 The argument of Counsel for the parties is set out at some length in the case report. The argument for the original owner was that the piece of paper which constituted the bank note was a chattel, quite distinct from the *chose in action* (ie the claim against the Bank of England) which it represented. The claim of the owner, therefore, related merely to his ownership of the piece of paper. He claimed that he remained the owner of it after the theft, whoever was in possession of it, unless the item had been transferred under one of the exceptions to the rule *nemo dat quod non habet*.[95] He said that none of the exceptions applied in this case.

5.96 Counsel for the innkeeper countered this argument as follows:

> But it is objected by Sir Richard, 'that there is a substantial difference between a right to the note, and a right to the money' but I say the right to the money will attract to it a right to the paper. Our right is not by assignment, but by law, by the usage and custom of trade. I do not contend that the robber, or even the finder of a note, has the right to the note: but after circulation, the holder upon a valuable consideration has a right.

5.97 Lord Mansfield agreed with him. He accepted that the rules which should apply to the bank note were those which would apply to money, and he explained why the rules relating to the ownership of cash were different from those that related to the ownership of other physical property:

> It has been quaintly said, 'that the reason why money cannot be followed is, because it has no ear-mark': but this is not true. The true reason is, upon account of the currency of it: it can not be recovered after it has passed in currency. So, in case of money stolen, the true owner cannot recover it, after it has been paid away fairly and honestly upon a valuable and *bona fide* consideration, but before money has passed in currency, an action may be brought for the money itself.

5.98 In the case of money, the incorporeal right to be paid by the sovereign attaches to the physical coin (cash) which represents it. That coin is transferrable more freely than other chattels. Although an owner may recover the property (the coin) from a thief, or someone who knows of

---

[94] (1758) 1 Burr 452.
[95] 'No-one can give away something that he does not have.' If the purported seller of a chattel does not own it, he cannot pass ownership to the buyer. There are, of course, many exceptions to this rule.

the theft, he cannot recover it once it has passed into circulation. The ownership of cash passes by delivery, as in the case of other goods, but without most of the conditions that would normally apply.[96]

5.99 Although this special regime applied to monetary claims against a sovereign, represented by coins, it did not apply to claims against private individuals. However, private individuals found a way to adapt the same process for business use. In the twelfth century, bankers in Florence began to issue bills of exchange.[97] The practice spread slowly to France, and even more slowly into England. At first, these instruments were not negotiable or capable of transfer, but merely gave the named beneficiary the right to be paid.

5.100 During the sixteenth and seventeenth centuries bills of exchange began to be recognized as capable of endorsement (that is, the right to be paid could be assigned by the named beneficiary, by his signature on the bill itself) and it also became common for bills to be made payable 'to bearer'. In 1680, in the case of *Shelden v Hentley*,[98] an action was brought on a promissory note made payable to bearer. The defence was that the note named no beneficiary who was capable of making a claim. The court held that the custom of merchants was such that a promissory note to bearer was recognized as conferring the right to claim on anyone who possessed the bill itself.

5.101 The legal basis of operation of bills of exchange, promissory notes, bank notes, and other instruments which embodied a claim for money was described by Cockburn CJ in *Goodwin v Robarts*,[99] when he referred to the reasoning in an earlier case, *Wookey v Pole*:[100]

> The judgment of Holroyd J, goes fully into the subject, pointing out the distinction between money and instruments which are the representatives of money, and other forms of property. 'The Courts', he says 'have considered these instruments, either promises or orders for the payment of money, or instruments entitling the holder to a sum of money, as being appendages to money, and following the nature of their principal'. After referring to the authorities, he proceeds: 'These authorities shew, that not only money itself may pass, and the right to it may arise, by currency alone, but further, that these mercantile instruments, which entitle the bearer of them to money, may also pass, and the right to them may arise, in like manner, by currency or delivery. These decisions proceed upon the nature of the property (ie money), to which such instruments give the right, and which is in itself current, and the effect of the instruments, which either give to their holders, merely as such, a right to receive the money, or specify them as the persons entitled to receive it.'

5.102 The same point was made more succinctly by Scrutton LJ in the early twentieth century:[101]

> At common law, a man who had no title himself could give no title to another. Nemo potest dare quod non habet. To this there was an exception in the case of negotiable chattels or

---

[96] See *Ilich v The Queen* (1987) 162 CLR 110, holding that money in circulation passes title 'because of the doctrine of negotiability—and negotiability was first attached to chattels in the form of money...'.
[97] See the detailed explanation of the history of the development of bills and exchange and promissory notes given by Cockburn CJ in *Goodwin v Robarts* (below).
[98] Show 160.
[99] (1875) 10 Exch 337.
[100] B & Ald 1.
[101] *Banque Belge v Hambrouck* [1921] 1 KB 321, at 329.

securities, the first of which to be recognised were money and bank notes: Miller v Race, and if these were received in good faith and for valuable consideration, the transferee got property though the transferor had none.

5.103 Bills of exchange, promissory notes, and bank notes were accepted in English law as capable of transfer by negotiation, with the effect of transferring the underlying *chose in action* or other property to which they related, because of their general acceptance in the commercial world by the 'law merchant'. Their status changed first with the Supreme Court of Judicature Act 1873.[102] As part of the assimilation of the common law and equity, the statute included provision for the assignment in writing of *legal choses in action*. This was subsequently re-enacted as s 136 Law of Property Act 1925. In 1882, the Bills of Exchange Act provided a comprehensive regime dealing, among other things, with the negotiation of bills of exchange and promissory notes.

5.104 The temptation is to see the law relating to bills of exchange and other negotiable instruments as being quite separate from that relating to other kinds of intangible property. In reality, the developed customs of the 'law merchant' relating to promissory notes and bills of exchange simply took a *chose in action* and attached it to a piece of paper. Thereafter, the rules allowed the ownership of the *chose in action* to be transferred along with the piece of paper, subject to the legal rules that governed the transfer of *choses in possession*, with amendments to facilitate the use of these special *choses in possession* for the purposes of trade. The Bills of Exchange Act provides a detailed code which embodies these rules. This analysis does not, of itself, have any consequence. Its significance lies in the fact that, throughout the world, amendments have been made, or at least discussed, to 'dematerialize' physical instruments, in order that they may be traded electronically.

5.105 Before such arrangements can be properly designed, it is important to understand what 'dematerialization' involves. It is not the case with promissory notes or bills of exchange that the property concerned is of its nature physical, so that any electronic means of retention and transfer must artificially exclude the physical nature of the property. Rather, the property is incorporeal in its nature. A promissory note, for example, is a *chose in action* which has been artificially attached to a physical thing (the piece of paper) so that it can be traded as a piece of paper. If one wishes to design a system for electronic transfer of such items, it may be unnecessary to 'dematerialize' the paper. It may be simpler, in concept and in practice, to miss out the step of 'materializing' the *chose in action* in the first place.[103]

Hybrid Rights

United States Uniform Commercial Code Article 8—Investment Securities

5.106 The identification and nature of ownership and other rights in *choses in action* is perhaps at its most difficult in relation to shares, bonds, and other securities which are held in clearing systems, or are otherwise held by financial institutions on behalf of customers. The days are

---

[102] See paras 5.55 and 5.56 above.
[103] In relation to the 'dematerialization' of bearer bonds, see paras 6.115 *et seq*.

long gone when the owner of a security could be identified by the fact that he held the share or stock certificate for it. Now, it is overwhelmingly likely that the security will be held for the investor by a financial institution.[104] The books of the institution record the fact that the investor owns a security. That security may be registered in the books of the issuer in the name of the institution itself, or may be held by another institution, whose books record that it holds the asset for the first intermediary. It is common now for an individual investor, who owns a share in a particular corporation, to trace his ownership through a great number of layers before there is any contractual link with the issuing company.

Each person in such a chain of holdings has a contractual relationship with the participant immediately above and the one immediately below him in the chain. The nature of his claim is, however, often difficult to identify, particularly if the chain passes through different jurisdictions which categorize the legal rights of holders and claimants in different ways. An analysis of this position is outside the scope of this book, and is indeed the subject of works devoted exclusively to it.[105] What can be said with a degree of certainty is that the interest of any particular claimant, whether a property interest in the securities themselves or a claim against another participant in the chain, will be a *chose in action*. **5.107**

In order to ensure the smooth working of a system of market dealing under which securities are held in chains of ownership, it is necessary to devise a regime under which the entitlement and interests of any participant may be predictably defined. It is of no use to the participant to be told that he has become an owner of a security upon purchase, subject to the fact that other people might have a claim to ownership of an equitable interest in the same assets, of which both the seller and purchaser are unaware. **5.108**

A solution to this problem has been found in the United States and is now set out in Article 8 of the Uniform Commercial Code. Article 8 creates a statutory claim called a 'security entitlement': **5.109**

'Security entitlement' means the rights and property interest of an entitlement holder with respect to a financial asset ... and

'Entitlement holder' means a person identified in the records of a securities intermediary as the person having a security entitlement against the securities intermediary ...

This claim is available to a holder shown in the records of a participant as having an entitlement against that participant.

The definition of 'securities entitlement' refers to 'rights and property interest' of the holder. However, that interest is a claim, arising under the terms of Article 8, against the particular participant whose books record its existence. Although there is no reason to object to the use of the phrase 'property right' to describe this claim,[106] it is hard to see that there is anything in the nature of the statutory claim that requires the use of the word 'property'. The entitlement does not include any right for the holder to claim, in respect of the security **5.110**

---

[104] The European Commission's *Summary of Responses re Legislation on Legal Certainty of Securities Holding and Transactions*, published in January 2010, estimated that 15 per cent of UK traded equities and 2 per cent of UK debt securities were held otherwise than in book-entry form. In other Member States, the percentages were even lower.
[105] See in particular J. Benjamin, *Interests in Securities* (Oxford University Press, 2000).
[106] See para 4.81 above, describing the use by Lord Hoffmann in *BCCI (No 8), Re* [1998] AC 214 of the word 'proprietary' in a wide sense.

concerned, against any person other than the book-keeping participant. The investor owns a *chose in action*, in the form of his claim against the book-keeping participant. He does not, however, have any property interest, by virtue of the Article, in any other asset. In particular, the investor is given no property interest in the underlying security. To say that he owns the property in a claim against his stockbroker adds nothing to the statement that he may claim against his stockbroker.

5.111 Article 8 sets out a complete regime for determining who is entitled to claim, and who is liable, in respect of dealings with securities held in a system. The effectiveness of the regime is produced not by its granting property rights in respect of the securities held in the system, but the opposite. The crux of the regime is found in Article 8-502 which provides:

> An action based on an adverse claim to a financial asset, whether framed in conversion, replevin, constructive trust, equitable lien, or other theory, may not be asserted against a person who acquires a security entitlement under Section 8-501 for value and without notice of the adverse claim.

5.112 The security of the system lies in denying the claims of anyone whose rights were acquired outside the regime. Section 502 does not do this by abolishing the rights concerned, for example by depriving an equitable owner of securities of his property rights in equity in those securities. Rather, it bars him procedurally from asserting those rights.

5.113 It might be said, therefore, that Article 8 creates a special kind of hybrid interest in *choses in action*. The Article grants special claims and liabilities among the named participants. Although there is a reference to the rights being 'property rights' it is hard to see that the word 'property' adds anything to the personal claims created by the Article. The statutory claims so created will defeat adverse claims arising outside of the regime not because the statutory regime creates property rights which will be superior to all other claims, but because all non-statutory claims are to be ignored. The structure underlying Article 8 can, therefore, be seen as a piece of very innovative thinking which avoids the need to create a hierarchy of property rights, or to re-categorize existing rights as personal rather than property rights.

6
THE LEGAL NATURE OF THE INTERNATIONAL BOND MARKET

Introduction

The incremental nature of market development

Commentators speak with awe about the world bond markets. A Bank for International Settlements paper in 2018 estimated the total debt outstanding on world bond markets at US$110 trillion.[1] The daily turnover in United States bond markets alone was US$822 billion in 2009.[2] The power that these numbers imply was summed up by James Carville, political advisor to President Clinton, as follows:[3]

6.01

> I used to think that if there was reincarnation, I wanted to come back as the President or the Pope ... But now I would like to come back as the bond market. You can intimidate everybody.

The word 'bond' has no technical meaning. It is used as a generic term to include all obligations and instruments which constitute or evidence long-term indebtedness, and which are traded between investors during the period between their issue and the date of redemption. The bonds may be in the form of documents or may consist of book entries, the benefit of which is traded. The indebtedness may be that of a central government or government agency, of a municipal authority, or of a company. The latter category includes issues by companies ('special purpose vehicles') which have no underlying business and the purpose of which is to borrow money as an issuer of debt securities into the bond market. The proceeds of the borrowing are then lent on to the company's sponsoring entity or are used to buy assets from that entity. The government and municipal bond markets are huge. For obvious reasons, they tend to be based in the country of the issuers concerned.

6.02

This chapter is concerned with the international bond market, into which entities from all over the world issue bonds, and which are bought by investors from equally diverse locations. Although it forms only one of the sub-divisions of the bond markets, the international market should not be dismissed lightly. The amount outstanding in international bonds was estimated in 2018 at US$24 trillion.[4] The issuers in this market are dominated by corporate entities (including financial institutions raising funds for their own purposes). It also includes governments which wish to raise long-term funds outside their own domestic

6.03

---

[1] Estimate of Bruno Tissot, Head of Statistics and Research Support, BIS.
[2] Estimate of The Securities Industry and Financial Markets Association.
[3] Reported on Bloomberg, 10 February 2009.
[4] Bank for International Settlements paper June 2018.

markets, and supranational bodies. The definition of an 'international bond' has changed over time. The definition now adopted by the Bank for International Settlements[5] states that an:

> ... international security is issued in a foreign market i.e. outside the market where the borrower resides.

The important thing to note about the definition is that it makes no reference to the currency in which the debt is denominated.

6.04 The international bond market is not only vast. It is growing and changing. A number of initiatives are now being taken to increase transparency within the market by introducing new exchanges and other trading platforms on which bonds can be bought and sold. In addition, market participants are keen to explore ways of bringing into the market retail investors in greater numbers. Because of the large minimum values in which bonds are regularly traded and the complex web of trading venues, the international bond market is currently accessible to retail investors, in practice, only through the medium of collective investment funds.

6.05 The legal issues affecting the international bond market are complex. There are two reasons for this. First, not all bonds are of the same legal nature. Individual securities issued as bonds may have different contractual and property elements. Investing in a bond involves much more than a simple purchase of a *chose in action* (ie the debt owed by the issuer). A bond is typically a web of relationships between the issuer, the investor, and several other entities who were parties to the original contractual documents which govern the issue and the nature of the obligation of the issuer. A further layer of relationships arises out of the trading of the bond and the separate obligations undertaken by sellers, buyers, and the brokers who act as agents for them.

6.06 The second reason for legal difficulty lies in the fact that the market is international. The complex web of relationships between parties often stretches across several national borders, and a number of different jurisdictions. It is not unusual at all to find a bond issued by, say, the Dutch subsidiary of a Japanese guarantor, where the investor is a Swiss mutual fund, which bought the bond through its London broker, which in turn acquired it from a selling broker in Frankfurt, who transferred it to the London broker through its accounts on a clearing system in Belgium, while the instrument which represents the underlying obligation is held on deposit in the vault of a bank in Paris. The analysis of the respective rights and obligations of the parties, both in relation to their contractual dealings and to their property entitlements, is difficult enough, if all parties are in the same jurisdiction. When the rights and obligations arise under the law of several different jurisdictions, the analysis can become almost impossible.

6.07 This chapter describes the roots from which the market grew and the legal nature of the bonds which developed with it. It then examines recent changes in the way in which bonds are structured, through 'immobilization' and towards 'dematerialization'. This evolution has been gradual. Change has been incremental, made by a series of small amendments to the existing structure, each doing the minimum necessary to accommodate the change in

---

[5] See the paper of June 2018.

market need. Until very recently, financial lawyers have not stood back and looked at the picture as a whole, to see if a radical change could lead to a structure which is simpler and more secure. When that overview is taken, the ways in which the legal structures can be simplified become clear.

The relationship between the nature of bonds and the market

In the case of most commercial markets, there is a direct link between the form of the trading activity and the nature of the commodity which is traded. For example, constraints are placed on the operation of the market in iron ore by the fact that ultimately the demand for it depends on the circumstances of companies who need it for steel-making. Traders might buy and sell as speculators, but the price and trading volumes are subject to the needs of the end user. The market has to develop taking into account the practical limitations of the commodity with which it is dealing.[6] In the case of international bond markets, however, there has not been such a constraint. The wish of issuers is merely to raise long-term borrowing. If investors would be more likely to subscribe, if the form of the instrument were changed (ie if the nature of the traded commodity were changed), there is no reason why issuers would not accommodate this. Accordingly, the development of the market (ie the trading in bonds between market participants) has shaped the form of the commodity in which they dealt. Put another way, the legal structure of bond issues and the way in which the rights are created and held has changed to meet the needs of the trading community.   6.08

The result is that the current legal form of many types of bond has evolved incrementally over a period in a series of responses to individual changes in the needs and preferences of those who wish to invest for trading purposes.   6.09

This adaptability has been the strength of the market, and has helped drive its growth. However, the legal nature of the bond market and dealings has become so complex that it risks inhibiting future development. Changes to facilitate further growth in the market will necessarily involve the participation of financial markets lawyers. Before such a change can even be contemplated, lawyers must understand the nature of bonds as they are currently constituted. In order to do this, it is necessary to go back to the time when companies first raised long-term debt finance, and from then to track the changes and developments of the legal instruments used for the purpose. An understanding of the form and nature of the securities concerned includes consideration of the reasons for their issue.   6.10

The Bond Market Pre-History

Since medieval times, European kings had borrowed money from overseas lenders in order to finance their wars with each other. It could not be said, however, that there was a healthy international trade in long-term sovereign debt during the Middle Ages. The most   6.11

---

[6] Arguably, the development of derivative products has allowed separate markets to develop in parallel with physical markets, thereby avoiding some of the limiting factors of physical markets.

appropriate point at which to begin consideration of the development of the modern bond market comes with the growth of the joint stock company during the nineteenth century.

6.12 Companies raised money for their commercial activities by inviting investors to subscribe for share capital. The money invested in this way entitled the subscriber to a 'share' in the capital of the company. The meaning of this phrase was determined partly by the terms of the Articles of Association of a company, partly by the terms of Companies Acts, and partly by decisions of the courts.

6.13 During the late nineteenth century, the courts wrestled with the task of deciding the nature of a share. In *Colonial Bank v Whinney*,[7] the Court of Appeal determined that a share was a *chose in action*, and Fry LJ further said:

> ... a share appears to me to be closely akin to a debt ...

6.14 This view was echoed a few years later by Lord MacNaughton in the leading case of *Trevor v Whitworth*,[8] when he drew attention to the provisions of ss 3 and 4 Companies Act 1877, which referred to the ability of a company:

> ... to pay off any capital which may be in excess of the wants of the company as if the share was principally a debt owing to the shareholder from the company.

6.15 It was clear, however, that the *chose in action* which comprised a share in a company was more than a simple debt. At the turn of the twentieth century, Farwell J had to consider the legal nature of a share in the case of *Borland's Trustee v Steel Brothers & Co., Ltd.*[9] In that case, an argument was advanced that a subscription of money for shares in a company resulted in the company holding the money concerned on a complicated series of trusts. This argument was firmly rejected:

> A share, according to the plaintiff's argument, is a sum of money which is dealt with in a particular manner by what are called for the purpose of argument executory limitations. To my mind it is nothing of the sort. A share is the interest of a shareholder in the company measured by a sum of money, for the purpose of liability in the first place, and of interest in the second, but also consisting of a series of mutual covenants entered into by all the shareholders inter se in accordance with s.16 of the Companies Act 1862. The contract contained in the articles of association is one of the original incidents of the share. A share is not a sum of money settled in the way suggested, but is an interest measured by a sum of money and made up of various rights contained in the contract, including the right to a sum of money of a more or less amount.

> Thus, although a share includes a right to receive money in certain circumstances (ie if the company is liquidated, its creditors have been discharged, and a surplus of cash remains), it also includes the benefit and the obligations set out in the contract between the company and the shareholders which is constituted by the Articles of Association.

6.16 Shares were transferable (or, more accurately, ownership of the *choses in action* constituted by the shares was transferable) by a written instrument. When that document was

---
[7] (1885) 30 Ch D 261, at 286, and see para 5.06.
[8] [1887] 12 App Cas 409.
[9] [1901] 1 Ch 279.

presented to the company, it would record the name of the transferee in its books as the person entitled to the *chose in action*, in place of the transferor. Parliament had an interest in requiring that transfers of shares were effected in this manner, since it levied stamp duty (a transaction tax on the value of property transferred by means of written instruments) on transfers of shares.

The issue of share capital was not the only method by which companies could raise funds to conduct their activities. They could, like any individual or other entity that was recognized by law as having a legal personality, borrow money by way of loan from banks or other lending institutions. If, however, companies wished to borrow for a long period (say, twenty or thirty years), they needed to look to a different kind of lender. Banks have traditionally been reluctant to lend for very long periods, because this operation involves the exposure to the risk of 'lending long and borrowing short'. Most commercial banks raise funds by taking deposits from retail customers or from other banks by way of deposits which are repayable on demand or within a short period. If the bank then lends those funds to customers, on terms that they cannot be called back by the bank for many years, the bank is exposed to the possibility of a liquidity squeeze, if it cannot replace its short-term borrowings as they fall to be repaid. 6.17

Companies which were looking to borrow funds long-term therefore sought either investors who were prepared to lend very long-term, or alternatively, those who wished to be able to realize the loan they had made by trading the indebtedness in the market. This meant, in practice, the same body of investors as those who were prepared to subscribe for companies' share capital and who could trade the shares through a stock exchange or other market mechanism. The investors who were prepared to lend long-term were the same people as the equity investors. 6.18

Accordingly, companies began to raise long-term borrowings in a form which closely resembled that of their share capital. In return for his subscription price, the lender would be issued with a certificate recording that he was entitled to be paid a certain amount of money at a specified date in the future, and in the interim would be entitled to receive interest at a specified rate, payable periodically. The terms of the loan would be set out in detail in a trust deed made between the company and a trustee appointed to act on behalf of all holders of indebtedness of the issue concerned. Under the trust deed, the company would agree with the trustee to conduct its business in accordance with detailed undertakings and subject to specified restrictions. The trustee would be given the right to sue the company, on behalf of the holders of the debt, in the event of any breach. The holders were, in equity, the owners of the *chose in action* constituted by the promises made by the company in the trust deed. 6.19

As an alternative, the company might enter into a unilateral deed, called a 'deed poll', directly in favour of the creditors, in which it made the same sort of promises. The deed would be expressed to confer benefits on all those who held parts of the indebtedness. On the whole, this method of issue was less popular with companies than the route which used a trust deed. Under the unilateral deed structure, each of the holders had the right to enforce his debt by action. In the case where a trust deed was used, only the trustee had the capacity to sue. The introduction of a trustee into the structure insulated the company from the possibility that it might need to deal with legions of creditors. All negotiations could be conducted through the trustee. 6.20

6.21 The benefits of each holder's part of the total subscribed loan were transferable in a manner very similar to that in which shares in the company's share capital could be transferred: the company kept a register of the holders of the indebtedness, who could transfer the benefit of their debts by a specified form of instrument. Under the terms of its unilateral deed or trust deed, the company would acknowledge as its creditor the person whose name was written in the register.

6.22 Forms of corporate indebtedness constituted in this way were known as 'loan stock' or 'debenture stock',[10] to differentiate them from the company's shares, or stock in its share capital.[11]

6.23 Although there were, clearly, differences between the sort of contractual rights given to a holder of loan stock, when compared to those given to a holder of stock in the share capital of the company, the structure and form of the legal obligations created was very similar. Loan capital can be seen as merely a different kind of company capital from that which is categorized as 'share capital'. The *Oxford English Dictionary* still defines 'loan capital' as:

> The part of the capital of a company or the like that is borrowed for a specified period.

At the start of the twentieth century, a leading legal textbook said that loan capital was:

> ...merely borrowed capital consolidated into one mass for the sake of convenience. Instead of each lender having a separate bond or mortgage, he has a certificate entitling him to a certain sum, being a portion of one large loan.[12]

6.24 The similarity between share capital and loan (or debenture) capital is preserved today in definitions in the Companies Act 2006:

> 'Debenture' includes debenture stock, bonds and any other securities of a company, whether or not constituting a charge on the assets of the company;[13]
>
> In this Chapter 'securities' means shares or debentures;[14]
>
> In this Chapter 'securities' means shares, debentures, debenture stock, loan stock, bonds, units of a collective investment scheme... and other securities of any description...[15]

Thus, at the beginning of the twentieth century, it was clear that corporate long-term indebtedness in the UK was usually constituted by a legal structure very similar to that of share capital.

---

[10] The complex arguments deployed in finding a definition of the word 'debenture' are set out in detail by the Court of Appeal in *Fons (HF) (In Liquidation) v Corporal Limited and Pillar Securitisation Sarl* [2014] EWCA Civ 304.

[11] Until 1929, companies were required by statute to allocate a unique identifying number to each share in their capital. When shares were transferred in any number, it was difficult to keep track of the individual numbers concerned. The practice developed of converting shares, as soon as they were issued, into 'units of stock', which were given, by the Articles of Association, exactly the same rights as the shares from which they derived. Crucially, there was no statutory requirement that they be numbered individually. The 1929 Companies Act removed the need to number shares, and with it the point of converting shares to stock units. There are now no listed companies whose share capital is divided into units of stock, although it is still common to talk of equity securities as 'stocks and shares'.

[12] W. B. Lindley, *Lindley on Companies* (6th edn, Sweet & Maxwell, 1902).

[13] Section 738.

[14] Section 755(5).

[15] Section 783.

Other countries, as their economies developed, evolved their own mechanisms and markets for raising long-term corporate debt. There was no reason for uniformity on this issue, because all markets were domestic. UK companies raised funds in the UK, American companies raised corporate debt on the US market from US investors, and so on. 6.25

Post-World War II

Growth of the markets

Before 1945, the holders of large amounts in any national currency were to be found in the state concerned. Thus, if a borrower needed US dollars (say to finance international trade priced in dollars), it would need to seek them from banks or investors based in the United States. If it needed to borrow sterling, it had no alternative but to look for lenders in London. The aftermath of World War II, however, saw an internationalization of holdings of currencies outside the country of issue. This particularly affected the US dollar. 6.26

The Marshall Plan, under which the United States financed the rebuilding of Europe after the war, resulted in European companies receiving large amounts of US dollars, for example as payment for carrying out construction work financed with US aid. These dollars were maintained as balances at banks in Europe. The banks concerned might have been European branches of US banks, or local banks. In addition, the Cold War of the 1950s and 1960s made the USSR and its allies reluctant to hold assets in the United States. This reluctance was driven by the fear of confiscatory action by the US government.[16] International trade, being conducted largely in US dollars, made the Soviet Bloc members reluctant recipients of US dollars. In order to avoid maintaining cash balances in banks in New York, they deposited their dollars in banks in Europe. Even if dealing with those funds would involve their transmission through the banking system in New York, the contractual relationship of the Soviet holders was with a bank in a less hostile jurisdiction.[17] Thus, the Eurodollar market was born. The large pool of US dollars held outside the US was available as an alternative source of funding for companies and governments which would otherwise have needed to borrow within the US in order to acquire that country's currency. 6.27

However, during the 1960s actions by succeeding US administrations had the unintended effect of turning the Eurodollar market into a preferred source of funding for non-US borrowers, rather than simply an alternative to the traditional New York source. 6.28

In 1963, concerned that too much available funding by US banks and investors was going abroad, in loans to non-US corporations and in the purchase of securities issued by non-US corporations, the Kennedy Administration introduced the Interest Equalization Tax.[18] This tax imposed a 15 per cent surcharge on interest received by US lenders and investors from non-US borrowers. The purpose was to persuade US lenders to concentrate on financing 6.29

---

[16] See paras 2.198 *et seq*.
[17] For a description of international payment mechanisms, see paras 3.33 *et seq*.
[18] Interest Equalization Tax Act of 1964, effective retrospectively to July 1963 (Public law 88-563, 78 Stat 809), extended by Executive Order 11198 of February 10, 1965.

US industry and to reduce capital outflows. The immediate effect of the tax, however, was that US lenders demanded increased interest payments from non-US borrowers, to compensate for the tax that would be payable on those receipts. Rather than pay this higher interest rate, non-US borrowers looked instead to acquire their dollars from the Eurodollar pool, where holders were not subject to the Interest Equalization Tax.

6.30 In 1965, in a further move to reduce capital outflows, the US Federal Reserve System introduced its voluntary Foreign Credit Restraint Program, which limited the amount of credit that US banks could make available to non-residents. This category included the overseas subsidiaries of US corporations. This tightening of US lending led to the predictable result that overseas companies which needed US dollars looked to the Eurodollar market to find them.[19]

6.31 In addition, the Federal Reserve Board regulated the interest rates payable by US banks on term deposits.[20] From 1966 the limit set by Regulation Q, the name given to the Federal Reserve measure concerned, became noticeably lower than the market rate would have fixed. Accordingly, holders of US dollars, who would otherwise have deposited them in New York, placed them in Europe, where Regulation Q did not apply, thereby swelling the pool of Eurodollars.

6.32 Thus, by the late 1960s a large market in US dollar deposits and loans was established in Europe, centred on London, but with substantial activity also in Zurich and Luxembourg. This dollar market was quite separate from the US domestic market and, most importantly, was largely immune from regulation by the US government.

6.33 Markets, of course, do not grow on their own, but expand only in response to the needs and appetites of their users. In the 1950s and 1960s, as the conditions for the development of the Eurodollar market unfolded, the numbers and needs of borrowers and investors also grew. The resurgence of the economies of continental European countries led to a growth in demand from companies, both for short-term Eurodollar loans to finance trading activities, but also for long- term corporate borrowing to finance infrastructure and investment. At the same time, a newly affluent middle class was enjoying the fruits of economic revival. Partly because of the experience of financial ruin brought about by World War II, newly prosperous professionals were cautious in the use of their wealth, and looked for long-term safe investment. Moreover, many members of the European middle class were reluctant to pay the taxes demanded by the public-sector renewal programmes of European states. The paradigm potential investor, usually referred to by commentators as 'the Belgian dentist', was not particularly interested in using his surplus earnings to buy US dollars, in order to place them in a deposit account with a bank. He would, however, be very interested in subscribing for a US dollar-denominated debt security, which could be held for the long term or sold for cash. He would be even more interested if the fact of his investment did not come to the attention of his national tax authorities.

---

[19] See R. Strauber, 'Voluntary Foreign Credit Restraint and the Nonbank Financial Institutions' (1970) 26 *Financial Analysts Journal* 3, pp 10–12.
[20] Under powers given by The Banking Act 1933 (in respect of banks that were members of the Federal Reserve) and The Banking Act 1935 (in respect of non-bank members).

Development of the form of bond

6.34 The conditions for the development of an international market in long-term debt were in place: large corporations wished to borrow US dollars on a long-term basis; large amounts of dollars were available in London and other European centres for this purpose; and there was a pool of retail investors, as well as institutional investors, ready to subscribe for long-term debt, provided that it could be traded easily. The missing element was a form of instrument which would satisfy the requirements of potential market participants.

6.35 The centre of activity and potential activity was London, which was the largest centre for US dollar deposits outside the United States itself. There was available under English law a well-established vehicle for the raising of long-term corporate debt. Loan stock and debenture stock had long been a part of the corporate landscape. However, this structure would not be appropriate for the developing international market. The majority of the borrowers would be outside the UK and would have corporate structures which might not readily accommodate the legal concepts which underlay conventional UK loan stock issues.

6.36 Further, although English law had long accepted the idea of loan stock issued to bearer,[21] UK practice from the end of the nineteenth century required, in effect, that securities issued by UK companies should be in registered form. The reason for this was that stamp duty levied on the transfer of securities was a valuable source of income, and successive UK governments were reluctant to permit the transfer of corporate securities without documentation on which the duty could be levied. By requiring the payment of stamp duty on the issue of bearer securities, English law forced the market to issue securities in registered form, so that tax could be levied on subsequent transfers.[22]

6.37 The stamp duty disadvantages were gradually eroded, until they were finally removed in 1986.[23] However, a fresh inhibition to the issue of bearer securities was created in 1947, by The Exchange Control Act of that year, which prohibited the issue of bearer instruments without the specific consent of HM Treasury. The requirement of Treasury consent was not removed until 1979.[24] In the result, the UK structure of registered loan stock was of no interest to those who had no reason to pay UK tax. In particular, it was not at all attractive to a Belgian dentist.

6.38 The requirement was for a form of legal structure under which the debt of the corporate borrower was capable of transfer in such a way that the change of ownership was not captured for tax purposes in any jurisdiction. The structure must also be recognized by all developed legal systems as transferring ownership of the debt concerned. Fortunately, such a concept was available. It had been used in trade throughout Europe, and subsequently the rest of the world, for several hundred years. The concept was the negotiable bearer instrument.

---

[21] See, eg: *Goodwin v Robarts* (1875) 10 Exch 337; and *Edelstein v Schuler & Co* [1902] 2 KB 144.
[22] Stamp Act 1891 s 109, as extended by Finance Act 1899 s 5(2).
[23] Finance Act 1986 s 79.
[24] By The Exchange Control (General Exemption) Order 1979 (SI 1979/1660).

Negotiable instruments

6.39 In the twelfth century, bankers in Northern Italy invented a means by which money could be transferred without the need to transport the coins which represented it. Their creation was the bill of exchange, a document under which the banker accepted, at the request of a customer who wished to transfer value, that he would pay a sum of money to a named transferee. This bill of exchange was acceptable to the named transferee/beneficiary, because he recognized the promise of the banker as giving him the same value as if he had received the coins.[25] These instruments involved the assumption by the payee of a credit risk on the banker who made the promise contained in the bill. However, merchants generally felt this risk to be acceptable. In thirteenth-century Europe, Florentine bankers were more creditworthy than most monarchs. Further, the bill of exchange eliminated the inconvenience and risks associated with transporting a large amount of coin, the only other way of discharging commercial debts.

6.40 With time, the forms of negotiable instruments became more diverse, in response to commercial needs. In 1680, in the case of *Shelden v Hantley*,[26] an English court was asked to consider the status of a promissory note (ie a simple written undertaking to pay) which was expressed to be payable to bearer. The maker of the promise argued that he could not be bound by it. Because the instrument named no person to whom the promise was owed, no-one had the capacity to enforce the promise. The court rejected the argument and recognized the note as conferring a right to claim on anyone who possessed the bill itself.

6.41 The legal basis for the recognition of bills of exchange and promissory notes by English law was the fact that the instruments concerned were treated as effective by the 'law merchant', the body of customs and practices among international merchants which was so secure and consistent that it created binding obligations by convention. English courts accepted that the law merchant formed part of the law of England.[27] Crucially, other major jurisdictions adopted the same view. The result was that the practices of international trade in using bills of exchange and promissory notes gave rise to legal rights and obligations which were consistent and sure in every major jurisdiction.

Negotiability

6.42 The legal concept which allowed these instruments to be regarded not only as creating binding relations between the parties to them, but as allowing the same rights to be transferred to other beneficiaries, is the concept of negotiability.

6.43 Negotiability was first used in connection with money, in the form of coins. The claim to payment from the issuing sovereign is embedded in the metal coin and passes to the person

---

[25] For an account of the development of the bill of exchange, see paras 5.92 *et seq* and also the explanation given by Cockburn CJ in *Goodwin v Robarts* (1875) 10 Exch 337.
[26] Show 160.
[27] See *Edie v East India Company* (1761) 2 Burr 1216, at 1226: 'The custom of merchants is part of the law of England; and Courts of Law will take notice of it, as such.' See also *Bechuanaland Exploration Co v London Trading Bank* [1898] 2 QB 658.

who is the owner of the coin. Ownership of coins, like other chattels, passes by delivery. However, to make their use in society possible, a rule must be imposed which is different from that which applies in the case of other chattels. Before someone will accept a coin as discharging a debt owed to him, he must be sure that he will become the owner of it by delivery. If there is a risk that a third party might claim it, say, on the basis that the coin was stolen from him some weeks before, a payee will not accept the coin unconditionally. The concept of negotiability therefore provides that, once the coin has been accepted by someone bona fide and for value, the coin is thereafter 'in circulation', and any former rights of ownership (eg the ownership of someone from whom the coin was stolen some time previously) are extinguished.

6.44 This was explained comparatively recently in the Australian case of *Ilich v The Queen*,[28] where the court pointed out that money which is stolen passes title, provided that it passes bona fide and for valuable consideration:

> ... that is because of the doctrine of negotiability, and negotiability was first attributed to chattels in the form of money...

6.45 The reason for the commercial success of bills of exchange and promissory notes lay in their negotiability. If the holder had taken the note in good faith and for value, he would be entitled to enforce the promise in the instrument, even if the person who gave it to him did not have good title to it.

Bond documentation

6.46 The form of documentation and instrument which evolved in the Eurobond market (now, more accurately, called the 'international bond market') was an agreement under which the borrowing company ('the issuer') would agree with subscribers that, in return for the payment of a sum of money, the issuer would give to each of them an instrument under which it promised to pay to bearer a stated amount at a fixed date in the future, perhaps a number of years after the date of issue. Each of those notes would have attached to it a series of 'coupons', each of which was itself a negotiable bearer instrument, and each of which represented an amount equal to interest for six months on the amount of the principal note. The notes which constituted the coupons would be payable at six-monthly intervals, starting on the date of issue and ending on the date of redemption. The coupons were physically detachable from the principal note, and therefore could be themselves traded separately from the principal note, or cashed on their stated payment date, as the holder chose.

6.47 Variations and elaborations swiftly developed. For example, bonds might be issued with warrants attached to them. Warrants were documents which gave the bearer the right to subscribe for other securities of the issuer at a future date, and at a stated price. That option could be exercised by extinguishment of part of the amount owed on the principal bond itself. Usually, however, the warrants were detachable and could be traded in the market

---

[28] (1987) 162 CLR 110.

as separate contractual rights. In other cases, coupons might be issued which provided for payment of an amount based on interest at a varying rate.

Temporary Global Notes

6.48 An unexpected influence on the structure of the Eurobond market lay in the provisions of the United States Securities Act of 1933, often referred to as 'the Securities Act'. The Securities Act was passed after the Wall Street Crash of 1929 in order to regulate the issue of corporate securities. The principal mechanism for this regulation, which has survived until today, is that securities which are to be issued to the public in the US must be registered with the Securities and Exchange Commission ('SEC').[29] Once registered, the issuer is required to comply with SEC rules on disclosure of information. Compliance with SEC registration requirements is intentionally a serious business. It is time-consuming and expensive. A non-US corporation which is issuing debt securities into the international bond market would wish to avoid the US registration requirements. It might be thought that this could be achieved by the simple expedient of the company not offering the securities for sale in the US. The position was, however, not that simple.

6.49 Section 5 of the Securities Act, which required registration of the securities offering with the SEC, was aimed at the protection of US investors. This included US nationals who lived outside the US. At the time when the international bond market was beginning to develop, the US had large numbers of troops stationed in Europe, who might have become investors in bond issues in the Euromarkets. In order to limit the protection of the Securities Act to US persons, Regulation S, made under s 5, provided a 'safe harbour' from registration requirements to foreign issues, but only if they excluded subscription or purchase by US persons. For this reason, it is usual to see in bond documentation a provision requiring any subscriber to represent to the company that he is not a 'US person'. If he does not make that declaration, his subscription will not be accepted.

6.50 On its own, however, this was not enough to safeguard US nationals from the sale of unregulated securities. Standard operations in the market were conducted on the basis that a small group of banks which agreed to underwrite the issue would themselves subscribe for all of the bonds on issue. They would then on-sell the bonds that they acquired to purchasers whom they had contacted beforehand. The purpose of the 'safe harbour' in Regulation S would be defeated if a European bank could subscribe for bonds on the date of issue, and sell them the next day to a US person, the sale having been arranged ahead of the issue.

6.51 The compromise was that the SEC would accept that the provisions of the 'safe harbour' would apply, provided that, in practice, US persons could not acquire bonds within 40 days of their issue. This period was known as the 'lock-up' period.

6.52 The bonds which constituted the securities were the bearer negotiable instruments produced by the issuer. If the issuer did not sign and deliver these negotiable instruments until the end of the 40-day period, it followed that no US person could acquire

---

[29] More accurately, the Securities Act requires the registration of offers or sales 'using the means and instrumentalities of interstate commerce', unless the law provides an exemption.

one before then. However, the market would have been uneasy with a situation where the underwriting banks paid to the issuer the total value of the issue on the date of issue, against only an undertaking by the issuer to produce a series of notes in 40 days' time. Accordingly, the practice developed of requiring the issuer, at the date of issue, to make a 'Temporary Global Note'. This was a note which set out the issuer's promise to pay an amount equal to the total of the principal value of the notes to be issued. Typically, the amount would be US$100 or 200 million. This Temporary Global Note would be placed with a bank, referred to as a 'Depository', which would agree to hold it on behalf of the underwriters until the end of the 40-day period. At that point, the company would produce 'definitive notes' in the smaller, tradable amounts. These definitive notes would in aggregate be the same value as the Temporary Global Note. On their production, they would be exchanged for the Temporary Global Note. This latter document would then be destroyed by the issuer, and the definitive notes distributed to those who had agreed to buy them.

Permanent Global Notes

The negotiable instrument had been, for centuries, a mainstay of international trade and the most efficient way of transferring value. However, by the 1960s, financial markets operated by telephone and book entry. Computers were even coming into use for recording transactions. For professionals, the pieces of paper which constituted the securities in which they dealt had become a hindrance. Professional dealers were happy to contract over the telephone to buy and sell a security, to confirm their agreement by telex, and to record the results in their respective books. They liked the situation that applied during a Eurobond lock-up period, when there was no definitive instrument to be passed. They could buy and sell bonds between themselves, knowing that they were represented by the Temporary Global Note, but without having to worry about transmitting pieces of paper, or losing them after they arrived. The Belgian dentist, of course, preferred to have the definitive note. As the market developed, however, the individual private subscriber became less and less important and the professional and institutional traders and investors began to dominate the market.

6.53

The state of affairs which the professionals preferred was that the Depository bank should continue to hold the Global Note. Trades in the bonds would take place according to the most efficient methods available to market participants, and the ownership of bonds would be recorded in the books of the professional dealers. As far as retail investors were concerned, the advantages of holding a definitive certificate diminished, as international tax regulation developed and the possibility of hiding ownership of assets from the tax authorities became less available. Private individuals who wished to access this market were content to do so through their broker, which would record in its books purchases made on behalf of the customer.

6.54

The market, therefore, moved to a system under which the Global Note delivered by the issuer on the date of issue was no longer temporary. It would remain in place throughout the life of the issue. Provision was usually made that, if a holder wished to have a definitive note of its own entitlement, such a note would be issued, and the Global Note physically

6.55

amended to record the reduction in the capital value represented by that instrument. In practice, the position developed where many issues had no definitive certificates produced in respect of them, but remained represented entirely by one Permanent Global Note, buried in a bank vault.

Immobilization and the Modern Era

The emergence of the ICSDs

6.56 With the domination of the international bond market by institutional investors and market professionals, there arose the need for systems through which market trades could be processed and settled. Two of these International Central Securities Depositories ('ICSDs') grew to dominate the market; Cedel Bank in Luxembourg (now called 'Clearstream Banking, SA'), and Euroclear Bank SA/NV, based in Brussels.

6.57 The function of the ICSDs is to settle trades in international bonds and other securities. In essence, this involves recording the effects of a transfer agreed between a buyer and seller, both of whom maintain accounts with the ICSD. These accounts show the ownership of securities, as between the ICSD and the account holder.[30] They also serve as a platform for the settlement of the trades by payment. Participants maintain cash balances with the ICSD, so that payment can be made through the accounts with the ICSD at the time when the transfer of securities takes place in the ICSD's records.

6.58 When a bond issue is launched, in those cases where no part of the issue is to be constituted by small definitive notes which are to circulate at a retail level, the issuer signs a single Permanent Global Note for a sum equal to the total proceeds of the issue. That Permanent Global Note is placed with a Depository. The Depository, which is a commercial bank, declares that it holds the note 'for' the ICSD. If, as is usually the case, it is intended that trades in the bonds should settle through both Clearstream and Euroclear, the Depositor declares itself to be the 'common depository' for both ICSDs.

6.59 When the subscription is made, the ICSD concerned records in its books entitlements to amounts of the bond issue, as instructed by the underwriters who have arranged the subscription. All intermediaries which participate actively in the market hold accounts with one or other of the ICSDs, so that this process simply involves the ICSD entering the amount of the entitlement in the account of the market participant concerned.

6.60 The issuer appoints a bank as its Paying Agent.[31] As and when money falls to be paid, whether by way of semi-annual interest or repayment of principal, the issuer puts the Paying Agent in funds for this purpose, and the Paying Agent pays over the total amount to the ICSDs, who credit the relevant part of it to each of the participants shown in their books as holding securities of the description concerned.

---

[30] The ICSD's records do not record the identity of the person for whom the account-holder is acting (see para 6.61 below).
[31] The Paying Agent is often, but not always, a branch of the bank which acts as the Depository.

6.61 The participants for whom accounts are held by the ICSDs may be acting on their own account. More likely, they will be acting on behalf of their own clients, for whom they will be holding the bonds concerned. The books of the participant will record the entitlements of the participant's clients. Those clients may, of course, themselves be intermediaries, holding on behalf of investors further down the chain.

6.62 The structure of relationships in a simple modern international bond issue (referred to in the market as the 'Classical Global Note' structure) might be represented as follows:[32]

Immobilization and the Modern Era

```
                    Payments of interest
                     and principal
    ┌──────────────┐◄─────────────────────┌──────────────┐
    │ Paying Agent │                      │   Issuer     │
    │(Bank in Zurich)│                    │(Italian Company)│
    └──────┬───────┘                      └──────┬───────┘
           │                                     │
   Payments of interest                          │
     and principal                               │
           ▼                                     ▼
    ┌──────────────┐   Holds Permanent Global  ┌──────────────┐
    │    ICSD      │◄──Note 'for' ICSD─────────│Depository Bank│
    │ (Euroclear   │                           │   (Paris)    │
    │  Brussels)   │                           └──────────────┘
    └──┬───────┬───┘
       │       └──────────────────┐
       ▼                          ▼
 ┌──────────────┐           ┌──────────────┐
 │ICSD Member A │           │ICSD Member B │
 │(Investment Bank,│        │   (Bank,     │
 │   London)    │           │ Amsterdam)   │
 └──┬────────┬──┘           └──┬────────┬──┘
    │        │                 │        │
    ▼        ▼                 ▼        ▼
 ┌──────┐ ┌──────────┐     ┌──────┐ ┌──────┐
 │Client C│ │ Client D │    │Client F│ │Client G│
 │(Lawyer)│ │(Individual)│  └──────┘ └──────┘
 └───┬──┘ └──────────┘
     ▼
 ┌──────────┐
 │Trustees of│
 │Settlement│
 │ Trust E  │
 └────┬─────┘
      ▼
 ┌──────────┐
 │Beneficiaries│
 │of Settlement│
 │  Trust H   │
 └──────────┘
```

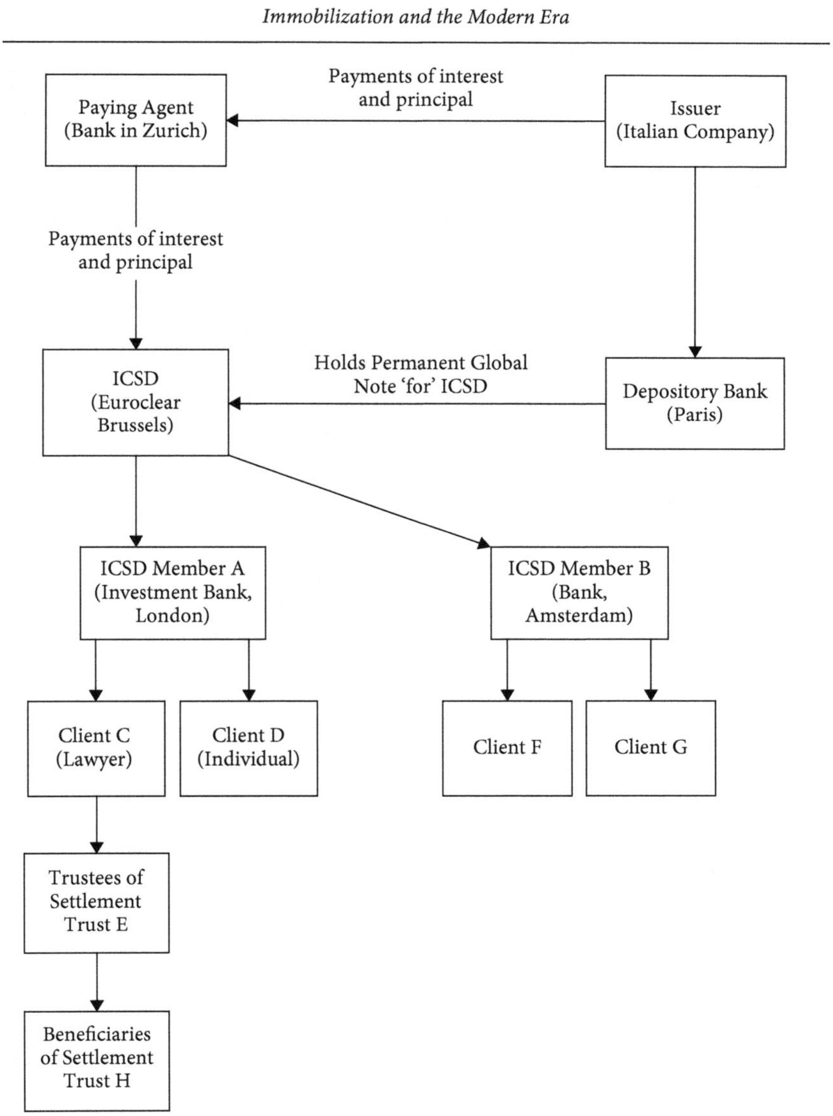

Figure 6.1 Relationships in a Classical Bearer Global Note Structure

[32] A variant is the 'Global Registered Note', where the Global Note is expressed to be payable to a named company, which is a nominee for the Depository. The name is a little misleading, since the 'registation' relates only to the name of the nominee.

6.63 The introduction of the ICSDs into the standard bond structure transformed fundamentally the operation of the market, not only in practice, but also in legal terms. It allowed the transfer of ownership of bonds to be dealt with swiftly and securely. A financial institution, whose holding was recorded in its account with the ICSD, could agree over the telephone to sell bonds to another dealer, and effect delivery by instructions to the ICSD to debit its securities account with the number of the bonds concerned and to credit them to the securities account of the buyer, in return for the debit and credit of the parties' cash accounts in the opposite direction.

6.64 The key to this leap in convenience of dealing lay in the immobilization of the bond itself. Under the Classical Global Note structure, the bond (ie the single instrument which embodies the debt owed by the issuer) is kept permanently in a bank vault, from which it is expected never to move. Further, the amount of the instrument represents the whole of the issue, and is therefore so large that it is incapable in practice of being traded. Burying (or 'immobilizing') the instrument in this way means that the market can deal with individual portions of the debt which the note embodies, free from worry that those dealings might be complicated by parallel transactions in the note itself.

6.65 From a legal point of view, the change to an immobilized structure involves a great irony. The genius of the legal structure adopted by the international bond market in its early days lay in the use of negotiable instruments; as the pieces of paper changed hands, the debt owed by the issuer passed with them. Under the immobilized system, the instruments, far from being the method by which the bonds were traded, became a potential embarrassment. The transfer of bonds through book entries at the ICSD is effective only if there is no possibility that the benefit of the debts could pass by any other method. It is therefore essential to ensure that the negotiable instrument is handled in such a way that it never can be negotiated. If there was any thought in the market that a Permanent Global Note might somehow escape from the vaults of the Depository bank, and actually be negotiated, no-one could trust the trading system set up through the ICSDs.

6.66 Under the immobilized system, the idea of negotiability, which allowed the international bond market to develop in the first place, has become a danger. The present system operates only if the concept of negotiability, which relates only to physical items, the ownership of which passes by delivery, is completely eradicated in practice. The question of whether, if negotiability is abolished in practice, it can continue in theory is considered below.[33]

New Global Note structure and New Safekeeping Structure

6.67 After the introduction of the euro as the common currency of many of the EU Member States, the European Central Bank became responsible for conducting money market operations in the eurozone, the group of countries which have adopted the euro as their

---

[33] See paras 6.81 *et seq.*

currency.[34] Central to those operations is the provision of liquidity to eurozone banks against the security of collateral. Subject to the fulfilment of relevant criteria, bonds traded on the international bond market are commonly used as collateral for the money market operations of central banks. The ECB, however, became concerned that the legal structure of bond issues, set out above, contained unacceptable risks for it as a collateral-taker.

6.68 In particular, the ECB was concerned about the lack of clarity in the legal significance of the fact that a Permanent Global Note was held, as Depository, by a commercial bank. The ECB would make liquidity available to commercial banks against collateral which was delivered via the book-entry system maintained by the ICSDs, both of which are located within the eurozone. In relation to the bonds concerned, however, the Permanent Global Note might well be held physically by a bank located outside the eurozone. The ECB's method of taking collateral was to arrange for the transfer into its name, or that of a nominee, of the bonds which were given as collateral, through book entries at one or other of the ICSDs. If the Depository bank located in, say, London went into liquidation, how safe would be the position of the holder of bonds, whose entitlement consisted of an entry in the records of one of the ICSDs? Could a liquidator of the Depository bank claim that he or she was the holder of a negotiable bearer instrument and therefore entitled to be paid by the issuer, inviting the holders shown in the records of the ICSDs to prove in the liquidation for the sums they claimed were due to them in respect of the bonds? If this was not a possibility in law, what was the point of the Permanent Global Note?[35]

6.69 The ECB therefore insisted that an amendment be made to the structure in respect of bonds which, after January 2007, were to be eligible as collateral for its money market operations. The amended structure, which uses only bearer instruments, is called the 'New Global Note' structure. The incremental amendments to the Classical Global Note structure are comparatively minor. The Global Bearer Note formerly held by a Depository bank is held under the New Global Note structure by a nominee of one of the ICSDs, the ICSDs themselves being appointed 'Common Safekeepers' of the note. The simple point about this change is that, if the instrument itself is held by the settlement systems, there is no-one who might compete with the interests of the owners who hold through the records of one of the systems.

6.70 A further change was made to the content of the Global Note under the new structure. Under the Classical Global Note structure, the Global Note stated the amount payable by the issuer, and made provision for this statement to be amended from time to time. For example, a holder might wish to take definitive notes in respect of his own holding, thereby reducing the amount represented by the Global Note; or some of the bonds represented by the Global Note might be repaid. Thus, the Note itself showed the amount outstanding at any time. Under the New Global Note structure, the Note simply states that the amount outstanding is the aggregate of the amounts shown in the records of the ICSDs as owned by members of the ICSDs. This is a sensible administrative change. It does, however, raise a fundamental legal question: even if a Classical Global Note can be argued to be a negotiable instrument, can the same ever be said of a New Global Note, where the amount of the debt which it embodies cannot be ascertained from the instrument, but only from the records of a third party?[36]

---

[34] Under the terms of the Treaty on European Union (the 'Maastricht Treaty'). For an explanation of the effect of the treaty, see paras 2.86 *et seq*.
[35] These questions are examined below at paras 6.79 *et seq*.
[36] This question is discussed in paras 6.85 *et seq* below.

6.71 The ECB introduced new requirements for collateral eligibility in respect of issue that used a registered form of Global Note. These changes took effect in June 2010. The only difference between the arrangements under the New Safekeeping Structure and those for a Classical Registered Global Note is that the note is described as being 'safekept' by one of the ISCDs (rather than 'deposited' with a Depository) and the name of the payee recorded in the issuer's records is that of a nominee for the ISCD.

Legal Analysis of Bond Structures

6.72 The law aims for predictability and consistency. Therefore, when any structure is known, it should be possible to analyse its effect and consequences. In the case of the structure of a bond issue, however, analysis faces a number of difficulties. First, bond structures, although they may share certain overall characteristics, have a number of variations which may be crucial in legal terms. For example, some issues include a trustee, which is given the benefit of various undertakings and covenants from the issuer, and which holds those rights as trustee for the bondholders. In other issues, there is no trustee, and the issuer makes the same covenants by means of a unilateral promise for the benefit of the bondholders. In each case, the effect is intended to be the same, but the legal nature of the rights of the bondholders is different.

6.73 Second, the main documents which constitute the issue arrangements, in particular the document which embodies the promises of the issuer by way of covenant to the bondholders, are often expressed to be governed by English law. However, issuers may elect to have their obligations governed by the law of any jurisdiction they choose. The choice may be influenced by the national identity of the issuer or of intended investors, or both. The choice of governing law is crucial in any analysis of the consequences of the document concerned.

6.74 Most importantly, the international nature of the market means that the facts in relation to the holding of any particular bond will vary, according to the countries involved. In the example given in para 6.62 above the Global Note is deposited with a bank in France. If the bank concerned were to become insolvent, the question would arise whether the ICSDs, for whom the Depository declares that it holds the note, or the bondholders could claim its delivery. Alternatively, the liquidator of the Depository bank might claim to be entitled to retain it, inviting other interested parties to prove in the liquidation for the amount that they claimed to be owed. An English lawyer analyzing this position cannot simply apply English law contractual provisions and English property law. As a matter of English law, questions relating to the ownership of property situated abroad are usually to be determined by an English court in accordance with the law of the place where the property is situated,[37] although this rule might not apply in relation to some questions concerning negotiable instruments. An English court might well need to take into account French law of property

---

[37] See Lord Collins and Prof. Harris (eds), *Dicey, Morris & Collins on the Conflict of Laws* (15th edn, Sweet & Maxwell, 2018), 33R-322 *et seq*.

when deciding the ownership of the Global Notes, although the necessity of this course this could be determined only after close examination of the facts.

The position is likely, in practice, to be even more complicated. Suppose, for example, that the Depository bank in Paris, shown in the diagram in para 6.62, was not incorporated in France, but was the Paris branch of a bank incorporated in The Netherlands. If the insolvency proceedings related to the whole of the bank's activities, the likelihood is that the insolvency proceedings in Holland would determine disputes between the parties about ownership of assets. The question therefore would fall to be considered by a Dutch court. That court would apply the principles of Dutch private international law in deciding which country's law should determine questions of ownership of the property concerned. Assuming that the rules of private international law adopted by Dutch law are the same as those that apply in English law, the Dutch court might well conclude that the ownership of the Global Note needed to be determined according to principles of French law, since the note was physically in France. In working out the effect of those rules, of course, the Dutch court would be bound to apply Dutch insolvency law.

6.75

The picture might change dramatically again if, in the event, it turned out that the Paris bank was the branch of an Italian bank which went into insolvency in Italy, or if, six months before becoming insolvency, the Dutch bank had closed down its Paris branch, and moved all the property deposited with it to the strongroom of its branch in Brussels.

6.76

The effect of individual rules of private international law, and the inter-relationship of the many such rules that are involved, is so important to any analysis of an international bond structure that it is impossible to predict what the effect of any structure will be, unless one knows the exact factual position at the time when the analysis will apply. Any analysis made in advance must always carry the caveat that the position will be different if the assumed facts change. And it is almost certain that they will change.

6.77

With the overriding proviso set out above, the following section of this chapter looks at certain questions about the structure of bond issues, from the point of view of English law. It assumes that English law applies to all legal questions which fall to be considered. In practice, this will not provide the answer to any of the questions. It is, however, a first step.

6.78

Question 1: Does the Global Note have any value?

The basis of the modern international bond issue is the assumption that the notes made by the issuer are negotiable instruments which constitute an obligation of the issuer to pay the sum stated. The benefit of that obligation is transferred by the delivery of the note, in the case of a bearer note, or endorsement of a 'registered' note. The concept of negotiability means that the recipient takes it free from any defect in title which might have arisen in the chain of ownership up to the point of transfer to him. All other rights arising out of the documentation of the issue are ancillary to that core obligation.

6.79

Practice has moved from the use of notes of comparatively small amounts to the use of a Global Note which is immobilized. The Global Note is of a very large value, and represents the whole of the issue. Immediately upon being made, it is handed to a Depository

6.80

174   THE LEGAL NATURE OF THE INTERNATIONAL BOND MARKET

or Common Safekeeper, whose principal function is to ensure that the note remains safely buried for the life of the issue and that it does not come into the hands of any other party.

6.81 The first point to consider is whether a Global Note is a negotiable instrument. Is it of such a legal nature that the debt which it embodies attracts the special rules about transferability which apply to such instruments? There are two possible bases on which a Global Note might, as a matter of English law, qualify for such treatment. It might be a promissory note, within the terms of the Bills of Exchange Act 1882, or it might be classified as a negotiable instrument in accordance with common law.

6.82 The Bills of Exchange Act 1882 s 83(1) defines a promissory note:

> A promissory note is an unconditional promise in writing made by one person to another signed by the maker, engaging to pay, on demand or at a fixed or determinable future time, a sum certain in money, to, or to the order of, a specified person or to bearer.

The Act deals with those bills of exchange and promissory notes which are intended to circulate freely as part of normal trade. The instruments designed for this use are intended to be self-contained, so that a transferee will recognize a document as having value, without the need to examine the background which gave rise to its being made. If the time of payment, the amount, or the currency of the obligation to pay can be ascertained only by reference to facts outside the terms of the instrument, the document cannot in practice be freely traded.

6.83 There are several respects in which the form of most Global Notes might take them outside the terms of the statutory definition. First, the promise to pay, contained in a Global Note, will rarely be 'unconditional'. It is usual to refer to the conditions set out in the issue agreements and covenants given by the issuer. There are numerous provisions in these documents which might have the effect of altering the terms of the payment set out in the Global Note. Among other things, these conditions might well affect the provision that a promissory note must be payable at a fixed or 'determinable future time'. It is usual for a Global Note to be stated to be payable at a particular maturity date. However, Global Notes usually go on to provide that the amount will become due earlier in accordance with the conditions attached to the issue. For example, agreed 'events of default' or other changes of circumstances might bring about an acceleration of the repayment obligation.

6.84 A promissory note must be a self-contained promise to pay. If it contains 'words which would be mysterious to anyone who did not know the full circumstances', the instrument cannot be a promissory note within the meaning of the Act.[38]

6.85 In addition, Global Notes usually provide for the alteration of the amount stated to be payable. If, for example, some holders require the issue to them of definitive notes, the issuer will normally undertake to produce such notes, and in that event the value of those notes will be deducted from the amount payable under the Global Note. The Global Note will be amended to reflect that change. It might be argued that this does not prevent the Global Note promising the payment of a 'sum certain in money' since, at any time, that amount can

---

[38] *Wirth v Weigel Leygonie & Co Ltd* [1939] 3 All ER 712.

be ascertained on the face of the note. However, in the case of New Global Notes issued to comply with the requirements of the European Central Bank,[39] this argument cannot apply. The requirement in the case of New Global Notes is that the amount payable should refer to the amount shown in the records of the ICSDs as the aggregate of bonds in issue. Looking at the note on its own, it is impossible to know the size of the amount that is promised. That can be found out only by looking at the records of the two ICSDs.

6.86 Most tellingly, an essential characteristic of a promissory note is that it should be intended by the maker to be a negotiable instrument (ie it should be capable of passing from hand to hand, with each transfer carrying the right to receive payment). If that element is absent, the instrument is not a promissory note.[40]

6.87 In light of the common intention that Global Notes should be kept securely, and under no circumstances should be negotiated, it seems highly unlikely that any Global Note would come within the definition of a 'promissory note' in the Bills of Exchange Act 1882. Accordingly, the attributes of negotiability given by that Act would not apply.

6.88 The Bills of Exchange Act 1882 did not create the idea of negotiability, but codified the consequences and applied them to certain specific instruments. Before that time, it had been recognized that certain instruments were, according to the law merchant, recognized as having special attributes of transferability. Cockburn CJ in *Goodwin v Robarts*[41] explained the special status of negotiable instruments by likening them to money. He said that it was well established by English cases that certain kinds of 'mercantile instruments' passed the right to receive payment in the same way that cash passed the same entitlement.[42] He quoted an earlier judge, Holroyd J:

> The courts have considered these instruments ... as being appendages to money and following the nature of their principal ... these decisions proceed upon the nature of the property (ie money), to which such instruments give the right ... and the effect of the instruments, which ... give to their holders, merely as such, a right to receive the money...[43]

6.89 The form of a modern Global Note could hardly be further from the 'near money' which the law merchant treated as negotiable. A Global Note is in an amount so large that it cannot conceivably be used in trade in the normal sense. Its terms are tied to the documents of issue, and the nature of the obligation to pay cannot be understood without full knowledge of those terms. Most importantly, there is no possibility of arguing that the purpose of the note was to allow its circulation as part of trading activity. The circumstances in which it is made, particularly relating to its deposit with a bank or safekeeper for the purpose of immobilization, show clearly the intention that it should never be traded or negotiated. The idea of immobilization is incompatible with the concept of negotiability.

---

[39] See paras 6.67 to 6.71 above.
[40] *Akbar Khan v Attar Singh* [1936] 2 All ER 545; *Claydon v Bradley* [1987] 1 WLR 521.
[41] (1875) 10 Exch 337.
[42] There was an inconsistency in relation to the recognition of promissory notes as negotiable instruments. In two cases, *Clarke v Martin* (1701) 2 Ld Raym 757, and *Buller v Crips* (1703) 6 Mod. 29, Lord Holt CJ had held that promissory notes were not negotiable instruments at common law. This position was reversed by a statute (3&4 Anne, c 8 of 1704), which was repealed by the Bills of Exchange Act 1882.
[43] See para 5.99.

6.90 It therefore seems difficult, as a matter of English law, to argue that a Global Note, whichever of the current structures is used, is a negotiable instrument.[44] Does it matter? The structure of the international bond market was originally based on the idea of negotiable instruments which could be, and were, traded by delivery, and where delivery passed title to the claim for payment by the issuer. Under present arrangements, where the Global Note is not traded, does it matter that a theoretical physical transfer might not itself pass the right to receive payment? In practice, there will be no chain of holders of the Global Note. It will be held only by the original Depository or Safekeeper, or possibly by a substitute for that body. The Depository/Safekeeper, having possession of the note, and being its first possessor, is never going to have to rely on its status as the holder of a negotiable instrument, in order to defeat the challenge of someone else who claims to be the owner of the physical note. Negotiability, therefore, is irrelevant. All that matters is that the promise to pay should constitute a *chose in action*, a debt enforceable against the issuer.

6.91 It is interesting to analyse the process by which the Global Note is created, in terms of English contract law. The issue arrangement is one under which the original subscribers, who may well be a group of underwriting banks, pay a large sum of money to the issuer. In consideration of that payment, the issuer undertakes that it will pay at a future date the same sum of money to the bearer of the piece of paper signed on that date, or to the named payee. That piece of paper will be given to the Depository/Safekeeper, the identity of which is known at the outset, and which it is intended should remain in possession of the paper until the repayment date. In the issue documentation, the issuer covenants with a trustee, for the benefit of the holders of the bonds from time to time, that it will make the payment promised in the Global Note. Although the capacity of the parties is not spelt out, it is known that the payment by the issuer at maturity to the Depository/Safekeeper (or named payee) will find its way into the hands of the bondholders, for whose benefit the issuer has promised to make the payment.

6.92 The point to consider is whether it would make a difference to the substance of the contractual obligations and rights of the parties, if the piece of paper ceased to exist.

6.93 During the Second Chechen War, Russian forces captured the capital of Chechnya, Grozny, in February 2000. During the course of the fighting a bank building in Grozny was destroyed by a bomb. The bank had been the Depository for the Global Notes in a number of bond issues by companies in the region. The issuers, bondholders, and market participants were faced with the question of whether the destruction of the Global Notes, and along with the notes the possibility that anyone could be the holder of them, meant that the issuers were no longer under an obligation to pay anyone in relation to the bond issue. If this were so, the entitlements of the bondholders, shown in the books of the relevant clearing systems, would be meaningless.

6.94 The consensus was that the issuers should still pay. They made out new notes, which were then deposited safely elsewhere. This story may be apocryphal. However, it clearly shows the view that the markets take of the rights and obligations of the parties. The issuers accepted that the original execution of the Global Notes did not discharge their obligations

---

[44] However, for a contrary view, see *Gore-Browne on Companies*, Update 78, para 29[2A].

under the contract with the issuers, and that they retained an obligation to pay at the maturity date irrespective of whether the piece of paper existed or not.

In legal terms, one might say that the subscription created a *chose in action*, the obligation of the issuer to pay at maturity. It had promised to pay 'the bearer' of a particular piece of paper, and it had undertaken to the subscribers, for the benefit of bondholders, that it would duly pay 'the bearer' of that piece of paper. At the time of the contract, everyone concerned knew the identity of the first 'bearer' (the Depository). It was not contemplated that, during the currency of the issue, the identity of the bearer would change. Certainly, the word 'bearer' had not been used in the expectation that the document would pass from hand to hand like a bank note. In fact, a reference to 'bearer' was merely a shorthand reference to the particular Depository which was expected to be the recipient of the money in due course, and which would then pass it on to the bondholders. In the circumstances, the piece of paper served only to identify the institution to which payment was to be made. Since the identity of that institution was known, even when the piece of paper had been destroyed, the contractual obligation of the issuer had not changed. **6.95**

Another way to put this is to contrast the situation where a creditor accepts the issue of a negotiable instrument in discharge of the debtor's payment obligation. For example, a customer whose account is in credit might ask his bank to supply him with a banker's draft (a promissory note made by the bank) for the amount of the credit. The issue of the draft, and the bank's assumption of liability on it, discharges the debt from the bank to the customer, constituted by the customer's account.[45] The bank's obligation to pay its customer has been replaced by its obligation to pay the draft on presentation. In the case of a bearer bond issue, the parties, including the maker of the Global Note, do not regard the making of the Note as a discharge of the issuer's repayment obligations under the bond documentation. They expect that the issuer will pay, at maturity, the possessor of the Note only if the possessor is the Depository. No-one other than the Depository could, in practice, be the legitimate holder of the Global Note, and accordingly no-one other than the Depository would be entitled to payment. **6.96**

This analysis is even clearer where the Global Note is in 'registered' form (ie the issuer undertakes to pay the nominee of the Depository/Safekeeper). If it is accepted that the Note is not a negotiable instrument, the Note does no more than repeat the promise made by the issuer in the agreement under which the issue was made. It is then seen merely as evidence of a term of a contract, an acknowledgement of the debt created by the subscription agreement. It is, however, evidence of something which is not in doubt. It is clear from all the rest of the documentation that the issuer has promised to make a payment to the payee at maturity. The Note is not, therefore, an essential element of the debt obligation. **6.97**

Question 2: What does the investor own?

When faced with this rather basic question, anyone other than a lawyer would answer that the investor owns a bond (or a debt security) of the issuer. The legal analysis of this **6.98**

---

[45] For this reason, bankers often speak of 'selling a draft' to the customer.

statement is, however, surprisingly difficult. Although a typical bond issue will involve the production of hundreds of pages of documentation, the answer to this question does not emerge with any clarity from it. The reason for the difficulty is the fact that the bond structure has evolved to accommodate the trading wishes of investors and the technology that enables those wishes to be put into effect, while the legal basis of the structure remains anchored in a different time.

6.99 The original concept was that the issuer created a series of simple assets: a number of negotiable instruments. The ownership of each of these assets passed by physical delivery, and carried with it the ownership of the debt which is embodied. At any time, the owner of the asset could be clearly seen. It was the person who had physical possession of it. It might be, of course, that he had obligations in relation to it in favour of third parties. The identity of the asset was, however, clear and it was easy to work out the rights that the parties had in it.

6.100 However, with the idea of immobilization, this simplicity and clarity disappears. The Global Note and the claim that it represents, if any, does not move. The trading of the bonds is now a quite separate matter from possession of the instrument. An analysis of the rights of the investor under a modern Global Note structure has to be based on legal principle, since there is no direct guidance from decided cases or from statute. What follows should, therefore, be regarded as tentative and as a stimulus for consideration, rather than firm conclusions. In addition, it should be remembered that in practice the parties will be based in several different jurisdictions, and questions of private international law will necessarily affect any analysis of their rights and obligations. For present purposes, the text assumes, quite artificially, that all aspects will be governed by English law.

If the Global Note is a negotiable instrument

6.101 If the Global Note is a negotiable instrument in law, whether by virtue of being a promissory note within the meaning of s 83 Bills of Exchange Act 1882 or because it is accepted at common law as one of the forms of negotiable instrument recognized by the law merchant, the Depository/Safekeeper (or its registered nominee) is the holder of the Global Note. This status has consequences, both in relation to the ownership of the paper and to the money claim that it embodies. The holder of the Note is the possessor of the piece of paper, and owner of the *legal chose in action* constituted by it (ie the right to claim payment of the sum concerned from the issuer).

6.102 The normal form of declaration by the Depository/Safekeeper is simply that it holds the Global Note 'as common depository (or common safekeeper) for the ICSDs'. This acknowledgement recognizes that, as between the Depository/Safekeeper and the ICSDs, the Depository/Safekeeper is not the owner of the Note. In English law, the piece of paper is a chattel, and the relationship between the Depository/Safekeeper and the ICSDs is best analysed as one of bailment (ie the Depository/Safekeeper has possession of the paper, but ownership of the paper rests with the ICSDs).

6.103 The use of the words 'as common depository (or safekeeper) for the ICSDs' might clarify the ownership of the piece of paper. It does not, however, identify the owners in equity of the *chose in action*. It is clear from the circumstances surrounding the issue that the ICSDs are not the beneficial owner of the bonds. However, as between the Depository/Safekeeper and them, they have the right in equity to claim the property which the Depository/Safekeeper declares itself to hold 'for' them. This comprises not only the paper itself, but also the *legal chose in action* that attaches to it.

6.104 The ICSDs, to the extent that they hold an *equitable chose in action* (the right to require, in equity, that the Depository/Safekeeper gives effect to its declaration in their favour), hold that asset themselves on trust for the benefit of their account holders. The account holders, in turn, hold their asset (the *equitable chose in action* constituted by their claim to an interest in the asset held by the ICSD, and also the *legal chose in action* constituted by their contractual rights against the ICSD to require it to fulfil its obligations to them as account holders) on trust for their clients.

6.105 The client of the account holder may, or may not, be the end investor. If the client is itself an intermediary, the right which it acquires through the chain described above will be held by it on trust for the entity whose intermediary it is. In this way, a chain of holdings is created in respect of the beneficial interest in the claim against the issuer. It is important to the note that the mechanism here is not the assignment of the equitable interest. Rather, at each link in the chain, the holder of an equitable interest retains that interest, but changes its capacity to that of a trustee of its interest in favour of the next person down the chain. This act creates a new equitable interest in the person at the next level down. The process creates a series of equitable interests, each one of which is dependent for its existence upon the existence of the one immediately above it.

6.106 This is not the end of the story. Even if the Global Note is a negotiable instrument, it is not the only asset created by the bond issue. In addition to executing the Global Note, the issuer also makes a number of contractual promises for the benefit of bondholders. For these purposes, 'bondholders' is usually defined as the body of person whose names are entered in the books at the ICSDs as holders of bonds. The methods by which the bondholders are given the benefit of the contractual promises may be directly, through the execution of a unilateral deed, which gives each of the bondholders an enforceable claim in respect of the contractual promise, or else through the mechanism of a trust deed between the issuer and a trustee, who acts for the bondholders. The trustee becomes the owner in law of the promises made by the issuer, and holds that *legal chose in action* on trust for the benefit of the bondholders, each of whom is the holder of an *equitable chose in action* (the ownership in equity of the promise made by the issuer, which is owed in law to the trustee).

6.107 Principal among the contractual promises made by the issuer is the undertaking to pay money to the bearer (the Depository/Safekeeper) or the registered payee (the Depository/Safekeeper's nominee) in accordance with the terms of the Global Note. Thus, the bondholders, either in law as a result of a promise made to them in the unilateral deed, or in equity through the promise made to the trustee, are the owners of a *chose in action*, the claim against the issuer to require the issuer to pay the principal sum to the Depository/Safekeeper or nominee (who is, of course, obliged to account for it to the ICSDs, who will distribute it among the bondholders).

6.108 The contractual promise to the trustee, or to the bondholders in the unilateral deed, enables him or them not only to ask a court for an order of specific performance, requiring the issuer to make the promised payment. If the issuer were to default, a simpler course would probably be for the bondholder to sue for damages, based on the issuer's breach of contract in failing to perform its promise to pay the Depositor/Safekeeper or nominee. In practice, this contractual claim, enforceable directly by bondholders or through the mechanism of a trustee for them collectively, provides a simpler and clearer right to payment than is available through a very complex chain of equitable interests.

If the Global Note is not a negotiable instrument

6.109 If, as seems likely, the correct analysis is that a Global Note does not have the characteristics necessary for it to be recognized in English law as a negotiable instrument, the Depository/Safekeeper or registered nominee cannot acquire, merely by virtue of its status as possessor of the Global Note, the rights given to the holder of a negotiable instrument. The Global Note does, however, contain a contractual promise. Whether that promise may be enforced by the Depository/Safekeeper or nominee is a difficult question to answer. Like any contractual promise, it needs to be supported by consideration. Whether the Depository/Safekeeper or nominee gave any consideration will be a question of fact, the answer to which will not be the same in every case. It is, at least, doubtful that a possessor would normally be able to enforce the promise as a matter of simple contract.

6.110 This is probably unimportant in practice. The bond issue involves the issuer promising to the trustee or directly to the bondholders that it will perform the promise set out in the Global Note. Because the promise to the trustee or bondholders is made by deed, questions of consideration are irrelevant. The crucial fact is that the bondholders, or the trustee (depending on the circumstances of the issue) will have a *legal chose in action* against the issuer in the form of a claim to enforce the promise to pay, or a claim for damages in the event of default.

Conclusion

6.111 If the analysis above is correct, then it matters not whether the Global Note is, or is not, a negotiable instrument. The important asset in a bond issue is the *chose in action* constituted by the promise of the issuer made to the trustee, or direct to the bondholders, to pay the principal amount in accordance with the note.

6.112 The owners of this *chose in action* are the bondholders. In the case of an issue which uses a unilateral deed, they are the owners of a *legal chose in action*, being a claim against the issuer of payment of the sums concerned. Where the bond issue uses a trustee structure, the bondholders will be the owners of an *equitable chose in action*, the ownership of the *legal chose in action* being owned by the trustee. Either way, the bondholders' position as owners of assets, and that of all investors in the chain beneath each bondholder, is secure.

6.113 In any language other than that of the most technical legal analysis, it is possible to say of any of the investors in the chain of holdings, up to the level of the account holder with an ICSD, that it 'owns a bond' or that it 'owns a debt security' of the issuer. In the case of everyone in the chain except the investor at the very bottom, its ownership rights need to be qualified by saying that it holds the security as trustee for the person below it in the chain.

6.114 A major consequence of the analysis is that the inclusion of the Depository/Safekeeper in the structure does not alter in any substance the rights of any of the other parties. It is merely a conduit for payments, which always belong to some other party. In practice, of course, payments do not flow through the Depository/Safekeeper at all but, as part of the contractual arrangements of the bond issue, are paid through the Paying Agent to the ICSDs, who pass them on to the bondholders. In the context of immobilization, the role of the Depository/Safekeeper is unnecessary, in any functional terms. Further, the existence of the Depository/Safekeeper serves to complicate the legal structure, and to make even muddier legal waters that would be murky in any event.

Dematerialization

The wish to move to dematerialization

The purpose of immobilization was to create circumstances in which bonds could be traded electronically, with the transactions in them being recorded on the computer records of the clearing systems and intermediaries involved. Such a system of trading clearly required that the negotiable pieces of paper which constituted the bonds should not also be circulating, with the possibility that the buying and selling of the bonds themselves might not correspond with the purchase and sales records of the intermediaries. Rather than create a structure for a bond issue which did not involve physical, potentially competitive instruments, the market chose, when inventing the idea of immobilization, to retain physical instruments as part of the structure. It removed their toxic ability to circulate by first ensuring that all of the bonds were consolidated into one enormous Global Note of an indigestible size, and then arranging that this note should be buried deep in a bank vault, with the bank being paid a fee to ensure that the Global Note would not under any circumstances ever be negotiated.

6.115

There was still a feeling within some parts of the market that the existence of the Global Note, however well it was isolated and however deeply it was buried, constituted a potential risk. It was for this reason that the European Central Bank, in sponsoring the New Global Note structure, required that the Global Note should not only be retained physically within the eurozone, but should be given into the possession of the ICSDs as 'safekeepers'. This change eliminates a perceived legal risk, that a Depository bank might become insolvent and that its liquidator might claim an entitlement to the deposited note, with the bondholders having only the right to prove in the liquidation of the Depository for the value of their interest. Whether or not such a legal risk is substantial, the changes demanded by the ECB are clearly effective to eliminate it.

6.116

The next step, and one which would simplify the structure of international bonds greatly, is to remove the Global Note from the structure altogether. This would have the effect of 'dematerializing' a bond issue. The only documents would be the agreements entered into at the time of the issue. All other aspects of dealing with the bonds, paying sums due in respect of them, and redeeming them in due course, would be dealt with electronically through the records of a clearing system.

6.117

Dematerialization in related markets

Although the international bond market has not yet evolved a structure which abandons paper in favour of complete reliance on electronic records and transfers, there are related markets in which progress has been faster. Most developed countries have a national

6.118

market in Money Market Instruments ('MMIs'), used by financial institutions, companies, and governments to obtain short-term and medium-term funds. These instruments include Certificates of Deposit, documents issued by banks, which acknowledge the deposit of money with them, and which are widely regarded as transferable by delivery and thus negotiable,[46] promissory notes, banker's acceptances, and various forms of government debt instruments. Although these MMIs do not share a single legal form with the Global Notes used in the international bond market, nor indeed with each other, they are all treated as if they are negotiable instruments.

6.119 A number of jurisdictions, including the United States, Canada, Australia, and Singapore have taken steps to change their practice and, in some cases, their law to allow the more efficient dealing with MMIs. This has taken the form of immobilization of the instruments and in some respects the dematerialization of the obligations concerned.[47] The detail of the issues varies from country to country. However, the underlying question is the same: if the structure dispenses with physical instruments, how should the law best ensure that the electronic regime which replaces them provides the result that the concept of negotiability gave to the use of negotiable instruments?

6.120 In the UK, the question was first addressed in the late 1980s. The Review Committee on Banking Services Law and Practice (usually called 'The Jack Committee', after its chairman, Professor Robert Jack) was asked to consider proposals for an immobilized system in which negotiable instruments would be held by a central depository and thereafter traded electronically. The report of the committee[48] said that the requirement was for legislation which replicated, in relation to screen-based trading, the effects that the Bills of Exchange Act 1882 produced for paper-based trading.

6.121 The Jack Committee, however, looked beyond the limited movement to immobilization. It foresaw a system of trading in which no instrument was created, and the obligation concerned existed only in a dematerialized form, in which:

> ... it would not simply be a question of trading an existing negotiable instrument without indorsement and delivery, but of trading an obligation which is not contained in any written instrument.

It recommended new legislation which would:

> ... contain provisions giving to transactions taking place in a screen based or book-entry depository (or dematerialised) system ... the same status as equivalent transactions in negotiable instruments generally.

6.122 The recommendations of the Jack Committee were not adopted immediately. However, the changes which it foresaw have been implemented, to a limited extent. In 1990, the Bank of England began to provide an immobilized trading service for MMIs through the medium

---

[46] Whether Certificates of Deposit (CDs) are, as a matter of law, promissory notes or otherwise negotiable, must be debatable. In practice, the nominal size of CDs, and the care with which they are safeguarded by their owners, means that the courts are not asked to consider whether a possessor of CD needs to be given the benefits of the status as a holder. In practice, the possessor is the owner.
[47] For a review of the measures involved, see the Australian *National Competition Policy Review of the Bills of Exchange Act 1909*, available on the website of the Australian Treasury: <http://www.treasury.gov.au>.
[48] (1989) Cm 622.

of its Central Moneymarkets Office (CMO). This relied on the existence of physical instruments held by a central depository, which were traded and settled between members of the CMO in electronic form. The arrangements were governed by the rules of the system, to which members assented by contract.

In 2003, the move to full dematerialization took place. The provisions of the Companies Act 1989 s 207, which had permitted the trading of equity shares in dematerialized form, were used to authorize the making of the Uncertificated Securities (Amendment) (Eligible Debt Securities) Regulations 2003.[49] Under these regulations, obligations (including the obligations of HM Treasury in respect of treasury bills) may be created in dematerialized form, and entered into the CREST trading system, the same system that is used for the holding of, and settlement of trades in, UK equity securities. No legislation was thought to be needed, in order to replicate the advantages given to negotiable instruments, because the statutory protection conferred on transfers within CREST was sufficient in practice.

6.123

The UK experience in relation to MMIs shows that a move to full dematerialization need not involve the legal complexities that have long been assumed. The dematerialization of the international bond market is, perhaps, a much easier process than has long been thought.

6.124

Dematerialization in the international bond market

It is arguable that the New Global Note structure achieves dematerialization, although it does not purport to do so. Under this new structure, the Global Note is a document which records the promise of the issuer to pay. It does not state the amount of the obligation. Rather, it quantifies the amount due as the aggregate of the amounts shown in the records of the ICSDs to be owing to individual account holders. The Global Note is given into the possession of the ICSDs for 'safe keeping'. At the time the Global Note is signed, the issuer covenants, either with a trustee on behalf of the bondholders or unilaterally in favour of bondholders, to make the payments referred to in the Global Note. That obligation is to pay to the ICSDs, for the account of their account holders, the amounts shown in the records of the ICSDs as owing to those members.

6.125

In the circumstances, it seems impossible to argue that the New Global Note constitutes a negotiable instrument and that the promise made in it is the *chose in action* around which the transaction centres. Rather, it is one of a number of contractual documents which record the obligation that the issuer has undertaken (ie to pay the relevant amounts of monies to the ICSDs on the due dates). If the Global Note were destroyed, the obligations of the issuer would not change. It would still be required to make the same payments to the same recipients, because it had contracted to do so in the trust deed or unilateral deed. Thus, although the New Global Note structure still involves a piece of paper, that material object is not an essential part of the structure.

6.126

The next step, and it is a very small one, is simply to dispense with the paper altogether. The issue would, in essence, consist of a contract under which the issuer, in return for the

6.127

---

[49] (SI 2003/1633).

payment to it of the subscription monies, would undertake, either by unilateral deed or by covenant in favour of a trustee, to make payments on the due dates to those bondholders whose names were recorded as such in the records of the ICSDs. There would need to be no Global Note, and no provision for the issue of any definitive notes at a later date. At that stage the issue could properly be regarded as dematerialized and free from any risks associated with the existence, loss, theft, or forgery of any pieces of paper.

6.128 Looking at an issue constructed on this basis, one has a strong sense of déjà vu. The structure is very similar to that which was adopted in the UK in the early twentieth century.[50] In this structure, a company would issue loan stock against receipt of subscription monies. It would, by entering into a trust deed with the trustee, undertake to pay certain sums of money at certain times to the loan stock holders, identified by their presence in a register of holders maintained by the company. Transfers of the loan stock were effected by a written instrument presented to the company, which would amend the register to reflect the terms of the transfer instruments.

6.129 An issue of international bonds under the New Global Note structure, without a Global Note, would look remarkably similar. The only substantive difference in the description would be that, rather than the issuer itself maintaining a record of holders setting out their entitlements, the record would be that which in any event is already maintained by the ICSDs.

6.130 In the international bond market, the use of negotiable instruments to constitute the debt obligation, rather than a formally recorded contractual undertaking, allowed the market to develop and flourish. It has, however, outlived its usefulness. The paper has, since the advent of electronic trading and computerized record-keeping become an embarrassment and a complication. The solution to which the market is moving, by small but inexorable steps, is a return to the point from which it began. In terms of simplicity, clarity and legal certainty, that is greatly to be welcomed.

---

[50] See paras 6.17 to 6.25 above.

7

FIDUCIARY DUTIES AND HOW THEY ARISE

> There are few legal concepts more frequently invoked but less conceptually certain than that of the fiduciary relationship.
>
> La Forest J[1]

The Perceived Risk

A fiduciary is someone who has entered into a relationship with another person in which the other party places trust and confidence in him. This relationship of trust and confidence gives rise to an obligation of loyalty.[2] The special relationship may follow from the nature of a contractual arrangement between the parties. For example, the appointment of a person as solicitor to the other will normally result in the solicitor being a fiduciary of his client, because the relationship of confidence and trust is inherent in the relationship of solicitor and client. The position of a fiduciary may also come about in non-contractual circumstances, the most obvious of which is that of a trustee, who is a fiduciary in relation to the beneficiaries of the trust.

7.01

When a fiduciary relationship exists, its most obvious consequence is that the fiduciary owes duties which extend beyond those explicitly undertaken. The detail of those fiduciary duties is framed by the overriding obligation of loyalty, seen in the context of the particular relationship. Thus, the special fiduciary duties may arise as implied terms in a contract of engagement between a professional and his client or as an obligation imposed by equity on someone because of his status or position.

7.02

There is nothing new about this branch of the law. Indeed, the insistence by equity that those in a position of trust, who had the power to influence or guide the affairs of others, were under particular duties of loyalty was inherent in the idea of equity itself. The existence of fiduciary relationships and duties was so fundamental that it was described, in a case of 1784, as being necessary for the 'preservation of mankind'.[3] Although this may be overstating the case a little, there is no doubt about the importance of fiduciary relationships and duties in English law and in all other common law systems.

7.03

In the past 30 years, the law relating to fiduciary relationships and the duties which flow from them has become a major topic for concern in financial markets and among financial institutions. The concern was, perhaps, triggered by a case heard by the High Court in

7.04

---

[1] *Lac Minerals Ltd v International Corona Resources Ltd* [1989] 2 SCR 574 (Canada).
[2] See Millett LJ in *Bristol & West Building Society v Mothew* [1998] Ch 1, at 18.
[3] *Wells v Middleton* (1784) 1 Cox 112, at 124–5.

London in 1995.[4] An Indonesian industrial group had entered into a series of swap transactions with a US investment bank. The swaps later turned out to be disadvantageous to the industrial company, and profitable for the bank. The customer claimed that the relationship between it and the bank was not that of two sophisticated commercial organizations contracting with each other on an arm's-length basis, but rather one in which the customer placed trust and confidence in the bank to protect its interests. The bank, it said, was the customer's fiduciary. The claimants did not succeed. Nonetheless, the fact that the claim could be made, and seemed to have a basis in English law, was felt to be disturbing.

7.05 At about the same time, the same bank, Bankers Trust Company, was faced with similar claims brought against it in the US by Proctor and Gamble, the consumer products group.[5] The claims, which were settled at an early stage, centred on the same assertions, that the bank was a fiduciary for its customer, rather than simply being a counterparty. Similar claims have continued to be asserted in the major common law jurisdictions.[6] Such claims, although they are almost always unsuccessful, continue to be made and are widely seen as a significant source of legal risk for financial institutions.

Fiduciary duties and financial institutions

7.06 Issues of fiduciary relationships and duties are not novel. However, cases in which they arose were, until the 1990s, generally confined to disputes about the conduct of trustees, solicitors, or agents. Until then, the law governing the relationship between banks and their customers had appeared to be straightforward, and based on established and clear common law principles of contract. *Foley v Hill*[7] established in 1848 that the relationship of banker and customer was primarily that of debtor and creditor, founded on the contract between them. It is important to consider why, at the end of the twentieth century, the banking industry began to worry that the law relating to fiduciaries might apply to relationships in the banking industry.

7.07 First, there was a major change in the structure of the banking industry in the UK, following the 'big bang' in 1986. Until that time, the capital and financial markets in the UK were divided into distinct compartments: stockbrokers, stockjobbers (wholesalers and market-makers in securities), commercial (deposit-taking) banks, and merchant banks (who provided advisory services to corporate clients and also carried out trade financing). In the securities industry, membership of the London Stock Exchange was limited to individuals. Stockbroking firms were, therefore, partnerships of individuals, as were stockjobbers.

7.08 In 1986, the London Stock Exchange, under pressure from the competition authorities and government, agreed to accept corporate members. This simple change altered radically the

---

[4] *Bankers Trust International plc v PT Dharmala Sakti Sejahtera* [1996] CLC 518. See the *Case Summary* published by The Financial Law Panel in January 1996.
[5] *The Proctor and Gamble Co v Bankers Trust Co and BT Securities Corp* Civil Action No C-1-94-735 (SD Ohio).
[6] See, eg, *JP Morgan Chase Bank v Springwell Navigation Corp* [2008] EWHC 1186 (Comm), a case brought in England and Wales, discussed in paras 8.92 et seq, and *Australian Securities & Investments Commission v Citigroup Global Markets Australia Pty Ltd* (ACN 113 114 832) (No 4) [2007] FCA 963, a case from the Australian Federal Court.
[7] (1848) 2 HLC 28.

structure of the financial industries in London. Banks, both local and from overseas, were able to acquire the business of London stockbroking firms and become members of the exchange through subsidiaries. Those subsidiaries had access to capital far in excess of that which could be raised by partnerships of individuals. At the same time, commercial banks began to acquire the businesses of the merchant banks, and to merge that activity with the business of their newly acquired stockbroking subsidiaries. By this route, the largest financial institutions combined businesses that were traditionally at arm's-length with their customers (eg commercial lending and trade finance) with businesses which were traditionally advisory (eg fund management and corporate advice). This blurred the distinction between the trading and advisory functions of banks. It was no longer always obvious whether a bank was merely a trading counterparty of its customer, or was also the customer's trusted advisor.

The same structural changes led to the introduction of the Financial Services Act 1986, and the regulatory regime embodied in it. The new structure quickly led to the development of detailed rules and guidance about the way in which those subject to the regime should conduct their businesses. Although the need to comply with numerous specific rules of conduct was not, in principle, incompatible with legal and equitable duties which were based on concepts of loyalty and 'conscience', there was considerable confusion about the relationship between the two. Did it follow, for example, that compliance with the detailed rules according to their letter would necessarily mean that an institution had also fulfilled any fiduciary duties to which it might be subject? These concerns led to a consultation paper from The Law Commission in 1992, which proposed statutory clarification of the relationship between the different duties imposed on financial institutions.[8]   **7.09**

The third factor which made the issue of fiduciary duties a particular problem for financial institutions was the growth in the early 1990s of complicated structured financial products, the nature and effect of which were often difficult to understand. Corporate customers which had entered into such arrangements with their banks would, if they proved profitable, regard themselves as extremely clever. If they lost money, they might assume that they had been misled by their banks, or at the very least that their banks had failed to give them the honest and disinterested advice to which they were entitled. This sense of grievance was heightened by the fact that, if a customer made a loss as a result of one these structured products, its bankers were usually the counterparty which made a corresponding profit. The concern is not confined to the common law world. A prosecution for 'aggravated fraud' was been initiated in Italy in March 2010 against four banks and a number of individuals, arising out of a financing in 2005 for the city of Milan, which consisted of a bond issue matched with an interest-rate swap. The allegation was that the municipality did not understand the risks involved, and was misled by its advisors. In December 2012, the defendants were convicted, having earlier settled the civil claims arising from the same events.[9] Similar claims have been made in recent years against banks with whom they entered into derivatives contracts by municipalities ranging geographically from Narvik in Norway to Jefferson County in Alabama, USA.   **7.10**

---

[8] *Fiduciary Duties and Regulatory Rules*, 1992, Cmd 129.
[9] Financial Times, 19 December 2012.

Uncertainties about fiduciary duties

7.11 Although it is quite easy to see why the possibility of the existence of a fiduciary relationship should have become an issue in the 1990s, this does not itself explain why it should be regarded in the financial industries as presenting a serious problem. There are several factors which mark out the question of fiduciary relationships as being particularly problematical.

7.12 First, the law is complex. This extends not only to the substance, but also to the situations in which it applies. In practice, it is not always as easy as one might suppose to determine whether a relationship is, or is not, fiduciary in nature. In *Satnam Investments Ltd v Dunlop Heywood & Co Ltd and others*,[10] the claimant, a property developer, appointed the defendants, a firm of surveyors, to advise in connection with the development of a site which was owned by a third party, but over which Satnam had a purchase option. The option could be terminated by the owner if, among other things, Satnam were to enter into receivership. As a result of cash-flow problems, Satnam's bank appointed an administrative receiver. Mr Murray, a director of Dunlop Heywood, who had been brought into the team advising Satnam, then approached another developer, Morbaine, and told them about the potential for development of the site. He assumed that Satnam would not be able to carry on with the development. The owners of the site terminated the option given to Satnam and entered into a new contract with Morbaine. Unexpectedly, Satnam's cash-flow problems were solved by the sale of certain properties that it owned, and it emerged from administrative receivership, feeling very aggrieved that it had lost the development opportunity.

7.13 Satnam sued Morbaine, claiming that it held the land on constructive trust for Satnam, and also sued Dunlop Heywood and Mr Murray, alleging breach of fiduciary duty. The Court of Appeal held that Morbaine were not constructive trustees of the property, but that Dunlop Heywood and Mr Murray were indeed in breach of fiduciary duties owed to Satnam and were liable to it accordingly. Although there is, perhaps, nothing remarkable in the decision, the point which is slightly disturbing is that the court offered no explanation of the decision that the relationship between Dunlop Heywood and Satnam, and Mr Murray and Satnam, had a special fiduciary nature. The court said simply:

> DH and Mr Murray had undertaken to act in the interests of Satnam. They clearly had both contractual and equitable obligations to Satnam and that has not been challenged ... It is plain that DH and Mr Murray were persons who owed fiduciary duties to Satnam.

No explanation was given as to the origin of the fiduciary obligations owed by Mr Murray to Satnam. Mr Murray had no personal contractual relationship with Satnam; he was merely a director of a company which had such a relationship. Nor is there any evidence that he had undertaken personally to Satnam any obligation of trust. The route by which, in equity, he came to owe employer's customer is not nearly so clear as the Court of Appeal seems to have assumed obligations of a fiduciary nature to his

7.14 The view apparently taken in the *Satnam* case is that the existence of a fiduciary relationship does not need to be explained, because it is obvious when it appears. On the facts of the case, this is not a cause for concern. However, it is a little disturbing, in the light of

---

[10] [1999] 3 All ER 652.

other cases where the courts have found a fiduciary relationship in circumstances where one was not readily predictable. Perhaps the paradigm of such cases is the Court of Appeal decision in *Reading v The King*.[11] Sergeant Reading was in charge of the medical stores at the main British hospital in Cairo throughout most of World War II. He was married to an Egyptian national, who ran a café in the city. Sergeant Reading was unusually affluent for an army sergeant. Only one soldier on the base, other than he, ran a private motor car. The colonel in charge had an Austin 7. Sergeant Reading drove a Cadillac. It was clear to the authorities that Sergeant Reading was misappropriating medical supplies, and regular audits were carried out to detect his theft. None was ever found. It was only at the end of the war that the source of his wealth came to light. Sergeant Reading had not stolen army property. However, in his off-duty hours, he had accompanied an Egyptian lorry driver as the lorry drove large amounts of contraband goods through Egyptian government customs posts. Because of Sergeant Reading's presence in the cab, dressed in his army uniform, the lorries were never stopped.

7.15 Funds belonging to Sergeant Reading, and claimed to be the sums paid to him by the black marketeers, were confiscated. Sergeant Reading sued in England for the return of the money. His claim was that, whatever the circumstances in which he had come by the money, the Crown had no claim to it and, as between the two of them, he was entitled to demand its return. At first instance, Denning J had accepted that there was no fiduciary relationship which was relevant. On appeal, however, the court took a different view. Delivering the judgment of the Court of Appeal, Asquith LJ said:

> ... 'fiduciary relations' exist (a) whenever the plaintiff entrusts to the defendant property, including intangible property as, for instance, confidential information, and relies on the defendant to deal with such property for the benefit of the plaintiff or for the purposes authorised by him, and not otherwise ... and (b) whenever the plaintiff entrusts to the defendant a job to be performed, for instance, the negotiation of a contract on his behalf or for his benefit and relies on the defendant to procure for the plaintiff the best terms available...

This statement is unremarkable, although one might think that it was not relevant to the facts of the case. However, the court went on to find that Sergeant Reading was in a fiduciary relationship with the Crown:

> ... as to the user of the uniform and the opportunities and facilities attached to it.

The finding that the wearing of an army uniform creates a relationship of 'trust and confidence' between the individual soldier and the Crown, not merely in relation to the soldier's activities in that capacity, opens the door to very wide interpretations of the circumstances in which a fiduciary relationship might arise. Although this may be an extreme case, and certainly the case has been heavily criticized on a number of grounds, it illustrates the fact that the prediction of the existence or non-existence of a fiduciary relationship is no easy matter.

7.16 The other major area of uncertainty, so far as financial institutions are concerned, relates to the remedies which are available for breach of fiduciary duty. The equitable rules dealing

---

[11] [1949] 2 KB 232.

with remedies for breach of the duties of fiduciaries have been developed mainly in situations where the breach was that of the duty of a trustee of a traditional trust. The remedies therefore centre on the idea of restoring the trust fund to the position in which it was before the breach, rather than on the provision of compensation for loss suffered,[12] and on requiring the fiduciary to account for profits wrongfully made.

7.17 The result of this, as far as a potential defendant is concerned, is not nearly so predictable as the calculation of damages under normal contractual rules. More importantly, the potential cost to a defendant can be much greater than that which it would suffer, if it were sued for damages. Where there is a finding of a deliberate breach of fiduciary duty of loyalty, the approach of equity is to deprive the fiduciary of his improper profit, regardless of the loss caused (or not caused) to the beneficiary. In *Murad v Al-Saraj*,[13] Arden LJ said:

> ... a loss to a person to whom a fiduciary duty is owed is not the other side of the coin from the profit which the person having the fiduciary duty has made: that person may have to account for a profit even if the beneficiary has suffered no loss.
>
> ...
>
> ... equity imposes stringent liability on a fiduciary as a deterrent – *pour encourager les autres*... in the interests of efficiency and to provide an incentive to fiduciaries to resist the temptation to misconduct themselves, the law imposes exacting standards on fiduciaries and an extensive liability to account.

This principle can be seen at work in *Reading v The King*. Sergeant Reading was ordered to pay to the Crown a sum equal to the payments that it was thought he had received by the improper use of his army uniform. However, there is no question that the Crown suffered any loss at all by virtue of his breach of fiduciary duty. The customs duties which were avoided were taxes payable to the Egyptian government, not to the Crown. In reality, the order had the effect of depriving Sergeant Reading of his gains, rather than restoring to the Crown anything that it had lost, or compensating it for any damage suffered. The flexibility and adaptability of equity's remedies is, in this case, a source of concern. The adaptability of the relief is seen as unpredictability, which leads to uncertainty.

The Fiduciary Relationship

The history of the concept

7.18 It is tempting to assume that the fiduciary relationship was a concept which grew out of the decisions of the courts of equity, rather than the courts of the common law. The need to control those who are in a position of trust and confidence, and who have the power to deal with the property and rights of those who are reliant upon them is central to the concept of equity and the purpose of the early Chancery courts.[14]

---

[12] See the explanation given by Lord Browne-Wilkinson in *Target Holdings Ltd v Redferns* [1996] 1 AC 421, at 430; and see Viscount Haldane LC in *Nocton v Lord Ashburton* [1914] AC 932, at 952.
[13] [2005] EWCA Civ 959.
[14] See paras 4.30 to 4.38.

7.19 While it is true that equity has always paid close attention to the position of fiduciaries, that is not the only source of the modern law. As equity developed its jurisdiction in relation to the obligations of trustees and others in similar positions, a number of parallel ideas were evolving within the forms of action recognized by the common law courts. The development was reviewed and explained in detail by Viscount Haldane LC in the case of *Nocton v Lord Ashburton*.[15]

7.20 Lord Ashburton was a rich man who had some experience of and interest in property development. Mr Nocton was a partner in the firm of solicitors used by the Ashburton family. He was the partner primarily responsible for dealing with Lord Ashburton's affairs. Mr Nocton had advised certain other clients of his in connection with the purchase by them of a building site in Kensington and the development of flats on the land. Mr Nocton himself had an interest in the development. He advised Lord Ashburton to lend £65,000 to the developers on the security of a first mortgage. Subsequently, financing of the development became difficult and Mr Nocton persuaded Lord Ashburton to release part of the site from his mortgage, in order to make it available to secure further borrowings. It was alleged that Mr Nocton had assured Lord Ashburton that his remaining security would be sufficient to cover his outstanding loan. It was further alleged that the effect of the release by Lord Ashburton of his mortgage on part of the site was to elevate the second mortgage on that property to the position of a first mortgage. Mr Nocton was interested in that second mortgage. Subsequently, the development failed and Lord Ashburton lost money as a result.

7.21 He sued Mr Nocton in deceit. He alleged that Mr Nocton knew that the courses of action that he was advising were not in the interests of Lord Ashburton. The claim was framed in deceit because, on the law as it then stood, a claim in negligence would have been statute-barred; although it would have been easier to prove negligence than to show deliberate fraud, it was necessary to allege deceit in order to overcome the statutory time-bar.

7.22 At first instance the claim failed. The trial judge found that, although Mr Nocton's advice had been very poor, and was no doubt negligent, there was no intention on his part to cheat his client, and accordingly a claim in fraud must fail. The Court of Appeal reversed this finding, holding that Mr Nocton did indeed intend to cheat his client. On appeal to the House of Lords, it was held that the Court of Appeal had been wrong to reverse the finding of fact about fraud. However, this did not prevent Lord Ashburton from succeeding. He was not limited to claiming in negligence. He had a separate claim against his solicitor, based on a breach of duty arising from a fiduciary relationship. Such a claim was not statute-barred.

7.23 In explaining the decision, Viscount Haldane LC reviewed the development of the law in this area from its earliest days. The court was not limited to choosing between two remedies: (1) the remedy for deceit, which, following the decision in *Derry v Peek*,[16] had required proof of intention to cheat; and (2) an action in negligence (which would in this case have been statute-barred). There was a third course:

> ... the old bill in Chancery to enforce compensation for breach of the fiduciary obligation.

---

[15] [1914] AC 932.
[16] [1889] 14 App Cas 337.

The decision in *Derry v Peak* had been taken, wrongly, as applying to claims for breach of duties imposed on fiduciaries by equity. The reason for this mistake was, said Viscount Haldane, that claims for the breach of the equitable duties were often referred to as claims for 'equitable fraud'. Accordingly, it had been assumed that the requirement to prove actual fraud, in the case of actions in deceit, extended also to claim for 'equitable fraud'. This was not so:

> In reality the judgment [in *Derry v Peek*] covered only a part of the field in which liabilities may arise. There are other obligations besides that of honesty the breach of which may give a right to damages. These obligations depend on principles which the judges have worked out in the fashion that is characteristic of a system where much of the law has always been judge-made and unwritten.

7.24 He enumerated the circumstances in which the courts have established doctrines requiring people in particular situations to exercise a duty of care. He referred to the development of the liability of an agent, of the implication of terms in contracts, and the claim to an account in the case of the passing off of goods. In addition, 'a man may come under a special duty to exercise care in giving information or advice'.

7.25 Lord Haldane then turned to the facts of the case before him:

> But in the appeal before us ... the only question which remains is whether there has been such a breach of duty as to give rise to liability. Now such a duty might arise either at law or in equity.
>
> ...
>
> Such a special duty may arise from the circumstances and relation of the parties. These may give rise to an implied contract at law or to a fiduciary obligation in equity.

7.26 Lord Dunedin, in the same case, makes the same point in a different way:

> Turning now to equity, here again, as I understand the situation, there was a jurisdiction in equity to keep persons in a fiduciary capacity up to their duty ... all the cases are based on the existence of a fiduciary relationship, and subsequently the breach of duty arising.
>
> Now, whenever we come to the idea of breach of duty we see how nearly the domains of law and equity approach, or perhaps more strictly speaking, overlap. Take the word negligence ... There can be no negligence unless there is a duty. That duty may arise in many ways. There are certain duties which all owe to the world at large ... So the man who leaves the loaded gun in a public place is liable for the accident ensuing, though it is not he that pulled the trigger. The common law gives a remedy. Then there are duties which arise from a contract, of which the solicitor's position gives an example ... he contracts to be professionally qualified and to be careful. Here again the common law will give an action for negligence. And then there are the duties which arise from a relationship without the intervention of contract in the ordinary sense of the term, such as the duties of a trustee to his cestui que trust or of a guardian to his ward. It is in this latter class of cases that equity has been particularly dominant, not, I take it, from any scientific distinction between the classes of duty existing and the breaches thereof, but simply because in certain cases where common justice demanded a remedy, the common law had none forthcoming ...

7.27 The House of Lords did not see the issue as a stark division between obligations and rights imposed by the common law, on the one hand, and different principles developed by equity, on the other. The intervention of equity was rather to provide remedies and recompense, rather than to establish a unique kind of liability. Lord Shaw of Dunfermline saw the issue more from the point of common law than from equity. For him, equity intervened to adjust a common law principle of duty. Equity will so intervene:

> ... where a representation has been made which binds the conscience of the party and estops and obliges him to make it good ... the representation in equity is equivalent to a contract and very nearly coincides with a warranty at law; and in order that a person may avail himself of relief founded on it he must shew that there was such approximate relation between himself and the person making the representation as to bring them virtually into the position of parties contracting with each other.[17]
>
> It is admitted in the present case that misrepresentations were made; that they were material; that they were the cause of loss; that they were made by a solicitor to his client in a situation in which the client was entitled to rely, and did rely, upon the information received. I accordingly think that that situation is plainly open for the application of the principle of liability to which I have referred, namely, liability for the consequences of the failure of duty in circumstances in which it was a matter equivalent to contract between the parties that that duty should be fulfilled.

Put simply, Lord Shaw regarded the fiduciary duty of the solicitor as an implied additional term of his contract with his client.

7.28 The existence of the fiduciary relationship and of the duties that flow from it are not exclusively the creation of equity. However, in practice, they will be seen when a claimant is seeking a remedy that is available only in equity. If the claimant is looking simply for damages, or another remedy available at common law, he may well assert his claim as one arising in negligence under a written or implied term of a contract. In this case, he has no need to invoke the concept of fiduciary relationships, nor to prove the existence of one. This does not imply that no fiduciary relationship exists.

The modern view of fiduciary relationships

7.29 Lord Browne-Wilkinson put the matter succinctly in *Henderson v Merrett Syndicates Ltd*:[18]

> The liability of a fiduciary for the negligent transaction of his duties is not a separate head of liability but the paradigm of the general duty to act with care imposed by law on those who take it upon themselves to act for or advise others. Although the historical developments of the rules of law and equity have, in the past, caused different labels to be stuck on different manifestations of the duty, in truth the duty of care imposed on bailees, carriers, trustees, directors, agents and others is the same duty; it arises from the circumstances in which the defendants are acting, not from their status of description. It is the fact that they have all

---

[17] Quoting an argument by counsel in *Peek v Gurney* LR 13 Eq. 79, at p 97.
[18] [1995] 2 AC 145, at 205F–G.

assumed responsibility for the property or affairs of others which renders them liable for the careless performance of what they have undertaken to do, not the description of the trade or position which they hold.

7.30 The development of the law relating to fiduciary relationships and fiduciary duties is not something which is uniquely the creation of equity, unknown to the common law; nor is it a common law doctrine which has been adopted by equity. The same relationship and facts might well give rise to a claim at common law, for example, for breach of an implied term in a contract or a claim for damages in tort, and at the same time might also give rise to a claim in equity for breach of the duties of fiduciary. As in *Nocton v Lord Ashburton*, the choice of which route to pursue will depend often on the nature of the remedy sought. If a claimant is looking for damages, he might well state his claim as one of breach of contractual duty. If, as was the case with Lord Ashburton, the claimant needs a remedy which only equity may give, the claim may be phrased as one for breach of a fiduciary duty. Lord Dunedin, in *Nocton v Lord Ashburton*, summed it up:

> If, then, we turn to the solicitor's position we may look at it in two aspects, which is not to look at two different things, but to look at the same thing from two different points of view. He has contracted to be diligent; he is negligent. Law will give a remedy ... But from the other point of view he may have put himself in a fiduciary position, and that fiduciary position imposes on him the duty of making a full and not a misleading disclosure of facts known to him when advising his client. He fails to do so. Equity will give a remedy to the client.

The Existence of a Fiduciary Relationship

7.31 If a fiduciary relationship exists, the fiduciary will owe duties to the other party, the breach of which might result in the payment of damages, or equitable compensation, or an order to account for profits improperly made or to restore property wrongfully taken. The duties may arise as implied terms of a contract, or as obligations imposed by equity separately from any contractual relationship between the parties. The common factor linking these duties is that they are unwritten. In the context of a financial transaction or relationship, it is difficult to rebut a claim that an institution is in breach of fiduciary duties to a customer or counterparty. The argument between the parties is not about the meaning or consequence of a written obligation, contained in a contractual term, statutory provisions, or regulatory rule. Rather the argument is about something intangible: would a court classify the relationship as 'fiduciary' and, if so, what duties would it find that the fiduciary owed? In practice, there is often considerable scope for disagreement on each of these two questions.

7.32 The first question is whether a fiduciary relationship exists. On this fundamental issue there appears to be a gap between the ease with which courts are able to answer the question and the difficulty it poses for practitioners and their clients. To judges, the identification of fiduciary relationships appears to be rather like the definition of an elephant: very hard to describe in detail, but 'you know one when you see one'. Practitioners find it more difficult to spot an elephant or, more accurately, to predict when the courts will spot one.

7.33 The difficulty in identifying a fiduciary relationship lies in the fact that a relationship assumes a fiduciary character because of the circumstances surrounding its creation and its execution, not because of its description. Lord Browne-Wilkinson made the point very clearly in the statement set out in para 7.29 above.

The established categories of fiduciary relationships

7.34 It is clear that the existence of a fiduciary relationship, or its absence, is a matter which is very sensitive to the facts in every case. Nonetheless, attempts have been made to classify situations in which a fiduciary relationship might be expected to arise. In its Consultation Paper of 1992,[19] The Law Commission divided fiduciaries into two categories: 'status-based fiduciaries' and 'fact-based fiduciaries'.[20] The former category, it argued, were those people who are considered to be fiduciaries, without further enquiry. In other words, it is to be assumed that the facts will always support the view that they are in a fiduciary relationship. The list of these relationships consisted of the following:

trustee/beneficiary;
solicitor/client;
agent/principal;
director/company;
partner/partner.

The latter category, fact-based fiduciaries, consists of those whom the court finds to be in a fiduciary position on the particular circumstances before it, even though they do not fall into one of the 'automatic' categories.

7.35 It is not clear that it is helpful to attempt to categorize in this way the circumstances in which fiduciary duties arise. The courts have not traditionally adopted this approach, and indeed, Lord Browne-Wilkinson in *Henderson v Merrett*, in the passage quoted above,[21] warned against such forms of categorization. The status as a fiduciary arises from the assumption of responsibility on the facts of the case, not from the description of the trade or profession of the claimed fiduciary.

7.36 In addition, the fact that someone is a fiduciary may not be relevant to the matter in dispute. For example, the relationship between a solicitor and his client is undoubtedly fiduciary in nature. As part of the relationship, the solicitor has an obligation to advise competently and with care. That obligation stems from the contract between him and his client and would be the same, whether or not the relationship had a fiduciary nature. The fact that a relationship can be described as 'fiduciary' is not necessarily relevant to consideration of everything that happens during the course of it.[22]

7.37 It is not clear what criteria the courts will apply in deciding whether the nature of the relationship is automatically classified as fiduciary. In the *Satnam Investments* case,[23] both the

---

[19] *Fiduciary Duties and Regulatory Rules*: Consultation Paper No 124, Cmd 129.
[20] See Consultation Paper, para 2.4.3.
[21] At para 7.29 above.
[22] And see paras 7.42 *et seq* below.
[23] See para 7.12 above.

trial judge and the judges in the Court of Appeal were in no doubt that Dunlop Heywood Ltd, the surveyors retained by Satnam in connection with its proposed development, and Mr Murray, a director of DH, were in a fiduciary relationship with Satnam:

> DH and Mr Murray had undertaken to act in the interest of Satnam. They clearly had both contractual and equitable obligations to Satnam and that has not been challenged ... we agree with the judge that it is plain that DH and Mr Murray were persons who owed fiduciary duties to Satnam.[24]

The nature of the relationship is not set out in any detail in the case report. In relation to DH, we are told that they were the surveyors of Satnam,[25] and that Satnam 'instructed DH to act for it in the acquisition of ownership or control of ... the site'. Mr Murray, we are told, was a director of DH who was brought into the team working for Satnam.[26] We are not told whether Mr Murray had any professional qualification. Nor is any indication given that there was any significance in the fact that he was a director of DH, rather than an employee or consultant.

7.38 The Court of Appeal held that both DH and Mr Murray were in breach of fiduciary duties owed to Satnam: (a) in disclosing to third parties information about the site which they had acquired as a result of acting on the Satnam development; and (b) in not telling Satnam about the proposals of the third party to usurp Satnam's position in the deal. No explanation is given, however, of the factors affecting DH and, more interestingly, Mr Murray that made their relationships fiduciary.

7.39 Satnam also asserted, unsuccessfully, a claim against the company which allegedly usurped its position, Morbaine, on the basis that Morbaine was liable as constructive trustee, having received information which was confidential, and which 'had been disclosed in breach of the obligations owed by DH and Mr Murray to Satnam'. Although the claim failed, the allegation seems to relate exclusively to the disclosure by DH and Mr Murray of confidential information.

7.40 It seems unlikely that the case supports an argument that surveyors, and those employed by them, are automatically in a fiduciary relationship with the clients of the surveyor's firm. More likely, the existence of the fiduciary duty arises from, and relates to the use of, confidential information. If that is so, it is unfortunate that the court did not explain the fact, but simply stated baldly that both DH and Mr Murray were fiduciaries.

7.41 It may be unhelpful to follow the distinction made by the Law Commission between 'status-based' and 'fact-based' fiduciaries. It might be better to take the view that in every case the decision of the court will depend upon whether the alleged fiduciary has, on the facts, assumed a responsibility and position which leads to the imposition on him of obligations which he would not have, were it not for the fiduciary nature of his relationship. However, there are certain relationships, for example, that of solicitor and client, or trustee and beneficiary, which will always involve reliance by one party on the other to some degree. In those

---

[24] [1999] 3 All ER 652, at 664f–j.
[25] At 655d.
[26] At 656f–g.

THE EXISTENCE OF A FIDUCIARY RELATIONSHIP   197

cases, the fiduciary will have obligations centred round the circumstances of the reliance. All fiduciary relationships are fact-based, but in some cases the facts are more obvious than in others.

Scope of the fiduciary relationship in the established categories

Even if the relationship between the parties is such as to give rise to an assumption that a fiduciary relationship exists, it does not follow that a particular individual transaction between the parties will be affected by the existence of that relationship. **7.42**

Not all of the duties owed by a fiduciary are fiduciary duties. The relationship between a solicitor and his client is undoubtedly a fiduciary relationship. The solicitor has, among other things, a duty to exercise skill and care in dealing with his client's affairs. That duty is not, however, a fiduciary duty. It arises because of the contract between the solicitor and the client, and not because the solicitor is a fiduciary.[27] **7.43**

It may even be the case that the transaction about which complaint is made, although it takes place between a fiduciary and his beneficiary, is simply outside the ambit of the matters in relation to which he is a fiduciary. An illustration of this can be seen in the leading case *In re Coomber*.[28] Arthur Coomber owned a business as a retailer of beer. One of the assets of the business was a valuable lease. For several years before his death, the business had been managed for him by his second son, Harry. When Mr Coomber died, he left all of his property to his wife. Harry continued to run the business for her. Three months after the death of Arthur Coomber, his widow assigned to Harry the lease of the premises, the goodwill of the business, and the licence to sell beer. The evidence was that, although Arthur had left all of his property to his wife, it has always been his intention that Harry should have the business. When Mrs Coomber died, the eldest son brought proceedings to set aside the transfer of the business to Harry. **7.44**

The elder son's argument was that Harry's relationship to his mother was a fiduciary one. He was either her agent or her employee in running the business. In either event, his relationship to her, as owner of the business, was a fiduciary one. It was to be assumed that, because of the fiduciary nature of the relationship, any gift to the fiduciary was brought about by the exercise of undue influence, and it was up to the fiduciary to show that no such undue influence had been involved. The elder son's counsel put it as follows: **7.45**

> In this case there was a fiduciary relation between the mother and son in regard to the particular property affected by the gift. Where such a fiduciary or confidential relation exists there is no need to prove undue influence. The Court will assume it, and a donee cannot support a gift unless he proves that there was no undue influence...

At first instance the claimant lost. The court accepted the argument that there was a presumption of undue influence, but found on the facts that the presumption had been displaced; it had been shown that Mrs Coomber had made the transfer to Harry without any **7.46**

---

[27] See *Henderson v Merrett Syndicates Ltd* [1995] 2 AC 145, at 205; and *Bristol & West Building Society v Mothew* [1998] Ch 1, at 18.
[28] [1911] 1 Ch 723.

undue influence on his part. In the Court of Appeal the decision was confirmed, but the court went further than the judge at first instance had gone. Cozens-Hardy MR thought that the proposition put forward by counsel for the claimant was 'in far too wide and general terms'. It was not correct to say that any fiduciary relationship between a donor and donee was sufficient to set up presumption of undue influence in relation to any transaction between them. Quoting a judgment of Lord Eldon,[29] he held that:

> There is no evidence of misrepresentation, or circumvention, or of any improper conduct leading Mrs Coomber to make this gift; it was the spontaneous fruit of her own generosity.

It had nothing to do with the duties owed to her by Harry as her agent or employee.

7.47 Fletcher Moulton LJ took the same view. After explaining the circumstances of the transfer, he went on:

> Under those circumstances what objection can be made to this transaction? It is said that the son was the manager of the stores and therefore was in a fiduciary relationship to his mother. This illustrates in a most striking form the danger of trusting to verbal formulae. Fiduciary relations are of many different types; they extend from the relation of myself to an errand boy who is bound to bring me back my change up to the most intimate and confidential relations which can possibly exists between one party and another where the one is wholly in the hands of the other because of his infinite trust in him. All these are cases of fiduciary relations, and the Courts have again and again, in cases where there has been a fiduciary relation, interfered and set aside acts which, between persons in a wholly independent position, would have been perfectly valid. Thereupon in some minds there arises the idea that if there is any fiduciary relation whatever any of these types of interference is warranted by it. They conclude that every kind of fiduciary relation justifies every kind of interference. Of course that is absurd. The nature of the fiduciary relation must be such that it justifies the interference. There is no class of case in which one ought more carefully to bear in mind the facts of the case, when one reads the judgment of the Court on those facts, than cases which relate to fiduciary and confidential relations and the actions of the Court with regard to them. In my opinion there was absolutely nothing in the fiduciary relations of the mother and the son with regard to this house which in any way affected this transaction.

7.48 The third Judge, Buckley LJ, made the same point in fewer words:

> It is not every fiduciary relation that calls this doctrine of equity into action. Between master and servant, between employer and bailiff or steward, there subsists, of course, a fiduciary relation; but there is no authority for the proposition that by reason of the existence of relations such as those a deed of gift from the one to the other can be set aside. This doctrine of equity does not rest upon the existence of a fiduciary relationship whatever be its nature. It rests upon the existence of such a fiduciary relationship as will lead the Court to infer undue influence, or knowledge in the one party concealed from the other, or other circumstances into which I need not go.

---

[29] *Harris v Tremenheere* 15 Ves 34.39.

7.49 Thus, the existence of a relationship which might be described as 'automatically' fiduciary in nature (or, in the words of The Law Commission, 'status-based') does not lead automatically to the conclusion that a court will find that the fiduciary was under obligations of a fiduciary nature in relation to the matter before it. The finding will depend upon the matter in dispute falling within the ambit of the relationship of trust and confidence which gives rise to the fiduciary relationship.

Ad hoc fiduciary relationships

7.50 It is relatively easy to start from the proposition that certain relationships (eg those of solicitor and client or agent and principal) are essentially fiduciary in nature, and then to consider whether the particular transaction falls within or outside the scope of that fiduciary relation. It is more difficult to examine a set of facts and then to predict whether a court would find that a fiduciary relationship has been created, when the relationship does not fall within one of the established fiduciary categories. The courts will find a fiduciary relationship on an *ad hoc* basis, if the elements of trust and confidence exist. The difficulty comes in predicting when the courts will detect those elements. To illustrate the difficulty, one need only examine the facts of three post-war cases.

7.51 In *Reading v Attorney-General*,[30] the facts of which are set out above,[31] Sergeant Reading sought to recover from the Crown money confiscated from him. The money had been paid to him by criminals, whom he had assisted to evade payment of customs duties levied by the Egyptian authorities who were, for these purposes, completely independent of the Crown. Wearing his uniform, he had accompanied the drivers of lorries which were smuggling black market goods into Cairo. His presence in the cab was thought to have allowed the lorries to pass unhindered through police checkpoints. There was clearly a wish, on the part of all the judges concerned, that Sergeant Reading should not be allowed to recover his money. However, the legal basis given by the judges for that conclusion differs.

7.52 At first instance, the court rejected the argument that Sergeant Reading had obtained the money as a result of a breach of a fiduciary duty. Although Denning J did not say that no fiduciary relationship existed between a soldier and the Crown, any such relationship was (as in *In re Coomber*) irrelevant to the facts of the case. The mere fact that Sergeant Reading was wearing a military uniform did not create a fiduciary relationship between the wearer and the Crown which was relevant to the circumstances:

> This man Reading was not acting in the course of his employment: and there was no fiduciary relationship in respect of these long journeys nor, indeed, in respect of his uniform.

The Crown succeeded on different grounds:

> ... if, as here, the wearing of the King's uniform and his position as a soldier is the sole cause of his getting the money, and getting it dishonestly, that is an advantage which he is not

---

[30] [1951] AC 507, reported at first instance and in the Court of Appeal as *Reading v The King*, respectively [1948] 2 KB 268 and [1949] 2 KB 232.
[31] At para 7.14.

allowed to keep. Although the Crown has suffered no loss, the court orders the money to be handed over to the Crown, because the Crown is the only person to whom it can properly be paid. The man must not be allowed to enrich himself in this way. He got the money by virtue of his employment, and must hand it over.

7.53 The reasoning is open to an obvious criticism. Sergeant Reading did not get the money because of his employment. He got it because he was wearing a British Sergeant's uniform. The effect would have been the same, if he had been a civilian who was merely posing as a British solider, and wearing a uniform with which he had no connection.

7.54 In the Court of Appeal, the reasoning of Denning J was not rejected. The court preferred, however, to rest its view on the existence of a fiduciary relationship. In order to reach this finding, the court defined the term 'fiduciary relation' much more widely than is usual:

> But the term 'fiduciary relation' in this connexion is used in a very loose, or at all events a very comprehensive, sense. A consideration of the authorities suggests that for the present purpose a 'fiduciary relation' exists (a) whenever the plaintiff entrusts to the defendant property, including intangible property as, for instance, confidential information, and relies on the defendant to deal with such property for the benefit of the plaintiff or for purposes authorised by him, but not otherwise ... and (b) whenever the plaintiff entrusts to the defendant a job to be performed, for instance, the negotiation of a contract on his behalf or for his benefit, and relies on the defendant to procure for the plaintiff the best terms available ...
>
> ...
>
> Assuming a fiduciary relation is necessary to enable the Crown to recover, we are of opinion, differing in this respect from the learned trial judge, that in the wide sense in which the terms is used in the relevant cases such a relation subsisted in this case as to the user of the uniform and the opportunities and facilities attached to it ...

7.55 The Court of Appeal went much further than the trial judge had done. Although Denning J had accepted that there might be a fiduciary relationship arising out of the wearing of the uniform, between the soldier and the Crown, he held that relationship did not apply when the solider was acting quite outside the scope of his military duties. The Court of Appeal, however, saw no such limitation. The mere fact that he was wearing the uniform meant that he was in a fiduciary relationship with the Crown, and owed to the Crown fiduciary duties which affected everything he did while wearing the uniform.

7.56 In the House of Lords, the judgments affirmed the view of the Court of Appeal and were, if anything, even more rigorous in their assertion that there was a fiduciary relationship between Sergeant Reading and the Crown. Lord Porter, with whom Viscount Jowitt LC agreed, took the view that there was a general principle that a servant who uses his master's property to obtain a benefit must account for that benefit. It had been claimed, following *In re Coomber*, that this principle applied only if it could be shown that there was a fiduciary relationship in relation to the matter concerned. On this point, Lord Porter was very robust:

> As to the assertion that there must be a fiduciary relationship, the existence of such a connexion is, in my opinion, not an additional necessity in order to substantiate the claim;

but another ground for succeeding where a claim for a money had and received would fail. In any case, I agree with Asquith, LJ [in the Court of Appeal] in thinking that the words 'fiduciary relationship' in this setting are used in a wide and loose sense and include, *inter alia*, a case where the servant gains from his employment a position of authority which enables him to obtain the sum which he received.

Lords Normand and Radcliffe simply agreed with the Court of Appeal. Lord Oaksey also agreed. However, he added a slightly different point. He argued that, for these purposes, a solider was a servant of the Crown, and that there is no difficulty:

> ... in imputing to a servant an implied promise that he will account to his master for any monies he may receive in the course of his master's business or by the use of his master's property or by the use of his position as his master's servant.

7.57 The case has been viewed as an extreme example of a situation where courts are prepared to stretch an existing doctrine in order to correct a perceived wrong. In the *Reading* case, the motivating concern of all the judges was that Sergeant Reading should not be able to recover his money; it did not matter that the Crown had no better claim to it than did he. In this respect, the reasoning of Denning J at first instance is to be preferred, as according with previous learning in relation to fiduciary duties. He specifically rejected the idea that there was a fiduciary relationship which was relevant to the matters under consideration. His grounds for refusing Sergeant Reading's claim for the money were quite different. The Court of Appeal and House of Lords' judges, in finding the existence of a fiduciary relationship in a 'very loose, or at all events a very comprehensive sense' have done no service to practitioners, who have to predict the reasoning of courts in future cases.

7.58 *Lloyds Bank Ltd v Bundy*[32] is another case which shows the courts casting wide the net of fiduciary relationships to catch situations which would not previously have been thought likely to be included. The case has been of particular significance to the financial industries because, perhaps for the first time, the court found a fiduciary relationship to exist between a high street bank and one of its private customers. The defendant was a retired farmer. His only asset was the house in which he lived. He had one son, who owned a company which hired out agricultural machinery. Mr Bundy had banked at the branch of Lloyds Bank in Salisbury for many years. His son and the son's company were also customers of the bank. When the son's company had first run into difficulties, Mr Bundy had been asked by the bank to guarantee the overdraft of the company up to the sum of £1,500, and to charge his house to the bank to secure his guarantee. He had done so. Later on, as the company's position worsened, the bank asked Mr Bundy to increase the level of his guarantee by £5,000, and to grant a further charge over his house to cover the increased amount. Mr Bundy had spoken about it to his solicitor, who advised him that he should not put at risk his assets above 50 per cent of the total value. On this basis, Mr Bundy executed the additional guarantee and charge. The company's position worsened. An assistant manager of the bank visited Mr Bundy, along with Mr Bundy's son, and said that the bank was prepared to maintain the company's overdraft only if Mr Bundy increased his guarantee by a further £11,000 and executed a further charge over his property. The

---

[32] [1975] 1 QB 326.

assistant manager described the problems of the son's company as 'deep seated'. Mr Bundy said that he was 100 per cent behind his only son, and signed the guarantee and charge on the spot. The company's business then collapsed, the bank called in the guarantee and sought an order to sell the house.

7.59 Resisting the application for an order for possession, Mr Bundy said that he 'always trusted' the bank and 'simply sat back and did what they said'. The County Court judge granted an order for possession, and Mr Bundy appealed to the Court of Appeal. The court allowed the appeal, finding that there was a fiduciary relationship between the bank and Mr Bundy. The bank was in a position, in relation to the final guarantee and charge, of conflict: it had a fiduciary obligation to advise Mr Bundy in his best interest, and also had its own financial interest in his entering into the documents. It ought to have resolved this conflict by advising Mr Bundy to seek the advice of his own solicitor. The guarantee and charge should therefore be set aside, as having been obtained through undue influence.

7.60 Lord Denning MR, whose judgment has attracted the most attention, did not cast his decision in terms of traditional analysis of fiduciary relationships. Instead, he said that there was a general principle, based on 'inequality of bargaining power'.[33] He said that there were four elements in this case that brought the principle into play:

1. The consideration given by the bank for the guarantee and charge was 'grossly inadequate'. The bank simply said that it would not call in the overdraft for the time being. 'All that the company gained was a short respite from impending doom'.
2. The relationship between the bank and Mr Bundy was one of trust and confidence.
3. Mr Bundy trusted his son and would naturally accede to any request by the son.
4. There was a conflict of interest between the bank and Mr Bundy.

According to the underlying principle, the court had jurisdiction to set the transaction aside. He finished his judgment by saying that, if he was wrong in his analysis of this new principle, he would still set the transaction aside on a basis which, one might say, was a traditional 'fiduciary relationship' basis:

> There was such a relationship of trust and confidence between them that the bank ought not to have swept up his sole remaining asset into its hands – for nothing – without his having independent advice.

7.61 The other two judges, Cairns LJ and Sir Eric Sachs, declined to find any principle of 'inequality of bargaining power'. Instead, they adopted a more traditional approach, based on the concept of fiduciary duty. Cairns LJ put the position very succinctly:

> I have had some doubt whether it was established in this case that there was such a special relationship between Mr Bundy and the bank as to give rise to a duty on the part of the bank ... to advise Mr Bundy about the desirability of his obtaining independent advice. In the end ... I have reached the conclusion that in the very unusual circumstances of this case there was such a duty. Because it was not fulfilled, the guarantee can be avoided on the ground of undue influence.

---

[33] At 339C.

Of the three judgments, it is perhaps that of Sir Eric Sachs which merits the most careful consideration. He analyses very carefully what is meant by 'fiduciary relationship', bearing in mind the unusual facts of the case. The points he makes are: **7.62**

1. The relationships which result in a duty of fiduciary care cannot be confined to predetermined categories. It is not the case that, in a relationship of confidence, 'the person owing the duty must be found clothed in the recognisable garb of a guardian, trustee, solicitor, priest, doctor, manager or the like'.[34]
2. It is neither feasible nor desirable to give a close definition of the relationship or its characteristics.
3. Without being prescriptive, however, it is possible to say that relationships tend to arise where someone relies on guidance or advice of another, where that other is aware of the reliance, and where that other obtains, or may obtain, a benefit from the transaction concerned. In addition, there must be shown to exist the element of 'confidentiality'.
4. Confidentiality is not the same as 'confidence'. 'Confidentiality' has something in common with 'confiding' and 'confidant'. It is one of the features of the element that, once it exists, influence naturally grows out of it.

The facts of the case show that the relationship between the bank and Mr Bundy was one of confidentiality. It was clear, on the facts, that Mr Bundy, who was very old, was quite confused and not well placed to make his own independent judgment. It was accepted that he relied implicitly on the bank and would do what they suggested he should do. It would be unusual for a customer of the bank to be in such a relationship. Nonetheless, the relationship existed here, and the bank, because of the conflict between its own interests and those of its customer, was under an obligation to ensure that Mr Bundy obtained independent advice before he acceded to its requests.

Lloyds Bank v Bundy is, as emphasized by the Court of Appeal, based on unusual facts. If one disregards the general principle put forward by Lord Denning and instead views the case as an illustration of the law relating to fiduciary relationships, as analyzed by Sir Eric Sachs, the decision is not surprising. It does, however, show that a fiduciary relationship might exist in an area where one might otherwise expect there to be only an arm's-length relationship between the parties. **7.63**

The third case that demonstrates the finding of the fiduciary relationship in circumstances where one might not expect it to exist, is the House of Lords decision in *Boardman v Phipps*.[35] Three individuals were the trustees of the trusts established by the will of Mr Phipps. They were his widow, who suffered from dementia and took no part in the affairs of the trust, his daughter, and his former accountant. One of the assets of the will trust was a holding of just below 25 per cent of the shares in a private textile company based in the Midlands, Lester & Harris Limited. The trustees received an approach, asking whether they would be prepared to sell their shareholding in the company. They consulted Tom Boardman, the solicitor to the trustees. After consideration of the company's accounts and other available material, Mr Boardman told the trustees that the shares in the company might have a real value considerably greater than had previously been thought. **7.64**

---

[34] Quoting Sir Raymond Evershed MR, in *Tufton v Sperni* [1952] 2 TLR 516, at 522.
[35] [1967] 2 AC 46.

7.65 Mr Boardman, along with Tom Phipps, one of the beneficiaries of the trust, attended the Annual General Meeting of the company, as proxies for the trustees, asked a number of questions and demanded a considerable amount of information. Over the following months they entered into correspondence with the directors of the company, again saying that they represented the trustees, and as a result of their enquiries acquired a great deal of information about the company's affairs. Tom Boardman and Tom Phipps concluded that the underlying assets of the company were in fact worth far more than the share price suggested. It would be a profitable transaction to acquire the shares that the trustees did not own, or a majority of them, use control of the company to liquidate the underlying assets, and distribute the profits to shareholders. The trustees saw merits in this. However, the trust did not have the legal powers to purchase any more shares. The will which established the trust did not permit it.

7.66 Mr Boardman therefore wrote to the beneficiaries, who included Mrs Norris, one of the trustees, and also Mr John Phipps, the respondent in the action. He outlined the negotiations that had taken place so far, explained that the trustees were not in a position to take forward the plan to buy the outstanding shares, and asked whether they had any objection to Mr Boardman pursuing the purchase of the outstanding shares on his own account. The beneficiaries raised no objection. Accordingly, Mr Boardman, together with Mr Tom Phipps, one of the beneficiaries, negotiated with the board and eventually acquired the majority of the shares. They pursued the policy of liquidating the assets and distributing the proceeds. In the event, Mr Boardman and Mr Tom Phipps made a substantial profit from the transaction. The trustees also did well financially, because their 25 per cent holding of shares in the company yielded a greater return than had been anticipated before Mr Boardman began his enquiries. That gain was brought about by the efforts of Tom Phipps and, in particular, Mr Boardman.

7.67 After the event, Mr John Phipps, one of the beneficiaries, brought proceedings against Mr Boardman and his own brother, Mr Tom Phipps, on the basis that they stood in a fiduciary relationship to the trustees, and were liable to account to the trustees for the profits that they had made out of their transactions in the shares of Lester & Harris Limited. The House of Lords held, affirming the decision of the Court of Appeal and of the first instance judge, that Mr Boardman and Mr Tom Phipps had placed themselves in a fiduciary relationship to the trustees, because of the way in which they had negotiated with the directors of the company. It was because of this special position that they had been able to conduct negotiations which gave them the opportunity to make the profit by acquiring shares in Lester & Harris Limited. They were accountable to the trustees for the profit so made, although they were allowed to retain a generous sum, as compensation for the work which they had done in obtaining the benefit which ultimately accrued to the trustees.

7.68 The fiduciary relationship in this case was an unusual one. Boardman was, of course, the solicitor to the trustees. The point is made by several of the judges, and there is no doubt that his capacity as solicitor placed him in a fiduciary position. However, the profits which he and Tom Phipps made did not relate to dealings between them and the trustees. Boardman did not buy property from the trustees, nor sell property to the trustees. In relation to the advice which he gave, he cannot be said to have breached any fiduciary duty. His first advice was that the trustees should not sell their shares when first approached. That advice turned out to be excellent. The trustees made far more money by retaining their shares than they would have made by selling. In relation to the purchase of other shares in Lester & Harris Limited, Boardman could not advise that the trustees should buy additional shares, because it was outside their legal powers to do so. As in *In re Coomber*, the fiduciary relationship did not concern the transactions under consideration. No claim for breach of a fiduciary duty can relate to Boardman's conduct as a solicitor.

In addition, Tom Phipps, who acted with Mr Boardman, was not a solicitor. The claim against him had to be based on a fiduciary relationship which was quite separate from that arising between a solicitor and his client. Lord Guest acknowledged this: **7.69**

> I make no distinction between the two appellants. They have never asked to be dealt with separately and they must be treated as co-venturers.

The fiduciary relationship between the trustees, on the one hand, and Messrs. Phipps and Boardman, on the other hand, must be different from that between the trustees and their solicitor. **7.70**

The question which has to be asked, therefore, is: what is it about the way in which Mr Boardman and Mr Tom Phipps behaved, which led to them being in a position of 'trust and confidence' or 'confidentiality' with the trustees? In the Court of Appeal,[36] Lord Denning MR and Pearson LJ had said that the fiduciary relationship arose out of the fact that Mr Boardman and Mr Phipps were 'self-appointed agents' of the trustees. Lord Guest, in the House of Lords, put the proposition more vaguely:

> Boardman and Tom Phipps ... placed themselves in a special position which was of a fiduciary character in relation to the negotiations with the directors of Lester & Harris Limited relating to the trust's shares.

It seems that the fiduciary relationship was found to exist because Mr Boardman and Mr Tom Phipps, through their positions as respectively solicitor to the trust and beneficiary under it, were able to represent themselves (imaginatively, if not untruthfully) as representing the trustees in their dealings with the directors of Lester & Harris Limited.

It should be noted that in Lord Guest's speech, and those of other of the judges, it is said that the existence of a fiduciary relationship gives rise to an obligation to account for any profit made: **7.71**

> Out of that special position and in the course of such negotiations they obtained the opportunity to make a profit out of the shares and acknowledged that the profit was there to be made. A profit was made and they are accountable accordingly.

The obligation to account in law arises only if the profit is a secret profit.[37] In this case, the finding of the judge at first instance was that the respondent, Mr John Phipps 'had only been told half the truth'. This element of concealment is an essential element of the liability to account, although not explicitly referred to in the judgment. Without the element of concealment as a constituent part of the breach, it is hard to see what duty Messrs. Phipps and Boardman could be said to have breached.

---

[36] [1965] Ch 992.
[37] See para 7.95 below.

7.72 There is a striking similarity between the reasoning in *Boardman v Phipps* and that in *Reading v Attorney-General*. In the latter case, Sergeant Reading was able to make a profit because he was in a position to represent himself implicitly as being a British soldier on military business and was therefore afforded advantages that would not otherwise have been available; he was allowed to pass through customs checkpoints unhindered. In *Boardman v Phipps*, Mr Boardman and Mr Phipps had first contacted the directors of Lester & Harris Limited as proxy representatives of the trustees at the AGM. They had subsequently claimed to be representing them in their dealings with the directors. If the directors had known that they were acting in a personal capacity, the directors might well have refused to give them the information which they sought. The directors would certainly have had no obligation to hand it over.

7.73 In both cases, there was an element of concealment which contributed to the ability of the fiduciary to make a profit for himself. In *Sergeant Reading's* case, the concealment lay in his giving the impression to customs officials that he was a British soldier on official business. In *Boardman v Phipps*, the concealment was achieved by the fiduciaries, after the first AGM, continuing to represent that they were acting on behalf of the trustees, when they had no such position. They were, as Lord Denning said, 'self-appointed agents'.

7.74 The point at which both cases step outside the mainstream of case law on fiduciary relationships is when, having found that a fiduciary relationship existed, the courts declined to examine the interest which this branch of the law seeks to protect. The purpose of enforcing strictly the duty of loyalty owed by fiduciaries to their beneficiaries is to protect the interests of the beneficiaries from abuse. In circumstances where such abuse cannot occur, no breach will be found. Thus, in *In re Coomber*, there was no breach of duty by the fiduciary, because the actions concerned had no bearing on the substance of the fiduciary relationship; the gift from mother to son was not influenced by the duties of employee to employer. In *Reading v Attorney-General*, the misuse of his uniform by Sergeant Reading had no connection with the matters in respect of which a soldier owes his allegiance to the Crown. In *Boardman v Phipps*, the protagonists had assumed a position of responsibility by attending the first AGM as representatives of the trustees. There was no suggestion that, in that limited capacity, they had failed to discharge their duties.

7.75 The facts of both cases seem to be quite far removed from the normal situation of a fiduciary relationship, as described by Sir Eric Sachs in *Lloyds Bank Ltd v Bundy*. In neither case was there a situation of reliance by the person to whom fiduciary duties were owed. Rather, the cases have a common characteristic, in that the fiduciary might be said to have misused an asset of the other party; in the *Sergeant Reading* case, the sergeant misused his military uniform, and in *Boardman v Phipps* the appellants misused their ability to represent themselves as acting on behalf of the shareholders, when in fact they were acting on their own account. On this basis, both cases might be seen as examples of the law relating to unjust enrichment, rather than a question of the protection of the interests of parties to whom a fiduciary duty is owed.

7.76 In both cases, although it is possible to say that the fiduciaries abused their positions of trust, it cannot be said that the interests of either the Crown or the trustees were abused. The courts were using the remedies for breach of fiduciary duty to punish the perceived wrongdoers, rather than to protect the vulnerable.

7.77 These three cases illustrate the concern felt by practitioners about this area of the law. They extended the reach of the legal concept of fiduciary relationships to areas where it had not been thought previously to apply. In particular, the introduction of the concept into the relationship between banker and customer in *Lloyds Bank Ltd v Bundy* seemed a radical change, and one which was disturbing for banks. For several years after the case was heard, it became common for those who wished to avoid obligations to their banks, particularly under the terms of guarantees, to claim that the guarantee was unenforceable because the customer had relied on the bank and trusted the bank in giving the guarantee. Such arguments were, on the whole, unsuccessful. Nonetheless, the case introduced into banking practice an element of uncertainty. On the positive side, it also led to a change in practice in high street banks, which began to take more care when dealing with customers who might be considered in any sense vulnerable.

7.78 In relation to financial markets, the possibility of finding fiduciary relationships in the context of bankers and their customers has been profound. Until the 1970s, banks had taken for granted that the relationship between banker and customer was one of debtor and creditor. They took comfort from the clear views expressed in *Foley v Hill*:[38]

> The money placed in the custody of a banker is, to all intents and purposes, the money of the banker, to do with as he pleases, he is guilty of no breach of trust in employing it; he is not answerable to the principal if he puts it into jeopardy, if he engages in a hazardous speculation; he is not bound to keep it or deal with it as property of his principal; but he is of course, answerable for the amount, because he has contracted.

Lloyds Bank v Bundy brought home to banks and their advisors that the position was not necessarily always so clear. From the beginning of the 1990s, when banks began to develop increasingly complicated products, the effects of which were often difficult to understand, attention was to focus again on the nature of the relationship between the bank and the customer.[39] Often, the word 'fiduciary' was not used; rather, the question was whether the bank was an arm's-length counterparty of its customer, or had assumed the role as 'advisor'. In reality, this is simply a change of language. The duties which an advisor owes to the recipient of the advice are, in most cases, the duties of a fiduciary.

The Nature of Fiduciary Duties

7.79 The identification of a fiduciary relationship does not, in itself, have any legal consequence. What matters are the duties that follow from the relationship, whether those duties are imposed by equity, or implied as contractual terms by the common law. The classic statement of the point was made by Frankfurter J in the leading US case, *SEC v Chenery Corp*.[40]

> To say that a man is a fiduciary only begins analysis; it gives direction to further enquiry. To whom is he a fiduciary? What obligations does he have as a fiduciary? In what respect has

---
[38] (1848) 2 HL Cas 28.
[39] See paras 8.85 *et seq*.
[40] (1943) 318 HS 80.

he failed to discharge those obligations? And what are the consequences of his deviation from duty?

7.80 It is not always easy to see clearly the nature of the fiduciary duties which are owed. Just as the existence and relevance of a fiduciary relationship depend upon the facts of the case, the nature of the duties which flow from the relationship will vary according to the circumstances. Lord Browne-Wilkinson said in *Henderson v Merrett Syndicates Ltd*[41] when discussing a fiduciary relationship which arose from a contract between the parties:

> The phrase 'fiduciary duties' is a dangerous one, giving rise to a mistaken assumption that all fiduciaries owe the same duties in all circumstances. That is not the case . . . the fiduciary duties owed, for example, by an express trustee are not the same as those owed by an agent. Moreover . . . the extent and nature of the fiduciary duties owed in any particular case fall to be determined by reference to any underlying contractual relationship between the parties.

7.81 To say that the detailed nature of the duties will depend on the facts of the fiduciary relationship is not to say that the nature of the duties is unpredictable in advance of an alleged breach. There are clear established rules against which the facts of any case may be evaluated. The clearest exposition of these rules in recent times is to be found in the judgment of Millett LJ in *Bristol & West Building Society v Mothew*.[42] The case is important not only for the exposition of the nature of fiduciary duties, but because it shows clearly why claimants, in order to obtain the relief they seek, may need to establish that a duty owed to them is fiduciary in nature.

7.82 Mr Mothew was a solicitor. In August 1988, shortly before the bursting of the house price bubble at the end of that year, he acted for the purchasers of a house in Romford. The purchase price was £73,000. In accordance with usual practice, he was instructed also by Bristol & West Building Society ('the Society') which had agreed to lend £59,000 to the purchasers. The purchasers had told the Society that the balance of the purchase price (£14,000) would be provided by them from their own resources, and they would not be taking a loan from any other source. The Society's agreement to provide the loan on the security of a first charge was conditional upon the purchasers providing the balance themselves, without recourse to further borrowings. When the Society instructed Mr Mothew, they made him aware of this condition, and required him to report to them, before they made the final advance, that, so far as he was aware, this condition had been fulfilled.

7.83 The purchasers intended to provide all the balance themselves. First, they needed to sell their existing house and to pay off the loan which had been taken to buy that property. They could then use the surplus to fund the £14,000 balance on the new house. However, they had a slight change of plan. They agreed with their previous banker, Barclays, to leave £3,350 of the earlier loan outstanding, and to secure this debt by a second charge in favour of Barclays over their new house. Mr Mothew was well aware of this arrangement, and indeed gave undertakings to Barclays in relation to the registration of their second charge over the new house.

---

[41] [1995] 2 AC 145, at 206.
[42] [1998] Ch 1.

7.84 In the event, Mr Mothew forgot to tell the Society about the second charge to be created in favour of Barclays. It is not clear whether he simply forgot that he had been instructed to report on the existence of any second charge, or whether he mistakenly thought that the Barclays arrangements did not fall within the matters about which the Society wished to be informed. In any event, it was accepted that his failure to tell the Society amounted to negligence on his part. There was, however, no suggestion of any intention by Mr Mothew to mislead the Society, or of any other improper behaviour.

7.85 Both the first charge in favour of the Society and the second charge in favour of Barclays were executed on 30 August 1988. On 25 November of that year Mr Mothew wrote to the Society requesting consent to the registration of the second charge in favour of Barclays. The Society gave its consent on 10 March 1989. The Society raised no objection to the existence of the second charge. Shortly thereafter the purchasers defaulted on their mortgage repayments to the Society, the Society exercised its rights under its mortgage, and the property was sold in February 1991 for £53,000. This left the Society with a loss of £6,000 plus interest and expenses. Barclays, as second chargee, received nothing.

7.86 The Society sued Mr Mothew, claiming to recover the whole of its net loss on the transaction. It based its claim on breach of contract, negligence, and breach of trust. There was no doubt that Mr Mothew had committed a breach of contract. His failure to tell the Society about the creation of the second charge was contrary to his instructions, and was a clear breach of his contractual duty to the Society. The Society could not, however, recover its losses, based only on a claim for breach of the duty of care inherent in its contract with Mr Mothew.

7.87 There had already been a series of cases arising out of the property collapse of the late 1980s, which had elaborated detailed rules for calculation of loss in situations where lenders had relied upon incorrect advice from solicitors or valuers.[43] The result of these rules was that, in order to succeed with its claim for contractual damages, the Society would need to show that, if Mr Mothew had properly performed his contractual duties and had told them about the creation of the second charge, the Society would have refused to lend money to the purchasers. Further, the loss which they could recover would be the loss which resulted from the existence of the second charge and the indebtedness to Barclays. On the facts, the second charge in favour of Barclays ranked after the charge in favour of the Society, and it would not be possible for the Society to show that it was damaged by the existence of the second charge.

7.88 Accordingly, it is clear that the Society, although it could show that Mr Mothew had committed a breach of contract, would not be able by this route to recover the money it had lost. In order to succeed, it would need to invoke equitable principles, which would make available to it a restitutionary remedy. The *Mothew* case is a prime illustration of the reasons why claimants often allege breaches of fiduciary duty in situations based upon contractual relationships, where there is a clear breach of contract that is itself actionable. Sometimes, a claim for breach of fiduciary duty is the only way in which the claimant can avoid the application of rules of causation and measure of damages which would deny it a recovery.

---

[43] See *Downs v Chappell* [1997] 1 WLR 426; *Banque Bruxelles Lambert SA v Eagle Star Insurance Co Ltd* [1997] AC 191; and *Mortgage Express Ltd v Bowerman & Partners* [1996] 2 All ER 836.

7.89 In order to bring itself within the protection of the equitable jurisdiction of the court, the Society alleged that Mr Mothew had committed a breach of trust. He had received from the Society the amount of the advance to be made to the purchasers on trust to apply that money in accordance with his instructions. He had failed to do this, and Mr Mothew's release of the money to the purchasers, to pay the purchase price of the property, amounted to a breach of trust for which he was liable. The court rejected this argument. The Society had given Mr Mothew authority to pay away the money on completion of the purchase. It had not made that authority conditional upon his having complied with all the other terms of his instructions at the time. Accordingly, the payment away of the money by Mr Mothew did not amount to a breach of trust.

7.90 This left only the claim that Mr Mothew's breach of duty, in failing to tell the Society about the creation of the second charge, was the breach not only of a contractual duty, but also the breach of a fiduciary duty. Accordingly, the Society argued, the court should make an order which restored the Society to the position it would have been in, had it not lent the money.

7.91 It is in this context that Millett LJ set out his description of the nature and content of fiduciary duties. It must be remembered that the context is that of the relationship between the solicitor and client. Although the principles transpose to other fiduciary relationships, the words chosen to express some of those principles relate specifically to the solicitor/client relationship.

7.92 Millett LJ begins at the beginning. A fiduciary:

> ... is someone who has undertaken to act for or on behalf of another in a particular matter in circumstances which give rise to a relationship of trust and confidence.

Fiduciary duties are those duties which are: (a) owed by a fiduciary; and (b) the breach of which attracts legal consequences which are different from those which follow from the breach of other duties which the fiduciary might have (eg his obligations under a contract of engagement).

7.93 In any fiduciary relationship, the fiduciary owes a large number of duties. Not all of those duties can be described as fiduciary duties. This description should be confined to those duties owed by the fiduciary which relate to the characteristics of the relationship which make that relationship a fiduciary one. Millett J quotes with approval from a Canadian case:[44]

> The word 'fiduciary' is flung around now as if it applied to all breaches of duty by solicitors, directors of companies and so forth ... But to say that simply carelessness in giving advice is such a breach is a perversion of words.

He then sets out a rather fuller explanation given by an Australian judge, Ipp J:[45]

> It is essential to bear in mind that the existence of a fiduciary relationship does not mean that every duty owed by a fiduciary to the beneficiary is a fiduciary duty.
>
> ...
>
> The director's duty to exercise care and skill [ie the duty of a company director owed by him to his company] has nothing to do with any position of disadvantage or vulnerability

---

[44] *Girardet v Crease & Co* (1987) 11 BCLR (2d) 361.
[45] *Permanent Building Society v Wheeler* (1994) 14 ACSR 109, at 157–8.

on the part of the company. It is not a duty that stems from the requirements of trust and confidence imposed on a fiduciary. In my opinion, that duty is not a fiduciary duty, although it is a duty actionable in the equitable jurisdiction of this court ...

7.94 Fiduciary duties are those duties which are special to fiduciaries. Their most important characteristic and consequence is that they attract remedies which are peculiar to equity and are intended to be restitutionary, rather than compensating the claimant for a loss suffered.

7.95 The core obligation of a fiduciary is that of loyalty:

> The distinguishing obligation of a fiduciary is the obligation of loyalty. The principle is entitled to the single-minded loyalty of his fiduciary.

This is perfectly clear. However, it is a high-level principle. It is not necessarily obvious what the principle will require the fiduciary to do in any particular situation. Millett LJ therefore sets out a number of 'facets' of this core liability. In considering these specific emanations of the principle, it must be borne in mind that the fiduciary relationship under consideration in *Mothew* was that of solicitor and client. A similar exercise in relation to, say, the agent/principal relationship might produce a slightly differently worded series of duties. The facets of the duty are:

1. a fiduciary must act in good faith;
2. a fiduciary must not make a secret profit out of his trust;
3. a fiduciary must not place himself in a position where his duty and his interest may conflict;
4. a fiduciary may not act for his own benefit or the benefit of a third person without the informed consent of his principal;
5. if the fiduciary deals with his principal, whether on his own behalf or on behalf of a third party, he must show that the transaction is fair and that he made full disclosure to his principal of all material facts; and
6. a fiduciary must take care not to be in a position where he has an actual conflict of duty, so that he cannot fulfil his obligations to one principal without failing in his obligations to the other (the classic dilemma which can arise when a solicitor is acting for both the lender and the borrower in the same transaction).

7.96 Millett LJ stresses that the list of the detailed obligations of the fiduciary:

> ... merely reflect different aspects of his core duties of loyalty and fidelity. Breach of fiduciary obligation, therefore, connotes disloyalty or infidelity.

The situation complained of before the court needs to be analyzed in the light of this core duty. In the circumstances, did the act (or default) which is complained of involve a breach of the core duty of loyalty? That is the matter of substance that lies at the heart of all claims for breach of fiduciary duty. The analysis cannot be accomplished by 'unthinking resort to verbal formulae'.[46]

---

[46] Fletcher Moulton LJ in *In re Coomber* [1911] 1 Ch 723, at 728.

7.97 Applying this reasoning to the facts before him, Millett LJ (with whom the other two judges agreed) decided that there was no breach of fiduciary duty by Mr Mothew. He had been negligent in failing to tell the Society of the creation of the second charge. It was also true that he was under a fiduciary duty to ensure that his obligation to the Society, as his client, did not conflict with that which he owed to the purchasers, who were also his clients. On the facts, however, the breach had nothing to do with the potential conflict of interest. The obligation he had breached was the contractual obligation to act competently. His failure to tell the Society did not flow from any wish to promote the interests of his purchaser clients over those of the Society. Although he was a fiduciary in relation both to the Society and to the purchasers, and owed both of them fiduciary duties of loyalty, it was not these duties which he had breached.

Summary

7.98 Although the law relating to fiduciary duties has a long and complex history, it is possible to summarize the current position in a few simple propositions:

1. A fiduciary relationship arises where one party has to repose trust and confidence in the other. The relationship may arise in the context of a contract between them, for example between a solicitor (or other professional advisor) and his client, or between an agent and his principal. It may, however, arise without the existence of a contract (eg between a trustee and the beneficiary of the trust).
2. Where a fiduciary relationship exists, the fiduciary owes a duty of loyalty to the person who places trust and confidence in him. He may have other duties, imposed by contract or by operation of law, which do not relate to the area of trust and confidence which gives rise to the fiduciary duty of loyalty. For example, a solicitor has a duty, in advising his client, to act competently. This is a matter of contract law quite separate from his fiduciary obligation of loyalty.
3. The fiduciary duty of loyalty, in any given situation, can be expressed as a more detailed obligation or set of obligations. For example, a solicitor's fiduciary duty of loyalty may, in a particular situation, involve an obligation not to put himself in a position where his interests conflict with his duty to his client. The nature of the specific fiduciary obligations will depend on the circumstances of the relationship.
4. If a fiduciary duty is breached, it will attract an equitable remedy, the aim of which is not to compensate for loss, but rather to restore the situation to where it was before the breach occurred, or to provide for restitution. A remedy, therefore, might be available in circumstances where a claim based on a breach of a non-fiduciary duty might not produce recompense.

7.99 The principles are deceptively simple. The difficulties arise in their application to situations; in particular, to their application to commercial and financial relationships. This issue is the subject of the next chapter.

8
FIDUCIARY DUTIES IN FINANCIAL MARKETS

Introduction

Chapter 7 described the circumstances in which fiduciary relationships are likely to arise and the consequences if they are found to exist. The establishment of a relationship, whether by contract or otherwise, in which one party has to place reliance and trust on the other is likely to give rise to special fiduciary duties. These take the form of obligations imposed by equity or, in those relationships established by contract between the parties, as additional implied terms of the contract. 8.01

The core duty arising from a fiduciary relationship is a duty to act loyally towards the person to whom the duties are owed. This basic obligation may take a number of specific forms, depending upon the circumstances of the case. Breach by a fiduciary of the duty of loyalty allows the wronged counterparty to seek access to the range of equitable remedies. In particular, he may seek restitution, or ask for an account of any gains wrongfully made by the fiduciary. He is likely to do this if a common law remedy for damages might be inadequate or would, in any event, yield less money for the claimant than would an equitable remedy. 8.02

This chapter examines the application of these processes to commercial relationships and specifically to relationships that arise in financial transactions. 8.03

One might assume that the concept of a fiduciary relationship would have little application in commercial life. Since the earliest days of its development, the common law adopted as a *leitmotif*—a theme which occurs and re-occurs throughout the structure—the idea that parties to commercial transactions must protect their own interests. The law would not interfere to protect those who had made bad bargains or who had tried to swim out of their depth. Self-reliance was encapsulated in the Latin phrase *caveat emptor* (let the buyer beware). 8.04

During the twentieth century, this principle has been very greatly eroded by consumer protection legislation, which recognizes the reality that, in practice, consumers often cannot protect themselves from a provider's greater bargaining position, no matter how wary they are. Apart from situations involving consumers, however, one would not expect the law to find in commercial activity the element of 'reliance and trust' or 'confidentiality'[1] that is the hallmark of the fiduciary relationship. In particular, one would not expect to find those factors in arm's-length dealings between large commercial enterprises. 8.05

---

[1] The word used by Sir Eric Sachs in *Lloyds Bank Ltd v Bundy* [1975] 1 QB 326.

8.06 However, even the most powerful, experienced, and sophisticated corporations may find themselves in situations where they have no choice but to rely on another organization or person to behave in a way which protects their interests. In this situation even a large and powerful company might have a vulnerability to abuse which will invoke the protection of equity.

8.07 There are three common business situations in which a commercial organization might find itself dependent on another. The first is to be found in joint venture arrangements. The nature of a joint venture, although different from that of a partnership, has a shared characteristic: often, one of the parties to the joint venture has the ability to deal with the fortunes or assets of the venture in a way which affects not only its interest, but that of its co-venturers. In this circumstance, all of the joint venturers are dependent upon the proper behaviour of the one which has the power to represent them.

8.08 The second situation, and the one which provokes most activity in the courts in this area, relates to confidential information. Very often, a commercial entity is obliged, for the purposes of a transaction in which it is engaged, to provide to another party confidential information about its activities or business. The recipient might be a business partner or a third-party advisor—its lawyers, bankers, or other professional firm. The receipt of confidential information in those circumstances creates an obligation on the recipient not to misuse that information. The obligation not to misuse the confidential information and to protect the interests of the owner of it often gives rise to a fiduciary duty.

8.09 The third situation is that where a commercial entity seeks advice from professionals, whether bankers, accountants, lawyers, fund managers, or others about its commercial affairs. The fact that it looks to others for help implies that it does not have the expertise within its own resources to make the decisions concerned. In seeking specialist advice, it is dependent upon the good faith, as well as the competence of its advisors.[2]

8.10 In relation to commercial activity, discussion of fiduciary duties in the cases, and the allegations made in pleadings, can be a little misleading. For example, a company claiming that its bankers persuaded it to buy a structured derivative product which it did not understand and which turned out to be very detrimental to it, may not mention the phrase 'fiduciary duties' in its claim. It may complain instead that the bank had assumed the position of advisor, rather than simply being the counterparty on the other side of a trade. Thus, the company might say, the bank had breached its contractual obligation as an advisor by giving improper advice, motivated by the fact that the bank would itself be the counterparty to the advised trade. This is, in substance, the same allegation as might be made by pleading that the bank had a fiduciary relationship with the company, and was therefore under an obligation not to allow a conflict between its obligation as advisor and its personal interest as potential counterparty.

8.11 Many of the complaints against professional advisors, and in particular accountants and lawyers, deal with the question of conflicts of interest when a professional firm seeks to act for a third party, whose interests are inimical to, or at least conflict with, those of a former

---

[2] For a detailed discussion of the law of fiduciary obligations in dealings in the securities industry, see Law Commission: Consultation Paper No 215 *Fiduciary Duties of Investment Intermediaries*, October 2013.

client. In practice, these cases usually turn on the duties owed by the firm to its former client, relating to confidential information. What often appears to be an argument about the detailed rules of professional procedure relating to conflicts of interest are, as far as the courts are concerned, about the protection of confidential information acquired by the firm in circumstances that give rise to fiduciary duties on its part not to misuse it.

Whether a court will find, or will not find, a fiduciary relationship in a particular situation depends on the facts. All of the law in this area flows from the finding by a judge that on the facts placed before him or her, one of the parties assumed a fiduciary relationship to the other. The cases examined below show examples of situations where the courts have made this judgment. From the point of view of a practitioner, the principal difficulty with this area of the law lies in predicting the judgment of the court on this fundamental question. The judgment is always fact-sensitive, and it is this which makes this area of the law particularly difficult for advisors. **8.12**

Fiduciary Duties in Commercial Transactions

The starting point for the modern approach of the courts to the imposition of fiduciary duties in commercial dealings is encapsulated in two sentences from the judgment in the New Zealand case *DHL International (NZ) Ltd v Richmond Ltd*:[3] **8.13**

> Arm's length commercial transactions rarely give rise to fiduciary obligations. They are matters of contract where the parties reasonably expect their contract to govern, rather than matters of conscience.

However, this is a generalization to which there are important exceptions. Simply to describe a transaction as 'commercial' does not decide whether it takes place within the context of a fiduciary relationship. The fact situations in commercial transactions and relationships are subject to an infinite range of subtle differences. It would be impossible to devise a number of categories and to assume that any potential set of facts would fall neatly within one of them. However, the attitude of the courts in recent years has shown a number of different trends: in some cases the courts have been ready to find a traditional form of fiduciary relationship and to order remedies accordingly; in others they have been much more reluctant to accept that a relationship of trust and confidence exists; and in others they have focused on one particular aspect of the commercial relationship which marks it as having a special flavour. The cases discussed under the sub-headings below do no more than indicate a shifting emphasis on the importance of the special duties that flow from a fiduciary relationship, depending on the type of situation with which the court is faced. **8.14**

Personal agency

Some relationships, although they arise in a commercial context, show an element of trust which is every bit as clear as that in the case of a trustee and individual beneficiaries. The **8.15**

---
[3] [1993] 3 NZLR 10.

commercial situation in which this relationship occurs is that of agency: where one person is given the authority to negotiate a transaction on behalf of another. The principal relies upon the agent to do the best that he can for the principal. The principal, particularly if he or she is commercially unsophisticated, is vulnerable to the possibility that the agent might breach this obligation of loyalty.

8.16 The principle can be seen with remarkable clarity in the 2009 decision of the Court of Appeal in *Imageview Management Ltd v Kelvin Jack*.[4] Mr Jack was a professional footballer. He was the goalkeeper for Trinidad and Tobago. In 2004 he decided that he wanted to play in the UK. He had some contact with Dundee United and asked a football agent, Mr Berry, to negotiate with the club for him. Mr Berry, acting through his company, Imageview Ltd, agreed to act as Mr Jack's agent for the purposes of negotiating a contract for him.

8.17 Mr Berry negotiated a two-year deal for Mr Jack. Mr Jack was to pay 10 per cent of his salary to Imageview. One year into his contract, Mr Jack discovered that, at the time the contract had been negotiated, Mr Berry had agreed with the club that Imageview would also be paid £3,000 by the club for its help in obtaining a work permit for Mr Jack. The permit was necessary because Mr Jack was not an EU citizen. When Mr Jack raised with Mr Berry the question of the commission which Imageview had been paid, he was told that it was none of his business. He stopped paying any part of his salary to Imageview. He sued for a return of the amounts that he had already paid, and also for an account of the £3,000 commission that Imageview had received from Dundee United.

8.18 In the first paragraph of his judgment, Jacob LJ put the issue very simply:

> What if a footballer's agent, in negotiating for his client, makes a secret deal with the club for himself on the side? That is what this case is about. It would not have happened if Mr Mike Berry (whose company, Imageview Ltd, was the footballer's agent) had been open. If he had told his client … that when he was going to negotiate for Mr Jack to sign for Dundee United, he was also going to make a deal with the club for himself about getting a work permit for Mr Jack, then, if Mr Jack had had no objection, there would have been no problem. Instead of doing that Mr Berry made a secret deal.

8.19 At first instance, the court had held that Imageview had committed a breach of fiduciary duty. When it chose to negotiate a deal for itself with the club, it had a clear conflict of interest. There was, at the very least, the possibility that the fees negotiated for itself with the club would reduce the amount that the club was prepared to pay Mr Jack. In addition, the existence of the commission arrangement was a reason why the agent might wish Mr Jack to sign for Dundee United, rather than for another club which had not agreed to pay any such commission. Jacob LJ agreed that acting in this way amounted to a breach of duty by Imageview:

> The law imposes on agents' high standards. Footballers' agents are not exempt from these. An agent's own personal interests come entirely second to the interest of his client. If you undertake to act for a man you must act 100%, body and soul, for him. You must act as if you were him. You must not allow your own interest to get in the way without telling him.

---

[4] [2009] EWCA Civ 63.

An undisclosed but realistic possibility of a conflict of interest is a breach of your duty of good faith to your client.

8.20 In support of this robust statement of the law, Jacob LJ referred to cases stretching back over a century and a quarter, to demonstrate that the fiduciary duties of a commercial agent are the same today as they have always been.

8.21 In *Boston Deep Sea Fishing v Ansell*,[5] the managing director of a company had, on behalf of the company, placed orders for fishing vessels. He had agreed with the shipbuilder that he would be paid a personal commission on the deals, and this arrangement was unknown to anyone else in the company. The Court of Appeal held that he was liable to account to the company for his commission. Bowen LJ said:[6]

> Now, there can be no question that an agent employed by a principal or master to do business with another, who, unknown to that principal or master, takes from that other person a profit arising out of the business which he is employed to transact, is doing a wrongful act inconsistent with his duty towards his master, and the continuance of confidence between them.

8.22 In the same case, Fry LJ used the language often adopted to describe wilful breaches of fiduciary duty as a form of 'equitable fraud':[7]

> In my judgment, the conduct of Ansell in so dealing was a fraud – a fraud on his principals – a fraud, not according to any artificial or technical rules, but according to the simple dictates of conscience, and according to the broad principles of morality and law ...

8.23 The principle is one which is to be tested objectively. It does not matter that the agent did not believe he was acting improperly, nor that such arrangements were common. As Fry LJ said:[8]

> We were invited to consider the state of mind of Mr Ansell; whether he thought it wrong; in other words we are invited to take as a standard for our decision the alleged conscience of a fraudulent servant. I decline to accept any such rule as one on which the Court is to decide such questions.

Accordingly, Mr Ansell was required to account to the company for the commission he had received, and was not allowed to claim unpaid salary to which he would otherwise have been entitled.

8.24 In *Rhodes v MacAlister*,[9] an agent had acted for a principal in finding a seller of certain mineral rights. The agreement was that, if the agent could find a seller who was prepared to accept less than £9,000, the agent would be entitled to a commission equal to half the difference between the price and £9,000. The agent found such a deal. However, he secretly negotiated with the seller to be paid a commission on the sale. The agent's claim to be paid commission by the principal failed. Scrutton LJ said:

> The law I take to be this: that an agent must not take remuneration from the other side without both disclosure to and consent from his principal. If he does take such

---

[5] (1888) 39 Ch D 339.
[6] At p 363.
[7] At p 368.
[8] At p 368.
[9] (1923) 29 Com Cas 19.

remuneration he acts so adversely to his employer that he forfeits all remuneration from the employer, although the employer takes the benefit and has not suffered a loss by it.

8.25 The consequence of a breach of fiduciary duty by an agent is extreme. Not only does he lose his right to be paid the fee or commission by his principal, he must also account for any secret profit that he has made. In the case of traditional dealings between trustees and beneficiaries, those remedies flow from the wish of equity to restore the position of the trust which has been damaged by the breach. As far as commercial transactions are concerned, the position can be put more simply. It is a policy decision by the courts. It is a way of enforcing commercial honesty. Jacob LJ said:

> The policy reason runs as follows. We are here concerned not with merely damages such as those for a tort or breach of contract but with what the remedy should be when the agent has betrayed the trust reposed in him – notions of equity and conscience are brought into play. Necessarily such a betrayal may not come to light. If all the agent has to pay if and when he is found out are damages the temptation to betray the trust reposed in him is all the greater. So the strict rule is there as a real deterrent to betrayal. As Scrutton LJ said in *Rhodes* at p 28: 'The more that principle is enforced, the better for the honesty of commercial transactions.'

8.26 The operation of the concept of fiduciary duties in these situations is very clear and easy to understand. 'If you undertake to act for a man you must act 100%, body and soul, for him. You must act as if you were him.'[10] Without the belief that this would happen, those engaged in commercial activity, whether individuals or corporations, would not have the confidence to give to agents the authority which they needed, in order for commercial transactions to proceed smoothly and efficiently. In this area, the view of the courts has not moved at all in the last century.[11]

Arm's-length investment

8.27 In recent decades, there has been a growth in the volume and reach of consumer legislation which imposes duties on suppliers and gives rights to their customers beyond those which would otherwise be available. Leaving aside such statutory provisions, however, the courts have shown a marked reluctance to accept that equity should step into matters of contract between private companies and individuals, when the issues in dispute between them have settled and predictable consequences under the law of contract. The clearest expression of this attitude is perhaps seen in the Privy Council decision in *Re Goldcorp Exchange Ltd*,[12] an appeal from the Court of Appeal of New Zealand.

---

[10] Jacob LJ in *Imageview v Jack*.
[11] See also *Wilson and another v Hurstanger Ltd* [2007] EWCA Civ 299, where the agent acting for mortgage borrowers received a commission from the lender. The Court of Appeal held that, even though the loan documentation disclosed the fact that the lender might pay a commission to the introducing broker, the failure to tell the borrowers the amount of the commission meant that the agent had received a 'secret' commission. He was liable for breach of his fiduciary duty. Further, the lender was itself liable to the borrowers, because the lender had assisted in the breach of fiduciary duty.
[12] [1995] 1 AC 74.

Goldcorp was a New Zealand company, which was a dealer in gold and other precious **8.28**
metals. It embarked on a programme of inviting members of the public to buy gold. Its brochures detailed two ways in which the purchase might be effected. The first method was by physical delivery, where the customer paid the purchase price for an amount of gold, and the gold was delivered to him by Goldcorp in the form of coins or ingots. It would then be a matter for the customer how he chose to safeguard his asset. The second approach was the so-called non-allocated method. One of Goldcorp's brochures described the process as follows:

> Basically you agree to buy and sell as with physical bullion, but receive a certificate of ownership rather than the metal. The metal is stored in a vault on your behalf.
>
> ...
>
> The metal stocks of Goldcorp are audited monthly by Peat Marwick, to ensure that there are sufficient stocks to meet all commitments.

Goldcorp's promise was that it would, at all times, hold stocks of bullion sufficient in size to allow it to deliver to all of its customers the amount of gold which they had contracted to buy, and for which they had already paid.

In the event, Goldcorp became hopelessly insolvent and a receiver was appointed by the **8.29**
Bank of New Zealand, which held a floating charge over all of the company's assets. It was discovered that the amount of gold owned by Goldcorp was nowhere near enough to satisfy its obligations to deliver metal to its customers. Indeed, there was not a sufficient value of gold to satisfy the claims of the floating charge holder.

There was no doubt at all that Goldcorp was in breach of contract in relation to each of its **8.30**
non-allocated customers. Their right to damages was, however, of no use to them, since the insolvent company would not have any money with which to pay, once the floating charge holder had taken all the assets that were available. The only hope of the non-allocated customers to recover anything was to persuade a court that they were the owners of Goldcorp's stock of gold (such as it was) as a matter of law. Failing this, they might persuade the court that equity should intervene to grant them a proprietary interest in the stock of gold as a restitutionary remedy.

The first question was whether a non-allocated customer acquired a property interest **8.31**
in gold by virtue of his contract of purchase with Goldcorp. The answer was that he did not. Section 18 of the Sale of Goods Act 1908 (New Zealand) provided that property in unallocated goods does not pass until the goods concerned are separated out and appropriated to the fulfilment of the contract concerned. As a matter of contract law, the non-allocated customers had no property claims in the gold assets of Goldcorp. Their only remedy lay in a claim for damages resulting from Goldcorp's failure to deliver gold to them as it had promised. This claim for damages would result in a fruitless proof in the liquidation of the company.

Accordingly, the non-allocated claimants deployed two other arguments, each of which was **8.32**
designed to show that they were entitled in equity to the ownership of the stock of metal. The first argument was that the promises which the company had made (ie to keep the stock safe and maintain a stock sufficient in size to meet its obligations) amounted to a declaration

of trust by the company in favour of the non-allocated customers, in respect of its stock of gold. The Privy Council rejected this argument. It simply did not accord with the terms of the contracts. When a customer agreed to buy gold, it was not suggested that the gold concerned was already owned by the company. The company merely promised that it would, when the customer asked for delivery, provide the amount of gold that he had bought. The contract of sale did not relate to the sale of specific gold which was identified at the time of the contract, or which was to be acquired by the company in order to fulfil its contractual obligations. It was a contract for the sale of 'generic' goods without stipulation as to the source from which they were to be obtained by the seller.

8.33 The non-allocated claimants therefore fell back on an argument based on the existence of a fiduciary relationship between Goldcorp and each of its non-allocated customers. Lord Mustill described the argument as follows:

> First, it is said that because the company held itself out as willing to vest bullion in the customer and to hold it in safe custody on behalf of him in circumstances where he was totally dependant on the company, and trusted the company to do what it had promised without in practice there being any means of verification, the company was a fiduciary. From this it is deduced that the company as fiduciary created an equity by inviting the customer to look on and treat stocks vested in it as his own, which could appropriately be recognised only by treating the customer as entitled to a proprietary interest in the stock.

8.34 The route by which an argument, which starts from the assertion that someone is a fiduciary, leads to a conclusion that the claimant is entitled to an equitable remedy is in three stages:

1. By virtue of the circumstances surrounding the relationship between A and B, A is a fiduciary for B.
2. The consequence of A being a fiduciary is that he owes certain duties, based on his obligations of loyalty, which are in addition to those which he would otherwise owe to B by virtue of their contractual relationship.
3. The breach of these fiduciary duties (but not the breach of any of his other contractual duties) invokes the assistance of equity and the availability of equitable remedies.

8.35 In the present case, the difficulty for the claimants lay in the fact that it was impossible to identify any duties which flowed from Goldcorp's relationship with its customers and which were not set out explicitly as one of the commercial terms of the agreement between them. Lord Mustill puts it as follows:

> But what kind of fiduciary duties did the company owe to the customer? None have [sic] been suggested beyond those which the company assumed under the contracts of sale read with the collateral promises; namely to deliver the goods and meanwhile to keep a separate stock of bullion (or, more accurately, separate stocks of each variety of bullion) to which the customers could look as a safeguard for performance when delivery was called for. No doubt the fact that one person is placed in a particular position vis-à-vis another through the medium of a contract does not necessarily mean that he does not also owe fiduciary duties to that other by virtue of being in that position. The essence of a fiduciary relationship is that it creates obligations of a different character from those deriving from the contract itself. Their Lordships have not heard in argument any submission which went

beyond suggesting that by virtue of being a fiduciary the company was obliged honestly and conscientiously to do what it had by contract promised to do ... It is possible without misuse of language to say that the customers put faith in the company, and that their trust had not been repaid. But the vocabulary is misleading; high expectations do not necessarily lead to equitable remedies.

Thus, it was impossible to argue that there was a fiduciary relationship. Since the duties which, it was argued, Goldcorp owed to its customers were only the ones which flowed explicitly from the terms of its contract with them, it was meaningless to say that Goldcorp was a fiduciary. Its relationship did not give rise to any special fiduciary duties. It followed that there could be no equitable remedies for their breach. **8.36**

Commercial agency

In some situations, an individual is required to appoint an agent who has a wide discretionary power to influence the affairs of his principal, or where circumstances make the principal particularly vulnerable. In these cases, the courts take a very robust view of their role in protecting a person whose trust might be abused. Examples of these kinds of relationship are those examined in the *Kelvin Jack* case and in *Wilson v Hunstanger Ltd*.[13] There are, however, a far greater number of situations where an agent is appointed to perform a very specific task. The principal makes the appointment in order to achieve a very limited objective, for example, the appointment of an agent to obtain and process a life insurance policy, or the appointment of an agent to sell a house. In these situations, the courts accept that the areas in relation to which the principal is vulnerable are quite limited. Although the relationship of agent and principal is essentially fiduciary in nature, the court will need to be convinced that the fiduciary has behaved badly, by the standards of normal commercial life, before it will authorize the grant of equitable remedies. **8.37**

This approach reflects the view of Millett LJ, expressed in *Bristol & West Building Society v Mothew*,[14] that the 'special' duties which the law requires a fiduciary to fulfil, in addition to those which he has specifically undertaken, whether by contract or otherwise: **8.38**

> ... merely reflect different aspects of his core duties of loyalty and fidelity. Breach of fiduciary obligation, therefore, connotes disloyalty or infidelity.

Whether a fiduciary has been disloyal is, of course, a question of fact in each case. However, the purpose of some agency relationships is so limited and circumscribed that the question of loyalty or disloyalty may arise only rarely.

This principle is set out in the Privy Council decision in *Kelly v Cooper*,[15] an appeal from the Court of Appeal of Bermuda. Mr Kelly owned a large detached house in Bermuda. The land included the frontage on a creek which opened out to the sea. He instructed the respondents, a well-known local firm of estate agents, to act as his agent in selling his house. They **8.39**

---

[13] See paras 8.15 *et seq* above.
[14] [1998] Ch 1.
[15] [1993] AC 205.

were to try to find a purchaser for his house. If they did so, he agreed to pay a commission based on a percentage of the sale price. At around the same time, the owner of the neighbouring house, a Mr Brant, instructed the same firm of agents to sell his house. Mr Brant's property fronted the other side of the creek. Together, the land attached to the two properties surrounded the creek.

8.40 The agents set to work. They showed the houses to various purchasers. One purchaser, Mr Ross Perot, made an offer to buy Mr Brant's house. Mr Brant accepted the offer. Mr Perot then approached the agents and offered to buy Mr Kelly's house. The agents notified Mr Kelly of the offer, but did not tell him that the same purchaser had already agreed to buy Mr Brant's house. Mr Kelly accepted the offer, and both sales were completed.

8.41 Mr Kelly then began proceedings against the agents. He said that their relationship was a fiduciary one, and that one of the fiduciary duties owed by an agent to his principal is to inform the principal of anything relevant to the agency which might affect the principal's interests. The agents had not told Mr Kelly that Mr Perot, when making his offer, had already agreed to buy the neighbouring house. Mr Kelly's contention was that one of the reasons for the purchase of his house was that Mr Perot, by making that purchase, would turn the creek into a private mooring basin, since he would own all land contiguous to it. That gave his land a special 'marriage' value which it would not have had for other purchasers. Had Mr Kelly known of Mr Perot's purchase of the neighbouring land, he could almost certainly have demanded and received a higher price. The agents, he said, were in breach of their fiduciary duty to him. He was entitled to damages for the breach of this duty. In addition, a consequence of the breach was that the agents should forfeit their right to commission on his sale.

8.42 The Privy Council found in favour of the agents. The court of first instance had found in favour of Mr Kelly. Its reasoning had started from the proposition that: 'An agent is, in general, under a duty to keep his principal informed about matters which are of his concern.'[16] One of the fiduciary duties of the agents to Mr Kelly was to inform Mr Kelly of the agreed purchase of the neighbouring property. The failure to pass on the information was a breach of fiduciary duty.[17] This was one of the fiduciary duties of the agents, and they were liable for their failure to comply with it.

8.43 The Board looked at the matter differently. Propositions such as that accepted at first instance might well be true, as a general guideline to the content of agency contracts. However, each contract, and each relationship that flowed from it, was different. The duties depended on the facts:

> In the view of the Board the resolution of this case depends upon two fundamental propositions: first, agency as a contract made between principal and agent; second, like every other contract, the rights and duties of the principal and agent are dependent upon the terms of the contract between them, whether express or implied. It is not possible to say

---

[16] F. M. B. Reynolds, *Bowstead on Agency* (15th edn, Sweet & Maxwell, 1985), p 147.
[17] The court at first instance had accepted that the agents owed a duty of confidentiality to Mr Brant, which precluded them from fulfilling their duty to Mr Kelly. Nonetheless, it held that, although they could not have been compelled to make disclosure to Mr Kelly, they were liable for their failure to do so.

that all agents owe the same duties to their principals: it is always necessary to have regard to the express or implied terms of the contract.

8.44 The relationship between estate agents and their principals appointed to sell a house is not necessarily the same as that between a principal and other kinds of agents. In the case of the estate agent, an appointor will normally choose the agent because the agent is well known to represent many sellers of the kind of house concerned. That reputation is the reason why potential purchasers would contact that particular agent when looking for a house. An appointor not only knows that the agent may be acting for other people selling similar properties, he usually chooses the agent because he acts for such other sellers. The agent does, of course, owe a duty to each of his principals to do his best for them. It is obvious, however, that his fulfilment of this duty in relation to principal A, to whom he directs a potential purchaser, will mean that he has not directed that purchaser to principal B. There is, of course, a conflict between the interests of the two clients. However, both of those clients know of this situation before they appoint the agent.

8.45 In the course of acting for each of its principals, an estate agent is likely to acquire information which is confidential to that principal. It cannot sensibly be said that the agent has a duty to disclose to each of its other principals information which it is bound, by its fiduciary duties to another principal, to keep confidential. The only way in which this position can be reconciled is by taking the view that the contract between an appointing principal and an estate agent recognizes that the agent has no duty to inform the principal of matters, in relation to which the agent is under a duty of confidentiality to another client. As Lord Browne-Wilkinson said:

> Accordingly, in such cases there must be an implied term of the contract with such an agent that he is entitled to act for other principals selling competing properties and to keep confidential the information obtained from each of his principals.

8.46 So far, the decision of the Board had related to the terms of the contract of agency. The existence or absence or particular obligations had been considered as a matter of contract law, in the light of the purpose and nature of the contract of agency. The question of fiduciary duties (in the sense of duties imposed by equity, rather than only as a matter of interpretation of the contract) was addressed differently, but led to the same result:

> Similar considerations apply to the fiduciary duties of agents. The existence and scope of these duties depends upon the terms on which they are acting.

To explain the interaction between the terms of the agency contract and the obligations imposed by equity because of the fiduciary nature of the relationship, the Board quoted the words of Mason J in an Australian case, *Hospital Products Ltd v United States Surgical Corp*:[18]

> That contractual and fiduciary relationships may co-exist between the same parties has never been doubted. Indeed, the existence of a basic contractual relationship has in many situations provided a foundation for the erection of a fiduciary relationship. In these situations it is the contractual foundation which is all important because it is the contract

---

[18] (1984) 156 CLR 41, at 97.

that regulates the basic rights and liabilities of the parties. The fiduciary relationship, if it is to exist at all, must accommodate itself to the terms of the contract so that it is consistent with, and conforms to, them. The fiduciary relationships cannot be superimposed upon the contract in such a way as to alter the operation which the contract was intended to have according to its true construction.

8.47 Combining these two lines of thought, the conclusion of the Board in relation to Mr Kelly's claim was that:

> ... the scope of the fiduciary duties owed by the defendants to the plaintiff (and in particular the alleged duty not to put themselves in a position where their duty and their interest conflicted) are to be defined by the terms of the contract of agency.

Accordingly, in the circumstances, the contract between Mr Kelly and his agents cannot have included terms which: (a) precluded the agents from acting for other vendors; or (b) requiring the agents to disclose to the principal information which was confidential to other clients. There was, therefore, no breach of fiduciary duty.

8.48 The case represents an admirably clear statement, in the context of an agency relationship, of the general proposition that the existence of the fiduciary duty and the formulation of the terms of it must depend on the nature of the relationships and the factual circumstances.[19] There is, however, a slightly confusing footnote. Mr Kelly had claimed not only damages from his agents, but also the right to withhold payment of their agreed commission. Although the Board found that there had been no breach of fiduciary duty, it said *obiter* that, even if a breach of fiduciary duty had been proved, they would not have lost their right to commission unless they had acted dishonestly. Although the matter did not arise, the Board approved the statement on the basis of the decision in *Keppel v Wheeler*.[20] The puzzling aspect of this statement is the acceptance that there might be 'honest' breaches of fiduciary duty, even though the breach of a fiduciary duty, as Millett LJ said, 'connotes dishonesty'.

8.49 The explanation lies in the fact that, although the exact formulation of a fiduciary duty will in each case be an emanation of a general duty of fidelity and loyalty, a specific duty as formulated becomes an objective obligation, whose identity does not include an element of honesty. Although the exact terms of the obligation spring from a duty to act honestly and properly, it does not follow that any breach must involve dishonesty.

8.50 In *Keppel v Wheeler*, estate agents acting for a seller had received instructions from him to accept an offer subject to contract. They had done so, but had later received a further offer from the same purchaser, for a larger sum. They did not pass on this later offer to their client, because of the mistaken view on their part that their obligations to the seller had terminated when he had accepted the original offer. Thus, they were in breach of their duty to keep him informed of matters touching his interests, but the breach did not come out of any dishonest intention on their part. In these circumstances, the court found that they were able to keep their commission.

---

[19] See *New Zealand Netherlands Society 'Oranje' Inc v Kuys* [1973] 1 WLR 1126, at 1129–30.
[20] [1927] 1 KB 577.

8.51 The remedies for breach of fiduciary duty are, being equitable in nature, a matter of discretion for the court. The *obiter* statement in *Kelly v Cooper* and the decision in *Keppel v Wheeler* should be taken as examples of situations in which the court would not grant a remedy, even if a breach of fiduciary duty had been found.

Joint ventures

8.52 A particular difficulty arises in analyzing the relationships between parties to a commercial joint venture. The phrase 'joint venture' embraces a very wide range of commercial activities. At one end of the spectrum, the relationship between joint venturers may be, as a matter of law, a partnership where each gives to the other a very wide discretion to commit the credit and resources of both parties. At the other end of the scale, a joint venture may be no more than a decision by two shareholders in a company that they should, in relation to certain corporate matters, vote their shares in the same way. Whether the arrangement gives rise to a fiduciary relationship is, of course, a matter of fact for the court to determine.

8.53 Further, the question is to be determined not merely by an examination of the terms of the joint venture agreement reached between the parties. A fiduciary relationship in relation to a joint venture may arise before any such agreement is concluded. During negotiations about its possibility, one of the parties may give to the other confidential information, the disclosure of which may itself create a fiduciary relationship. In *United Dominions Corp Ltd v Brian Pty Ltd*,[21] a decision of the High Court of Australia, the court said:

> A fiduciary relationship can arise and fiduciary duties can exist between parties who have not reached, and who may never reach, agreement upon the consensual terms which are to govern the arrangement between them. In particular, a fiduciary relationship attendant to fiduciary obligations may, and ordinarily will, exist between prospective partners who have embarked upon the conduct of the partnership business or venture before the precise terms of any agreement have been settled. Indeed, in such circumstances, the mutual confidence and trust which underlie most consensual fiduciary relationships are likely to be more readily apparent than in the case where mutual rights and obligations have been expressly defined in some form of agreement.

8.54 The difficulty faced in predicting whether a court will find such a relationship to exist can be seen clearly by examining two cases, one in England and the other in Canada.

8.55 The case of *Murad v Al-Saraj*[22] came before the High Court in 2004. Mr Al-Saraj had been born in Iraq, but had lived in England for many years. He was a businessman with interests in several countries. One of his businesses consisted of locating in the UK property investments for non-residents, and managing those investments. In 1995, Mr Al-Saraj acted on behalf of a Kuwaiti national, Mr Al-Abrash, in connection with the purchase of a hotel in Clapham. Following the acquisition of the hotel, Mr Al-Saraj took responsibility for the management on behalf of the owner. In 1997, Mr Al-Abrash decided to sell the hotel. Mr Al-Saraj was interested in buying it for himself. He had met, a couple of years before, Mrs

---

[21] (1985) 157 CLR 1.
[22] [2004] EWHC 1235 (Ch).

Murad. She lived in Bahrain and, along with her sister, had inherited a large amount of money from her father. She had spoken to Mr Al-Saraj about the possibility of acquiring a property investment in England.

8.56 After discussion, an arrangement was concluded under which Mr Al-Saraj, Mrs Murad, and Mrs Murad's sister would establish a jointly owned company to acquire the hotel. The company would buy the hotel for a total price of £4.1 million. The Murad sisters would contribute £1 million, Mr Al-Saraj would contribute £500,000, and the remainder would be raised by bank borrowings. The hotel would continue to be managed by Mr Al-Saraj, the three joint venturers each receiving one-third of the profit. On any subsequent sale of the hotel, the profit would be split equally between the Murad sisters on the one hand, and Mr Al-Saraj on the other.

8.57 The sale proceeded. However, the transfer price quoted was not £4.1 million, but rather £3.6 million. No part of this cash was contributed by Mr Al-Saraj. Unknown to the Murad sisters, Mr Al-Saraj had negotiated that he should receive an introductory commission from Mr Al-Abrash of £369,000. In addition, it was claimed that he was entitled to other payments of £131,000 from Mr Al-Abrash. Accordingly, the £500,000 which Mr Al-Sarah had agreed to contribute to the joint venture was in fact provided by way of set-off. Most of the set-off related to a commission which Mr Al-Saraj had negotiated without the knowledge of his co-venturers.

8.58 The hotel was ultimately sold for a substantial profit. The Murad sisters then claimed that Mr Al-Saraj was in breach of fiduciary duties owed to them, and that they were entitled to an account of the profit which he had received.

8.59 The court held that there was, indeed, a fiduciary relationship and a breach of fiduciary duty:

> ... Mr Al-Saraj did owe fiduciary duties to the claimants in relation to the joint venture to acquire the Hotel ... prior to the proposal by Mr Al-Saraj for the acquisition of the Hotel, the relationship between Mr Al-Saraj and Mrs Murad was one in which Mrs Murad, who lived abroad, looked to Mr Al-Saraj, who was an Iraqi businessman living and working in England, to make appropriate recommendations to her and to assist her in connection with possible investments in England. The reality was, as Mr Al-Saraj was well aware, that the Claimants were wholly dependent upon Mr Al-Saraj for his advice and recommendation in relation to the Hotel, and for the negotiations with Mr Al-Abrash ... [and] the instruction of professionals on their behalf, including in relation to the structure of the transaction and the documentation. The relationship between them was a classic one in which the Claimant reposed trust and confidence in Mr Al-Saraj by virtue of their relative and respective positions.

8.60 One might, at first sight, question the last sentence in the passage quoted above. The court found that the Murads trusted Mr Al-Saraj 'by virtue of their relative and respective positions'. One might argue that the Murads trusted Mr Al-Saraj because they chose to do so. In most fiduciary relationships, the person who reposes the trust has no practical alternative but to do so. A client who goes to a solicitor for advice, or the beneficiary of a trust who relies upon the trustee to carry out his trust properly is vulnerable to abuse by the fiduciary and cannot in practice avoid this. In the present case, the Murads chose to trust Mr Al-Saraj in relation to all matters connected with their business dealings. It was not necessary that they should have done so. They could have instructed solicitors, or another third party, to check that what they were being told was correct. Had they done this, they would not have been deceived. One might conclude that, far from being a classic case of a fiduciary relationship, this is an unusual situation, perhaps akin to that in *Lloyds Bank Ltd v Bundy*,[23] where, on unusual and special facts, a fiduciary relationship exists.

8.61 However, there is another way to see the facts. Although the description by the court of the arrangement as a 'joint venture' connotes an arm's-length commercial arrangement, the court may have seen the arrangement rather as an investment by the Murad sisters, for the purposes of which they had enlisted the help of an advisor, on whom they had relied to find the investment for them. The fact that he represented that he proposed to be a co-investor with them did not alter the 'quasi-agency' nature of their relationship.

8.62 When the case came to the Court of Appeal[24] the questions in dispute did not concern the existence of a fiduciary relationship. The finding of fact that there was such a relationship was accepted by all parties. The dispute in the Court of Appeal related to the consequences of that finding. Once again, the argument was about the availability of equitable remedies. It was not disputed that Mr Al-Saraj had made misrepresentations in relation to his contract with the Murads. Nor, indeed, was it disputed that those representations were fraudulent. The matter for debate was whether he should be required to hand over to the Murads all of the profit which he had made on the sale of the hotel. It was held that the trial judge had been correct to order that he should. Arden LJ said:

> It would be tempting to jump to the conclusion ... that in this case the judge took the novel step of awarding the equitable remedy of account for the common law tort of deceit ... but that is not in my judgment the true interpretation of the judge's judgment. The judge gave a remedy of account because there was a fiduciary relationship. For wrongs in the context of such a relationship, an order for an account of profits is a conventional remedy. The Murads considered that that remedy will be more beneficial to them because, if they were awarded damages at common law, they would simply be entitled to recover the difference between the profit share to which they agreed and that which they would have negotiated if the true position had been disclosed to them.

8.63 The Court of Appeal agreed that the appropriate remedy in this case was an order for an account of profits. It was quite clear that the purpose behind this order was not one of compensation for the breach of duty concerned. It had the object of clawing back from the defaulting fiduciary any profit that he had made. Arden LJ said:

> Equity recognises that there are legal wrongs for which damages are not the appropriate remedy. In some situations therefore, as in this case, a court of equity instead awards an account of profits ... the purpose of the account is to strip a defaulting fiduciary of his profit.

She quoted with approval a statement of Morritt LJ in *United Pan-Europe Ltd v Deutsche Bank AG*:[25]

---

[23] [1975] 1 QB 326, and see paras 7.58 *et seq*.
[24] [2005] EWCA Civ 959.
[25] [2000] 2 BCLC 461.

... it is not in doubt that the object of the equitable remedies of an account or the imposition of a constructive trust is to ensure that the defaulting fiduciary does not retain the profit; it is not to compensate the beneficiary for any loss.

Jonathan Parker LJ was of the same view:

It is thus clear on authority, in my judgment, that the 'no conflict' rule is neither compensatory nor restitutionary: rather, it is designed to strip the fiduciary of the unauthorised profits he has made whilst he is in a position of conflict.

In this case, therefore, the consequences of the finding that there was a fiduciary relationship between the parties to the joint venture were far more severe for Mr Al-Saraj than would have been the case, had the court found only that he had committed a fraudulent misrepresentation in connection with a commercial contract.

8.64 A contrasting case dealing with joint venture relationships is the decision of the Supreme Court of Canada in *Lac Minerals Ltd v International Corona Resources Ltd*.[26] The case is important for two reasons. First, two of the judgments in the case explore in detail the extent to which fiduciary relationships can exist in a commercial setting, particularly in the context of joint venture arrangements between corporations. In addition, the case examines the close relationship between claims for breach of confidence and claims for breach of fiduciary duty.

8.65 Corona, described in the report as a 'junior' mining company, was exploring property which it owned in search of gold deposits. It published some of its data, indicating that it might well have located a valuable source of gold. In response to the publication, Corona was approached by Lac, referred to as a 'senior' mining company. A meeting was held between executives of the two companies, in which Corona explained in more detail the information which it had published. It also shared with Lac other information which had not been published. This further data indicated that major deposits were to be found on adjacent land. Particularly promising was land owned by Mrs Williams. The Lac executives advised Corona that Corona should buy the Williams' land if at all possible.

8.66 Following the meeting, various exchanges took place between Lac and Corona, which explored the possibility of forming a joint venture for the exploitation of the potential deposits. Although Corona had the expertise to exploit the opportunity, it did not have the financial muscle to do so. In the event, the proposed joint venture did not proceed. Corona, which had by this stage acquired other backers, approached Mrs Williams with an offer to buy her land. She told them that she had already received an offer for the land, but invited them to make a formal proposal in writing. They made such a formal offer, which was rejected on the basis that the alternative proposal was higher. It then emerged that the other buyer was Lac.

8.67 Corona brought proceedings against Lac, arguing its case on two bases. First, the relationship between the two companies, which were exploring the possibility of a joint venture,

---

[26] [1989] 2 SCR 574 (Canada).

was a fiduciary one, and Lac's profiting from the knowledge which it gained through its fiduciary position was a breach of its fiduciary duty to Corona. Alternatively, Corona had a claim for breach of confidence at common law. Lac had been given information which it knew to be confidential, solely for the purpose of evaluating the possibility of a joint venture with Corona. It had used that information for its own purposes to the detriment of Corona and was liable accordingly.

All members of the court found that Lac was liable to Corona in respect of its misuse of confidential information. On the question of fiduciary duty, three of the judges held that there was no fiduciary relationship arising out of the negotiation of the proposed joint venture. One held that there was such a relationship. The fifth held that no fiduciary relationship existed by virtue of the negotiations, but that the divulging of confidential information during those negotiations created a fiduciary relationship in relation to that information. The misuse of the information was therefore also a breach of fiduciary duty. **8.68**

Issue 1: The existence of a fiduciary relationship
Sopinka J stressed that there was a general reluctance on the part of courts to make a finding that a fiduciary relationship existed in a commercial context unless it was essential. In such a situation, the parties have the opportunity to set out their mutual obligations. The contractual remedies available to them, in the event of breach of any of those obligations, should be sufficient. To describe one of the parties as a fiduciary exposes him potentially to a variety of equitable remedies, many of which were not designed to provide compensation to the wronged party in a commercial transaction, but to deprive the wrongdoer of his gain. Not only are the equitable remedies for breach of fiduciary duty a 'blunt tool',[27] but its overuse would damage the effectiveness of equitable remedies. On this latter point, he quoted Lord Selborne LC in *Barnes v Addy*:[28] **8.69**

> It is equally important to maintain the doctrine of trusts which is established in this court, and not to strain it by unreasonable construction beyond its due and proper limits. There would be no better mode of undermining the sound doctrines of equity than to make unreasonable and inequitable applications of them.

Sopinka J's approach is encapsulated in the sentence:

> In my opinion, equity is a blunt tool and must be reserved for situations that are truly in need of the special protection that equity affords.

While stressing that situations are always fact-sensitive, Sopinka J concluded that the situations where a fiduciary obligations has been imposed have three general characteristics: **8.70**

1. The fiduciary has scope for the exercise of some discretion or power.
2. The fiduciary can unilaterally exercise that power or discretion so as to affect the beneficiary's legal or practical interest.
3. The beneficiary is peculiarly vulnerable to or at the mercy of the fiduciary holding the discretion or power.

---

[27] Quoting from Professor E. Weinrib, 'The Fiduciary Obligation' (1975) 25 *University of Toronto LJ* 1, 4.
[28] (1874) 9 Ch App 244, at 251.

8.71 In the present case, the telling factor was that the element of vulnerability was missing:

> While it is perhaps possible to have a dependency of this sort between corporations, that cannot be so when, as here, we are dealing with experienced mining promoters who have ready access to geologists, engineers and lawyers.

He quoted with approval a statement by Wilson J in *Frame v Smith*:[29]

> Vulnerability arises from the inability of the beneficiary (despite his or her best efforts) to prevent the injurious exercise of the power or discretion combined with the grave inadequacy or absence of other legal or practical remedies to redress the wrongful exercise of the discretion of power. Because of the requirement of vulnerability of the beneficiary at the hands of the fiduciary, fiduciary obligations are seldom present in the dealings of experienced businessmen of similar bargaining strength acting at arm's length: ... The law take the position that such individuals are perfectly capable of agreeing as to the scope of discretion or power to be exercised, i.e., any 'vulnerability' could have been prevented through the more prudent exercise of their bargaining power and the remedies for the wrongful exercise or abuse of that discretion or power ... are adequate in such a case.

In the present case, Sopinka J was clear that no such vulnerability existed.

8.72 La Forest J took a different view. He divided the categories of fiduciary relationships into three. The first consists of those situations which almost always give rise to a fiduciary obligation (eg solicitor and client, directors and companies, trustees and beneficiaries). The second is composed of those cases where a fiduciary obligation arises as a matter of fact out of the specific circumstances. The third use of the word is, in his view, a misuse. It occurs when a court feels that the remedy available to it is inadequate, unless the relationship is defined as fiduciary. If it is so described, the remedies of equity become available. Accordingly, the relationship is described as fiduciary in order to bring about the availability of equitable remedies:

> In my view, this third use of the term fiduciary, used as a conclusion to justify a result, reads equity backwards. It is a misuse of the term.

In the present case, the question was whether the situation fell within the second category (ie whether, on its facts, a fiduciary relationship had been established). On this point, La Forest J disagreed with Sopinka J about the importance of the presence or absence of the factor of 'vulnerability'. In his view:

> ... the issue should be whether, having regard to all the facts and circumstances, one party stands in relation to the other such that it could reasonably be expected that the other would act or refrain from acting in a way contrary to the interests of that other.

In any event, in his opinion Corona was vulnerable to Lac. He rejected the argument that Corona could, had it wished, protected itself against misuse of the power which Lac was given by disclosure of the information.

---

[29] [1987] 2 SCR 99, at 137/138.

There is not a great deal of difference of argument among the judges in the *Lac Minerals* case. All are agreed that, in commercial dealings between arm's-length parties, a fiduciary relationship will not normally arise. The difference is one of degree. The majority took the view that the essential element of a fiduciary relationship was vulnerability, and that this would not exist if the party which was alleged to be vulnerable had the capacity and the opportunity to protect itself. The fact that it had chosen not to do so did not invoke the protection of equity. La Forest J, on the other hand, did not regard vulnerability as the key test, but rather focused on the expectation of behaviour on the part of the party claiming protection. In any event, he felt that Corona was, on the facts, vulnerable.   **8.73**

Issue 2: Confidentiality

All of the judges found that the use of the information provided to Lac by Corona was a breach of confidence and was actionable. The question at issue was the appropriate remedy to be granted. Sopinka J took the view that a claim for the misuse of confidential information did not rest solely on one of the traditional bases for action—contract, equity, or property—it involved elements of all three. The court had considerable flexibility in fashioning a remedy for breach. In most cases, damages would be an appropriate remedy and should apply here. There was no need to go so far as to imposing a constructive trust on Lac in relation to the property that it had acquired through misuse of confidential information.   **8.74**

La Forest J, with whom two other judges agreed, took a different view. Although the law relating to confidential information and that relating to fiduciary obligations are not the same, they are not distinct. They spring from the same origins. The two branches of law, although different, are intertwined. The main difference between the two, in practice, is that a claimant for breach of confidence must show that the information has been misused to his detriment. In the case of a claim of a fiduciary obligation, the object is to enforce the duty of loyalty of the fiduciary, and there is no need to show that the beneficiary suffered any detriment by virtue of the breach.   **8.75**

A further difference between the two branches of law is that, in the case of confidential information, both legal and equitable remedies are available, while only equitable remedies are available for the breach of a fiduciary duty. In the present case, it was appropriate that Lac should be subject to a constructive trust of the property purchased as a result of the misuse of confidential information, rather than simply being liable in damages.   **8.76**

Summary

Modern cases throughout the common law world show a clear view of the superior courts that the concept of fiduciary relationships or fiduciary duties in the context of arm's-length commercial dealings.[30] On the other hand, claimants will often wish to allege that the circumstances of their case are outside the norm. If a court can be persuaded that the relationship between the parties is a fiduciary one, any breach of a fiduciary duty will allow the imposition of equitable remedies—disgorgement of gain, constructive trust, etc, which might produce a much more lucrative result for the claimant. The difficulty for companies   **8.77**

---

[30] See the extensive list of references given by Sopinka J and La Forest J in the *Lac Minerals* case.

entering into commercial arrangements, who might see themselves a potential defendants, lies in predicting the factors which will most influence the court in deciding how to categorize the situation. For the majority in the *Lac Minerals* case, the weightiest factor was the vulnerability of the claimant, and in particular the inability of the claimant to protect himself against an abuse of power. The powerful dissenting voice of La Forest J, however, did not regard the test of vulnerability as nearly so important and, in any event, the judge thought that the claimant in that case was in fact vulnerable, notwithstanding that it could have protected itself against the abuse of the power given to the other party.

8.78 It is not only cases between large corporations that show the attitude of the commercial courts. In the *Goldcorp* case, the claimants were private individuals who had paid money to Goldcorp in the expectation that it would do as it had promised, and maintain a stock of gold sufficient to meet its obligations to all investors. In one sense, the claimants were extremely vulnerable. They relied on the company doing what it had promised to do. They had, in practice, no way of checking whether this was being done, or protecting their interests. Nonetheless, the Privy Council did not regard the relationship as a fiduciary one:

> Many commercial relationships involve just such a reliance by one party on the other, and to introduce the whole new dimension into such relationships which would flow from giving them a fiduciary character would (as it seems to their Lordships) have adverse consequences far exceeding those foreseen by Atkin LJ in *In re Wait*. It is possible without misuse of language to say that the customers put faith in the company, and that their trust has not been repaid. But the vocabulary is misleading; high expectations do not necessarily lead to equitable remedies.

8.79 The cases where the courts seem much more ready to find a fiduciary relationship are those which concern the misuse or protections of confidential information. As La Forest J pointed out in the *Lac Minerals* case, the relationship between a claim for breach of confidence and a claim for breach of fiduciary duty arising out of the misuse of by a fiduciary of confidential information is a very close one. The finding by a court of a breach of duty in such a case[31] should not be seen as a deviation from the general principle set out in the *Goldcorp* case and in *Kelly v Cooper*.

8.80 The case which seems, at first sight, to be at variance with the trend is *Murad v Al-Saraj*. The court at first instance had found that a fiduciary relationship existed. On appeal, the appellant accepted this finding, and there was no discussion of it in the Court of Appeal. The discussion concerned the appropriate remedy for a breach. The court in *Murad v Al-Saraj* took the view that the Murads were entirely dependent upon Mr Al-Saraj to protect their interests. It was his duty to do so, and he breached that duty. Another court might have taken the view, on the same facts, that the Murads and Mr Al-Saraj were entering into a joint venture with each other, and that the Murads should have expected that Mr Al-Saraj would look after his own interests first. He would protect their interests only to the extent that they were co-extensive with his own. It may well be that the use of the phrase 'joint venture' is here slightly misleading. It gives the impression that there are two parties, each of whom decides

---

[31] As, eg, in the *Satnam Investments case* discussed in paras 7.12 *et seq.*

on its own and for its own purposes to enter into an arrangement, in circumstances where each is normally capable of protecting its own interests.

It may be that, despite the use of the phrase, the judge in this case took the view that the arrangement between the Murads and Mr Al-Saraj was closer to the appointment of an agent or a professional advisor. They had asked Mr Al-Saraj to help find investments for them in the UK. It may have been thought coincidental that the investment found was one in which Mr Al-Saraj would also himself invest. On this basis, the arrangement can be seen not as a commercial joint venture between the Murads and Mr Al-Saraj, but rather a purchase by the Murads of a property investment, on which they were advised by Mr Al-Saraj, and in relation to which he also acted as their agent. **8.81**

This is, of course, speculation. The judgment in *Murad v Al-Saraj* does not explain the basis on which the court concluded that there was a fiduciary relationship. However, like the difference of view of the judges in the *Lac Minerals* case, it shows that the existence of a fiduciary relationship is not always easy to detect: confidentiality is sometimes in the eye of the beholder. **8.82**

Fiduciary Duties in Financial Transactions

Transactions between banks and other financial institutions, on the one hand, and individual retail customers, on the other, can clearly involve relationships in which the retail customer has to place trust and confidence in its advisor. In those situations, one would not be surprised to see the courts finding that fiduciary duties were owed and granting equitable remedies in respect of their breach. The obvious example of such a situation is that found in *Lloyds Bank v Bundy*,[32] although it should not be assumed that the court will be enthusiastic to find a fiduciary relationship merely because the claimant is an individual. In *Rehman v Santander UK plc and BNP Paribas Real Estate Advisory and Property management UK Ltd*[33] customers applied for a loan to their longstanding relationship bank. It was to be secured on property owned by the borrowing entity and guaranteed by the individuals. The bank required a valuation of the property. It arranged this valuation and showed a copy to the proposed guarantors. When the borrower defaulted and the guarantees were called, the question arose whether the bank had a duty of care to ensure that the valuation was accurate. The court held that, in an 'ordinary commercial transaction' such as the one in issue, no such duty of care arose. Further, and in contrast to the situation in *Lloyds Bank v Bundy*, the fact that the customers had a longstanding relationship with the bank and trusted it did not convert the normal banker–customer relationship into a fiduciary one. **8.83**

Where the parties concerned are large commercial organizations which can be assumed to be able to protect their own interests, one would not normally expect duties to be imposed which are outside the terms of the explicit contractual arrangements between the parties. There are, however, three situations where, even between sophisticated and knowledgeable **8.84**

---

[32] See para 7.58 above.
[33] [2018] EWHC 748 (QB).

market participants, it is sometimes argued that one of the parties is entitled to the protection which equity gives to those to whom fiduciary duties are owed. The first is the case where the product being sold by one party to the other is complicated and outside the experience of the buyer. The second is where a sophisticated client seeks to prevent a former professional advisor from acting for another party, relying on the fiduciary duties owed by that professional to its former client. The third category of potential situations is that where one party, during the course of a relationship or transaction, does not have the information necessary for it to monitor the behaviour of the other party and accordingly to protect its own interests.

8.85 Generally speaking, the courts have been reluctant to find fiduciary duties in arm's-length commercial dealings between financial institutions and their customers or counterparties. Nonetheless, it is worth examining those situations where the existence of such duties has been alleged, and the reaction of the courts to the allegations.

Derivatives transactions between banker and customer

8.86 In the 1970s, commercial banks began to develop swaps and other kinds of financial instruments for use as risk management tools. In time, these structures became more complex and dependent on very sophisticated mathematical modelling. Customers who had entered into these contracts with their bank as a way of hedging risks in their business, or as a way of generating income through speculation, discovered that the instrument did not produce the result which they had expected but, in the event, resulted in them owing large amounts to their banker/counterparty.

8.87 In these circumstances, it is to be expected that the customer will seek to avoid its obligations under the contract. The basis of the escape attempt is usually to argue that the relationship between the bank and its customer was not simply an arm's-length commercial arrangement. Banker and customer were not merely debtor and creditor.[34] Because of the complex nature of the product, only the bank understood how the product would perform. The customer was entirely dependent upon the bank in any decision to enter into a complex financial engineering arrangement.

8.88 Quite often, the word 'fiduciary' does not appear at all in the customer's legal pleadings. The dispute usually arises when the bank informs the customer that the customer is obliged to make large payments to the bank under the terms of their contract, and the customer does not wish to pay. In these circumstances, the customer does not need any remedy which is the preserve of equity; the customer will be quite satisfied with a judgment for damages and/or rescission. Accordingly, the claim is often framed in contractual terms: that the relationship between the parties was such that the bank was not an arm's-length counterparty of its customer, but was an advisor. As an advisor, it owed contractual duties to its customer to ensure that the customer fully understood the risks of the contracts into which it was advised to enter and that the advisor should not take advantage of its position by concealing or misrepresenting facts to the customer. Although the duties

---

[34] See *Foley v Hill* (1848) 2 HL Cas 28.

claimed will often be asserted as contractual duties implied into the contract between banker and customer, they are in essence the same duties of loyalty that would be recognized by a court of equity as 'fiduciary'.

The first case in which this issue was raised before the English courts was *Bankers Trust International plc v PT Dharmala Sakti Sejahtera*.[35] Dharmala was an Indonesian industrial company. At the beginning of 1994 it had entered into a swap contract with BT. Some three months later this was cancelled by mutual consent and a new swap contract entered into on different terms. The effect of the second contract was that, if US dollar interest rates remained low for a substantial period, large net amounts would be due from BT to Dharmala. If, on the other hand, interest rates rose and remained high, payments would be due the other way. Within a few weeks, interest rates had moved in such a way that the mark-to-market value was a negative amount against Dharmala of US$45 million. It purported to rescind the contract at this point. Eventually, the case came before the commercial court in England, in the form of an action by Bankers Trust claiming the sum of US$65 million due under the contract.

8.89

Dharmala resisted the claim on a number of grounds. Relevant to the issue under discussion here are the following three points:

8.90

1. BT had misrepresented the effects of the swaps, leading Dharmala to believe that the contracts were safe and suitable for it, and that its likelihood of incurring a loss was very low.
2. The misrepresentations were, moreover, made fraudulently, entitling Dharmala to rescind the contract.
3. BT was under a duty of care to Dharmala, as an advisor to it. It was in breach of this duty, since it had failed to warn Dharmala of the risks which were being undertaken, had failed to satisfy itself as to Dharmala's competence in this area, its objectives or its understanding of what was proposed, had failed to advise it on any other possible steps it could take, other than entering into the swap contract with BT, and had failed to advise Dharmala to take independent advice.

Although there was no claim that BT was a fiduciary, the detailed obligations which it was claimed had been assumed by BT are in substance the obligations of a fiduciary. In particular, the claimed obligation to advise the customer to take independent advice is clearly a fiduciary duty.[36]

The key to the decision in this case, as in all similar cases, is the view which the court takes of the nature of the relationship between the parties. The judge, Mance J, put it succinctly. Dharmala's claims:

8.91

> ... necessitate a close analysis of the parties' relationship and circumstances leading to the relevant transactions ... the relationship under examination is not the conventional banker-customer relationship, although that too may on occasions be affected by representations, undertakings or the assumption of an advisory role. The bank here was marketing to existing or prospective purchasers derivative products of its own devising which were both

---

[35] [1996] CLC 518.
[36] See *Lloyds Bank Ltd v Bundy* [1975] 1 QB 326, discussed in paras 7.58 *et seq*.

novel and complex. The analysis of the relationship is in the circumstances one of some delicacy.

8.92 On the facts, all of Dharmala's claims failed. The court was not persuaded that BT had assumed a relationship which led to fiduciary (or 'advisory') duties. If the facts had been slightly different, however, the court's answer might have been different.

8.93 Similar points arose in a case that came before the High Court in 2008. In *JP Morgan Chase Bank v Springwell Navigation Corp*,[37] Springwell, the investment vehicle of a wealthy Greek ship-owning family, had entered into contracts with the bank to purchase large quantities of complex debt instruments linked to emerging markets. When those markets collapsed in 1997/98, Springwell suffered losses, thought to be in excess of US$500 million. It sued the bank in order to recover the money it had lost.

8.94 There were three claims:

1. The bank was an advisor to Springwell and owed it a duty of care to advise appropriately on investments.
2. The bank had misrepresented to Springwell the risks involved in buying products and was liable under s 2 Misrepresentation Act 1967.
3. The bank owed fiduciary duties to Springwell and was liable to account for all gains that it had made on instruments where it was the counterparty to Springwell.

8.95 The judgment runs to almost 300 pages. The facts and evidence were very complex. The conclusion, however, was that the bank was not liable to Springwell. There was no written agreement between the bank and its customer which provided that the bank should give advice to the customer. On the facts, there was no evidence that it had assumed a position of advisor which would have given rise to contractual obligations to protect the customer's interests in giving advice. On the facts, the court held that there was no misrepresentation in relation to the instruments sold.

8.96 As far as the fiduciary relationship was concerned, the court held that no such relationship existed. The basis of the decision was the earlier finding that there was no advisory contract in existence between the two parties. The bank had not undertaken to act as advisor in the interest of its customer as a matter of contract, and the facts did not support an argument that it had assumed such a position without having the contract. The claim that a fiduciary relationship existed could not succeed, once the court had found that there was no contractual obligation to provide advisory services. In an evidential sense, an advisory relationship was co-extensive with a fiduciary relationship.

8.97 In the last few years, banks have become aware of the dangers of allowing situations to develop in which it might be said that they had assumed the position of a fiduciary. Accordingly, in dealing with structured and other complex products, banks will now usually insist that the relationship is governed by contractual terms which specifically deny that there is any fiduciary relationship or that the customer has relied upon the bank's advice outside those situations specifically covered by written contract. In *Titan Steel Wheels Ltd v*

---

[37] [2008] EWHC 1186 (Comm).

Royal Bank of Scotland plc,[38] a dispute between the bank and its customer included the allegation that the bank acted as an advisor in relation to the purchase of derivative products which turned out to be unfavourable to the customer.

The 'terms of business' which the bank had sent to the customer stated that the bank would not provide advisory services and that no opinions expressed by the bank constituted investment advice. Titan was to take independent advice if it considered that such advice was necessary. In addition the specific terms of each transaction contained written provision that Titan was to seek independent advice if required, and an acknowledgement that Titan placed no reliance on the bank for advice or recommendations. The court relied on the Court of Appeal decision in *Peekay v Australia and New Zealand Banking Group*,[39] to the effect that in a commercial contract a party who agrees to an express acknowledgement of fact is generally bound by it. The exclusion of the duty of care was therefore binding upon Titan. The court noted also that the same approach had been adopted in the *Springwell Navigation* case.[40] It went on to say that an alternative approach for the court would have been to have concluded that the exclusions of liability and the acknowledgements of non-reliance on advice and representations were not only effective to exclude a duty which might otherwise have existed. They would also be taken as evidence to refute the claim that a duty of care had been owed. The effect would the same either way.

8.98

In the *Springfield Navigation* and *Titan Steel Wheels* cases, the exclusion clauses confirmed that the relationship between the bank and its customer had no fiduciary element and (which had the same effect) that the bank had not assumed the position of advisor. In Australia the courts have taken a similar approach to exclusion clauses, even more robustly. In *Australian Securities and Investments Commission v Citigroup Global Markets Australia Pty Limited (ANC 113 114832) (No.4)*[41] Citigroup acted as investment banking advisors to a company that was proposing to make a takeover bid for another listed company. The contract with the customer consisted of an engagement letter, the terms of which denied that there was a fiduciary relationship between them. Dealings in the shares of the target company by a different division of Citigroup prompted proceedings by the Commission alleging, among other things, the existence of a fiduciary relationship between Citigroup and its customer and the breach of duties that flowed from that relationship. The court saw the matter as very clear-cut:

8.99

> ... All of the [relevant] claims ... depended upon the existence of a fiduciary relationship ... However, the claim failed at the outset because the letter of engagement under which [the customer] retained Citigroup as its adviser specifically excluded the existence of such a relationship. The Court held that the law does not prevent an investment bank from contracting out of a fiduciary capacity.

The *Citigroup* case perhaps goes further than the English cases in an important respect. The English cases look at situations where the contractual arrangements between the parties might, or might not, denote a fiduciary relationship according to the view taken of the facts.

8.100

---

[38] [2010] EWHC 211 (Comm).
[39] [2006] 2 Lloyd's Rep 511.
[40] See also *Trident Turbo Prop (Dublin) Ltd v First Flight Couriers Ltd* [2008] 2 Lloyd's Rep 581.
[41] [2007] FCA 963.

In those cases the parties have chosen to state that their relationship is not a fiduciary one, or is not of a nature that would automatically impute fiduciary duties (eg that of professional advisor and client). The courts have accepted the description of their relationship given by the parties in their contract. In the *Citigroup* case, on the other hand, the relationship was that of advisor and client. Arguably, it is incapable of being an arm's-length commercial arrangement. The subject-matter of the contract is the giving of advice from someone with expertise to a counterparty who needs his help. In this respect, the relationship resembles that of solicitor and client. It is hard to imagine that a court would accept a clause in a solicitor's engagement letter that purported to exclude all of the solicitor's fiduciary duties to his client. The *Citigroup* case should, perhaps, be approached with caution.

Conflicts of interest for professionals

8.101 The relationship between solicitor and client, and also that between other professionals (eg accountants) and their clients is inherently of a fiduciary nature.[42] One of the ways in which the core duty of loyalty of the fiduciary manifests itself is in the 'no conflict' rule, that the fiduciary should not put himself in a position where his duty to his client conflicts with his own interest or with his duty to another client.[43] Where a solicitor or other professional has a continuing relationship with a client, it is clear that his fiduciary duty prevents him from beginning to act for another whose interests are contrary to those of the first client. The position is absolutely clear:

> ... a fiduciary cannot act at the same time both for and against the same client, and his firm is in no better position. A man cannot without the consent of both clients act for one client while his partner is acting for another in the opposite interest. His disqualification ... is based on the inescapable conflict of interest which is inherent in the situation.[44]

8.102 The more difficult situation arises where a professional firm accepts instructions to act for a client against the interest of a former client. The objection of that former client is likely to centre around the fact that the professional, by virtue of his earlier fiduciary relationship, possesses confidential information about the affairs of the former client. The argument would be that his fiduciary duties to that former client continue, notwithstanding the end of the relationship, and the fiduciary is precluded from acting for anyone else contrary to the interest of the former client, if this might involve the use of confidential information. In these situations, the law relating to fiduciary obligations and that relating to confidential information become entwined.[45] In *Bolkiah v KPMG*,[46] the House of Lords considered an application by Prince Jeffri Bolkiah, the younger brother of the Sultan of Brunei, to prevent his former accountants from acting for his brother in connection with an investigation into the way in which Prince Jeffri had managed certain assets of the state. The argument for KPMG was that they had put in place information barriers—so-called 'Chinese walls'—which would

---

[42] See paras 7.34 *et seq*.
[43] For an explanation of this rule, see paras 7.95 and 7.96.
[44] *Per* Lord Millett in *Bolkiah v KPMG* [1999] 2 AC 222, at 234H.
[45] See the discussion of this point in the *Lac Minerals* case, discussed in paras 8.64 *et seq* above.
[46] [1999] 2 AC 222.

ensure that no information about work done for Prince Jeffri in the past would become available to those individuals who were advising his brother in the proposed investigation.

8.103 The House of Lords regarded the situation as being, in essence, the same as that which would apply in the case of solicitors. The duty of confidentiality imposed on solicitors by their fiduciary relationship with a former client was extremely strict. It was based not only on the protection of the confidential information, but also on the possibility that the information might be privileged, in legal terms, as well as confidential, in commercial terms. Accordingly, as long as there was the slightest risk of prejudice to the former client, his former lawyers would not be allowed to act contrary to his interests. Lord Millett said:

> It is in any case difficult to discern any justification in principle for a rule which exposes a former client without his consent to any avoidable risk, however slight, that information which he had imparted in confidence in the course of a fiduciary relationship may come into the possession of a third party and be used to his disadvantage. Where in addition the information in question is not only confidential but also privileged, the case for a strict approach is unanswerable. Anything else fails to give effect to the policy on which legal professional privilege is based. It is of overriding importance for the proper administration of justice that a client should be able to have complete confidence that what he tells his lawyer will remain secret. This is a matter of perception as well as substance. It is of the highest importance to the administration of justice that a solicitor or other person in possession of confidential and privileged information should not act in any way that might appear to put that information at risk of coming into the hands of someone with an adverse interest.

In the case of lawyers and, by analogy, certain other professionals, the nature of the client relationship is such that the confidentiality of information will be protected, even in situations where the law relating to the protection of commercial confidential information would offer no protection.

8.104 The rule relates to the fiduciary duties of the solicitor, but centres on the obligation to keep information confidential. Lord Millett said:

> This would run counter to the fundamental principle of equity that a fiduciary may not put his own interest or those of another client before those of his principal. In my view no solicitor should, without the consent of his former client, accept instructions unless, viewed objectively, his doing so will not increase the risk that information which is confidential to the former client may come into the possession of a party with an adverse interest.

On this basis, Prince Jeffri was granted the injunction he sought.

8.105 The point came before the Court of Appeal again in *Marks & Spencer Group plc v Freshfields Bruckhaus Deringher*.[47] Freshfields were instructed by a consortium of interests which launched a bid to acquire the share capital of M&S. M&S immediately applied to the High Court for an injunction to restrain Freshfields from acting for or advising the bidders in connection with the acquisition. The basis of the application was that Freshfields had in the past acted for M&S on a number of complex litigation matters, as a result of which members

---
[47] [2004] EWCA Civ 741.

of the firm were in possession of detailed and sensitive information about the business of M&S. In addition, Freshfields had advised M&S in relation to the commercial arrangements with Mr George Davis, who designed the company's most profitable range of clothing. The information about the terms of those arrangements was said to be extremely sensitive and confidential.

8.106 M&S argued that Freshfields, as fiduciaries for them, would be in breach of the 'no conflict' rule if they were to act for the consortium of bidders, because that would involve the use of information that was confidential to M&S. As a separate point, it was argued that Freshfields were in possession of information which was of its nature confidential, and they could not act for the consortium in circumstances where that confidentiality might be breached. Freshfields argued that they were putting in place arrangements which would, in fact, ensure that no confidential information became available to those advising the consortium.

8.107 The Court of Appeal confirmed the decision and the reasoning of the first instance judge. As regards the question of conflict of interest, the judge had taken the view that there was 'a real or serious risk of conflict'. This was not based on the use of confidential information by Freshfields, but rather on the fact that the offer for the shares might very well involve the bidders making public statements critical of the performance of M&S management in relation to matters on which Freshfields had advised them. The duty of loyalty which Freshfields owed to M&S as part of their fiduciary relationship required that they should not be in a position where they assisted public criticism of their former client, in relation to matters on which they had advised.

8.108 As a separate matter, the judge had been unconvinced that Freshfields could put in place systems which must inevitably safeguard against the misuse of confidential information which was in its possession:

> So far as confidential information is concerned, it [sic] is obviously a huge amount of confidential information within Freshfields in relation to Marks & Spencer's affairs through acting for it over the years, some of which may be material to the bid, if only to be discarded. I cannot see, even with a firm the size of Freshfields, that effective information barriers can be put in place given the very large number of people involved, even on the two matters. There must be very many Freshfields people with knowledge of Marks & Spencer's confidential information. In those circumstances I am satisfied the Chinese Walls cannot be or be seen to be sufficient.

Accordingly, the Court of Appeal confirmed the granting of the injunction to prevent Freshfields acting.

8.109 Although it is clear that the question of conflict of interest is separate from issues of confidential information, it is hard to see situations where a former client of a professional firm would wish to prevent the firm for acting against him, but which did not involve the improper use of confidential information. In the *Freshfields* case, one of the reasons for granting the injunction was the possibility that Freshfields would, when acting for the bidders for M&S, be involved in making criticisms of their former client's management, in relation to matters on which they had advised. Although that rationale does not refer to confidential information, any potential implied criticism by Freshfields of their former client would only have significance if it was thought that their criticism was based on information, and that information would have come to them in circumstances of confidentiality. Claims about conflicts of interest that involve professionals will almost inevitably be disputes about the protection of confidential information.

Situations of inequality of information

A number of transactions in financial markets involve the establishment of relationships in which one or more of the parties cedes a discretion or a power to another in respect of important financial matters. Examples are to be found at the bond market, where commonly bondholders will appoint a trustee for the purpose of dealing with the issuer of the bonds. The trustee is given an exclusive right to bring an action on behalf of the bondholders. The individual bondholders are dependent upon the trustee behaving conscientiously in order to protect their interests. 8.110

In the syndicated loan market, lending banks will usually appoint one of their number to be the agent for the purpose of dealing with the borrower. The agent is the exclusive channel for payment of sums to the lenders by the borrower and often is the only channel of communication in relation to information about the status of the credit (eg discussions with the borrower about its compliance with financial covenants). In all forms of collective financing arrangement, it is common to see a trustee appointed to hold security for those entitled to the benefit of it. 8.111

These situations of agency and trusteeship are relationships which traditionally have been regarded as fiduciary. However, the purpose in the creation of such arrangements in financial transactions is usually very limited. The investors or lenders are usually highly sophisticated organizations which are quite capable of looking after their own interests. Their reason for delegating part of their power is one of convenience. Laurence Collins LJ explained this point in *Elektrim SA v Law Debenture Trust Corp plc*:[48] 8.112

> The use of a trustee is an effective way of centralising the administration and enforcement of bonds. Bondholders act through the trustee, and share *pari passu* in the fortunes of the investment, and do not compete with each other. The trustee represents and protects the bondholders, who are treated as forming a class, and who give instructions to the trustee through a specified percentage of bondholders. Such a scheme promotes liquidity. Individual bondholders rely on the trustee as the exclusive channel of enforcement and can be confident that on enforcement principal and interest will be distributed *pari passu*.

A similar explanation could be made for the use of other agency and trustee structures in financial transactions. The institutions undertaking these functions, whether they are trust corporations formed specifically to provide such functions, or one of the lending institutions which is pressed into performing this role, see themselves as carrying out a mechanical exercise. They do not accept responsibility for (and, just as importantly, are not remunerated for) protecting the overall interests of their appointors. Accordingly, the contractual arrangements that govern such appointments usually take great pains to exclude any duty of

[48] [2008] EWCA Civ 1178.

care beyond the matters specifically set out in the agreement. Further, there is often a denial of any fiduciary relationship.

8.113 In the area of fiduciary relationships, the facts of individual cases are always crucial. However, it is possible to make the generalization that the courts will usually be reluctant to go beyond the wording that has been agreed between the parties. The Privy Council in *Kelly v Cooper* made it clear that the scope of any fiduciary duties must be seen in the light of the terms of the contract between the parties. Thus, if the contract between a group of banks and their appointed agent makes it clear that the duties of that agent are limited to a series of specified activities, the courts will not normally be prepared to find that the agent had additional duties beyond those agreed.[49]

8.114 In the *Titan Steel Wheels* case[50] and in the *Springwell Navigation* case,[51] the court accepted the effectiveness of documentation which specifically excluded liability or limited the duties which might otherwise be implied. Both cases referred with approval to the views of the Court of Appeal in *Peekay v Australia and New Zealand Banking Group*.[52] In that case, a bank employee had misrepresented the nature of an investment product. However, the agreement between the bank and its customer contained provisions to the effect that the customer knew the true nature of the products being offered and had decided that such product was suitable for it. There was also a statement that the customer had taken independent advice and was not relying upon the bank. Moore-Bick LJ said that there was an important principle of English law to the effect that a person who signs a document knowing it is intended to have a legally effect is generally bound by its terms. This, he said: 'underpins all commercial life'. Accordingly, even though, in that case, it was not true that the customer had taken independent advice, and was untrue that the customer understood the true nature of the contract, the customer had contractually bound itself to act on that basis. It could not now resile from it.

8.115 This thinking will apply in the case of most financial contracts other than those involving consumers. In the *Elektrim* case, Laurence Collins LJ dealt robustly with the suggestion that a trustee for bondholders owed fiduciary duties, notwithstanding clear limiting language in the document. He pointed out that 'bondholders are expert investors who look after their own interests' and went on to say:

> It is surprising to find an allegation that the Trustee of a bond issue (whose main functions is administrative and ministerial) has the duties which are pleaded ... [ie fiduciary duties beyond those set out] and I am satisfied that ... there are no such duties in the circumstances of this case under English law ...

8.116 It seems clear that the courts will give effect to contractual arrangements which limit the application of the law relating to fiduciary relationships in this area. However, there are situations in which the courts might be expected to take a different attitude. In some situations, one party to a relationship may not be in a position to protect its own interests, however

---

[49] For a detailed explanation of this area of law, see *Torre Asset Funding Limited & anr v The Royal Bank of Scotland plc* [2013] EWHC 2670 (Ch).
[50] See para 8.97 above.
[51] See para 8.93 above.
[52] [2006] 2 Lloyd's Rep 511.

sophisticated and conscientious it is. This is because the other party is the only one which has the information and hence the capacity to protect the interests of the more vulnerable of the two. Examples of such relationships might be:

1. In the case where a lender has sold in the secondary market a 'silent participation' in a loan,[53] the purchaser will often have no access at all to information from the lender. Indeed, it is often the case that such participations are 'silent' because the loan agreement precludes the transfer of the indebtedness. In these circumstances, the purchaser of the interest is entirely dependent upon the seller, who remains the lender of record as far as the borrower is concerned, to protect its interests in dealing with the borrower.

2. In the last thirty years, it has become common for the holders of large amounts of securities to appoint a bank as 'global custodian' of the investments. A small number of banks specialize in this activity, which consists of administering the purchases and sales of investments in the portfolio, the collection of dividends, tax credits, etc, and the mechanics of sales and purchases, including the conversion of purchase monies or sales receipts. Although these activities are 'administrative and ministerial', they involve the exercise of considerable discretion by the custodian. For example, conversion of sale proceeds from one currency to another is usually effected by a sale of currency from the custodian bank to the customer, carried out by the custodian bank itself. The customer has, in practice, no way of monitoring the precise details of such transactions and is reliant almost entirely on the custodian to carry out such tasks in the best interests of the customer. Further, the information given to the custodian as part of the relationship may often give to the custodian the opportunity to trade for its own account and make considerable profits, perhaps at the cost of its own customer.

It is quite easy to foresee that a court might take the view that, in such circumstances, the organization which had the power to protect the interests of the other, or to act to its own advantage against those interests, should be fixed with the duties of a fiduciary, even if the governing contractual documents purported to limit its liability or to deny the fiduciary nature of the relationship.[54]

8.117

Regulatory Rules for Retail Customers

There is a general reluctance for courts to identify a fiduciary relationship in commercial and financial arrangements between sophisticated entities. Where private individuals are concerned, there is a greater readiness to accept that the private customer might be vulnerable

8.118

---

[53] For a description of this arrangement, see paras 5.72 *et seq*.
[54] In one case in California, state pension funds began proceedings against their global custodian alleging, among other things, breach of fiduciary duty by the custodian. The state Attorney-General, the Dept. of Justice and the Securities Exchange Commission, intervened in the case, alleging breaches of criminal statutory provisions: *California v State Street Corp* 34-2008-00008457-CU-MC-GDS. On 26 July 2016 The Boston Globe reported that State Street had agreed to pay penalties and compensation of $382m and had reserved a further $147.6m to settle class actions arising from the same facts.

in a financial or commercial relationship.[55] In addition to the potential protection afforded by equity, statute has introduced a regime for the protection of private customers in investment transactions, the effect of which follows closely the protections provided by equity.

8.119 Section 138D Financial Services and Markets Act 2000[56] provides in subsection (1):

> A contravention by an authorised person of a rule[57] is actionable at the suit of a private person who suffers loss as a result of the contravention, subject to the defences and other incidents applying to actions for breach of statutory duty.

8.120 The highest level in the hierarchy of rules which apply to those carrying on investment business are those set out as Principles for Business in the FCA Handbook. Some of these principles have a striking resemblance to the formulation of the fiduciary duties given by the courts:[58]

> 1. Integrity
> A firm must conduct its business with integrity.
> ...
> 6. Customers' interests
> A firm must pay due regard to the interests of its customers and treat them fairly.
> ...
> 8. Conflicts of interest
> A firm must manage conflicts of interest fairly, both between itself and its customers and between a customer and another client.
> 9. Customers: relationships of trust
> A firm must take reasonable steps to ensure the suitability of its advice and discretionary decisions for any customer who is entitled to rely upon its judgement.

The obligations imposed by the FCA Principles are not noticeably wider or more onerous than fiduciary duties which might be imposed on an institution dealing with a customer to whom such duties were owed. However, the advantage to a potential claimant is that it may be easier to show that the claimant falls within the class of persons referred to in the FCA Principles than it would be to convince a court that, on the particular facts of the case, a relationship of trust and confidence existed. Those who fall within the protected classes are entitled to the protection given. This is so, even in circumstances where the individual concerned is an experienced and sophisticated investor, who might struggle to convince a court that he needed the special protection of equity.

8.121 Section 138D applies only for the benefit of someone who is a 'private person'. The phrase is defined[59] to include any individual, unless he suffers the loss in the course of a regulated activity which he is himself carrying on. The definition also includes corporations and other entities, unless the loss concerned was incurred 'in the course of carrying on the business of any kind'.

---

[55] See, eg, *Lloyds Bank Ltd v Bundy*, paras 7.58 *et seq*, and *Murad v Al-Saraj*, paras 8.54 *et seq* above.
[56] As amended by Financial Services Act 2012.
[57] As defined in Financial Services and Markets Act 2000 s 417(1) (as amended).
[58] FCA Handbook PRIN 2.1.1R.
[59] Article 3, Financial Services and Markets Act 2000 (Rights of Action) Regulations 2001 (SI 2001/2256).

8.122 It is not surprising that attempts have been made to bring a claim within the ambit of s 138D by claimants who were not private individuals. In the *Titan Steel Wheels* case,[60] Titan had suffered losses as a result of the purchase from its bank of structured products which speculated on the movement of currencies. It argued that it fell within the definition of 'private person' for the purposes of s 150 Financial Services and Markets Act 2000 (the relevant provision before the addition of s 138D), because the speculation was not related to its business as a manufacturer and seller of industrial products. The court held that Titan was not a 'private person', given the frequency with which it entered into currency transactions, and the fact that its business relied on the export of goods, and accordingly dealing in currencies was a necessary part of its business in any event. Although claims by corporations under s 138D will be very difficult to mount, it does not follow that all commercial entities will, in all the circumstances, fall outside the ambit of the section.

8.123 The existence and terms of the statutory claim given by s 138D cast an interesting light on the issue of fiduciary duties generally. Section 138D has not, in practice, proved to be a major headache for investment businesses. Those who conduct their relationships with customers in accordance with accepted standards and statutory obligations do not often find themselves sued for breach of this statutory duty. As far as potential claims for breach of fiduciary duty are concerned, the same rule applies. The banks and other institutions which take care to draft their contractual arrangements to reflect clearly what is expected to happen, and then abide by the terms of the contracts which they have formed, will rarely find themselves in a situation they will be found to owe duties beyond those which they have anticipated. Although the idea of fiduciary duties is detailed and conceptually difficult, it is not a trap for a financial institution which conducts its business and its dealings with others in an honest and sensible way.

---

[60] See paras 8.97 *et seq* above.

9
CREDIT SUPPORT IN FINANCIAL MARKETS

9.01 In financial markets, as in all other commercial settings, a creditor is often unwilling or unable to rely solely on the fact that his debtor has a legally enforceable obligation to pay. The reluctance may be based on the financial fragility of the debtor; it may stem from doubts about his trustworthiness; or it may arise from concerns about the possible difficulty of enforcement if, for example, the debtor is resident in a different jurisdiction. Whatever the cause, it is very common that a creditor will look for a way to reinforce the debtor's obligation to pay.

9.02 The forms of reinforcement can be divided into two main categories. First, there is a range of mechanisms under which the creditor is given, or otherwise obtains, recourse to an asset of the debtor or of a third party which can be used as a source of repayment, in the event that the debtor's personal obligation to pay is not met. These mechanisms might be termed 'security arrangements'. They are discussed in Chapter 10. The second category of repayment-enhancement devices can be given the generic title 'credit support'. In this category, the personal obligation of the debtor is enhanced by additional personal undertakings given by, or changes to the legal position of, a third party or parties.

9.03 There are a number of ways in which a third party may enhance a debtor's obligation. Support may be provided by the fact that more than one person becomes liable for the debt, so that the creditor may look to a second promise, should the first, that of the debtor, fail. A third party might agree to reinforce an obligation which is not his own by becoming a surety for the debtor. In some cases the third party might not be willing to go so far as to undertake to pay the debt, in the case of default by the debtor, but might accept a form of obligation short of an outright guarantee, by giving a 'comfort letter' or 'almost guarantee' in respect of the debtor's obligations. In some circumstances, a debtor may arrange for commercial providers to support its promise, through the provision of a performance bond. The creditor might arrange its own protection by buying credit insurance, or by purchasing a credit derivative contract which will compensate it, if its debt is not paid. Finally, a creditor might obtain support for its position by arranging for another creditor of the debtor (eg an associated company of the debtor which is owed money on inter-company account) to agree to subordinate its position to that of the first creditor, thereby elevating the chance of payment of the first debt.

9.04 It is common to find that credit support and security mechanisms are used together. For example, a third party might guarantee payment of a debt, and thereby assume a personal liability to the creditor. He may then grant to the creditor a security interest over one of his assets, in order to secure the personal obligation that he has undertaken in his guarantee. For reasons for simplicity, this chapter deals only with questions of credit support through dealings with personal obligations.

Multiple Obligors

9.05 The chances of a debt being paid are increased if several promisors take responsibility for the same obligation. In the event of default, the creditor can choose to sue the one, or ones, of the multiple promisors which can most easily be made to pay. English law recognizes three different kinds of multiple contractual liability. When structuring contractual obligations it is important to be clear about the different legal and practical consequences which flow from choosing each of the categories. It should be stressed that the treatment below deals only with the question of multiple contractual liability; different rules apply where more than one person is liable in respect of a tort. It must also be remembered that situations can arise where damage is suffered as a result of default by more than one person, but where the default of one may be a breach of contract, and the liability of the other might arise because of commission of a tort. Consideration of these issues is outside the scope of this chapter.[1]

9.06 A financial lawyer structuring a transaction or documenting a proposal is likely to be concerned only with the contractual aspects of the arrangement under which multiple promisors accept liability for an obligation. The principles apply, of course, to any contractual obligation. For the sake of clarity, however, this chapter assumes that the obligation concerned is the payment of a debt. The three forms of liability are: several liability; joint liability; and joint and several liability.

Several liability

9.07 Several liability arises when two or more people make separate but identical promises to the same obligee. It does not matter whether the promises are included in the same or different documents. A simple example is where each of A and B promises to C that he will pay C £100. Each of A and B is liable to pay £100.[2] The two promises are cumulative, and C is entitled to be paid £200 in total. Payment by one of A and B does not discharge the other in respect of his separate (several) debt.

9.08 It would not be usual to see a structure under which obligations involving several liability were used as credit support. In the example above, the promise by B to C does not 'support' the promise by A to C. It is an additional and quite separate matter. The situation in which the concept is regularly encountered, however, is in syndicated lending, where a group of banks undertakes to make loans available to a borrower. Each of the banks commits to lend, on request by the borrower, a specific amount. In aggregate, the amounts committed by the banks are the total amount of the facility which the borrower needs. It is made clear in the documentation, however, that the obligations of the banks to advance funds are separate individual obligations. If one of the banks fails to advance funds as it has undertaken to do, the other banks cannot be compelled to lend in its place.

---

[1] See generally H. Beale (ed), *Chitty on Contracts* (33rd edn, Sweet & Maxwell, 2018), Ch 17.
[2] See *Mikeover Ltd v Brady* [1989] 3 All ER 618.

Joint liability

Joint liability arises where two or more people jointly promise to do the same thing. The classic example is where A and B jointly promise to pay £100 to C. In this case, there is only one debt owed to C, of £100.[3] Each of A and B is, however, liable to make the payment, and C can sue whichever one he chooses. Payment by A or B discharges the other of them, because there is only one debt. When it is paid by one of the joint debtors, there is nothing left for the other to pay.

9.09

Joint liability is subject to a number of technical rules of law, which have been developed by the courts over the years. Many of these rules are unlikely to be relevant in the case of substantial financial transactions. For example, a joint promise made by an adult and a minor is enforceable against the adult, although it may be voidable by, or at least unenforceable against, the minor.[4] However, other of the rules may impact on financial transactions.

9.10

A person cannot, under normal circumstances, contract with himself, and accordingly, at common law, a contract between A and B, on the one hand, and A (or A and C) on the other hand was void.[5] This very harsh rule was altered by the Law of Property Act 1925 s 82. Under that section, an agreement concluded by any person with himself and others (eg where an individual contracts with a partnership in which he is himself a partner) is to be construed as if the body which constituted the counterparty did not include himself.

9.11

Because an obligation owed jointly by a number of people is a single obligation, it was formerly necessary that any proceedings against defendants who were jointly liable should include all of the people who had any liability. Under current rules of procedure,[6] the position is much more flexible, but is still complex.

9.12

If the group of people who are jointly liable includes an individual who then dies, his liability ceases. It does not pass to his personal representatives.[7] This may, of course, radically alter the strength of the promise, if the individual who dies is the substantial member of a group of joint obligors. Of course, when the number of joint obligors is reduced by death to one, the obligation will become the obligation of that person alone and, in accordance with normal rules, will bind his estate if he dies. To this rule there is a statutory exception. In the case of partnerships,[8] the estate of a dead partner remains liable for the debts of the partnership which arose at the time when he was a partner, subject to the prior settlement of his non-partnership debts.

9.13

Until 1978, a judgment obtained against one joint debtor had the effect of preventing any action against other joint debtors, even if the judgment could not be satisfied.[9] The rationale appears to be that the debt has become 'merged' with the judgment. In other words, the judgment replaced the original debt, and it was therefore no longer possible to sue a

9.14

---

[3] See *King v Hoare* (1844) 13 M&W 494.
[4] *Gibbs v Merrill* (1810) 3 Taunt 307.
[5] *Mainwaring v Newman* (1800) 2 Bos & P 120.
[6] Civil Procedure Rules 1998.
[7] *White v Tyndall* (1888) 13 App Cas 263.
[8] Partnership Act 1890 s 9.
[9] *King v Hoare* (1844) 13 M&W 494.

different joint obligor on the same debt, since it had disappeared. The rule was abolished by s 3 of the Civil Liability (Contribution) Act 1978.[10]

Joint and several liability

9.15 Joint and several liability arises when two or more people, in the same document, jointly promise to do the same thing, and also make individual promises to do that thing. If A and B 'jointly and severally' promise to pay £100 to C, they have created a joint obligation to pay £100. They have also created two separate obligations to pay £100. The creditor in this case is in the position that, to recover his £100, he can sue the two of them together on the joint promise they have made. Alternatively, he can elect to sue A on his several promise or B on his several promise.

9.16 Of course, the obligations of joint and several obligors are not cumulative. C has three separate promises, each of which is to pay him £100, which he can pursue. However, performance of any one of those obligations discharges all the others. C is not entitled to recover more than £100 in total.[11]

9.17 The advantage of multiple liability which is expressed to be 'joint and several', when compared with that which is merely joint, is obvious. If recovery by the creditor in respect of the joint liability is impeded or prevented by one of the technical rules relating to the enforcement of joint liability, the creditor can instead choose simply to pursue one of the several promises given by the obligors.

Creation of multiple obligations

9.18 It is clear that, in most cases, a creditor will be better placed if an obligation which is owed to him by more than one person is owed on the basis that they are jointly and severally liable, rather than merely jointly liable. Care needs to be taken in drafting to make it clear that (if it is the case) the intention of the promissors is that they should be severally, as well as jointly, liable.

9.19 The presumption is that a promise made by more than one person is joint. Thus, a debt contracted on behalf of a partnership is a joint liability of the partners. If a bill of exchange contains the signatures of two or more acceptors, drawers, or endorsers, the liability of those parties to the holder of the bill is a joint liability.[12] Whether the presumption that liability is intended to be joint is ousted, so that liability will be joint and several, is a matter of construction of the contract concerned. Some of the cases in this area turn on very fine distinctions. In the case of promissory notes, little help is given by statute. Section 85(1) Bills of Exchange Act 1882 provides only that when a note is made by two or more makers, their liability will be joint, or joint and several, 'according to its tenour'. Rather more assistance

---

[10] There is an argument that s 3 applies only to court decisions, and not to awards in arbitration.
[11] *Banco Santander SA v Bayfern Ltd* [2000] 1 All ER (Com) 776, at 780e.
[12] *Other v Iveson* (1855) 3 Drew 177; *Re Barnard* (1886) 32 Ch D 447.

is given in one specific case. Where a promissory note is made with the words 'I promise to pay' and is signed by more than one person, their liability is joint and several.[13]

The only safe course in drafting is to use the phrase 'jointly and severally', if it is intended that the liability should be of that nature. The use of other expressions may force a court to make an interpretation which may turn on a very fine point. For example, if A and B promise 'for themselves that they or one of them will pay £100', the obligation is joint. If, however, they promise 'for themselves or either of them that they will pay £100', the promise is joint and several.[14]

9.20

Care needs to be exercised, however, in the use of the phrase 'jointly and severally' in order not to change by accident the nature of an obligation which is not intended to fall into that category. In *AIB Group (UK) Ltd v Martin*,[15] M & G had both borrowed money from a bank. Some of the borrowings were joint, but others were loans taken on an individual basis. After the loans were established they entered into a mortgage deed with the bank, in which M & G were together described as 'the mortgagor'. That expression was said to refer to 'all and/or any one' of them. M & G covenanted to pay to the bank all sums due from 'the mortgagor', and agreed that their liability should be 'joint and several'. The question of construction for the court was whether G's joint and several liability to the bank was limited to the advances which had been made to the two of them together, or whether his liability extended also to the loans made to M alone. The House of Lords held reluctantly that G had agreed to become severally liable to the bank in respect of advances made to M alone.

9.21

Contracts of Suretyship

The distinction between guarantees and indemnities

The previous section discussed the circumstances in which two or more promissors are liable to pay the same debt. In terms of financial transactions, joint liability, or joint and several liability, will arise in the case of liabilities incurred by two or more people acting together (eg obligations undertaken by the members of a partnership). Multiple liability may also arise, however, where an obligation is incurred (whether by one party or by several people acting together) and a third party agrees to become the surety in relation to the obligation incurred by the principal promisor(s). The formation of a contract of suretyship may, therefore, lead to a position where the surety and the principal promisor are jointly and severally liable to the creditor. It is usual, however, to consider contracts of suretyship as a separate issue, since this relationship is subject to a number of special rules, in addition to those which flow directly from the fact that it involves multiple obligations.

9.22

As far as financial transactions are concerned, contracts of suretyship are usually divided into two classes: contracts of guarantee; and contracts of indemnity. The discussion in this chapter will follow that division. It is important to bear in mind, however, that this division

9.23

---

[13] Bills of Exchange Act 1882 s 85(2).
[14] *Wilmer v Currey* (1884) 2 De G & Sm 347; *Levy v Sale* (1877) 37 LT 709.
[15] [2001] UKHL 63.

does not reflect a technical legal analysis. Indeed, a contract of indemnity is not, strictly speaking, a contract of suretyship at all.

9.24 Suretyship is the generic term for contracts under which one person (the surety) agrees with a creditor to ensure that a third party who owes an obligation to the creditor (the principal debtor) will duly perform his obligations.[16] As a matter of construction, the usual assumption is that the surety has gone further than simply undertaking to pay (in the case of a financial obligation) if the principal debtor does not pay. The surety is deemed to have undertaken to ensure that the principal debtor does indeed pay. Important consequences can flow from this fine distinction. In particular, if damage results from the principal debtor's failure to pay, in addition to the non-receipt of the debt concerned, the surety will be liable to the creditor in damages in addition to the amount of the debt in respect of which he is the surety.[17]

9.25 A contract of indemnity is a different matter. The word 'indemnity' is used widely to describe an obligation which one party has to make good loss suffered by another party. That obligation may not be the consequence of a contract at all, but may instead be based on some other legal principle and arise by operation of law. The term 'contract of indemnity', although obviously narrower than the first usage, is also used to describe a wide variety of contracts. It is used, for example, in the insurance industry to describe a number of different kinds of insurance contracts. For the purposes of this chapter, however, it is used in a strict sense. For these purposes, a contract of indemnity is a contract between a promisor (the indemnifier) and a creditor who is owed money by a third party (the principal debtor). The indemnifier promises that, if the principal debtor does not perform his obligation to pay the creditor, then the indemnifier will make good the loss suffered by the creditor as a result of the principal debtor's failure to pay. The promise may, at the choice of the contracting parties, be framed in narrower terms than this. For example, the promise may be only that, if the principal debtor does not promptly pay the amount owed, the indemnifier will pay the amount of the debt on first demand. In this case, he will not have promised to make good any damage which flows from the debtor's failure to pay, above the amount of the unpaid debt.

9.26 The Court of Appeal in *Marubeni Hong Kong and South China Ltd v The Mongolian Government*[18] pointed out the essential difference between a guarantee and an indemnity:[19]

> The distinction between the two contracts is, in brief, that in a contract of guarantee the surety assumes a secondary liability to answer for a debtor who remain primarily liable; whereas in a contract of indemnity the surety assumes a primary liability, either alone or jointly with the principal debtor.

---

[16] In *Moschi v Lep Air Services Ltd* [1973] AC 331, Lord Diplock at 347 said that the obligation of the guarantor:
... is not an obligation himself to pay a sum of money to the creditor, but an obligation to see to it that another person, the debtor, does something.
But see Lord Reid at 344–5, where he points out that it is not 'a general rule applicable to all guarantees'. Parties may agree whatever terms they choose, and each must be construed on its merits.
[17] *Moschi's* case above.
[18] [2005] EWCA Civ 395.
[19] Quoting with approval H. Beale (ed), *Chitty on Contracts* (29th edn, Sweet & Maxwell, 2004), Vol 2, para 44.013.

In practice, it can be difficult to decide whether a particular contract, on its true construction, should be regarded as a contract of guarantee or as one of indemnity. The legal consequences of a contract being in one category, rather than the other, can be great. Accordingly, it has been the practice for many years in financial transactions for lenders, who are looking for credit support in respect of an obligation that is to be incurred to them, to use a form of contract which includes both a contract of guarantee in respect of the obligations concerned, and also a contract of indemnity for the same obligation. The purpose is that, should one of the many technical rules of law relating to guarantees operate to invalidate or otherwise adversely affect the guarantee, the contract of indemnity (which is subject to far fewer potential legal mishaps) will ensure that the payment obligation of the surety/indemnifier remains in place.

Contracts of guarantee

9.27 In a contract of guarantee, the surety promises the creditor to be responsible, in addition to the principal debtor, for the due performance by the principal debtor of his existing or future obligations to the creditor. The exact terms of the promise are a matter of contract between the parties. There are, however, three characteristics which all guarantees share.

9.28 First, a guarantee obligation gives rise to a secondary liability on the part of the surety. There must be a principal obligation, the performance of which is being guaranteed. For this reason, if the obligation of the principal debtor is discharged, whether by payment or as a result of it being invalidated, the contract of guarantee will normally come to an end. In *Western Credit Ltd v Alberry*,[20] a surety guaranteed due performance by the principal debtor of his obligations under a hire purchase agreement. The principal debtor then terminated the agreement in accordance with its terms and paid the termination amount then due. This was much less than the full amount that would have been payable, had the contract run its course. It was held that the surety had been discharged by the early termination of the contract on the part of the principal debtor. Because the principal debtor had no further obligations, the surety could no longer have a secondary obligation to ensure that the primary obligation was met. However, if the surety has expressly agreed that he will remain liable, even if the principal debtor has been released, his liability will continue, notwithstanding the fact that the principal debtor's obligation no longer exists.[21]

9.29 Second, in order to bring about the application of the legal rules relating to suretyship as between the creditor and the surety, the creditor must be a party to the contract of suretyship. This may seem an obvious point. However, it is perfectly possible to have a contract of suretyship as between the principal debtor and the surety, without the creditor being aware of the fact. For example, A and B, who are in partnership, might contract with C to pay £100 to C. Without further agreement, A and B will be jointly liable as principals to pay £100 to C.[22] However, A might have agreed with B that, as between the two of them, B's liability should

---

[20] [1964] 1 WLR 945.
[21] *Perry v National Provincial Bank* [1910] 1 Ch 464; *Union Bank of Manchester (Ltd) v Beech* (1865) 3 H & C 672; and *Cowper v Smith* (1838) 4 M & W 519.
[22] See para 9.19 above.

be that of the surety, that A will discharge the debt of £100, and that if B is called upon to pay to C, A will reimburse B. As far as C is concerned, the contract is not one of suretyship, and none of the technical rules which might prevent his recovering from A on the basis that A is a surety will operate to prevent him claiming against A on the basis of A's position (under the contract between C, A, and B) as a joint principal debtor.

9.30 There is one major exception in financial markets to the rule that the creditor must be a party to the contract of suretyship. In a bond issue, the guarantor of the obligations of the issuer may enter into a contract with a trustee for the bondholders, under which he guarantees the obligations of the issuer. The benefit of the contractual obligation is then held by the trustee on behalf of the people who are the bondholders at any given time. In this case the creditor (the trustee of the promise for the benefit of the bondholders) is a party to the contract of guarantee. However, an alternative approach is that the surety gives his guarantee under the terms of a unilateral deed (a so-called 'deed poll'). The covenant under seal is made for benefit of anyone who is a bondholder at any time, and is enforceable by those bondholders, even though they were not originally parties to a contract with the surety.[23]

9.31 The third characteristic shared by all guarantees is that the contract must be in writing or evidenced by a written memorandum, and that the contract or memorandum must be signed by or on behalf of the surety. This requirement is derived from s 4 Statute of Frauds 1677, which provides that:

> ... no action shall be brought ... whereby to charge the defendant upon any special promise to answer for the debt default or miscarriage of another person ... unless the agreement upon which such action shall be brought or some memorandum or note thereof shall be in writing and signed by the party to be charged therewith or some other person thereunto by him lawfully authorised.

9.32 Section 4 does not use either of the words 'surety' or 'guarantee'. This section applies if the alleged surety has promised 'to answer for the debt default or miscarriage of another person'. The courts look to the substance of the promise which is being made, in order to decide whether it is one to which the formalities of the Statute of Frauds apply. Thus, in a case where the chairman of a company (the principal debtor) told the creditor that he 'would make sure that the money owed would be forthcoming', he had in substance promised to 'answer for the debt' of the company. Accordingly, the promise, because it was not evidenced in writing, was not enforceable.[24]

9.33 In addition to the possibility that a contract of guarantee may be unenforceable because of a failure to comply with the formalities of the Statute of Frauds, there are a number of other technical rules of law which might lead to the discharge of a surety before the creditor has been paid in full. Many of these rules can be excluded by the explicit contrary agreement of parties. For this reason, most bank standard forms of guarantee run to many pages; most of the provisions are designed to ensure that such rules do not apply.[25]

---

[23] See para 6.20 for a description of the use of a deed poll in an issue of loan stock.
[24] *Motemtronic Ltd v Autocar Equipment Ltd*, unreported, 20 June 1996; and see also *Actionstrength Ltd v International Glass Engineering INGLEN SpA* [2001] EWCA Civ 1477.
[25] See generally H. Beale (ed), *Chitty on Contracts* (33rd edn, Sweet & Maxwell, 2018), Ch 44.

Contracts of indemnity

From the point of view of a creditor, one of the most pleasing characteristics of the contract of indemnity is that it does not fall within the terms of s 4 Statute of Frauds 1677, and does not therefore require to be signed by the indemnifier, nor even to be in writing. Section 4 relates to promises that are 'to answer for the debt of another person'. It can apply, therefore, only when the liability of the surety is secondary, and someone else (a principal debtor) is primarily liable for the debt concerned. The section does not apply where the surety assumes a primary liability.[26]

9.34

In drafting a contract of suretyship for use in connection with a financial transaction, the safest course to follow, and the one which is invariably followed in the standard forms of guarantee used by most lending institutions, is to require the surety to promise as guarantor and also to promise separately, usually in the same document, as an indemnifier. Unfortunately, there is no form of words which will inevitably produce the result that the document will be construed as an indemnity, rather than a guarantee, if that should become necessary.

9.35

When a court is asked to decide whether a particular form of words evidences a guarantee or an indemnity:

9.36

> ... every case must depend upon the true construction of the actual words in which the promise is expressed.[27]

There are certain obvious markers in the terms of the contract which will aid construction. In *Clement v Clement*,[28] the Court of Appeal said that the use of the word 'guarantee' is not itself conclusive, but in doubtful cases it may provide some guidance, especially if the word is repeated a number of times in the document.

Pointing in the opposite direction, towards the contract being an indemnity, is the case where the creditor's rights against the principal debtor and against the guarantor, or indemnifier, are not co-extensive. If the promisor might be liable for a greater amount than the principal debtor, or liable in circumstances where the principal debtor is not himself liable, the contract is probably one of indemnity. In *ABN Amro Commercial Finance PLC v McGinn & Others*,[29] directors of a company had entered into a deed of indemnity with the bank that had agreed to provide finance to the company. They argued that their liability was that of sureties. Accordingly, they could rely on any defense that was available to the company to reduce its liability as a debtor. The Court held that, on a true construction of the contract of indemnity, they had agreed to make payments as primary obligors. Of particular importance in this respect, the contract contained a 'conclusive evidence' clause, under which the promisor accepted as conclusive a statement of the amount owing, given by the bank. This was the amount that would be payable by the promisor in any event, even if the sum payable by the principal debtor turned out to be lower. The existence of this clause was

9.37

---

[26] *Birknyr v Darnell* (1805) 1 Salk 27.
[27] Per Lord Diplock in *Moschi v Lep Air Services Ltd* [1973] AC 331, at 349.
[28] (1996) 71 P&CRD 19.
[29] [2014] EWHC 1674 (Comm) and see also *IIG Capital LLC v Van Der Merwe* [2008] EWCA Civ 542 [2008] 2 Lloyd's Rep 187.

strong evidence that the promisor had intended to assume a primary obligation, and not merely a secondary one.

9.38 All matters of construction depend on the individual terms of the contract and the circumstances in which it was concluded.[30] The primary rule in drafting must be to give the court as much help as possible. If the intention is that the surety should be liable both as a guarantor and also as an indemnifier, this should be spelt out as clearly as possible.

'Almost Guarantees' and Comfort Letters

9.39 In a financial transaction, it is common to find that the principal debtor is a member of a group of companies, the collective financial strength of which is much greater than that of the principal debtor itself. The contracting entity may even be a special purpose vehicle, formed specifically for the purposes of the transaction concerned. Such an entity will have no more substance than that conferred by the transaction itself. In such a situation, the creditor will naturally think first of asking for guarantees from a parent and/or associated companies of the principal debtor.

9.40 However, there are a number of reasons why a parent or other associated company might be unwilling to give support in the form of a guarantee:

1. The transaction under which the liability of the principal debtor arises may have been structured to be 'off-balance sheet', as far as the parent company is concerned. The intention is that the transaction should stand alone, and the potential liability arising from it should not affect the financial position of the rest of the group. The accounting regime in most countries requires a guarantee to be noted on the accounts of the guarantor company or companies. In effect, this brings the potential liability of the transaction concerned back into the consideration of the financial stability of the group as a whole. Such a consequence might defeat the purpose of having an off-balance sheet structure.
2. Loan agreements and bond documentation concluded by a parent company or other substantial members of the group will almost certainly contain financial covenants. In these undertakings, the company concerned will usually have undertaken to limit its borrowings to an agreed level. This figure is often delineated as a multiple of the value of the company's share capital and reserves. It is also usual in such covenants for the principal value of any guarantees which have been given to be included as if they amounted to borrowings by the guarantor.
3. In the case of most large companies, and certainly in the case of UK listed corporations, the constituting documents of the company may limit the power of the directors to borrow money above a stated level. Again, this level is often fixed by reference to the company's share capital and reserves, and again it is usual to find that the maximum amount contingently payable under a guarantee is treated as a borrowing for these purposes.

---

[30] See Chapter 11.

4. The giving of guarantees may be prohibited under the laws or regulation of the place of incorporation of the company which is asked to give credit support. The circumstance which most often gives rise to this problem is the existence of exchange control regulations which prohibit the giving of guarantees, or which make the giving of guarantees impracticable.

In addition, there may be circumstances where the parent company or affiliate is simply not prepared to give a guarantee.

9.41 If the issue is not the unwillingness of the parent or affiliate to give a guarantee, it may be possible to enter into a different form of contract which has the same economic effect as a guarantee. In the 1970s, regulations in Japan made it very difficult for Japanese companies to issue guarantees in respect of borrowings by their overseas subsidiaries. This extended to subsidiaries which had been formed in low-tax jurisdictions for the sole purpose of raising money for the group by issuing bonds. Although the Japanese regulations prevented a guarantee, the parent companies concerned were able to enter into 'keep whole' agreements. These agreements were simply an unconditional promise to ensure that the subsidiary would remain in existence and would be in a position to honour its financial obligations. The promise was made to the bondholders or to a trustee for the bondholders. If, by reason of insolvency or lack of liquidity, the subsidiary was unable to fulfil its obligations, the parent company would be liable in damages.

9.42 The arrangement is perfectly satisfactory from the point of view of the creditor, subject to two reservations. First, the essence of a guarantee at common law is that the surety undertakes to ensure that the principal debtor will perform its obligations. The surety does not simply undertake to pay, if the principal debtor does not pay. Because the reason for the use of a 'keep whole' agreement is to avoid the giving of a guarantee, care must be taken to ensure that the agreement does not run the risk of being construed as a guarantee. The parent company should not, for example, undertake to ensure that the subsidiary *will* meet its obligations. It should go no further than promising to make sure that the subsidiary *is able* to do so.

9.43 Second, a 'keep whole agreement', if drafted to avoid the effect of guaranteeing the obligation of the subsidiary, is narrower than a contract of suretyship. It will usually be limited to an obligation by the parent or associate that the subsidiary will be kept in a position where, in financial terms, it is able to perform its obligations. The wording would not normally assist the creditor in a situation where the subsidiary, although financially sound, was unable to perform for some other reason. For example, payment by the subsidiary might become unlawful under the law of the country in which the subsidiary itself was incorporated. Thus, even though it had the funds to pay, it would be unable to pay. It might well be that if the parent had given a straightforward guarantee the creditor would be able to look to the parent under that guarantee. In the event, the creditor might not be paid, despite the fact that the parent had complied with its obligations under the 'keep whole' agreement.

9.44 The 'keep whole' agreement between a parent company and the creditors of its subsidiary should not be confused with the situation illustrated in *Carillion Construction Ltd v Hussain*,[31] where an Indian parent company in 2006 acquired the share capital of an English company, which was itself the parent of the company concerned in the case, Simon Caves

---

[31] [2013] EWHC 685 (Ch).

Ltd. Caves had a balance-sheet deficit. In the three years following the acquisition, the deficit grew to more than £200 million. In order to give the directors of Caves the confidence that they could continue to trade in the belief that the company would be able to meet its debts, and to persuade the company's auditors that they could certify the accounts on a 'going concern' basis, the parent company wrote a letter, addressed to the directors of Caves. In it, the parent company confirmed:

> ... that we shall provide the necessary financial and business support to [Caves] to ensure that the Company continues as a going concern.

It wrote a similar letter in each of the next two years.

9.45 Unfortunately, Caves went into administration and the administrators sold its business, leaving a large deficit. The company went into liquidation. Carillion Construction was a creditor. It could not claim directly against the Indian parent, since there was no contractual or other link between the two of them. Rather, it argued that the letters contained an enforceable contractual promise made to Caves itself. Carillion sought to compel the liquidators of Caves to sue the parent on its promise.

9.46 The High Court held that there was no contract between the parent company and Caves. First, the letters had been addressed to the directors, in their personal capacity, and not as agent for the company. Further, there had been no consideration given for the promise.

9.47 The *Carillion* case shows that, if lenders or other creditors decide to use an indirect route to ensure the financial support of a parent or other affiliate, they must pay careful attention to the exact contractual form.

9.48 In other situations where the parent cannot, or will not, enter into a 'keep whole' agreement or give a guarantee, the parent may be prepared to write a 'comfort letter' or 'almost guarantee'. This letter confirms the intention of the parent to support its affiliate, without unequivocally undertaking to do so. The position is intrinsically uncomfortable: the creditor wishes to argue (perhaps to an internal audit committee, or perhaps to external regulators) that the obligation of the principal debtor has the enforceable financial support of a third party; that third party wishes to argue that it has not undertaken a binding obligation. Again, it may need to make this argument to its auditors, to persuade them that the existence of the support given does not require a note to be made to the accounts, since the company has undertaken no binding obligation.

9.49 The inescapable problem with a comfort letter is that one party argues that it evidences an agreement to create a legal obligation, while the other argues that it is evidence of agreement that no such obligation be created. Only one of the arguments can be correct. A comfort letter attempts to look enforceable from one point of view, but to appear unenforceable when seen from the other side of the negotiating table.

9.50 Whatever the parties may say about the status of a comfort letter, when discussing its significance with auditors or regulators, its enforceability can be decided only by a court. The issue then becomes a matter of construction of the contract embodied in the comfort letter.[32]

---

[32] See Chapter 11.

9.51 An English court considering a comfort letter will apply the same principles of interpretation and construction as would be applied to any commercial contract. There is, however, one variation from the normal approach. The principal objective of construction of a commercial contract is to find out what a disinterested spectator, looking at the words of the contract in the context in which it was made, would conclude that the parties intended. Because the construction focuses on the objective meaning of the words of the contract, the court is not concerned with what the parties might say that they meant when they used the words concerned. The meaning that the words actually convey to a reader, rather than the meaning intended by the author, is what matters.

9.52 One consequence of this approach is that consideration of pre-contractual negotiations between the parties is normally excluded.[33] Knowledge of these negotiations might cast light on the intention of the parties, but will not illuminate the objective meaning of the discussions that led to the production of the words used. In the case of comfort letters, however, it is usually impossible to ignore the intentions of the parties. With a comfort letter, the only point at issue is usually whether the parties did, or did not, intend to create a binding obligation beyond the literal meaning of the words used. This question cannot be answered satisfactorily without looking at their discussions at the time.

9.53 The leading case in England is that of *Kleinwort Benson Ltd v Malaysian Mining Corp Bhd*.[34] In this case, a parent company which had given a comfort letter in respect of its subsidiary argued that it had not intended to create any binding obligation. The relevant sentence of the agreement was:

> It is our policy to ensure that the business of [the subsidiary] is at all times in a position to meet its liabilities to you ...

The Court of Appeal held that the letter had honestly and correctly stated the policy of the parent company at the date when it was written. The letter had not said that the parent company's policy would not change in the future, if circumstances changed. There was no question that the parent company had misrepresented its own view at the time the letter was written. The only question was whether it had undertaken that it would not change its policy. In reaching the conclusion that it had made no such promise, the Court of Appeal was heavily influenced by the fact that, in negotiations, the parent company had refused repeatedly to give a guarantee. In other words, it had not been prepared to accept a continuing obligation of support, even though that support was in accordance with its policy at the time.

9.54 In contrast to the *Kleinwort Benson* case, a case heard in Australia in the same year reached a different conclusion. In *Banque Bruxelles Lambert SA v Australian National Industries Ltd*,[35] the parent company issued a letter, the relevant sentence of which read:

> We ... take this opportunity to confirm that it is our practice to ensure our affiliate ... will at all times be in a position to meet its financial obligations as they fall due.

---

[33] See paras 11.72 *et seq*.
[34] [1989] 1 WLR 379.
[35] [1989] 21 NSWRL 502.

In this case, the court held that the comfort letter created a binding obligation. It was, in effect, a 'keep whole' agreement. The argument was that the letter expressed itself to be a confirmation of a practice. In other words, it referred to a continuing and consistent approach, without any suggestion that it would change. In addition, there was no evidence that, during negotiations, the parent had refused to accept legal liability for its undertakings in the letter.

9.55 Consistent with this approach is the decision in *Re Atlantic Computers plc (in administration), National Australian Bank Ltd v Sowden*.[36] In this case, the letter from the parent company to the bank said that the parent would ensure that the subsidiary's obligations would be met. However, it went on to state that the obligation, apparently expressed in the letter, was an:

> ... expression of present intention by way of comfort only.

The court took the view that these words removed any implication that the statement of intention would continue and would be a binding obligation.

9.56 When construing letters of comfort, courts are often placed in an almost impossible position. They are asked to interpret a document which the parties say represents an agreement between them, in circumstances where often the parties never had the same intention at all. A lawyer advising either of the parties to such an agreement must be very careful. The intentions or wishes of one of the parties to the contract at the time it is made may be a very poor guide to the conclusion to be reached by a judge in the case of dispute several years later.

9.57 A further point to be borne in mind is that in a situation where a parent gives a letter of comfort, in order to persuade a creditor to enter into a transaction with its affiliate, there could be a liability in deceit, or in respect of a negligent mis-statement under the rule in *Hedley Byrne v Heller & Partners*.[37] If a parent states that it is its intention or policy to support its subsidiary, at a time when (as evidence may subsequently show) that was not group policy, it may be liable in damages to the creditor, if its mis-statement induced the creditor to lend.

Commercial Credit Support

9.58 The mechanisms described above all involve support being given to a principal debtor by a person or company which has its own interest in the success of the credit arrangement. The supporter is either a business partner or associate of the principal debtor, or else it has a group shareholding relationship which gives it an interest in the success of the arrangement. There is, however, an equally important series of mechanisms under which an independent third party, usually a bank, insurance company, or government department, provides its own creditworthiness in support of the obligations of a principal debtor. This is done, of course, in return for a fee or other payment. The payment may be made by the creditor, which is protecting its own interest in being paid, or by the principal debtor, which buys the support in order to obtain business from the creditor. There is a wide variety of such arrangements. Those most frequently encountered in financial markets are set out below.

---

[36] [1995] BCC 696.
[37] [1964] AC 465.

Performance bonds

9.59 It is very common in contracts for the international sale of goods for payment to be made through the medium of a documentary credit. The buyer arranges for its bank to promise the seller that, on delivery to the bank of the bill of lading for the goods, showing that they have been loaded onto a vessel for dispatch to the purchaser, the bank will pay to the seller an amount equal to the purchase price. This arrangement gives rise to a contract between the bank and the seller, which is quite separate from the contract for the sale of the goods. The bank, having paid the seller under its letter of credit, then looks for reimbursement from the purchaser, at whose request the letter of credit was opened.

9.60 A similar mechanism is available to support obligations other than a simple payment obligation owed by a purchaser of goods. These arrangements are known variously as performance bonds, on-demand undertakings, on-demand securities or performance guarantees. As so often in financial law, the terminology can be misleading. In particular, the use of the word 'guarantee' in this context is unhelpful. As will be seen below, the liability under these instruments is not usually a secondary liability as guarantor, but a primary obligation of the company which makes the promise concerned.

9.61 The structure of a performance bond can be moulded to support a number of different kinds of potential payment obligation. It is not possible to give an all-embracing definition. However, as a working description, a performance bond might be said to be a promise to pay a specified amount to a named beneficiary on demand or on presentation of specified documents.[38] The document called for might be a certification of default by an independent expert. It might, however, be merely a written claim by the beneficiary that it is entitled to be paid.

9.62 The undertaking, usually given by a major commercial bank, is a direct primary obligation of the maker. It is not a secondary obligation undertaken as a surety. In order to induce the bank to give such an undertaking, its customer (the principal debtor) will agree to pay a fee, and will also undertake to indemnify the bank in the event that its undertaking is called upon. The customer may, of course, be required by the bank to grant security for the indemnity which it has given to the bank.

---

[38] The International Chamber of Commerce Uniform Rules for Demand Guarantees (ICC Publication 458, October 1992) contains a more elaborate definition:

... a demand guarantee (hereinafter referred to as 'Guarantee') means any guarantee, bond or other payment undertaking, however named or described, by a bank, insurance company or other body or person (hereinafter called 'the Guarantor') given in writing for the payment of money on presentation in conformity with the terms of the undertaking of a written demand for payment and such other document(s) (for example, a certificate by an architect or engineer, a judgment or an arbitral award) as may be specified in the Guarantee, such undertaking being given:
  (i) at the request or on the instructions and under the liability of a party (hereinafter called 'the Principal'); or
  (ii) at the request or on the instructions and under the liability of a bank, insurance company or any other body or person (hereinafter 'the Instructing Party') acting on the instructions of a Principal,
To another party (hereinafter 'the Beneficiary').

9.63 At first sight, the arrangement is puzzling. It is quite common to find banks giving undertakings to foreign parties in respect of large amounts of money, payment being triggered merely by the uncorroborated statement of the foreign entity that it is entitled to be paid money by the principal debtor. In the case of a letter of credit used to pay for goods, one does at least know that goods of description concerned have been loaded onto a ship and dispatched. Although there may later be a dispute about the goods, there is at least some substance at the time of the payment by the bank. In the case of performance bonds, there may be no more than a mere statement from the payee that it is entitled to be paid.

9.64 One might wonder why banks are prepared to give such undertakings and, more importantly, why their customers are prepared to pay to have them do so. To understand this, one needs to look at the kind of commercial activity, in connection with which such performance bonds are given. It is very common, for example, to see the giving of performance bonds in large international construction contracts. Suppose that the government of Ruritania wishes to construct a highway between two of its major cities. It puts the proposal out to tender, and appoints as principal contractor a UK construction company with experience and a reputation in road building. The Ruritanian government will agree to pay for the road as and when it is constructed, say on completion of every 50 kilometre stretch. Completion will be deemed to have occurred when an independent engineering expert confirms that the stretch of road has been finished to the contracted standard. However, roads take time to build and require the use of expensive equipment and a great deal of labour. The contractor may well have insufficient liquidity to permit it to fund the completion of the first stretch of road, before it is paid anything at all. It needs, in effect, a cash 'float' throughout the period of the contract, in order to meet the payments which it must make before contract payment is made to it. The obvious source of that liquidity is the Ruritanian government. Accordingly, the contractor might ask for, and be given, a deposit, or prepayment, equal to the contract price for the first stretch of highway.

9.65 From the point of view of the Ruritanian government, it might well be prepared to give this liquidity to the contractor, provided that it is paid a fee for the use of its money, and also that it has the chance to unwind the arrangement in the event of dispute. Accordingly, the Ruritanian government might agree to pay a deposit, against the provision by the contractor of a performance bond from a major bank. The bond would take the form of a direct undertaking by the bank to the Ruritanian government that, forthwith upon demand by the Ruritanian government, the bank would pay a specified sum (say, equal to the amount of the deposit paid at the start of the contract). The performance bond is thus not, in commercial reality, any support for the due performance of the obligations of the contractor. It is, rather, a source of repayment of a working-capital loan made to the contractor.

9.66 Performance bonds are by no means confined to the international construction industry, but are used in many kinds of commercial transactions. In many ways, performance bonds can be best seen, like letters of credit, as payment mechanisms separate from the operation of the contract in respect of which they were given.

9.67 A number of cases about the calling of performance bonds came before the English courts in the 1970s. They usually involved an attempt by a bank's customer to prevent the bank complying with its obligation to pay under a performance bond, on the grounds that demand had been made by the creditor, either fraudulently or at least without justification.

The courts took a consistently clear view that, except in unusual circumstances, performance guarantees should be enforced in accordance with their strict terms. They should really be regarded as payment instruments, rather than as part of a complex contractual arrangement which had fallen into dispute.

9.68 The leading case is *Edward Owen Engineering Ltd v Barclays Bank International Ltd*.[39] Edward Owen were the manufacturers of commercial greenhouses. They received a contract from a Libyan state entity to construct a large number of greenhouses in Libya. In connection with the contract, they arranged for Barclays Bank to give a performance bond, in terms that Barclays would pay to the Libyan purchaser's bank the sum of £50,203 'on demand without proof or conditions'. After the greenhouses had been delivered to Libya, the purchaser failed to pay for them. The supplier told the buyer that it was treating the failure to pay as a repudiation of the contract, and that the performance bond would not be honoured. The Libyan purchaser then made demand under the performance guarantee. Edward Owen sought to injunct its bank to prevent payment (which would, of course, have triggered the indemnity obligation which Edward Owen had given to the bank).

9.69 The court was clear that the question of whether Edward Owen was in breach of contract was irrelevant. All that the performance bond required was that the Libyan beneficiary should make demand. If it did so in accordance with the terms of the bond, the bank must pay. Lord Denning MR said:[40]

> So, as one takes instance after instance, these performance guarantees are virtually promissory notes payable on demand. So long as the Libyan customers make an honest demand, the banks are bound to pay: and the banks will rarely, if ever, be in a position to know whether the demand is honest or not. At any rate they will not be able to prove it to be dishonest. So they will have to pay.
>
> All this leads to the conclusion that the performance guarantee stands on a similar footing to a letter of credit. A bank which gives a performance guarantee must honour that guarantee in accordance with its terms. It is not concerned in the least with the relations between the supplier and the customer; nor with the question whether the supplier has performed his contractual obligations or not; nor with the question whether the supplier is in default or not. The bank must pay according to its guarantee, on demand, if so stipulated, without proof or conditions.

9.70 The position is not quite as clear-cut as the *Edward Owen* case suggests. There are circumstances in which the bank might be prevented from payment, or might not be able to recover from its customer if it does pay. For example, if the terms of the undertaking require the beneficiary to state that a particular circumstance exists (eg that the principal debtor is in breach of contract) and the bank has actual knowledge that the statement so made has been made fraudulently; it may be prevented from paying.[41]

---

[39] [1978] QB 159.
[40] At pp 170H–71B.
[41] See the *Edward Owen* case, *per* Lord Denning MR:

> The only exception [to the general rule that the bank must pay in accordance with the terms of the guarantee] is when there is clear fraud of which the bank has notice.

See also *United City Merchants (Investments) Ltd v Royal Bank of Canada* [1983] 1 AC 168.

9.71 Cases in the last few years appeared to move towards the position that a debtor could restrain its bank from paying, if the debtor alleged that the call of the performance guarantee was in breach of an express restriction in the underlying contract and the restriction had been '*positively established*'.[42] In later cases the position appeared to move even further in favour of a debtor who claimed that the guarantee had been wrongly called. One case suggested that, in some circumstances, it might be sufficient for the debtor to establish only that it had '*a reasonable prospect of success*' in showing a breach of a condition in the underlying contract, in order to obtain an injunction against payment by its bank.[43]

9.72 However, a case in 2015[44] preferred the '*positively established*' test. Whatever the fine detail of the test required to show the claimant's right to prevent payment by a bank that has given a performance guarantee on its behalf, the position remains that a performance bond is much closer in terms of its legal effect to a letter of credit than it is to a normal form of guarantee.

9.73 The customer which has arranged the issue of a performance bond is given a degree of protection against wrongful call by a further rule. The court will presume that a contractual document was not intended to take effect as an on-demand undertaking, unless the undertaking has been given by a bank in connection with an international commercial transaction.[45] The uncompromising nature of the liability is confined within tightly drawn boundaries.

Export credit guarantees

9.74 An exporter of goods, whether capital goods such as ships or heavy manufacturing machinery, or manufactured goods, has a payment risk which it does not encounter when it sells in its domestic market. Because the purchaser is outside the jurisdiction, the enforcement of the buyer's payment obligation becomes much more difficult. There are several ways in which an exporter may guard against non-payment:

1. It may require that payment is made by means of a letter of credit in its favour opened by a bank in the exporter's country. Alternatively, a letter of credit opened by a bank abroad may be confirmed to the exporter by a bank in the exporter's country.
2. It may require that the purchaser produce a bank guarantee of its payment obligation.
3. The exporter may take out insurance, either against non-payment or against the occurrence of events which might lead to non-payment (eg the insolvency of the buyer or the imposition of exchange controls in the buyer's country which prevent payment).

Traditionally, however, there has been a reluctance on the part of commercial banks and insurers to accept certain kinds of risk. In particular, the political risk of changes in the purchaser's country which prevent payment is an area which commercial organizations have traditionally found difficulty in evaluating.

---

[42] *Sirius International Insurance Company v FAI General Insurance Ltd* [2003] EWCA Civ 470.
[43] *Doosan Babcock v Comercializadora De Equipos Y Materiales Mabe Limitada* [2013] EWHC 3201 (TCC).
[44] *MW High Tech Products v UK Ltd v Biffa Waste Services Limited* [2015] EWHC 949 (TCC).
[45] See *Carey Value Added SL v Grupo Uvesco SA* [2010] EWHC 1905 (Comm).

In order to create the facilities for their industries to export, industrial countries many years ago stepped into the market gap, by establishing state enterprises, the function of which was to provide the kind of financial support which was not available in the commercial market. In the UK, the Export Credits Guarantee Department was established in 1919. The department, which operates under the name 'UK Export Finance', is now governed by the Exports and Investment Guarantees Act 1991 (as amended). **9.75**

The concept of state-owned entities, the function of which is to provide financial assistance to companies incorporated in the country concerned has, over the years, become a sensitive issue. Clearly, in an international market place the provision of financial assistance to some industrial companies by their home-state governments is likely to lead to a distortion of competition. Within the European Union, the restriction of State Aid is seen as a vital element of the creation of the single market. The operation of the various Export Credit Guarantee Departments of the Member States has been the subject of close scrutiny over many years. The result is that the facilities that such departments are able to offer have been restricted, and the terms on which they deal with customers are less flexible or inventive than they might otherwise be. **9.76**

In the UK one of the major effects of competition concerns has been that the short-term (ie, under two years) business of ECGD was privatized in 1991, and sold to a private sector insurer. The medium and longer-term business, however, remains. **9.77**

In the context of support for exporters in relation to the payment obligations of their overseas customers, there are three kinds of facilities offered by ECGD:[46] **9.78**

1. Export Insurance Policy (EXIP)
   This is a traditional insurance policy, covering the possibility of non-payment by an overseas purchaser. The policy can also be structured to cover loss to the exporter which arises from an improperly-called performance bond.[47] The terms of an Export Insurance Policy prohibit assignment of the policy, whether absolutely or by way of charge. Accordingly, it cannot be used by the exporter to obtain finance.
2. Supplier Credit Bills and Notes Facility
   Under this arrangement, the overseas buyer of goods pays for them by drawing bills of exchange, payable at a future date, in respect of the purchase price. It hands these to the exporter, who sells the bills to a commercial bank, in exchange for cash. At the request of the exporter, ECGD guarantees to the bank that the bills will be met by the buyer on presentation. The transaction is represented in Figure 9.1.
3. Bond Insurance Policy
   This facility is available when an exporter has been required to procure a performance bond in favour of an overseas purchaser.[48] The bank which provides the performance bond will, of course, need to have assurance that, if the bond is called and the bank pays the buyer, the bank will be able to recoup the cost from its customer, the exporter.

---

[46] Technically, ECGD contracts are insurance policies, even if sometimes described as 'guarantees'. See Hobhouse LJ in *Credit Lyonnais Bank Nederland NV v Export Credit Guarantee Department* [1998] 1 Lloyd's Rep 19, at 38.
[47] For a description of the performance bond, see paras 9.59 to 9.73 above.
[48] A description of the circumstances in which this might arise is given in para 9.64 above.

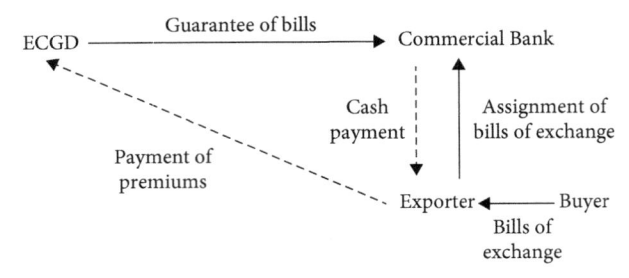

Figure 9.1 Supplier Credit Bills and Notes Facility

However, the exporter may not be able to provide adequate security to the bank as cover for the exporter's indemnity obligation to the bank. Under a Bond Insurance Policy, ECGD agrees with the exporter, in exchange for the payment of the premium, that it will indemnify the bank against the consequences of the bank's performance bond being called. Under the terms of the insurance, ECGD will have no right of recourse against the exporter if the exporter can establish that the call of the performance bond was unjustified or that the circumstances which gave rise to the call (eg the exporter's failure to perform its contractual obligations) resulted from *force majeure.*

Credit insurance

9.79 Insurance companies have for many years been prepared to insure their commercial customers against non-payment of debts owed to them. In the UK domestic market, this form of insurance is most often taken out by small trading companies which supply goods on credit to other small traders. They do not have the resources to make detailed credit assessments of new customers, nor to devote time to the recovery of payment, if a default is made. It is worth their while, therefore, to pay a premium to an insurance company which is able to make an assessment of the creditworthiness of the customer and is prepared to pursue defaulting debtors, using its rights of subrogation.

9.80 On an international level, Export Credit Guarantee Department offers insurance to exporters.[49] The circumstances in which private sector credit insurance has been used to support financial transactions have been more limited. These facilities, which were more common in the past than they are now, are limited in scope, but large in capital value.

Bond insurance

9.81 In this context, a bond is an instrument that creates or evidences indebtedness for borrowed money.[50] Bond insurance is an arrangement under which the issuer of a bond pays a premium to an insurance company, in return for which that company undertakes to make payments to bondholders, in the event that the issuer fails to do so. Alternatively, where the issuer of the bond is a special purpose vehicle, its ability to pay interest and capital is dependent upon receipt by it of income from its sponsor. In this case, the insurance policy may provide for an amount equal to the relevant income to be paid to the bond issuer itself, in

---

[49] See para 9.78 above.
[50] For a fuller description of the form of a bond, see paras 6.02 *et seq.*

the event that it has not received the income to which it is entitled. The insurance proceeds can then be used to pay to bondholders the sums to which they are entitled.

Bond insurance first began in the early 1970s. Municipalities and regional authorities in the United States regularly borrowed funds from the US domestic bond markets. The interest rate which they were required to pay depended on the perceived creditworthiness of the relevant issuer. If the bond could be enhanced by the addition of insurance, provided by a company whose credit rating was higher than that of the issuing municipality, markets would be prepared to lend at the rate applicable to the insurer. Accordingly, specialized corporations, intended to attract very high credit ratings for their own obligations, were formed to insure municipal bonds.   **9.82**

As the volume of insured municipal bonds grew, general insurance companies entered the market in competition with the specialized bond insurance companies. This situation lasted until 1989, when the New York State Insurance Law[51] effectively separated bond insurance from general insurance business.   **9.83**

During the 1990s, the specialized financial guarantee insurers, which were known as 'monoline' insurers, because of the restricted nature of their business, expanded into the insurance of certain aspects of structured financial products, particularly those that were based on an underlying pool of domestic mortgages. In 2006, it has been estimated, the total value of paper insured by monoline insurers reached US$3.3 trillion.[52] This contingent liability was supported by a collective equity capital base of US$34 billion.[53]   **9.84**

Before 2007, there is no record of any monoline insurer either defaulting on an obligation, or having its own credit rating downgraded. However, following the sub-prime crisis in that year, and the subsequent loss of confidence in structured financial products, many of the monoline insurers suffered credit downgrading, and some defaulted. As a result, the issuance of bonds supported by a policy of a monoline insurer has become severely curtailed. Whether, and when, it will rebound remains to be seen.   **9.85**

The UK position
The market for bonds issued by local authorities was largely confined to the US. In Europe, the ability of local authorities or other public bodies to raise money outside the control of central government is severely limited.[54] The monoline insurers therefore developed no meaningful business in Europe; nor did European insurers become involved in this business. However, there are pockets of activity which have involved insurance companies as part of the design of the structure. The economic reason behind this is probably that, as certain markets have expanded, they have exhausted the appetite for risk within the usual banking or investment community. Structures have therefore been devised to allow   **9.86**

---

[51] Section 6904(a), which provides that 'financial guaranty insurance' may be transacted in the State of New York only by the corporation licensed under the Act. In addition, s 6902(a)(1) prohibits such a licensed guaranty insurer from transacting almost all other kinds of insurance business.
[52] *The Economist*, 26 July 2007.
[53] Estimate of the Association of Financial Guaranty Insurers.
[54] See, eg, Local Government Act 2003, Pt 1 ch 1, which prohibits almost all borrowing by local authorities outside limits set by central government. In particular, s 2(3) prohibits borrowing by local authorities in currencies other than sterling without the consent of HM Treasury.

insurance companies to take part of the risk which traditional financiers have been unable, or unwilling, to assume.

Insuring bank advances

9.87 During the 1980s, insurance companies became involved in insuring the risks that banks were taking in lending on commercial property developments and also on film financing. In the latter case, money was typically lent by a bank to a film production company to cover the amount need to produce films (less the amounts already received or receivable through 'pre-sales' of distribution rights). The money for repayment of the loan was expected to come from the sales proceeds of the film. The production company then took out an insurance policy against any deficiency in those sale proceeds. Usually, it assigned the policy to the bank as security. Alternatively, the bank might take out its own policy. In the film industry, these policies were called 'Time Variable Contingency Policies' or 'Pecuniary Loss Indemnity Policies'.

9.88 In the commercial property business, a similar structure applied. A bank would lend money to a developer, based on a valuation of the property under construction. The bank would take security over the property to protect its loan. It would also take out a policy with an insurance company, to cover any shortfall between the amount outstanding, in the event of default by the borrower, and the realized value of the security.

9.89 In the film finance industry, the idea was developed further in the 1990s in order to permit the securitization of film production programmes. In this case a special purpose vehicle ('SPV') undertook to fund the production of a series of films. The SPV raised the money by issuing bonds to investors. The bondholders' security for repayment was a charge over the films themselves, plus an insurance policy taken out by the SPV, in an amount which covered any deficiency in the ultimate sale proceeds of the films to be made.

9.90 In both film financing and property financing, problems arose when claims were made under the policies. Often, the insurance company would claim that, at the time the policy was placed, an important piece of information had been withheld or misrepresented, either by the insured entity or by its placing brokers, acting as its agent. The insurance company would claim, using accepted and well-established principles of insurance law, that it could avoid the policy for non-disclosure of material facts.

9.91 The controversy arose because, almost always, this possibility had been foreseen, and the lawyers drafting the financing structure had gone to some lengths to exclude the ability of the insurance company to avoid the policy on any grounds whatsoever.

9.92 The issue is a difficult one, and complete clarity in the drafting of the relevant contracts is difficult to achieve. In one of the film finance cases which resulted in complex litigation, *HIH Casualty and General Insurance Ltd v Chase Manhattan Bank*,[55] Lord Hoffmann remarked of this kind of business:

> It is a form of insurance in which the players need to have their wits about them.

[55] [2003] 2 Lloyd's Rep 61.

The difficulty of negotiation and drafting stems from a problem similar to that which makes comfort letters so difficult to interpret.[56]

In the case of comfort letters, one party wishes to see the arrangement as creating a binding obligation, while the other wishes to see it as not having this effect. In the case of the use of insurance policies in financing structures, the insured wishes to see the insurance policy as a 'cash equivalent' obligation, rather like a performance bond.[57] Whatever the circumstances, it wishes the insurance company to have an obligation to pay immediately and in full. The insurance company, on the other hand, wishes to view these kind of policies as having the same basic nature as all other insurance policies, and as subject to the same defences and same legal principles as other insurance policies. 9.93

The drafting process usually involves some form of compromise between these two points of view. The wording which is ultimately concluded allows the insured to say that it has an unequivocal right to be paid, but allows the insurer to take the view that it has the defences and protection provided by general insurance law. If a loss occurs, this uneasy compromise is a recipe for litigation. 9.94

Credit derivatives

Credit derivatives first appeared in the early 1990s, as a tool by means of which banks and investors in financial markets could manage financial risk. Within a short period the form of the instruments themselves and the uses to which they were put had grown greatly in sophistication and vastly in usage. The increase in complexity of the investment instruments which were created on the basis of credit derivative contracts is widely thought to have contributed to the severity of the financial crisis which began in 2007/2008. The public focus is now on ways of controlling the speculative use of such instruments and in making analysis, both for investment and regulatory purposes, more certain. At a more basic level, credit derivatives still remain a major resource for risk management and for the support of obligations arising under financial transactions. 9.95

The simplest form of credit derivative is a contract under which a 'protection buyer' pays a sum of money, or agrees to pay a periodic fee, to a 'protection seller'. In return, the protection seller agrees to pay a much larger sum of money if a 'credit event' occurs in relation to a named entity or class of entities. For example, the protection seller might agree that if X, a listed oil company, enters into insolvency proceedings, it will pay an agreed amount to the protection buyer. A simple extension would be where the event was not the entry into insolvency proceedings of X, but rather an event which affected X's creditworthiness (and consequently the value of its publicly traded bonds or other securities). Thus, the 'credit event' might be the downgrading of X's public debt by a named credit rating agency. A further simple extension might be to name a number of oil companies along with X, and provide that the payment should become due if any of the named group of companies suffered a credit downgrade. 9.96

---

[56] See paras 9.39 *et seq* above.
[57] See paras 9.67 to 9.73 above.

9.97 The uses of such instruments in risk management are clear. If an investor holds securities of X in its portfolio, it is at risk of a drop in value of the portfolio if X's creditworthiness drops. A credit derivative which results in a payment to the investor in the event of the downgrade of X's public debt can be used to 'hedge' the value of a portfolio of securities which includes X's bonds.

9.98 In structuring financial transactions, therefore, it is often comparatively simple for a creditor to obtain support for an obligation of a principal debtor by buying credit protection in the form of a credit derivative.

9.99 At its simplest, a credit derivative can be used as a form of insurance against the decline in creditworthiness of a particular principal debtor. The flexibility of the instrument, however, allows the credit derivative to be structured so as to target the particular source of risk in the transaction in hand. For example, a bank which is helping to finance the development of a major coal mine is at risk if the joint venture company, formed for the purpose of developing and operating the mine, is unable to pay its debts. It may be thought that the real risk of non-payment in such a case will only come about if the project's viability is called into question by an unexpected drop in the world price of coal, the result of which is to make the operation unprofitable. The obligation of the joint venture company to repay may then be most efficiently supported by an instrument under which payment is made by the protection seller either in the event that the commodity price drops below a particular level, or if the credit rating of a group of named coal producers declines. The rationale for the latter trigger is that a decline in the credit rating of the world's coal producers is likely to be attributable to a drop in the world price in coal.

9.100 At their inception, credit derivatives were hailed as a panacea for the dangers of credit risk. Any organization which took risk on financial instruments or financial situations could now hedge that risk and reduce its size to the level with which the investor was happy. The excess risk could be transferred to other organizations with the appetite and capacity to accept the financial risk concerned. In this way, it was said, financial risk could be spread around the world market so that it resided only with those institutions which were comfortable to accept it. There need never be any financial crashes brought about by failures of credit: risk would be held only by institutions able to absorb it.

9.101 The fault with this argument was that it assumed that the total amount of risk would be the same, whether or not it had been spread around the market by the use of credit derivatives. In reality, the flexibility and ease of construction of credit derivatives allowed the development of so-called 'synthetic' instruments, under which payment obligations were undertaken, in return for a fee, which bore no relation to any underlying risk on a genuine transaction or investment. The synthetic instruments had the effect of creating risk where none existed before. That risk was then, of course, spread around the market through sales and hedging mechanisms. The result, arguably, was that credit derivatives allowed risk to be spread efficiently, but they also allowed the total amount of risk to be multiplied many times. Thus, rather than a situation where a few vulnerable institutions held an unsustainable amount of risk, they produced a situation where very many institutions held an unsustainable amount of risk.

9.102 The response to this problem is a matter of public law and regulation. The legal issue in relation to credit derivatives which affects the financial lawyer is much more specific. The industry has been concerned for some years with the possibility that a credit derivative contract might be held to be an insurance contract. If this were the case, it might be unenforceable. This is a very technical and specific point. It does, however, have its origins in the legislative response to an earlier problem which has very strong echoes of the issues surrounding the growth of credit derivatives.

9.103 The modern insurance industry developed in Europe from the sixteenth century onwards. The two areas on which the market focused were life assurance and the insurance of ships and their cargoes. While the markets were seen to have very obvious and clear benefits commercially, there was widespread concern that they offered the opportunity for speculation and gambling and could produce other undesirable social effects. For periods in the sixteenth and seventeenth centuries, life assurance was banned in France, Holland, and Sweden. A notorious case is cited from the nineteenth century in Pennsylvania, where six men insured the life of an elderly neighbour. In order to speed up payment under the policy, they murdered him.[58]

9.104 In the UK, statutory control of the perceived danger took the form of provision in two statutes. The Life Assurance Act 1774 governs not just life assurance, but all forms of insurance other than marine insurance.[59] Section 1 of the Act provides:

> From and after the passing of this Act no insurance shall be made by any person or persons, bodies, politick or corporate, on the life or lives of any person, or persons, or on any other event or events whatsoever, wherein the person or persons for whose use, benefit, or on whose account such policy or policies shall be made, shall have no interest, or by way of gaming or wagering; and every assurance made contrary to the true intent and meaning hereof shall be null and void to all intends and purposes whatsoever.

9.105 The Life Assurance Act 1774 contains no definition of the word 'interest'. In the case of marine insurance, the statutory provisions are a little more helpful. The governing statute, the Marine Insurance Act 1906, begins by defining 'contract of marine insurance' as:

> ... a contract whereby the insurer undertakes to indemnify the assured ... against marine losses, that is to say, the losses incident to marine adventure.[60]

Section 4 of the Act renders void every contract of marine insurance made by way of gaming or wagering. It deems to be a gaming contract every contract of marine insurance where the assured has no 'insurable interest'.

9.106 Section 5 of the Act, which defines 'insurable interest', begins unpromisingly:

> (1) Subject to the provisions of this Act, every person has an insurable interest who is interested in a marine adventure.

Fortunately, subsection (2) expands on this:

> (2) In particular a person is interested in a marine adventure where he stands in any legal or equitable relation to the adventure or to any insurable property at risk therein, in

---

[58] Cited by W. C. Spalding in 'Insurable Interest' in *Insurance Fundamentals* <http://thismatter.com>.
[59] Life Assurance Act 1774 s 4 excludes 'Insurances bona fide made by any person or persons on ships, goods or merchandises'.
[60] Marine Insurance Act 1906 s 1.

consequence of which he may benefit by the safety or due arrival of the insurable property, or may be prejudiced by its loss, or by damage thereto, or by the detention thereof, or may incur liability in respect thereof.

9.107 The relevance of these provisions to credit derivatives is easy to see. If a credit derivative contract is a contract of insurance, it will be void unless the protection buyer can show that it had an insurable interest in the subject-matter of the credit derivative. In some cases this might be comparatively easy to do. For example, the protection buyer might be able to show that it held bonds issued by the company, by reference to which the credit derivative was structured. If that reference entity defaulted, the protection buyer stood to lose money. It therefore had an insurable interest in the creditworthiness of the reference entity.

9.108 However, there are many situations where the relationship between the risk which the protection buyer is trying to cover and the creditworthiness of the reference entity will not be so clear. The protection buyer may not be able to show that it will be prejudiced by the default of the reference entity, or will benefit from the non-default of that entity.

9.109 The important point, in practice, is not whether the protection buyer has an insurable interest in the subject-matter of the credit derivative, but whether the credit derivative is a contract of insurance at all. If the credit derivative is not an insurance policy, there is no need to show any 'insurable interest'. Despite the fact that the question whether a particular instrument is, or is not, a contract of insurance has arisen regularly in commercial disputes, the courts have been reluctant to formulate any all-embracing definition.[61] The reason is that the factor which differentiates contracts of insurance from other kinds of contract is the purpose for which the contract was made.

9.110 The purpose of insurance is to cover the assured against a detriment which he would suffer, if the insured event were to happen. Whether such detriment might, or might not, occur is not something which would necessarily be known to the other party. For example, the promoter of an open-air concert might stand to lose a great deal of money, if it rained on the day of his concert. He might wish to hedge this risk by placing a bet with a bookmaker that it would rain on that day. If it rained, he would lose money on his concert, but would be compensated by his winning bet. As far as the bookmaker is concerned, this is a simple wagering contract. As far as the concert promoter is concerned, however, the gaming contract is an insurance against a risk which, if it materializes, will cost him a great deal of money. The bookmaker may well be completely unaware of this motivation. It would be quite unrealistic to suggest that the bookmaker had, by taking a bet in circumstances where the punter had an 'insurable interest' in the subject-matter of the bet, begun to carry on an insurance business without the requisite authorization under the Financial Services and Markets Act 2000.

9.111 Whether a credit derivative contract is a contract of insurance (and the consequences that follow from this) is, in practice, not a question of the categorization of the contract itself, but of the categorization of the parties. If the protection seller is a bank, or other entity which is

---

[61] See, eg, *Prudential Insurance Co v Inland Revenue Commissioners* [1904] 2 KB 658; *Fuji Finance Inc v Aetna Life Insurance Co* [1997] Ch 173; and generally J. Birds, S. Milnes, and B. Lynch (eds), *MacGillivray on Insurance Law* (14th edn, Sweet & Maxwell, 2018), Ch 1.

authorized by the Financial Services Authority to conduct the relevant kind of business, and that business is not classified by the FSA as insurance business, there is in practice little concern that a court might subsequently say that the business was in fact insurance business,[62] and that the contracts made as part of it were insurance contracts.

Subordination

9.112 A fundamental principle of the insolvency law of the UK, and of most other common law jurisdictions, is that the assets of an insolvent company (and also of a bankrupt individual) should be distributed among its creditors in proportion to the value of debts owing to them. The *pari passu* principle is subject to statutory provisions granting preference to certain kinds of payments, and to the rights of secured creditors. The principle is stated very clearly in the Insolvency Rules:

> Debts other than preferential debts rank equally between themselves in the winding up and, after the preferential debts, shall be paid in full unless the assets are insufficient for meeting them, in which case they abate in equal proportions between themselves.[63]

9.113 The purpose of a creditor in looking for support for the obligation of a principal debtor is first to arrange that, in the event of the insolvency of the principal debtor, the creditor will be more likely to receive payment in full than will the other creditors who share in the *pari passu* distributions. An obvious way in which the creditor might attempt to achieve this result would be to put in place a contractual arrangement with the principal debtor that, in the event of the insolvency of the latter, the creditor would be paid before other creditors. Unfortunately, such a contractual arrangement runs contrary to the mandatory provisions of insolvency law, which require the distribution of assets *pari passu*.

9.114 In *British Eagle International Airlines Ltd v Compagnie Nationale Air France*,[64] the House of Lords considered the operation of the clearing house operated by IATA. Airlines which were members of the organization undertook with each other to carry passengers who had purchased a ticket from another member. Thus, if someone had purchased a ticket from airline A, but could not travel on a convenient flight provided by that airline, he could use his ticket on a flight to the same destination operated by airline B. Under the clearing arrangements, airline A agreed that it would reimburse airline B for the cost of the flight which it had provided to the holder of airline A's ticket. The accounting arrangements for the clearing house system operated on a monthly basis. At the end of each month, an accounting was made of the amounts due by way of reimbursement to each member from all other members, and of the aggregate amount which each member owed to other members. In the case of each member, the net figure so calculated was then payable by or to the clearing house.

9.115 Thus, if airline A owed £100 to airline B, because airline B had carried one of airline A's customers, and airline A was owed £100 by airline C, because airline A had carried an airline C

---

[62] See Financial Law Panel, *Credit Derivatives: The Regulatory Treatment* (May 1997).
[63] Insolvency Rules 1986, r 4.181(1). This Rule applies to compulsory winding up proceedings. In relation to voluntary winding ups, a similar provision is contained in Insolvency Act 1986 s 107.
[64] [1975] 1 WLR 758.

passenger, the clearing operated so that airline A neither paid nor received anything. In effect, the £100 owed to A by C was diverted to satisfy the payment of £100 due from A to B.

9.116 If airline A went into liquidation before the accounting has been made, the effect of allowing the clearing to proceed would be that B, which was owed money by A, would be paid out of the debt owed to the insolvent company by C. An asset of the insolvent company (the £100 owed by C) would not be available for distribution to creditors in accordance with the *pari passu* principle. Instead, it would be used to satisfy the debt owing from the insolvent to B. B would be thereby elevated above the other creditors of A in terms of payment. The House of Lords held that this was contrary to the statutory terms of insolvency law that unsecured creditors should be paid *pari passu*. It was not open to parties to agree among themselves contractual arrangements which altered the mandatory provisions of the statute.[65]

General subordination

9.117 Following the *British Eagle* case, it was clear that the *pari passu* principle was mandatory. It was not open to a company to agree that some of its creditors should be elevated, in the event of its insolvency, above its other creditors. However, in order for it to be advantaged in an insolvency, it is not necessary that a creditor should be allowed to step forward to the head of the queue. It will be equally effective that other creditors should step back. Such an effect is achieved by the mechanism of general subordination, in which a creditor, say a parent company of the principal debtor which is owed a large amount by way of inter-company loan, agrees with the principal debtor that, in the event of the insolvency of the principal debtor, its debt should be paid only after debts owed to the other creditors had been settled in full.

9.118 This contractual arrangement, if effective, has, like the arrangement in the *British Eagle* case, the effect of elevating some creditors (all creditors other than the parent company) above the creditor or creditors which has or have agreed to be subordinated. In normal commercial terms, there seems to be no objection to an arrangement under which one creditor voluntarily agrees to stand aside for the benefit of the others. However, the *ratio* of the *British Eagle* case was that the *pari passu* provisions of the insolvency legislation were mandatory, and it was not open to parties to contract out of the statutory provisions. The concern was that this might apply when the creditor agreed to stand back, just as when it wished to jump the queue.

9.119 The matter came before the High Court for consideration in two cases in the early 1990s. In *In re Maxwell Communications Corp plc (No 3)*,[66] the insolvent company had been a party to bond documentation, in respect of a bond issued by its subsidiary. The insolvent company

---

[65] Following the *British Eagle* case, IATA re-wrote its rules so that they excluded any liability or right of action for payment between member airlines. Each member was a debtor only of IATA itself. This arrangement was considered by the High Court of Australia in *International Air Transport Association v Ansett Australia Holdings Ltd* [2008] HCA 3, (2008) 234 CLR 151, and held to be effective. See Lord Mance's endorsement of the decision in the *Belmont Park* case (referred to below at para 9.122) at para 165 of the judgment.
[66] [1993] 1 WLR 1402.

had guaranteed the payment of the bond 'on a subordinated basis'. The question for the court was whether the *pari passu* principle required that this arrangement, agreed between the bondholders and the guarantor, should be ignored, with the effect that the bondholders would prove for the whole of their debt, along with all other unsecured creditors of the insolvent company.

9.120 The court held that the liquidator could take notice of the agreement for subordination, and that distribution by him in accordance with that arrangement to the other creditors would not offend against the *pari passu* provisions of the Insolvency Act. This case confirmed a decision a year earlier in *In re British & Commonwealth Holdings plc (No 3)*.[67]

9.121 The result of the decision in the *Maxwell Communications* case is sensible and helpful. There are many cases where finance is to be provided to a subsidiary of a large company, which may itself be of little substance and may in fact be a special purpose vehicle, with no business at all outside the transaction concerned. Quite often, such a company is dependent for support on finance provided by its parent company. If the parent company is unwilling or unable to guarantee the debts of the subsidiary, an agreement under which the parent agrees to subordinate all inter-company indebtedness may be as effective in providing support to the covenant of the subsidiary.

9.122 It has to be said that the reasoning behind the decision in the *Maxwell Communications* case is not particularly convincing. The court based its decision on the following argument:

> Of course, a loan can be effectively subordinated if the creditor constitutes himself a trustee for other unsecured creditors ... or he may contract to assign the benefit of his debt to other unsecured creditors without in either case affecting the ordinary process of proof in the liquidation or the application of the company's assets *pari passu* amongst creditors whose proofs have been submitted. However, to recognise subordination by these means, and not by a direct contract between the company and the creditor would represent a triumph of form over substance.

It is true that the economic effect of subordination arrangements may well be the same as would come about by the parent company granting security to other creditors, by way of charge, over its own asset (the debt owed to it by the subsidiary). But it is hardly true to say that the two arrangements are merely a difference of form rather than substance. They may have the same economic effect, but they are quite different legal mechanisms. However, it is now accepted that there is no principle of insolvency law which precludes the operation of general subordination arrangements agreed as a matter of contract between a creditor and the debtor company. Indeed, the principle set out in the *Maxwell* case has been endorsed and re-stated (in slightly different terms) by Lord Mance in *Belmont Park Investments Pty Ltd v BNY Corporate Trustee Services Ltd and Lehman Brothers Special Financing Inc*:[68]

> ... the principle in British Eagle ... does not preclude creditors from agreeing inter se on the distribution inter se of their pari passu shares.

---

[67] [1992] 1 WLR 672.
[68] [2011] UKSC 38, para 148.

Ad hoc subordination

9.123 In the case of general subordination, the debts owing to the subordinated creditor (the 'junior creditor') are stated to be subordinated to the claims of *all* other unsecured creditors. Often, however, this is not the intention of the arrangement. It is wished that the claims of the junior creditor should be subordinated only to the claims of the creditor who is seeking support (the 'senior creditor'), but to no other. If the junior creditor should be paid only after the senior creditor had been paid in full and the senior creditor ranked equally with a larger number of other creditors, it would follow that the junior creditor would be subordinated to all creditors, and all creditors (rather than just the senior creditor) would benefit from the postponement of the junior creditor. Often, the agreement between the junior creditor and the senior creditor is that the senior is to have the benefit of any sums that would otherwise be paid to the junior creditor in an insolvency. The senior creditor does not wish to share the benefit of those sums with other unsecured creditors. From the point of view of the junior creditor, it has agreed not to take any benefit from the liquidation until the senior creditor has been paid. However, once this has happened, it wishes to share any other sums equally with the other creditors.

9.124 Such a private arrangement could be made by agreement between the two creditors alone, without the involvement of the principal debtor company. This was the arrangement that Lord Mance had in mind in the *Belmont* case.[69] The junior creditor might, for example, agree to assign to the senior creditor its claims on the debtor, such agreement to take effect on the insolvency of the debtor. It might simply charge to the senior creditor the debt due to the junior creditor from the debtor company as security for payment in full of the amounts owed to the senior creditor by the debtor company.

9.125 However, there may be reasons why the senior creditor is not prepared, or is unable, to grant security over its debt to the senior creditor. An alternative in this situation is a subordination arrangement made by agreement between the two creditors and the debtor company. Such an arrangement does not envisage that the junior creditor will be subordinated to the claims of all unsecured creditors generally. It is not the intention that the junior creditor should be entitled to receive nothing by way of distribution until all of the creditors have been paid. Instead, the intention is that the sums which are payable to the junior creditor in respect of its debt should be diverted to the senior creditor. When the senior creditor has received sufficient funds by way of distribution (whether out of distributions in respect of the debt owed to the senior creditor or out of distributions in respect of the debt owed to the junior creditor) to satisfy in full the debt owed to it, further distributions in respect of the junior creditor's debt should be for its own benefit.

9.126 Accordingly, an agreement between the senior and junior creditors and the debtor company will usually provide that, upon the insolvency of the debtor company, the debts owed to the junior creditor should be postponed and subordinated to the debts owed to the senior creditor. The agreement then provides that, if the junior creditor receives any sums by way of distribution from a liquidator of the debtor company, which it has been agreed should be paid to the senior creditor, it will hold those funds on trust for the senior creditor and account to the senior creditor for them.

---

[69] See para 9.122 above.

9.127 Such *ad hoc* subordination arrangements, although clear in their commercial intent, raise a question of difficult legal analysis. Does the arrangement, under which a distribution payable to the junior creditor is diverted to the senior creditor, and/or the use of the 'turnover trust' amount to the creation of a charge, which might be registrable as a charge over a 'book debt'?[70] The analysis will, of course, depend on the wording of the subordination agreement. For the purposes of this chapter, however, it is assumed that the agreement provides simply that the liabilities owed to the junior creditor should, in the event of the insolvency of the principal debtor, 'be postponed and subordinated' to the debts owed to the senior creditor. It is further assumed that the agreement provides that, in the event that any sums are received by the junior creditor by ways of distributions, those sums will be held on trust for the senior creditor.

9.128 The expectation of commercial people would be that the junior creditor should receive no payment in respect of the indebtedness owed to it by the debtor company until such time as the senior creditor had received payment to discharge all of the indebtedness owed to it by the debtor company. Assume that, at the point when the subordination agreement becomes effective, both the junior and senior creditors are owed £100 by the debtor company. Before the insolvency event occurs, it is the intention that the debtor company should pay both creditors in the normal course, without reference to the subordination agreement. If the intention is that, on insolvency, the senior creditor shall be entitled to claim a sufficient amount from the debtor company to ensure that its total receipts by way of dividend are £100, there are two bases on which the diversion of the payments might happen:

1. The junior creditor might assign to the senior creditor, on the occurrence of the trigger event, the benefit of its £100 debt, so that the debtor company is then under an obligation to pay £200 to the senior creditor, and is no longer under an obligation to pay anything to the junior creditor. In the insolvency, the senior creditor would prove for £200 and the junior creditor would be entitled to prove for nothing at all.
2. The effectiveness of the agreement between the parties does not involve the transfer of claims from one creditor to the other. Rather, the junior creditor has agreed that the terms of its contractual right to payment from the debtor company has changed, so that sums which would have been paid to the junior creditor by way of dividend should instead be paid to the senior creditor in discharge of the indebtedness to the senior creditor of the debtor company. Any payments so made would reduce the debt of £100 owed to the senior creditor. The payment of those funds would not, however, affect the indebtedness outstanding to the junior creditor, which would remain at £100. In other words, sums payable by way of distribution by the debtor company should be used to discharge the debt owed to the senior creditor, rather than the debt owed to the junior creditor.

9.129 Of the two alternatives, the first seems rather implausible. It is unlikely that the parties intended that there should be an assignment of indebtedness owed to the junior creditor. Had it been the intention that the senior creditor should be entitled to prove in the liquidation for £200, and that the junior creditor should have no debt for which it could prove, one would expect to see a provision for reassignment of the junior creditor's original debt (which had

---

[70] Companies Act 2006 s 860(7)(f).

been assigned to the senior creditor as part of the subordination) at the point when the dividends received by the senior creditor had totalled £100.

9.130 A much more likely interpretation is that the parties intended that both the junior and senior creditors would prove for £100, but that the liquidator of the debtor company should discharge the obligation to the senior creditor before discharging that to the junior creditor. Further, if the intention was to assign the benefit of the junior debt to the senior debtor, there would be no need for the company to be party to the contractual arrangement. It could simply be told that the indebtedness had been assigned.

9.131 If there were, in reality, an assignment of the junior indebtedness, it would certainly be arguable that the assignment amounted to a charge. The commercial arrangement is that the senior creditor should be entitled to the benefit of indebtedness owed to the junior creditor, only to the extent necessary to ensure that the senior debt is repaid in full. Once that has occurred, the intention is clearly that the junior debtor should be entitled once again to the benefit of its debt.

9.132 Further, the existence of the 'turnover trust' may evidence an arrangement which is in reality a charge. The argument would be that the junior creditor has, by virtue of the declaration of trust, granted property rights to the senior creditor in respect of property belonging to the junior creditor (cash actually received in respect of debts owed to the junior creditor). That property interest, it would be argued, amounted to a charge, because its purpose was to ensure that the proceeds can be used to repay the indebtedness of the debtor company to the senior creditor.

9.133 The better view is that the arrangement does not evidence the creation of a charge. The normal form of subordination agreement, referred to above, evidences an arrangement that money which would otherwise be payable to the junior creditor shall instead be paid to the senior creditor in discharge of liabilities owed to the senior creditor. Any moneys so paid belong to the senior creditor absolutely. If, for whatever reason, those sums are not paid to the senior creditor, but are instead paid to the junior creditor, it must follow that they are received by the junior creditor on trust for the true owner, the senior creditor. The provision does not, therefore, create a trust. The property received by the junior creditor is not received by it in its own right. It does not, therefore, create a trust over its own property in favour of the senior creditor. Rather, it acknowledges a legal consequence which flows from the contractual arrangements. Once the senior creditor has received dividends of £100 in total, its debt will have been discharged, and any further dividends which fall to be paid will be payable direct to the junior creditor in its own right.

9.134 Although analysis suggests that the normal form of *ad hoc* subordination agreement does not involve the creation of a registrable charge, it must be stressed that the point is a fine one, and turns on the exact wording of the agreement concerned. Care should be taken, therefore, in drafting to ensure that as much assistance as possible is given to a judge who, at some point in the future, might be asked to decide the point. If there remains any lingering doubt, consideration should be given as to whether it is possible or desirable to effect registration of the arrangements as a charge.

10
SECURITY INTERESTS

> What's in a name? That which we call a rose
> By any other name would smell as sweet;
>
> Shakespeare: Romeo and Juliet, II ii, 43–44

Reasons for Taking Security

10.01 Financial transactions are almost always concerned with the creation of a personal obligation to pay money. This may be the repayment of a loan, the redemption of a bond, payment of the purchase price of an asset, or the discharge of some other obligation undertaken by contract. In a perfect world, it would be enough for financial lawyers to structure transactions and systems so that the payment obligations were valid and enforceable as a matter of law. All concerned could assume that the obligations would then be performed in accordance with their terms.

10.02 Sadly, the world is not so benign. An obligor might not have the resources with which to perform its obligations, might be prevented from paying by governmental action,[1] or might simply refuse to do what it has promised. To safeguard itself in this situation, an obligee has two potential courses of action: first, it can arrange an additional or substitute promisor;[2] or it can put in place an arrangement which gives it the ability to use an asset, which may or may not belong to the obligor, as the source of repayment.

10.03 Although the wish to guard against the consequences of a default by a promisor is the most obvious reason for taking security, it is possible to identify a number of other motivations.[3] Of particular significance in financial transactions, one might mention the following:

1. Legal regimes for corporate insolvency make provision for the utilization of assets of the insolvent estate, in order to spread as fairly as possible the deficit resulting from the insolvency. The regime may give priority to certain kinds of claims or particular categories of claimant. For example, in the UK priority is given to some claims of employees, and in the case of insolvent insurance companies priority is given to those claims which form part of their insurance business. In addition, almost all insolvency regimes allow priority to claimants who have enforceable rights which relate to specific assets of the insolvent estate.

---

[1] For a discussion of these circumstances, see paras 3.60 *et seq.*
[2] See Chapter 9.
[3] See generally the discussion in Ch 1 of G. McCormack, *Registration of Company Charges* (3rd edn, Jordans, 2009).

2. In project finance, the institutions which provide the money are often dependent upon the success of the project as the only source of repayment. In this event, their interest in the assets of the project lies not so much in the ability to sell them if the project fails (in which event the assets may have comparatively little value), but rather to allow the financiers to take control of the operation of a project, if it is felt that the obligor is not handling it in a responsible and efficient way.
3. In international transactions, an obligee may find it very difficult in practice to enforce its personal rights against an obligor, if enforcement has to take place in a jurisdiction other than its own. In this case, the possibility of recourse to an asset located in a more convenient jurisdiction may discourage any possible default by the obligor.
4. In securities markets, financial assets provided as security for obligations owed to a lender may, with the consent of the owner of those assets, be used by that lender as if it were itself the owner.[4] The security-taker (the lender) may then use the assets to provide security to third parties for loans which it has itself taken. The lender in this case takes security not only to cover itself against the possibility of default by its borrower, but also to give itself a source of liquidity, which it may use to fund the loan which it has itself made.
5. In the case of banks, their capacity to lend is constrained by capital requirements set by their regulators. Banks are required to ensure that their assets (ie the loans which they have made) are supported by capital on the bank's balance sheet. Those capital requirements usually distinguish between different kinds of loan asset. Thus, a loan by the bank which is secured on property of the borrower is often treated as less risky than one which is unsecured. Such a loan is required to be supported by less capital than an unsecured loan. For a bank, therefore, taking security may be motivated only in part by the fear of default, and perhaps even more by the wish to reduce funding costs by lending in the way which requires the least capital.

The task of structuring financial transactions therefore needs an understanding not only of the legal mechanisms available, but also of benefits or needs of taking security in the first place, and the reasons why some forms of security may be more advantageous than others.

Terminology

Meaning of 'security'

10.04 When discussing the topic of security and the concepts that are encompassed by it, it is necessary to take even greater care than usual about the use of technical terms. First, the word 'security' itself is a nebulous term, with no very precise meaning. At its widest level, it can be used to mean:

Something which makes the enjoyment or enforcement of a right more secure or certain.[5]

---

[4] See Reg 16, Financial Collateral Arrangements (No 2) Regulations 2003 (SI 2003/3226), implementing the 2002 Directive on Financial Collateral Arrangements (EC 2002/47). The provision is not a novel departure in English law. It has always been open to a principal to agree that his agent might represent that he was himself the principal, or to the owner of an asset to allow his bailee to sell the asset as if it were his own.

[5] Jowitt's *Dictionary of English Law* (4th edn, Sweet & Maxwell, 2015).

Thus, early cases used the word 'security' to mean not only a document or arrangement which is collateral or supplementary to an obligation. In some circumstances, 'security' could refer to the instrument which created the primary obligation.[6]

10.05 The underlying idea was that the existence of the instrument made enforcement of the intangible rights easier and more convenient and therefore more 'secure'. Thus, the term 'securities' began to be used as a generic name to cover many forms of financial instrument, for example share or bond certificates, which constituted or evidenced an underlying intangible obligation.

Interchangeability of terms

10.06 The legal mechanisms by which security interests are constituted are all precise. They embody a series of specific and recognized legal rights and obligations, combined in a consistent way. Thus, mechanisms such as 'lien' or 'charge' consist of quite different sets of rights and obligations. However, it is common in matters of legal security for clients and also lawyers to treat as interchangeable terms which describe quite different concepts.

10.07 The concepts of mortgage and charge are quite different.[7] In England since 1925 the mortgage has been replaced as a security mechanism for real property by the charge. However, it is still common for both laymen and lawyers to talk about someone granting a mortgage over his house to his bank. The Law of Property Act 1925, having replaced the concept of mortgage with that of charge, provides in s 87(1) that a charge will have the same effect as a mortgage, provided that it is expressed in the document to be given 'by way of legal mortgage'. To a pedant, this might appear similar to saying that 'dog' shall indicate the same creature as 'cat' provided that it is referred to as a 'dog by way of cat'. This semantic confusion does not amount to a pitfall, provided that one remembers that a reference by someone to his having granted a mortgage over his house actually means that he has granted a charge.

10.08 To embody this confusion even further in statute, the Companies Act 2006 provisions dealing with registration of charges[8] provide that 'charge' includes 'mortgage'. In the Law of Property Act 1925,[9] 'mortgage' includes 'any charge or lien on any property for securing money or money's worth'. Accordingly, it is not safe to assume that, when someone says that a mortgage has been granted over property, this is a technical description of what has happened. It may well be that the interest created takes another legal form, but carries the name 'mortgage'.

10.09 The word 'lien'[10] denotes a form of security under which someone in possession of property belonging to another is entitled to retain that property until a particular obligation is

---

[6] See *Jones v IRC* [1895] 1 QB 484; *British Oil & Cake Mills Ltd v IRC* [1903] 1 KB 689.
[7] See paras 10.46 to 10.60 below.
[8] Section 859A(7).
[9] Section 205(1)(xvi).
[10] See paras 10.65 to 10.68 below.

discharged. However, the word is quite often used much more loosely than this in relation to financial transactions. In particular, the phrase 'banker's lien' refers to a contractual right to combine accounts. There is no property of the customer capable of being retained.[11] The use of the phrase has been criticized by the courts.[12] Nonetheless, the phrase is still used in the banking industry to describe a security arrangement which does not have the legal characteristics of a lien.

10.10 One of the most common cross-uses of terminology is the description of security over shares or bonds as a 'pledge of shares' or 'pledge of bonds'. Pledge,[13] like lien, is a security concept that relies upon the security-taker having possession (either actual or constructive) of a physical item. Again, it cannot apply in concept to a share or a bond, which is intangible in nature. When reference is made to a 'pledge of shares', almost certainly the form of security to which it relates is either a mortgage of the shares or a charge over them. The use of the words 'pledge' seems to have originated in the practice of depositing as security the certificates which represented the intangible shares. The courts would see the security as relating to the physical property of the certificate, and would then describe it as a form of pledge.[14]

Local authority borrowing

10.11 The lax use of technical terms, and the possibility of misunderstanding which follows from it, is something which needs to be remembered. It is not usually something which is likely to embody a significant risk. However, there is one example of such a misunderstanding which could have given rise to serious problems. In the 1980s, trade surpluses in Japan resulted in Japanese banks taking large amounts on deposit from their domestic bases. They were anxious to lend this out in ways which were very low risk, and where the sums involved were substantial. One of the markets which they identified was that of loans to UK local authorities. In common with many countries, the UK restricts quite severely the ways in which local authorities can raise funds, otherwise than from the central government or through levying local taxes. Nonetheless, certain kinds of borrowing are permitted. The Local Government Act 1933, which then governed the ability of local authorities to borrow, was at pains to point out that all borrowings should rank *pari passu*, that no class of borrowings should be given priority over another class, and certainly no assets of the local authority should be put at risk through the grant of mortgages or other security. The Act, therefore, required that all borrowings should be treated equally in relation to payment, all being paid out of the income of the local authority without differentiation. It expressed this in rather archaic language:

---

[11] However, for the purposes of the Financial Collateral Directive 2002/47/EC, implemented in the UK by the Financial Collateral Arrangements (No 2) Regulations 2003, SI 2003/3226 (as amended), the Court of Justice of the European Union has ruled that a bank which owes money on current account to a customer can, in some circumstances, be 'in possession or control' of the customer's asset constituted by the account. See *Private Equity Insurance Group SIA v Swedbank AS*, a judgment of the CJEU, under number C-156/15 made on 10 November 2016 on a reference from the Supreme Court of Latvia.
[12] *National Westminster Bank Ltd v Halesowen Presswork Ltd* [1972] AC 785 and see paras 3.20 to 3.26.
[13] See paras 10.61 to 10.64 below.
[14] See, eg, *Halliday v Holgate* (1868) LR 3 Exch 299.

Borrowed money shall be charged indifferently on all the revenues of the authority.

10.12 One of the non-legal meanings of the verb 'to charge' is 'to entrust'. This is the sense in which the word is being used in the 1933 Act. One could paraphrase the provision:

> The revenues of the authority shall be used to repay borrowed moneys without differentiating between the borrowings concerned.

The provision requires that no lender should have priority in repayment. The Parliamentary draftsman would no doubt have argued that it followed automatically from this that no creditor could be granted a charge, mortgage, or other security interest, which would have the effect of giving greater priority of payment to its debt.

10.13 Nonetheless, a number of Japanese banks lent to local authorities on the basis that their loans would be treated as secured lending for the purposes of calculating capital requirements placed on them by their home regulators. They were, apparently, advised that the wording gave them a security interest in the income stream of the local authority, because the revenues were 'charged' to pay their loans.

10.14 This error was recognized, and legislation, when recast, intended to make it clear that there was no possibility of any lender acquiring a security interest in any income or revenue of a local authority. The Local Government Act 2003 s 13(1) now reads:

> Except as provided in subsection (3), a local authority may not mortgage or charge any of its property as security for money which it has borrowed or which it otherwise owes.

One might think that this wording had categorically and finally removed any confusion. No-one will have a charge (or a mortgage) over any property of a local authority to secure debts of that authority.

10.15 However, the statute immediately reintroduces the confusion. Subsection (3) of 13 reproduces the provision from the 1933 Act:

> All money borrowed by a local authority … shall be charged indifferently on all the revenues of the authority.

Subsection (1) begins with the words 'except as provided in subsection (3)'. Accordingly, the *pari passu* provision in subsection (3) is described as an exception to the rule that no-one may have a mortgage or charge over the property. Subsection (3) can only constitute an exception to the rule if the activity which it describes does indeed constitute a 'mortgage or charge' of the property of the local authority. The reference to the terms of subsection (3) as an exception to the rule in subsection (1) should not be taken too literally. At the most technical level, it cannot be an exception. In subsection (3), it is the statute which declares that the property should be 'charged', while subsection (1) prohibits a voluntary act by the local authority, of granting a charge. Since the act in subsection (3) is not a voluntary act of the authority, it cannot logically be an exception to the prohibition against such voluntary acts.

10.16 The significance of the terms of s 13 lies in the fact that it illustrates the ease with which it is possible to cause confusion in this area by the imprecise use of language.[15]

---

[15] Section 13(4) compounds the confusion. Having made clear that all security given by a local authority in breach of the statutory prohibition shall be unenforceable, the section then goes on to say:

Cross-border insolvency

10.17 In financial transactions, the possibility that an obligor might become subject to insolvency proceedings is made more complicated by the fact that those proceedings might take place in a jurisdiction which is different from that of the lender's residence. Further, security taken by the lender over assets of the borrower might relate to assets which are situated outside the country where the insolvency proceedings take place. The assets might be in the country of the lender or in a third country.

10.18 The security arrangement concluded between the lender and the borrower will have taken the form which it seemed to them most appropriate at the time the arrangement was made. For example, an Italian company borrowing money from a bank in London might secure repayment by granting security over land in Scotland and over the shares of its French subsidiary. The parties will have drafted documentation which granted the form of security most appropriate in Scotland for dealing with Scottish land, and that which was thought appropriate in France for granting security over rights in a French company. If the borrower were to begin insolvency proceedings in Italy, one of the questions for the lender would be: will the Italian court, applying Italian insolvency legislation, recognize the lender's rights under security documentation governed by French law (in the case of the shares) or Scottish law (in the case of the land)?

10.19 This is one of the most important and most difficult questions to come before a lawyer who is drafting the documentation for an international financial transaction. There is no simple answer. However, the European Union has sought to deal with the issue, so far as concerns arrangements where the jurisdictions concerned are all within the EU. The Regulation on Insolvency Proceedings of 2015[16] deals with the question of the law that governs the conduct of insolvency proceedings. One of the major issues with which it has to deal is the question of the extent to which insolvency proceedings in an EU Member State should recognize the forms of security granted under laws of other Member States, even when those specific detailed legal structures have no relevance under the law of the jurisdiction where the insolvency proceedings are taking place.

10.20 The solution adopted in the Regulation is that the general rule should be that the law applicable to insolvency proceedings and to the effect of those proceedings should be that of the Member State where the proceedings take place. However, on certain matters, the courts of that Member State are required to recognize the effect of rights acquired under other legal systems. These include matters relating to set-off, reservation of title, contracts relating to land, and, most importantly, the rights described in Article 8 as the 'rights in rem of creditors or third parties'. The principle is set out in Recital (68) of the Regulation:

> There is a particular need for a special reference diverging from the law of the opening State in the case of rights *in rem*, since such rights are of considerable importance for the

All securities created by a local authority shall rank equally without priority.
Here, of course, the word 'security' is being used in the wide sense described in paras 10.04 and 10.05 above.

---

[16] Regulation (EU) 2015/848, replacing Council Regulation (EC) No 1346/2000.

granting of credit. The basis, validity and extent of such a right *in rem* should therefore normally be determined according to the *lex situs* and not be affected by the opening of insolvency proceedings. The proprietor of the right *in rem* should therefore be able to continue to assert its right to segregation or separate settlement of the collateral security.

Accordingly, Article 8.1 provides: **10.21**

The opening of insolvency proceedings shall not affect the rights *in rem* of creditors or third parties in respect of tangible or intangible, moveable or immovable assets, both specific assets and collections of indefinite assets as a whole which change from time to time, belonging to the debtor which are situated within the territory of another Member State at the time of the opening of proceedings.

This raises a question which is crucial not only to the draftsman of the Regulation, but to every lawyer who advises on the structuring of security arrangements in an international transaction: what are 'rights *in rem*'? The Regulation does not offer an exhaustive definition. It does however give a list of rights which would be considered to be 'rights *in rem*': **10.22**

2. The rights referred to in paragraph 1 shall in particular mean:
   (a) the right to dispose of assets or have them disposed of and to obtain satisfaction from the proceeds of or income from those assets, in particular by virtue of a lien or a mortgage;
   (b) the exclusive right to have a claim met, in particular a right guaranteed by a lien in respect of the claim or by assignment of the claim by way of a guarantee;
   (c) the right to demand the assets from, and/or to require restitution by, anyone having possession or use of them contrary to the wishes of the parties so entitled;
   (d) a right *in rem* to the beneficial use of assets.
3. The right, recorded in a public register and enforceable against third parties, under which a right *in rem* within the meaning of paragraph 1 may be obtained, shall be considered a right *in rem*.

The terms 'lien', 'mortgage', and 'guarantee' are left undefined.

The draftsmen of the Regulation had an extremely difficult task to perform. They needed to describe a category of legal concepts which were to be excluded from the general rule that the law to be applied was that of the place where the proceedings were taking place. This group of excluded concepts would, however, include a widely varying list of legal mechanisms, each of which was derived from the rules of a different legal system. The report which preceded the first draft of a proposed treaty, which later became the Regulation on Insolvency Proceedings 2000,[17] says, at para 100: **10.23**

Article 5[18] refers to 'rights in rem' but does not define what these are. The Convention does not intend to impose its own definition of a right in rem, running the risk of describing as rights in rem legal positions which the law of the state where the assets are located does not

---

[17] M. Virgos and E. Schmit, 'Report on the Convention on Insolvency Proceedings', reproduced as an appendix to G. Moss, I. Fletcher, and S. Isaacs, *The EC Regulation on Insolvency Proceedings: A Commentary and Annotated Guide* (2nd edn, Oxford University Press, 2009).
[18] The Article corresponding to Article 8 on the 2015 Regulation.

consider to be rights in rem, or of not encompassing rights in rem which do not fulfil the conditions of that definition....

For this reason, the characterisation of a right as a right in rem must be sought in the national law which, according to the normal pre-insolvency conflict of laws rules, governs rights in rem...

10.24 Thus, the intention behind the drafting of the Article is to indicate the nature of the characteristics of a legal concept which are considered to produce 'rights *in rem*' to a court which is asked to consider whether the exemption applies. The task is, in theory at least, a difficult one and involves a number of conceptual problems.[19] In practice, the problems do not appear to have been very great. Courts throughout the EU seem to have little difficulty in recognizing a right *in rem* when they see one.

10.25 The significance of Article 8 for the draftsman of financial security documentation lies in the emphasis it gives to the way in which a particular concept works. The effectiveness, in terms of cross-border enforceability, of a particular security concept depends on an analysis of its effect, rather than on the name given to it. In this sense, the Regulation is very pragmatic, and some might say that it follows a traditional common law path.

Registration

10.26 An understanding of the precise nature of security interests is essential not only for the purpose of assessing their significance in relation to cross-border transactions. The issue is crucial for purely domestic purposes. The UK, like most developed countries, has a system of registration for security interests. The purpose behind all such systems is to guard against the danger of 'false wealth'. If the assets which appear to belong to an individual or a corporation are subject to property interests owned by third parties, a misleading impression about the creditworthiness of the owner might be given. Although there are limits to the protection that can be given to the public against this misunderstanding, most legal systems adopt a policy of public registration of adverse interests.

10.27 In England and Wales, the system of registration of security interests is fragmented and complicated. In relation to individuals, Victorian legislation relating to the registration of 'bills of sale' required the registration of some instruments which created a security interest over chattels owned by a security-giver.[20] Security interests in land are required to be registered under the terms of Part 5 of the Land Registration Act 2002 and the Land Charges Act 1972. Security interests in aircraft are recorded in a register maintained by the Civil Aviation Authority,[21] and security over ships in a separate register of ship charges.[22]

---

[19] See the discussion in M. Virgos and F. Garcimartin, *The European Insolvency Regulation: Law and Practice* (Kluwer Law International, 2004), pp 91–108.
[20] See Bills of Sale Acts 1878 and 1882.
[21] See The Mortgaging of Aircraft Order 1972 (SI 1972/1268).
[22] See Merchant Shipping (Registration of Ships) Regulations 1993 (SI 1993/3135).

10.28 From the point of view of financial transactions, the most important registration provision is to be found in Companies Act 2006. Many attempts have been made over the years to produce a coherent and wide-ranging system of registration of security interests created by companies incorporated in England and Wales. However, attempts for an all-embracing definition of 'security interest' on which to base registration requirements have always come to nothing, because of problems of detail..

10.29 Until 2013, the requirement for registration by companies was determined by examining the security interest concerned (or, sometimes, the property over which the security was given) and comparing it against an eclectic list set out in the Companies Act. This gave rise to disputes, usually between a security-taker and the receiver of an insolvent security-giver, over whether an unregistered instrument evidenced the creation of a charge and, if it did, whether it fell within the detailed list of registrable charges.

10.30 The usual reason for the dispute between interested parties was that the failure to register a charge that ought to have been registered resulted in the charge being void, as against a receiver of the chargor company. Much intellectual effort was devoted to the task of deciding whether the security at issue was a charge, or was instead some other security interest that fell outside the ambit of the registration provisions. If it was a charge, the argument shifted to the question whether the charge was within the list set out in the legislation.

10.31 Perhaps the best-known case in this area is the *Charge Card* case,[23] discussed in Chapter 4, which concerned the legal nature of a 'charge-back'. This is an arrangement under which a creditor (eg a depositor with a bank) grants a charge over the debt to the debtor himself (in this example, grants a charge to the bank with which the deposit has been made). The charge secures a debt owing in the opposite direction (say, indebtedness arising from a loan by the bank to the depositor). In the *Charge Card* case, Millett J said that such an arrangement was not a charge, since it was conceptually impossible to charge a debt in favour of the debtor. Accordingly, the arrangement could not be void for want of registration. However, in a later case[24] the House of Lords held that it was possible to describe such an arrangement as a 'charge'.

10.32 The registration regime for security interests created by UK incorporated companies has been simplified by amendments[25] to the relevant provisions of the Companies Act 2006, made in 2013. Now, all charges created by a UK company are registrable, unless a specific exemption is given by statute.[26] For these purposes, 'charge' includes mortgage.[27] The creation of any registrable charge is to be notified to the Registrar of Companies within 21 days.[28] If registration is not effected as required by the Act, s 859H(3) provides that the charge is void, so far as it creates security over the property of the company, against a liquidator, administrator, or creditor of the company.

---

[23] *In re Charge Card Services Ltd* [1987] Ch 150.
[24] *In re Bank of Credit and Commerce International SA (No 8)* [1998] AC 214.
[25] See Companies Act 2006 (Amendment of Part 25) Regulations 2013 No 600.
[26] As far as financial markets are concerned, the most important exemption is probably that for financial collateral covered by the Financial Collateral Arrangements Regulations (No 2) 2003.
[27] Companies Act 2006 s 859A (7).
[28] Companies Act 2006 s 859A(4).

10.33 The changes in the registration regime made in 2013 have undoubtedly helped to simplify practice in this area. However, in contrast to Article 8 of the 2015 EU Regulation on Insolvency Proceedings, the UK legislation does not start from a generalized concept of 'security interest' or 'right *in rem*'. It relates only to charges and mortgages. Forms of security interest which do not fall into either of those categories are not registrable. The UK regime still leaves scope for uncertainty.

10.34 To lawyers who are not practitioners in the financial markets, the great concern caused by this issue is somewhat puzzling. The obvious response is that if there is any doubt as to whether the arrangement is indeed a 'charge', the safe course is simply to register the security. However, very often in practice this is not possible. A security-giver, for good commercial reasons, may refuse to agree to registration of an arrangement. For example, an arrangement between a securities clearing house and its members might well include security arrangements in favour of the clearer over sums owing from the clearer to its customer. A customer would, however, be very reluctant to see that arrangement, which it regards as a purely commercial off-setting provision, to be registered against it as a charge which it has granted.

10.35 Another reason for reluctance to accept registration is that the party entering into the arrangement may have given negative pledge covenants in various loan transactions or bond documents. It may have covenanted with its lenders or bondholders that it would not grant security to a third party. If an arrangement, which it does not regard as being a grant of security in the normal sense, is to be registered as a charge on a public register, this could have adverse commercial implications.

10.36 Nor should it be thought that the registration process is necessarily very simple. In a complex financing arrangement, a borrower might be a member of a group of companies with hundreds of subsidiaries, many or all of which are involved in the financing arrangements as guarantors or joint obligors. If it is decided that a particular arrangement is registrable under the terms of the Companies Act, this might involve the registration of charges against hundreds of companies. In a complex financing which is subject to adjustment and amendment at regular intervals, the process of registering charges can become a full-time activity in itself. If it is possible to structure the arrangement in such a way that the need for registration does not arise, life can be made very much easier. The determination of these issues can be made only if there is a very clear understanding of the legal nature of the security arrangements which are available.

Kinds of Security

10.37 It is natural for any discussion of security in English law to address the question by itemizing and describing the separate legal concepts that share the characteristic of being 'security'. However, there are three things which must be remembered. First, terminology in this area is notoriously and dangerously fluid, so that the name given to a particular legal mechanism can be misleading.[29] Second, the cases in which classifications of security have

---

[29] See paras 10.04 to 10.10 above.

been given or discussed inevitably look at the issue from the point of view of the facts under consideration and can rarely be taken as an exhaustive review of the subject. Third, it must be remembered that the common law on commercial matters is concerned primarily with practicalities. What matters is the effect of an arrangement, rather than its conceptual basis. As Lord Hoffmann explained in *In Re Bank of Credit and Commerce International SA (No 8)*:[30]

> ... the law is fashioned to suit the practicalities of life and legal concepts like 'proprietary interest' and 'charge' are no more than labels given to clusters of related and self-consistent rules of law. Such concepts do not have a life of their own from which the rules are inexorably derived.

10.38 An illustration of the second of these points can be seen in the case of *Halliday v Holgate*,[31] heard by the Court of Exchequer Chamber, shortly before the fusion of the administration of law and equity by the Supreme Court of Judicature Act 1975.[32] In this case an individual had bought shares in a mining company. To raise money, he had issued a promissory note in favour of a lender, and handed over the share certificates as security for payment of the promissory note. He then became bankrupt. The holder of the certificates sold them and, out of the proceeds of sale, reimbursed himself for the money owed. The assignee in bankruptcy objected to this, and claimed that the lender was liable to him in tort, because he had sold the certificates without first making demand for repayment of the loan.

10.39 The court rejected this argument. In coming to the conclusion that no wrong had been committed by the security-holder, the court said:

> There are three kinds of security: the first, is simple lien; the second, a mortgage, passing the property out and out; the third, a security intermediate between a lien and a mortgage – viz., a pledge – where by contract a deposit of goods is made a security for a debt, and the right to the property vests in the pledgee so far as is necessary to secure the debt.

The case was heard by a court of common law, rather than a court of equity. It is, perhaps, unsurprising that no mention was made of the concept of a charge or that of an equitable mortgage. As far as the court was concerned, it was clear that the intention of the deposit of the share certificates was to create a security for the payment of the debt. According to the classification then adopted at law, the description of the arrangement produced must be that it was a pledge. The pledge gave the security-taker, as the possessor of the share certificate, the right to dispose of that share certificate to realize cash. The value of the security, of course, lay in the fact that its transfer also operated to assign the ownership of the *chose in action* of which it was evidence. Thus, the court was content that a pledge of the certificate itself gave the security intended.

10.40 Had the case come before a chancery court, rather than a court of common law, the view might well have been taken that the deposit of the share certificate as security was an attempt to create a mortgage over the shares. In the eyes of equity, this should be regarded

---

[30] [1998] AC 214, and see paras 4.80 *et seq*.
[31] (1868) LR 3 Exch 299.
[32] See paras 4.30 to 4.38.

as an equitable mortgage, or as a charge over the underlying *chose in action*. The outcome would have been the same.

10.41 In 1998, long after the fusion of law and equity, Millett LJ reviewed the same point in *In Re Coslett (Contractors) Ltd*.[33] He said that there were four kinds of security: mortgage, pledge, equitable charge, and consensual lien. In this, he was not disagreeing with the earlier case, but simply adding to it the additional product of equity. The application of this classification to the facts of *Halliday v Holgate* would produce no different outcome, although the security granted by the deposit might have been described as an equitable charge. Placing the arrangement in the category of 'charge' rather than that of 'pledge' would not affect the rights of the parties.[34]

10.42 The flexible approach adopted by courts to the classification of types of security has a practical consequence for a financial lawyer concerned with the drafting or review of security arrangements. It is often unfruitful to seek to draft a 'charge' or a 'mortgage', starting with the chosen classification for the security arrangement. It is usually more profitable to decide on the terms of the security to be given, and thereafter to analyze the effect that the arrangements will have as a matter of law.

10.43 This can be done in a series of three questions:

Question 1:
Is the arrangement effective, as between the security-giver and the security-taker, to produce the effect that is intended?

Question 2:
What is the effect, as against third parties? The rights of the security-taker must be such that they will survive challenge, not only from the security-giver, but also from others who claim an interest in the subject-matter of the security. In particular, this would include third parties who claim to have acquired ownership of the asset concerned, or who claim themselves to have taken security over it. Most importantly, the security must be effective, notwithstanding the insolvency of the security-giver.

Question 3:
(In cases which have a cross-border element.) If a court in a foreign jurisdiction has to consider the security arrangements, will it recognize the rights of the security-taker? In particular, if the security-giver enters into insolvency proceedings elsewhere in the EU, will the arrangements fall within one of the exceptions to the basic rule in the Regulation on Insolvency Proceedings 2015,[35] so that the effect of the security arrangements which will be recognized is that produced by the governing law of the documentation?

10.44 The following sections of this chapter summarize the kinds of security mechanism which are effective in English law. Each of these concepts is capable of forming the subject of a text book in its own right. Some of them do. The summary below should be taken, therefore, as a menu, rather than a meal in itself.

---

[33] [1998] Ch 495.
[34] At the time of *Halliday v Holgate* there was no requirement for the registration of a security such as the one then created. The significance of any distinction would have been felt, however, if (as is the case now) the registration of charges had been required, but that of pledges had not. See paras 10.26 *et seq* above.
[35] See paras 10.17 to 10.25 above.

The obvious main division between kinds of security is that between the concepts which are based on the security-taker acquiring some form of property interest in an asset belonging to the security-giver, and those in which the rights of the security-taker are constituted by contract alone.[36] Most forms of security involve the security-taker being granted a form of property interest in an asset which belongs to the security-giver, but this is not always so. As will be seen below, there are a number of mechanisms which deal with the ownership of the asset concerned in a different way, but in the end produce the same economic result. For a lawyer structuring a transaction or drafting documentation, these mechanisms can properly be regarded as security arrangements, although their form and substance is different.

10.45

Title-based security

Mortgage and charge

Mortgage and charge are separate legal concepts, one being the product of the common law, and the other of equity. They are, however, so closely related that for many purposes the terms are interchangeable, and it is therefore convenient to deal with them together.

10.46

As early as Saxon times, it was accepted that land, like chattels, could be pledged. A lender would be allowed to take possession of the land, and in the event of non-payment of the sum due, he would become the owner of it.[37] By the sixteenth century, a mortgage could take one of two forms. It could consist of a transfer by the security-giver to the security-taker of the whole of his ownership interest in the land, accompanied by a proviso that, if he repaid the debt in accordance with its terms, the security-taker would retransfer the property to him. The alternative form was that the security-giver would grant to the security-taker a lease of the land, with the proviso that the lease should be surrendered if the debt was paid in accordance with its terms. The first of these mechanisms, outright transfer with a proviso for retransfer on redemption, was used also to grant security over the other kinds of asset recognized by the common law – personal moveable property (chattels) and legal *choses in action*.

10.47

By the early nineteenth century, the use of a lease to take a mortgage of land had largely died out. By the end of the century, Lindley MR could describe a mortgage as follows:[38]

10.48

> A mortgage is a conveyance of land or an assignment of chattels as a security for the payment of a debt or the discharge of some other obligation for which it is given.

Mortgages of chattels are governed by the Bills of Sale Acts 1878 and 1882. The legislation stipulates particular forms of documentation for the grant of security over chattels and certain kinds of incorporeal property. The provisions are complex and registration requirements are very onerous. However, the Acts have now very little practical effect, since most commercial activity is conducted through corporate entities, to whom the Acts do not apply. However, there are situations in which individuals grant security as part of significant

10.49

---

[36] Lord Hoffmann's comments about the importance of the word 'proprietary', referred to in para 10.37 above, must always be borne in mind.
[37] For a discussion on the early forms of mortgage, see W. Clark (ed), *Fisher & Lightwood's Law of Mortgages* (14th edn, LexisNexis, 2014).
[38] *Santley v Wilde* [1899] 2 Ch 474, CA.

financial transactions. For example, the tax treatment of film finance means that production is quite often conducted through partnerships of individuals. Since the security in film financing almost always involves the physical fruits of the activity (ie prints of films, props, etc), care must be taken to ensure that the security package does not fall foul of the terms of the Acts.

10.50 The Law Commission proposed in November 2017[39] the repeal of the Bills of Sale Acts, and their replacement with a system of mortgages over goods. It remains to be seen whether this recommendation will be adopted.

10.51 From the point of view of financial transactions, the creation of security by companies is overwhelmingly more important than security given by individuals. Companies Act 2006 s 859A provides that all charges are registrable if created by a company. For these purposes, 'charge' includes 'mortgage'.[40]

10.52 The Law of Property Act 1925 provides a statutory mechanism for the mortgage of debts and other 'legal *choses in action*'. Although s 136 of that act deals only with 'absolute' assignments and specifically excludes those 'purporting to be by way of charge only', it has been decided that for these purposes an assignment of the *chose* with a proviso for reassignment, in the classic form of a mortgage, is within the terms of the section.[41]

10.53 The Law of Property Act 1925 made a major change to the form of legal mortgage of land. Section 85 creates the concept of a 'charge by way of legal mortgage'. This term is included within the definition of 'legal mortgage' contained in s 205(1)(xvi) of the Act. Since 1925 a legal mortgage of land can be created only by the grant of a lease to the security-taker or by the grant in his favour of a 'charge by way of legal mortgage', subject to the provision that the charge should cease to apply when the mortgage is redeemed. Transfer of the ownership of the land is no longer involved. In the case of land, therefore, a legal mortgage is no longer a mortgage at all, but a charge which says that it is a mortgage.

10.54 As far as registered land is concerned, the concept of a mortgage by grant of lease has been abolished by the Land Registration Act 2002. Section 23 gives an owner of land the power:

> to charge the estate at law with the payment of money.

By s 51 of the Act, such a charge has the same effect as a 'charge by way of legal mortgage'. It is not only practitioners who find the technical details of the law relating to mortgages of land confusing. In 1991 the Law Commission[42] recommended that the existing methods of mortgage and charge over land should be abolished and should be replaced by two standardized forms of mortgage, the 'formal land mortgage' and the 'informal land mortgage'. These proposals have not, however, been implemented.

10.55 Thus, a mortgage of moveable property or intangible property involves the transfer of the property concerned to the security-taker, with contractual provision for retransfer on payment of the secured debt. In the case of land, title is not transferred to the security-taker.

---

[39] In a Report entitled *From Bills of Sale to Goods Mortgages*, Law Com No 376.
[40] See para 10.32 above.
[41] See *Tancred and others v Delagoa Bay and East Africa Railway Co* (1889) 23 QBD 239; and see paras 5.56 to 5.59 above.
[42] *The Transfer of Land-Mortgages*, Law Com No 204, 13 November 1991.

Instead, he has a special form of charge under which he is, by statute, given the rights that he would have, if he had taken a mortgage in the traditional form.

10.56 A charge is, in concept, quite different from a mortgage. At its most basic, a charge is simply the dedication of property to the performance of a particular obligation. Thus, the Local Government Act 2003 s 13[43] provides that all borrowings of a local authority 'shall be charged indifferently on all the revenues of the authority'. This simply means that the revenues of a local authority shall be used to repay its borrowings (without, of course, providing that they should not be used for other purposes). The provision gives no legal interest in those revenues to lenders to the authority. The section does not confer on the lender to a local authority any security. He has no right to claim or deal with the revenues of the local authority which are 'charged'.

10.57 But that is not the end of the matter. In consensual arrangements devised with the object of providing security, equity will enforce the dedication (charging) of the property for the discharge of the debt. It will do this by granting rights to the security-taker to deal with the property and use the proceeds for payment of the debt. Millett J said in the *Charge Card* case:[44]

> ... the essence of an equitable charge is that, without any conveyance or assignment to the chargee, specific property of the chargor is expressly or constructively appropriated to or made available for payment of a debt, and the chargee is given the right to resort to the property for the purpose of having it realised and applied in or towards payment of the debt. The availability of equity remedies has the effect of giving the chargee a proprietary interest by way of security in the property charged.

10.58 Thus, 'mortgage' and 'charge' are very different in concept. In the case of a mortgage, the security-taker acquires a proprietary interest because he becomes the owner of the property, subject to the security-giver's right to redeem and demand a retransfer. In the case of a charge, however, the agreement to grant the charge confers itself no property interest on the security-taker. He acquires this by virtue of the availability to him of equitable remedies. This entitlement creates a transmissible interest in the asset.[45]

10.59 Despite this divergence in concept, the result of the two mechanisms is, for most purposes, identical and the terms are often used as interchangeable. In *Downsview Nominees Ltd v First City Corp Ltd*,[46] Lord Templeman said:

> A mortgage, whether legal or equitable, is security for repayment of a debt. The security may be constituted by a conveyance, assignment or demise or by a charge on any interest in real or personal property. An equitable mortgage is a contract which creates a charge on property but does not pass a legal estate to the creditor.

10.60 In English law, the concept of the floating charge is of vital importance in the structuring of security arrangements, where the security-giver is a corporation. The idea of a floating charge, first recognized in the nineteenth century, is that a company may grant a charge

---

[43] See paras 10.11 *et seq* above.
[44] *In Re Charge Card Services Ltd* [1987] 1 Ch 150.
[45] Per Millett LJ in *Re Coslett (Contractors) Ltd* [1998] Ch 495.
[46] [1993] AC 295, at 311.

which 'floats' over all of its assets or an identifiable class of its assets. Until such time as it 'crystallizes', the company can deal with those assets free of any interest of the security-taker. On crystallization, however, the charge attaches to all the assets owned by the company in the class concerned, as a fixed charge. Lord Templeman in the *Downsview* case said:

> The security for a debt incurred by a company may take the form of a fixed charge on property or the form of a floating charge which becomes a fixed charge on the assets comprised in the security when the debt becomes due and payable.

In the past, the distinction between a fixed charge and a floating charge was often of vital importance. One reason for the importance was that a floating charge was registrable under the terms of the Companies Acts, while a fixed charge over the same assets might not be. Since the amendments made in 2013 to the registration regime,[47] all charges, whether fixed or floating, are subject to the same registration requirements. The distinction between fixed and floating remains significant in some circumstances, but issues of registration have gone.

Pledge

10.61 Pledge is one of the oldest forms of security known to English law. A pledge, or pawn, is created by a contract. The contract is put into effect by the security-giver handing physical possession to the security-taker, on terms that the latter may retain possession of the asset until the debt is discharged. Ownership of the asset remains with the security-giver, but the security-taker may on default sell the asset concerned.[48] The proceeds of sale will be used to satisfy the debt, any excess being held by the security-taker on trust for the original owner.[49]

10.62 Because the security relies on the physical possession of the asset, pledge is an inappropriate mechanism in the case of land, and also in the case of intangibles. It is argued that a pledge of documents evidencing ownership of an intangible asset, such as a share certificate, might have the effect of pledging the certificate itself, but cannot amount to a pledge of the shares concerned. Being intangible, they are incapable of being possessed. A purported pledge of shares in this way might, however, amount to an equitable mortgage or charge over the shares.[50]

10.63 Because the concept of pledge relates only to chattels, its application in modern financial transaction is limited. However, the concept is sometimes used in film financing transactions, where the physical product of the project (ie film prints, etc) hold a great deal of the value of the assets and can be easily taken into possession by financiers or their agents. In addition, it is perfectly possible for possession to be held by the agent of a security-taker, rather than the security-taker itself. Thus, if the security for a transaction consists of goods which are in a warehouse, it is possible to arrange for the warehouse owner to 'attorn' to a security-taker. This he does by accepting, at the request of the owner of the goods, that

---

[47] See paras 10.29 to 10.32 above.
[48] See *Re Morritt* (1886) 18 QBD 222.
[49] *Matthew v Sutton Ltd* [1994] 4 All ER 793.
[50] This argument is set out in detail in *Paget's Law of Banking* (15th edn, LexisNexis 2018) para 16.2. But, for a case where a common law court had no difficulty in accepting the efficacy of a pledge over shares, see *Halliday v Holgate* (1868) LR 3 Exch 299, discussed in paras 10.38 to 10.40 above.
  This analysis of common law concepts of property is muddied a little by the intervention of EU Community law in the form of the Financial Collateral Directive, which provides for the idea of 'possession or control' of incorporeal things (see footnote 11 to para 10.09). This should be seen as an exception to the rules of the common law, rather than as an amendment of them.

he holds the goods for the account of the security-taker. He thus has possession of them as agent for that party, whose possession can be used to support a pledge of the goods concerned.[51]

By far the most important use of pledge in financial transactions is its use in trade finance. Bills of lading of goods are recognized at common law as having an unusual status. The possession of a bill of lading to goods is treated as possession of the goods themselves. Transfer of the bill of lading is equivalent to the transfer of the goods. By pledging to a financier a bill of lading which represents goods in transit, the owner pledges the goods themselves.[52] **10.64**

Lien

The word 'lien' is used to describe several diverse types of arrangement. The classic common law lien is a right which arises by operation of law, rather than as a result of any agreement between the parties that it should exist. A common law lien is a passive right; the right to retain possession of a physical asset, as against the owner, until a debt has been paid. The holder has merely the right to retain possession, and has no right to sell or otherwise deal with the property.[53] An example of a common law lien is the solicitor's lien, where the solicitor has a right to retain papers belonging to a former client until outstanding fees are paid. **10.65**

An equitable lien is a similar right, which arises under a doctrine of equity, rather than being created by contract between the parties. For example, a vendor of land has an equitable lien on it until the purchase price is paid.[54] **10.66**

In addition, the courts have recognized the existence of the so-called 'consensual lien'. This arises where the security-taker already has possession of property belonging to the security-giver and the latter agrees that he should be entitled to retain possession until the debt is paid. It will normally be coupled with an agreement that the security-taker should be able to sell the property in default of payment. The effect is very similar to that of a pledge. Millett LJ described it as follows in *Re Coslett (Contractors) Ltd*:[55] **10.67**

> A pledge and a contractual lien both depend on delivery of possession to the creditor. The difference between them is that in the case of a pledge the owner delivers possession to the creditor as security, whereas in the case of a lien the creditor retains possession of goods previously delivered to him for some other purpose.

For financial lawyers, the importance of lien is negative rather than positive. It is not a concept that is often used in order to facilitate financial transactions. It can, however, pose a problem which must be avoided. It is common to find in financial arrangements the existence of a 'negative pledge', an undertaking by a borrower that it will preserve the position of an unsecured creditor by ensuring that no other creditor is granted security. Thus, the unsecured creditor, although he has no priority himself, can be satisfied that he will at least rank equally with all other creditors. From the point of view of the borrower, it is possible to comply with this negative undertaking by ensuring that no other creditor is given a charge **10.68**

---

[51] See *Dublin City Distillery (Great Brunswick Street, Dublin) Ltd v Docherty* [1915] AC 823, HL.
[52] On this topic, see generally *Paget's Law of Banking* (15th edn, LexisNexis 2018), paras 16.3 to 16.12.
[53] *Mulliner v Florence* (1878) 3 QBD 484.
[54] See *Sookraj v Samaroo* [2004] UKPC 50.
[55] [1998] Ch 495.

or mortgage or pledge. However, because common law and equitable liens arise by operation of law, and come into operation without the acquiescence of the security-giver, it is not possible to prevent them arising. For example, in any situation where a company has a solicitor's bill outstanding, the solicitor has a lien over the client's papers. It does not matter that the lien may never be exercised; it comes into existence as soon as a bill is delivered by the solicitor and remains until the bill is discharged. In agreeing to the wording of negative pledge clauses, borrowers should take care to exclude liens arising by operation of law in the ordinary course of business.

Declaration of trust

10.69 An arrangement sometimes found in cross-border lending is that where a corporate borrower declares itself trustee of its assets, or a certain class of its assets, for the benefit of creditors (say, a syndicate of lending banks) until such time as the loans have been repaid. The declaration of trust is not an independent security device, but amounts, in law, to an equitable charge over the property concerned.[56] Its use has little advantage over the straightforward grant of a charge over the assets concerned. It is used in those situations where there is likely to be a shifting class of beneficiaries of security (eg members of a syndicate of banks where the interests might be traded) and where, for some reason, it is thought inappropriate to appoint a trustee who can take the benefit of a charge on behalf of the security-takers. By using the declaration of trust, the security-giver, in effect, constitutes itself the trustee of the security.

Ownership as security

10.70 One of the oldest forms of security, the mortgage, is based on the idea that the ownership of the asset is transferred to the security-taker, with the security-giver retaining a right to demand retransfer, when the secured debt was repaid. Over time, the law has recognized this arrangement as one of shared ownership, with the security-taker becoming the owner of the property in the eyes of the law, but with the security-giver retaining an 'equity of redemption', which is itself a right of property. In relation to land, the concept of the mortgage has evolved even further, to the stage where it does not involve a transfer of title at all.[57] In security structures, the law has moved away from the idea of the transfer of ownership as a form of security. However, there are a number of structures which are very commonly used in financial transactions, which have the same economic effect as the grant of security in property, but which rely upon the acquisition or retention of ownership.

10.71 In the wider commercial world, retention of title is one of the most important forms of security, in the sense of being a mechanism to protect against the consequence of non-payment. Under this arrangement, a supplier of goods grants credit to a customer, by agreeing that the customer should pay for the goods some time after they have been delivered into his possession. The seller covers himself against the possibility of non-payment by agreeing with the customer that title to the goods should not pass until the purchase price has been paid (or, perhaps, until all sums owing to the seller on any account have been paid). Thus, rather than taking a charge over assets of the debtor, the creditor simply retains the ownership of the goods he has agreed to sell.

---

[56] See para 10.57 above. See also *Goode and Gullifer on Legal Problems of Credit and Security* (6th edn, Sweet & Maxwell, 2017), Ch 1–57.]
[57] See paras 10.47 to 10.48 and para 10.53 above.

10.72 The reservation of title structure is, in English law, very secure, although it has limitations. First, it is rarely of assistance if the goods have been sold by the customer, before he has paid for them. Nor is the mechanism effective if the goods are such that they are mixed with other items and not capable of being identified as the property of the seller. Nor is the mechanism useful if the goods are consumed as part of the manufacturing process, so that they cease to exist in their original form, and simply become part of the different asset.[58] Notwithstanding these limitations, reservation of title to goods remains a vitally important mechanism by which suppliers may, in effect, secure themselves against non-payment.

10.73 In the securities markets, a similar mechanism exists, in the form of the sale-and-repurchase, or repo, agreement. A broker/dealer who needed to balance its books at the end of the trading day would have either surplus cash or a cash deficit. In the latter case, a convenient way to acquire the cash, rather than borrowing it on security, would be to agree with another broker/dealer, who had surplus cash, that the former would sell securities to the latter, for immediate payment. Because the cash so acquired was needed only until the next trading day, the agreement would provide that, on the following day, the purchasing broker would sell the securities back to the selling broker, the resale price being slightly higher than the purchase price, to reflect the use of the money overnight.

10.74 The economic effect of a repo agreement is, of course, the same as the borrowing of money, against the grant of a mortgage or charge over shares belonging to the borrower. The form, however, is different. The mechanism used in a standard repo has become more sophisticated over time, and has been adapted to other situations. For example, the transaction known as 'stock lending' operates on the same basis. A broker which needs to acquire shares or bonds, usually in order to fulfil an obligation to a third party to deliver those securities under a contract of sale, may agree with someone who owns the securities concerned that it will 'borrow' the securities for a period. The use of the words 'lend' and 'borrow' are very misleading. The agreement between the parties is that the 'lender' transfers ownership of the specified securities to the 'borrower'. The 'borrower' agrees to transfer, at a specified date in the future, the equivalent securities (ie securities of the same number and the same description) to the 'lender'. It also agrees to pay a fee for the provision of the facility by the 'lender'.

10.75 If the 'lender' is motivated to use this facility by the need to raise cash, the stock lending agreement can stipulate that, when the stock is first transferred, a purchase price is paid for it, and when the 'borrower' transfers equivalent stock back to the 'lender' the latter will also pay a purchase price. If cash changes hands in this way, the arrangement is, from the point of view of the 'lender' the equivalent of borrowing money against a mortgage of shares.

10.76 The only difference between these mechanisms and a mortgage is that, in the case of the stock-lending arrangement and the repo agreement, the shares which are transferred back to the original owner are not the same shares as were originally transferred by him. They are equivalent securities. In the case of a mortgage, however, the securities would be the same, because the original owner would never have parted with the title to them.

---

[58] See *Borden (UK) Ltd v Scottish Timber Products Ltd* [1981] Ch 25.

10.77 Repo, stock lending, and other similar arrangements are now very commonly used internationally as the way of raising liquidity in securities markets. The legal concern has always been that a court might take the view that these transactions were not transactions of sale and purchase, but rather secured lending. This concern leads to the worry that the security would be vulnerable to attack if, for example, registration provisions had not been observed.

10.78 On the basis of the standard forms normally used in the market for such transactions, this fear has been laid to rest. The area was reviewed in detail by the Federal Court of Australia in *Beconwood Securities Pty Ltd v Australia & New Zealand Banking Group Ltd*.[59] In this case, Beconwood entered into a securities lending agreement with OPS Prime Stockbroking Ltd. The agreement was based on one of the market standard agreements for stock lending. The question that came before the court was whether the true character of the securities lending agreement was that of a mortgage, pursuant to which Beconwood borrowed money from OPS and put up shares by way of security.

10.79 The judge, Finkelstein J, reviewed the cases on the nature of security and concluded that the arrangement was one of sale and purchase, rather than that of mortgage or charge. Although it may often be difficult to differentiate between a sale and repurchase and a mortgage, the essential difference is that, in the case of an outright transfer, there is no right on the transferor to redeem the property which he has transferred. He quotes Romer LJ in the English case *Re George Inglefield Ltd*:[60]

> In a transaction of sale the vendor is not entitled to get back the subject-matter of the sale by returning to the purchaser the money that has passed between them. In the case of a mortgage or charge, the mortgagor is entitled, until he has been foreclosed, to get back the subject matter of the mortgage or charge by returning to the mortgagee the money that has passed between them.[61]

10.80 This reasoning points out why the mechanisms of repo and securities lending are convenient in the securities markets. Securities are fungible, in the sense that one share or bond in a particular series of a given issuer is exactly the same as every other share or bond in that series. It makes no difference to a transferor whether he receives back exactly the same securities as he transferred, or whether those which he receives back are merely of the same description. The interchangeability of the assets means that the identity of the particular assets is not important.

10.81 Another form of financial structure which has been widely used for many years, and which also relies for its effect on the transfer of title to assets, rather than the granting of security over them, is the practice known as 'debt factoring'. Debt factoring in turn has a variation known as 'invoice discounting'.[62] In debt factoring, a company, whose business involves the fact that it will become entitled to sums of money from its customers (receivables), agrees with a financier to sell its receivables to the financier. As each receivable is created (say, by the company selling goods to a customer), the company sells it to the financier, and assigns it absolutely to the financier. The financier agrees that the purchase price will be the face

---

[59] [2008] FCA 594.
[60] [1933] 1 Ch D 1.
[61] See also *Alderson v White* [1858] 2 De G & J 97.
[62] For a discussion of this arrangement in a different context, see paras 4.58 to 4.73.

value of the debt, and that the price will be paid at the end of the specified period (the selling company's normal debt collection period). If, at the end of that period, the debt has not been paid, the financier will reassign to the company the debt which is unpaid, again at its face value, the amount of this obligation being set off against the purchase price of the same amount originally agreed to be paid by the financier. This arrangement, of course, provides no financing advantage to the selling company. This benefit is obtained by a separate agreement that the financier will pre-pay for the debts, the pre-payment price being a discounted version of the purchase price for the debt concerned, reduced to take account of the early payment period.

The effect of this arrangement is the same as would have been achieved if the trading company had borrowed from the financier the amount of the pre-payment, against the grant of a charge over the receivables as security. However, for similar reasons to those which governed the *Beconwood Securities* case, this agreement takes effect as a sale and purchase, rather than a secured lending transaction.[63]

10.82

Contract-based security

Security is connected, in the thought processes of almost all lawyers, with the idea of a property interest in an asset belonging to someone else. That interest might consist of ownership (in the case of a mortgage), possession coupled with a contractual right of sale (in the case of pledge), or a contractual arrangement which gives a right to sell the asset and use the proceeds (in the case of a charge). There are, however, a number of mechanisms which rely solely on contractual arrangements to produce the same effect. Because of the way the contract operates, there is no need for the security-taker to claim any rights of property, in order to obtain the economic benefit of the asset concerned. Arrangements under which one party can look to an asset to discharge a debt owed to it can be regarded, for practical purposes as a form of security, notwithstanding that no property interest is claimed.

10.83

Chapter 3[64] described the mechanisms of contractual set-off, netting, running accounts, and the banker's right of combination of accounts. They were examined as examples of mechanisms which were the equivalent of payment. The establishment of a mechanism which, when put into effect, will be the equivalent of payment can be equally well described as an arrangement to secure the payment of money.

10.84

The common characteristic of these mechanisms is that a debt owing from A to B (which may, of course, be described as an asset belonging to B) is used to discharge a debt owing from B to A. Provided that there is no legal doctrine which prevents the operation of such a mechanism, the legal basis for the concept does not matter. A does not care whether he is allowed to use B's asset (the debt due to B from A) (i) because he (A) has the benefit of a charge over the debt owing by him to B; or (ii) because the contract between him and B says that he may set off the debt owed to B against the sum that is owed by B to him. This, it can

10.85

---

[63] See *Lloyds & Scottish Finance Ltd v Prentice* (1977) 121 SJ 847.
[64] Paras 3.07 to 3.26.

be said, is the outcome of the debate about the nature of a 'charge-back' which culminated in the House of Lords' decision in *Re Bank of Credit and Commerce International SA (No 8)*.[65]

10.86 The House of Lords held that the grant by B in favour of A of the right to set off a debt due from A to B against indebtedness owing from B to A could properly be described as a charge, granting to A property rights in respect of the debt which it owed to B. This did not prejudice the view taken by the Court of Appeal in the same case, that the arrangements operated as a matter of contract to produce the same effect. A's ability to use his contractual rights to set off his liability to B against the amount which B owed to him produced exactly the same result in economic terms as a claim by A to have a property interest in B's asset (the amount owed by A to B), which A could realize by setting the amount of it off against sums that B owed to A.

10.87 In relation to charge-backs, as well as in relation to the other mechanisms discussed, what matters is the outcome. Whether the security-taker reaches his goal by the exercise of contractual rights or by the exercise of property rights makes no difference.

10.88 The view that contractual rights can produce a position for a security-taker which is as favourable as that which follows from his having a property interest is subject to one major reservation: that it should not fall foul of any legal doctrine which would affect the operation of the contractual terms. In the minds of financial lawyers, the principal such concern is the so-called 'anti-deprivation principle'. The main purpose of taking security in financial transactions is to guard the security-taker against the consequence of the security-giver becoming insolvent, and unable to discharge its contractual obligations. Crucial to the usefulness of any security arrangement, therefore, is the fact that it should operate notwithstanding the insolvency of the security-giver.

10.89 It has been a guiding principle of insolvency legislation in England for many centuries that, on an insolvency, the assets of the insolvent should be available to satisfy the debts of creditors *pari passu*, subject only to priorities given by statute and to the claims of secured creditors (ie those creditors who have a property interest by way of security in the assets of the insolvent). In 1880, Cotton LJ said:[66]

> There cannot be a valid contract that a man's property shall remain his until bankruptcy, and on the happening of that event go over to someone else, and be taken from his creditors.

The concern with the drafting of arrangements which, as a matter of contract, produce the same effect as the grant of a property interest by way of security is that the arrangement will be seen by a court to fall foul of this principle. In the drafting of any contractual arrangements, great care must always be taken to ensure that the arrangement cannot be seen to operate as a deprivation of property.

10.90 An example of an arrangement constructed specifically with the view of avoiding this danger is a concept developed in the 1970s and then called 'flawed asset'. In the mid-1970s, large corporations with international operations faced an annoying accounting problem. If a company based in the UK had acquired a major overseas asset (say, the share capital of a

---

[65] [1998] AC 214. See paras 4.75 to 4.89.
[66] *Ex parte Jay* (1880) 14 Ch D 19.

company in the United States), the UK accounting rules required that, on consolidation, the value of the US asset should be stated in sterling, the currency conversion being made at the time of consolidation. The effect of this was to produce large annual swings in the value of overseas assets, which reflected the movements between the two currencies concerned, rather than the performance of the overseas assets in commercial terms. This could, of course, be noted on the accounts in order to inform readers of the reason for the apparent increase or decrease in value of overseas assets. Such a note did not, however, achieve much more than telling readers that the accounts did not really mean what they said.

10.91 A better form of presentation, it was thought, was to eliminate from the accounts the effect of the currency fluctuations. This was achieved by way of a mechanism known as a 'parallel loan'. In this arrangement corporation A, which owned a US asset valued at, say, US$100 million would borrow US$100 million from a counterparty. The counterparty, a US corporation with UK assets, would borrow an equivalent sterling amount from the English company. From the point of view of the English company, it had altered the position from one in which it owned an asset worth US$100 million to one in which it had (i) an asset worth US$100 million, balanced by (ii) a liability of US$100 million under its loan from the US corporation, and (iii) a sterling asset, being the amount of the debt owed to it by the US corporation. The effect, for accounting purposes, was that the UK company had neutralized the effect of its asset being overseas.

10.92 As a matter of law, however, the English company had created a situation where it owed US$100 million to its counterparty, and was owed in return an equivalent sterling amount. Although the transaction had achieved its purpose of making the corporate accounts slightly clearer, this was hardly worth doing, if the cost was to take on a substantial financial risk. If the US counterparty were to become insolvent, the English company must be certain that it could not be forced to repay the US$100 million it had borrowed, while being compelled to prove in the insolvency for the sterling equivalent amount which was owed to it. Although there was little doubt at the time that a contractual set-off mechanism would have been effective in insolvency,[67] there was thought to be a need for an additional arrangement which was not open to challenge.

10.93 That mechanism was produced by ensuring that each of the two loans in the arrangement (the US dollar loan to the English company, and the sterling loan by it to the US corporation) was made on terms that the loan was repayable only simultaneously with repayment of the other identified loan. If the first loan was not repaid, the second loan was not repayable. Thus, if the UK corporation were to become insolvent, or were for any reason unwilling or unable to pay its debt, neither it nor its liquidator could demand repayment of the sterling loan from the US corporation unless he was prepared to repay the full amount of the dollar loan. This gave rise to the name of the arrangement: the loan asset of each company as 'flawed' in the sense that it was repayable only if a condition precedent was met (the repayment of the linked loan).

10.94 The view was accepted that the arrangement could not be said to contravene the no-deprivation principle. It was not the case that, in the event of insolvency of one of the parties,

---

[67] Because of the mandatory set-off provisions in the Insolvency Rules (now Rule 14.25 of The Insolvency (England and Wales) Rules 2016).

its asset (the loan owing to it) ceased to be payable or became payable on different terms. It was part of the nature of the asset that it was repayable only in certain circumstances (ie on repayment of the countervailing loan). The security for the non-defaulting party did not lie in any rights which it had in relation to the asset; its security lay in the nature of the liability that it had to the counterparty. The insolvent counterparty was in no sense 'deprived' of its asset; nor was the asset in any way altered by the insolvency. The liquidator was entitled to be paid in exactly the same circumstances as the counterparty had, before its insolvency.

10.95 The anti-deprivation principle has been examined by the courts, in relation to a different kind of mechanism that has become common in complex financings. Sometimes an arrangement has only one source of cash-flow. It might be, say, the proceeds of sale of the energy produced by a power station, or the income received by an SPV from securities bought with the funds raised by a bond issue. The commercial terms may involve an agreement that receipts should be used to pay the creditors in a particular order of priority. It is common to find that, if one of the creditors (which may itself owe continuing obligations under the structure) should become insolvent or suffer some other adverse event, the order of priority is to change, to protect other participants against the consequence of that event. The question is whether the change of priority, to the detriment of the insolvent party, amounts to a deprivation of its property, and so offends against the principle.

10.96 The Court of Appeal considered the principle in two separate cases which were heard together, *Perpetual Trustee Co Ltd v BNY Corporate Trustee Services Ltd and another*; and *Butters and others v BBC Worldwide Ltd and others*.[68] The *Perpetual* case arose out of a structured finance product created by Lehman Brothers. Under the arrangements a Lehman Brothers company acted as the swap counterparty with a Special Purpose Vehicle (an 'SPV') established for the purpose of the arrangement. Under the terms of the security arrangements, the assets of the SPV were to be used, in the event of default, in paying sums due to the Lehman swap counterparty, and thereafter any surplus was to be paid to investors in the notes of the SPV. However, if the reason for the default was a failure of the swap counterparty, rather than of the SPV (as happened in the event), the arrangements provided that the priorities should be reversed. The available assets should be used first to pay the noteholders, and only thereafter to pay the swap counterparty. The switch in priorities was called 'the flip clause'.

10.97 The argument on behalf of the liquidators of the swap counterparty was that the arrangements offended against the anti-deprivation principle, because they operated to demote the priority of the swap counterparty on its bankruptcy. They had the effect of taking away one of its assets which should otherwise be available to its creditors.

10.98 The *BBC Worldwide* case had a very different factual background. It concerned a joint venture between BBC Worldwide and certain associated companies, on the one hand, and media subsidiaries of the Woolworth Group on the other. The arrangements related to the production and dissemination of programmes produced by the BBC. Under the joint venture agreement, the BBC was entitled to acquire the interest in the joint venture of the Woolworth companies, in the event that any of them suffered an 'insolvency event'.

[68] [2009] EWCA Civ 1160.

In addition, the licence of intellectual property rights to the joint venture contained a provision that the licence would terminate immediately if any of the Woolworth companies suffered an insolvency event and the BBC served notice to acquire the shares in it. When Woolworths failed, BBC Worldwide served a notice to acquire an interest in the companies, and the licence terminated. The administrators of the Woolworth companies contended that the result of the provisions was to offend the anti-deprivation principle. The termination of the licence in the event that the BBC decided to acquire the shares in the joint venture meant that, in the event of the insolvency of the Woolworths companies, the asset which they were obliged to sell to the BBC became immediately less valuable.

10.99 The Court of Appeal held that the anti-deprivation principle did not operate to invalidate any of the arrangements in either of the cases. In the *BBC Worldwide* case, it was pointed out that it was very common for licences to contain a provision under which they would terminate on insolvency. This was also the case in relation to commercial leases. If this happened, it was not correct to say that the event had operated to deprive the licensee or tenant of his asset. The nature of the party's interest in the lease or the licence was such that it existed only until the occurrence of an event that brought it to an end.

10.100 In the *Perpetual* case, Patten LJ adopted a similar explanation. The interest of the swap counterparty in the payments to be made by the SPV was always subject to the terms on which it was granted. The alteration on insolvency was part of the nature of the asset itself:

> The reversal of the order of priority ... was always a facet of the security designed to regulate competing interests over the collateral ...

10.101 The issue came before the Supreme Court in *Belmont Park Investments Pty Ltd v BNY Corporate Trustee Services Ltd and Lehman Brothers Special Financing Inc*,[69] another case arising from the demise of Lehman Bros. The facts were very similar to those in the *Perpetual Trustee* case. It is important to note that the effect of the flip clause was referred to throughout the *Belmont* case as a 'flawed asset', described by Lord Collins as existing:

> ... where it is an inherent feature of an asset from the inception of its grant that it can be taken away from the grantee (whether in the event of his insolvency or otherwise) ...

This is crucially different from the 'flawed asset' described in paras 10.90 to 10.93 above. In that case, the rights and obligations of the parties are not changed in any way by reference to the insolvency of either party. There is no way in which a party which becomes insolvent can be said to have been deprived of any property. Once again, a phrase is being used to describe two quite different things.

10.102 The members of the Supreme Court in the *Belmont* case were unanimous in holding that the flip clause did not offend against the anti-deprivation principle. However, their reasons were not the same as those of the Court of Appeal in the *Perpetual Trustee* case. Lord Collins rejected the idea that a 'flawed asset' structure (as defined in the case) must always be valid:

> But it does not follow that any proprietary right which is expressed to determine or change on bankruptcy is outside the anti-deprivation rule, still less that a deprivation which has

---

[69] [2011] UKSC 38.

been provided for in the transaction from the outset is valid. If it were so, then the anti-deprivation rule would have virtually no content.

10.103 The court preferred to rest its decision on the fact that the contract, and the flip clause contained in it, had been negotiated 'in good faith' for sound commercial reasons. The flip clause should be upheld:

> ... the anti-deprivation principle is essentially directed to intentional or inevitable evasion of the principle that the debtor's property is part of the insolvent estate and is applied in a commercially sensitive manner, taking into account the policy of party autonomy and the upholding of proper commercial bargains...

10.104 The resounding affirmation of the courts' wish to support sensible commercial decisions and provisions is reassuring. One should perhaps add a word of caution. The intention of the parties in including provisions such as flip clauses or other 'flawed asset' mechanisms (as that expression is used in the *Belmont* case) is that, on the occurrence of adverse events, the most easily foreseeable being the insolvency of the counterparty, the contracting party should be protected, by having access to assets of the counterparty which would not otherwise be available to it. If the provisions are valid, the assets concerned will not be available to the insolvent's other creditors. One might say that the core purpose of a flip clause is the 'intentional... evasion of the principle that the debtor's property is part of the insolvent estate'. The intention is that property which would otherwise go to the insolvent party should instead go to the 'secured' party.

10.105 Clearly, courts in England will apply the principle with a view to supporting commercial transactions which they regard as proper. In any individual case, however, the outcome can be determined only after close examination of the facts. There is always the possibility, however remote, that a judge will strike down a particular provision because he or she does not approve the motives of the parties. Many practitioners would prefer to draft on the basis of the more formal view taken by the Court of Appeal in the *Perpetual Trustee* case. Nonetheless, the *Belmont* case confirms the usefulness of flip clauses and similar forms of contract-based security in financial transactions.

Reverse Security

10.106 The purpose of security is to enhance the position of the security-taker by providing a means by which a debt owed to it is more likely to be paid. However, security structures can be arranged with the opposite purpose: to limit the liability of the security-giver. There are three common commercial situations in which the granting of a security by a security-giver has the effect of limiting the risk of the debt which it is undertaking.

Special Purpose Vehicles

10.107 In securitizations and in project financing it is common for the economic originator of a transaction to arrange for the transaction to be conducted through a separate company (a Special Purpose Vehicle, or SPV). For example, a football club wishing to raise money on the strength of future ticket receipts might establish an SPV for this purpose. The club would assign to the SPV the right to future ticket receipts for the period of, say, five years. The price might be an immediate cash payment. The SPV would raise the money to make the cash payment by selling bonds to investors. The security granted to the investors would be a charge over the assets of the SPV (ie the future ticket receipts, which had been assigned to the SPV by the club).

From the point of view of the investors, the debt owed to them by the SPV is secured on assets which, they have decided, are worth more than the amount of the debt. From the point of view of the club, it has limited the amount which it can be required to repay in respect of the money raised by way of loan. The liability to the bondholders is that of the SPV. The club's risk has been limited. If, in the event, the receipts for ticket sales are less than the amount of the debt, it is the bondholders who will suffer the shortfall. The club will have no liability to the bondholders to repay the difference between the amount of the money the bondholders have lent and the value of the asset used to repay them. 10.108

Thus, the structure is a form of secured lending for the bondholders. Viewed from the position of the club, however, the structure is a way of limiting its liability in respect of the loan. Put in a different way, the structure provides a form of insurance to the club against a dramatic shortfall in the value of its ticket receipts. 10.109

Third-party security

The classic explanations of security emphasize the action of the security-giver in making an asset available to the security-taker for the payment of a debt. They do not require that the debt should be owed by the security-giver. Thus, in the *Coslett* case,[70] Millett J described the essence of a charge as follows: 10.110

> ... a particular asset or class of assets is appropriated to the satisfaction of a debt or other obligation of the charger or a third party, so that the charge is entitled to look to the asset and its proceeds for the discharge of the liability.

In practice, the use of 'third party' security is very common. In this arrangement, A charges in favour of B a property which he owns, to secure a debt owed to B by C. A does not undertake any personal obligation to B.[71] He merely makes his property available to satisfy the payment of an obligation owed by C. 10.111

Providers of finance will usually, in negotiation, ask that the provider of the security should also undertake a personal obligation. This will usually take the form of a guarantee by the security-giver of the obligations of the borrower. The security provided by the security-giver will then be conferred to secure the guarantee obligation undertaken by the security-giver. From the point of view of the security-taker, there is a double benefit. Not only does it 10.112

---

[70] *In re Coslett (Contractors) Ltd* [1998] Ch 495 and see paras 10.41 *et seq* above.
[71] Unless, on a proper construction of the agreement, he intended to assume a personal obligation as well as to grant a charge: see *Tan Wing Chuen and another v Bank of Credit and Commerce Hong Kong Ltd* [1996] BCC 388.

have resort to the property given as security, it also has the right to a personal claim against the security-giver, should the security not be adequate.

10.113 From the point of view of the security-giver, however, the effect of limiting its involvement to the provision of a third-party security is to put a cap on its potential liability. Whatever the size of the debt owed by the borrower to the security-taker, the security-giver can never lose more than the value of the property charged.

10.114 Third-party security arrangements are very common in domestic financial arrangements. An individual will often be asked by his bank to grant a charge over his house to secure loans to him, or to secure a guarantee that he has given of the indebtedness of a company which he owns. However, he may have a spouse who lives in the house and who has an interest in it as co-owner. The bank will usually ask the spouse, in this case, to grant a charge over her interest in the house, as security for the loan to her husband or his company. Such an arrangement allows the bank to have security over the house, while limiting the spouse's liability to the value of only one of her assets.

10.115 The grant of third-party security does not, by itself, involve any assumption of personal liability by the security-giver, even to the extent of the value of the property.[72]

Non-recourse and limited recourse lending

10.116 The use of special purpose vehicles to isolate a borrower from some of the economic effects of a loan is very common. Less common in the UK, but frequently used elsewhere, is the use of non-recourse, or limited recourse lending.

10.117 Under these arrangements the borrower grants security for the loan (say, in the form of a mortgage of real property) and agrees with the lender that, if the lender wishes to enforce payment, the borrower's liability shall be limited to the realized value of the secured asset (non-recourse lending) or to a specified amount in excess of that value (limited recourse lending). The effect of this arrangement is to alter the amount of the personal liability of the borrower on the debt so that it corresponds with the value of the property, or is related to the value of the property. The economic effect, of course, is the same as that achieved in a securitization by the use of an SPV, where in practice the amount of the debt is limited to the value of the assets of the SPV, or to that value plus the amount of an additional limited guarantee given by the promoter of the SPV.

10.118 A spectacular recent use of non-recourse financing was seen in the United States, following the collapse of the investment bank, Bear Stearns. The US government encouraged JP Morgan Chase & Co to purchase the troubled bank. To facilitate this, the Federal Reserve System made available to JP Morgan Chase a non-recourse loan of US$30 billion, secured on the less liquid assets of Bear Stearns. The effect of that arrangement is that the Federal Reserve will bear the loss, to the extent that the assets concerned turn out to be worth less than US$30 billion. The value of the remaining assets will accrue to the purchaser.

---

[72] *In Re Bank of Credit and Commerce International SA (No 8)* [1998] AC 214. For a discussion of the effect of third-party security in that case, see paras 4.75 to 4.84.

10.119 One of the side-effects of non-recourse borrowing through the medium of an SPV is to make the SPV 'insolvency-remote'. If its liabilities (the amount that it owes to bondholders) are limited to the value of its assets, it follows that it cannot become insolvent, in the sense that its liabilities exceed its assets. Thus, there is no practical possibility that the bondholders might lose control of the situation through the appointment of an administrator or liquidator, nor that the insolvency of the SPV might contaminate the affairs of the originator by cross-default. However, the High Court decision in *In re Arm Asset Backed Securities SA*[73] casts doubt on this. The judge held that the court had power to make an order for liquidation of an SPV whose only borrowings were non-recourse:

> As a matter of ordinary language, I would take the view that if a company has liabilities of a certain amount on bonds or other obligations which exceed the assets available to it to meet those obligations, the company is insolvent, even though the rights of the creditors to recover payment will be, as a matter of legal right as well as a practical reality, restricted to the available assets, and even though, as the bonds in the case provide, the obligations will be extinguished after the distribution of available funds.

It may be, therefore, that one of the perceived beneficial side-effects of non-recourse borrowing structures may not after all be available.

10.120 Again, non-recourse and limited recourse lending can be seen as ways in which the borrower is secured against unexpected consequences of the lending transaction. In particular it is attractive to borrowers for the finance of assets whose value may be volatile. This has been seen at its most dramatic in the collapse of the US housing market. In some states, a large proportion of the lending was made on a non-recourse basis. In times of steep upward movement in asset prices, banks were prepared to lend 100 per cent of the purchase value of a property, on the assumption that its value would exceed the amount outstanding on the loan within a very short period of time. However, when the housing bubble burst, and asset values dropped dramatically, borrowers simply declared themselves in default and handed the keys of the property over to the bank, leaving the bank to bear the shortfall on the sale of the property. The effect, when banks were prepared to lend up to 100 per cent of valuations of property, was that the banks were taking the whole of the risk on any future downward movement of the housing market. As far as the borrowers were concerned, of course, the effect of a non-recourse arrangement was that their risk of a loss on the capital value of their houses had effectively been eliminated.

10.121 Until recently, non-recourse loans were unknown in the UK housing market. However, they have recently begun to appear, banks and insurance companies have introduced a product known as an 'equity release mortgage', aimed at affluent homeowners. The lender advances a sum of, say, 30 per cent of the current value of the customer's house on terms that interest will be at a fixed rate and will be accumulated until the death of the borrower, when the total of principal and accrued interest will be payable, and the house sold. Crucially, the contract usually contains a provision that the total amount payable can never exceed the realized value of the house. The loan is without further recourse to the borrower or his estate.

---

[73] [2013] EWHC 3351 (Ch).

10.122 The attractions to borrowers are easy to see. They can take in cash immediately part of the value of their homes. They might wish to spend it, or to pass it to their children, who would otherwise have to wait for their inheritance until their parents' death. Additionally, the release of capital might be used as a way of reducing the amount of inheritance tax payable on those deaths. Under UK tax law, a gift of the cash released will remove that amount from the value of the estate, provided that the borrowers live for a further seven years. The amount of the gift, plus all interest on it, will be a liability of their estate when they die, and will reduce the value of the estate that is charged to tax.

10.123 At the same time the risks to a lender are obvious: if the borrowers live longer than anticipated, and/or interest rates rise to greater heights than foreseen, and/or the value of the house falls dramatically, the lender will bear the cost of the shortfall.

11
THE CONSTRUCTION OF FINANCIAL CONTRACTS

> Oh, wad some Power the giftie gie us,
> To see oursels as others see us,
> It would frae monie a blunder free us
> An' foolish notion.[1]

Contracts in financial markets are almost always drafted and negotiated by transactional lawyers. However, on the rare occasions when a dispute arises or the operation of the contract is disrupted by insolvency or by some extraneous event, the legal consequences will be determined, not by transactional lawyers, but in a court process conducted by litigators and judges.

11.01

Litigators understand the complex and sophisticated processes that the courts follow and the principles that they apply in the search to find the meaning of the agreement under consideration. They are familiar with the mass of case law that deals with the subtleties of difference between the meanings of expressions which are almost identical. Financial transaction lawyers, on the other hand, have rarely been trained in this aspect of the legal process. If a contract that they have drafted or negotiated comes before a court for interpretation, they are unlikely to be involved.[2] This stark separation of function between lawyers means that those who draft and negotiate the terms of complex documents are often unaware of the way in which their work will be analyzed by a court, in the event of later litigation.

11.02

This chapter is designed for the benefit of transactional lawyers who, it is to be hoped, will never become involved in arguments before a court about the meaning of documents that they have drafted. Drawing their attention to the basis on which a court might approach their drafting might help them to avoid some of the pitfalls which await them. In Burns' words, it might free them *'frae monie a blunder... An' foolish notion'*.

11.03

The Meaning of Contracts

Modern principles

In *Re Sigma Finance Corp*,[3] Lord Mance identified four House of Lords decisions which restated the principles that a court should use to interpret a financial document. The cases

11.04

---

[1] Robert Burns, *To a Louse*.
[2] In large part, because of the rule that excludes consideration of the subjective intent of the drafter. See paras 11.72 to 11.81.
[3] [2009] UKSC 2.

were *Charter Reinsurance Co Ltd v Fagen*,[4] *Mannai Investment Co Ltd v Eagle Star Life Assurance Co Ltd*,[5] *Investors Compensation Scheme Ltd v West Bromwich Building Society*,[6] and *Chartbrook Ltd v Persimmon Homes Ltd*.[7] The statements of principle set out in these cases are clear. However, the difficulty in interpreting some of them mirrors ironically the problems of interpreting contracts which they are intended to solve.

11.05 The starting point for any discussion of the modern principles of contractual interpretation is usually taken to be the summary by Lord Hoffmann in the *Investors Compensation Scheme* case. It is best to set this out in full:

> The result has been, subject to one important exception, to assimilate the way in which such documents are interpreted by judges to the commonsense principles by which any serious utterance would be interpreted in ordinary life. Almost all the old intellectual baggage of 'legal' interpretation has been discarded. The principles may be summarized as follows:
>
> (1) Interpretation is the ascertainment of the meaning which the document would convey to a reasonable person having all the background knowledge which would reasonably have been available to the parties in the situation in which they were at the time of the contract.
> (2) The background was famously referred to by Lord Wilberforce as the 'matrix of fact', but this phrase is, if anything, an understated description of what the background may include. Subject to the requirement that it should have been reasonably available to the parties and to the exception to be mentioned next, it includes absolutely anything that would have affected the way in which the language of the document would have been understood by a reasonable man.
> (3) The law excludes from the admissible background the previous negotiations of the parties and their declarations of subjective intent. They are admissible only in an action for rectification. The law makes this distinction for reasons of practical policy and, in this respect only, legal interpretation differs from the way we would interpret utterances in ordinary life. The boundaries of this exception are in some respects unclear, but this is not the occasion on which to explore them.
> (4) The meaning which the document (or any other utterance) would convey to a reasonable man is not the same thing as the meaning of its words. The meaning of words is a matter of dictionaries and grammars; the meaning of the document is what the parties using those words against the relevant background would reasonably have been understood to mean. The background may not merely enable the reasonable man to chose between the possible meanings of words which are ambiguous but even (as occasionally happens in ordinary life) to conclude that the parties must, for whatever reason have used the wrong word or syntax (see *Mannai Investments Coast Co. Ltd v Eagle Star Life Assurance Co. Ltd* [1997] AC 749).
> (5) The 'rule' that words should be given their 'natural and ordinary meaning' reflects the common sense proposition that we do not easily accept that people have made

---

[4] [1997] AC 313.
[5] [1997] AC 749.
[6] [1998] 1 WLR 896.
[7] [2009] UKHL 38.

linguistic mistakes, particularly in formal documents. On the other hand, if one would nevertheless conclude from the background that something must have gone wrong with the language, the law does not require judges to attribute to the parties an intention which they plainly could not have had. Lord Diplock made this point more vigorously when he said in *The Antaios Compania Neviera S.A. v Salen Rederierna A.B.* [1985] A.C. 191, 201:

> … if detailed semantic and tactical analysis of words in a commercial contract is going to lead to a conclusion that flouts business commonsense, it must be made to yield to business commonsense.

11.06 The most important part of Lord Hoffmann's restatement of the principles, so far as drafters of financial documents are concerned, is the concentration on the objective meaning of the words. The reason why common law courts choose to look for the objective meaning was explained elegantly by Patten LJ in *Kookmin Bank v Rainy Sky SA and others*:[8]

> In a commercial contract (like any other contract) the parties have chosen to define the limits of the obligations which they have undertaken by the language they have used. The purpose of the contract is to provide an objective record of what they have agreed so as to regulate the legal relationship between them. The Court's function is to give effect to those obligations by respecting the terms in which they are cast.

11.07 The concentration on the words used in the contract, to the exclusion of the parties' later statements about their intention in using those words, has been the basis of the common law approach to contractual interpretation for centuries. One of the greatest common law jurists, Oliver Wendell Holmes, wrote in 1897:[9]

> In my opinion no one will understand the true theory of contract or be able even to discuss some fundamental questions intelligently until he has understood that all contracts are formal, that the making of a contract depends not on the agreement of two minds in one intention, but on the agreement of two sets of external signs – not on the parties' having meant the same thing but on their having said the same thing.

The matrix of fact

11.08 Despite the clarity and certainty of the main object of interpretation, there remain areas of difficulty in the application of the principles. Detailed examination of these is outside the scope of this chapter. However, there are two issues that transactional lawyers should bear in mind when drafting. The first point arises from the fact that, although the object of the search is the meaning of the words used by the parties, the courts have always accepted that the meaning cannot be found in the words seen in isolation. In *Charington & Co Ltd v Wooder*,[10] Lord Dunedin spoke of the meaning seen in the context of 'the surrounding

---

[8] [2010] EWCA Civ 582.
[9] 'The Path of the Law' (1897) 10 *Harvard Law Review* 457.
[10] [1914] AC 71.

circumstances'. In 1971, Lord Wilberforce preferred to refer to the 'matrix of fact'[11] in which the words were used. This phrase has been widely used in subsequent cases.

11.09 The formulation in the *Investors Compensation Scheme* case used to describe the relevant matrix of fact is extremely wide. Lord Hoffmann's statement that 'It includes absolutely anything which would have affected the way in which the language of the document would have been understood by a reasonable man' has been taken by many advocates as an invitation to them to introduce into argument about interpretation extraneous facts that would not otherwise be accepted as relevant. While this practice seems to have died down to some extent, the *Investors Compensation Scheme* case is one of the most-cited cases before the English courts.

11.10 Although the *Investors Compensation Scheme* case opens the possibility that an extremely wide body of facts might be deemed to be relevant for interpretation, there is a very strong line of judicial thinking that limits the scope of the background which forms the matrix. In *Bank of Scotland v Dunedin Property Investment Co Ltd*,[12] a Scottish case, Lord Kirkwood referred to:

> Facts which both parties would have had in mind and known that the other party had in mind, when the contract was made.

Staughton LJ in *Scottish Power plc v Britoil (Exploration) Ltd*[13] described the relevant background as:

> ... what the parties had in mind ... what was going on around them at the time when they were making the contract.

11.11 The inclination of judges seems now to limit consideration of matters other than the words themselves to those which affect consideration of the document as a whole. The context in which the words are considered is that of the document in which they appear, rather than in the context of 'absolutely anything' which is relevant. In the *Sigma Finance* case, Lord Collins (with whom Lords Mance and Hope agreed) looked at the issue in the context of a security document, the parties to which had become adherents over a long period of time, and each in different circumstances. He said:

> Consequently, this is not the type of case where the background or matrix of fact is or ought to be relevant, except in the most generalised way. I do not consider, therefore, that there is much assistance to be derived from the principles of interpretation re-stated by Lord Hoffman in the familiar passage in *Investors Compensation Scheme Ltd v West Bromwich Building Society* [1998] 1 WLR 896, 912–913. Where the security document secures a number of creditors who have advanced funds over a long period it will be quite wrong to take account of circumstances which are not known to all of them. In this type of case it is the wording of the instrument which is paramount. The instrument must be interpreted as a whole in the light of the commercial intention which may be inferred from the face of the instrument and from the nature of the debtor's business. Detailed semantic analysis must give way to business common sense: *The Antaios* [1985] AC 191, 201.

---

[11] *Prenn v Simmonds* [1971] 1 WLR 1381.
[12] 1998 SC 657.
[13] The Times, 2 December 1997.

11.12 In the same case, Lord Walker, while not going so far, supported a restrictive view of the context:

> ... I completely agree that it is necessary to construe the language of clause 7.6 of the deed 'in the landscape of the instrument as a whole' (in the words of Lord Mustill in *Charter Reinsurance Co Ltd v Fagan* [1997] AC 313, 384H).

It may be, therefore, that one should see the later cases as restricting the ambit of the 'matrix' of relevant facts mentioned in the *Investors Compensation Scheme* case.

11.13 The other aspect of Lord Hoffmann's formulation in the *Investors Compensation Scheme* case that has proved controversial, and that drafters need to keep firmly in mind, is the qualification to the 'natural and ordinary meaning rule', that the meaning must be made to yield to 'commercial commonsense', if the rule otherwise led to a different conclusion.[14]

11.14 Like the 'matrix of fact' element, this qualification to the interpretation process proved to be an invitation to litigators to argue that, when a literal interpretation of a disputed clause produced a result unfavourable to their client, the interpretation did not accord with 'business commonsense', and must be rejected. The approach had sound support in case law. In the *Rainy Sky* case, when it reached the Supreme Court,[15] Lord Clarke said:

> If there are two possible constructions, the court is entitled to prefer the construction which is consistent with business common sense and to reject the other.

11.15 However, the Supreme Court has subsequently made clear that the 'matrix of fact' element and the 'business commonsense' factor are aids to interpretation, and do not push aside the basic principle that interpretation should follow the ordinary and natural meaning of the words:

> ... the reliance placed in some cases on commercial common sense and surrounding circumstances ... should not be invoked to undervalue the importance of the language of the provision that is to be construed.[16]

11.16 In *Wood v Capita Insurance Services Limited*[17] the Supreme Court sought to reconcile the apparent conflict between the 'ordinary and natural meaning' approach, and the 'surrounding circumstances/business commonsense' approach. Lord Hodge, with whom all of the other judges agreed, said that the two approaches are not in conflict. They are tools which a court can use to find the objective meaning of the language that the parties have used. Which of the tools will prove the more useful will depend on the circumstances of the contract under consideration.

11.17 The judgment in the *Wood* case is clear. However, it may be that it will merely shift the ground in the battle of interpretation between competing parties. The argument will now be about the identity of the tool that the court should choose in its task of interpretation.

---

[14] See para 11.05 above.
[15] *Rainy Sky SA and others v Kookmin Bank* [2011] UKSC 50.
[16] *Arnold v Britton and others* [2015] UKSC 36 per Lord Neuberger. See also *Marley v Rawlings* [2014] UKSC 2.
[17] [2017] UKSC 24.

The Common Law and Civil Law Approaches

The difference between the two

11.18 A comparison between the approach to the interpretation of contracts which is adopted by civil law systems and that followed by common law systems looks, at first sight, like an interesting academic exercise, rather than a practical guide to drafting. However, the difference in approach is fundamental and can lead to interpretations being placed on a contractual term which vary widely, according to the location of the court which addresses the issue. Since many financial contracts involve parties based in, or transactions which take place in, different jurisdictions, the drafter of a financial contract must bear in mind the location of the courts which might consider the terms of the contract, and should be aware of the difference in the approach that courts might adopt when searching for the meaning of the contract.

11.19 Lord Hoffmann drew attention to the different bases of interpretation of contracts adopted by French law (which, for these purposes, is taken as being representative of that adopted by all civil law systems) and that adopted by English law, in *Chartbrook Ltd v Persimmon Homes Ltd and others*.[18]

11.20 Both approaches start with the same objective. As Sir Christopher Staughton put it:[19]

> ... the task of the judge when interpreting a written contract is to find the intention of the parties. Insofar as one can be sure of anything these days, that proposition is unchallenged.

Both civil and common law systems look to find that intention. Despite the use of the same word in both cases, however, they are not looking for the same thing.

11.21 In civil law systems, contractual intention is the actual intention of the contracting individuals, referred to as their '*volonté psychologique*'. It is an entirely subjective matter. This idea is so central to French contract law that it is explicitly included in the Civil Code.[20]

11.22 Legal rules dealing, for example, with matters of evidence or illegality operate, in civil law countries, on that subjective intention to limit its effect or significance. Thus, for example, the existence of a rule which makes illegal a particular activity will have the effect of shaping and limiting the intention of the parties to perform that act. There is a strict separation between the fact of the parties' intention and the legal rules which operate on that intention.[21]

11.23 English and other common law systems, on the other hand, take the view that the intention of the parties is not to be found in their subjective view, expressed at a later date after a dispute has arisen. Rather, it is an objective matter. The parties are assumed to have meant what they said. The intention of the parties is taken to be that which a reasonable outside observer

---

[18] [2009] UKHL 38.
[19] 'How Do the Courts Interpret Commercial Contracts?' (1999) 58 *Cambridge Law Journal* 2, 303–13.
[20] Article 1156 C.c. 'One must in contracts seek to ascertain what was the common intention of the contracting parties, rather than stop at the term's literal meaning.'
[21] See generally Professor C. Valcke, 'On Comparing French and English Contract Law: Insights from Social Contract Theory' (2008), available at <http://ssrn.com/abstract=1328923>.

would have understood their intention to be, based on what they said in the contract. There are two reasons for the adoption of this objective approach.

First, the basis of contract law is that the contract embodies the 'common' intention of the parties. It may sometimes be a fiction to suggest that all the parties to a contract share the same intention. An enquiry into the actual intent of each of the parties might reveal that there was, in fact, no shared intention at all. It is less artificial for the court to look for the objective meaning of a particular term, and then to attribute to the parties an intention to signify that meaning, than to seek the subjective views of all the parties, with the risk that it would then be forced to reject the statement of one, and find that he intended the same thing as the other party, despite his denial.

11.24

The common law is, perhaps surprisingly, more in tune with modern linguistic theory than is the civil law. Semiotics treats words as 'signifiers', which have no validity in themselves, but rather point to something that is in the mind of the speaker. Thus, if someone says 'dog', the importance of the word is that a listener will interpret its utterance as a sign that the speaker has in his mind the image of a member of the canine species. That is the 'meaning' of the word: the listener understands that the intention of the speaker is to signify the idea of a dog. What matters is the understanding by the listener of the word used, rather than the wish of the speaker.[22]

11.25

The second reason for the adoption of the objective approach is purely practical. It is likely, after a dispute has arisen, that each party will give evidence that his intention at the time was that which best suits his case in the dispute. As Sir Christopher Staughton put it:[23]

11.26

> ... nothing or not very much would be gained by listening to self-serving evidence of both of them.

It has long been accepted that the result of the objective approach is that the court will sometimes find the intention of the parties, based on the meaning of the words used, to have been something quite different from their actual intent. Over a century ago, Justice Holmes said:

11.27

> ... nothing is more certain than that parties may be bound by a contract to things which neither of them intended, and when one does not know of the other's assent.[24]

In more recent times, Lord Hope interpreted a termination provision in a commercial contract and concluded with the words:

> I have reached this conclusion with regret. It seems to me most unlikely that the parties to this agreement intended that it should be capable of being terminated by reason only of the non-fulfilment on the condition ...[25]

One consequence of the objective view is that the rules relating to admissibility of evidence or illegality, which under the civil law system are a quite separate matter which is applied once the intention of the parties has been found, becomes in the English system entangled

11.28

---

[22] See the explanation of Oliver Wendell Holmes set out in para 11.07 above.
[23] 'How Do the Courts interpret Commercial Contracts?' (1999) 58 *Cambridge Law Journal* 2, 303–13.
[24] 'The Path of the Law'.
[25] *Total Gas Marketing Ltd v Arco British Ltd* [1998] 2 Lloyd's Rep 209, at 223.

with the question of finding the parties' intention. If, for example, a particular act is prohibited by statute a reasonable outsider, looking at ambiguous words used in a contract, might decide that they could not have intended the meaning which led to something which was illegal. The outsider would, therefore, conclude that they had intended the act signified by the alternative interpretation.

11.29 The difference between the civil and common law approaches has been recognized internationally. It has also been accepted that the two approaches cannot be subject to a compromise: every legal system must choose one or the other. The Principles of European Contract Law,[26] the fruits of an attempt to produce a uniform code for contract law to be adopted throughout the EU, opts clearly for the civil law approach, falling back on the common law approach only if it is impossible to find the subjective meaning of the contract.[27] Article 5:101 says:

(1) A contract is to be interpreted according to the common intention of the parties even if this differs from the literal meaning of the words.
(2) If it is established that one party intended the contract to have a particular meaning and at the time of the conclusion of the contract the other party could not have been unaware of the first party's intention, the contract is to be interpreted in the way intended by the first party.
(3) If an intention cannot be established according to (1) or (2), the contract is to be interpreted according to the meaning that reasonable persons of the same kind as the parties would give to it in the same circumstances.[28]

11.30 A similar approach is taken by the Principles of International Commercial Contracts adopted by Unidroit:[29]

(1) A contract shall be interpreted according to the common intention of the parties.
(2) If such an intention cannot be established, the contract shall be interpreted according to the meaning that reasonable persons of the same kind as the parties would give to it in the same circumstances.

Neither the European Principles nor the Unidroit Principles have any binding effect, and it is unusual for parties to choose to incorporate them into normal commercial contracts.

11.31 Almost invariably in financial contracts, the parties choose the national law which they wish to govern the contract. An important point to bear in mind when drafting international

---

[26] 1998 Revision.
[27] It is hard to see that para (3) is anything other than a sop to common law sensitivities. The civil law approach will always produce a result, even if it might be difficult to do so and the result might be incorrect. It is hard to think of a civil law judge concluding that he or she is unable to work out what the contract means, and that he or she should therefore adopt the common law approach to finding the meaning.
[28] The European Commission adopted on 1 July 2010 a Green Paper which proposed a number of ways in which contract law across the EU could be made 'more coherent'. The options range from the publication of model contract rules which might be adopted by parties at their option, through to the enactment of a European Civil Code which would replace national rules of contract law. The project was open for consultation until January 2011. No further proposals have been brought forward. See the press release at <http://europa.eu>, ref: IP/10/.595.
[29] 2016 Revision Art 4.1.

financial contracts is that the choice of governing law is often a matter of negotiation. Sometimes it becomes a contentious issue. The clause of the contract which fixes the governing law is usually in the terms:

> This agreement shall be governed by *and construed in accordance with* the laws of []

The choice between the law of a civil law jurisdiction and that of a common law jurisdiction is not simply between the substantive rules of law relating to the subject-matter of the contract. The choice will affect fundamentally the way in which a court will address the task of finding out what the contract means. The common law drafter of a financial contract may be alarmed to find that his painstakingly crafted wording is being treated by the court in the civil law jurisdiction as comparatively unimportant, in its quest to find what the parties really meant. A party from a civil law jurisdiction may be equally alarmed to find that a common law judge regards as irrelevant his categorical statements of what he meant.

The objective approach and financial contracts

11.32 The words used in a contract to express the intention of the parties can be no more than a reflection of their intention. One might think, therefore, that the subjective approach, which looks beyond the reflection of the parties' intention to find the reality of the intention, would be preferable to the objective approach, which starts with the reflections of reality embodied in the words of the contract, and then looks for the thing of which the contract might be thought, by an objective observer, to be the reflection. That thing is then deemed to be the reality of the parties' intention, whether or not it was in fact.

11.33 Both the Unidroit Principles and the European Principles[30] choose the subjective approach. In each case, the objective approach is only to be used if the former is not available. On examination, however, the objective approach adopted in common law jurisdictions is itself much more suitable for the interpretation of modern commercial, and in particular financial, contracts. There are a number of reasons for reaching this conclusion.

11.34 In the case of commercial contracts, and particularly contracts relating to financial transactions, the parties are usually corporate entities rather than individuals. A corporate entity does not have a mind and is incapable of forming any *volonté psychologique*. To overcome this problem, legal systems have developed rules which have the effect of attributing to the inanimate corporate entity human attributes, such as intention and motivation. If one is looking for the actual intention of a corporation, following the subjective approach to interpretation, one is looking for something which is inevitably artificial (ie the intention of an employee or agent which is by law attributed to the corporation itself).

11.35 The objective common law approach, which starts with the words used by the corporation in its contract, and then seeks to find what 'must have been intended' is no more artificial. Arguably, the subjective approach often involves a greater degree of artificiality. In the case of any complex contract, a number of individuals are involved on behalf of the corporation in deciding upon and concluding the terms of the contract. The individual who formally

---

[30] See paras 11.29 and 11.30 above.

signs or concludes the contract or who takes the final decision that it should be signed, may not have been involved in the negotiation or discussion of the term which, in the event, proves to be contentious. It is therefore artificial to look for the intention of that person. It is, arguably, more realistic to take the objective approach in deeming the company itself to have an intention and looking to find the content of that intention through the words that the corporation used.

11.36 Second, many financial contracts, whether made between market entities or made by an institution with a consumer, are concluded wholly or partly on standard terms. For example, an individual asked to give a guarantee to a bank of the obligations of one of its customers, will be presented with a printed document running to many clauses spread over several pages. The content of the guarantee will be highly technical, drafted largely to avoid the effect of legal rules which might serve to avoid the liability of the guarantor. The bank employee who presents the form for signature, and who signs it on behalf of the bank, is unlikely to have a detailed knowledge of the content, and certainly not of the technical legal purpose behind much of the drafting. The guarantor who signs the document will, despite the presence in the document of representations by him that he has read and understands all of it, probably not have read the document at all. If he or she has read it, it will be without any comprehension of most of the terms.

11.37 One of the premises of contract law, whether in civil law or common law system, is that a contract represents the agreement of the parties to it. In the example given above, and in the case of many contracts concluded on standard terms, it is a fiction (although a necessary one) to say that all the parties agreed on each of the terms, the wording of which is reflected in the written form of contract. The objective approach to interpretation takes this fiction no further. Having said that the parties agreed on the wording of the contract, it simply then assumes that they must have meant what they said. The subjective approach, on the other hand, starts with the fiction that they agreed upon the written terms, and compounds the artificiality by then seeking to find their subjective intent in doing something (reaching agreement) which they did not, in reality, do at all.

11.38 Third, the objective approach is clearly preferable in the many situations where the formation of the contract involves a long period of time or different circumstances. This can arise in two ways. A standard form of contract is drafted by lawyers appointed by a financial institution, or by a trade association of such institutions. It may be used thereafter for many years, with amendments to detail made periodically over that period. When a contract is concluded on such standard terms, the intention behind the choice of words is in reality not that of the individuals who signed the contract, but that of a lawyer who selected the words, perhaps decades before they were used by the parties.

11.39 Alternatively, the parties may be divorced from the choice of words used in the contract by different practical circumstances. In *Re Sigma Finance Corp*,[31] the Supreme Court was asked to consider the meaning of a term in a security deed granted by Sigma, a special purpose vehicle used in a structured financing transaction. The security deed was a document under which the assets of Sigma were charged in favour of counterparties with whom it

---

[31] [2009] UKSC 2.

did business. As each individual transaction was concluded, Sigma's counterparty became a party to the security deed. When Sigma went into administrative receivership, there were a number of parties to the security deed, who had become parties at different times and in different factual circumstances, as a result of separate individual transactions. The consideration of the meaning of the disputed term in the deed centred on the extent to which the court should look at surrounding circumstances when construing the words used. Lord Collins pointed out that the parties to the deed had become adherents over a 13-year period in different circumstances. Since the meaning of the clause concerned must be the same in each case, it followed that the court should not look, save in the most general terms, at the circumstances surrounding the grant of security. It should confine itself, so far as possible, to consideration of the words themselves:

> Consequently this is not the type of case where the background or matrix of fact is or ought to be relevant, except in the most generalised way... Where a security document secures a number of creditors who have advanced funds over a long period it will be quite wrong to take account of circumstances which are not known to all of them. In this type of case it is the wording of the instrument which is paramount. The instrument must be interpreted as a whole in the light of the commercial intention which may be inferred from the face of the instrument and from the nature of the debtor's business.

In these situations, the subjective approach is unlikely to produce a sensible result. In the case of a market standard form of contract, it might lead to the conclusion that the parties had no intention at all, and that the only intention relevant was that of a drafter who had produced the wording a decade before the contract was signed. In the second case, the conclusion might be that the parties all had different intentions when entering into the contract. In both cases, the law will be required to invent a further rule in order to give effect to the contract. The objective approach, however, as demonstrated by Lord Collins, does not require any further gymnastics. It treats the words used as embodying the intention of all parties and there is no need for further inquiry or amendment. **11.40**

In modern commercial and financial usage, there is a fourth reason why the objective approach to interpretation is to be preferred to the subjective. Many commercial and financial transactions involve the transfer of contractual rights. The sale of shares or debt securities involves the transfer of the benefit of the agreement which constituted the issue. When a purchaser buys a bond, he acquires the benefit of the promises made at the time of the issue in the contract between the issuing company and the trustee, or alternatively, he may acquire direct rights given to bondholders under the terms of the unilateral deed. In the international loan market, participations in loan agreements are bought and sold. The purchase often involves the transfer of the benefit of the original loan agreement. For these purposes, it does not matter whether the transfer of a financial asset is by way of assignment or novation. The important point is that the purchaser becomes entitled to the benefit of a contract, the terms of which were written and concluded by different parties before he became involved. **11.41**

In these circumstances, the objective approach is the one which makes the most sense. When the prospective purchaser of, say, an international bond reviews the terms of the security arrangements or of the repayment provisions, he must be able to work out what it **11.42** means, before he can become a party to it. If its meaning is dependent on the intention of the parties who concluded the wording and signed it some years before, the purchaser can never be sure that the document means what it says. The only way on which an assignee of a financial contract can be sure that its meaning is that which he attributes to it is to know that the meaning will be assessed without reference to extraneous information. In particular, he needs to know that he will not be wrong-footed by learning, after he has taken an assignment of contractual rights, that the original contracting parties intended the meaning to be something quite different from that which he has assumed the words to convey. If the purchaser could not rely on the wording of the document, he would not know what he was buying. The comments of Lord Collins in the *Sigma Finance* case, although made in a slightly different context, apply equally in situations where contractual rights are traded.[32]

11.43 It is not the case, of course, that legal systems which adopt the subjective approach are incapable of dealing adequately with the interpretation of commercial contracts where standard forms have been used, or contractual rights have been traded to parties other than the original contracting entities, or where the contracting party is a corporate entity without its own mental processes. However, in order to do so, any system which starts with the subjective approach to interpretation must apply a number of legal rules which are artificial and complex. The objective approach, on the other hand, by making the single assumption that the parties intended what they said in the contract, simplifies (in theory at least) the task of deciding the meaning of the words chosen. It represents the most appropriate starting point for any search for the meaning of a contractual term.

The Difference between Meaning and Effect

11.44 When a court looks to find the meaning of an agreement, its search is for something specific and limited. It is trying to discover the nature of the facts described by the words used or of the acts which the words describe. In common speech, however, it is quite usual to use the word 'meaning' to encompass not only that which is described by the words used, but also the consequence or effect of that description. For example, if it is announced that the rate of income tax will be raised, television reporters might well ask the viewer 'What does this mean for you?' In this context, the reference is clearly to the practical consequences which will follow from the rise in the tax rate, rather than any attempt to interpret the meaning of the government announcement.

11.45 In the drafting of commercial contracts, it is important to bear in mind the difference between meaning and effect. Freedom of contract requires that, in general terms, parties are free to describe, as they choose, matters that affect them alone. However, the effect of what they have agreed may impact on third parties. These consequences are not a matter for the contracting parties alone, but for the law.

11.46 A may agree with B that he will sell to B the watch which he is wearing, and that title should pass on the following day. The watch, in fact, belongs to C for whom A is holding it. The meaning of the contract is quite clear. It is open to A and B to agree that A should sell the

---

[32] See also *National Bank of Sharjah v Dellborg* [1997] EWCA Civ 2070.

watch and should pass ownership to B. It is unaffected by the fact that A does not own the watch at the date of the contract and is not then in a position to fulfil his contractual obligations. He will be liable to B for breach of contact if he fails to pass title to B at the contracted time.

The question whether he can pass title, however, is not a matter for A and B alone. When a court comes to examine the term '… and title shall pass to B tomorrow', it will not be considering the meaning of the words used, but rather the effect. Did the agreement between A and B (that title in the watch should pass to B) have the effect that they intended? The answer is not a matter of interpretation of the words, because the answer to it will affect a third party. If the effect of the words is to pass title to B, C will no longer be the owner. **11.47**

There are, of course, circumstances in which the effect of the words would be to transfer title in the watch to B. For example, A might have the actual authority of C to deal with the watch as if it were his own. Alternatively, the facts may be such that the general rule that only an owner may pass title to an asset does not apply.[33] However, when the effect of an agreement between the parties to a contract is to alter the legal position of others, the involvement of the law goes beyond merely deciding what the parties to the contract intended. **11.48**

When lawyers draft commercial contracts, they are not concerned simply with recording an agreement between the parties about what they will do. They look also at the effect of that agreement. Usually, the purpose of the chosen words is to bring about a particular effect. For example, an agreement by a borrower that the lender should have property rights over an asset of the lender, which he may exercise if the loan is not repaid, records not only the position between the lender and the borrower, but is intended to grant to the lender rights which will affect the position of third parties. If the grant of the charge is effective, unsecured creditors of the borrower will be disadvantaged, as against the lender, in the borrower's insolvency. A statement in the document that the lender is to have a charge over the property is not the end of the matter, however clearly drafted. A court will be concerned to decide whether the words used had the effect of conferring a charge. **11.49**

Recharacterization

A distinction between the meaning of words used in a contract and their effect is fundamental to consideration of an issue which has assumed importance in recent years in the practice of financial law. When drafting documents in financial transactions, it is often of crucial significance that the rights conferred should have a particular legal character. For example, it might be critical that the charge granted by a security agreement should be a fixed charge, rather than a floating charge, or that the provisions of a subordination agreement creating a 'turnover trust' should not create a charge.[34] **11.50**

To make clear the result which the parties intend, contractual documents will often state specifically their intention. Very commonly, the creation of a charge will include the words 'by way of fixed charge'. Or, a document might state that the arrangements set out do not **11.51**

---

[33] See, eg, Sale of Goods Act 1979 ss 21–5 and Factors Act 1889 s 2.
[34] For an analysis of the 'turnover trust', see paras 9.126 to 9.134..

involve the grant of a charge. There is, of course, the danger that a court which subsequently considers the effect of the documentation might analyze it differently. Notwithstanding that the document states that a charge is to be a fixed charge, or says that the contractual arrangement does not involve the grant of a charge, the court might decide that the charge described as 'fixed' is in fact floating, or that the arrangement which was said to create no charge did indeed create a charge.

11.52 This possibility is often described as 'recharacterization risk'. This is, perhaps, an unfortunate phrase. It implies that the security arrangement has a particular legal character, chosen and described by the parties in their contract, and that this is subsequently disrupted by a court, which decides to change the character given to the arrangement by the parties and to substitute another.

11.53 At its extreme, this 'recharacterization risk' can be seen as judicial interference with the parties' freedom of contract. Such a view is a misunderstanding of the judicial process. This in turn can lead to basic mistakes in drafting.

11.54 The point can best be illustrated by the examination of an issue which came before the courts during the 1990s. A charge over property gives the chargee the ability to resort to that asset for payment of the sums owing to it from the owner of the property, in priority to claims of other creditors of the owner which are not secured in the same way. The security given to a chargee may, however, be reduced, or even eliminated, in some circumstances. For the purposes of the issue under consideration, two are relevant. First, certain 'preferential' creditors will have priority over the claims of the chargee, if the charge, in the form in which it was created, can be described as a 'floating charge'.[35] Second, under the law as it then stood, if the charge, when created, was a 'floating charge', it would have been void against a subsequent administrator or liquidator and against some third parties, if its creation had not been noted on the public register.[36]

11.55 The classification of a charge as 'floating' will not always be important: preferential claims may not be large enough to have a significant effect on the distribution of assets, and it will often be possible to register the creation of a floating charge, as required by the Companies Act. However, as a general proposition it is true that a charge may be less valuable to a chargee if it is floating than if it is fixed.

11.56 The distinction between a fixed and a floating charge is not always easy to see. To understand why this is so, it is necessary to consider briefly the history of the floating charge. The charge, as a concept, is a creation of equity. Its essence is the dedication of property by its owner to the payment of a particular obligation owed to a creditor.[37]

11.57 The charge was a very efficient way for a security-taker to replace the owner as controller of an asset, without the need to transfer ownership to him, and without the need to remove the asset from the possession of the owner. All that was needed was for the chargee to exercise practical control of the asset (eg by denying to the owner the right to sell the asset without

---

[35] Insolvency Act 1986 s 40(2) and ss 175–176ZA.
[36] The relevant parts of the Companies Act were amended in 2013 to change substantially the registration requirements. See paras 10.29 to 10.36 above.
[37] For a fuller explanation of the nature of a charge, see paras 10.56 to 10.60.

the consent of the chargee). However, one defect in the structure was exposed by the growth in the nineteenth century of manufacturing and trading companies, the asset value of which was represented not only by capital items, but also by their stock and work-in-progress. It was impracticable to charge to lenders these important classes of assets, because the owner needed to retain for itself the ability to control sales and to deal with the assets as part of its normal trading activities. A trading company could not operate if, before it could sell an item of stock to a customer, it needed to ask its bank to exercise the right of sale given to the bank by the charge or, alternatively, to release the item of stock from the ambit of the bank's charge.

11.58 The answer to the problem was the floating charge. Under this arrangement, the agreement between owner and chargee did not give to the chargee, in place of the owner, the ability to exercise all of the owner's rights of control in the assets. Rather, it left with the owner such of those rights as were necessary to allow him to deal with the assets in the way his business required. Only on liquidation or enforcement would the charge 'crystallize' and would those rights of control be taken away from the owner and handed over to the chargee.

11.59 It is difficult to identify with precision the differences between a floating charge and any other kind of charge. A charge is 'floating' if enough of the rights of the owner have been left with the chargor to enable it to control the asset as owner for the purpose of its business. The identity of the precise rights which is sufficient for these purposes depends on the nature of the business and of the surrounding facts. For this reason, cases have never attempted a definition of a floating charge, but rather a description of its characteristics. Hoffmann J in *In re Brightlife Ltd*[38] explained why this was so:

> ... a floating charge, like many other legal concepts, [is] not susceptible of being defined by the enumeration of an exhaustive set of necessary and sufficient conditions. All that can be done is to enumerate its characteristics. It does not follow that the absence of one or more of those features or the presence of others will prevent the charge from being characterised as 'floating', there are bound to be penumbral cases in which it may be difficult to say whether the degree of deviation from the standard case is enough to make it inappropriate to use such a term.

11.60 Accordingly, the question whether the arrangements between chargor and chargee in a particular case mean that the charge can be described as 'floating' will depend on whether the chargee has allowed the chargor to retain enough of the capacity to exercise ownership rights to ensure that the chargee does not itself have the powers of a mortgagee.

11.61 Often, the documentation which creates the security will itself describe a charge arrangement as 'fixed' or 'floating'. The use of the description may be seen either as an attempt to help a future judge to decide the nature of the charge, or as an attempt to pre-empt the need for the judge to reach any conclusion at all.

11.62 In *In re New Bullas Trading Ltd*,[39] the Court of Appeal considered the terms of a debenture which dealt in unusually elaborate detail with the question of security over book debts. Usually, a company which gives security over book debts will grant a charge to its bank.

---

[38] [1987] Ch 200.
[39] [1994] 1 BCLC 485.

The bank normally provides current account banking services as well as loans. Accordingly, any charged book debts, when they are paid, will result in an increase in the balance on the company's current account with the bank. The bank's security interest, once the money has been paid to it for the account of its customer, will be constituted by its right of consolidation of accounts.[40] The bank's interest in its trading customers' book debts for security purposes lasts only so long as the debts are unpaid.

11.63 The position is different if the chargee is not the company's banker. In the *New Bullas* case, the chargee was a venture capital company which did not operate bank accounts for the chargor. The chargee was interested in taking security over the debts owing to the chargor from its customers, and also in obtaining security over the proceeds of those debts, when they had become cash in the hands of the company's bankers. Accordingly, it entered into an agreement with the company under which the company purported to give it a charge over unpaid book debts, which was described as 'fixed', and a separate charge over the contents of the company's bank account.

11.64 The purpose of this drafting was to make the best out of a difficult position. The company needed to have access to the money in its bank account, in order to trade in the ordinary course. If the charged property consisted of all amounts which were owed to the company, whether from its customers or from its bankers, a court might well take the view that the degree of ownership control which was left with the company by the arrangements (ie its freedom to deal with the money in its current account) was such that the charge must be described as floating in nature. If, however, the property could be described as two separate items (unpaid debts owing from the customers, and debts owed by the bank which were the fruits of customer's debts after they had been paid), the two items could be dealt with separately. The unpaid customer's debts could be subject to mortgage-like strict control by the chargee; and the paid debts could be subject to much less stringent control, with the acceptance that this would result in the charge over them being only a 'floating' charge.

11.65 The Court of Appeal upheld this approach, and found that the charge over the unpaid book debts was fixed in nature, while the charge over the company's bank account constituted a floating charge. Lord Millett subsequently described the decision of the Court of Appeal in the following way:[41]

> The principal theme of the judgment, however, was that the parties were free to make whatever agreement they liked. The question was therefore simply one of construction; unless unlawful the intention of the parties, to be gathered from the terms of the debenture, must prevail. It was clear from the descriptions which the parties attached to the charges that they had intended to create a fixed charge over the book debts while they were uncollected and a floating charge over the proceeds. It was open to the parties to do so, and freedom of contract prevailed.
>
> However, the case was widely criticized and in *Agnew v Commissioner of Inland Revenue* the Privy Council found that it had been wrongly decided. The decision was, they said, 'entirely destructive of the floating charge'. The item of property charged was in fact a single asset.

---

[40] See paras 3.20 to 3.26.
[41] In *Agnew v Commissioner of Inland Revenue* [2001] 2 AC 710.

It did not matter that the asset consisted of a debt owed from a trading company, or its replacement (the debt owned by the bank which had collected it). There was only one item of property, and there could be only one charge over it.

More importantly, the Privy Council disagreed with the process of analysis which they had said, had been adopted by the Court of Appeal, and which is set out above. In doing so, the Board explained how a court decides the effect of contractual arrangements chosen by the parties to an agreement. It is worth quoting this explanation in full: **11.66**

> Their lordships considered this approach to be fundamental mistaken. The question is not merely one of construction. In decision whether a charge is a fixed charge or a floating charge, the Court is engaged in a two-staged process. At the first stage it must construe the instrument of charge and seek to gather the intentions of the parties from the language they have used. But the object at this stage of the process is not to discover whether the parties intended to create a fixed or floating charge. It is to ascertain the nature of the rights and obligations which the parties intended to grant each other in respect of the charged assets. Once these have been ascertained, the Court can then embark on the second stage of the process, which is one of characterisation. This is a matter of law. It does not depend on the intention of the parties. If their intention, properly gathered from the language of the instrument, is to grant the company rights in respect of the charged assets which are inconsistent with the nature of a fixed charge, then the charge cannot be a fixed charge however they may have chosen to describe it. A similar process is involved in construing a document is to see whether it creates a licence or tenancy. The Court must construe the grant to ascertain the intention of the parties; but the only intention which is relevant is the intention to grant exclusive possession: see *Street v Mountford* [1985] AC 809 at p 826 *per* Lord Templeman. So here: in construing a debenture to see whether it creates a fixed or floating charge, the only intention which is relevant is the intention that the company should be free to deal with the charged assets and withdraw them from the security without the consent of the holder of the charge; or, to put the question in another way, whether the charged assets were intended to be under the control of the company or the charge holders.[42]

In the context of this explanation, one can see the danger in speaking of the risk of 'recharacterization'. There may be in the use of the word an implication that it is within the power of the parties not only to describe what they intend to do, but also to decide how that act should be characterized as a matter of law. The Privy Council in *Agnew* made it clear that this is quite wrong. The question of the characterization of the legal effect of an agreement reached by the parties to a contract is a matter of law for a court to decide. **11.67**

From the point of view of those involved in drafting documents in financial markets and devising transaction structures, the risk which needs to be assessed is not that a court will, at **11.68**

---

[42] See also, on the analysis of whether a charge is fixed or floating, Fletcher Moulton LJ in *Evans v Rival Granite Quarries Ltd* [1910] 2 KB 979, where he said that the answer:

> ... did not depend upon the special language used in the particular document, but upon the essence and nature of the security.

See also McCarthy J in the Supreme Court of Ireland in *Re Keenan Bros Ltd* [1986] BCLC 242:

> ... one must look, not within the narrow confines of such term, not to the declared intentions of the parties alone, but to the effects of the instruments whereby they purported to carry out that intention.

a later date, 'recharacterize' an arrangement to which the parties have legitimately ascribed a character. Rather, the risk is that the draftsman of the document, when including a prediction of the characterization of the legal effect which will be decided by a court later (eg by describing a charge arrangement as 'fixed') have wrongly predicted the court's decision. Put more simply, the danger is not that a court will undo what the draftsman has done, but that the draftsman will be found to have got it wrong.

11.69 This has a major implication in financial markets. It is part of the strength of English commercial law that it seeks to give effect to the intention and expectations of the commercial world. However, it does not follow that courts will necessarily be willing to ascribe to market arrangements the effect which is desired by the draftsman of standard documents. In the cases of charges over book debts, it is clearly more desirable to financing institutions that the charge which they take should be fixed, rather than floating. They may include in their standard documents statements that this is the effect of the charge created by those instruments.

11.70 However, it should not be assumed that the meaning or effect of standard documents is that which the drafters say they intended. The attitude of the courts is neatly summarized by Briggs J. in one of the cases arising from the collapse of Lehman Bros. In *Anthracite Rated Investments (Jersey) Ltd v Lehman Brothers Finance SA in Liquidation*,[43] he said of the ISDA Master Agreement:[44]

> It is probably the most important standard market agreement used in the financial world ... It is axiomatic that it should, so far as possible, be interpreted in a way that serves the objectives of clarity, certainty and predictability, so that the very large number of parties using it should know where they stand ...

The overriding object is clarity.

11.71 In every case that involves interpretation of a standard document, the court will apply the same principles and approach as it would apply to any other contract. The fact that the drafter or drafters of a standard document intended it to have a particular effect will, in itself, be no more relevant than in the case of any other contract.[45] However, the views of the lawyers involved in drafting the standard form might be relevant in establishing the 'matrix of fact' that is the context of interpretation.

Exclusion of pre-contract negotiations and subjective intent

11.72 One of the five principles laid down in the *Investors Compensation Scheme* case is that the 'matrix' of background facts excludes 'the previous negotiations of the parties and their declarations of subjective intent'. It is a consequence of the adoption of the objective approach that the courts, when looking for the meaning which the words of a contract would convey to a reasonable onlooker, should exclude the parties' statements about what they meant and

---

[43] [2011] EWHC 1822 (Ch).
[44] Quoting himself in *Lomas and others v JFB Firth Rixon Inc and others* [2010] EWHC 3372 (Ch).
[45] See paras 11.72 *et seq* below.

also evidence about their individual intent which might be gleaned from their negotiations before the contract took place.

The rule which excludes consideration of pre-contract negotiations has been justified partly on the basis that it is necessary to preserve objectivity, and also on the basis of practicality. As early as 1604, Popham CJ[46] had warned against the dangers of accepting oral evidence of what parties had intended when signing formal documents: **11.73**

> It would be inconvenient, that matters in writing made by advice and on consideration, and which finally import the certain truth of the agreement of the parties should be controlled by averment of the parties to be proved by the uncertain testimony of slippery memory.

In 1822 in *Millers v Miller*,[47] Lord Eldon declined to consider correspondence which preceded the making of a marriage contract: **11.74**

> My Lords, all the previous correspondence I lay entirely out of the case, because I cannot conceive that any thing can be more dangerous than the construing deeds by the effect of letters and correspondence previous to the execution of them.

The issue was considered fully in *Inglis v John Buttery & Co*.[48] The House of Lords affirmed the principle that, in considering the meaning of the contract, the court was to be placed 'in the position in which the parties stood before they signed'. In other words, the court should take into account the matrix of fact available at the time. However, Lord Blackburn rejected the idea that this should include consideration of pre-contract negotiations. He referred to the opinion of Lord Gifford in the same case: **11.75**

> … where parties agree to embody, and do actually embody, their contract in a formal written deed, then in determining what the contract really was and really meant, a Court must look to the formal deed and to that deed alone. This is only carrying out the will of the parties. The only meaning of adjusting a formal contract is, that the formal contract should supersede all loose and preliminary negotiations – that there shall be no room for misunderstandings which may often arise, and which do constantly arise, in the course of long, and it may be desultory conversations, or in the course of correspondence or negotiations during which the parties are often widely at issue as to what they will insist on and what they will concede. The very purpose of a formal contract is to put an end to the disputes which would inevitably arise if the matter were left upon verbal negotiations or upon mixed communings partly consisting of letters and partly of conversations. The written contract is that which is to be appealed to by both parties, however different it may be from their previous demands or stipulations, whether contained in letters or in verbal conversation. There can be no doubt that this is the general rule …

This rule has been affirmed more recently by the House of Lords and the Supreme Court on several occasions.[49]

---

[46] *Countess of Rutlands Case* (1604) 5 Co Rep 25b, at 26a.
[47] (1822) 1 Sh App 309.
[48] (1878) 3 App Cas 552.
[49] See *Prenn v Simmonds* [1971] 1 WLR 1381, at 1384 *per* Lord Wilberforce; *Chartbrook Ltd v Persimmon Homes Ltd and others* [2009] UKHL 38 *per* Lord Hoffmann, at para 28; and *Arnold v Britton and others* [2015] UKSC 50.

11.76 Lord Wilberforce in *Prenn v Simmonds* explained that the reason for excluding evidence of prior negotiations was that such evidence was unhelpful. In the course of discussions before a contract, parties inevitably take a 'negotiating position' which does not necessarily reflect that which they expect to be in the contract which they will ultimately sign. Knowledge of the parties' discussions during this period is just as likely to mislead about their intention as it is to illuminate the position.

11.77 The same reasoning led, even more strongly, to the exclusion of evidence from the parties about their individual understandings of the words. Lord Wilberforce said:

> Far more and indeed totally, dangerous is it to admit evidence of one party's objective – even if this is known to the other party. However strongly pursued this may be, the other party may only be willing to give it partial recognition, and in a world of give and take, men often have to be satisfied with less than they want. So, again, it would be a matter of speculation how far the common intention was that the particular objective should be realised.

11.78 The rule has been subject to criticism in the recent past.[50] It remains, however, undisturbed.

11.79 The exclusion of evidence about what was said during the course of negotiating an agreement for the purpose of deciding the meaning of words used in the contract does not mean that evidence of those negotiations will always be irrelevant. The court's objective in interpreting the contract is to find the meaning that would have been attributed to it by a reasonable observer, who had the knowledge that was available to the parties at the time they concluded the contract. Things said in negotiation might very well form part of that body of knowledge, against which the meaning of the words must be placed. For example, the parties to a financial contract might have discussed the subject-matter on the shared assumption that interest rates would not rise during the term of the agreement, and that provision needed to be made only for the situation where interest rates fell. If there is a subsequent difficulty in interpreting the clause, a court would not admit evidence from a party that the clause had been intended to apply only if interest rates fell. The court might, however, accept as relevant evidence that the clause had been negotiated against a shared assumption of all the parties that interest rates would not rise. A reasonable man who was aware of this background fact might conclude that the words were not intended by the parties to apply to a situation where interest rates rose. The background facts and assumptions which shaped the intention of the parties, as they expressed them in the contract, are a relevant issue to be taken into account.[51]

11.80 In relation to many contracts in the financial markets, it is somewhat artificial, however necessary it might be, to talk about the contract embodying the intention of the parties. Many contracts are extremely complicated and highly technical in their drafting. The wording of the contract which is signed is often the product of years of development in the precedent banks of the law firm of one of the parties, or through various drafting committees of trade associations. Such standard documents are taken as a starting point for negotiations, which are often conducted largely through lawyers, arguing about highly technical issues. It is very

---

[50] See the review of the arguments by Lord Hoffmann in the *Chartbrook* case, at paras 34 to 40.
[51] See Lord Hoffmann in the *Chartbrook* case, at para 42.

common to find that the parties agree a 'term sheet' which sets out on one piece of paper the commercial terms of the deal with they propose. This may be a swap transaction, a syndicated loan, or a complex financing structure. The term sheet is then handed over to the lawyers, and the pile of documents which subsequently emerge for signature may have involved comparatively little consideration by the parties who then sign them.

11.81 It is a premise of common law systems that this pile of document embodies the agreement between the parties on whose behalf they were signed. Interpretation is the attempt to find the deemed intent of those parties. The courts exclude from this consideration any evidence of the subjective intent of the signatories. A salutary point for financial markets' lawyers to remember is that the rule shuts out, even more firmly, consideration of the intention of the lawyers who were responsible for the production of the final documents, or who drafted the precedents on which they were based. While it is obvious that this must be the case, it can be a shock to the system of the draftsman to be told that a document means X rather than Y because the parties cannot have intended it to mean Y, when he has drafted the document with the very specific intention that it should mean Y. It points to a stark and unchanging rule for all draftsmen: what you mean to say is irrelevant; all that matters is what you are taken to mean.

Rectification

11.82 There is an established situation in which a court will be prepared to consider negotiations and correspondence between the parties, which took place before the written agreement was concluded. One party to a contract may claim that part of that contract should be 'rectified'. This involves an assertion that the parties had reached an agreement or understanding, but that the written document, by mistake, does not reflect the agreed position. Although the meaning of the words used in the written contract might be quite clear, they do not accurately represent the intention of the parties, and the court is asked to amend the words of the contract, before ascribing a meaning to it.

11.83 Often the meaning of the contract, applying normal rules of construction, is quite clear. Properly speaking, the rules relating to rectification are not concerned with the meaning of the contract. More accurately, the court examines the contract or other arrangement which the parties had concluded *before* the written contractual document was signed. When the court has decided, using its usual criteria of interpretation, what the original contract meant, it amends the written embodiment of that contract to accord with its finding.

11.84 Although rectification is not a matter of construction of a contract, it is sometimes easy to confuse it with the process referred to as 'correction of mistake by construction'. The difference between the two is that, in the case of rectification, the written contractual document is internally consistent and is capable of being interpreted according to normal criteria of construction. The allegation, however, is that this, apparently correct, record of the parties' intentions is inaccurate as a result of a mistake. In the case of correction by construction, the mistake is apparent from the document itself. At its most simple, a document which refers on a number of occasions to an event which is to happen on '1 Jan 2010' may, in one place, refer to '1 Jan 2011'. It may be obvious, on reading the document, that this was a typographical error. If this happens, the court will correct the internal mistake as part of the process of constructions.

11.85 Brightman J in *East v Pantiles (Plant Hire) Ltd*[52] set out the conditions required before the court will correct an error as part of the construction process:

> Two conditions must be satisfied: first there must be a clear mistake on the face of the instrument; secondly, it must be clear what correction ought to be made in order to cure the mistake. If those conditions are satisfied, then the correction is made as a matter of construction.[53]

11.86 The process of rectification is quite different. It involves the court concluding that the written contract did not reflect the arrangement which had been agreed, and then amending it to conform with the prior understanding. In *Oceanbulk Shipping & Trading SA v TMT Asia Ltd and others*,[54] Lord Clarke said:[55]

> In principle, the remedy of rectification is one permitted by the Court, not for the purpose of altering the terms of an agreement entered into between two or more parties, but for that of correcting a written instrument which, by a mistake in verbal expression, does not accurately reflect their true agreement.

11.87 Until 1970, there was an argument that the process could be applied only when the parties had earlier concluded a contract, and the document before the court was simply the written statement of the existing oral contract. However, in *Josclyne v Nissen*,[56] the Court of Appeal confirmed that the process could be applied also in a case where there was no enforceable prior agreement, but only a concluded common intention on a matter which was subsequently embodied in the agreement.

11.88 When a court decides that rectification might be possible, its task is to examine the contract or arrangement which existed before the written document was produced, and decide upon the meaning of that agreement or understanding. In reaching a conclusion, it will apply the same objective approach as it applies to the interpretation of written contracts. In *Frederick E Rose (London) Ltd v William H Pim Jnr & Co Ltd*,[57] Denning LJ said:

> Rectification is concerned with contracts and documents, not with intentions. In order to get rectification it is necessary to show that the parties were in complete agreement on the terms of their contract, but by an error wrote them down wrongly; and in this regard, in order to ascertain the terms of their contract, you do not look into the inner minds of the parties – into their intentions – anymore than you do in the formation of any other contract. You look at their outward acts, that is, at what they said or wrote to one another in coming to their agreement, and then compare it with the documents which they have

---

[52] [1981] 263 EG 61.
[53] See also *KPMG LLP v Network Rail Infrastructure Ltd* [2007] Bus LR 1336, quoting with approval Levinson, *The Interpretation of Contracts* (Sweet & Maxwell, 2004), Ch 9.01:

> As part of the process of construction the court has power to correct obvious mistakes in the written expression of the intention of the parties. Once corrected, the contract is interpreted in its corrected form.

[54] [2010] UKSC 44.
[55] Quoting Slade LJ in *Agip SpA v Navigazione Alta Italia SpA* [1984] 1 Lloyd's Rep 353 at 359.
[56] [1970] 2 QB 86.
[57] [1953] 2 QB 450.

signed. If you can predicate with certainty what their contract was, and that it is, by a common mistake, wrongly expressed in the document, then you rectify the document; but nothing less will suffice.[58]

11.89 Although, in an action for rectification, the court's task is to decide the objective meaning of the contract or arrangement which existed before the written document was produced, there may be circumstances where the court will be prepared to consider evidence from the parties about their subjective understanding of what had been agreed. This is not to change the nature of the interpretation process; rather, the understanding of the parties may be evidence which helps the court decide on the objective meaning of the arrangement between the parties. This is particularly so when the arrangement which preceded the written contract was wholly or partly oral: the only way to find out what the parties had agreed may be to ask them. Lord Hoffmann said in the *Chartbrook* case:

> In a case in which the prior consensus was based wholly or in part on oral exchanges or conduct, such evidence may be significant. A party may have had a clear understanding of what was agreed without necessarily being able to remember the precise conversation or action which gave rise to that belief. On the other hand, where the prior consensus is expressed entirely in writing ... such evidence is likely to carry very little weight. But I do not think it is inadmissible.[59]

Estoppel by convention

11.90 Another situation in which a court may decide not to apply the rule that pre-contractual negotiations should be ignored when interpreting a contract is that where the doctrine called 'estoppel by convention' applies. At its most stark, the doctrine becomes relevant, not in relation to the interpretation of the words used in a contract, but where the parties to a contract have forgotten that a particular term was included at all. In *Christopher Charles Dixon and EFI (Loughton) Ltd v Blindley Heath Investments Ltd and others*[60] the shareholders in a private company had agreed on its formation that they should have pre-emption rights, in the event that others of them wished to sell shares. Mr Dixon had, at one point, transferred shares to a company that he controlled. Neither he nor any other shareholder raised the existence of the pre-emption rights at that time. All had, apparently, forgotten about their existence and behaved as if they did not exist. Later, another of the shareholders wished to transfer his shares. At this point Mr Dixon raised the existence of the pre-emption rights, having just remembered it. The Court of Appeal took the view that, all the shareholders having forgotten about the pre-emption term (or, at least, having behaved on the assumption that it did not exist) it would be inequitable for Mr Dixon now to rely on the contractual term to the disadvantage of the proposing transferor.

11.91 The concept of 'estoppel by convention' can also arise where the parties have a shared view that the words of a contract bear a particular meaning, even though an objective view of the

---

[58] See also *Olympic Pride (Etablissements) Georges et Paul Levy v Adderley Navigation Co Panama SA* [1980] 2 Lloyd's Rep 67; and *George Cohen Sons & Co Ltd v Docks and Inland Waterways Executive* (1950) 84 Lloyd's Rep 97.
[59] See also *Carmichael v National Power plc* [1999] 1 WLR 2042, at 2050; and *Cambridge Antibody Technology Ltd v Abbot Biotechnology Ltd* [2005] FSR 590.
[60] [2015] EWCA Civ 1023.

wording would lead to a different interpretation. In this situation, a court might hold that it would be inequitable for one of the parties to deny the parties' chosen interpretation, and to assert an objective view. Although this is often treated as separate from the process of rectification, it can most easily be seen as a variation of it.

11.92   In *Swainland Builders Ltd v Freehold Properties Ltd*,[61] the Court of Appeal set out clearly the conditions which must be met before rectification could be granted:

> The parties seeking rectification must show that:
> (1) the parties have a common continuing intention, whether or not amounting to an agreement, in respect of a particular matter in the instrument to be rectified;
> (2) there was an outward expression of accord;
> (3) the intention continued at the time of the execution of the instrument sought to be rectified;
> (4) by mistake, the instrument did not reflect that common intention.[62]

It may be, however, that the mistake was not the insertion into the written contract of words other than those which the parties had agreed to use. The 'mistake' might lie in the fact that the parties used a particular word, or words, in a sense which they shared, but which was different from that which would be attributed to those words by a reasonable outsider. Although both parties were in agreement as to the meaning of the words used, an objective outsider would understand them to mean something other than that which they had intended.

11.93   In the circumstances, estoppel by convention might apply.[63] The process does not involve the court in changing the wording of the contract. Instead, it precludes either of the parties from arguing that the objective meaning of the words is the correct meaning. Lord Hoffmann explained the process briefly in the *Chartbrook* case:

> If the parties have negotiated an agreement upon some common assumption, which may include an assumption that certain words will bear a certain meaning, they may be estopped from contending that the words should be given a different meaning.

Whether one treats this doctrine as a variation on the process of rectification, or as a separate issue, it represents a second situation in which the courts will go outside the general rule that they will not consider pre-contract negotiations when considering the meaning of commercial contracts.

Implied Terms

The two kinds of implied term

11.94   During the lifetime of a contract, it is common for a situation to arise which is not specifically contemplated by the written contract. During discussion between the parties at this

---

[61] [2002] 2 EGLR 71.
[62] For a slightly different formulation, see Briggs J in *HMRC v Benchdollar Ltd* [2009] EWHC 1310 (Ch), adopted by the Court of Appeal in *In the Matter of Lehman Brothers International (Europe) (in administration)* [2011] EWCA Civ 1544.
[63] See *Amalgamated Investment & Property Co Ltd v Texas Commerce International Bank Ltd* [1982] QB 84.

point, it will almost inevitably be said by one of them that 'a term must be implied' to give effect to the wishes of that party. In fact, the rules for the implication of terms are much more restricted than many drafters imagine.

The courts have developed clear principles about the circumstances in which they are prepared to imply terms into contracts, and the nature of the terms so implied. The guiding light in this area is that the courts will not become involved in rewriting for the parties a contract which they had already made. It is not possible to use the implication of terms as a way of adjusting a contract to deal with situations which have not been contemplated by the parties.[64] **11.95**

In *Luxor (Eastbourne) Ltd v Cooper*,[65] Lord Wright pointed out that there were two distinct kinds of implied term. First, there are terms implied by law. Statutes, particularly in relation to consumer affairs, provide that certain terms are to be implied in the class of contracts with which the statute deals. Thus, for example, the Sale of Goods Act 1979 implies into contracts for the sale of goods warranties on the part of the seller as to title and as to the fitness of the goods for their intended purpose. The common law also implies terms into certain types of contracts. For example, the leading case of *Lister v Romford Ice and Cold Storage Co Ltd*[66] decided that all contracts of employment include an implied term that an employee owes a duty to take reasonable care of the employer's property and to take reasonable care in the performance of his duties. **11.96**

The second type of implied term, with which this section is concerned, consists of those terms which, in the words of Lord Wright, are 'based on an intention imputed to the parties from their actual circumstances'. **11.97**

Implied terms based on presumed intention

In *BP Refinery (Westernport) Pty Ltd v Shire of Hastings*,[67] Lord Simon set out five conditions which must be fulfilled, before the court will imply a term in a contract, on the basis that the parties were to be presumed to have intended that it should be there. The conditions for the implication of a term are that: **11.98**

1. it must be reasonable and equitable;
2. it must be necessary to give business efficacy to the contract, so that no term will be implied if the contract is effective without it;
3. it must be so obvious that 'it goes without saying';
4. it must be capable of clear expression; and
5. it must not contradict any expressed term of a contract.

---

[64] It has been a matter of some doubt whether the law about the implication of terms is part of that dealing with the construction of contracts at all. See Lord Pearson in *Trollope & Colls Ltd v North West Metropolitan Regional Hospital Board* (1982) 149 CLR 337. In practice, the distinction does not have a great deal of significance. The Supreme Court in *Marks and Spenser plc v BNP Paribas Securities Services Trust company (Jersey) Limited* [2015] UKSC 72 has concluded that the two processes, of implication and construction are separate.
[65] [1941] AC 108. See also *Geys v Societe Generale* [2013] 1 AC 523 para 55.
[66] [1956] AC 555.
[67] [1978] 52 ALJR 20.

11.99 Conditions 1, 4, and 5 pose few problems in practice. The difficulty comes in relation to Conditions 2 and 3. Although the two conditions are often combined, so the impression is given that there is a single 'business efficacy' test, it is important to remember that there are two separate issues, both of which must be resolved. First, it must be shown that that it is necessary that a term be implied, which is not expressed in the written contract, in order that the contract should continue to have business efficacy in the circumstances which have exposed the gap in the written contract. Second, it must be clear what that term is. The court will not become involved in making commercial choices for the parties.

11.100 The 'business efficacy' test originated with the decision in *The Moorcock* in 1889.[68] Bowen LJ said:

> In business transactions such as this, what the law desires to effect by the implication is to give such business efficacy to the transaction as must have been intended at all events by both parties who are business men ...

11.101 At this stage, the 'business efficacy' test did not involve the court in consideration of the content of the term which should be implied. The test merely described the purpose which the court would have, were it to imply a term into the contract. That purpose would be to give efficacy to a contract which would not otherwise have it.

11.102 A series of judgments delivered by Strutton LJ, the great commercial lawyer, in the early part of the twentieth century gave the impression that the consideration of the exact wording of the term sought to be implied was part of the same exercise as the decision whether any term needed to be implied. In *Reigate v Union Manufacturing Co*,[69] he said:

> A term can only be implied if it is necessary in a business sense to give efficacy to the contract; that is, if it is such a term that it can be confidently said that if at the time the contract was being negotiated someone had said to the parties 'What will happen in such a case?', they would have replied: 'Of course, so and so will happen; we did not trouble to say that; it is too clear.'

This passage conflates the decision that the parties, had they addressed at the time the contract was made the question that subsequently arose, would definitely have reached a particular conclusion, with the question whether it is necessary to imply a term at all.

11.103 In practice, the two points are not co-extensive. An unexpected event often happens, as a result of which the terms of a commercial contract produce a result which is different in economic terms from that which either party would have expected at the time when the contract was made. It might also be possible to identify, with the benefit of hindsight, what the parties would have decided to insert in the contract at the outset, had they foreseen the event. This is not to say, however, that it is necessary to insert such a term in order to give 'business efficacy' to the contract. If the contract continues to be workable without the term being added (even if the effect is not what the parties would have provided, had they foreseen the change of circumstances) no new term will be implied. It must be remembered that the matter will come before a court only if the parties cannot agree how to deal with

---

[68] (1889) 14 PD 64.
[69] [1918] 1 KB 592.

the change of circumstances. If they are in agreement, it is open to them to amend their contract.

Courts are conscious of the need to avoid exercising the power to imply a term, merely to substitute their view of what is commercially sensible for the conclusion to which the words written in the contract would otherwise lead. Sir Thomas Bingham said:[70] **11.104**

> ... the implication of contract terms involves ... the interpolation of terms to deal with matters for which, ex hypothesi, the parties themselves have made no provision. It is because the implication of terms is potentially so intrusive that the law imposes strict constraints on the exercise of this extraordinary power.

In *Mosvolds Rederi A/S the Food Corp of India*,[71] Steyn J identified the test as a two-stage process. First, it must be necessary to imply a term in order to give business efficacy to the contract, in the sense that 'the contract is unworkable without it'. Second, it is not permissible for a court to imply a term simply because the court considers it to be reasonable. It is possible to imply a term only if: **11.105**

> ... reasonable men ... would without hesitation say: 'Yes, of course that is so obvious that it goes without saying'.

Although the two parts of the test are not the same, they are inextricably linked. A court will need to be satisfied, not only that it is necessary, in order to make the contract workable, that an unspoken term should be included. It must also be clear beyond doubt what the parties would have intended that term to be. Sir Thomas Bingham MR explained the two-stage test:[72] **11.106**

> And it is not enough to show that had the parties foreseen the eventuality which in fact occurred they would have wished to make provision for it, unless it can also be shown either that there was only one contractual solution or that one of several possible solutions would without doubt have been preferred.

The modern law on the implication of terms has been set out by Lord Neuberger in *Marks and Spencer plc v BNP Paribas Securities Services Trust Company (Jersey) Limited*.[73] He begins by confirming the position as set out in the *BP Refinery* case[74] and expanded in the *Philips Electronique* case.[75] He goes on to add six comments on the tests laid down in the *BP Refinery* case: **11.107**

1. In deciding what the parties would have agreed at the time that the contract was concluded, the court looks at the decision that would have been taken by notional 'reasonable' people, not necessarily the decision that the contracting parties would actually have made.
2. A term should not be implied merely because it appears fair, or merely because the court thinks that the parties would have included it, had it been suggested to them at the time.

---

[70] *Philips Electronique Grand Public SA v British Sky Broadcasting Ltd* [1995] EMLR 472.
[71] [1986] 2 Lloyd's Rep 68.
[72] The *Philips Electronique* case, above.
[73] [2015] UKSC 72.
[74] See para 11.98 above.
[75] See para 11.104 above.

3. The requirement for reasonableness and equitableness is probably redundant. If a term satisfies the other tests, it will almost certainly be reasonable and equitable.
4. The requirements of 'business necessity' and obviousness' are alternatives, in the sense that only one needs to be satisfied. However, if one of them is satisfied, it is likely that the other will also be met.
5. It is necessary to formulate the question that the objective outsider would ask (ie the form of the term to be implied) with the utmost care.
6. The so-called 'necessity for business efficiency' would be better expressed by saying that a term can be implied only if, without that term, the contract would lack commercial or practical coherence.[76]

11.108 Heated discussions about the possible implication of terms into contracts frequently take place when arrangements run into commercial difficulties. In practice, the firm reliance by the courts on the wording of the contract mean that it is difficult to persuade a commercial court to insert a term into a contract merely because the circumstances have changed since the original contract was negotiated.

---

[76] An illustration of the court's examination of the requirement for the 'business necessity' of an implied term is to be found in *Concord Trust v Law Debenture Trust Corp plc*. In that case, it was sought to prevent the trustee of a bond issue from calling the acceleration of repayments under the issue on the basis of breach of the terms by the issuer. It was argued that the issuer had committed no breach, and that the call by the trustee would be invalid. The mere fact of the call, however, could have a damaging effect on the company's business. It might, for example, trigger cross-default clauses in other arrangements. It was argued that the contract under which the issue was made included an implied term that the trustee would not make an invalid call for acceleration. The argument was rejected on the grounds that a call, if it was invalid, would have no contractual effect. In order for the contract (ie the terms of the bond issue) to be effective and workable, there was no need to imply a promise that the trustee would not do something which was of no contractual effect. Although, if one had asked the parties at the outset whether it was their intention that the trustee should not call an acceleration without proper grounds, they would no doubt have agreed that this was the intention. However, the inclusion of such a term was not necessary even though, had they thought about it, the parties might have included a term to that effect.
See also *Sparks v Biden* [2017] EWHC 1994 (Ch).

INDEX

accounts
    banker's right of combination of 10.84
    consolidation of 3.20–3.26
    running 3.18–3.19
agency 8.111–8.112
almost guarantees 9.02, 9.39–9.57
anti-deprivation principle 10.88, 10.94–10.99, 10.102–10.103
anti-federalism 2.108
Argentinian bond case 3.80–3.98
    see also pari passu principle
arm's-length investment 8.05, 8.13, 8.27–8.36, 8.77, 8.85, 8.87–8.88, 8.100
assets
    customer 10.09
    disposing of diminishing 3.22, 3.102
    freezing of 2.196, 2.198, 3.22, 3.60, 3.68
    liability and 2.07, 2.32, 2.73
    ownership of *see* property rights
    see also financial assets
audit 7.14, 9.44, 9.48, 9.50
Australia
    MMIs 6.119
    securities lending agreement 10.78–10.79
aviation industry 9.114–9.122, 10.27

Balkan wars (1993) 2.08
bank accounts 5.18
Bank for International Settlements (BIS) 6.01, 6.03
bank loans 5.73–5.87, 6.17–6.19, 7.83, 10.03
bank notes 5.02
    definition of 2.24–2.25
    function and structure of 2.24
    historical origins 2.25
    legal status of 2.24
    see also notes and coin
Bank of England 2.12
    asset holding 3.144
    clearing process 3.32, 3.36, 3.39–3.40
    notes 2.22, 2.27–2.32, 2.36–2.38, notes 5.94
    obligation to pay 2.45–2.49
    sterling clearing services 2.205
banker's
    acceptances 6.118
    draft 3.06, 3.68–3.69, 6.96
    lien 3.20, 3.26, 4.57, 10.09
    payments 3.68
    right of combination 3.20, 3.22–3.23
    right of consolidation 3.20, 3.25, 4.56
    right of set-off 3.20, 4.56
    right to take security over sums 4.57
    see also consolidation of accounts
Bankers Trust Company 7.05, 8.89
banking crisis (2008)
    regulatory response to 1.21

bankruptcy 3.21, 10.38
    dividends declared on 5.18
banks
    customers, relationships with 7.77–7.78
    global custodian role of 8.116
    'having money in the bank' 2.10
    private banking 2.26
    trading vs advisory functions 7.08
Banque de France 2.111
    clearing process 3.36, 3.39–3.40
Banque Nationale de Belgique 2.113
Barclays Bank 3.53, 3.104–3.105, 7.83–7.85, 7.87, 9.68
bare rights 5.06, 5.13
bargaining power
    inequality of 7.60–7.61
Bear Stearns 10.118
bearer securities 2.182, 6.36, 6.95
bearer shares 3.147
Belgian central bank 2.113
Belgian *Cour de Cassation* 2.114
Belgian dentist 6.33, 6.37, 6.53
Belgium
    banks 2.113
    constitution 2.113
    currency 2.113
big bang of 1986 7.07
bills of exchange 5.15, 5.18, 5.43–5.44, 5.99, 5.101, 5.103–5.105, 6.39–6.41, 6.45, 6.81–6.82, 6.87–6.88, 6.101, 6.120, 9.78
bills of lading 5.44, 10.64
bills of sale 10.27, 10.49–10.50
Bitcoin 2.127–2.130, 2.136, 3.117
    definition of 2.156
    forking of 2.147
    mining process 2.155, 2.157
Blackstone, William 5.01
blockchain 2.128, 2.139–2.141, 2.148, 3.130
    see also Distributed Ledger Technology (DLT)
BNP Paribas 2.203
bona fide purchasers 2.54
bond insurance 9.81–9.85
    definition 9.81
    origins 9.82
Bond Insurance Policy 9.78
bond issues 2.95, 4.93–4.95, 9.30, 11.107
bonds 5.02
    certificates 10.05
    definition of 6.02
    documentation 9.40
    indenture 3.81–3.82
    see also international bond market
bondholders 4.93, 4.95, 5.02, 6.106–6.108, 6.110, 8.115, 9.30, 10.109, 10.119
    holdout 3.80–3.81
book debts 4.66, 11.62

INDEX

breach of contract *see* contract, breach of
Bretton Woods Agreement 2.189–2.191, 2.193
building contracts 5.46
building societies 2.12, 3.31–3.32, 5.18, 7.82
Bundesbank 2.111
business commonsense approach 11.14–11.16
business efficacy test 11.99–11.101, 11.103, 11.105–11.107
business necessity 11.107

calling-in procedure 2.48–2.51
Canada
   joint venture relationships 8.64–8.76
   MMIs 6.119
capital sums 5.19
care, duty of 7.24, 7.29, 7.86, 8.98
carousel fraud 3.101
Carville, James 6.01
cash equivalent obligation 9.93
cash-dollar bills 3.68–3.69
cash-flow problems 7.12
causation, rules of 7.88
caveat emptor (let the buyer beware) 8.04
Cedel Bank (Luxembourg) 6.56
central bank money 2.10
Central Moneymarkets Office (CMO) 6.122
Central Securities Depositories (ICSDs) 6.56, 6.85, 6.125–6.127, 6.129
   emergence of 6.56–6.66
   function of 6.57
Certificates of Deposit (CDs) 2.12, 3.68–3.69, 6.118
Chancery courts 4.36, 4.38, 7.18, 10.40
CHAPS payment 3.28, 3.104
charge-back arrangement 4.54–4.57, 10.31, 10.85, 10.87
charge(s) 1.20
   concept of 10.06–10.08, 10.12, 10.32, 10.37, 10.39, 10.110
   conferral of 11.49
   equitable 10.41–10.42
   fixed vs floating 11.51, 11.54–11.69
   mortgage and charge, concepts of 10.46–10.60
   registration of 10.08, 10.51
charterhire 3.43, 3.65–3.67
charterhire (non-payment) 3.48–3.52
chattel(s) 2.56, 5.01, 6.43, 10.27, 10.47–10.49
chattelisation 2.182, 5.92–5.105
Chechen War (Second, 2000) 6.93
cheques 2.190–2.191, 3.05, 5.18
China
   cryptocurrency 2.184
CHIPS 3.68–3.69
choses in action 5.04–5.11
   assignability 5.36–5.52
   bank loans 5.73–5.87
   bank notes 5.94–5.97
   bonds 6.05
   charge-backs 4.55
   chattelization 5.92–5.105
   coins 5.93, 5.98–5.99
   Colonial Bank v Whinney case 5.06–5.10, 5.13, 5.21, 5.28, 5.31
   company shares 6.16, 6.19
   cryptocurrency 2.157, 2.159, 2.168, 3.126, 5.39–5.42
   dealings with 5.53–5.105
   definition of 5.07, 5.26
   equitable 5.14, 5.16, 5.22, 5.30, 5.54, 6.104, 6.106, 6.112
      assignment 5.64–5.71
   financial assets 5.17–5.24
   Global Notes 6.90, 6.95, 6.101, 6.103, 6.106–6.107, 6.110, 6.112, 6.126
   hybrid rights 5.106–5.113
   identifying 5.12–5.16
   Investors Compensation Scheme case 5.29, 5.37
   legal 5.11, 5.14–5.15, 5.22, 5.43, 5.45, 5.64, 5.69–5.70, 5.89, 5.103, 6.101, 6.103–6.104, 6.106, 6.110, 6.112, 10.47, 10.52
      assignment 5.54–5.63
   nature of 5.25–5.26
   novation 5.88–5.91
   owners/bearers 5.34–5.35
   partnership agreements 5.51–5.52, 5.68
   property, other types of 5.27–5.35
   right to sue 5.28
   security interests 10.39–10.40
   subject to equities 5.63
   sub-participation 5.72–5.87
      funded participation 5.75
      participation by guarantee 5.75
      sale of part of the debt 5.75
   US Uniform Commercial Code 5.106–5.113
choses in possession 5.04–5.11, 5.104
   definition of 5.05
   ownership of 5.27
civil law
   common law and 11.18–11.43
      differences 11.18–11.31
   legal concepts 1.18
   personal and property rights, distinction between 4.18–4.29
Civil Procedure Rules (CPR) 3.12, 3.108, 9.12
clearing houses/arrangements 9.114–9.122, 10.34
clearing systems 6.117
   outside US 3.68–3.69
   see also TARGET2 settlement system
Clearstream Banking, SA 6.56, 6.58
coal production 9.99
coins
   bronze 2.22
   counterfeiting of 2.57–2.61
   gold 2.22
   legal tender and legislation 2.22, 2.23
   Royal Mint, production by 2.22, 2.23
   silver 2.22
   see also notes and coin
Cold War 6.27
collective investment funds 6.04, 6.24
comfort letters 9.02, 9.39–9.57, 9.93
commercial agency 8.37–8.51
commercial banks 7.07
commercial commonsense 11.13
   see also business commonsense approach
Commercial Credit (CC) 4.60–4.67
commercial credit support 9.58–9.111
   credit derivatives 9.95–9.111

credit insurance 9.79–9.94
  bond insurance 9.81–9.85
  insuring bank advances 9.87–9.94
  UK position 9.86
  export credit guarantees 9.74–9.78
    Bond Insurance Policy 9.78
    Export Insurance Policy (EXIP) 9.78
    Supplier Credit Bills and Notes Facility 9.78
  performance bonds 9.59–9.73
  see also **credit support in financial markets**
commercial honesty 8.25
commercial lending 7.08
commercial loan agreement 5.02
commercial paper 5.02, 5.72
commercial responsibility 1.21
commission, payment on 8.17, 8.24, 8.26, 8.39–8.51
common law
  civil law approaches and 11.18–11.43
    differences 11.18–11.31
  contract, principles of 7.06
  courts 4.38, 7.19, 10.40
  development of 1.10–1.12
  economic change and 1.07
  equity and, relationship between 4.39–4.43, 7.27–7.28, 7.30
  judicial precedent 1.11
  jurisdictions 7.05
  legal concepts 1.18
  money, concept of 2.04
  money, nature of 2.01
  objective approach 11.23, 11.26–11.28, 11.72
  other legal systems vs 2.02
  personal and property rights, distinction between 4.18–4.29
  rule of law 1.11–1.12
Commonwealth countries 3.108
companies
  Articles of Association 6.12, 6.15, 6.22
  Companies Acts (UK) 6.12, 6.14, 6.22, 6.24, 6.123, 10.28–10.29, 10.32, 10.36, 10.51, 10.60, 11.55
  director's duty to exercise care and skill 7.93
  dividends 5.18
  DLT systems 3.139
  incorporation and credit support 9.40
  inter-company account 9.02
  parent companies, liability of 9.41, 9.44–9.47, 9.54–9.55, 9.57, 9.117–9.118, 9.121–9.122
  share capital 5.15, 5.83, 6.12–6.17, 7.64–7.68, 9.40, 10.38
  winding-up of 3.13
compensation 8.117
  equitable 7.31, 7.98
computer technology 1.08
conceptual impossibility 4.80, 4.86
confidentiality 8.05, 8.82
  confidence vs 7.62, 7.70
  confidential information 7.39, 8.08, 8.11, 8.45, 8.79, 8.102–8.109
  joint ventures 8.74–8.76
conflicts of interest
  for professionals 8.101–8.109
  for retail customers 8.120

conflicts of laws 1.18
Confucius 2.132, 2.171
construction of financial contracts 11.01–11.108
  common law and civil law approaches 11.18–11.43
    differences 11.18–11.31
  definition of contracts 11.04–11.17
  estoppel by convention 11.90–11.93
  financial contracts 11.32–11.43
  implied terms 11.94–11.108
    based on presumed intention 11.98–11.108
    types of 11.94–11.97
  matrix of fact 11.08–11.17
  meaning and effect, difference between 11.44–11.93
  modern principles 11.01–11.07
  objective approach 11.32–11.43
  pre-contract negotiations, exclusion of 11.72–11.81
  recharacterization 11.50–11.71
  rectification 11.82–11.89
  subjective intent 11.72–11.81
constructive trusts 5.111
consumers
  consumer affairs 11.96
  products 7.05
  protection legislation 8.05, 8.27–8.36
continuous linked settlement 3.111
contraband goods 7.14
contract
  breach of 5.20, 7.86–7.87, 8.30, 8.34, 11.46
  definition of financial 11.04–11.17
  law 1.20
  obligations of 2.92
  rights 5.02, 5.19, 11.42
contract-based security 10.83–10.105
conversion theory 5.111
conveyancing 3.140–3.142
copyright law 2.169, 5.23
  see also **intellectual property rights**
corporate advice 7.08
corporate collective investment vehicle 4.98–4.99
correction of mistake by construction 11.84–11.85
  see also **rectification**
correspondent bank transfer 3.68
counterfeit money 2.57–2.61
  definition 2.58
  see also **forgery**; **fraud**
coupons 6.46–6.47
Court of Justice of the European Union (CJEU) 10.09
covenant of a suretyship under a lease 5.19
credit card payments 2.18, 3.05
credit derivatives 9.02, 9.95–9.111
credit event 9.96
credit insurance 9.02, 9.79–9.94
  bond insurance 9.81–9.85
  insuring bank advances 9.87–9.94
  UK position 9.86
credit or performance guarantee 5.18
credit rating agency (CRA) 9.96
credit risk 9.100–9.101
credit support in financial markets 1.20, 9.01–9.134
  almost guarantees 9.39–9.57
  comfort letters 9.39–9.57
  multiple obligations, creation of 9.18–9.21

credit support in financial markets (*cont.*)
  multiple obligors 9.05–9.17
    joint liability 9.09–9.14
    joint and several liability 9.15–9.17
    several liability 9.07–9.08
  subordination 9.112–9.134
    ad hoc 9.123–9.134
    general 9.117–9.122
  suretyship, contracts of 9.22–9.38
    guarantee, contracts of 9.27–9.33
    guarantees and indemnities, distinction between 9.22–9.26
    indemnity, contracts of 9.34–9.38
  see also **commercial credit support**
creditors 3.90, 8.87, 9.01–9.02, 9.30
  junior vs senior 9.123–9.133
  preferential 11.54
creditworthiness 9.96, 9.97, 9.108
CREST trading system 6.123
crime, financial *see* **counterfeit money; fraud; money laundering; organized crime; proceeds of crime; theft**
cross-border insolvency 10.17–10.25
cross-border lending 10.69
cross-default clauses 3.78, 10.119, 11.107
Crown currency 2.23
  see also **Royal Mint**
cryptoassets 2.127–2.131
  definition of 2.178
  legal nature of 2.148–2.159
  other than cryptocurrencies 2.178–2.183
Cryptoassets Taskforce 2.178–2.179, 2.184–2.185
cryptocurrency 2.05, 3.117–3.121
  chose in action 2.157, 2.159, 2.168
  court's approach 2.154
  cryptosecurities distinguished 2.180
  definition of 2.178
  digital record 2.162
  economic uses 2.177
  financial crisis (2008) 2.184
  forking process 2.145–2.147
  governmental and regulatory response to 2.184–2.186
  holders of 2.172–2.173
  intangible assets and 2.159
  language and terminology 2.132–2.135
  as a medium of investment 2.130, 2.143
  modes of dealing with 2.174–2.177
  money laundering 2.155
  nature of 2.15
  property law 2.153, 2.159
  regulatory treatment of 2.184
  risks and challenges 2.184–2.185
  systems of 2.130
  tax implications 2.150, 2.154, 2.186
  theft and 2.150, 2.154, 2.164–2.165
  trading of 2.171–2.173
  transferring ownership and digital 'wallets' 5.39–5.42
  units of as property 2.160–2.170
  see also **bitcoin; Distributed Ledger Technology (DLT); Ethereum**
cryptosecurities
  corporate securities distinguished 2.182
  cryptocurrency distinguished 2.180
  definition of 2.178, 2.181
  security tokens 2.179
  utility tokens 2.179
cryptosystem
  address 2.137–2.138, 2.158, 2.172
  input and output messages 2.138–2.144, 2.151, 2.158, 2.172–2.173, 3.120
  nodes 2.141–2.142, 2.145
  operation of a 2.136–2.147
  private keys 2.137–2.138, 2.172, 2.175
  verification process 2.139, 2.141
  wallet-holders 2.144, 2.176, 3.129, 3.136
crystallization 10.60
Cuba
  sanctions 2.203
currency
  in circulation 2.19, 2.51
  currency note 2.20
  inconvertible 2.76
  indexes 2.95
  movement of 8.122
  national identity and rights, as an assertion of 2.206
current coin, definition of 2.61
customers
  assets 10.09
  interests 8.120
  relationships of trust 8.120
  see also **retail customers**
customs checkpoints 7.51, 7.72

damages 8.25, 8.30–8.31, 8.74
  Banco de Portugal case 2.78–2.82
  contractual 7.87
  measure of 7.88
  payment of 7.31
  in tort 5.20
  unliquidated 5.20
databases 2.167–2.169
debenture 5.18, 11.62, 11.65–11.66
  definition of 6.22, 6.24
  stock 6.22, 6.24, 6.35
debt 1.18
  factoring 10.81
  financial assets 5.18
  instruments 8.93
  Iranian debt crisis 3.75–3.79, 3.98
  securities 5.02, 5.15
debtors 3.90, 8.87, 9.01–9.02
deceit, remedy for 7.23
decentralization 3.122
Declaration of Trust 10.69
deed poll 6.20, 9.30
deeds 3.140–3.142
dematerialization in international bond market 5.104–5.105, 6.07, 6.115–6.130
  international bond market 6.125–6.130
  related markets 6.118–6.124
  wish to move to 6.115–6.117
  see also **international bond market**
demonetization 2.38–2.51

Denmark
  euro currency 2.86
Depository/Safekeeper 6.52, 6.54, 6.58, 6.62, 6.65, 6.68, 6.69, 6.71, 6.74–6.75, 6.80, 6.90, 6.91, 6.93, 6.95–6.97, 6.101–6.104, 6.107, 6.109, 6.114, 6.116, 6.120–6.122
derivatives contracts 2.95, 7.10
derivatives markets 2.95
derivatives transactions between banker and customer 8.86–8.100
design rights 5.23
deutschmark LIBOR 2.95
discharge of obligation to pay money 3.04–3.26
  agreed method of payment 3.05–3.06
  consolidation of accounts 3.20–3.26
  netting 3.15–3.17
  running accounts 3.18–3.19
  set-off 3.07–3.14
    independent 3.12
    insolvency 3.13–3.14
    transactional 3.11
  see also payment
disintermediation 3.122
Distributed Ledger Technology (DLT) 1.08, 2.129, 2.131, 2.139–2.140, 2.146, 2.148–2.149, 2.153, 2.178, 2.183, 3.117–3.118
  benefits of 3.128
  effect on legal principles and practices 3.138–3.152
  geographical location 3.150–3.151
  permissioning 3.121, 3.125, 3.131, 3.135, 3.144, 3.150
  potential uses of 3.122–3.132
  regulatory challenges 3.133–3.137
  see also blockchain; cryptocurrency
distribution rights 9.87
dividends
  bankruptcy 5.18
  company shares 5.18
documentary credit 9.59
documentation, effectiveness of 8.114
Dodd-Frank Act 1.21
drafts payable to bearer 5.44
drug trafficking 3.99, 3.102
duty, breach of 7.90, 7.98, 8.19, 8.25–8.26

Economic and Monetary Union (EMU)
  process of 2.84, 2.86, 2.91, 2.93
economic change 1.07–1.09
electronic trading 1.19
electronic transfer of funds 2.05
English Civil War (1642–1651) 2.03
entitlement holder, definition of 5.109
equitable assignment 5.64–5.71
equitable charges 4.69, 4.81, 4.83, 10.41, 10.57, 10.69
equitable fraud *see* fraud
equitable interest 5.02
equitable lien 5.111
equitable rights 5.22
equitableness 11.107
equity
  common law and, relationship between 4.39–4.43, 7.27–7.28, 7.30
  concept of 7.18
  legal and equitable ownership 4.30–4.38
  principles of 7.88
  registrable charges 4.64, 4.67, 4.69
  rules 4.36–4.37
  securities 5.02, 6.22
  trusts and equitable ownership 4.44–4.53
estoppel by convention 11.90–11.93
Ethereum 2.147
euro
  change in economic value 2.96–2.97
  contractual issues 2.98
  eurozone Member States 2.119–2.126
  introduction of 2.86–2.98
  issuance of euro notes and coins 2.110–2.116
  market stability 2.96
  open questions 2.99–2.103
  ownership issues 2.104–2.109
  Participating Member States 2.88, 2.90, 2.99, 2.105, 2.106, 2.108–2.109, 2.116
  payment through TARGET2 3.40
  Rome Treaty 2.99, 2.102, 2.106, 2.110, 2.115
  settlement arrangements 2.117
  sovereignty issues 2.101, 2.106–2.107, 2.116
  transitional period 2.88–2.89, 2.95
Euroclear Bank SA/NV (Brussels) 6.56
Eurodollar market 3.96–3.97, 6.27–6.33
European Central Bank (ECB)
  clearing process 3.34–3.40
  collateral, security of 6.67–6.69, 6.71, 6.85, 6.116
  euros, issue of 2.88–2.89
  financial crisis (2008) 2.120, 2.122, 2.124
  German base 2.117
  issue of euro bank notes 2.110, 2.112, 2.115–2.116
  role and function 2.106
European Civil Code, proposals for a 11.29
European Commission (EC)
  contract law, coherence of 11.29
European Communities 2.03
European Currency Unit (ECU) 2.03, 2.87, 2.95, 2.99
European Financial Stabilisation Mechanism (EFSM) 2.125
European Single Currency 2.84–2.186
  see also cryptoassets; cryptocurrency; cryptosystem; euro
European Stability Mechanism (ESM) 2.123–2.125
European System of Central Banks 2.88
European Union (EU)
  cross-border insolvency 10.19, 10.43
  euro currency 2.107–2.108
  sanctions 2.08, 2.198
  State Aid, restriction of 9.76
exchange bonds 3.80–3.81
exchange contracts 2.191–2.194
exchange control 2.189–2.194
Export Credit Guarantee Departments 9.75–9.78, 9.80
export credit guarantees 9.74–9.78
  Bond Insurance Policy 9.78
  Export Insurance Policy (EXIP) 9.78
  Supplier Credit Bills and Notes Facility 9.78
Export Insurance Policy (EXIP) 9.78
exportation of services 2.201
extraterritoriality 2.204

fact-based fiduciaries 7.34, 7.41
fact-sensitive judgments 8.12
false wealth 10.26
falsification of records 2.202
FCA Handbook Principles for Business 8.120
   conflicts of interest 8.120
   customer relationships of trust 8.120
   customers' interests 8.120
   integrity 8.120
Fedwire 3.68–3.69
fiat money 2.14, 2.127, 2.130, 2.153, 3.132
fiduciaries
   definition 7.01, 7.93
   obligations of 7.95–7.98
fiduciary duties/relationships 1.21, 7.01–7.99, 8.01–8.123
   ad hoc 7.50–7.78
   arm's-length investment 8.05, 8.13, 8.27–8.36, 8.77, 8.85, 8.87–8.88, 8.100
   breach of 7.88
   commercial agency 8.37–8.51
   commercial transactions 8.13–8.76
   concept of 1.21, 8.123
      historical context 7.18–7.28
      modern approaches 7.29–7.30
   confidentiality 8.74–8.76
   conflicts of interest for professionals 8.101–8.109
   damages 7.17
   definition 7.54, 7.92–7.94, 7.98
   derivatives transactions between banker and customer 8.86–8.100
   duty of loyalty, breach of 7.17, 7.22–7.23
   established categories of 7.34–7.41
   existence of 7.31–7.78, 8.69–8.73
   fiduciary relationship 7.18–7.30
   financial institutions 7.06–7.10
   financial transactions 8.83–8.117
   inequality of information 8.110–8.117
   joint ventures 8.52–8.76, 8.80–8.81
   military duties vs 7.55–7.57, 7.74
   nature of fiduciary duties 7.79–7.97
   overview 8.01–8.12, 8.77–8.82
   perceived risk 7.01–7.17
   personal agency 8.15–8.26
   preservation of mankind 7.03
   profit 7.71–7.73
   remedies 7.16
   retail customers, regulatory rules for 8.118–8.123
   scope of 7.42–7.49
   self-appointed agents of trustees 7.70, 7.73
   uncertainties about 7.11–7.17
film industry 9.87, 9.89–9.90
   film finance, tax treatment of 10.49
financial assets 5.17–5.24
   contractual rights 5.19
   debts 5.18
   equitable rights 5.22
   intellectual property 5.23–5.24
   rights of action 5.20
   shares 5.21
   see also *choses in action*
financial contracts 2.95
   see also construction of financial contracts

financial covenants 9.40
financial crisis (2008) 2.85, 2.118–2.126, 2.184, 9.95
financial engineering arrangement 8.87
financial institutions 7.06–7.10
financial law
   legal practice vs 1.02
   transnational nature of 1.06
Financial Services Act 1986 7.09
Financial Services Authority (FSA) 9.111
Financial Stability Board (FSB) 3.133
flawed assets 10.90, 10.101
flip clauses 10.96, 10.101–10.105
floating charges
   concept of 10.60
   fixed charges vs 11.51, 11.54–11.69
   holders 8.29–8.30
force majeure clauses 3.59, 9.78
Foreign Credit Restraint Program 6.30
foreign policy 2.08
FOREX dealing 2.193
forgery 6.127
   bank notes 2.40, 2.44
   see also counterfeit money
forward currency contract 2.93
France 6.75, 9.103
   Civil Code 11.21
   contractual interpretation 11.19
   euro 2.104–2.105
   francs 2.95
   livres 2.02
   monetary law 2.01
   security rights 10.18
fraud 2.05, 3.28, 7.22
   aggravated 7.10
   Banco de Portugal case 2.62–2.83
   carousel 3.101
   equitable 7.23, 8.22–8.23
fraudulent misrepresentation 8.63, 8.90, 8.94, 8.114
freedom of contract 11.45
freezing injunctions 3.108, 4.16
freezing orders 3.108
freezing regulations 2.08
French Revolution (1789) 2.02
frustrated contracts 3.72–3.73
fund management 4.98–4.99, 7.08
funded participation 5.75
future sums 5.19

gaming contracts 9.104–9.105, 9.110
geography 1.08
Germany 2.117
   banks 2.03
   deutschmark 3.110
   hyper-inflation in Weimar Republic 2.03
   monetary law 2.01
gift, deed of 7.48, 10.122
global custodian 8.116
Global Notes 6.62, 6.115–6.118, 6.125–6.127, 6.129
   Classical Bearer Global Note Structure 6.62, 6.64, 6.69–6.71
   as a negotiable instrument 6.101–6.108
   New Global Note Structure 6.67–6.71
   as not a negotiable instrument 6.109–6.110

permanent 6.53–6.55
temporary 6.48–6.52
value of 6.79–6.97
see also **international bond market**
global unenforceability provision 2.193
globalization 1.09
gold 8.27–8.36
bullion 3.145, 4.07–4.08
good faith 2.54, 8.19
government
action 10.02
debt instruments 6.118
embargo legislation 3.60
stock 5.21
Greece
euro 2.104
guarantee(s) 10.22
of bills 9.78
contracts of 9.23, 9.27–9.33
demand 9.61
indemnity, distinction with 9.22–9.26, 9.36
obligation 9.28
participation by 5.75
performance 9.60
Statute of Frauds 9.31–9.33
guarantors 11.36

hedge funds 4.10–4.11
hedging risk *see* **risk**
Herstatt risk 3.109–3.112
HM Treasury 2.29–2.30, 2.34, 2.178, 6.37, 6.123, 9.86
holdout bondholders 3.80–3.81
HSBC 3.103–3.105
human instincts 1.10
hybrid rights 5.106–5.113
hyper-inflation 2.03

ICSDs *see* **Central Securities Depositories (ICSDs)**
immobilization 6.07, 6.56–6.71, 6.89, 6.100, 6.115
Classical Bearer Global Note Structure 6.62
ICSDs, emergence of 6.56–6.66
New Global Note Structure 6.67–6.71
New Safekeeping Structure 6.67–6.71
see also **international bond market**
implied terms 11.94–11.108
based on presumed intention 11.98–11.108
types of 11.94–11.97
see also **construction of financial contracts**
indemnity
contracts of 9.34–9.38
definition 9.25
guarantee, distinction with 9.22–9.26, 9.36
indemnity, contracts of 9.23
definition 9.26
index-linking prices 2.03
inequality of information 8.110–8.117
inflation 2.03
see also **hyper-inflation**
inheritance tax 10.122
in-house transfer 3.68
insider trading 4.44
insolvency 6.75, 9.112, 10.88, 11.49
ad hoc subordination arrangements 9.123–9.128

corporate, legal regimes for 10.03
cross-border proceedings 10.17–10.25
event 10.98
proceedings 9.96, 10.43
proprietary interests 4.06–4.16
remote 10.119
risk of 3.109–3.110
Scottish and Northern Irish banks 2.36
set-off 3.13, 3.16–3.17
UK law 9.112–9.122
see also **anti-deprivation principle; Herstatt risk; liquidation; winding-up of companies**
insurance
bank advances 9.87–9.94
business 9.111
companies 9.79, 9.87, 9.90–9.91
contracts 3.02, 9.25, 9.111
industry 9.103
legal principles 9.90, 9.94
policies 5.15, 5.19, 9.93
see also **bond insurance; credit insurance**
intangible assets 1.18
cryptocurrency and 2.159, 2.168
intangibles as property 1.18, 5.01–5.113
hybrid rights 5.106–5.113
see also **choses in action; choses in possession**
intellectual property rights 1.18, 2.169, 3.104, 5.19, 5.23–5.24, 5.43, 10.98
see also **copyright law; patents; registered designs**
interdiction 2.195–2.206
legislation 2.197, 3.99–3.107
Interest Equalization Tax 6.29
interest on money held on trust 5.16
interest rates 9.82
euro currency 2.93, 2.95
mortgages 10.121, 10.123
swaps 7.10
US dollar 8.89
international bond market 1.19, 6.01–6.130
definition 6.03
historical background 2.182, 6.01–6.10
bond market pre-history 6.11–6.25
ICSDs (International Central Securities Depositories) 6.56–6.66
immobilization 6.56–6.71
investor ownership 6.98–6.114
legal analysis of bond structures 6.72–6.114
legal issues 6.05
lock-up period 6.51, 6.53
market development, incremental nature of 6.01–6.07
nature of bonds and the market, relationship between 6.08–6.10
World War II, after 6.26–6.55
bond documentation 6.46–6.47
development of the form of bond 6.34–6.38
growth of the markets 6.26–6.33
negotiability 6.42–6.45
negotiable instruments 6.39–6.41
permanent global notes 6.53–6.55
temporary global notes 6.48–6.52
see also **bonds; dematerialization in international bond market; Depository/Safekeeper; Global Note; immobilization; safekeeping**

International Monetary Fund (IMF) 2.189
international payments 3.33
International Swaps and Derivatives Association 3.15
international trade 1.07, 2.08, 4.100
international transactions 2.06, 10.03
interpretation, principles of contractual 11.05–11.07, 11.11
intra-Eurosystem obligations 3.37
investment banking 8.99–8.100
investment in illiquid assets 3.145
invoice discounting 10.81
Iran
   debt crisis (1979) 3.01, 3.75–3.79, 3.98
   sanctions 2.201, 2.203
Iraq
   aggravated fraud 7.10
   asset freezing 2.198
Italy
   exchange contracts 2.192
   insolvency legislation 10.18
   lira 2.95

Jack Committee (Review Committee on Banking Services Law and Practice) 6.120–6.122
Japan 9.41, 10.11, 10.13
joint and several liability 9.06, 9.15–9.17, 9.22
joint liability 9.06, 9.09–9.14, 9.22
   death and 9.13
joint ventures 8.52–8.76, 8.80–8.81
   arrangements 8.07, 9.99, 10.98
   confidentiality 8.74–8.76
JP Morgan Chase 3.121, 3.125, 3.127, 10.118
Judicature Acts 4.42, 4.51
jumbo syndicated loans 3.77
jus ad rem / jus in personam (personal rights) 4.25
jus in rem (rights of ownership) 4.25

keep whole agreements 9.43–9.44, 9.48, 9.54
Keynes, J. M. 1.01
King's Council 4.34
Kuwait
   asset freezing 2.198
   Iraqi invasion of (1990) 2.08

land
   law 1.20, 4.44
   option to purchase 5.19
   ownership 3.140–3.142
   registration 10.27
   see also property; tenancy law
Law Commission 7.09, 7.34, 7.49, 10.50, 10.54
law merchant 5.44, 5.103, 6.41, 6.88
lawyers 1.01
   financial 1.04–1.06, 1.14–1.15
      challenges for 1.13–1.15
   litigation 1.03, 1.05
   transactional 11.01–11.03
leases 7.44
legal advice in financial markets 1.03–1.06
legal assignment 5.54–5.63
legal *choses in action* see *choses in action*
legal developments 1.07–1.09

legal ownership 4.30–4.38
legal remedies 5.04
legal rights
   concept of 4.21
   enforcement of 5.04
legal tender 2.16–2.22
Lehman Brothers International (Europe) 4.10–4.15, 10.101, 11.70
leitmotif 8.04
lenders of record 5.78, 5.86
'lending long and borrowing short' 6.17–6.19
letters of credit 9.63, 9.66, 9.69
lex monetae rule 2.92
liability
   assets and 2.07, 2.32, 2.73
   forms of *see* joint liability; joint and several liability; several liability
   fraud and 2.69
libertarianism 2.129
Libra 3.130–3.132
Libya 9.68–9.68
   Libyan Arab Foreign Bank case 3.61–3.74, 3.95–3.97
licenses 7.44
lien 4.75, 4.78
   banker's 3.20, 3.26, 4.57
   concept of 10.06, 10.08–10.10, 10.22
   consensual 10.41, 10.67
   definition of 4.57
   equitable 5.111, 10.66, 10.68
   possessory 2.167
   security interests 10.65–10.68
   solicitor's 10.65
life assurance 9.103–9.104
limited recourse lending 10.116–10.123
liquidation 3.53, 4.07, 9.45, 9.116, 9.122–9.123, 9.126, 9.129–9.130, 10.119, 11.70
   Bank of Credit and Commerce International SA (No 8) case 4.75–4.86
   Charge Card case 4.58–4.87
   see also insolvency
liquidity squeeze 6.17
Lloyds Bank 2.201–2.203, 3.69, 7.58
loan agreements 2.95, 9.40
loan capital, definition of 6.23
Loan Market Association 5.76
loan stock 6.22, 6.24, 6.35–6.36, 6.128
local authority borrowing 10.11–10.16, 10.56
London Dollar Clearing System 3.58, 3.68–3.69, 3.97
London Metal Exchange 2.192
London Stock Exchange 7.07–7.08
loyalty, breach of duty of 7.17, 7.22–7.23
Luxembourg 6.32

M0 and M4, definition of 2.12
Maastricht Treaty (Treaty on European Union) 2.86–2.88, 2.102, 2.114, 2.126
manufactured goods and commodities 5.01
Mareva injunction 3.108
marine industry 10.27
marine insurance 5.43–5.44, 9.103–9.106
   contract of, definition 9.105
   insurable interest 9.105–9.110

marker on account 3.105
market development *see* international bond market
market master agreements 3.17
marriage
    contracts 11.74
    settlement 5.48
Marshall Plan 6.27
mathematical modelling 8.86
matrix of fact 11.05, 11.08–11.17, 11.71, 11.72, 11.75
meaning and effect, difference between 11.44–11.93
Medieval England 4.32–4.34
memoranda 9.31
mercantile instruments 6.88
merchant banks 7.07
mere chose 5.09, 5.36, 5.41
misappropriation 7.14
mistake *see* rectification
monetary law 2.01
money 2.01–2.206
    ability of states to control use of 2.187–2.206
        exchange control 2.189–2.194
        interdiction 2.195–2.206
        sanctions regulations 2.195–2.206
    in the courts 2.52–2.83
    as currency 2.55, 2.61
    central bank 2.10
    characteristics of 2.12
    concept of 1.17, 2.14
    definitions of 2.09–2.15
    fiat 2.14, 2.127, 2.130, 2.153, 3.132
    importance of understanding 2.01–2.08
    intangible assets 5.02
    as a means of exchange 2.12–2.13, 2.56
    as a measure of value 2.12–2.13
    measures of 2.12
    as medal 2.55, 2.61
    nature of 2.09–2.15
    private 2.26
    quantity theory of 2.11
    societal theory of 2.100, 2.109
    state theory of 2.100–2.102, 2.104, 2.109
    state theory of 2.187
    statutory treatment of 2.16–2.51
        demonetization 2.38–2.51
        legal tender 2.16–2.22
        Northern Ireland, position in 2.33–2.37
        notes and coin 2.23–2.32
        Scotland, position in 2.33–2.37
    stolen 2.53–2.54
    supply of 2.10
    tangible and intangible concepts 2.10
    transmission of *see* payment
    see also cryptocurrency; European Single Currency
money laundering 3.99, 3.107, 3.136, 4.44, 2.129
    cryptocurrency 2.155
Money Market Instruments (MMIs) 6.118–6.119, 6.122
monoline insurers 9.84–9.86
Montesquieu 4.19
mortgages 1.20, 4.68, 7.20, 10.15, 10.22
    of chattels 10.49
    choses in action 5.16, 5.20, 5.38, 5.60
    commission 8.26, 8.39–8.51

    concept of 10.07–10.08, 10.32, 10.50–10.58, 10.70, 10.74–10.76, 10.78–10.79, 10.83
    debts 5.18
    deeds 9.21
    definition of 10.48
    equitable 10.40–10.42
    equity release 10.121
    formal land 10.54
    informal land 10.54
    joint and several liability 9.21
    legal 10.53
    monoline insurers 9.84–9.85
    mortgage and charge, concepts of 10.46–10.60
    repossession 7.59
    right of rescission of 5.38
    UK housing market 10.121
    US housing market 10.120
    see also property: development
multiple contractual liability 9.05
multiple liability 9.22
multiple obligations, creation of 9.18–9.21
multiple obligors 9.05–9.17
    joint liability 9.09–9.14
    joint and several liability 9.15–9.17
    several liability 9.07–9.08
multiple ownership 4.90–4.99
    bond issues 4.93–4.95
    fund management 4.98–4.99
    project finance 4.96–4.97
    syndicated lending 4.91–4.92
municipal bonds 9.82–9.83

natural and ordinary meaning rule 11.05, 11.13, 11.16
negligence 7.21
    action in 7.23
    breach of 7.86
    negligent mis-statement 9.57
negotiability 6.42–6.45
    coins, ownership of 6.43
    concept of 6.79, 6.87–6.90, 6.119
    see also international bond market
negotiable instruments 5.18, 6.39–6.41, 6.90, 6.96–6.97, 6.99, 6.119, 6.130
negotiations, pre-contractual *see* pre-contractual negotiations
nemo dat quod non habet rule 2.54, 5.95, 5.102
Netherlands 9.103
    insolvency law 6.75
    private international law 6.75
netting 3.09, 3.15–3.17, 10.84
    close-out 3.15–3.16
    contractual 3.16–3.17
    payment 3.15–3.16
new payment technologies 3.113–3.121
nominalism, principle of 2.02
non-disclosure of material facts 9.90
non-performance of a contractual obligation 3.150
non-recourse lending 10.116–10.123
Norman Conquest (1066) 4.31
Northern Bank Limited 2.41
Northern Ireland
    notes as legal tender 2.16, 2.19–2.20, 2.33–2.37

Norway
  derivatives contracts 7.10
  notes and coin 2.23–2.32
    definition of money 2.10, 2.13
    see also bank notes; coins
  novation 3.37, 5.88–5.91

objective approach (financial contracts) see construction of financial contracts
obligation to pay 2.45–2.51
  Banco de Portugal case 2.80–2.83
obviousness 11.107
off-balance sheet structure 9.40
off-setting provisions 10.34
oil companies 9.96
OMT (Outright Monetary Transactions) programme 2.122, 2.124
on-demand securities/undertakings 9.60
oral evidence 11.73
ordinary commercial transactions 8.83
organized crime 3.99
ownership
  investor 6.98–6.114
  legal and equitable 4.30–4.38
  as security 10.70–10.82
  trusts and equitable 4.44–4.53
  of unreasonable things, concept of 4.27
  see also multiple ownership

Pakistan
  exchange control 2.190
paper currency see bank notes; notes and coin
parallel loan 10.91
pari passu principle 8.112, 9.112–9.122, 10.11, 10.15, 10.89
  see also **Argentinian bond** case
partnerships
  agreements 5.51–5.52, 5.68
  joint liability 9.13
  shares 5.16, 5.22
patents 5.23–5.24
  see also intellectual property rights
Paying Agents 6.60, 6.62
payment 3.01–3.152
  actually paid, definition of 3.02
  agreed method of 3.05–3.06
  between payer and payee 3.41–3.57
  chose in action and contractual rights 5.33
  concept of 1.17–1.18
  court injunctions against 3.60
  cross-border 3.84, 3.118
  definition of 3.02
  as the discharge of an obligation to pay money 3.04–3.26
  international 3.03
  new payment technologies 3.113–3.121
  organizations 3.131
  payment-versus-payment basis 3.111
  punctuality of 3.47, 3.51, 3.89
  as the transmission of money 3.27–3.152
  UK banking system 3.31–3.32
  see also discharge of obligation to pay money; transmission of money, payment as
Pecuniary Loss Indemnity Policies 9.87

peer-to-peer lending 3.123, 3.129
penalties 8.117
pension funds 1.21, 2.93, 5.45, 8.117
performance bonds 9.02, 9.59–9.73, 9.93
  commercial transactions 9.66, 9.73
  definition of 9.61
  structure of 9.61
performance guarantees 9.60
performance of contracts 2.117
Permanent Global Note 6.58, 6.65, 6.68, 6.74–6.75
  see also Global Notes
personal agency 8.15–8.26
personal and property rights, distinction between 4.01–4.101
  Bank of Credit and Commerce International SA (No 8) 4.75–4.86
  bond issues 4.93–4.95
  Charge Card case 4.58–4.87
  charge-backs 4.54–4.57
  civil law systems 4.18–4.29
  common law and equity, relationship between 4.39–4.43
  common law systems 4.18–4.29
  current position 4.85–4.89
  equitable ownership 4.30–4.38
  fund management 4.98–4.99
  importance of distinction 4.01–4.17
  legal ownership 4.30–4.38
  multiple ownership 4.90–4.99
  nature of the distinction 1.18, 4.18–4.53
  practice, distinction in 4.54–4.89
  project finance 4.96–4.97
  structuring security arrangements 4.100–4.101
  syndicated lending 4.91–4.92
  trusts and equitable ownership 4.44–4.53
pleadings 8.10
pledge(s) 10.39, 10.41
  of bonds 10.10
  concept of 10.10
  negative pledge clauses 10.68
  of shares 10.10
  of stock 2.171
  title-based security 10.61–10.64
Portugal 2.11
positively established test 9.71–9.72
power
  abuse of 8.77
  concept of (*dominium*) 4.21, 4.25–4.26
pre-contractual negotiations 11.90, 11.93
  exclusion of 11.72–11.81
pre-emption rights 5.19, 11.90
premiums, payment of 9.78, 9.79
Prime Brokerage Agreement 4.10
Principles of European Contract Law (PECL) 11.29–11.30, 11.33
Principles of International Commercial Contracts (PICC) 11.30, 11.33
private banking 2.26
private international law
  rules of 3.149, 3.151
private law 4.20
private money 2.26

private persons 8.122
proceeds of crime 2.196–2.197, 3.100, 3.103, 3.107
Proctor and Gamble 7.05
professional expertise/advice 8.09, 8.11
profit 7.71–7.73
    secret 7.71
project finance 10.03
    arrangements 4.96–4.97
promisors 10.02
promissory notes 2.45, 5.18, 5.44, 5.100–5.101, 5.103–5.105, 6.118, 6.40–6.41, 6.45, 6.81, 6.82, 6.86, 9.19, 10.38
    definition of 6.82, 6.84, 6.87
proof of intention to cheat 7.23
property
    agricultural 7.58
    charges 7.83–7.87, 7.97
    collapse in the late 1980s 7.87
    cryptocurrency as 2.153, 2.159
    development 7.12, 7.20, 9.87, 9.88, 9.90
    electronic databases 2.167–2.169
    family 4.44
    guarantees 7.58
    intellectual 5.23
    investment 8.55–8.63
    military 7.14
    physical 1.18, 5.01
    rights 1.18, 5.110–5.113, 11.49
    wrongdoing 4.44
    see also intangibles as property; land; mortgages; personal and property rights, distinction between
proprietary interest
    concept of 10.37
    property 4.81
protected coin 2.20
protection buyer 9.96
protection seller 9.96
public funds 5.21
publicly traded bonds 9.96

quantity theory of money 2.11

reasonable care 11.96
reasonableness 11.107
recharacterization 11.50–11.71
    risk 11.52–11.53, 11.67
record-keeping
    centralized records 1.08
    electronic 6.130
rectification 11.82–11.89, 11.91–11.93
    see also correction of mistake by construction
registered designs 5.23
    see also intellectual property rights
registration of charges *see* charges
registration of security interests 10.26–10.36
Regulation Q 6.31
Regulation S 6.49–6.50
reliance and trust 8.05
remedy
    equitable 7.98, 8.25, 8.32, 8.34–8.37, 8.51, 8.62–8.63, 8.72, 8.83, 10.57–10.58
    restitutionary 7.88

replevin 5.111
repo (sale-and-repurchase) agreement 10.73–10.77, 10.80
reputed ownership 5.10
restitution 7.88, 7.98
retail banking
    bank accounts 3.18
    European Currency Units 2.03
retail customers
    conflicts of interest 8.120
    customers' interests 8.120
    integrity 8.120
    regulatory rules for 8.118–8.123
    trust, relationships of 8.120
reverse security 10.106–10.123
    limited recourse lending 10.116–10.123
    non-recourse lending 10.116–10.123
    Special Purpose Vehicles (SPVs) 10.107–10.109
    third party security 10.110–10.115
    see also security interests
Review Committee on Banking Services Law and Practice *see* Jack Committee
rights of action 5.20
rights in rem of creditors or third parties 10.20–10.24, 10.33
risk
    bond market 9.86
    hedging 9.97
    Herstatt 3.109–3.112
    housing market 10.123
    management 3.14, 3.16, 8.86, 9.97
    perceived 7.01–7.17
    political 9.74
    recharacterization 11.52–11.53, 11.67
Roman law 2.11, 4.19, 4.22–4.28
Royal Mint 2.22
rule of law
    common law 1.11–1.12
    financial lawyers 1.14–1.15
running accounts 3.18–3.19, 4.61–4.62, 4.64–4.65, 10.84
'Ruritania' 2.205, 4.03, 9.64–9.65
Russia 2.08, 2.198

safe harbour 6.49–6.51
safekeeping 6.67–6.71
    see also Depositary/Safekeeper; Global Notes; international bond market
sale of goods warranties 11.96
sale of part of debt 5.75
sanctions 2.08
    regulations 2.195–2.206
Scotland
    bank notes, as legal tender 2.16, 2.19–2.20, 2.33–2.37
    security rights 10.18
    set-off 3.09
secret deals 8.18, 8.24
secured lending 10.77, 10.82, 10.109
Securities and Exchange Commission (SEC) (United States) 6.48, 8.117
securities industry 7.07
securities markets 10.03

348 INDEX

security arrangements/mechanisms 5.59, 9.02, 10.43, 10.45
   structure of 4.100–4.101
security entitlements 5.30, 5.111
   definition 5.109–5.110
security interests 10.01–10.123
   contract-based security 1.20, 10.83–10.105
   property-based security 1.20
   reasons for taking security 10.01–10.03
   registration 10.26–10.36
   reverse security 10.106–10.123
     limited recourse lending 10.116–10.123
     non-recourse lending 10.116–10.123
     Special Purpose Vehicles (SPVs) 10.107–10.109
     third party security 10.110–10.115
   terminology 10.04–10.25
     cross-border insolvency 10.17–10.25
     interchangeability of terms 10.06–10.10
     local authority borrowing 10.11–10.16
     security, definition of 10.04–10.05
   title-based security 10.46–10.82
     Declaration of Trust 10.69
     lien 10.65–10.68
     mortgage and charge, concepts of 10.46–10.60
     ownership as security 10.70–10.82
     pledge 10.61–10.64
   types of security 10.37–10.45
seigniorage 2.31, 2.37
set-off 3.07–3.14
   agreement 3.102
   banker's right of 3.20, 4.56
   contractual right of 3.16, 3.22, 3.26, 4.65, 4.71, 4.85, 10.84, 10.86, 10.92
   English law 3.08
   global 3.16
   independent 3.12
   insolvency 3.13–3.14
   mandatory provisions 4.78–4.80
   Scotland 3.09
   transactional 3.11, 3.14, 3.20
settlement of securities trades 3.112
several liability 9.06–9.08
share(s) 5.43
   capital, definition of 6.23
   certificates 10.05, 10.38–10.40
   financial assets 5.21
   option to purchase 5.19
   see also companies; partnerships
ships 1.07
   commercial hire of 5.01
   see also marine insurance
silent participation in a loan 8.116
Singapore
   MMIs 6.119
smuggling black market goods 7.51
social security benefits 5.45
societal theory of money 2.100, 2.109
sovereignty
   euro currency 2.101, 2.106–2.107, 2.116
Spain
   euro 2.105
special entities, definition of 1.21

special position of financial law 1.03–1.22
   common law, development of 1.10–1.12
   economic change 1.07–1.09
   financial lawyers, challenge for 1.13–1.15
   legal advice in financial markets 1.03–1.06
   legal developments 1.07–1.09
   topics, choice of 1.16–1.22
Special Purpose Vehicles (SPVs) 5.46, 6.02, 9.89, 10.95–10.96, 10.100, 10.107–10.109, 10.117, 10.119
specialist advice 8.09
stablecoins 2.153, 2.178, 3.125, 3.144
stamp duty 3.147, 6.37
State Aid 9.76
state theory of money 2.100–2.102, 2.104, 2.109, 2.187
state-owned entities, concept of 9.76
statutory assignment 5.54, 5.59, 5.63–5.65, 5.70
statutory treatment of money 2.16–2.51
   demonetization 2.38–2.51
   legal tender 2.16–2.22
   Northern Ireland, position in 2.33–2.37
   notes and coin 2.23–2.32
   Scotland, position in 2.33–2.37
steam engines 1.07, 3.113
sterling 3.69, 3.97
   cheques 2.190–2.191
   clearing services 2.205
   domestic payment 3.32
stock lending 2.171, 10.74–10.77
stockbrokers 3.21, 7.07–7.08
stockjobbers 7.07
stocks and shares 6.22
structuring security arrangements 4.100–4.101
sub-participation (*choses in action*) 5.72–5.87
   funded participation 5.75
   participation by guarantee 5.75
   sale of part of the debt 5.75
subjective approach (financial contracts) 11.32–11.35, 11.37, 11.40, 11.43
subjective intent 11.72–11.81
subordination 9.112–9.134
   ad hoc 9.123–9.134
   general 9.117–9.122
subsidiaries (fiduciary duties/relationships) 7.08
Sudan
   sanctions 2.201, 2.203
suing 8.17
   right to sue oneself 4.69
Supplier Credit Bills and Notes Facility 9.78
supply of money 2.10
suretyship, contracts of 9.22–9.38
   definition of 9.24
   guarantee, contracts of 9.27–9.33
   guarantees and indemnities, distinction between 9.22–9.26
   indemnity, contracts of 9.34–9.38
swap contracts 8.86, 8.89–8.92
swap transactions 7.04, 11.80
swaps business 1.21
swaps dealers 1.21
Sweden 9.103
Switzerland 6.32
syndicated agreement 3.78

INDEX

syndicated lending 4.91–4.92
   loan market 8.111, 11.80
   syndicate of lending banks 10.69
synthetic instruments 9.101

TARGET2 settlement system 3.40, 3.34–3.40
taxation
   corporate 2.07
   cryptocurrency 2.150, 2.154, 2.186
   evasion 3.136
   income, rise in 11.44
   inheritance 10.122
   international regulation 6.54
   personal 2.07
   raising of 2.03
technology
   changes in trading patterns 1.07
   computer 1.08
   new payment 3.113–3.121
   organizations 3.130–3.131
   see also Distributed Ledger Technology (DLT)
telegraphic transfer 3.28
Temporary Global Notes 6.48–6.52
tenancy law 4.39–4.41
   see also land
term sheet 11.80
terms of business 8.98
terrorism 3.99
theft 2.53–2.54, 3.28
   cryptocurrency and 2.150, 2.154, 2.164–2.165
things in action 5.05
things in possession 5.05
third-party security 10.110–10.115
Time Variable Contingency Policies 9.87
title-based security 10.46–10.82
   Declaration of Trust 10.69
   lien 10.65–10.68
   mortgage and charge, concepts of 10.46–10.60
   ownership as security 10.70–10.82
   pledge 10.61–10.64
tokenisation 3.144–3.147
topics, choice of 1.16–1.22
tort 9.05, 10.38
trade 1.07
   associations 5.76, 11.80
   finance 7.08
   see also international trade
transactional lawyers 11.01–11.03
transactional set-off 3.11, 3.14, 3.20
Trans-European Automated Real-time Gross-settlement Express Transfer *see* TARGET2 settlement system
transfer, in whole or in part 4.91, 5.35
transfer of money
   acquisition of property belonging to another 2.05
   electronic 2.05
transmission of money, payment as 3.27–3.152
   Argentinian bond case 3.80–3.98
   disruption in the process 3.58–3.79
      Iranian debt crisis (1979) 3.75–3.79, 3.98
      Libyan Arab Foreign Bank case 3.61–3.74, 3.95–3.97

Distributed Ledger Technology (DLT):
   effect on legal principles and practices 3.138–3.152
   potential uses of 3.122–3.132
   freezing orders 3.108
   Herstatt risk 3.109–3.112
   interdiction legislation 3.99–3.107
   international payments 3.33
   new payment technologies 3.113–3.121
   payment between payer and payee 3.41–3.57
   payment through UK banking system 3.31–3.32
   regulatory challenges 3.133–3.137
   Sterling Domestic Payment 3.32
   TARGET2 3.34–3.40
   US Dollar International Payment 3.34
   see also payment
Treaty on European Union *see* Maastricht Treaty
Treaty of Rome (Treaty establishing the European Community) 2.88, 2.99, 2.102, 2.106, 2.110, 2.115
triple cocktail arrangement 4.88–4.89
trust, breach of 7.86, 7.89
trust deeds 6.19, 6.126, 6.128
trustee/trusteeship 4.92, 8.112
trusts
   beneficial interests 5.22
   definition of 4.44
   equitable ownership and 4.44–4.53
   law of 1.21
   Medieval origins 4.45–4.49
turnover trust 9.132, 11.50

Ukraine 2.08, 2.198
undue influence 7.45–7.48, 7.59, 7.61
Unidroit Principles 11.30, 11.33
unit trust arrangement 4.98–4.99
United Kingdom (UK)
   accounting rules 10.90
   constitutional system 4.19
   corporate debt 6.24–6.25
   credit insurance, position on 9.86
   equity securities 6.123
   euro currency 2.86
   exchange control 2.193–2.194
   Export Credits Guarantee Department 9.75–9.78
   HM Treasury bills 6.123
   HMRC and taxation 2.186
   housing market 10.121
   insolvency law 9.112–9.122, 10.03
   Jack Committee 6.120–6.122
   joint venture relationships 8.55–8.63
   life assurance 9.104–9.105
   listed corporations 9.40
   loan stock issues 6.35–6.37
   loan stock issues 6.128
   local authority borrowing 10.11
   MMIs 6.120–6.124
   overseas assets 10.90
   payment through UK banking system 3.31–3.32
   property valuation 8.83
   sanctions 2.201, 2.205
   security interests 10.33
   tax law 10.122
   UK Export Finance 9.75

350 INDEX

United Nations (UN)
  resolutions 2.08
United States (US)
  Argentinian bond case 3.80–3.98
  bond market turnover 6.01
  clearing process 3.34
  constitutional drafting 4.19
  corporate debt 6.25
  derivatives contracts 7.10
  dimes, used in Canada 2.57–2.61
  dollars 2.92, 2.107, 2.201, 6.26–6.27, 6.34–6.35, 10.93
    deposits and loans 6.32
    interest rates 8.89
    International Payment 3.34
  domestic bond markets 9.82
  Eurodollar market 6.28, 6.30, 6.33
  executive orders 3.62, 3.76, 3.78, 3.86–3.87, 3.91
  Federal Reserve Bank of New York 3.67
  Federal Reserve Board/System 6.30–6.31
  Foreign Credit Restraint Program 6.30
  freeze regulations 2.08
  housing market 10.120
  independence, declaration of 2.03
  Iranian debt crisis (1979) 3.75–3.79, 3.98
  IRS and taxation 2.186
  Libyan Arab Foreign Bank case 3.61–3.74, 3.95–3.97
  life assurance 9.103
  measures of money 2.12
  MMIs 6.119
  monoline insurers 9.84–9.85
  mortgages, sub-prime crisis 9.84–9.85
  New York State Insurance Law 9.83
  overseas assets 10.90
  overseas subsidiaries of US corporations 6.30
  sanctions on Russia 2.08
  sanctions regulations 2.198, 2.200–2.204
  SEC registration requirements 6.48–6.49
  Uniform Commercial Code (UCC) 5.30, 5.106–5.113
  see also **Cold War; Interest Equalization Tax; Marshall Plan**
units of stock 6.22
unjust enrichment 7.75
unsecured credit 11.49
USSR 6.27

Value Added Tax (VAT) 3.101
virtual currency *see* **cryptoassets; cryptocurrency; cryptosystem**
volonté psychologique 11.21, 11.34
Von Savigny, Friedrich Carl 4.19–4.20, 4.30
vulnerable individuals 1.21

Wall Street Crash (1929) 6.48
warranties 4.93, 7.27, 11.96
warrants 5.02, 6.47
Wendell Holmes, Oliver 11.07
wills 5.16
winding-up of companies 3.13
  see also **insolvency**
World War II 6.26, 6.33, 7.14
  post-war international bond market *see* **international bond market**
writs 4.32–4.35
written contract 8.97, 11.20, 11.75, 11.82–11.89, 11.92, 11.94, 11.99
written memorandum 9.31
wrongful acts 8.21